An Exposition of the book of Solomon's Song

JOHN GILL, D.D.
1697-1771

AN EXPOSITION

OF THE BOOK OF

SOLOMON'S SONG

COMMONLY CALLED

CANTICLES.

WHEREIN THE AUTHORITY OF IT IS ESTABLISHED AND VINDICATED AGAINST OBJECTIONS, BOTH ANCIENT AND MODERN; SEVERAL VERSIONS COMPARED WITH THE ORIGINAL TEXT;

The different Senses both of Jewish and Christian Interpreters considered;

AND THE WHOLE OPENED AND

EXPLAINED IN PROPER AND USEFUL OBSERVATION.

"Canticum canticorum spiritualis quaedam sanctarum est voluptas mentium, in conjugio illius regis and reginae civitatis, quod est Christus and ecclesia; sed haec voluptas allegoricis tegminibus involuta est, ut desideretur ardentius, nudeturque jucundius, and appareat sponsus, cui dicitur in eodem cantico, aequitas dilexit te and sponsa quae ibi audit, charitas in deliciis tuis." –Aug. de Civ. Dei, 1. 17, c. 20.

BY JOHN GILL, D.D.

LONDON:
WILLIAM HILL COLLINGRIDGE; LONG LANE, ALDERSGATE STREET.
1854

The Baptist Standard Bearer, Inc.
No. 1 Iron Oaks Drive • Paris, Arkansas 72855

*Reprinted
by*

THE BAPTIST STANDARD BEARER, INC.
No. 1 Iron Oaks Drive
Paris, Arkansas 72855
(479) 963-3831

THE WALDENSIAN EMBLEM
lux lucet in tenebris
"The Light Shineth in the Darkness"

ISBN #1-57978-490-9

TABLE OF CONTENTS

Preface . . . . .Page iii

Prefatory Address . . . . .Page v

To The Reader . . . . .Page vii

Chapter 1 . . . . .Page 1

Chapter 2 . . . . .Page 65

Chapter 3 . . . . .Page 110

Chapter 4 . . . . .Page 133

Chapter 5 . . . . .Page 177

Chapter 6 . . . . .Page 233

Chapter 7 . . . . .Page 259

Chapter 8 . . . . .Page 292

PREFACE.

The following Exposition was delivered in one hundred and twenty-two sermons, to the Congregation where God in his providence has placed me, and were designed only for their use, profit, and edification. Had I had any thoughts of publishing it to the world when I entered upon it, perhaps it might have appeared with some little more advantage than now it does; nor had it appeared now, had not the importunity of the people to whom I minister, with others, obliged me to it; to which I the more readily complied, considering that the authority and usefulness of this book are called in question in this loose and degenerate age; in which, not only this, but all scripture is ridiculed and burlesqued, and the great doctrines of faith therein contained treated with the utmost sneer and contempt; and therefore would willingly contribute all I can towards the vindicating of this, or any other part of the sacred writings; which, being given by inspiration of God, are " profitable for doctrine, for reproof, for correction, and for instruction in righteousness."

I have in the performance of this work, consulted the original text, with the versions of several learned men; and have taken notice of them where they have differed from our translation, or have furnished out a proper and useful observation. I have also inspected several interpreters upon this book, both Jewish and Christian, and have collected their several senses together; and generally, if not always, have humbly given my opinion which is the most eligible. The versions which I have made use of, are those of the Septuagint, the Vulgate Latin, the Tigurine, Junius and Tremellius, Arias Montanus, Pagninus, &c. The writings and interpreters which I have consulted, of the Jewish, are Shirhashirim Rabba, Targum, Jarchi, Aben Ezra, Alshech, and Yalcut Simeoni, together with the books of Zohar and Rabboth, which are interspersed with the senses of various passages in this book. Of Christian interpreters, Alcuin, Foliot, Mercerus, Cocceius, Sanctius, Ainsworth, Brightman, Cotton, Durham, Patrick, &c., from all which I have received profit and advantage; and from none more than from the short notes of the incomparable Ainsworth, and the sweet observations of the excellent Durham; I mention these authors, not by way of ostentation, but as in duty bound to acknowledge by whom I have profited; for, as Pliny says,[*] "Est benignum et plenum ingenui pudoris, fateri per quos profeceris." Where two or more senses of any passage have offered agreeable to the analogy of faith, I have considered them all, and have made what improvement of them I was capable of, leaving the reader to judge for himself, which of them is most preferable; this I thought to be a much better way than to be too positive and dogmatical in the sense of a text, especially in such a part of scripture which is so very mystical and obstruse. If I should be thought in any

---
[*] Præfat. in Nat. Hist.

part of this work to have stretched the metaphors too far, I hope it will be imputed to an honest zeal, and a hearty desire to set forth the glory of Christ's person, and his exceeding great love to his church and people; to do which, all tropes and figures, all the flowers of rhetoric, fall abundantly short. I have been obliged to contract what I delivered sermon-wise, lest the work should swell to too large a bulk, but the substance of it is here contained.

I would only observe, as to this edition * of the work, that I have made various additions to it; having, since the publication of the second edition met with an objection or two to the antiquity and authority of the book itself, I thought it necessary to consider them, and remove them; being unwilling that any thing should lie against a book so grand, so sacred, and useful. I have also given a summary of the contents of each chapter, which was wanting in the former editions; and though I had in many parts of the work, attended to the literal sense of passages, yet not so frequently as I have in my shorter notes on this book published in my Exposition of the whole Bible: I have therefore inserted from thence many things relating to the literal sense, with many others added, which will greatly enrich this edition, and make it more entertaining; and will greatly serve to show the propriety of the allusions, figures, and metaphors made use of throughout the whole; and to illustrate and confirm the spiritual meaning of this sublime and mysterious book. I have left out at the end of it, the Targum or Chaldee paraphrase, with my notes thereon, which were in the former editions, they being of little use and benefit, especially to common readers.

---

* Preface to third edition.

PREFATORY ADDRESS,

TO THE CHRISTIAN READER.

THE immortal Toplady has truly declared, that, " while true religion, and sound learning, have a single friend in the British Empire, the WORKS and name of GILL will be precious and revered."

My esteemed friend and Christian brother, Mr. Doudney, has *accomplished* his arduous undertaking, and presented us with a beautiful edition of " Dr. Gill's Commentary," at an amazingly low price. The Christian Minister has now a sound and learned gospel Exposition of the sacred Scriptures. We have also Gill's *whole mind*, in doctrine, experience, and practice, in his elaborate " Body of Divinity ;" a new edition of which I carefully revised for the press in the year 1839. And if the reader would be acquainted with a sterling work, that plucks up by the roots the *Arminian* heresy, and wrests the sacred Word out of the unhallowed hands of *Pelagian* Expositors, then let him consult " Gill's Cause of God and Truth." But there *yet* remains (I trust) a great number of plain and *precious disciples* of the meek and lowly Jesus, that are *not* ministers, and who have also but little time, or perhaps taste, for *polemical* and *critical Divinity*, who nevertheless *have* a relish *for*, and an appetite to feed at a table well spread with *rich experimental provisions*, and are glad to partake of " *old* wines well refined." I am truly thankful that *these* persons, who are " heirs of God and joint-heirs with Christ," are not *passed over*, but that our good brother has catered for *them* also, in re-publishing " Dr. Gill's Exposition of Solomon's Song ;" a most blessed work, originally delivered in 122 sermons. It is very scarce, and exceedingly valuable. I know not a work containing more experimental savour, written by man. I have, during more than forty-five years spent in the Christian Ministry, repeatedly obtained *marrow and fatness* from a perusal of its pages. Nothing from Gill's pen has perhaps been made *so* useful to *devotional* Christians as *this ;* so that I can *well* recommend it to all those who would cry out with the Spouse, " Let *Him* kiss me with the kisses of his mouth: for thy love is better than wine " (Song i. 2.) Reader ! take the exposition of this verse, as a commencing *sample*.

The celebrated James Hervey was a very great admirer of this work. In his " *Theron* and *Aspasio*," we have the following high encomium (not too high) upon Gill on the Song :—" It has such a copious view of sanctified invention running through it, and is also interspersed with such a variety of delicate brilliant images, as cannot but highly entertain a curious mind. It presents us also with such *rich and charming displays of the glory of Christ's Person, the freeness of his grace to sinners, and the tenderness of his love to the church*, as cannot but administer the most *exquisite delight* to the believing soul. Considered in *both* those views, I think the work resembles the *paradisaical* garden, described by MILTON, in which

> ' Blossoms and fruits at once of golden hue
> Appear'd, with gay enamell'd colours mix'd.' "

This Exposition has stood the test of exactly 130 years, (the sermons were preached in the year 1724;) it has obtained the meed and high approval of the truly wise and good; so that *now* all that *modern* men may allege, in *depreciating*, will be but as the paper pellets of a school-boy against a well-constructed fortification. Gill's works " praise him in the gates, " Prov. xxxi. 31.

I need add no more: but, I shall consider a long ministerial life to be *well* closed, in recommending " Gill on Solomon's Song " to the " Generation following." Psal. xlviii. 13.

J. A. JONES.

London, March 8th, 1854.

TO THE READER.

BELOVED!—We are not fond of blank leaves, and therefore, as otherwise there would be a blank leaf in this introductory sheet, we venture to intrude upon the reader with a few remarks.

With what our aged Friend and Fellow-labourer has said of this invaluable Exposition, we fully concur. Circumstances have occurred during its passing through the press, to prevent our paying the same close attention to it as to the voluminous Commentary. It has been read and revised mostly by others. But as far as the proof-sheets have fallen into our hands, we have found, not a close, clear, searching scrutiny of the doctrine of the text merely, but in addition, a savour and a power for which we were scarcely prepared. We love sound, full, so-called high-doctrine; but where the grace and the dew of the doctrine is there too, under the teaching, power, and application of the Holy Ghost, it fixes that doctrine in the heart and conscience; and we defy men or devils thence to uproot it. An unctious word dropped by the Holy Ghost upon the heart is like "cold water to a thirsty soul;" and whilst it exalts and endears a precious Christ, in his person, work, and offices, it is the most deadly artillery with which Satan and all the powers of darkness can be attacked.

We are of opinion that many of these savoury sweets, beloved, will drop from this honey-comb into your heart; and thus make

"Sovereign mercy dear to you,
And Jesus all in all."

One difficulty ofttimes presents itself in reading Solomon's Song—it is the difficulty to ascertain who is the speaker, whether Christ or the Church. But to our mind there is a blessedness and a satisfaction in this very difficulty. It tends specially and powerfully to set forth the unions the oneness, the identity that subsists between Christ and his Church—the Bridegroom and the Bride. This very union in name, as well as in nature, is sweetly expressed by the prophet Jeremiah; in the 23rd chapter and 6th verse it is written, "And this is HIS name whereby HE shall be called [Jehovah-tsidkenu] the Lord our righteousness;" and again in the 33rd chapter and 16th verse it is recorded, "And this is the name wherewith SHE shall be called, [Jehovah-tsidkenu] the Lord our righteousness."

During the publication of Dr. Gill's invaluable writings, we have had repeatedly to combat the scruples and objections of those who have marvelled that we, as a member and a minister of the Church of England, could publish the works of one who was opposed to that Church. To the great and grand essentials—which are sound doctrine, and "the fruits of good living," as evidencing the sincere and hearty reception of sound doctrine—which are the very bulwarks of the Church of England—Dr. Gill was *not* opposed. With regard to minor points of discipline we differ and agree to differ. We view these as non-essentials—the mere scaffolding of the true spiritual temple. "Let every man be fully persuaded in his own mind." There are things in the Church of England which we could desire altered: and from the mass of its ministers we differ as widely as light from darkness; but what men of truth in the Establishment may say and feel, that men of truth out of the Establishment equally say and feel. We have as much freedom and liberty—yea, infinitely more—within her pale, than others have without her pale. *We* have no interference where *they* have interference. *They* are subjected to a caprice and dictation to which *we* are not subjected.

But with respect to the writings of Dr. Gill, and men of the same school, if there be light, if there be life, if there be power, we stay not to ask—for we care not to do so—who they are, and what they are in point of relative position before men. We care not a straw whether they are Episcopalian or non-Episcopalian. It is enough for us that they are taught of God, blessed by God; and as such we hold out to them the right hand of fellowship, and wish them good luck in the name of the Lord." And this is not in mere word. Those who are acquainted with the " Gospel Magazine," originally edited by the immortal Toplady, can testify that these are the principles upon which we have, through grace, conducted it for fourteen years.

Finally, brethren, we say these are not times for contention: this is not a day for splitting hairs about straws; it little behoves us now to ask, " Who is of Paul, or who of Apollos?" The enemy is at our very gates—yea more, he has scaled the walls,—made a breach,—and is, apparently at least, upon the very point of taking possession of the citadel. Up then, " to the help of the Lord, to the help of the Lord against the mighty." Print, preach, and practice (as God shall give you grace) " the truth, the whole truth, and nothing but the truth." Let press, and pulpit, and parlour, echo and re-echo, with a living testimony for covenant love, covenant blood, and covenant salvation: and this shall be found the most effectual means of counteracting the artifices of Satan, and the cunning devices of Pope, Puseyite, and all such sanctimonious but hypocritical pretenders.

One word more. It does at times cheer our ofttimes drooping heart to reflect, that when our head shall be laid low, the hand that now writes shall be paralyzed in the long sleep of death, and our body be mouldering in the silent grave; these precious testimonies for God and truth shall be circulating far and wide, even to the very ends of the earth. It does cheer us—'mid much darkness and many doubts—to think, that there have been, through our feeble instrumentality, two thousand two hundred and fifty sets (or thirteen thousand five hundred volumes) of the incomparable Commentary printed, and nearly all in circulation, from this little, dark, desolate, Popish village! And not only Gill, but the immortal Hawker, though dead, yet speaks afresh to us from the same quarter. Five thousand of his Morning and Evening Portions are at this moment passing through this Village-press.

Gracious Lord, crown the same with thy covenant blessing: and, when we shall depart this life, oh grant that our children and our children's children—grant that these little poor benighted villagers—the present helpers in this great work—may rise up to call Thee blessed; and that *they* may sing of *us*, as *we* now sing of *ours*.

> " We are travelling home to God,
>   In the *Way* our fathers trod;
> *They* are happy now, and we
>   Soon their happiness shall see."

Beloved, we are yours to serve in the kingdom and patience of Jesus Christ,

David Alfred Doudney,
Curate of Monksland.

Bonmahon, Co. Waterford,
April 7, 1854.

An Exposition
of the book of
Solomon's Song

AN EXPOSITION
OF THE
SONG OF SONGS

In this chapter, after the general title of the book, ver. 1; *the church expresses her strong desires and most ardent wishes for some fresh discoveries of the love of Christ to her, and for communion with him,* ver. 2; *and having tasted of his love, and smelled a sweet savour in his grace, and enjoyed fellowship with him in his house,* ver. 3, 4, *she observes her blackness and uncomeliness in herself, and comeliness in him, the trials and afflictions she met with from others, and her carelessness and negligence of her own affairs,* ver. 5, 6; *and entreats her beloved to direct her, where she might meet with him feeding his flocks and giving them rest; to which he returns a kind and gracious answer, and gives proper instructions where to find him,* ver. 7, 8; *and then commends her beauty, sets forth her amiableness and loveliness by various metaphors, and makes promises of more grace and good things to her,* ver. 9, 10, 11; *when she declares what a value she had for Christ her beloved; and how precious he was unto her, like a bundle of myrrh, and a cluster of camphire,* ver. 12, 13, 14; *and Christ again praises her beauty, and particularly takes notice of her eyes, and her modest look,* ver. 15; *and she returns the encomium back to him, and expresses her pleasure and satisfaction in the house he had built for her, and the furniture of it,* ver. 16, 17.

Verse I. *The Song of Songs, which is Solomon's.*

INTENDING by the assistance of God, to open and explain this mysterious part of the sacred writings, it will be proper—
I. To enquire into, and establish the authority of this book.
II. Show the nature of it; it being a *Song.*
III. The excellency of it; it being called the *Song of Songs.*
IV. The penman of it; which is *Solomon.*

I. I shall endeavour to prove the divine authority of this book, and vindicate it from those exceptions which are made against it; and
1st. It was always received by the ancient Jews, to whom *the oracles of God were committed,* as a very valuable part of the sacred writings; and has been continued in the canon of the scriptures by the Christians in all ages to this very day. The Jews had always a very venerable esteem of it, calling it *the holy of holies;* forbidding their children the reading thereof, as well as the first chapter of *Genesis,* and the beginning and end of the prophecy of *Ezekiel,* until they were thirty years of age,[a] because of the mysteriousness and sublimity of it. They say,[b] that *Solomon,* when he was old and near death, the Holy Ghost dwelt upon him, and he compassed the books of *Proverbs, Song of Songs,* and *Ecclesiastes.* Their ancient book of *Zohar*[c] asserts, that *Solomon* composed it "by the inspiration of the Holy Spirit;" as does also the *Turgum* upon this book, and *R. Solomon Jarchi,* and *R. Aben Ezra,* in their prefaces to their commentaries upon it; the latter of which has these words; "God forbid, God forbid," says he, "that the *Song of Songs* should be *written or understood* of things obscene; but it is entirely parabolical, and had it not been of very great excellency, it had not been written in the catalogue of the holy scriptures; for of it there has been no controversy, that it defiles the hands;"[d] for though there was once a controversy[e] among the wise men concerning the books of *Proverbs* and *Ecclesiastes,* who afterwards, as it became them, changed their minds; yet there never was any concerning this, as appears from their *Misnah;* where they say,[f] that "all the scriptures are holy, but the *Song of Songs* is the holy of holies: and if the wise men have had any controversy, it has been only concerning *Ecclesiastes;*" so that this book appears to be authentic, according to the mind of the ancient as well as of the modern Jews; and as for the Christians, they have always looked upon it as a part of the holy scripture, a few only excepted, and have all along continued it in the canon as they found and received it. The ancient fathers and councils have always esteemed it sacred and venerable, not to take notice of authorities of a later date. The opinion of *Theodorus* of *Mopsuest,* who called the divine authority of this book into question, was condemned in

---

[a] Hieron. Præfat. in Ezekiel. Origen. Prolog. Cant. Cantic. [b] Seder Olam Rabba, p. 41. [c] In Exod. fol. 59. col. 3. Edit. Sultzbac. [d] Vide T. Bab. Megillah, fol. 7. 1. Maimon. Hilch. Abot Hatumaot, c. 9. sect. 6. [e] Vide Vorst. not. in Maimon. Yesode Hattorah, c. 6. sest. 12. [f] Tract Yadaim, c. 3. sect. 5.

the second council of *Constantinople*, which was held about the year 553. This book also appears in the catalogue of the canonical books of scripture, established in the council of *Laodicea*, Can. 59, held about the year 364. It is likewise in *Origen's* catalogue, recorded by *Eusebius*,[g] as well as in that which *Melito*[h] brought from the East, and sent to his friend *Onesimus*, who flourished about the year 140. So that thus far, at least we can trace up the authority of this book among the Christians: not to take notice of the canons of the apostles, in which it stands as a part of canonical scripture: nor the Constitutions of the Apostles with the larger epistles of *Ignatius*, in which citations are made from this book; which, if genuine, would prove the reception of it in the Christian church still more early; but because they are generally looked upon to be spurious, they are not to be insisted on. And it may be farther observed, that not only *Origen*, but *Hippolytus* in the third century,[i] *Carpathius*, *Gregory Nyssene* in the fourth, and *Theodoret* in the fifth, and others in the following centuries, wrote commentaries upon this book; and *Eusebius*[k] ascribes it to *Solomon*, and so does *Athanasius*.[l]

2ndly. This book was written by one that was θεόπνευστος, divinely inspired; as appears by his being the penman of the books of *Proverbs* and *Ecclesiastes;* for why he should not be under the inspiration of the same Spirit in writing this, as he was in writing those, there appears no reason to conclude. The objection against it, taken from his great fall into lewdness and idolatry, produced by a late author,[m] avails but little; especially, if, as some think, it should appear that it was written before; or if, with others, it is taken to be written after his fall, it will lie as strongly against the book of Ecclesiastes, which is generally allowed to be written after, as it does against this: besides, it has pleased the all-wise God, who gives no account of his matters to his creatures, to make use of men, after very great falls into sin, as amanuenses of his Holy Spirit, and penmen of the sacred scriptures, as David and Peter.

3rdly. The dignity and sublimity of the matter contained herein, show it to be no human composure; for *never man spake* or wrote like unto it; it is therefore called the *Song of songs*, being the most excellent of songs; which cannot be equalled by any, but surpasses all others, not only human but divine; it is preferred to all scriptural songs, which, as one[n] observes, would be blasphemous to do, was it not of a Divine rise and authority.

4thly. The majesty of its style bears a testimony to the divine original of it, which cannot be equalled by the most elaborate performances; it defies all the art and wisdom of man to come near it; and plainly shows itself to be the language of God himself, whose *voice is powerful and full of majesty.*

5thly. The power and efficacy which it has in and over the hearts of men, is another evidence of its being the Word of God; which is *quick and powerful, and sharper than any two-edged sword, piercing even to the dividing asunder of soul and spirit, and of the joints and marrow, and is a Discerner of the thoughts and intents of the heart.* This book has been *profitable for doctrine, for reproof, for correction, for instruction in righteousness;* which are so many arguments of its being *given by inspiration of God;* it *effectually works in them that believe;* it has been useful to thousands who have had their spiritual senses exercised, for the comfort of their souls, the raising of their affections, the increase of their faith, and their instruction in divine things: the reading and expounding of this excellent portion of Scripture have been owned by God for the good of multitudes, who are so many sealing evidences of the authority of it.

6thly. The impartiality of it is another evidence of its divine original: the bride is here frequently introduced proclaiming her own weaknesses and infirmities, as in chap. i. 5, 6, and iii. 1, and v. 2, 3. Now was it a mere human composure of *Solomon's*, celebrating the amours between him and *Pharaoh's* daughter, would it be reasonable to suppose, that he should so manifestly and openly declare the defects and imperfections of his bride? But to consider it as a divine poem, expressing the mutual love between Christ and his church, it agrees very well with the other parts of the sacred writings, wherein the infirmities of God's own people are not concealed; not even of those who were themselves the penmen of them; which is a strong proof of their divine authority.

7thly. There is a very great agreement between this and other portions of Scripture. Now this has been always looked upon as a considerable evidence of the authority of the sacred writings, that though they have been delivered *at sundry times, and in divers manners*, yet there has been always an entire harmony between them; the which also appears in this part of Scripture; for though it is delivered in a mysterious and figurative style, yet it admits of senses which are very agreeable to the *proportion* or *analogy of faith;* nay, in many places of the New Testament, there seems to be manifest allusions to this song, as will be hereafter more particularly observed: but notwithstanding all these evidences of its divine original, there have not been wanting persons who have called in question its sacred authority; as Theodorus of Mopsuest, whose opinion was, that it was not written by inspiration, but was only designed by Solomon to celebrate his amours between him and

---

[g] Eccles. Hist. l. 6. c. 25. [h] Ibid. lib. 4. c. 26.
[i] Euseb. Eccl. Hist. l. 6. c. 22. 32. [k] Contra Marcellum, l. 1. c. 2. [l] Synops. S. Script. l. 16.
[m] Mr. Whiston's supplement to his essay towards restoring the text of the old Testament, p. 11. 12.
[n] Durham Clav. Cant. p. 5.

Pharaoh's 'daughter.; which opinion of his was condemned in the sixth century by the second council of Constantinople, as has been before observed: Castalio in the sixteenth century was condemned for the same opinion, by the senate of Geneva, and was ordered to depart the city upon it: Grotius in the last century seemed to be much of the same mind; and Mr. Whiston in this has attempted in a set tract to weaken the authority of it, and make it appear to be a loose, profane, and amorous song: his proposition is this: "The book of Canticles is not a sacred book of the Old Testament; nor was it originally esteemed as such, either by the Jewish or Christian church;" with what truth this is asserted, will in some measure appear from what has been already said. The arguments by which he endeavours to confirm and establish this proposition, are as follow, which I shall particularly consider.

I. Because as he asserts, "It was not written in his younger days, or when he was the good, the wise, the chaste, and the religious man; but long afterwards, when he was become wicked and foolish, and lascivious, and idolatrous." And he affirms, that there are some very plain and particular chronological characters in this book, which determine it to belong to the latter and worse part of his life, and to that only. And,

The first passage in it, which he mentions to confirm this, is Cant. i. 9, where the church is compared to *a company of horses in Pharaoh's chariots;* which he imagines refers to those horses and chariots which Solomon, contrary to an express command, Deut. xvii. 16, had brought unto him out of Egypt, 1 Kings x. 28, 29; when he began to degenerate from his former piety: in answer to which, it may be replied, that the comparison in the text under consideration, is not made to a company of horses brought out of Egypt, which ran in Solomon's chariots; but to a company of horses in Egypt, which ran in Pharaoh's chariots; so that the text falls very much short of proving what it is produced for.

His other chronological evidence of this book's belonging to the loose and vicious part of Solomon's life, is Cant. vii. 12, where mention is made of *the chariots of Amminadib;* in which he supposes there are more proofs than one of what he contends for; the first is, that here are chariots referred to, as used in Judea, which, he says, we only meet with once before, since the days of Moses, namely, 2 Sam. viii. 4; though that appears to be a mistake; for Absalom prepared himself chariots and horsemen, 2 Sam. xv. 1; as did Adonijah, 1 Kings i. 5; both which were before Solomon's accession to the throne. His other proof from this text is, that this Amminadib was one of the twelve rulers of provinces, who married Taphath the daughter of Solomon, 1 Kings iv. 11; and therefore he concludes that Solomon could not be a very young man when he wrote this book. To which I answer,

1st. That it is not Amminadib but Abinadab, that is there mentioned.

2ndly. That it was not Abinadab, but the son of Abinadab, that married Solomon's daughter.

3rdly. It is not likely that King Solomon's son-in-law should be a chariot driver, as this Amminadib is thought to be by many interpreters, who was famous for his skill, courage, and swiftness in driving.

4thly. This is not the proper name of any person, but are two words, as R. Aben Ezra, and R. Solomon Jarchi observe, and should be rendered, *the chariots of my free* or *princely people;* and therefore afford no chronological character of any part of Solomon's life whatever.

The last chronological evidence he mentions, page 10, and which he takes to be the principal and most evident one, which shows in what particular time of Solomon's life this book was written, is chap. vi. 8, 9; where mention is made of *sixty queens,* and *eighty concubines,* and *virgins without number;* which he thinks refers to Solomon's wicked practice of polygamy, expressly forbidden, Deut. xvii. 17. To which I reply,

1st. That the allusion does not seem to be made to the number of Solomon's queens and concubines, but to the custom of some princes in the East, which Solomon had in view; for the number of queens and concubines here does not agree with the number of Solomon's, recorded 1 Kings xi. 3, where he is said to have *seven hundred wives, and three hundred concubines,* which is vastly different from the account which is given here: and if it should be said, that though when he wrote this book, he had not arrived to that prodigious pitch of wickedness in the practice of polygamy, to which he afterwards did; yet he had begun, and gone a great way in it, and had at the time he wrote it, such a number of wives and concubines as are here mentioned, which he refers to. I answer,

2ndly. That it is not likely that Solomon should prefer one of his wives, and praise her above all the rest; which would have been the way to have alienated their affections from him, and made her the object of their envy, as well as have raised such domestic feuds and quarrels, which would not easily be laid. Besides,

3rdly. It does not seem reasonable to suppose that those other queens and concubines of Solomon's should speak so much in the praise and commendation of his lawful wife, as these are said to do here; which is not usual for such sort of persons to do. As to those other texts referred to, namely, chap. i. 3, 5, and ii. 7, and iii. 5, 10, 11, and v. 8, 16, and vi. 9, and viii. 4, 6, 7; produced by Mr. Whiston, to prove that the person, who is the bridegroom in this song, loved many other women and virgins, of which his spouse is jealous; I need only say, that those texts do indeed express the love of the daughters of Jerusalem to him, and the notice which the spouse took of them, for whom she appears to have a very great value and affection, to whom she often points out her beloved, and directs them to observe the transcendent excellencies and beauties of his person, as well as strictly charges them to give him no disturbance: yet she also signifies her very great love and regard to him; but no where insinuates any wandering affection or wanton love in him unto others, or that she was jealous of him upon that account.

II. His next reason, page 12, 13, is, "that there is no foundation for an allegorical, or mystical sense of this book; there being not the least sign of a sober, virtuous, or divine meaning therein, nor any thing that in the least concerns morality or virtue, God or religion, the Messiah or his kingdom;" which, if true, would indeed go a great way against the authority of it; but I hope the following Exposition will make it appear that there is a good foundation in it for a mystical or allegorical sense, agreeable enough to the analogy of faith; as well as show that there are many things in it which encourage morality and virtue, promote the cause of God and religion, and concern the Messiah and his kingdom; and Mr. Whiston has not thought fit to give any one instance which discovers the contrary.

III. He says, page 13, that "the introduction of double or mystical senses of Scripture among the Jews, is much later than the days of Solomon, and cannot therefore be supposed to belong to any book of his writing:" but this does not appear to be true, for surely the speech of Jotham to the men of Shechem, recorded in Judg. ix., must be understood in an allegorical or mystical sense; and Nathan's parable, 2 Sam. xii. 1, which was delivered before Solomon's time. Moreover, the forty-fifth Psalm is of the very same strain, and bears a very near resemblance with this song, which was written by David, Solomon's father; besides, suppose this allegorical and mystical way of writing had not been used before by the inspired writers, it is no argument that it should not be used now, as it was afterwards in the writings of the New Testament, as Mr. Whiston confesses, page 22.

IV. Another reason which he produces, page 23, is, that "neither the contemporary nor succeeding writers of the Old Testament, ever quote or allude to this book of Canticles, nor to any part thereof, upon any occasion whatsoever." The same may be said of many other books of the Old Testament, whose authority was never yet called in question; nor can this be looked upon by judicious persons, a sufficient reason why any of them should.

V. He says, page 24, "The apocryphal writers of the Old Testament, never quote nor allude to this book, nor to any part thereof, upon any occasion whatsoever." Which I persuade myself, will be no ways shocking or stumbling to any thoughtful Christian, nor be looked upon by them as a sufficient objection against the authority of it; had they expressly opposed it, it could not have been very considerably improved against it, much less will their silence have any force to explode it; and yet after all, in Eccl. xlvii. 18, Solomon is admired for his Songs, Proverbs, and Parables.

VI. He urges, page 25, that "Philo, the eminent Alexandrian Jew, who was not contemporary with Christ and his earliest apostles, and who was prodigiously fond of mystical or allegorical senses of Scripture, does yet never cite nor allude to this book of Canticles, nor to any part of it, on any occasion whatsoever." Be it so, that it is not once cited or alluded to in his writings; for though they are voluminous, there are but few citations of Scripture in them; yet it does not follow from thence that it must be spurious. Many books in the canon of Scripture, whose authority is unquestionable, would yet stand upon a very precarious foundation, if citations out of them and allusions to them in human writings, were absolutely necessary to their continuance in it.

VII. What he lays a considerable stress upon, and makes the main foundation for the exclusion of this book, is, that Josephus not only neither cites nor alludes to it, but has also left it out in his catalogue of the sacred writings. That he should neither cite nor allude unto it, in writing a history, need not be wondered at; but if it can be made to appear that it is not to be found in his catalogue, it will indeed be a considerable objection against it. Now the account which Josephus[o] gives of the sacred writings among the Jews is only this, namely, that they had only two-and-twenty books, five of which are books of Moses, thirteen written by the prophets, and the other four contained holy hymns and moral precepts. Now in this account he seems to have regard to the division of books of the Old Testament into three parts,[p] used by the Jews; which was first, the Law; secondly, the Prophets; and thirdly, the Hagiographa; which our Lord also takes notice of, Luke xxiv. 44, where he saith, *These are the words which I spake unto you, while I was yet with you, that all things must be fulfilled, which were written in the law of Moses, and in the Prophets, and in the Psalms, concerning me;* where by the Psalms is meant the whole third part called the Hagiographa, because it began with that book; which also contained the most plain and manifest testimonies, of the person, office, and sufferings of Christ; more than any other book in that part did. Now the order of the books, according to this division of them, which Josephus had a regard to, was this, namely,

In the Law, which was the first division, stood

---

[o] Contr. Apion. l. 1.
[p] Buxtorf. Tiberias, c. 11.

These are the five books of Moses, according to Josephus.
1. Genesis.
2. Exodus.
3. Leviticus.
4. Numbers.
5. Deuteronomy.

In the Prophets, which was the second division, stood

These are the thirteen books of the prophets, according to Josephus.
1. Joshua.
2. Judges, with Ruth; which make but one book.
3. Samuel I. and II. but one book, hence Samuel is called a prophet, Acts xiii. 20.
4. Kings I. and II. but one book.
5. Isaiah.
6. Jeremiah, with the Lamentations, but one book.
7. Ezekiel.
8. Daniel.
9. The twelve minor prophets, but one book. See Mark i. 2, Acts vii. 42.
10. Job.
11. Ezra and Nehemiah, but one book.
12. Esther.
13. Chronicles I. and II. but one book.

In the Hagiographa, which was the third division, stood

These are the four books containing holy hymns and moral precepts, according to Josephus.
1. Psalms.
2. Proverbs.
3. Ecclesiastes.
4. Solomon's Song; in all twenty-two.

From hence it appears, that there is no force in this objection; nor has Mr. Whiston any reason to charge Dean Prideaux with forcing this book of Solomon's Song into Josephus's catalogue; for his twenty-two books cannot be made up without it; though the Dean had no manner of reason to leave out the book of Chronicles, seeing Ezra and Nehemiah, which he makes to be two books, are comprehended in one by the Jews, which he himself also observes.ᵃ The Jews indeed, at this present time, reckon the books of the Old Testament to be twenty-four, and that by making Ruth, which is a continuation of the history of the book of Judges and the Lamentations, which were written by Jeremy, and so properly belong to him, two books distinct by themselves; and even in this account of theirs of the sacred writings, this book of Canticles keeps its place, nor did they ever pretend to exclude it.

VIII. Another argument used by Mr. Whiston,

page 29, is, "our blessed Saviour himself does never once make the least allusion to this book, or to any part of it, on any occasion whatsoever." To this I reply, that it appears plain and manifest, that several phrases used by our Saviour bear a near resemblance with, are allusions to, and seem to be taken out of this book: thus the efficacious grace of God is expressed by drawing, John vi. 44, agreeable to Cant. i. 4. In his discourse with Nicodemus, he compares the Holy Spirit to the wind, John iii. 8, which metaphor is used, Cant. iv. 16; likewise he seems manifestly to allude in Matt. xiii. 52, where *the instructed Scribe* is said to bring forth *things new and old*, to Cant. vii. 13; where the very phrase is used: as also his comparing the church to a *vineyard*, and *letting it out* to husbandmen, are very agreeable to, and are the very phrases used, Cant. viii. 11, 12. To all which might be added, several other resemblances and allusions, which are to be found in the evangelic history, as Matt. xxv. 1, 5, compared with Cant. v. 2, and Matt. ix. 13, John iii. 29; where Christ is called *the bridegroom*, and the disciples *the children of the bride-chamber*, agreeable to the several parties in this song.

IX. He says, page 30, that "when St John, the beloved disciple, came at the end of his Revelation, to this very matter of *the marriage of the Lamb*, or Messias; yet have we not a word of it; that is, this book, nor the least allusion to it, nor to any part of it, whatsoever." That John, in his book of Revelation, refers and alludes to this of Solomon's song, seems undeniable; every one may easily observe what a likeness and resemblance there is between the description which the spouse gives of her beloved in Cant. v. and that which John gives of Christ in Rev. i. Moreover, the phrase of Christ's *standing at the door, and knocking*, Rev. iii. 20, manifestly refers unto, and plainly appears to be taken out of Cant. v. 2; where the spouse says, *It is the voice of my beloved that knocketh, saying, Open to me*, &c. Besides, what John says of the marriage of the Lamb, and the preparation of the bride for it; if it is not an allusion to, yet it is a confirmation of what is said in this book, where the church is represented as beautifully arrayed and adorned, and as passionately wishing for the consummation of the marriage; nay, this is spoken of as completed, Cant. ii. 16; and the glory and pomp of the solemnity described, Cant. iii. 11; with the joy that was expressed on that occasion: for there the *day of his espousals* is called *the day of the gladness of his heart;* also it deserves our notice, that those two books of Revelation and Solomon's Song, conclude much in the same manner. John closes his book of the Revelation, and with it the canon of the scriptures, with a passionate wish for Christ's second coming, saying, *Amen: even so, come, Lord Jesus;* and the church concludes the book of Solomon's Song thus: *Make haste, my beloved, and be thou like*

ᵃ Connexion of the history of the Old and New Testament, part. 1. book 5. p. 332. 8vo.

to a roe, or to a young hart upon the mountains of spices.

X. As what he thinks will much prejudice the authority of this book, he says, page 30, that "the writers of the known books of the New Testament, with their earliest companions, the apostolical fathers of the first century; St. Matthew, St. John, St. Peter, St. Paul, St. Mark, St. Luke, St. James, St. Jude, St. Clement in his epistles, St. Barnabas, that prodigious allegorizer, and St. Hermas; I may add, says he, and St. Polycarp also, one of their later companions, do never once cite or allude to this book of Canticles, or to any part of it, on any occasion whatsoever." That the evangelists, Matthew and John, either in using their own, or in recording the words of Christ, have alluded to some passages in this book, I have already shown: and the same may be said of the other evangelists, Mark and Luke, who mention several of the very same things; for which see Mark ii. 19, 20, and xii. 1, Luke v. 34, 35, and xx. 9; and it seems very evident, the apostle Paul has reference to it in many passages of his writings, as will appear from comparing 2 Cor. ii. 14, 15, 16, Eph. v. 2, with Cant. i. 3, as also Col. ii. 16, 17, Heb. x. 1, with Cant. ii. 17, and iv. 6, to which may be added Eph. v. 27, compared with Cant. iv. 7. So that seeing there are so many passages in several of the writers of the known books of the New Testament, which bear so near a resemblance, and have so manifest an allusion to some parts of this book, it need not much concern us that Clement, Barnabas, Hermas, and Polycarp take no notice of it.

XI. What he thinks will much prejudice the authority of this book, is, "that the Apostolical Constitutions give no manner of reason to suppose that this book of Canticles was then looked upon as a book of scripture, but the direct contrary." Now those books called The Constitutions of the Apostles, by Clement, Mr. Whiston looks upon to be truly authentic and apostolical; when they appear manifestly to be spurious, entirely destitute of apostolical authority, are of a much later date than the times of the apostles, and contain several things and doctrines directly opposite unto them. As for nstance, praying with the face to the east is enjoined, l. 2, c. 57, and l. 7, c. 44. Trigamy is asserted to be an indication of incontinency; and such marriages as are beyond the third, are called manifest fornication, and unquestionable uncleanness, l. 3, c. 2. Anointing with oil in baptism is enjoined, l. 3, c. 15, 16, and l. 7, c. 27, 41, 42. The keeping of the day of Christ's nativity, Epiphany, the Quadragesima, or Lent, the feast of the passover, and the festivals of the apostles, l. 5, c. 13, and l. 8, c. 33. Fasting on the fourth and sixth days of the week. l. 5, c. 15. Baptizing of infants, l. 6, c. 15. Singing for the dead, and honouring of their relics, l. 6, c. 30. Nay, praying for saints departed, l. 8, c. 41, 42, 43, 44. As also crossing with the sign of the cross in the forehead, l. 8, c. 12. Moreover the Lord's Supper is called an unbloody sacrifice, l. 8, c. 23, and l. 8, c. 5, 46. It is likewise asserted, that Christ, in the celebration of that ordinance, mixed wine and water in the cup, l. 8, c. 12. Nay, concubines, continuing so, are allowed an admittance to a participation of that sacred ordinance, l. 8, c. 32; with many other things which appear foreign enough from the simplicity of the apostolic age, doctrine, and practice. And now who that reads and considers these things, will ever think that those writings can furnish out an argument sufficient to prejudice the authority of the book of Solomon's Song? Had anything been said in them, which was expressly against it, it would scarce have deserved consideration, much less should their silence about it be improved as an evidence against it. And yet after all, it is pretty to observe how much Mr. Whiston himself is foiled with two passages in them, which appear to be allusions and references to a passage in this book: the one is in l. 6, c. 13; where the false apostles are called ἀλωπέκων μερίδες καὶ χαμαιζήλων ἀμπελώνων ἀφανσταὶ, *the portion of foxes, and the spoilers of the low vineyards.* And again in the same book, c. 18: where those same persons are said to *spoil the church of God*, ὡς ἀλώπεκες μικροὶ ἀμπελῶνας, *as the little foxes do the vineyards;* which are manifest references to Cant. ii. 1; and over-against the latter of which passages Mr. Whiston himself has placed this text as referring to it in the edition of the Constitutions which he has published. Now to evade the force of this, he is obliged to make this part of the work to be of a later date than the rest, even later than the destruction of Jerusalem; lest this book of Canticles should appear to have obtained authority too early in the world. He acknowledges that it is in the catalogue of the sacred writings mentioned in the Canons of the Apostles, Can. 85; which he looks upon to be genuine and authentic, though he questions its being in the original copies of those Canons; he allows, that Ignatius, in his larger epistle to the Ephesians, cites Cant. i. 3, 4; and is very willing to grant it a place in Melito's catalogue, which I have before mentioned: so that from the whole it appears, that the Apostolical Constitutions are so far from making against the authority of this book, that they rather make for it; though their testimony is good for nothing, the whole being a spurious work, and carries in it evident marks of falsehood and impiety, and was condemned as false and heretical by the sixth general synod held at Constantinople,ʳ about the year 680.

ʳ Vide Carranzæ Summ. Concil. Conc. Constantinop. 6. Can. 2. ˢ Since I wrote this, I have met with an answer to these arguments of Mr. Whiston by the very learned Carpzovius, Professor of Divinity in the University of Leipseck, published in his Critica Sacra, par. 3, which was printed in the year 1728, the same year my Eposition of this Book first came out. In the year 1729 was published a translation of the Critica Sacra into English, so far as it is concerned with Mr. Whiston, by Moses Marcus, a converted Jew.

Thus have I considered the several arguments and objections produced by Mr. Whiston to disprove the sacred authority of this book, which, notwithstanding, appears to have a divine stamp upon it.[s] There is one objection more made against it, which I think Mr. Whiston has taken no notice of, and that is, that no proper name of God is to be found in this Song. To which I reply, in the words of Mr. Durham;[t] 1. "That it is so also in other scriptures, as in the book of Esther; the scripture's authority doth not depend on naming the name of God, but on having his warrant and authority. 2. This Song being allegorical and figurative it is not so meet nor consistent with its stile, to have God named under proper names, as in other scriptures: Yet, 3. There are titles and descriptions here given to an excellent person, which can agree to none other but Christ, the eternal Son of God: as, *The King; O thou whom my soul loveth; the chief of ten thousands; the Rose of Sharon,* and the like; whereby his eminency is singularly set out above all others in the world." And yet after all, the name of God, Jah, the same with Jehovah, and a contraction of that, is mentioned in it, which is the greatest of the divine names, and is expressive of the being, eternity, and immutability of God. It is in chap. viii. 6, שלהבתיה, *the flame of God,* or *Jehovah,* which we render *a most vehement flame*; the sense being increased by the word Jah being added, as the word God to *mountains* and *cedars,* in Psal. xxxvi. 6, and lxxx. 10 ; for these are not one word, as Ben Asher thinks ; but two, according to Ben Naphtali and Aben Ezra; see the exposition of the place.

Since the second edition of this Exposition was published in 1751, I have met with two learned gentlemen; I am sorry for it, and that I am obliged to take notice of them, who think that this book is of a later date than the times of Solomon, and so of course none of his, and which must sap the authority of it. The one observes,[u] that the word David, from its first appearance in Ruth, where it is written דוד, without the yod, continues to be so written through the books of Samuel, Kings, Psalms, Proverbs, Isaiah, Jeremiah, and Ezekiel, but appears with a yod דויד, in the books of Chronicles, Ezra, Nehemiah, and Zechariah; wherefore he suggests, that if it was customary to write this word without a yod till the captivity, and with one after it; then he thinks a strong argument may be drawn from hence against the antiquity of the Canticles, and its being made by Solomon, since this name is written with a yod in Cant. iv. 5 ; the only place in it in which it is used. But in answer to this, it must be said, it is not fact that the word is universally used without the yod in the books mentioned, particularly in the book of Kings : for the authors of the Masorah have observed on 1 Kings iii. 14, that it is five times written full, as they call it, that is, with a yod, דויד, three of the places in the book of Kings I have traced out, 1 Kings iii. 14, and xi. 4, 36 ; and have found it so written in all the printed copies I have seen ; and so it is read by the Eastern Jews in Ezek. xxxvii. 24 ; and in several printed editions of Ezek. xxxiv. 23. This learned man is aware that it is so written once in Hosea, and twice in Amos ; books written two hundred years before the captivity ; but then he observes that in the two last places in Bomberg's edition it has a little circle (o) to mark it for an error, or a faulty word, though none over the word in Hosea: But it should be known, that that circle in hundreds of places is not used to point out any thing faulty in the copy, but is only a mark referring to the margin, and to what is observed there: and be it, that it does point out an error or a faulty word, the same circle is over the word in Canticles, and consequently shows it to be faulty there, and to be corrected and read without the yod, which observation destroys the argument from it; and so it is read in that place in the Talmud[w] without it, and in the ancient book of Zohar ;[x] and indeed it seems as if it was read without the yod in the copies seen by the authors of the Masorah, since in their note on 1 Kings iii. 14 besides the five places where it is written full, or with the yod, they say it is so written throughout the Chronicles, the twelve minor prophets, and Ezra, which includes Nehemiah, but make no mention of Solomon's Song; which one would think they would have done, had it been so written there in the copy or copies before them : so that upon the whole, the argument, if it has any force in it, turns out for, and not against the antiquity of Solomon's Song. But this matter stands in a clearer light by observing the larger Masorah on 1 Kings xi. 4, and on Ezek. xxxiv. 23, in which the five places are mentioned where this word is written full, 1 Kings iii. 14, and xi. 4, 36, Cant. iv. 4, Ezek. xxxiv. 23 ; in which places this word was originally so written, as well as throughout Chronicles, the twelve prophets, and Ezra ; so that in all these places it is marked not as a faulty word, but as rightly written, though different from what it is in other places. The other learned man,[y] forms his argument from the use of the word שלהבת, in Job xv. 30, and in this Song, chap. viii. 6, his words are, "I am much deceived if this word be not a strong proof of the age of this poem, (the book of Job) for it is not found but in Ezekiel and the Song of Solomon, the one written during the captivity, and the other after it." This proceeds upon a false piece of criticism in a twofold respect; for he adds, "its construction which is evidently ש for אשר, and להבת, the constructive form of להבה, *flamma,* shows very clearly its age ; since that manner of abbreviation is not found in the books undoubtedly written before the captivity." For 1st, this abbreviation appears in books much more

---

[t] In Clav. Cant. p. 5.   [u] Dr Kennicot, Dissert. 1. p. 20, &c.   [w] T. Bab. Beracot. fol. 30. 1.   [x] In Gen. fol. 114. 3.   [y] Heath, Comment. on Job xv. 30.

ancient than that not only in the book of Solomon's Song, the antiquity of which is not only to be set aside by this observation, but frequently in the book of Ecclesiastes, undoubtedly written by Solomon, and in the Psalms of David his father before him; for it is not only in psalms without a title, all which are supposed by some to be David's, as in Psalm cxxix. 6, 7, cxxxv. 2, 8, 10, cxxxvi. 23, and cxlvi. 5; but also in psalms which bear his name, as in Psal. cxxii. 3, 4, cxxiv. 2, 6, cxxx. iii. 2, 3, and cxliv. 15; yea, it was in use long before the times of David, even in the times of the Judges. Deborah has it in her song, עד שקמתי שקמתי, Judges v. 7, and in other places in that book, chap. vi. 17, and vii. 12, and viii. 29. 2ndly. It is a mistake that the construction of the word שלהבת, is ש for אשר, and להבת; for ש in that word is not servile but radical, as Aben Ezra and Ben Melech observe; it is an addition to the Hebrew word after the Chaldee manner, and its derivation from a root in the Chaldee or Syriac language, שלהב, which signifies to *kindle, inflame*, and *burn*, as appears, not only from all the Syriac and Chaldee Lexicons, but from the frequent use of the word in the Syriac version of the Old Testament; nor is this the only Chaldee or Syriac word in Solomon's Song; see chap. i. 17, and ii. 11. Though perhaps as this writer from[a] the Chaldaisms, Syriasms, and Arabisms in the book of Job, argues its being a production of a later age than what is usually assigned to it; so another of the same way of thinking and reasoning may conclude from some Chaldee words used in Solomon's Song, that it must be of a later age than his: but why may not Solomon be thought to make use of Chaldee or Syriac words as well as his father David, who makes use of words in the Syriac signification of them, as in Psal. li. 4, compared with Rom. iii. 4, and Psal. lx. 4, and with Syro-chaldaic affixes, Psal. ciii. 3, 4, 5, and cxv. 7, 10? and why may not David and Solomon be thought to understand Chaldee or Syriac as well as Hezekiah's courtiers? see 2 Kings xviii. 26; and certainly Solomon must understand it, if what is said of him is true, though I lay no stress upon it, that he wrote the book of Wisdom in the Chaldee language,[a] though not by inspiration. Moreover, since the Hebrew, Chaldee, Syriac, Arabic, &c., are supposed to be dialects of the same language, why may not a word in one dialect less frequently used in a book appear in it without determining the age of it? since one dialect may be as early or nearly as early as another, and can be no evidence of a book being of a later production than is generally thought, or of it being written when the purity of the Hebrew language began to decline, and after the dispersion of the Jews throughout the East, when it began to receive a taint of the other dialects, as this writer suggests; for what taint of the other dialects, as he calls it, did the Hebrew language receive in the captivity, and by the dispersation of the Jews? what appearance is there of Chaldaisms, Syriasms, &c., in the book of Haggai, Zechariah, and Malachi, excepting the names of the months, books written after the captivity, more than in any books before, or even so much? are they not written in as pure Hebrew as any of those books, which may be thought to be written when that language was in its greatest purity? and if so, a few words in another dialect here and there in a book, is no rule to judge of a book by, and determine the age of it. Upon the whole, it is irresistibly clear, that the sacred and divine authority of this book remains firm and unshaken, notwithstanding the above objections made against it; nor is there any reason for persons to scruple it, much less to reject it from the canon of the scriptures, nor to question in the least the antiquity and authenticity of it. I proceed,

Secondly. To consider the nature and subject of this book; it being a *Song* in which the bride and bridegroom, with their friends and companions, and daughters of Jerusalem, bear their several parts; and it being a divine song, is, no doubt, intended for the glorifying of Christ, the cheering and refreshing of his church, and also the edification of others; for it is the duty of saints to be *teaching* and *admonishing one another in psalms, and hymns, and spiritual songs; singing with grace in* their *hearts to the Lord*. I shall not enter into the consideration of the controversy, whether singing of the praises of God vocally, is an ordinance to be used under the New Testament, though I firmly believe it to be so; nay, that it is one of the most noble, and most glorious branches of religious worship, it being that which comes nearest to the employment of saints in a glorified state; and what requires a great deal of light, knowledge, experience, faith, and love to perform in a right way and manner; nor shall I need to observe those several cases of conscience concerning singing, which have a very good solution from this song; such as these, namely, whether the distressed cases of God's children may be sung, or they sing when in distressed circumstances: whether complaints of their sins, failings and infirmities, may be put into their songs: whether cases different from theirs, yea, such as they have not attained unto, may be sung; as also whether it is lawful to sing the praises of God in mixed assemblies; all which may be answered in the affirmative, and for which this song affords a sufficient foundation; the church here bringing her sorrows and distresses into this song as well as her comforts and privileges, chap. i. 6, and iii. 1, and v. 7, nay, her sins and failings, chap. i. 5, 6, and v. 2, 3, 4. Very different cases are also here sung; yea, such, which, if taken in a strict sense, she had not fully attained to, as in chap. viii. 12. Moreover, she sings in the presence of, and joins with the virgins, and daughters of Jerusalem, who seemed in a great measure to be ignorant of Christ.

---

[a] Preface, ibid. p. 11.

[a] R. Azarias, Imre Binah, c. 57. fol. 175. 2.

chap. v. 8, 9, and vi. 8, 9, 10; all which are largely and judiciously insisted upon by the excellent Mr. Durham, in his Exposition of this place, to which I refer the reader. I proceed more particularly to consider the nature and subject of this song; which,

1st. Is not a celebration of the amours between Solomon and Pharoah's daughter, which has been the opinion of some, as has been already observed; for there are some things in it which are spoken of this bridegroom, which cannot be applied to Solomon, as that he was both a *king* and a *shepherd*, as in chap. i. 4, compared with v. 7, that he was his wife's brother, and she his sister, chap. v. 2, and viii. 1. Nor is it likely that Solomon would ever give such commendations of himself, as are mentioned in chap. v. 10, &c. There are also many things spoken of the bride, which by no means agree with Pharoah's daughter, as that she was *a keeper of the vineyards*, chap. i. 6, and yet *a prince's daughter*, chap. vii. 1; that she should be represented as running about the streets in the night, unattended, chap. iii. 2; and be exposed to the blows and contempt of the watchmen, chap. v. 7; besides, several of the descriptions here given of her, if taken in a literal sense, would rather make her appear to be a monster than a beauty, as chap. iv. 1—5, and chap. vii. 1—5; all which agree very well, when understood of Christ and his Church. Nor

2ndly. Is it typical, that is to say, this book does not express the amours and marriage of Solomon and Pharoah's daughter, as typical of that inexpressible love and marriage-union between Christ and his church; it is true, there is some resemblance between natural and spiritual marriage, as is manifest from Eph. v. 23, 24, 25, 29, 31, 32; nor is it altogether to be denied, that Solomon was a type of Christ, in some respects, in his marriage of that person; but that this book is an epithalamium, or nuptial song composed by him on that occasion, and that in such a manner, as at the same time also to be expressive of the love of Christ to his church, must be denied; for Solomon's marriage with Pharoah's daughter was at least twenty years before this book was written, as appears from chap. vii. 4; where mention is made of the *tower of Lebanon*, by which seems to be meant, *the house of the forests of Lebanon*, or some tower near unto it; now he was seven years in building the temple, 1 Kings vi. 38, and thirteen more in building the temple, 1 Kings vii. 1, after which he built this, v. 2. From hence it may be reasonably concluded, that this book was not penned on any such occasion; for Solomon would never write a nuptial song twenty years after his marriage, which should have been sung the same night he was married. M. Bossuet[b] has an ingenious conjecture, though it seems to be without a solid foundation, that whereas the nuptial feast with the Hebrews was kept seven days, this song is to be distributed into seven parts, a part to be sung on each day during the celebration. The first day, chap. i. ii. 6; the second day, chap. ii. 7—17; the third day, chap. iii. v. 1; the fourth day, chap. v. 2—vi. 9; the fifth day, chap. vi. 10—vii. 11; the sixth day, chap vii. 12—viii. 3; the seventh day, chap. viii. 4—14. Nor,

3rdly. Is this book prophetic, expressing the state of the church and kingdom of Christ in the several ages of the world, with regard to particular historical facts and events, which had befel or should befal it, either under the Old or New Testament-dispensation; this way indeed go most of the Jewish interpreters, as the Targum, R. Solomon Jarchi, and R. Aben Ezra; who have been followed by many Christian writers, though with more judgment and greater regard to the analogy of faith, as well as to the times of the New Testament: and who consider this book as describing the state of the church of God, whether the church under the legal dispensation, from the times of David and Solomon; and before, and in, and after the captivity to the birth and death of Christ; or the church under the gospel-dispensation, in its beginning, progress, various changes, and consummation, as Brightman and Cotton. Others interpret this book as pointing to the several ages and periods of the Christian church, in agreement with the seven churches of Asia, as Cocceius, and those that follow him, Horchius, Hofman, and Hennischius; which last writer makes this distribution of them : 1. The church at Ephesus, Cant. i. 5—17; from the ascension of Christ to heaven, A. C. 33, to 370. 2. The church at Smyrna, Cant. ii. 1—17, from A.C. 371 to 707. 3. The church at Pergamos, Cant. iii. 1—11, from A. C. 708 to 1045. 4. The church at Thyatira, Cant. iv. 1, to chap. v. 1, from A. C. 1046 to 1383. 5. The church at Sardis, Cant. v. 2, to chap. vi. 8, from A. C. 1384 to 1721. 6. The church at Philadelphia, Cant. vi. 9, to chap. vii. 14, from A. C. 1722 to 2059. 7. The church at Laodicea, Cant. viii. 1—14, from A. C. 2060, and onwards. But hereby the book is made liable to arbitrary, groundless, and uncertain conjectures, as well as its usefulness for the instruction and consolation of believers, in a great measure, is laid aside; for then such and such parts of it, which regard the church and believers, in such an age or period of time, can only be applied to them that lived at that time, and not to others; whereas all, and every part of this song, the first as well as the last, is applicable to believers in all ages of the world, which is a manifest proof that it cannot be historical, or prophetical. But

4thly. The whole is figurative and allegorical, abounding with a variety of lively metaphors, and allusions to natural things; and so may be illustrated by the various things of nature, from whence the metaphors are taken, and to which the allusions be, and by the language and behaviour of

---

[b] *Vide* Lowth. de Sacr. Poef. Heb. Prælect. 30. p. 393, 394. and Not. Michael. in ibid. p. 156—159.

natural lovers to each other, and which are to be observed in love-poems, though here expressed more decently and beautifully. This divine poem sets forth in a most striking manner the mutual love, union, and communion, which are between Christ and his church; also expresses the several different frames, cases, and circumstances which attend believers in this life; so that they can come into no state or condition, but here is something in this song suited to their experience: which serves much to recommend it to believers, and discovers the excellency of it. Which,

Thirdly. Comes next to be considered, it being called the *Song of songs*, for this reason, because it is the most excellent of songs; so the *holy of holies* is used for the most holy, and the *King of kings* and *Lord of lords*, for the greatest King and chiefest Lord. This song is more excellent than all human songs; there is no comparison between them, either in the subject, stile, or manner of composition: it has the ascendant of all those thousand and five songs which Solomon himself made, of which we read 1 Kings iv. 32, nay, is preferable to all scriptural songs; the subject of it being wholly and purposely the love of Christ to his church; its style is lovely and majestic; the manner of its composition neat and beautiful; and the matter of it full and comprehensive, being suited to all believers, and their several cases: This song indeed contains all others in it, and has nothing wanting and deficient therein. The Jews say in their ancient book of Zohar,[c] that "this song comprehends the whole law; the whole work of the creation; the secret of the fathers; the captivity of Egypt, and the coming out of Israel from thence; the song that was sung at the sea; the covenant of mount Sinai; the journey of the Israelites through the wilderness; their entrance into the land of Canaan; the building of the temple; the crown of the holy name; the captivity of Israel among the nations, and their redemption; the resurrection of the dead; and the sabbath of the Lord, which is, and which was, and which is to come."

Fourthly. The author or penman of this song is said to be Solomon; *the Song of songs, which is Solomon's*; that is, which is *of*, or *concerning* Solomon,[d] as the words may be rendered; and so respect the subject of this song, which is Christ, the true Solomon, of whom Solomon was an eminent type, as is at large shown in several particulars, on chap. iii. 7. Now it is he that this song treats of; the transcendent glories and excellencies of his person; his inexpressible love unto, care of, and concern for his church and people, together with the nearness of access unto and sweet communion and fellowship with himself, which he indulges them with, are here particularly expressed and set forth; so that it may well be called *the Song of songs, which is concerning* Solomon; though perhaps, the words may regard Solomon as the author and penman of it, who was used by the Holy Ghost as his amanuensis therein, which was no small honour to him; his wisdom, riches, and grandeur, did not set him above an employment of this nature; nay, his being concerned herein, was a greater honour to him than all the rest: and it may not be amiss to observe, that his royal title, as *king of Israel*, is here omitted, which yet is put at the beginning of both his other books, Proverbs and Ecclesiastes; the reason may be, either because such a title, expressive of majesty, would not as well have suited a *song of loves*; or else it is purposely omitted, lest he should be thought to be the *king*, so frequently spoken of in this song; or rather because that the subject of this song is *the King of kings*; and therefore, whilst he is speaking of *the things* which he had made, *touching the king*, he lays aside his own royal title, veils his majesty, and casts his crown at the feet of Him, by whom *kings reign*, and *princes decree justice*. The time of his writing this book does not appear very manifest; some think that he wrote it in his youthful days, the subject being love, and the manner of its writing being poetry, both which the youthful age mostly inclines to, and delights in; but it appears from what has been already said, that it was not written until twenty years after his marriage, when he could not be a very young man; and so might be written in the middle part of his life, when in the most flourishing circumstances as to body, mind, and estate. Dr. Lightfoot[e] is of opinion it might be written in the thirtieth year of his reign, about ten years before his death, after he had built his summer-house in Lebanon, to which he supposes he alludes in chap. iv. 8, and vii. 4; and upon his bringing Pharaoh's daughter to the house prepared for her, 1 Kings ix. 24. The Jewish chronologer[f] says, that the books of Proverbs, the Song of songs, and Ecclesiastes, were all written in his old age, as indeed the last seems to be; and perhaps he wrote this also a little before his death, after his fall and repentance, when he had had a larger discovery of the love of God unto his own soul, notwithstanding all his sins, failings, and infirmities; and so a proper person for the Holy Ghost to use in setting forth the greatness of Christ's love to his people, and the several different states, conditions, cases, and circumstances, which they are, at one time or another, brought into in this life, of which he had had a very great experience. But from the title, I shall now proceed to the consideration of the book itself; which thus begins,

Verse 2. *Let him kiss me with the kisses of his mouth; for thy love* is *better than wine.*

HAVING considered the title, now follows the song itself, which begins with these words; and it

---

[c] In Exod. fol. 59. col. 3. [d] לשלמה de Solomone Cocceius. so Midrash in loc. [e] See his works, vol. 1. p. 76. [f] In Seder Olam Rabba, c. 15. p. 41. so Shir Hashirim, fol. 3. 3.

being dialogue-wise, where several parties are concerned, and do interchangeably speak, it will be therefore necessary, in order to explain them, to consider,

I. Who the person is that speaks and begins the song.

II. To whom this speech is directed.

III. The nature of the request that is made. And,

IV. The reason of it.

I. Let us consider who the person is that speaks; it appears clearly to be the church and bride of Christ, who here begins and continues speaking to ver. 8. She first directs her speech to Christ, in this and the two following verses; in ver. 5, 6, she turns herself to the daughters of Jerusalem; and then again to Christ, in ver. 7, she begins the song, which,

1st. Does not suppose that she was first in her love to Christ: she was not beforehand with him, neither in her love, nor in the expressions, and manifestations of it; for he had loved her with an everlasting love, and therefore had thus sweetly *drawn* her with the *bands of love*, to himself. Christ is first, both in his love and in the discovery of it; for *we love him because he first loved us*; it is the manifestation of Christ's love to our souls, which causes us to love him again, and in some way or other to show it.

2ndly. Neither does it suppose, that her love to Christ, and desires of his presence and company, were more ardent than his were to her; for as Christ's love is prior to ours, so it far exceeds, and is much superior to it; neither can believers be more desirous of Christ's company than he is of theirs. But,

3rdly. It shows that she was impatient of delay, and could not bear his absence any longer; she was sick of love; for *hope deferred maketh the heart sick*; she had, perhaps, been hoping, waiting for, and expecting his presence a considerable time, and he was not come; therefore growing impatient, breaks out in this abrupt manner, *Let him kiss, &c.*, or, " Oh, that he would kiss me with one of the kisses of his mouth! I cannot be easy unless he does."

4thly. She speaks as one who had had experience of Christ's love; she knew how sweet the kisses of his mouth were, and how delightful his company had been to her in time past; she had *tasted that the Lord was gracious*; and therefore was so earnestly desirous of the returns of these love-visits, venting her heart and soul in these passionate wishes and desires. And,

5thly. Though Christ gives the first discoveries of love on his part; yet when the church is espoused unto him, it highly becomes her to show an affectionate regard unto him, and strong desire after his company.

II. It will be proper to take notice of the person to whom this speech is directed, and that is Christ; and the form of speech here used, is also worthy our regard; here is no particular mention made of any person; no one particularly named, whose company she desired; but only *him, let him kiss me, &c.*, it is a relative without an antecedent, of which we have many instances in scripture, as Ps. lxxxvii. 1, Isa. liii. 2, Lam. iii. 1, unless we suppose that the antecedent to it is Solomon, in ver. 1, *let him*, that is, Solomon, or Christ, who is Solomon's antitype, whose song this is, and who is the subject of it: *Let him*, I say, *kiss me with the kisses of his mouth*; though the connection seems rather to be with the thoughts of her heart, than with any words before expressed: she had had him so much in her thoughts, and her love was so fixed on him, she knew him so well, and had had so much converse with him, that she thought there was no need to mention his name; but that every one must very well know who she designed; as Mary Magdalen, at Christ's sepulchre, when Jesus said unto her, "Woman, why weepest thou? whom seekest thou?" she supposing him to be the gardener, saith unto him, "Sir, if thou have borne him hence, tell me where thou hast laid him, and I will take him away," John xx. 15. Suppose he had been the gardener, how should he have known who this *him* was she meant? But she was much in the same frame as the church is here, who speaks of Christ as if there was no other in the world besides him; and indeed he is a *nonsuch*, the most eminent person in the world, in the believer's esteem; whose language is, Whom have I in heaven but thee? and there is none upon earth that I desire besides thee," Psal. lxxiii. 25. Christ then is the person here spoken of, whom she intends, and to whom she directs her speech.

III. Having taken notice of the person speaking, and to whom this speech is directed, we will now consider the request itself, which is here made, " Let him kiss me," *&c.*, and this may be considered, either,

First. As the request of the church under the Old Testament. And that,

1st. For the manifestation of Christ in the flesh; than which nothing was more passionately longed for, and earnestly desired; many kings and prophets greatly desired it; yea, all the Old Testament saints did more or less pray, as David did, " O that the salvation of Israel were come out of Zion," Psal. xiv. 7, and this they were so vehemently desirous of, because they knew hereby redemption from all evil would be obtained, the curse removed, and all spiritual blessings procured for them; Christ's incarnation being, like kisses, a pledge and indication of his love, was very desirable to the church, and as appears by her expressions, would be exceeding grateful to all those who were " waiting for the consolation of Israel." He had sent his prophets, and by them had spoken unto her " at sundry times, and in divers manners;" yet she is not easy and contented herewith, but would have greater displays of his grace, by his appearing in his own person to kiss her with the kisses of his mouth.

2ndly. For the doctrines of the Gospel, in opposition to the law. Most of the Jewish[s] writers understand, by the kisses of his mouth, the words of the law, which God spake to the people face to face; but that dispensation was not so desirable a one; for "they that heard that voice of words, entreated that the word should not be spoken to them any more; for they said unto Moses, Speak thou with us, and we will hear; but let not God speak with us, lest we die," Exod. xx. 19. The words of the law contain sharp and severe rebukes for sin; pronounce the sinner guilty before God; curse and condemn him, and are the killing letter to him; therefore these are not the kisses of Christ's mouth, which the church here desires; but rather they are the sweet and comfortable doctrines of the Gospel, which may be so called.

1. Because they come from him; they are the words of his mouth, which drop from him "like sweet smelling myrrh;" he is the author of them, he has spoken and delivered them; they proceed alone from him, and it is he that owns, blesses, and makes them useful to men.

2. As kisses they carry in them intimations of his love to souls, to whom they come "in power, and in the Holy Ghost;" the love of Christ is the great subject of the Gospel; it fills all the doctrines thereof, which give a noble display of it, and lead into a farther acquaintance with it.

3. As the kisses of a friend, they are grateful and acceptable to believers; they are more valuable to them than their necessary food, and are preferred by them to all that is dear in life, yea, to life itself, however they are slighted and despised by the men of the world.

4. As kisses, they raise the affections and fill the soul with love to Christ; kisses, as they are indications of, so they are incentives to love. When the truths of the Gospel come with power upon a sinner's heart, they let in, not only a great deal of light, but also a large measure of love; faith comes hereby, and that works by love, both to Christ and to his Gospel. Or,

Secondly. We may consider this request as the request of the church, or of every particular believer, for the enjoyments and manifestations of Christ's love is very desirable to believers, who would always have it if they could; this is their heaven on earth, and the beginning of glory to them; this comforts them in all their troubles, and is preferred by them to all earthly enjoyments, and may be called the kisses of Christ's mouth.

1st. Because kisses are evidences and pledges of love amongst nearest relations: Christ stands in and fills up all relations to his people, and has affections for them suitable to them all; he is a kind and indulgent father, a tender husband,

an affectionate brother, and loving friend; of all which he has given, and continues to give, full and incontestible proofs; of which the kisses of his mouth are plain and undeniable evidences.

2ndly. Kisses are tokens of reconciliation and agreement. Now though reconciliation is made by the blood of Christ, and believers have the comfortable application of it to their souls; yet every time that Christ withdraws his presence from them, they are ready to think that he is angry with them, and is not reconciled unto them; but when he shows himself again, and manifests his love, then they can behold him, and God in him, as reconciled unto them.

3rdly. Kisses are incentives to love: there is nothing raises believers' love higher to Christ, than the flowing in of his love into their souls; this warms it when cold and chill, raises it to a flame, quickens it when dull, puts it in motion, and sets it at work.

4thly. By this expression the church intends that nearness and familiarity in communion with Christ, which her soul wanted; which was not only to show himself to her, feed and feast her, and take his walks with her; by all which phrases communion with Christ is sometimes expressed; but to be kissed with the kisses of his mouth, which is yet nearer still: well may the saints be said to be "a people near to the Lord;" what wondrous and surprising grace is this, that Christ should condescend to kiss such vile and sinful creatures as we are! to receive us into such near communion with himself! It is a bold request the church makes, and yet she is in it no bolder than welcome. These are called *kisses*, in the plural number.

1. To show the various ways Christ has to manifest his love, sometimes by one providence, and sometimes by another! sometimes in one ordinance and sometimes in another; he is not tied to one way, but has divers ways, and makes use of various means to show himself unto his people; he is never at a loss when he thinks fit to do it.

2. To denote the frequent and repeated actings of his love to her soul which she was desirous of; she was for having, not one kiss, but many; one discovery and manifestation of his love and grace after another; yea, many visits from him, until she arrived to the full enjoyment of his love, with himself, in glory. Or,

3. The words may be read thus, *Let him kiss me with* one of *the kisses of his mouth.*[b] See chap. iv. 9; and then the sense is, "O that I had but one glimpse, one view, one discovery more of his love and grace unto my soul, but one kiss more from his mouth, which *is most sweet, and altogether lovely;* how great a satisfaction would it be to me, could I have but this request granted!" which way of speaking shows how exceeding grateful the manifestations of Christ's love are to believers. Moreover it may be observed, that

---

[s] Midrash, Targum, R. Sol. Jarchi, and R. Aben Ezra, in loc.

[b] מנשיקות פיהו uno tantum, vel altero de osculis oris sui, Michaelis; so Gusset. Comment. Heb. p. 446.

kisses with the ancients were not frequent, but rarely used, and but *once* when persons were espoused, and as a token of that; and then they were reckoned as husband and wife; on which account it may be it is here desired; since it was after this we hear of the spouse being brought into the nuptial chamber, and of the keeping of the nuptial feast, ver. 4—12. Again, These are also said to be the "kisses of his mouth;" which is not to be looked upon as a mere Hebraism, or as a redundancy in expression; but this heaping up of words shows,

1. The vehemency of her affection, how much her heart was set upon, and how eagerly desirous she was of communion with Christ; and therefore pours out words, that she might fully express her mind; "for out of the abundance of the heart, the mouth speaketh."

2. She mentions the kisses of "his mouth," in contradistinction to any other; she valued the kisses of no other mouth but Christ's: the kisses of any mouth were not desirable to her, none but the kisses of his mouth were.

3. She hereby expresses the singular satisfaction she should take herein; "Let him kiss me with the kisses of his mouth;" "his mouth, which is sweet and delightful to me; his mouth, whom my soul loves, whom I value and esteem above all others, and in the enjoyment of whom I place my chiefest happiness." Or,

4. It may point out that particular way and manner in which she was desirous that he would manifest his love unto her, that is, by his word of promise in the Gospel; as if she should say, "O that he would manifest himself, and break up his love and grace to my soul, in some kind promise or other, which may drop from his mouth, and be brought home unto me by the Spirit of grace."

Fourthly. She assigns a reason for this request, "for thy love is better than wine;" here is a sudden change of person, from the third to the second; before she said, "let him kiss me," &c., now she says, "for thy love," &c.; the reason of which, perhaps is, because he was absent before, but now present; she had lost sight of him, and speaks of him as at a distance from her; but now he is in view, at the very sight of whom her faith is increased, and her soul fired with love; and having greater nearness to him, grows in her familiarity and boldness with him.

Here we shall, 1. Take notice of the *love* of Christ, and give some account of the nature and excellency of it: And, 2. Show in what respects it is preferable to *wine*.

First, Let us consider this love of Christ, which is so highly commended by the church; in the Hebrew text it is in the plural number, loves,[k] to show,

1st. The various ways in which Christ has discovered it; he showed it by his suretyship-engagements for the elect in the everlasting covenant of grace and peace, of which he is the Surety, Mediator, and Messenger; he showed it in his assumption of human nature in time; he has given a full display of it in laying down his life for the sheep, in giving himself a ransom for many, and in offering himself a sacrifice for the sins of all his chosen ones; he has loved them and died for them, loved them and shed his precious blood for them, and in that blood has washed them from all their sins; he now shows that he loves them, by appearing in the presence of God for them, acting as an advocate with the Father, and preparing glory for them; and he will, ere long, come again to take them to himself, that where he is, there they may be also.

2rdly. It may intend the various effects of it; all the blessings of grace flow from it, such as vocation, sanctification, justification, adoption, and glorification: all spring from this boundless and matchless love of Christ.

3rdly. Being in the plural number, may denote the aboundings of it; it is superabounding love; love that has heights, and depths, and lengths, and breadths; it is immeasureable and inconceiveable; it passeth the perfect knowledge of men and angels.

4thly. The frequent discoveries of it, which are made to the saints: and which, like the waters in Ezekiel's vision, increase and rise from the ancles to the knees, and from the knees to the loins, and from thence become waters to swim in, a river, an ocean of love which cannot be passed over.

5thly. The great esteem the church had of Christ's love, which she shows by calling it "loves," in the plural number, as well as by saying that it was "better than wine:" the excellency of which will farther appear, if we consider the nature and properties of it, which are as follow:

1. As to the original of it, it is free and sovereign; it does not take its rise from any thing in us, or done by us; nothing of this nature moved him to it, but he loved us, because he would love us: nothing out of himself moved him to it; it was not because we were better than others, for we "are by nature children of wrath," even as others; he loved us when unlovely; he died for us while we were yet sinners, and ungodly in ourselves, and enemies to himself; our love to him is not the cause of his loving us, but his love to us is the cause of ours: in this he is entirely free and sovereign; he has pitched his love and grace on whom he will, and these he loves freely; he was not moved or influenced by foreseen faith or works, or any deserving of ours whatever; for we neither deserved nor desired his love, neither indeed could we have expected it.

2. As to the time of its commencement, it is from eternity; before the mountains were formed,

---

i Salmuth in Pancirol. Memorab. Rer. par. 1. tit. 46. p. 215.

k דודיך amores tui, Pagninus, Montanus, Junius and Tremellius, Piscator, &c.

and the highest part of the dust of the earth was made, he was " rejoicing in the habitable part of his earth, and his delights were with the sons of men ;" that he loved his people from eternity, is manifest from his engaging as a Surety for them ; his becoming the Mediator of an everlasting covenant; in which he agreed to take care of their persons, and by dying to redeem their lives from destruction, and to bring them to eternal glory ; as also from his receiving all grace for them before the world began ; all which manifestly show that he had a love for them, for all the after-actings of his love and grace are but the openings and breakings forth of this love of his, which he bore towards them from everlasting.

3. As to its duration, it is to eternity; " having loved his own, which were in the world, he loved them unto the end," John xiii. 1 ; his love is invariable, unalterable, and unchangeable: it is like himself, " the same yesterday, to-day, and for ever ;" all the waters of sin and corruption cannot extinguish it ; nor can any creature in heaven, earth, or hell, separate his people from it.

4. As to the degree of it, it is the greatest love, " greater love hath no man than this, that a man lay down his life for his friends, " John xv. 13 ; but Christ's love is greater than this, for he hath laid down his life for enemies, and even whilst they were such ; here is great love for great sinners, shown by a great person, one who " thought it no robbery to be equal with God ;" and this he showed by giving " himself a ransom" for them ; such is the greatness of this love, that it cannot fully be expressed by men or angels.

5. As to the quality of it, it is the nearest; that of the nearest relations and friends to each other, as of a parent to a child, of an husband to a wife, of brothers, or friends, to each other, are but faint resemblances and mere shadows of this; all fall short of painting and expressing to the life the nature of this love.

6. As to the pattern or form of it, it is as the Father's love to him ; " as the Father hath loved me; (says he) so have I loved you ;" John xv. 9 ; as the Father loves Christ, as Mediator, with an everlasting, unchangeable, and inseparable love, so does Christ love his people. What surprizing grace is this, that Christ should love us with such a love ; when there is no comparison between him, who is the object of the one, and them, who are the objects of the other ; when we contemplate this amazing love conceptions fail us to comprehend it, words fall short of expressing it; in eternity only will those surprising mysteries of grace be unfolded to us.

7. As to any instance of love, none can be compared with it, it is unparalleled ; that of Jonathan's to David, of one friend's dying for another, and of those brave Romans who died for their country, which history furnishes us withal, can by no means equal or come near it; *scarcely for a righteous man will one die, peradventure for a good man some would even dare to die*, says the apostle, Rom. v. 7, 8; where he alludes[1] to the division of the Jewish nation into three parts, which were these ; *First*, There were עדיקים, or righteous persons, who kept to the external letter of the law, and did, as they imagined, what that required, but would do no more. *Secondly*, There were others called חסידים, or good men, who were bountiful and liberal to the poor, and did more than the law required in repairing the temple and maintaining of sacrifices, &c. But, *Thirdly*, there were another sort who were called רשעים, or wicked or ungodly persons, who had no regard to the law, profligate wretches, the refuse of the people. Now for one of these righteous ones, says the apostle, scarce any would die, because what he had done, he was obliged by the law to do; peradventure for one of these good men, one to whom he had been kind and liberal, a person would even dare to die ; but who will die for the other sort, the wicked and ungodly? not one ; *but God commendeth his love towards us*, in *that while we were yet sinners, Christ died for us*; O matchless and unparalleled love !

8. As to its effect upon the hearts of sinners, it is surprising, comfortable, and rejoicing ; for souls, when but just let into it, begin that wonder which will last throughout an endless eternity; they now place an *ecce*, a *behold* before it, and say as the Jews did of Christ, in regard to Lazarus, *behold how he loved him*; O how has he loved me, and me! says one and the other; what manner of love is this! it is surprising, *wonderful, passing the love of women*, as David said concerning Jonathan's ; and it being *shed abroad* in the heart by the Spirit of God, fills the soul with an universal pleasure, *with a joy unspeakable and full of glory*; the manifestations and discovery of it bear up the soul under all the trials of life, and make it long to be in glory, that it may have its fill thereof, wherefore it is no wonder the church here prefers it to wine.

Secondly, We shall now consider. The church had a real value for Christ's person, and therefore must needs esteem his love; his person being, to her, the *chiefest among ten thousand*, his love must be preferable to all others; she hath tasted a real sweetness in it, and hath seen the vanity and emptiness of all earthly enjoyments, and therefore prefers it to wine ; by which is intended the most sumptuous banquet, with all the dainties, and delightful entertainments thereof: nothing is so valuable as the love of Christ ; *O how excellent is thy loving-kindness*, says the Psalmist, it is *better than life*, Psal. xxxvi. 7, and lxxiii. 3 ; and all the comforts, pleasures, and profits thereof. I will now endeavour to show, in a few particulars, wherein this love of Christ is *better than wine*.

---

[1] *Vide* Godwin's Moses and Aaron, l. 1. c. 9.

1st. It is preferable to it for its antiquity; good old wine is accounted the best; and therefore Christ says, *No man having drunk old wine, straightway desireth new: for he saith, the old is better*, Luke v. 39. Age makes wine better, but not oil, as Plutarch observes.[m] Now no wine is comparable to this of Christ's love, for its antiquity; for, as has been already shown, it is a love which commences from everlasting; it does not bear date with time, but was before time was, and will be when time shall be no more. The Jews[n] often speak of wine, that has been reserved in the grape ever since the creation of the world, which they imagine, they shall drink in the earthly kingdom of the Messiah; but this wine of divine love was laid up and reserved in the heart of Christ long before the creation of the world: this excels all other wine for its antiquity.

2udly. It is preferable to wine for its purity; no wine so pure and unmixed as this of Christ's love; it is wine *on the lees well refined*, free from all dregs of deceit, hypocrisy, and dissimulation; it is a *love unfeigned, a pure river of water of life.*

3rdly. It is better than wine, and is preferable to it for its freeness and cheapness: wine is not every one's liquor, every one's purse cannot reach it, especially in some countries; but this wine of Christ's love, is to be had *without money, and without price*, than which nothing can be cheaper; nor is any thing freer, for it is freely *shed abroad* in the hearts of God's people, by the Spirit.

4thly. For the plenty of it, it is preferable to wine; wine, as it is dear, so it is scarce in some places; but this as it is cheap, and to be had freely; so there is plenty of it: in the marriage at Cana of Galilee, there was want of wine; but there is no want thereof in this feast of love, which Christ has made for his spouse and bride: this is a river, nay, an ocean of love, which flows forth in plentiful streams to poor sinners.

5thly. It is preferable to wine in the effects of it.

1. Wine will revive and cheer a man that is of a heavy heart, and therefore it is advised to be given to such, Prov. xxxi. 6; yet it will not bring a man to life that is dead; but such is the nature of Christ's love, that when it is conveyed into the heart of a sinner, *dead in trespasses and sins*, it makes him alive; for whenever it is *a time of love* to a poor sinner, it is also a *time of life*; nay, it not only conveys life, but it maintains and supports it, and keeps souls from dying; he that has had it *shed abroad* in his heart, by the Spirit, shall never die *the second death*.

2. Wine may remove a worldly heaviness, or a sorrow on the account of worldly things, the things of time; but not a spiritual heaviness, or a sorrow on the account of the things of another world, the things of eternity; but the manifestation of Christ's love to the soul, can remove this sorrow and heaviness, and fill it with a *joy unspeakable and full of glory*, and give him that ease, and comfort, and satisfaction of mind, he is wishing for.

3. If a man drinks never such large draughts of the wine of Christ's love, it will never hurt him; when other wine, with excessive drinking of it, not only wastes the estates, but consumes the bodies, and destroys the health of men; but of this a man may drink freely and plentifully, without doing himself any hurt; nay, it will be of considerable advantage to him, and therefore says Christ, in chap v. 1, *Eat, O friends, yea, drink abundantly, O my beloved.*

No wonder then that the church was so desirous of enjoying Christ's presence, and having the manifestations of his love to her soul, seeing his love is thus *better than wine*; besides, it may be observed that she makes use of this as an argument with him to obtain her request; and in so doing, shows what a value she had for the love of Christ, how much she esteemed it, as also what it was she expected and sought after, in desiring communion with him.

Verse 3. *Because of the savour of thy good ointments, thy name is as ointment poured forth; therefore do the virgins love thee.*

THE church having mentioned the excellency of Christ's *love*, as the reason why she desired such intimate communion with him, proceeds in these words to take notice of his savoury *ointments* and precious *name*; which were both so delightful, fragrant, and odorous, that even the *Virgins*, those chaste creatures, were ravished, and had fallen in love with him; and therefore it was no wonder that she, who was his spouse and bride, should express her love to him, and be so desirous of his company. In these words we have,

I. The savour of Christ's ointments expressed.

II. The fragrancy and preciousness of Christ's name declared.

III. The influence that all this has upon the hearts of the virgins, in attracting their love to Christ: *therefore do the virgins love thee.*

I. The savour of Christ's ointments is here expressed by the church, as having knowledge of them herself, and as having observed the effect of them upon the hearts of others. By *ointments* we are to understand the graces of the Spirit of God, that *oil of gladness* with which Christ, as Mediator, is *anointed above his fellows*; this was poured out without measure upon him; it is *like the precious ointment upon Aaron's head, that ran down upon his beard, and went down to the skirts of his garments*; for this being poured upon Christ, the head, descends to all his members; from him they receive that *anointing, which teacheth all things,*

---

[m] Sympos. l. 7. p. 702.   [n] Targum in Cant. 3. 2. and Zohar in Gen. fol. 81. 4.

In explaining these words, I will endeavour,

First. To show why the graces of the Spirit in Christ, or in his members, are compared to *ointments*.

Secondly. Why they are called *Christ's* ointments.

Thirdly. In what sense they are said to be *good*. And,

Fourthly. What is meant by the *savour of them*.

First. I shall endeavour to show why the graces of the Spirit, either in Christ or in saints, are compared to *ointments*.

1st. With the holy anointing oil, which was made according to a divine prescription and direction, kings, priests, and prophets were formerly anointed, and thereby installed into their several offices: thus *Saul, David*, and *Solomon* were anointed to be kings; thus *Aaron* and his sons were anointed to be priests; and thus *Elisha* was anointed prophet in the room of *Elijah*; now, as with this anointing oil these were anointed, and thereby installed into their offices; so Christ, with the anointing oil of the Spirit, was anointed, and thereby installed into those offices which he has taken upon him, and bears for the good of his people; it is with this he is anointed to be king, and is set over God's *holy hill of Zion*; it is with this he is *consecrated* a priest for evermore, to offer sacrifice, and make intercession for transgressors; and this same Spirit being upon him, he is anointed therewith a prophet to "preach good tidings to the meek." Christ, as the glorious God-man, was anointed and installed into his office as Mediator, from eternity; his human nature was anointed with the Holy Ghost, at the time of its conception in the virgin's womb; and more visibly at his baptism, when the Spirit descended upon him as a dove; and still more gloriously at his ascension to, and session at the Father's right hand, when he received from him the promise of the Spirit, and was made or declared to be both Lord and Christ: and it is with the same unction that saints are by him made kings and priests unto God; kings, because grace reigns in their hearts now, and they shall reign with Christ in glory, for ever hereafter; priests, "to offer up spiritual sacrifices acceptable to God by Jesus Christ."

2ndly. With this holy anointing oil, all the vessels of the tabernacle were anointed and made fit for use; to which saints may be compared, who are chosen vessels, vessels of mercy, that were foreordained for glory; now these, in their natural state, are not fit for their master's use: yet when anointed with this unction, they are not only fit for their master's present use here, but are prepared for glory hereafter: the saints having the oil of grace, as well as the lamps of profession, are ready to go in with the bridegroom, whenever he comes and calls for them.

3rdly. Anointing with oil was made use of for ornament; "it makes the face to shine," as the Psalmist says, Psal. civ. 15; Christ, as man and Mediator, is adorned with the grace of the Spirit; he is "fairer than the children of men," and the reason is, because "grace is poured into his lips:" he has a larger measure of this "oil of gladness" than others, and therefore is "the perfection of beauty;" he is "white and ruddy, the chiefest among ten thousand;" and as Christ is, so the saints are adorned herewith, and become beautiful in his eye, being "all glorious within:" by this grace they are purified and prepared, and so presented as a chaste and beautiful virgin to Christ.

4thly. Anointing with oils or ointments was used for cheering and refreshing guests at festivals, being very useful for this purpose in hot countries; the smell of which was very delightful and pleasing;° hence Solomon says, "Ointment and perfume rejoice the heart," Prov. xxvii. 9, and for this reason Mary brought ointment and anointed the feet of Jesus, to cool and refresh them while he sat at meat: these ointments, or graces of the Spirit, are the *oil of gladness*, both to Christ and to his people; in the exercise of them, he, as man, was delighted and refreshed, and so are his saints; the grace of the Spirit is, to them, *the oil of joy for mourning*; he, by his sweet influences and delightful operations on their souls, powerfully draws forth grace into exercise, and thereby administers much comfort to them; they are oftentimes filled *with joy and peace in believing*, being made to *abound in hope through the power of the Holy Ghost*.

5thly. Ointments are useful for mollifying and healing wounds, Isa. i. 6; these being applied, soften hard tumours, break them, and then heal them; the hearts of sinners are hard and obdurate, being swelled with pride, vanity, and conceit of themselves; but the ointments of divine grace being applied, softens them, breaks these hard swellings, makes their hearts contrite, and then heals them: Christ, the great Physician, acting herein, like the good Samaritan, who had compassion on the wounded man, and bound up *his wounds, pouring in oil and wine*.

Secondly. We will now consider why these ointments are said to be Christ's.

1st. They are of his making; as he is God, he has an all-sufficiency of grace in himself, underived from any other, and is the Author of all grace; this excellent composition is all his own; this ointment is made and prepared by his own hand; the holy anointing oil, though of God's prescribing, yet it was not of his making, though according to the composition of it, no other was to be made; but these ointments are not only prescribed, but made by him, that is God: and none can make according to the composition thereof; which shows the excellency of them.

2ndly. He is the subject of them; as God, he is the Author and Maker, but, as Mediator, they are communicated to him; they are poured into him, and upon him without measure; *it pleased*

° Non te illius unguentorum odor, non vini anhelitus, &c. Cicero. Orat. 2s. c. 7.

the Father, that in him should all fulness dwell; they are his, not only because made by him, but because they are in his possession; he is anointed with them *above his fellows*.

3rdly. They are his, because he has a right to dispose of them; they are his own as God, being the Maker of them; and they are his own as Mediator, being given to him; wherefore he may do what he will with them, as indeed he does; he gives these ointments to whom he will, and he gives them freely and plentifully; he has a fulness of all grace in himself, and from thence saints receive grace for grace. This ointment being poured plentifully upon the head, runs down freely to all the members; these ointments are first Christ's, and then they are ours; he composed them as God, for our use and service, and they were given to him as Mediator, for that purpose; grace in Christ, and grace in us, are of the same nature, though not of the same degree: grace in us is as in its streams, but grace in Christ is as in its fountain; it is but a small measure we have, but it is an infinite, and inexhaustible fulness that is in him; which may serve to recommend Christ to us, and direct us where to go for these oils or ointments.

Thirdly. They are said to be good ointments, or oils; some oils are better than others, and some places produced better than others: *Tekoah* was the chief place for oil in *Judea*, and the next to it was *Regah* beyond *Jordan*;[p] no doubt but *Solomon* had the best. The oils or ointments of the true Solomon are best of all. And of ointments there were various sorts,[q] as of roses, lilies, almonds, nard, myrrh, saffron, &c.; and *Syria*, a neighbouring country to *Judea*, was famous for some sorts of ointments, from whence *Solomon* might be supplied.

1st. They are good in their own nature—are an excellent composition, there is no ingredient in them but what is good; grace, as wrought in us, is called *some good thing toward the Lord God of Israel*; it is a *good work*, which being begun, shall be performed until the day of Christ.

2ndly. These ointments are both made, and applied by a good hand; for he that has made them, and he that anoints us with them, is God. The ingredients are not only good, but they are put together by a skilful hand; this unction is made by, and received from *the Holy One*.

3rdly. They are good in their effects: they are good to *make the face to shine*, to adorn the saints, revive and refresh them; they are good to soften hard hearts, and heal wounded spirits; they are good to anoint the eyes with, and thereby recover, continue, and increase sight.

4thly. They are good in the believers' esteem; they have had experience of their nature and effects, and can write *probatum est* upon each of

them; and therefore highly value them, and with very good reason. For,

5thly. These ointments are exceedingly rich and costly. The holy anointing oil was rich and costly, being made of the principal spices, but not to be compared with these; the ingredients of which are preferable to gold and silver, to rubies, and all things that can be thought of or desired; these are precious, rich, and costly ointments indeed.

6thly. Which makes them still more valuable, they never lose their efficacy; *dead flies cause the ointment of the apothecary to send forth a stinking savour;* corrupt it so, that it loses its virtue, and becomes good for nothing; grace cannot be lost and perish in the saints; the anointing which they receive, abides in them; it is an immortal seed, a well of living water, springing up into eternal life; and notwithstanding the dead flies of their sins and corruptions, yet they cannot make the ointment of grace send forth a stinking savour; corruptions do, but grace never will; it is not indeed always in exercise, but it never will lose its nature or its virtue; the saints' lamps shall never go out, being supplied with oil from that fulness of it that is in Christ.

Fourthly. These ointments are said to have a *savour* in them; precious ointments have a fragrancy,[r] a sweet savour in them, very delightful; a greater savour has the grace of Christ to a believer, who savours not the things of men, but the things of God; for, as the natural man, *he receiveth not*, that is, he savours not, *the things of the Spirit of God, for they are foolishness,* unsavoury and insipid things *unto him*; these ointments can no more be savoury to a carnal man, than food can be relishing to a man of a vitiated taste, or music be delightful to a deaf man, or colours pleasant to one that is blind; for as the one wants his taste, the other his hearing, and the third his sight, so this man wants his smelling, and therefore these ointments cannot be savoury to him; but they are so to the believer, who has his spiritual smelling; now by the *savour* of these ointments, is intended the manifestation of Christ's grace unto the soul; the sense and perception which souls have of it, and their interest in it, fill them with pleasure and delight; and it was this which made the virgins love Christ, and the church so desirous of his company. There is an emphasis on the word *thy; thy good ointments,* none so odorous, so savoury, and of so grateful a smell as his; as lovers used to admire and commend each others ointments, by which they sought to recommend themselves.[s]

II. The church in these words declares the fragrancy and preciousness of Christ's name, when she says, that his *name is as ointment*

---

[p] Misn. Menachot. c. 8. s. 3.   [q] Athenæi Deipnosophist. l. 15. c. 11. p. 688, 689. Clement. Alex. Pædagog. l. 2. p. 183.   [r] Abundant vino, unguentorum fragrantia. Valer. Maxim. l. 9. c. 1. extern. 1.   [s] Nam omnium unguentium odos præ tua nautea est. Plauti Curculio, act. 1. sc. 2. v. 5.

poured forth. It will be proper to enquire what is intended by the name of Christ, and in what sense that may be said to be as *ointment poured forth.*

1st. By the name of Christ may be meant his person, this being not an unusual way of speaking in the scripture; thus in Rev. iii. 4, "Thou hast a few names," that is, persons, "even in Sardis," &c., and in Matt. xii. 21: "and in his name shall the Gentiles trust," that is, in the person of Christ shall the Gentiles trust; so here *thy name is as ointment poured forth,* that is, thy person is as delightful, grateful, and odorous to me, as the pouring forth a box of ointment; thou art *altogether lovely* to me, thy whole person is so; every thing in thee is engaging, and thou hast every thing to render thee desirable to me; all beauty, power, wisdom, and grace, are in thee, that it is no wonder the virgins love thee; for not only thy mouth, but all of thee is lovely and desirable.

2ndly. By it may be intended some one, or any one of those names by which he is called. As,

1. The *Messiah* or *Christ*, which signifies anointed. So that in comparing it to ointment, there may be an allusion to the signification of the name itself, and may more particularly point out which name is intended, even the name *Messiah*, to which *Christ*, in the new Testament, answers; which, though not very frequently met with in the Old Testament, yet was well known to the ancient Jews, as appears from their *Targums*, where it is made use of in upwards of sixty places, in which the Redeemer is treated of;[1] and as it was well known, so it was highly esteemed of by them; they expected him who was to redeem *Israel*, under this title and character; and when he was come, and had revealed himself unto some, in an exulting manner they said one to another, *We have found the Messiah, which is, being interpreted, the Christ;* that name had been always precious to the saints, who waited for the *consolation of Israel,* and was then like a box of *ointment poured forth,* exceeding grateful, delightful, and refreshing to them.

2. Another name by which Christ is called, and which may be said to be as "ointment poured forth," is the name Jesus, which signifies, a Saviour, and was given him, because he "saves his people from their sins." Christ is, in the everlasting Gospel, revealed as a Saviour; it is therein declared, that the design of his coming into the world was to save sinners, and that he has obtained eternal salvation for them, and is both able and willing to save the chief of them; the discovery the Gospel makes of him is exceeding delightful and pleasant to awakened sinners. This name Jesus, a Saviour, how sweet is it to such who have seen the exceeding sinfulness of sin, themselves lost and undone thereby, and in a perishing state and condition! the news of a Saviour are good news and glad "tidings of great joy" unto them; the discovery of it is like the breaking open a box of ointment, and pouring it out; it at once removes the filthy stench of sin from the sinner's nostrils, and that sadness and sorrow of heart which arise from the guilt of it upon the conscience.

3. Christ's name, Immanuel, may be said to be as "ointment poured forth," which signifies "God with us;" and there are two things in it which make it like "ointment poured forth," that is, exceeding odorous and grateful to believers.

1. That he is God; hence they know, and are well assured, that he is able to save them; that the work is not too heavy for him; that he has not undertaken that which he is not able to accomplish, which they would have reason to believe, if he was only a creature: from hence they comfortably conclude, as well they may, that all he did was efficacious, and answered the purposes for which it was done; as that his sacrifice was effectual to atone for and expiate sin; his blood to procure the pardon of it, and thoroughly cleanse from it; his righteousness to justify from all sin, and render them acceptable in the sight of God; and all this, because they are the sacrifice, blood, and righteousness of one that is God. From this name they also gather, that he having taken the care and charge of them, "is able to keep them from falling;" and that none is able to pluck them out of his hands, no more than they can separate them from his heart, which they could not be so assured of, was he a creature.

2. Another thing which makes this name like "ointment poured forth," is, that he is "God with us;" God dwelling and conversing with us, God in our nature, God manifest in the flesh; hence it appears, that He who is the great God, and our Saviour, is near akin to us, and we to him; being "flesh of his flesh, and bone of his bone," we are both of one and the same nature, and therefore he is not ashamed to call us brethren; and his assuming our nature, gives him a right, as well as makes him a proper person to be our *Goel* or Redeemer, whereby all the blessings, which he procured in this nature, are communicated to us, and not to angels; now what makes this name still more sweet, savoury, and delightful, is, that he, who is Immanuel, God with us, God in our nature, is, and will be on our side; and if God be with us, and *for us,* who shall be *against us?*

4. Christ's name, "the Lord our righteousness," may be said to be as "ointment poured forth," by which he is called, Jer. xxiii. 6; this is exceeding grateful, sweet, and precious to a poor sinner; one who has seen his own righte-

---

[1] *Vide* Buxtorf. Talm. Lex. p. 1268, 1269, &c.

ousness as filthy rags, and as an unclean thing, how does he value Christ as the Lord his righteousness! he counts all things but loss and dung, in comparison of him, and desires only to be found in him, and in his righteousness, and not in his own; but what makes this so exceeding precious to him, is, because it acquits from all sin, and secures from all wrath and condemnation, and renders him spotless, unblameable, and irreproveable in the sight of God.

5. Any, or all of those names of Christ, in Isa. ix. 6, may be said to be as "ointment poured forth," they being exceeding precious and delightful to believers; such as *Wonderful, Counsellor*, the *Mighty God, the everlasting Father*, and *Prince of peace*. Christ's name " Wonderful," is so; he being wonderful in his incarnation and grace, in his person and offices, in his works, relations, and characters; this emits a sweet odour to believers, even like a box of ointment opened to them: and so is his name " Counsellor;" under which character he acted from everlasting, consulting with the other two persons, our eternal welfare in the ancient council of peace; and still continues to bear this character, which he makes good, by giving to us the best advice and most wholesome counsel, and this he does freely and faithfully: his name, " the Mighty God," carries in it as much sweetness and comfort to the believer, as it does greatness and majesty; and that endearing title, the " everlasting Father," who, as such, loves his children with an everlasting love, and has made everlasting provisions for them, and takes everlasting care of them, fills those he stands thus related to, with the utmost pleasure: and that noble character, the " Prince of peace," which he bears on the account of his having obtained peace by " the blood of his cross," for rebellious sinners, so sweetly diffuses the odour of his grace, that it charms and captivates the believer's heart. The names of true lovers are dear to each other, to which the allusion is ; they love to hear their names mentioned, &c., which are as precious ointment, as delicious nectar." Or else,

3rdly. By Christ's *name*, we may understand his Gospel; thus, the apostle Paul is said to be *a chosen vessel, to bear the name* of Christ *before the Gentiles*, that is, to preach his Gospel to them; he was a vessel full of the precious ointment of the Gospel, and his preaching of it was the pouring of it forth, which was exceeding grateful to poor sinners. The Gospel to some is like a box of ointment shut up; it is hid unto them, they know it not, it is a sealed book, a hidden mystery, an unpleasant story, and unsavoury words; it sends forth no other savour than that " of death unto death ;" but unto others, it is like a box of ointment opened, and poured forth, which diffuses and spreads a sweet and delightful odour abroad. The ministers of the Gospel make manifest the savour of Christ's knowledge in every place where they are sent, and become to some the " savour of life unto life ;" they open the box, and pour forth the ointment of the Gospel, which coming with power, is received with pleasure; and being " worthy of acceptation," it meets with it in the hearts of awakened sinners.

4thly. By the *name* of Christ, may be intended the fame which was, and still is spread abroad of him: some Jewish writers^w expound it of a good name or good report which Solomon says, " is better than precious ointment," Eccl. vii. 1; and then the sense is this, " such is the fame that is spread abroad of thee, of thy greatness and goodness, of thy beauties and excellencies, that even those who have only heard of thee by the hearing of the ear, and to whom, at present, thou art not known by sight, have fallen in love with thee." In the days of Christ's flesh, his name was renowned, his fame was spread far and near, for the good he did to mankind, in healing the sick, and curing all manner of diseases ; for the surprising miracles which he wrought, and for the work of the ministry, which he was engaged in ; his matter being excellent and divine, words of grace and wisdom, such as " never man spake ;" and his manner of delivery being with power and authority : and now his fame is great, and an excellent report is spread abroad of him, through the preaching of the everlasting Gospel, for the mighty achievements of his grace, and what his arm of Almighty power has done, in working out, and bringing in salvation for poor sinners; as also for those peculiar blessings of grace, which souls daily receive from him, as well as for those personal excellencies which are in him; now such a report going abroad of him, his *name* being thus " as ointment poured forth," the virgins love him, souls flock after him, and come unto him. Which brings me to consider,

III. The influence that all this has upon the hearts of others; " therefore do the virgins love thee." In explaining which clause, I shall endeavour,

1st. To show who are meant by the *virgins*.

2ndly. Give some account of the nature of their love and affection to Christ.

1st. Let us consider who are intended by *the virgins*. Some think carnal professors are here meant, who are called virgins in scripture, though foolish ones ; but their love is not real, such as this seems to be in the text : others have thought that they are the uncalled and unconverted among the Gentiles, who are not yet espoused to Christ ; but they rather appear to be true believers in Christ, by their love to him, for " faith works by love ;" and, perhaps, persons lately converted are

---

" Nomen nectari dulcius beato. Martial. Epigr. l. 9. ep. 9.

^w R. Sol. Jarchi in loc. So *Lyra. Vide* Targum in loc.

intended, whose love to Christ is generally warm and lively, and their affections strong, not having as yet met with those chills, nor attended with that coldness and indifference, which too often, and too soon, befal God's children: the first love is the best and strongest, but oftentimes doth not last long, warm and lively, being gradually chilled with the aboundings of corruption within, and the snares of the world without; though, perhaps, all true believers, whether of a later or of a longer standing, may be understood here, and may be justly called *virgins*.

1. For their chaste and strict adherence to Christ, their only husband, to whom they are espoused; "I have espoused you to one husband," says the apostle, "that I might present you a chaste virgin to Christ," 2 Cor. xi. 2; these being betrothed to him, "in righteousness, in lovingkindness, in mercies, and in faithfulness," know, own, and acknowledge him as their Lord and Husband, and steadfastly adhere to him as such; he is a Head, both of eminence and influence to them; to him they hold, and him alone they submit unto as such; he is the Saviour of the body, the church, and they acknowledge him to be theirs, and will have no other. Their language is, "Ashur shall not save us, neither will we say any more to the works of our hands, Ye are our gods." They make use of none, as the mediator between God and them, either as a mediator of redemption, or of intercession, but the Lord Jesus Christ; him they know and love, to him they have given up themselves, and by him they will abide, as their Head and Husband, their Saviour and Mediator.

2. For the singleness of their love and affection to Christ. Their love is not common to all; it is not bestowed upon any creature, but purely reserved for him who alone deserves it; they can every one of them say, "Whom have I in heaven but thee? *and* there is none on earth that I desire besides thee," Psal. lxxiii. 25. Christ requires all their love, he will admit of no rival in it, and they are heartily willing to bestow it all upon him. Those who love any creature, or creature-enjoyment more than Christ, or equally with him, are not worthy of him, nor worthy to be called by the name of *virgins*.

3. For their incorruptness in the doctrine of faith: this is what the apostle seems to have a regard to, when he declared his fervent desire to present the Corinthians, as a chaste virgin to Christ; he was jealous, lest they should be seduced through the subtilty and craftiness of ill-designing men, and their pure minds be corrupted and drawn aside "from the simplicity that is in Christ;" lest they should be polluted with error, and so not answer the character of virgins, which they had hitherto borne, and which he earnestly wished might continue with them. Now virgins are such, who having received, "hold fast the faithful word, as they have been taught;" whose souls having been "nourished up in the words of faith," and of good doctrine, and established therein, cannot be moved from thence, but will earnestly contend, and strive together "for the faith once delivered to the saints."

4. For the truth and sincerity of their worship: they are such who "worship God in Spirit and in truth;" who make the word of God, and his will therein revealed, the rule to act by, in all solemn and social worship, and not the authorities, customs, and inventions of men; and when they are concerned in any part of religious worship, their desires are, that their hearts and souls may be engaged therein, they are not of those who "draw near to God with their mouths, and with their lips honour *him*, but have removed their hearts far from *him*, and their fear towards *him*, taught by the precepts of men;" for as they have not committed spiritual whoredom, which is idolatry, so they serve the Lord with pure spirits; they desire that whatsoever they do, more especially in divine worship, might be done in faith, from a principle of love to God, and according to his word and will: these are they who are said not to "be defiled with women, for they are virgins; these are they which follow the Lamb whithersoever he goeth," Rev. xiv. 4; in every ordinance and institution of his, which he in his word has pointed out unto them, and marked out for them.

5. For the purity of their lives and conversations; they hold "the mystery of the faith," not merely notionally and by a profession of it, but "in a pure conscience," and hereby "adorn the doctrine of God, our Saviour;" their garments are, in some measure, kept from being spotted with the "pollutions of the world," and which they also frequently wash and make "white in the blood of the Lamb." Besides, "that grace of God, which bringeth salvation," Tit. ii. 11, 12; that is, the doctrines of grace, which bring the news of salvation by Christ, to poor sinners, "teach *them*, that denying ungodliness and worldly lusts, *they* should live soberly, righteously, and godly, in this present world;" which through the mighty power of God's grace, they are in some measure enabled to do.

6. For their fairness and beauty. Virgins being fair and beautiful, believers are therefore compared unto them; for though they are *black* in themselves, yet they are *comely* in Christ; though full of spots in themselves, yet, as considered in him, they are "all fair, and there is no spot" in them: through that comeliness, which he has put upon them, they are a perfection of beauty, and being so, are the delight of Christ, and wonder of angels.

7. For their gay and costly attire, and yet modest behaviour. Virgins, in their youthful days, if modest, though their attire is gay and splendid, suitable to their age, yet are of decent and becoming behaviour. Believers are richly attired: these virgins appear in cloth of gold, "in raiment

of needlework," curiously wrought, which cannot be matched; they are decked with all kinds of ornaments, with bracelets, chains, rings, and Jewels; they have on the glorious robe of Christ's righteousness, and are adorned with the various graces of the Spirit, which make their behaviour decent and modest; for they are not proud and haughty, one of their ornaments being that " of a meek and quiet spirit;" they have low, mean, and humble thoughts of themselves; suitable to their character is their carriage and deportment; for though they are so richly clothed, and so nearly related to the King of kings, yet, like their Lord, are *meek* and *lowly*.

Secondly. I shall now proceed to give some account of the love which these virgins bear to Christ; in doing which I shall,

1st. Give some account of the nature of it.
2udly. Show from whence it arises. And
3rdly. How it manifests itself.

1st. Let us consider the nature and properties of it.

1. It is a superlative love which souls bear to Christ; it exceeds and excels their love to all creatures, or creature-enjoyments. Christ loves them above all others, and they love him more than all persons or things besides; of all that claim a share in their love, as none deserves, so none has a greater interest therein than himself.

2. It is universal; they love all of Christ, and all that belong to him; they love him in his Person, and in all his offices, relations, and characters, which he has taken upon him, and by which he is pleased to manifest himself unto them: they love all his saints, be they high or low, rich or poor, and by whatsoever character or denomination, they are distinguished, if it appears that his grace is but wrought in their hearts, and they bear his image and superscription; they love all his commands, ordinances, and institutions; they "esteem his precepts concerning all things to be right," and are not partial in their obedience thereunto.

3. It is, or at least ought to be, constant and faithful, as his is to them, and as *Jonathan's* was to *David*; we should love him in adversity as well as in prosperity, at all times; nothing should separate our love from Christ, as nothing can separate his love from us.

4. It is, or ought to be, fervent and ardent; and so it is usually at first conversion, as has been already observed; and this is called in scripture, the "first love," which the church at *Ephesus* was blamed for leaving; not that she had lost her love to Christ, but the fervency thereof was much abated; she began to grow cold and lukewarm in her affections, which is too often the case of God's people, through the prevailing of corruptions, and an immoderate desire and pursuit after the things of this world; "because iniquity shall abound," says Christ, "the love of many shall wax cold," Matt. xxiv. 12.

5. Where there is true love to Christ, it is always hearty and unfeigned; the virgins, true believers, love him "with all their heart, *and* with all their soul;" they love him "in sincerity," and from their very hearts can appeal to Him, who is the heart-searching and rein-trying God, as *Peter* did, and say, "Lord, thou knowest all things, thou knowest that I love thee," John. xxi. 17. Here is no deceit, dissimulation, or hypocrisy in their love; though it may be sometimes weak and languid, yet whenever it exerts and shows itself, it is real and hearty; these love not " in word only," neither in tongue, "but in deed and in truth."

2ndly. It will be proper to enquire into the springs and causes of this love, and to observe from whence it arises. And,

1. It springs and arises from a sight of Christ's loveliness: an unbeliever sees no beauty in Christ, wherefore he should desire him; there is nothing in him lovely to a carnal eye; but one that is "made light in the Lord," and has but a glimpse of "the King in his beauty," his heart is won, his soul is ravished and drawn forth in love to him; he admires and desires him above all, and cannot be easy without an interest in him.

2. From a view of his suitableness, as a Saviour; the believer not only sees personal and transcendent excellencies in him, which ravish him, but special blessings, which are proper for him; he beholds him as "full of grace and truth;" he smells a sweet savour in his ointments, and that name *Jesus*, a Saviour, becomes exceeding precious to him; he views all righteousness and strength, peace and pardon, light and life, joy and comfort, grace and glory, and all things appertaining to salvation, every thing to make him comfortable here, and happy hereafter, in Christ; and therefore says, as *David* did, "I will love thee, O Lord, my strength," Psal. xviii. 1.

3. From a sense of his love and manifestation of it to their souls; "we love him," says the apostle, "because he first loved us," 1 John iv. 19; our love is not the cause of his, but his is the cause of ours; and it is not merely his loving us, but the shedding it abroad in our hearts by his Spirit, which draws out our love to him; for though he loved us, yet if he had not some way or other manifested it to us, and overcome our hearts with it, we should still have remained enemies to him; but his giving us the sense and perception of it in our hearts, is what has drawn us to himself, and will keep us there.

4. From a view of union and relation to him; how can persons do otherwise than love him, when they see themselves so nearly united to him, as to be "members of his body, of his flesh, and of his bones?" How can they but love him, when they view him standing in and filling up the relations of an indulgent Father, a tender Husband, a loving Brother, and faithful Friend unto them?

5. This is more and more increased by enjoying

communion with him; the more intimate a believer is with Christ, the oftener he sees him, the more frequent visits he receives from him, and the greater acquaintance and fellowship he has with him, the more he loves him; every sight of him, visit from him, and enjoyment of his presence, add fresh strength and fervency to his love; *John*, the beloved disciple, who leaned on Christ's bosom, and had intimate communion with him, had his heart filled with love to him, and wrote the most largely of it. But,

3rdly. I shall now endeavour to show how this love manifests itself; and it does so,

1. By a regard to Christ's commands and ordinances; "If ye love me," says Christ, "keep my commandments; for he that hath my commandments and keepeth them, he it is that loveth me," John xiv. 15—21; that is, he that hath my commandments written upon his heart, by the finger of the Spirit, according to the tenor of the covenant of grace, and is enabled to keep them by the assistance of my grace and Spirit, he it is that shows his love to me; and therefore, as you say, you love me, show it by an observance of my commands: and all that love Christ will do so, according to the measure of grace received; they will love the place of divine worship, and have a respect to all his ordinances and institutions; for all his *tabernacles* are *amiable* and lovely to them.

2. By a regard to his truths, the doctrines of the Gospel; they receive the truth in the love of it, and value it more than their "necessary food;" they highly esteem the preachers of it, and cannot bear to hear one truth of the Gospel spoken against.

3. By a regard to his people; they love the saints, who love Christ, they delight in their company, and take pleasure in conversing with them; they are the "excellent in the earth, in whom is all their delight;" and indeed, where there is no love to the saints, there can be no true love to Christ; for, as the apostle *John* says, "he that loveth not his brother, whom he hath seen, how can he love God, whom he hath not seen?" 1 John iv. 20.

4. By a regard to his presence; a soul that loves Christ, values the presence of Christ; nothing so desirable to him as that is: and when he has lost sight of Christ, cannot be easy without him, but seeks here and there until he has found him whom his soul loves: he thinks himself never more happy than when he has Christ's presence, and never worse than when he is without it.

5. This love manifests itself, by parting with and bearing all for Christ: a soul that truly loves Christ, will part with all that is near and dear to him, for him; he will forsake his own kindred, and his father's house; he counts Christ "the pearl of great price," and is therefore willing to quit all he has, that he may but enjoy that; he leaves all, as the disciples did, and follows Christ; and resolves, come what will, that Christ's God shall be his God, and Christ's people his people, and where Christ lodges he will lodge, and where he goes he will follow, and cleave close to him, as *Ruth* did to *Naomi*. Moreover, he is not only willing to leave and lose all for Christ, but also to bear all for him, that he is pleased to lay upon him, and call him to; he is willing to suffer reproaches, afflictions, and persecutions for the sake of him and his Gospel, and to bear any cross whatever he thinks fit to enjoin him: all which he would never be willing to submit to, was not his soul filled with love to Christ; and such a love as this, which springs from such causes, and manifests itself in these ways, is exceeding grateful to Christ, as appears from chap. iv. 10.

Verse 4. *Draw me, we will run after thee: The King hath brought me into his chambers. We will be glad and rejoice in thee: We will remember thy love more than wine: The upright love thee.*

THE church having taken notice of the excellency of Christ's love, the savour of his ointments, and preciousness of his name, which made the virgins, her companions, love him; she persists in and continues her request, for communion with him, in these words; in which we have,

I. A petition; "draw me."

II. An argument which she makes use of to obtain this request; "we will run after thee."

III. The request granted to her, which is acknowledged by her; "the king hath brought me into his chambers."

IV. The effects thereof, or the influence which this had upon her; "we will rejoice," &c.

I. Here is a request or petition made by the church to Christ; "draw me." What she intends hereby will be proper to consider. And,

1st. There is a powerful efficacious drawing of souls to Christ, at conversion, when God calls a poor sinner by his grace, brings him to Christ, enables him to venture upon him, and believe in him for life and salvation; which is what Christ speaks of in John vi. 44, when he says, "No man can come to me except the Father which has sent me, draw him." A soul's coming to Christ for life, is not the produce of power and free-will in man, but of the grace of God in drawing, though it is not effected by force or compulsion; it is true, the sinner, in his natural estate, "is stout-hearted, and far from righteousness," averse to Christ and the way of salvation by him; but by mighty grace, this stout heart is brought down, and made willing to submit to God's way of salvation; this obduracy is removed, and hardness of heart taken away by him, who has promised to take away the "stony heart, and give a heart of flesh." Unconverted sinners are indeed unwilling to come to Christ for life; but those who belong to the election of grace, are made "willing in the day of

Christ's power:" the manslayer did not more willingly flee from the avenger of blood, to the city of refuge, than a sinner, sensible of sin, and the danger of his state, does to Christ for salvation; for though a soul is not brought to Christ, by the power of his free-will, yet he is not brought against his will: drawing does not always suppose force and compulsion; there are other ways of drawing besides that. Thus the fame of a skilful physician draws many people to him; thus music draws the ear; love the heart; and pleasure the mind; as the poet says, "Trahit sua quemque voluptas." Nor is this done by mere moral suasion, which is what ministers use; knowing the terrors of the Lord, they persuade men: but if the mighty power of grace does not attend their ministry, not one soul will ever be converted; though they represent the joys of heaven and the terrors of hell, in never such a lively manner; speak in never such moving strains, and use the most powerful arguments to win upon souls; yet they will stretch out their "hands all the day, to a gainsaying and disobedient people;" they will return with a "who hath believed our report? the arm of the Lord" not being "revealed" unto them. God does not act as a mere moral cause in man's conversion; he does not only propose an object, and then leave the will to choose, but powerfully and effectually works both "to will and to do of his own good pleasure;" for this drawing is accomplished by the secret and invisible power of his mighty grace: and in this sense is the word used, in Judges iv. 7, when *Deborah* tells *Barak*, that the Lord had promised, saying, "I will DRAW unto thee, to the river Kishon, Sisera, the captain of Jabin's army, with his chariots and his multitudes, and I will deliver him into thine hands;" that is, I who have the hearts of kings, generals, and captains of armies in my hands, and can turn them "as the rivers of waters, whithersoever I will," will powerfully and invisibly work upon, move, and incline *Sisera's* heart to lead his army to the river *Kishon*, where I will give an instance of my power and goodness in delivering him into thine hands. Thus God powerfully and invisibly works upon the hearts of sinners, bends their wills, slays the enmity of their minds, allures and draws them to Christ, "suavi omnipotentia, and omnipotente suavitate," "by a sweet omnipotence, and an omnipotent sweetness;" and this he does by revealing Christ unto them, in all his beauty and loveliness, discovering the love of Christ unto their souls; by the kind invitations of his grace, the precious and encouraging promises of the gospel, and the special teachings of his Spirit; all which is an evidence of his everlasting love; for it is, because he hath "loved them with an everlasting love; therefore "with loving kindness" he hath "drawn" them; this is also a fruit of Christ's death; "I, if I be lifted up from the earth," says he, meaning his elevation upon the cross, "will draw all men unto me," John xii. 32; that is, all that the Father hath given me, and has promised, shall be gathered to me, and whom I shall shed my blood for. Moreover, it is likewise an indication of the weakness and impotence of sinners, seeing they cannot come unless they are drawn; and sufficiently destroys the notion which advances the free-will and power of the creature in conversion: but I apprehend that this is not the drawing intended in this petition, for thus the church had been already drawn.

The *Septuagint* read it, "They have drawn thee: at the smell of thine ointments, will we run;"[x] that is, the virgins have loved thee, and shown their love to thee; and this has so taken with thine heart, that it has drawn thee after them, they have thy company, which I want; but by the smell of those ointments, which thou carriest about with thee, I, and others, will run after thee, till we find thee: so that Christ, according to this version and sense of the words, is the *person drawn*, and not the person petitioned to, to draw; though the latter seems best to agree both with the *Hebrew* text, and the sense of the words.

R. Aben Ezra thinks that they are the words of the virgins, who, every one of them, desire, saying, "draw me; we," every one of us, "will run after thee;" but they seem rather to be the words of the church, desirous of more intimate communion with Christ; for there is,

Secondly, A drawing to nearer communion with Christ, which believers oftentimes want, and are desirous of, and which the church had enjoyed; as appears from the following clause in this verse; in which she declares that "the king had brought her into his chambers," where he conversed with her, and disclosed the secrets of his heart to her: now this petition of hers for nearer communion with him, supposes,

1. A distance between Christ and her; not a distance with regard to union; for believers being one with Christ, they never are, nor can be distanced from him; they are always in this sense, "a people near unto the Lord;" nor is there a distance of affection, for "having loved his own, which were in the world, he loves them to the end;" they can never be separated from his love, seeing they are engraven as a seal upon his heart: but this is a distance as to communion; and, in this sense, Christ does sometimes stand at a distance, and hides himself from his people; as appears by their frequent complaints of it, they then thinking themselves forsaken and forgotten by him.

2. This petition shows her uneasiness in this condition, and therefore she says, "draw me;" not but that sometimes believers are lukewarm and indifferent; for falling asleep upon a bed of security, they become insensible of their condition, and therefore unconcerned about it; but when

---

[x] Ἑιλκυσάν ϛε, &c. Sic legunt Origen. Theodor und Ambros. in Sanct. in loc.

they are awakened, and find their beloved gone, their souls are troubled, and being impatient of delay, though in the night, as the church in chap. iii., arise from their beds, and in "the streets and broad ways" seek him, whom their souls love.

3. This request shows the sense she had of her own inability to attain to a state of nearer communion with him: "when he hides his face, who can behold him?" when he stands at a distance, who can come near him? if he is pleased to withdraw his presence, there is no commanding it; the light of his countenance, the enjoyment of his presence, and fellowship with him, are as much the instances of his distinguishing and sovereign grace, and as much depend upon his sovereign pleasure, as the first workings of grace itself; we can no more enjoy the one at pleasure, than we could effect the other; the same Spirit that wrought grace in us at first, must give us access into Christ's presence; we need now the same bands and cords of love to draw us to Christ, as then we did.

4. It signifies the apprehension she seems to have of danger; *draw me*, or I shall be drawn away: believers may be sometimes under fearful apprehensions of being drawn away by the corruptions of their nature, the snares of the world, and the temptations of Satan, though they can never be drawn totally and finally from Christ. He has, by the cords of love, drawn them to himself; and though they may not always experience it, yet he will never leave his people till he has brought them safe to glory.

5. It shows that high value and esteem she had for communion with Christ, which makes her so earnestly importune that blessing, and use such pressing and repeated instances for the enjoyment of it; this was the "one thing" she earnestly desired and sought for, yea, preferred to all other enjoyments. Moreover,

II. Here is an argument made use of to obtain this request, "We will run after thee:" or else it may be considered as the end of her asking this favour, "draw me," that *we* may "run after thee.ʸ" Lord, do thou draw, that we may run, which we cannot do, unless thou dost; but if thou wilt, we shall run after thee. Here is a change of persons in these words; first she says, draw *me*, and then *we* will run after thee; by whom are meant, she, and the virgins, her companions; the church, and particular members: every one in their stations would act with more life and vigour upon such drawings. "We will run after thee;" this is not a running *to* Christ, as sinners do under apprehension of danger, as to a city of refuge, and saints, as to a place of protection, safety, and security; but this is a running *after* him: Christ is the *fore-runner* who has gone before us, and left us an example, both in doing

and suffering, as the Fulfiller of righteousness, and the great Captain of our salvation; and we must follow him, the Lamb, whithersoever he goeth; and not only follow, but run. Our life is frequently, in scripture, called a *race;* Christ is the *mark* we must press after: heaven is the *prize* we should have in view; and the way or *stadium* in which we should run, are Christ's commandments; though our running therein, or performing them, is not the cause of our obtaining the prize; for "it is not of him that willeth, nor of him that runneth, but of God that showeth mercy;" yet running herein is our duty; which supposes,

1st. Cheerfulness, readiness, and willingness; then, says David, "will I run the way of thy commandments, when thou shalt enlarge my heart," Psal. cxix. 32; that is, I shall observe them more cheerfully, readily, and willingly; it will remove that backwardness that is in me to duty.

2ndly. Swiftness; "I made haste, and delayed not, to keep thy commandments," Psal. cxix. 60, says the same psalmist; such obedience as this, though far more perfectly than we are capable of, do the angels perform in heaven.

3rdly. Strength; and this we have not; but there is fulness of it with Christ; who, whilst we are waiting on him, is pleased to *renew* our *strength*, so that we "mount up with wings as eagles, and run and are not weary, and walk and do not faint." Now this is the effect of that drawing, without which there is no running; we cannot set one step forward unless he speak to us, much less can we run, unless he draw us.

III. Here is an account of the request being granted, which she observes with pleasure, "the King hath brought me into his chambers;" though others read it, "Let the King bring me,* or, O! that the King would bring me," &c. and so take it as a continuation of her desires after communion with Christ; but this is for want of knowledge in the *Hebrew* language, as *Mercer* observes: others think that the past tense is put for the future, and so read it, "The King shall or will bring me," &c., as being expressive of her faith, that she should enjoy what she was desirous of. *Junius* renders it, "When the King shall have brought me," &c., and so carries in it the nature of a promise, as to her and her virgins future behaviour upon the enjoyment of such a blessing; though I think it is much better rendered by our translators, "The King hath brought me," &c., and so signifies her enjoyment of the mercy she sought after. Wherein are three things to be considered,

1st. Who this *King* is, that brought *her* into his chambers.

2ndly. What *chambers* those are, which he brought her into.

3rdly. What is meant by his bringing there, or what this phrase is expressive of.

ʸ נרוּצָה ut curramus, so some in Marckius.

* Εισαγαγετω με, Symmachus; introducat me, Marckius.

1st. Who this *King* is, not *Solomon*, for "a greater than Solomon is here;" but the Lord Jesus Christ, who is κατ' ἐξοχην, by way of eminency, called, "The King:"[a] who is the King of the whole word, the King of the kings of the world, and the King of saints; he has, as he is God, an universal empire over all worlds, heaven, earth, and hell; and as Mediator, has a kingdom given him by his Father, which he has purchased with his own blood, and by the mighty conquests of his grace, has brought into subjection to himself; in this kingdom he enacts laws for the subjects thereof, by which they are governed and kept in order; he subdues all their enemies, sin, Satan, and the world; protects them from all dangers; encourages his loyal and faithful subjects; courteously receives them, graciously takes notice of all their petitions, and supplies them with every thing needful for them: now this kingdom, which Christ as Mediator, is possessed of, is of a spiritual nature, and managed in a spiritual way; it is kept in peace, being governed in wisdom and righteousness; and will continue for ever, when all other rule and authority shall be thrown down. But,

2ndly. What *chambers* are these which this king is said to bring her into? Not the temple, into which *Solomon* introduced the people of *Israel*, which is the same sense[b] some give of the words; though there may be an[c] allusion to the temple, and the chambers thereof, of which mention is made, 1 Chron. xxviii. 11, 12; and more especially to the holy of holies, which was inaccessible to any but the high priest; as that, which was typified by it, is to any but Christ the High-priest, and those who belong to him, to whom he gives access, and who have boldness and liberty to enter into the holiest of all, by the blood of Jesus: nor do I think that by them are meant those everlasting mansions of peace and rest, which are in Christ's Fathers's house, which he is preparing for his spouse, and bride, and into which he, ere long, will introduce her, where they will keep an everlasting nuptial feast; for at present she could not say, that she was brought thither, though she might be assured of it, that she should, by those kind intimations of his love unto her; therefore it seems better to understand them either,

1. Of those chambers of intimate communion and fellowship, which Christ sometimes brings his people into, and of which they are exceeding desirous; this inestimable blessing Christ frequently grants to his people in his ordinances; for he does not always suffer them to stand without, in the outer courts, but sometimes takes them into his inner chambers, where he discloses the secrets of his heart unto them, gives evident intimations of his love, and fills their souls with divine consolation: or else,

2. The doctrines of the Gospel, which contain the unsearchable riches of Christ, and the mysteries of his grace, which he brings his people gradually into, and shows them those things which eye hath not seen, neither hath ear heard, nor the heart of man conceived of:[d] He took me, as if she should say, into his chambers, and there more thoroughly instructed me into his mind and will; gave me to know more fully the *mysteries of the kingdom;* opened all the treasures of his grace, and showed me all his riches, and glory contained therein. Now this sense suits well with a practice much used by the *Jews*, who frequently taught in chambers, where they also met together to converse about, and determine matters in religion, as fully appears from their writings;[e] and we have many hints in the New Testament, which confirm it; it was in such a chamber that Christ kept the passover, and instituted the Lord's Supper, and gave there a discovery of the nature of his death and sufferings to his disciples: in such a room the disciples met together, after his ascension; and in such an one *Paul* preached till midnight. But,

3rdly. What is meant by being brought into these chambers; or what does this phrase import, or express?

1. On Christ's part.

(1). An acknowledgement of her to be his bride; he having espoused her to himself, and solemnized the marriage among her friends, which was the Jewish custom, takes her home to himself as his spouse and bride, to live and converse with him; leads her into his chambers, and there unlocks all his treasures; shows her all his riches and glory, and puts her into the possession of them.

(2). It imports wonderful condescension in him, that he, who is the King of kings, should vouchsafe to regard such a worthless creature, as the church is in herself; and much more espouse her to himself, and in such a kind, loving, and familiar manner, give her access to his person, and all he has, and grant her such intimate communion and fellowship with him.

(3). It shows us, that all our nearness to, and communion with God, are in and through Christ; it is he that gives us " access into the grace wherein we stand," and leads us into the presence of his Father; he is our only way of access unto him, and acceptance with him.

2. On her part, they being her words, show,

(1). That she does not ascribe this to herself, but to his powerful and efficacious grace; she was conscious of her own inability, and therefore makes application to him, and, having obtained her desires, acknowledges it to the glory of his grace; who " brought, *or* caused her to come," as the[f] word may be rendered, notwithstanding all diffi-

---

[a] So the Cabalistic Doctors interpret the King, when put alone, of Tiphereth, the bridegroom, Lexic. Cab. p. 536. [b] Brightman and Cotton, in loc. [c] *Vide* Bishop Patrick, in loc. [d] So Theodoret. and Tres Patres, in loc. Targum in Cant. 3. 4. and Tract. Sabbat. in Misnah, c. 1. §. 4. [e] הביאני me venire fecit. [f] *Vide*

culties and obstructions which lay in the way.

(2). This she does with thankfulness, in an exulting manner, as this way of speaking testifies, and the following words declare: what was before matter of prayer, is now the subject of praise; she owns, with gratitude, as became her, the mercy she had received.

(3). It seems to be in a boasting way and manner that she speaks. Believers are allowed to glory in the Lord, and boast of what he has done for them, and manifests to them, that his grace may be magnified, others take notice of it, and they be encouraged in their addresses to him: the church here might have an eye to the virgins or daughters of *Jerusalem*.

IV. We have, in these words, the effects or consequences of the church's enjoying this valuable blessing, as they appear in her own members, or her daughters, "the virgins."

1st. Gladness and rejoicing in Christ; "we will be glad and rejoice in thee." The several clauses of this text, some think, should be considered thus;* the first clause, "Draw me," as the words of the church; the next, "We will run after thee," the chorus of the virgins; then the church again says, "The King hath brought me into his chambers;" and after that the virgins, "We will be glad," &c., but whether the church, or the virgins, or both, are here intended, it is certain, that this is the language of believers, of whose joy Christ is the object: they rejoice, not in themselves, neither in their works, nor graces, nor frames, but in the Lord Jesus Christ; this is one part of the character which the apostle gives of true believers; they are such who "rejoice in Christ Jesus, *and* have no confidence in the flesh," Phil. iii. 3.

1. They rejoice in his person, in his greatness, fitness, fulness, and glory, as he is God and man in one person; for, being so, he is able to be their Saviour, a proper person to be a Mediator, has all fulness of grace treasured up in him, and appears to be "the brightness of his Father's glory, and the express image of his person;" a view of, and communion with, such an one, must needs fill the believer with "a joy unspeakable and full of glory."

2. They rejoice in what he has done for them; he is the Lord Jehovah, "who has done great things for them, whereof they are glad;" he engaged as their Surety in the everlasting covenant, and in the "fulness of time" assumed their nature, finished and made reconciliation for their sins, satisfied Divine Justice, fulfilled a righteous law, brought in and clothed them with an everlasting righteousness, procured the pardon of all their sins; and, in short, has secured all grace and glory for them; and when they consider all this, they cannot but be glad and rejoice in him.

3. They rejoice also in what he is unto them, as well as in what he has done for them; he stands in and fills up all relations to them; he is their "everlasting Father," their kind and loving Brother, their tender and indulgent Husband, their constant and faithful Friend, and indeed, their "all in all;" he is every thing unto them, for he "of God is made unto *them*, wisdom, righteousness, sanctification, *and* redemption;" and when they consider him under all these endearing characters and relations, it is no wonder that they are heard to say, "I will greatly rejoice in the Lord, my soul shall be joyful in the God of my salvation," &c.

2ndly. Another effect of the church enjoying such intimate communion with Christ, is a remembrance of his love; "We will remember thy love more than wine." I have already, on ver. 2, shown you the preferableness of Christ's love to wine, and shall not here repeat it, only show,

1. What it is to remember Christ's love.
2. Why we should, and every believer will do so.

1. What it is to remember it.

1. It is so to record it in our minds, as not to forget it; we should, with *David*, call upon our "souls, *and* all that is within us, *to* bless his holy name, *and* forget not all his benefits," Psal. ciii. 1, 2; and more especially we should not forget his love, from whence they all spring.

2. We should often meditate upon it; which would not only serve to advance the glory of divine love; but would sweetly ravish our souls, raise our affections, inflame our love, and quicken our faith.

3. We should constantly observe that ordinance, which Christ has appointed for this purpose, namely, the Lord's supper: it being his design in the institution of it, that we should remember him, his broken body and precious blood, and particularly his special love, which appeared in all.

4. We should so remember it, as to have our desires more strongly after it, and our affections more firmly fixed upon it: Christ's love is excellent and valuable; it is preferable to life itself, and all the comforts of it; and a frequent revolving it in our minds will enlarge our desires after a greater knowledge of it, and heighten our value for, and esteem of it.

5. We should so remember it, as to exercise faith in it; for it will bring us but little comfort, and do us but little service, unless we can, in some measure, appropriate it to ourselves, saying, with the apostle, "He hath loved me, *and* hath given himself for me;" it will afford us no solid joy and comfort, that he has loved others, if we have no reason to hope and believe that he hath loved us; for it is faith's viewing a peculiar interest in this love, that fixes a sense of it more firmly upon the mind.

6. It then appears, that this is uppermost in our minds, when we speak and make mention of it to others; and, indeed, that should be the subject of our discourse now, which will be the de-

---
* Vide Bishop Patrick in loc.

lightful theme of glorified saints to all eternity. But,

2. Why should we, and why will every believer remember Christ's love, value and esteem it more than wine?

1. Because it is worthy of remembrance, in its own nature, and in its effects, as has been already shown; it is " better than wine;" it is great and glorious, stupendous and unparalleled, matchless and boundless, everlasting and unchangeable; it " passeth knowledge, and is the source and spring of all the grace we now receive, and of all the glory we are expectants of.

2. It would be ungrateful in us not to remember it; should we be unmindful of, and forget this love, and the benefits which spring from it, we should be justly chargeable with the vile sin of ingratitude; and it might be very pertinently returned upon us, what *Absolom* said to *Hushai*, " Is this thy kindness to thy friend?" 2 Sam. xvi. 17.

3. Because he hath remembered us, and that " in our low estate, because his mercy endureth for ever;" even when we were in the depths of sin and misery, could not help ourselves, and were so far from having any love to him, that we were in open rebellion against him; yet such was his amazing love to us, that he raised us " beggars from the dunghill, washed us from our sins in his own blood," and made " us kings and priests to God and his Father;" and shall we not remember? can we be forgetful of this love?

4. A remembrance of it promotes our own comfort and edification, serves to make sin odious and detestable, and is oftentimes useful to excite and revive grace, to banish our doubts and fears, and make the person of Christ more precious to us.

3rdly. Another effect or consequence of the church's being brought into the chambers of near fellowship and communion with Christ, is, that the love of his church and people is the more drawn forth to him, who here go under the character of upright ones, " the upright love thee;" or according to the Hebrew text, " uprightnesses love thee;"[h] the abstract for the concrete; which intends upright men, or men of uprightness, as being the persons who love Christ; unless with *R. Sol. Jarchi*, we take it to be expressive of the sincerity of their love, and so read it, " in uprightnesses, *or* with an upright love they love thee:" R. Aben Ezra thinks it is the adjective of *wine*, before-mentioned, and intends the excellency, sweetness, and incorruptness of it, as in chap. vii. 9; and the sense then is this, " we will remember thy love more than wine, yea, more than upright wine," or wine that goes down sweetly, " do they love thee:" though I rather think it intends the character of the persons who love Christ. I have already, on the preceding verse, shown the nature of this love, with which souls love Christ, from whence it springs, and how it manifests itself: and shall now only consider the character of those persons who are here said to love him, namely, upright ones; and they are.

1. Such who are said to be " upright in heart," of whom mention is made in Psal. cxxv. 4, " Do good, O Lord, to them that be good, *and* to them that are upright in their hearts;" such are they who have a work of grace wrought upon their souls; whose hearts are right with God, and desire to worship him with their whole hearts; who live by faith on Christ, and his righteousness, and whose words and actions are without dissimulation; such are " Israelites indeed, in whom there is no guile."

2. Who are of an upright conversation, as in Psal. xxxvii. 14. These are they who walk according to the rule of God's word; they are not partial in their observance of his commands, but have a regard to them all; they make a conscience of avoiding lesser, as well as greater sins; and in all their obedience to the divine will, seek the honour and glory of God: and what they do, they do in faith, and from a principle of love to God and Christ. *Junius* understands this clause of the sincerity and uprightness of the love of the church and her friends to Christ, and reads it in connection with the former thus, " We will remember thy love more than wine, *and* whosoever most uprightly love thee;"[i] that is, whoever bear a sincere affection to thee will do the same.

Verse 5. *I am black, but comely; O ye daughters of Jerusalem, as the tents of Kedar, as the curtains of Solomon.*

THE church in the preceding verses had directed her speech to Christ, where we have observed the request she makes, and the success of it, and also the comfortable and grateful frame of Spirit produced by it: here she turns herself to " the daughters of Jerusalem," and gives an account of her person and state, and delivers her mind to them in this and the following verse. Wherein may be considered.

I. The persons she speaks to, " the daughters of Jerusalem."

II. The character which she gives of herself.

III. The reason of her so doing.

I. The persons she speaks to, are " the daughters of Jerusalem:" and seeing these are frequently mentioned in this Song, it will be necessary to consider who are meant by them. *R. Sol. Jarchi* would have them to be the Gentiles, who, he says, are so called, because *Jerusalem* shall be the metropolis of all nations, according to Ezek. xvi. 61, " I will give them unto thee for daughters;" and that they are, in the same sense, " the daughters of Jerusalem," as the towns of *Ekron* are called in Josh. xv. 45, " the daughters of Ekron;" but it is much better to understand them of particular churches, of which, " Jerusalem that is above," or that general assembly, *and* church of the first-born,

---

[h] מישרים εὐθύτης, Sept. Rectitudines. Ar. Mont.   [i] Quicunque rectissime diligunt te, Jun.

whose names are written in heaven," is the mother; though I rather think, young converts are intended by them, who, perhaps, had not as yet joined themselves to the church, though they had a very great respect for her, as is manifest from chap. v. 9; they seem to be very weak, and their knowledge of Christ but small, yet desirous of knowing him and seeking him with her. (See chap. v. 8, and vi. 1.) And it is very evident, that not only the church, but Christ also, had a very great respect for them, from chap. iii. 9, 10, 11. They were her friends and companions, distinct from mothers' children, mentioned in the following verse, and were far from being enemies either to Christ or his church.

II. To these persons she gives a character of herself.

1st. She makes a concession that she was *black*.
2ndly. Notwithstanding asserts that she is *comely*. And.

3rdly. Uses some similes to express both by, "as the tents of Kedar, the curtains of Solomon."

1st. She ingenuously and frankly acknowledges, that she was *black*. This is not to be understood literally of *Pharaoh's* daughter, whom *Solomon* had married; and whose mother, *Grotius* conjectures, might be an *Arabian*, and so these words be expressive of her natural complexion; but this is not intended, nor, perhaps, is there so much as an allusion to it; but rather to a shepherdess, or keeper of vineyards, made black by lying in the fields, as the following verse seems to intimate. The *Targum* applies it to the people of *Israel*, when they made the calf, and says, that then " their faces became as black as the Ethiopians, that dwell in the tents of Kedar, but when they returned, by repentance, and were forgiven, the brightness of the glory of their countenances was increased, as the angels:" but the words are expressive of the spiritual estate and complexion of the church of Christ, and of all believers in him; who may be said to be *black*, and *comely*; *black* by sin, *comely* by grace:[k] *Black*.

1. Upon the account of many spots, blemishes, and infirmities; for though they are fair and spotless, as considered in Christ, yet they are black and full of spots, as considered in themselves; sin dwells in them, and they are sometimes overcome, and carried captive by it; it is always present with them; this body of sin and death, they carry about as their burden; neither will they be rid of it in this life; for " if we say that we have no sin, we deceive ourselves, and the truth is not in us;" the most holy and righteous man on earth is not without it; every one is both disturbed and defiled with it, and therefore in this sense may be said to be *black*; and so the[l] Jewish doctors expound it, of the sinful actions and evil works of the congregation of *Israel*.

2. The church of Christ may be said to be *black*, oftentimes on the account of those swarms of hypocrites and heretics that appear in it; there have always been more or less of them in the church, in all ages, which have been "spots in their feasts of charity." There was a Cain in Adam's family, a Ham in Noah's, an Ishmael in Abraham's, an Esau in Isaac's, and a Judas among Christ's disciples; these goats have always been among Christ's sheep, these tares grow up among his wheat, and will do so, till he shall divide the sheep from the goats, and take his fan in his hand, and thoroughly purge his floor. Now upon the account of these, and the several heresies, schisms, and divisions, which frequently arise, and are made in the church of Christ, she may be said to be *black*: And also,

3. By reason of the persecutions and reproaches of the world, which the church of Christ, and all believers in him sustain; for they that "will live godly in Christ Jesus must suffer persecution" of one kind or another; if not confiscation of goods, fines, imprisonments, racks, tortures, yea, death itself, which in some ages of the world, have been the lot of God's children, yet, at least, loss of their good name, credit, and reputation; for if they are loved by Christ, they must expect to be hated by men; if they have peace in him, in the world they must have tribulation; they may be sure of being vilified by the world, and backbited and reproached by carnal professors; and this is what the church seems to ascribe her blackness to, in the following verse. So in Zohar,[m] this blackness is by the Jews, expounded of the captivity of the people of Israel.

4. She may be said to be black, with sorrow and mournings; black colour not only being the habit of mourners, but does also, in scripture, express grief and sorrow itself. See Jer. viii. 21, and xiv. 2. The sins and corruptions of God's people, oftentimes put them in this mourning habit; as David says, when he was under a sense of his manifold iniquities, "I go mourning all the day long," Psal. xxxviii. 6, or nearer the Hebrew, " I go in black all the day long;"[n] the coldness, hypocrisy, and formality of professors, give them much uneasiness: the many errors and heresies among them, and the persecutions and reproaches, both of the world and carnal professors, produce this black hue and mournful colour.

5. They are black in the eyes of the world, which indeed is no wonder: for the men of the world see no beauty nor comeliness in Christ himself, and therefore not any in his people; they being, in their eyes, mean, abject, and contemptible, despised by them, and accounted as the refuse and " off-scouring of all things." But notwithstanding all this she could say,

---

[k] Nigra per naturam, formosa per gratiam, Aug. de Tempore, Serm. 201, p. 354. tom. 10. Fusca per culpam, decora per gratiam, Ambros. in Ps. 118. octon. 2. col. 881. tom. 2. [l] R. Sol. Jarchi and R. Aben Ezra, in loc. in Lev. fol. 25. 1. [m] In Exod. fol. 6. 1. and Jun. [n] קדר הלכתי atratus pergo,

2ndly. That she was *comely*, that is, beautiful and desireable, having graceful features, and a just symmetry and proportion. Now the church, and every believer in Christ, may be said to be comely.

1. By the imputation of Christ's righteousness, whereby they are justified from all sin, and stand spotless and irreprovable in God's sight; their own righteousness is as filthy rags, and rather detracts from, than adds to their comeliness; but Christ's righteousness being that "fine linen, clean, and white," with which being arrayed, they are "adorned as a bride for her husband," they appear perfectly *comely through* the *comeliness which* Christ has *put upon* them; they are no ways comely in themselves, but in Christ they are a *perfection of beauty*.

2. By the sanctifying grace of the Spirit, whereby they are made new creatures; Christ is formed in their hearts, and they are conformed to him, who is the "first-born among many brethren;" his image is impressed upon them, and all the parts of the *new man* are in a just proportion in them, though not grown up to their perfection; and thus being made partakers of the divine nature, and appearing in the beauties of holiness, they are *all glorious* and comely *within*.

3. Believers are so in their church-state, having fellowship with Christ, and with one another, walking together in, and according to the commands and ordinances of Christ Jesus: a church of Christ, in gospel order, is beautiful for situation; all her tabernacles are amiable and lovely; and enjoying the presence of Christ in them, is "beautiful as Tirzah, comely as Jerusalem, and terrible as an army with banners." O how comely are the saints in their goings in Zion! a more lovely sight than this can scarce be seen; they are then like a "company of horses in Pharaoh's chariots."

However black believers may be in the eyes of the world, they are certainly comely in the eyes of Christ; who often, in this song, calls his church, his "fair one," and "the fairest among women;" however undesirable she was to others, she was very desirable to him; her eyes, cheeks, lips, teeth, head, hair, neck, &c., are commended and praised by him; so much beauty and comeliness appeared in her, that his heart was even ravished with her; and so long as he thinks her comely it matters not what opinion others entertain of her.

3rdly. She makes use of some similes to express both her blackness and her comeliness, "as the tents of Kedar, as the curtains of Solomon."

Some think that these refer to both parts of her character; and suppose that the tents of Kedar, though they were mean and abject without, yet were full of wealth and riches within; and a number of them together made a fine appearance, as Dr. Shaw relates they now do; and that Solomon's curtains or hangings had an outward covering, which was not so rich and valuable as that within; and so are both designed by the church to represent unto us, that though she was mean and abject in the eyes of the world, yet she was rich, glorious, and beautiful within: the outside of a believer is only seen by the world, and they judge of him accordingly; his inside is hid from them, as the riches of *Kedar's* tents, and the fineness of *Solomon's* curtains were from those who viewed the outside only; though I rather think her blackness is designed by the one, and her comeliness by the other.

1. For her blackness she compares herself to the *tents of Kedar*. *Kedar* was the second son of *Ishmael*, Gen. xxiv. 13, whose posterity dwelt in the desert of *Arabia*, Isa. xliii. 11, and their employment being to feed cattle, Isa. lx. 7, they dwelt in tents, Psal. cxx. 4, 5, which were made of hair-cloth, and that of goat's hair; which being always exposed to the sun and rain, were very black, looked very mean and contemptible: they had no other houses but these; and because they always dwelt in them, removing and pitching them at pleasure, therefore they were called *Scenites*. Now the church compares herself to these mean, black, and despicable tents, on the account of the sins and infirmities of herself, the carnality and hypocrisy of others, the many errors and heresies she was vexed with, as well as the persecutions and reproaches of men, which oftentimes oppressed her, as has been already observed.

2. For her comeliness, she compares herself to the *curtains of Solomon*. The Septuagint read it, ὡς δέῤῥεις Σαλωμών, *as the skins of Solomon*; and so the *Vulgate Latin* likewise; which version *Gilbert Foliot* following, in this exposition of this place, says, it is not to be understood of the skins of sheep, goats, or any other animal, but of the very skin of *Solomon* himself; who being a rich king, and living deliciously, he supposes was very comely and beautiful: to whose fine skin he thinks the church here compares herself, to set forth her comeliness: but this is much better referred by *Alcuin*, his countryman, to the skins of slain beasts, of which he thinks *Solomon* made tents for himself; though it seems rather to intend those rich hangings of tapestry, which *Solomon* had, either about his bed, or in the several

---

° נאוה optabilis, Pagninus, Montanus, Tig. Vers. Mercer. So Aben Ezra.   Mercer. in loc.
q Travels, p. 222. ed. 2.   r *Vide* R. Sol. Jarchi, and R. Aben Ezra in loc.   s Nomadas, infestatoresque Chaldæorum, Scenitæ clandunt, et ipsi vagi, sed a tabern aculis cognominati, quæ ciliciis metuntur, ubi libuit, Plin.1. 6. c. 28. Arabes nobiles monte Casio, qui Scenitæ causam nominis inde ducunt, quod tentoriis succedunt, nec alias domos habent; ipsa autem tentoria cilicina sunt; ita nuncupant velamenta é caprarum pilis texta. Solin. Polyhist. c. 46.
t This Gilbert Foliot was bishop of London, and lived in the 12th century, in the reign of King Henry II. whose Exposition, together with the Compendium of Alcuin, his countryman, were published by Patricius Junius, p. 1638.

apartments of his house; which, no doubt, were very rich, costly, and glorious, he being so great and wealthy a prince: or his garments, as *Theodoret*, see Matt. vi. 29; and therefore the church, on the account of her perfect comeliness, through Christ's righteousness put upon her, and the curious and embroidered work of the Spirit of God in her, as also her walk in Gospel-order, compares herself to these curtains or hangings Moreover, by a metonymy, may be understood, both in this and the preceding comparison, the persons who dwelt in *Kedar's* tents, and *Solomon's* courtiers, who lived in those apartments of his which were so richly hung; the former being black, and the latter dwelling in the palace of a wealthy king, and faring deliciously, were no doubt, plump and comely: though neither *Solomon* nor any of his courtiers, could come near the church for beauty and comeliness; and to this sense agrees *Junius's* version of the text." But

III. Let us now consider the reason of her giving this account of herself to the daughters of *Jerusalem*: her design seems to be to obviate what might be objected by, and remove whatever might be discouraging in her to the daughters of *Jerusalem*, those young converts; they might object to her. Thou talkest of being brought into the king's chambers, and having nearness of access unto him, how can it be, that one so black as thou art, should be taken notice of by so great a person, and have such nearness to him, who appears to be so mean and so unworthy thereof? To this she answers, by granting, that she was black in herself, but yet was comely, through his comeliness; in him she was *prepared as a bride adorned for her husband*; and it was this that gave her the favour and acceptance she had with him.

Again, It might be objected, How canst thou be cheerful, when thou art so black, loaded with persecutions and afflictions, and hated and despised by all? This she obviates by observing, that the world could not see her inward glory, and therefore passed a wrong judgment upon her: and that the unseen glory, riches, beauty, and perfection in Christ, supported her under all reflections, persecutions, and reproaches.

Also, the sins and infirmities which they saw in her, as well as the suffering she was exposed unto, might stumble those young converts, and be a means to deter them from the ways of Christ, and joining with his church and people; and seeing there was danger of this, therefore she informs them of her beauty as well as of her blackness; of her grace, as well as of her corruptions; of her glory, as well as of her sufferings; and in doing this, her design is to engage and encourage them to go with her; in all which, she discovers her strength of faith in Christ, and his righteousness, notwithstanding all her sins and sufferings; of which she gives a further account in the following verse.

Verse 6. *Look, not upon me, because I am black, because the sun hath looked upon me: My mother's children were angry with me; they made me the keeper of the vineyard; but mine own vineyard have I not kept.*

THE church, here continues her discourse to the daughters of *Jerusalem*: And,

I. Desires of them, not to look upon her.

II. Gives a reason why she should not have them do so, *because I am black*; of which blackness she assigns several causes; some of which are more near, others more remote.

1st. "Because the sun *had* looked upon her."

2ndly. "*Her* mother's children were angry with *her*."

3rdly. "They *had* made *her* the keeper of the vineyards."

4thly. This occasioned a neglect of her own; *mine own vineyard have I not kept*; all which produced this blackness in her; for it was not her true and native colour.

I. She desires the daughters of *Jerusalem* not to *look upon* her; which may be understood, either, 1. Of a look of scorn and disdain:ᵃ she was now in suffering circumstances, surrounded with a variety of enemies, exposed to a multitude of troubles, and liable to many failings and infirmities; for which reasons she might be jealous of falling under their scorn and contempt, and therefore says, *Look not upon me*. The meanness, poverty, and sufferings of the saints, render them contemptible to the world; and the failures and imperfections of their lives are oftentimes thrown in their teeth, and this, too often, by professors themselves; but this we should be very careful of, that we do not treat our fellow Christians after such a manner: we should be far from slighting a believer under sufferings, or carrying with a disdainful air to a fallen saint; for we should consider, that we also are *in the body*, and liable to the same temptations. Or else, 2. It means a curious and prying look into her failings and infirmities; conscious she was to herself of them, but knew it was not their duty, though perhaps they too often made it their business, to look into them. There are some who are never better, than when thus employed, in exposing of the saints; they watch for their haltings, and are glad to report and spread a tale of the infirmities of their brethren; their eyes pierce like vultures, and fasten upon nothing else but corruption: but such a curious, prying look as this, is condemned by Christ, Matt. vii. 3, 4, 5, "And why beholdest thou the mote that is in thy brother's eye, but considerest not the beam that is in thine own eye," &c. If God did as strictly observe and mark our iniquities, as we are too apt to mark one another's, what would become of us! This con-

ᵘ Similis sim Scenitis Kedarenis, at similis sum inhabitantibus aulæu Schelomonis. *Vide* Joseph. Antiq. l. 8. c. 2. ᵃ *Vide* Alshech in loc.

sideration should deter us from a practice so vile in itself, so dishonourable to religion, and which is so highly resented by Christ. 3. It may also signify a looking with delight and pleasure at her afflictions and falls, which perhaps, she was suspicious of: this was what Edom was blamed for, in Obad. v. 12, 13, "but thou shouldest not have looked on the day of thy brother," that is, with joy and pleasure, as the following words show; "neither shouldest thou have rejoiced over the children of Judah, in the day of their destruction," &c.; believers should be so far from such a temper as this is, that they should rather sympathise with them in their sufferings, and falls, than triumph over them; for "let him that thinketh he standeth, take heed lest he fall." Or, 4. She would not have them look upon her as persons astonished and amazed at her present sufferings, as though some strange and unaccountable thing had happened to her; for they need not be surprised, when they consider, that Christ, her Head and Husband, the holy and the harmless one, was treated after the same, yea, after a much worse manner; that the sufferings which she underwent, were but what were appointed for her, and would all end in God's glory, and her own good, therefore she would have them not be startled at them, nor be discouraged by them from joining with her. 5. She would have them not to look at her blackness only, but also at her beauty; it is true, she was black in herself, and that she acknowledges; but then she was comely in Christ, and that she would have them take notice of, as well as the other: she would have them look upon Christ, who is "white and ruddy, the chiefest among ten thousand," who is altogether lovely and exceeding comely, and consider her in him, and not as she was in herself, for that might be frightening and discouraging to them.

II. She proceeds to give the reason why she would not have them look upon her, because, says she, "I am black:" she had said this before; but here she uses the same word in another form, which some think is to diminish the signification of it, and that she was not so black as they thought her to be, or had represented her; and read it "blackish," or "somewhat black;"[a] though the doubling of the radicals seems rather to increase the signification, as in other places, see Psal. xlv. 5, Prov. viii. 3t-; and therefore should be read, "because I am very black;" or exceeding black;[b] and this she here mentions again with this addition, that she might have an opportunity to give account of the particular reasons thereof; which reasons are as follow.

1st. She declares, that one reason of her blackness was, "because the sun had looked upon her." The Ethiopic version has it, "because the sun hath not looked upon me," that is, not kindly and gently, which would be pleasant and delightful; but severely, as to scorch her, and therefore looked black: and so Ambrose[c] reads the words; but interprets them of the Sun of righteousness, who had not shone upon her, being deprived of which, she had not attended to her devotion and observance of the commands, which had brought blackness upon her. 1. The Targum expounds this of the congregation of Israel, which was made black by the idolatrous worship of the sun and moon; against this, a law was provided, it was strictly prohibited by God, Deut. xvii. 3; but yet was very early in the world; most nations under the sun fell into it; some worshipped the sun under one name, and some under another, and all paid a regard unto it; this idolatrous worship seems to have obtained in Job's time, see Job. xxxi. 26, 27; and the Jewish nation was not exempt from it; they frequently fell into it, and were blackened by it, see 2 Kings xxiii. 5—11, Ezek. viii. 16; for idolatry, error, and superstition, will make the church black. 2. Others understand it of Christ,[d] "the Sun of righteousness;" and that she was made black, either by suffering for him, or else by being in his company, in whose presence, all other beauty, but his own, vanishes and disappears. Thus a person that is not of a fair complexion, being in the company of one that is, looks abundantly worse than if viewed alone: Christ's beauty infinitely exceeds any that is in us; there is no comparison between them; we look black, exceeding black, when compared to Christ. But, 3. I should rather choose to understand it of the sun of persecution, for under this name it goes in Matt. xiii. 6, compared with v. 21, and this seems to suit better with the church's present state and circumstances; and, indeed, every one "that will live godly in Christ Jesus, shall suffer persecution," from the tongues, if not from the hands of men: and this persecution, which the church underwent, seems to be a very vehement one, in that she compares it to the looks and scorchings of the sun; and it must continue some time upon her, to make and leave such visible marks and impressions upon it; and yet she patiently endured all, and bravely "bore the heat and burden of the day," and seems to be more ashamed of her sufferings, than she was of the person and cause for whom she suffered. The allusion is to persons burnt with the sun,[e] and so made black or swarthy, as in some countries; and especially to such who are much in the fields, and employed in rural work, as the church is represented as a keeper of vineyards and of flocks of sheep, in the following words.

2ndly. Her "mother's children were angry with

---

[a] שְׁחַרְחֹרֶת μεμελανωμήνη, Sept. Subnigra, Junius and Tremellius, Piscator, Mercerus, Cocceius; paululum denigrata, Pagninus; so Ainsworth and Aben Ezra. [b] Valde fusca, Bochart. prorsus vel valde et tota nigra, Marckius, Michaelis. [c] De Isaac. c. 4. [d] Foliot and Cocceius in loc. [e] Perusta solibus Pernicis uxor, Horat. Epod. Ode 2. v. 41, 42. Αλιοκαυστον, Theocrit. Idyll. 10. v. 27.

her." To her outward persecutions were added intestine broils; it is therefore no wonder she looked so black as she did: oftentimes a man's worst enemies are those of his own house. The Targum by *mother's children* understands the false prophets, who taught the congregation of Israel to serve idols, and walk in the statutes of the people; by reason of which, she served not the Lord, neither walked in his statutes, nor kept his precepts and his laws. R. Sol. Jarchi thinks the Egyptians are intended, among whom the Israelites were brought up; many of whom came along with them out of Egypt, and were frequently the cause of their falling into sin: but rather we are to understand by *mother's children*, either, 1. Indwelling sins and corruptions, which are produced with nature: lust conceived, as soon as we were conceived; nay, we were conceived with it, and in it, as the Psalmist says, Psal. li. 5, " Behold I was shapen in iniquity, and in sin did my mother conceive me;" which brought forth sin in us as soon as we were brought forth into the world; and these indwelling lusts and corruptions proclaim war against us; these war against the soul, and sometimes " bring it into captivity to the law of sin which is in the members;" they frequently draw us away to the performance of sinful actions, making us the keepers of other vineyards, and often divert us from our duty, and cause us to neglect it; they hinder us from doing the good we would; for " when we would do good, evil is present with us;" and so we may be said not to keep our own vineyard. Or else, 2. Carnal professors may be here intended, who are members of the same society, externally children of the same mother, who profess themselves of the holy city, are pretenders to godliness, but enemies to it; such are they, who have " a form of godliness, but deny the power thereof," in themselves, and hate it in others; which, perhaps, may be one reason why these children that were born after the flesh, these false brethren, were angry with the church here; as they frequently are at her zealous defence and vindication of gospel-truths and ordinances, in the power and purity of them, and at her faithful reproofs and admonitions to them and others; throwing all the scandal and reproach upon her that possibly they can: now these are generally her most bitter and implacable enemies, are thorns in her side, and give her the greatest uneasiness; causing more grief and trouble to her, than all her sufferings and persecution from the world; for hereby they blacken and lessen her reputation and character, more than any other whatever; and yet bear it she must, and patiently she ought to endure it; Christ himself was not free from it; for who were more bitter and implacable enemies to him and his Gospel, than the Jews, God's professing people, and the chief among them, the high-priests and Pharisees?

3rdly. She says " they made her the keeper of the vineyards," as an effect of their anger to her, and this, no doubt, added to her blackness; for being obliged to lie abroad in the fields, to keep the vineyards, she was exposed to the scorching sun-beams, and thereby got the hue she appeared with: this employment being not only very slavish, but base, mean, and reproachful; it was what was usually done by the poorer sort, and was much below the honour and dignity she was raised unto. By *vineyards* may be meant false churches; and by her keeping them, her falling in with their corrupt worship, and observance of the vain traditions and ordinances of men: which Christ complains of, and condemns in the Jewish church, who " made the commandment of God of none effect by their traditions." But this the church was obliged unto by her mother's children; her compliance does not seem to be voluntary, but forced, and she complains of it as an imposition; " they made me," that is, forced and obliged me to do it. And this produced,

4thly. A neglect of her own vineyard, " but mine own vineyard have I not kept;" which still increased her blackness; through outward persecution, intestine brolls, and a sinful compliance to human traditions, arising either from fear or weakness, or both, her own vineyard, the church, or her own soul, was neglected, and the affairs of it; her duty and business incumbent on her, the religious exercise she ought to have been employed in: with the Romans, neglect of fields and vineyards came under the notice of the censors, and did not go unpunished.[d] Every believer has talents more or less given him to occupy, grace to exercise, gifts to use, and a part assigned him in the Lord's vineyard, to labour in; and when these things are neglected by him, either through the fear of men, or the corruptions of his own heart, he may be said, not to have kept his vineyard; which, perhaps, sometimes is like his who was " void of understanding, which was all grown over with thorns, and nettles had covered the face thereof;" but when he is sensible of it, he will acknowledge and bewail it, as the church does here; she does not go about to extenuate her sin, by the anger of her mother's children, nor by their obliging her to keep other vineyards, but ingenuously acknowledges that it was her fault to neglect her own; which, as it was prejudicial to herself, so it was highly resented by Christ, who thereupon removed his presence from her; for she seems to be at a loss to know where he was, as is manifest from the following words.

---

* So Horace calls his own works Vineta, Epist. l. 2. epist. l. v. 220.

[d] A. Gell. Noct. Attic. l. 4. c. 12.

Verse 7. *Tell me, (O thou whom my soul loveth), where thou feedest, where thou makest thy flocks to rest at noon; For why should I be as one that turneth aside by the flocks of thy companions?*

THE church having, in the two former verses, directed her speech to the daughters of Jerusalem, and given them an account of herself, and present condition, with the reasons thereof, which she did, in order to solve their objections, and remove all discouragements from them that might arise from thence; and being sensible of her weakness and sinfulness in complying with, and embracing the traditions and doctrines of men, in which she found no solid food for her soul; she therefore makes application to Christ, the great Shepherd of the sheep, that he would feed, refresh, guide, direct, and restore her wandering soul. In these words are,

I. A request made unto him.
II. Some arguments used by her to prevail upon him.

I. Here is a request made by the church of Christ, which consists of two parts. *First*, To know where he feedeth; "Tell me where thou feedest." *Secondly*, That he would inform her where he rested and refreshed his flock in the heat of the day, "where thou makest thy flocks to rest at noon;" both which we shall enter into a consideration of.

First. She desires to know where Christ fed: which is to be understood not passively, where he himself was fed, or where he fed himself; but actively, where he fed others, namely his flock; which, though not expressed in the original text, must be understood; and it may be observed here, that God's own children sometimes may be at a loss to know where Christ feeds; which may arise, either from the prevailings of corruptions in them, whereby they have stepped out of the ways of Christ; or from the hidings of God's face, and the withdrawings of the Sun of righteousness, or from the violent temptations of Satan, and fierce persecutions of the world; but when they are hungry, and desirous of spiritual food, they will enquire after it, and are very jealous, lest they should not be fed by Christ, and with the wholesome words of faith and sound doctrine: therefore in these straits they make their application to Christ, and him only, who "feeds his flock like a shepherd;" which branch of Christ's work and office we shall now consider; and shall endeavour to show, 1st. What this phrase supposes and intends, as referred to Christ. 2ndly. What he feeds his flock with. 3dly. How, after what manner, and by what means he feeds them. 4thly. Where he does so.

1st. It will be proper to enquire what is supposed and intended by Christ's feeding souls.

1. It supposes that Christ is a Shepherd; and he calls himself so, in John x. The scriptures, both of the Old and New Testament, do abundantly testify that he bears this character, and stands in this relation to his people, where he is called God's Shepherd, "Awake, O sword, against my Shepherd, and against the Man that is my fellow, saith the Lord of hosts," Zech. xiii. 7: now he is so called because he is the Shepherd, whom God the Father hath approved of, chosen, appointed, set up, and sent to be the Shepherd of the sheep; who, as such, died for the sheep and rose again, and as such must give an account unto the Father, of all the sheep which he has intrusted him with; he must bring in the full number, yea, must not have one of them wanting. He is also called the Chief Shepherd; "And when the Chief Shepherd shall appear, ye shall receive a crown of glory which fadeth not away," 1 Pet. v. 7, which title he well deserves; for he that is God's shepherd, is also God's fellow, entirely equal to him in the dignity of his nature, and in the fulness of his power and glory; all other shepherds are under him, they receive their commissions from him, have their several flocks assigned to them by him, are furnished with abilities from him to feed them; to him, at last must they give an account of themselves, their work, and the flocks that were put under their care, and from him shall they receive the never-fading crown of glory. He likewise calls himself the good Shepherd; "I am the good Shepherd; the good shepherd giveth his life for the sheep," John x. 11; and he may very justly call himself so, for so he was to him that employed him, and so he is to those who are made his care and charge; he was faithful to his Father, that appointed him, and is merciful and compassionate to, careful and tender of, the sheep committed to his trust; of which, a greater proof cannot be given, than his laying down his life for them. He is called the great Shepherd; "Now the God of peace, that brought again from the dead our Lord Jesus, that great Shepherd of the sheep," Heb. xiii. 20; which will manifestly appear, if we consider the dignity of his Person, being the Son of God; the nature of his flock, the souls of men, therefore he is called "the Shepherd and Bishop of souls;" and also the largeness of his abilities for this work; he has an exquisite knowledge of them, he can call them all by name; he is endued with infinite wisdom and prudence to manage and order his flock aright; has an Almighty arm to protect and defend them from all their enemies; is furnished with large supplies of grace for them, and bears an inexpressible love unto them. Finally, he is the One, and the only Shepherd; "I will set up one Shepherd over them, and he shall feed them," Ezek. xxxiv. 23; not but that there are other shepherds, which are under Christ, and whom he employs in his service, to feed his flock; but Christ is the Chief and Principle; God the Father never did, nor ever will set up any other; he is the only Shepherd that owns the flock,

D

having purchased it with his own blood, and he alone is able to take care of it.

2. Feeding being applied to Christ, not only supposes that he is a Shepherd, but also that he has a flock to feed; "He shall feed his flock like a shepherd," Isa. xl. 11. All the elect are Christ's flock, they are "his people, and the sheep of his pasture;" the Father has given them to him, and has put them into his hands : he has also purchased them with his blood, and calls them by his grace: hence they know his voice, follow his steps, believe in him, and therefore shall never perish, but have everlasting life. Which flock is, 1. A distinct one; it is distinguished from all others, by electing, redeeming, and efficacious grace; Christ's sheep are distinct from the world's goats, and Satan's wolves in sheep's clothing, and will one day be separated and manifestly distinguished, not only from the open enemies of Christ, but also from all painted hypocrites, and carnal professors. 2. Though this flock is divided into many parts and branches, yet it is but one flock; for, as there are but "one fold and one shepherd," so there is but one flock under the care of this shepherd; though there are many particular flocks or churches here on earth, yet there is but "one general assembly and church of the first-born, whose names are written in heaven." 3. This is but a little flock; "Fear not, little flock," &c., Luke xii. 32. Christ's flock of sheep are little and contemptible in the eyes of the world; and are low and mean in their own eyes; they are few in number, when compared with the world's goats, though when all appear together in glory, they will be a "great multitude, which no man can number." 4. It is called a flock of slaughter. Thus said the Father to the Son, "Feed the flock of the slaughter," and he replied, "I will feed the flock of the slaughter, even you, O poor of the flock," Zech. xi. 4--7; and it is so called, because it is exposed to the cruelty and barbarity of open and avowed enemies, and to the ravenings of wolves in sheep's clothing; the saints, for the sake of Christ and his gospel, have been "killed all the day long, and accounted as sheep for the slaughter," Rom. viii. 36. 5. Nevertheless it is a beautiful flock, as the people of the Jews are called in Jer. xiii. 20; the saints are beautiful in Christ's eyes, being clothed with his spotless righteousness, washed in his precious blood, and sanctified by his Spirit; therefore, however black they may be in their own eyes, or in the eyes of others, they are comely and delightful in the eyes of Christ.

3. This act of feeding, takes in and comprehends the whole work and business of a faithful shepherd towards his flock: all which Christ fully and exactly performs. 1. He knows them distinctly, and takes a particular account of them; he knows them so, that he can call them all by name: he knew them full well in his Father's gift of them to him, and so he did when he shed his precious blood for them; he knew distinctly all that he died for; and in effectual calling, he sets his mark, stamps his image on them, that it may also appear, both to themselves and others, to whose flock they belong; he took a particular account of them, when the Father put them into his hands, and made them his care and charge, and they shall "again pass under the hands of him that telleth them :" for he will take care that not one of them shall be lost, but shall be all safely folded in heaven. 2. He not only, as a shepherd, takes a particular account of his flock, but he also leads them out, goes before them, and they follow him; he leads them out of the barren pastures of sin, and leads them into the green pastures of his love and grace; he goes before them as an example to the flock, of love, meekness, humility, patience, &c., and they follow him, in an observance of his ordinances, and in obedience to his commands, till he has safely conducted them to glory. 3. He protects them from all their enemies; Christ's flock is exposed unto, and surrounded by many a roaring lion; ravenous wolves, and snarling dogs stand ready to devour it, had they but as large a permission, and as good an opportunity as they desire; but as David defended his father's sheep from the lion and the bear, so does Christ defend his; he has power enough to do it, and there is not wanting in him, either will, courage, or diligence. 4. He restores his sheep, when they have wandered and strayed from the fold; as it is natural for sheep to go astray, so it is common to Christ's sheep, not only before, but after conversion; "I have gone astray like a lost sheep," says David, Psal. cxix. 176. "Seek thy servant;" Christ does so, when his sheep go astray, he seeks every where until he has found them; when he lays them upon his shoulders, and brings them into his fold again, rejoicing; he restores their souls to their former life and liveliness, and "leads them in the paths of righteousness, for his own name's sake." 5. He heals all their diseases; there are many diseases which sheep are liable to, and therefore had need to be well looked after: so there are many diseases which Christ's sheep are liable to, but they are all healed by him; he binds up the broken hearted, strengthens the weak, heals the sick and wounded; none ever die of their diseases; he is a sovereign, free, universal, and infallible Physician. 6. He watches over them in the night seasons, as the shepherds of Bethlehem did over their flocks; he watches over them night and day, in the dark and cloudy day, in the night of affliction, temptation, and desertion; he never leaves them, nor forsakes them. 7. In short, he makes all necessary provisions for them; so that they shall not, neither can they want any good thing; he takes care that they shall have the best of food, and what is most suitable and proper for them; he has all fulness of grace treasured up in him, and he freely distributes it among them as they stand in need.

Having thus taken notice of what is supposed

and intended in this act of feeding, I shall now consider

2ndly. "What Christ feeds his flock with," and that is, 1. With himself, who is "the Bread of Life," which being fed upon by faith, supports and maintains the life of God's children; and such are the nature, virtue, and efficacy of it, that if a man eat thereof, he shall never hunger after the sinful pleasures of this life, so as he has heretofore done; he shall also never die the second death, but shall live spiritually here, and eternally with Christ hereafter. Christ's "flesh is meat indeed, and his blood is drink indeed;" and the believing soul tastes a sweetness therein, and receives nourishment from hence. Christ is the hidden manna, the food of the wilderness, which faith lives upon, whilst travelling through it. O how richly are the saints fed, whose food is Christ himself! 2. He feeds them with the Gospel, the doctrines and promises of it; the doctrines of the Gospel are "the wholesome words of our Lord Jesus Christ," in which believers are nourished up; these are sweet to their taste, the joy and rejoicing of their hearts, and are esteemed by them more than their necessary food; the promises of the Gospel are "exceedingly great and precious;" faith often lives upon them; the whole Gospel furnishes the believer with a variety of food; in it are milk for babes and meat for strong men; there is what is suitable to the dispositions, tastes, and constitutions of all God's children. 3. He feeds them with the discoveries of his love and grace; he brings them into his "banqueting-house," and his "banner over them is love;" there he gives his best wine, and revives and refreshes their fainting and drooping souls with it; he not only feeds them with himself, "the Bread of Life," but he also sheds abroad his love in their hearts, which is "better than wine;" and thus, with both these from time to time, does he regale them; and in making such comfortable repasts for them, which they largely feed upon, they "grow stronger and stronger," until, at length they become perfect men in Christ Jesus. But,

3rdly, "How, after what manner, and by what means does Christ feed his flock?" This is the part of the church's request; for so the words may be read, "Tell me how thou feedest, and how thou makest thy flocks to rest at noon." Now, Christ feeds his flock: 1. By his ministers, who are his under-shepherds, to whom he gives commissions to feed his flock, saying, as he did to Peter, John xxi. 15—17, "Feed my lambs, feed my sheep;" who receive food from Christ, the great Shepherd, and have suitable gifts and graces bestowed upon them, that they may feed souls "with knowledge and understanding," that is, with the doctrines of the Gospel; which is the food Christ would have his fed with, as has been shown already. 2. He feeds them by his ordinances, which are "breasts of consolation" to his people, out of which they suck, and are satisfied. Christ oftentimes makes a feast for his people, in his ordinances, and bids them welcome, and says, "Eat, O friends, yea, drink abundantly, O beloved;" and their faith feeds heartily upon "the goodness and fatness of his house." 3. He does all this by his Spirit: it is the Spirit of Christ that takes Christ, and the things of Christ, and sets them before us, for faith to feed and live upon; it is he that applies the doctrines, and seals the promises of the Gospel to us; and it is he that sheds abroad the love of Christ in us; the ministry of the word, and the ordinances of the Gospel, are the means of feeding souls; but these would be dry breasts, and would fall short of satisfying and refreshing them, were they not attended with the Spirit of Christ.

4thly. The last enquiry is, Where does Christ feed? To this I answer, in the gardens, his several and particular churches, according to chap. vi. 2, "My beloved is gone down into his garden, to the beds of spices, to feed in the gardens." Would any, with the church, know where Christ feeds? It is where his Gospel is powerfully preached, his ordinances purely administered, and the laws of his house faithfully put in execution: this may then serve as a direction to such enquiring souls, who would be glad to know where Christ feeds, that they may feed with him; let such seek after a Gospel ministry and sit under it; or a church in Gospel-order, and give up themselves unto it, to walk with the saints, in all the ordinances, and commands of Christ. So much for the first part of the request. It remains to be observed,

Secondly. That the church is also desirous to know where Christ "makes his flock to rest at noon;" and there was a great deal of reason for her to make such a request as this, for it was noon with her; the sun was in its meridian, in its full strength, and had looked upon her, as she declares in the former verse. The allusion is to shepherds in hot countries, leading their flocks to some shady place, where they may be sheltered from the scorching heat of the sun; which, as Virgil says, was at the fourth hour, or ten o'clock, two hours before noon.[f] We read of προβατια μεσεμβριαζυντα, sheep nooning themselves, or lying down at noon, under a shade by a fountain asleep.[g] Some by *noon* understand the noon of the everlasting day of the saints' happiness and felicity in heaven, where Christ feeds his elect with joys that will never end;[h] "leads them to fountains of living water, wipes all tears from their eyes,' and gives them an everlasting rest from all their toil and labour; but I think, by it we are rather to understand, either, 1. The noon

---

* איכה תרעה quomodo pascas, Tigurine version. So the Syriac version. and Jarchi, *Vid.* Ainsworth in loc. f Inde, ubi quarta sitim coeli collegerit hora, Georgic. l. 3. v. 327. g Plato in Phædro, p. 1230. h Hieron. et Bernard. in Sanct. et Diodat; in loc.

D 2

of temptation, which is sometimes very hot, fierce, and violent; Satan throws his fiery darts, thick and fast, which oftentimes give the believer much uneasiness; he is "in heaviness through manifold temptations;" but Christ makes him to lie down quietly, and rest safely; which he does, either by shading him from the violent heat thereof, or by supporting him under it, or else by giving him deliverance from it. Christ has sweet resting-places for his people, in the time of temptation, and would you know where and what they are? I answer, the fulness and all-sufficiency of grace, which is in him, is what he makes a believing soul sweetly to rest in, at such a time; when he is pleased to say unto it, as he did to the apostle Paul, when in such a case, "My grace is sufficient for thee;" such sweet resting-places, in times of temptation, are also his precious blood, which always speaks peace and pardon, and is of an eternal efficacy; his spotless righteousness, in which, as neither law nor justice, so neither can Satan find any flaw: as likewise, his atoning sacrifice, by which he has effectually "put away sin, and perfected for ever them that are sanctified;" and so is his advocateship and intercession, in the discharge of which, he pleads the believer's cause, answers all Satan's charges and accusations exhibited against him, and prays for him, "that his faith fail not;" moreover, the covenant of grace is another resting-place, which stands firm and sure, and the promises thereof are absolute, unconditional, and shall never fail. Now these are some of those sweet resting-places, in which Christ causes his people to lie down and rest in the noon-time of temptation: or else, by noon may be meant, 2. The noon of affliction, which is sometimes very sharp and severe upon God's children: so that as Job says, chap. xxx. 30, "their skin is black upon them, and their bones are burnt with the heat thereof;" they have generally a large share of afflictions in this world; this sun oftentimes smites them very severely: but Christ has his resting-places for them, where he makes them lie down and rest, which are such as the world know nothing of: he grants them his presence, and goes along with them, when they walk through the fire, or through the water, so that the one shall not kindle upon them, nor the other overflow them; he puts underneath his everlasting arms, and supports them under all their trials; he makes their beds in their affliction, so that it becomes easy to them; he discovers his love and grace to their souls, and gives them views of their interest in him; he remembers his word of promise to them, on which he has caused them to hope; lets them see that all their afflictions are in love, that they are all working for their good, and when he thinks proper, he delivers them; and upon such pillows, and in such resting-places as these, does he cause his people to lie down, where "he gives his beloved sleep," in the noon-time of affliction: Or else, 3. By the *noon* may be meant the noon of persecution; and this, indeed, seems to be the case of the church here; the sun of persecution had scorched her; and her "mother's children were angry with her;" and therefore, being in distress and anguish of soul, she desires to know unto what cooling and refreshing shades Christ used to lead his flock at such a time. It is an allusion to shepherds, as before observed, who, in those hot countries, used to lead their flocks in the heat of the day, which is at noon, to some cool and shady place, where they might repose themselves and be preserved from the vehemence of the scorching sun. Most of the Jewish writers[1] interpret it of the captivity of the people of Israel, which was a time of tribulation and distress unto them: the heat of persecution seems chiefly intended, which fiery trial oftentimes befals God's children; but Christ has his resting-places for them, at such a time, and under such a trial; he will "recompense tribulation to them that trouble his people," but to those that are troubled, that is, with persecution, he will "give rest with us," says the apostle, 2 Thes. i. 6, 7; rest here, and rest hereafter; he give liberty of soul when in prison, and fills with an unspeakable joy, even when both their goods and good names are spoiled, and taken away from them; he gives them a peace under all the racks and tortures, cruelty and barbarity, that are exercised upon them by their enemies, which passeth all understanding: they find such rest, satisfaction, and contentment in the person, blood, and righteousness of Christ, that they choose rather with Moses, "to suffer affliction with the people of God, than to enjoy the pleasures of sin, which are for a season," Heb. xi. 25.

Thirdly. The arguments she makes use of to obtain her request, which are these, 1st. She argues from her strong love and affection to him; "Tell me, thou whom my soul loveth;" it is true these words may be considered as an endearing title which she gave to him; but yet they seem more strongly to express her singular esteem of him, and her sincere and unfeigned love and affection to him, than those usual titles, *my love*, or *my beloved*, do: which love of hers might be very well improved as an argument to obtain her request, thus: "O thou who art the great Shepherd of the sheep, tell me in what pastures thou art graciously pleased to feed thy flock, and to what cooling shades thou dost lead them, in the heat of the day, to screen them from the scorching sun. She who makes this humble request unto thee, though mean and unworthy of thy notice, yet is one that loves thee with all her heart and soul; who, though of late, through the weakness and sinfulness of her own heart, and through the fear and force of others, has stepped aside from thy commandments to the doctrines and traditions of men; yet, being made sensible of her weakness and folly therein, cannot be easy to

---

[1] *Vide* Targum et R. Sol. Jarchi in loc. So Lyra.

continue among those false teachers and worshippers; and therefore, from a real love to thy person, a respect to thine ordinances, and a regard to thy glory, humbly desires to be informed of these things." Now though the church knew full well that her love to Christ could merit nothing, nor deserve a gracious answer from him; yet she was sensible that expressions of love were very pleasing to him, and therefore she takes this method. The nature, causes, and actings of a soul's love to Christ have been shown on ver. 3. 2ndly. She argues and expostulates with him, on the account of her present case, and what was likely to befal her, if he did not give her some speedy directions; "for why should I be as one that turneth aside by the flocks of thy companions?" There is much difficulty and difference in the rendering of the Hebrew word, which we translate "as one that turneth aside;"[k] some render it "as one covereth herself, or is covered,"[l] either as an harlot:[m] so Tamar covered herself, which made Judah take her to be an harlot, Gen. xxxviii. 14; or as a widow in mourning,[n] it being the custom of mourners to cover themselves, Ezek. xxiv. 17, 22; and then the sense is, "Why should I be suspected to be an harlot, and looked upon as an unchaste woman, that has left her own husband to follow strangers; when thou who art the Searcher of hearts and Trier of reins, knowest that I love thee in sincerity, and are heartily desirous of following thee in thine own ways;" or else the sense is, "Why should I appear in a widow's dress, and go mourning and sorrowing as if I had no husband: O tell me where thou art, and where I may enjoy thy presence, and be delighted with thy company." Junius and Tremellius translate the words thus, "Why should I be as one that spreadeth the tent with the flocks of thy companions?" and give this as the sense, "Why should I? I would not, though but for a time, have any conversation with such persons, who pretend to be thy friends, and are not; I cannot bear it, my soul abhors and detests the thoughts of it, though, perhaps, through my weakness and infirmities, I may do it; O therefore, tell me quickly, speedily, where thou feedest." Others render it "as one that wanders about, declines, or turns aside by the flocks of thy companions:"[o] this agrees with our version: and from these words we may observe, 1. That there are some who would be the associates and companions of Christ, who indeed are not: these were not really so, but usurped to themselves an equal power and authority with Christ; such are those who take upon them an arbitrary and lordly government of Christ's flock, who make and impose laws on the consciences of men, which Christ never established, and who teach doctrines contrary to those which Christ taught, and which are derogatory to his honour and glory: such rivals with, and pretended companions of Christ, are, the pope of Rome, who exalts himself above all that is called God; Arians, who deny Christ's Divinity; Socinians, that oppose his satisfaction; and all self-justiciaries, that advance the doctrine of justification by works, in opposition to justification by his imputed righteousness: but such Christ will not own as his friends, nor suffer to be his rivals and companions; for as his own arm brought salvation to him, so the government is alone upon his shoulders, as he was alone in the purchase and salvation of his flock, so he will be in the government and feeding of it; for his glory which arises from thence, he will not give to another. Christ never did, nor never will empower any to make new laws, nor coin new doctrines for his church and people. 2. These false and pretended friends and companions of Christ, who are no other than wolves in sheep's clothing, have their flocks. Heretics and false teachers, in all ages, have had their followers, and sometimes large numbers have been drawn away after them; and this God suffers in a judicial way: he gives men up to believe a lie, because they love not the truth; but having itching ears, grow weary of it and want something new: also these are permitted to have their flocks by themselves, that Christ's little flock might be distinguished from them, and that those who are chosen, loved, and approved by God, might be made manifest; as also to animate and excite the faithful ministers of the Gospel to be constant and assiduous, bold and faithful to preach the doctrines of Christ, and to oppose errors. 3. Believers are very fearful, lest they should, and are very desirous that they might not, go aside from the ways of Christ; they are jealous of their own hearts, and are sensible that there is in them a propensity thereunto; they know that Satan uses all the crafty methods, and takes all the opportunities he can to draw them aside, and corrupt their minds "from the simplicity that is in Christ;" they are apprized of their own weakness, and know that they are not kept by their own power, but that if they are left to themselves, they shall soon divert to crooked paths; and the present case of the church also manifestly shows that God may, for a time, suffer his own children to be carried away with the error of the wicked; but when they are made sensible of it, they will be filled with an holy indignation against it, and make it their principal request at the throne of grace to be delivered out of it, and that their feet may be guided and directed in the paths of Christ: now those who are desirous that they may be kept from turning aside unto, and joining with the flocks of false teachers, who vainly pretend to be the friends and companions of Christ, should abide

---

[k] Vide Aben Ezram in loc. [l] כעטיה ὡς περιβαλλομήνη, Sept. siuct amicta vel operta, Michaelis; quasi operiens se, Piscator; ut obnubens. Cocceius; sicut obvelaus se, Marckius. So Zohar, in Lev. fol. 7. 3. [m] So Mercer in loc. R. Sol. Jarchium in loc. David Kimchi in lib. Shorash. rad. עטה. [n] Vide Yalkut and Targum in loc. R.

in the Lord's inheritance, keep close to Christ's ways and ordinances, and not believe every spirit, but try them according to the word of God, as the noble Bereans did; they should earnestly beg that the gospel which is preached unto them might effectually work in them, and make deep impressions upon them; so shall they not be "like children tossed about with every wind of doctrine." But let us hear what directions Christ himself gives to the church in the following words.

Verse 8. *If thou know not, O thou fairest among women! go thy way forth by the footsteps of the flock, and feed thy kids beside the shepherd's tents.*

SOME think[p] that these are the words of the chorus of virgins or daughters of Jerusalem, by whom she is called the "fairest among women," in chap. v. 2, and vi. 1; who here instruct and direct her where she might find and come at the sight of her beloved; but the note of R. Solomon Jarchi is much preferable, which is, that "this is the answer of the shepherd;" for it was to him, and not to the virgins, that she made her application; nor were they capable of giving her any directions in this case, but rather stood in need of some from her, as is manifest in chap. iv. 9, and vi. 1. In this answer of Christ's unto the church, are these three things:

I. The commendation he gives her; "O thou fairest among women!"

II. A supposition of her ignorance; "if thou know not."

III. A direction to her; "go thy way," &c.

I. Christ in these words gives the church an excellent commendation, "O thou fairest among women;" in what sense the church is fair and comely has been shown, on ver. 5; who, though black in herself, and in her own eyes, yet having Christ's righteousness imputed to her, and his grace wrought in her, is fair and comely: which commendation here, both in itself, and as it follows upon the account which she gave of herself and state, in the preceding verses, may teach us the following things: 1. That the beauty of the church is very great and exceedingly admired by Christ; as some men are eminent for their strength, courage, and valour, so are some women for their beauty and comeliness: and she being said to be "the fairest among women," shows that her beauty must be excellent and surpassing; as he is fairer in her eyes than all the sons, so she is fairer in his than all the daughters of Adam. 2. That believers are fairest in Christ's eyes, when blackest in their own; she had asserted of herself, in ver. 5, that she was black; but here Christ says, that she was "the fairest among women." The humble believer that has low and mean thoughts of himself, on the account of the corruption of his nature, the imperfection of his obedience, the weakness and insufficiency of his righteousness, is much more esteemed and valued by Christ, than the proud, haughty, and vain-glorious Pharisee; an instance of this we have in Luke xviii. 13, 14. An humble soul is one that looks upon itself as the least of saints, and the chief of sinners; the countenance of such an one blushing at its sins and infirmities, is beautiful and comely in the eyes of Christ, and is a sight exceeding desirable to him; and therefore he says, in chap. ii. 14, "Let me see thy countenance, let me hear thy voice, for sweet is thy voice, and thy countenance is comely." 3. That Christ's thoughts of believers are not according to those which they have of themselves, nor according to those which the world entertains of them; he "seeth not as man seeth," neither does he look upon, or judge according to the outward appearance: the believer oftentimes looks upon, and judges of himself, according to his indwelling corruptions, and the inward frames of his soul, and draws black conclusions against himself: the world looks upon the outward, mean, and abject appearance of the saints, and so they become black and contemptible in their eyes; but Christ views them in himself, and in his own righteousness, and considers them in all that glory in which he saw them in the glass of his Father's purposes and decrees, which glory he has fully resolved on, and designed to bring them to the actual possession of; and on this account they appear exceeding fair and beautiful in his eyes. 4. This excellent commendation of the church given by Christ, shows his amazing and unalterable love to her; he loved her now as well as ever; notwithstanding all her blackness through sins and sufferings, she was as fair in his eyes as ever, nay, surpassingly fair, fairer than all others; though she had been negligent of her duty, and had sinfully complied with false and superstitious worship, with the doctrines and traditions of men, and thereby wandered from Christ and his ways, and knew not where he fed and caused his flock to rest; yet upon her first application to him, he gives her such a character, as expresses much love and tenderness, as well as manifests a very great regard to her, in directing and instructing of her: O matchless love! boundless grace!

II. Here is a supposition of her ignorance, "if thou know not:" which is not to be understood, either by way of hesitation or reprehension, as if Christ either doubted of her ignorance, or reproved her for it, but by way of inference from what she had suggested; for this particle *if*, is not always hypothetic or conditional, but is sometimes illative, see Phil. ii. 1, and thus the words may be rendered, "seeing thou knowest not," so Junius; or "because thou knowest not;" and may be considered as a reason why Christ gave her the following direction and advice, and will lead us to observe these two things: 1. That believers may, in some measure, be ignorant of a

---

[p] Sanct. in loc. and Psellus in ibid.

great many things in this life; this life is a state of imperfection, both with respect to holiness and knowledge; the greatest believer knows but in *part*, and sees things but *through a glass darkly;* he is ignorant of himself in a great measure, though he may know much of the plague of his own heart, of the corruptions and treachery of it, yet he does not know all; for the heart is " deceitful above all things, and desperately wicked, who can know it?" These words may be rendered from the Hebrew text, thus,ᵠ " If thou know not to thee, or, for thyself;" so Ainsworth; or, " if thou knowest not thyself;" it is generally looked upon as a pleonasm, yet it may intend, not only the ignorance which was in herself, but also her ignorance of herself. Again, a believer may be in some measure ignorant of Christ and his Gospel; he may not so fully know his relation and union to him, and interest in him: many of those truths, which concern Christ's person, grace, and kingdom, may be but obscurely revealed unto him; he may have but a small insight into them: though he may have been long in Christ's school, yet he may be but a babe in knowledge, and need to be taught " the first principles of the oracles of God;" our knowledge of these things at best is but imperfect, and when compared with that which saints shall have in glory, is very dark and obscure: also believers sometimes may be at a very great loss to know where Christ feeds his church and people; and this has been the case of the saints, as it was the church here, in times of persecution, darkness, and superstition; they have not only been at a loss for his presence, but they have also been at a loss for his ordinances; they have not not only been ignorant where he was, but also they have not known where his gospel was preached in the power, and his ordinances administered in the purity of them. 2. That though Christ's people are ignorant of a great many things, and of such which, as one would think, they should not be ignorant of, but should make it their principal business to be acquainted with, yet Christ does not upbraid them with it; for " he has compassion on the ignorant, and on them that are out of the way;" as their merciful and faithful High-priest, he has atoned for their sins, both of ignorance and presumption; and as their prophet he instructs them by his word and Spirit, and " guides their feet in the way of peace;" and therefore the most ignorant soul need not be discouraged from going to Christ for wisdom, counsel, and direction; but let him that "lacketh wisdom, ask it of him who giveth liberally to all men, and upbraideth not, and it shall be given him," Jam. i. 6.

III. Here is a direction which Christ gives her, in answer to her request, which consists of two parts; First, To " go forth by the footsteps of the flock." Secondly, to "feed her kids beside the shepherd's tents."

First. The first thing which Christ directs and advises her to, is, to " go her way forth by the footsteps of the flock." Some consider these words, not as a direction to the church, but as spoken by way of resentment to her. Christ, observing the church was growing uneasy under her trials and temptations, and, as it were, threatening that if he did not relieve her, she would join herself to the flocks of his companions; being ignorant, both of her own beauty, which she had received from him, and of that relation which she stood in to him; as also, that she must expect to meet with more troubles, temptations, and trials with him and for him; Christ, I say, observing and resenting this froward temper of hers, and the ignorance that was in her, bids her be gone from his presence, and follow the steps of those flocks which she had mentioned, and see what would be the consequence of it, and whether she would find her account in it or no; and " feed her kids," that is, give a loose to, and indulge her carnal lusts and corruptions among those persons whom she seemed to have an inclination to: but they seem rather to be spoken by way of direction than resentment; and there are some, who, though they look upon the words as a direction of Christ to the church, yet by " the footsteps of the flock," understand the paths and ways of those sheep and shepherds, among whom she was, and by whom she was in danger of being carried away, and read the words thus, " Go out of those footsteps of the flock,⁎ " so Junius and Tremellius. But though, no doubt, the church is here directed and exhorted to depart from the ways of sin, to leave all superstition and idolatry, and come out from among false worshippers; yet I cannot but think that the " footsteps of the flock " are the rule and mark by which she was to go, and keep her eye upon, in finding Christ: and it may be enquired, 1st. What is meant by "the flock." 2ndly. What by " the footsteps" of it, by, and in which the church was to go.

1st. What is meant by " the flock;" and by it we are to understand, the flock which the Father has committed into the hands of Christ, which he has purchased with his own blood, and continually feeds like a shepherd; this is called *a flock* in the singular number, in opposition to the numerous flocks of those other shepherds mentioned in ver. 7; for as there is but one shepherd, who is Christ, so there is but one flock, which is the church; of which flock I have given a more large account on the former verse.

2ndly. By " the footsteps of the flock," are meant the ways and ordinances in which saints by faith walk, in obedience to Christ Jesus; he has left us an example that we should follow his steps; so far as believers walk therein, we should follow and walk in the steps of the same faith which they have done, and in so doing, may, and

---

ᵠ אִם לֹא תֵדְעִי לָךְ ἐὰν μὴ γνῷς σεαυτήν, Sept. nisi cognoveris te, Ar. Montanus. ʳ Foliot and Alcuim in loc. ⁎ Egredere a vistigiis illis gregis; but then it should have been בְּעִקְבֵי and not בְּעִקְבוֹ.

shall find the presence of Christ Jesus. From whence may be observed, 1. That we have no reason to expect a new gospel or new ordinances; but we should enquire for *the good old way*, which the saints in all ages have trodden; no new lights nor new revelations, that have no foundation in the word of God, are to be regarded by us; for "we have a more sure word of prophecy, to which we do well if we take heed." Christ has in his word established the order of his churches, fixed the ordinances thereof, till his second coming, and marked out the paths in which he would have his people walk; and these are the footsteps of the flock, which saints in all ages should go by. 2. That the faith and obedience of God's children, as to the substance of them, have been the same in all ages: There is but "one faith, one Lord, one baptism;" the object of faith has been always the same; so have the Spirit and Author of faith, and also the grace itself, as to its nature and actings; there has been but one Lord, who has established laws and ordinances, has a power to require obedience, and to whom, in all ages, it has been given by his saints, both in a way of doing and suffering. 3. That the practices of former saints, both as to their faith and obedience, are to be imitated by us: see Heb. vi. 12, and xiii. 7; but always with this limitation, given by the apostle Paul, "Be ye followers of me, even as I also am of Christ," 1 Cor. xi. 1; and indeed, no farther should we follow the most eminent saints, for faith and holiness, than as they have trodden in those steps which Christ has marked out for them and us. 4. In so doing, we may expect to have our souls fed and nourished, as theirs were, and to enjoy the presence of Christ, as they did; for though our faith and obedience deserve none of all this, yet in walking in Christ's ways, we have most reason to expect it, being encouraged both by Christ's promises, and by those many instances and clouds of witnesses that have gone before us. The Targum and R. Sol. Jarchi, understand this part of the direction, of the righteous, in whose steps those that come after should tread.

Secondly. The other part of the direction is, to feed her kids beside the shepherds' tents. It was common in the eastern countries, as Philo says of the Arabs,[t] not for men only to keep flocks, but women also and young virgins; of women keeping flocks see Gen. xxxix. 2, Exod. ii. 16; the same Josephus says of the Troglodites,[u] and it was an early custom for shepherds to have tents where they fed their flocks: they were so early as the days of Jabal, who was the inventor of them, Gen. iv. 20. Hence the Arabian shepherds, who dwelt in tents, and moved them from place to place for the sake of pasturage, were called *Scenites*; and

1st. By *shepherds* may be meant such who are called *the companions* of Christ in ver. 7;[w] who only had the appearance of shepherds, but were inwardly ravenous wolves: the words may be rendered, "Feed thy kids above the shepherds' tents, or above the tents of other shepherds;" so R. Aben Ezra and Junius; that is, go beyond their tents, and do not pitch thine where theirs are, but carry thy kids farther, into other pastures, and feed them with better and more wholesome food than they can give: or else by them, may be meant the ministers of the Gospel, who are Christ's under-shepherds, whose business is to feed Christ's sheep and lambs, with the soul-refreshing doctrines of the everlasting Gospel; who receive their commission from Christ to feed the flock, are furnished with abilities from him for that work, and must give an account unto him; and by, or near the tents of these shepherds,[x] the church is directed to feed her kids. 2. By the tents of these shepherds, may be meant those places of divine worship, where the ministers of Christ usually preach his Gospel, and administer his ordinances; which tents or tabernacles are amiable and lovely to believers: the Jewish writers generally understand them of their schools or synagogues.[y] It is an allusion to shepherds' tents, which are usually pitched where they feed their flocks. 3. By kids may be meant young converts, who, though they are desirous of the sincere milk of the word, that they may grow thereby, yet are but weak in faith, and have but a small degree of knowledge; and therefore should be near the shepherds' tents, that they may be under their immediate care and inspection; as Christ himself has the strongest affection for these, and takes a special care of them, as in Isa. xl. 11; so he would have his ministers and churches be particularly careful and tender of them: these kids R. Aben Ezra calls קטני אמנה ὀλιγοπίστους, "persons of little faith;" the very character which Christ gives of his disciples, Matt. vi. 30; young converts are not only called kids, because of their faith and knowledge; but kids being young goats, lascivious, and of an ill smell,[z] may intimate, that notwithstanding the grace which is wrought in them at conversion, yet there still remains sin and corruption in them, disagreeable to themselves and others; as also, that being called by divine grace out of the world, and having separated from the men of it, they did *male olere*, smell ill, and were become abominable and contemptible to them; and therefore needed much refreshment and encouragement from the church and ministers, that they might not be discouraged and cast down at their own corruptions, nor at the frowns and reproaches of the world. This direction to the church, to feed her kids beside the shepherds' tents, where the Gospel was preached by Christ's ministers, shows the necessity

---

[t] De Vita Mosis, l. 1. p. 610. [u] Antiqu. l. 2. c. 11. s. 2. [v] *Vide* R. Sol. Jarchium, Junium and Ainsworth in loc. [x] Juxta, V. L. Piscator, Michaelis; apud, Mercerus, Cocceius. [y] Targum in loc. and Zohar in Lev. fol. 7. 3, and in Num. fol. 69. 4. and 80. 1. [z] Hoedi petulci, Virgil. Georgic. l. 4. v. 10. lasciva capella, Bucolic. eclog. 2. v. 64. Horat. Carmin. l. 2. ode. 15. v. 12. olet Gorgonius hircum, Horat. Satyr. l. 1. sat. 2. v. 27.

and perpetuity of the Gospel ministry, and of Gospel ordinances; and what a value saints should have for them, and also what use they should make of them, as well as informs us of the wretched mistake of those persons who think themselves above hearing the word, and regarding ordinances.

Verse 9. *I have compared thee, O my love, to a company of horses in Pharaoh's chariots.*

CHRIST having returned a suitable answer, and given proper directions to the church in her present difficulties, enters upon a commendation of her, which is begun in this verse, and continued in the following one. In these words are,

I. An affectionate title given to her; " O my love."

II. A comparison which Christ makes of her, " to a company of horses in Pharaoh's chariots." And,

III. It may be enquired why such a comparison is made and mentioned in this place.

I. Here is a very loving and endearing title given unto her, " my love;" it may be rendered " my friend;"[a] there is a mutual friendship between Christ and believers: the church owns Christ to be her beloved and her friend, and Christ welcomes his church and people to the entertainments of his grace, under the characters of his beloved, and his friends, saying, " Eat, O friends; drink, yea, drink abundantly, O beloved;" and he not only calls them so, but uses and treats them as such; he converses with them, and discloses the secrets of his heart unto them; he is a friend to them at all times, in adversity as well as prosperity, and has given the most incontestible proofs of it in his suffering and dying for them. The Septuagint renders it, " my neighbour:" the church is Christ's neighbour; they dwell near to each other; he dwells in their hearts by faith, and they by faith dwell in him: he shows, that he regards his church as his neighbour, by loving her as himself; nay, he has so loved her, as to give himself for her. Again, if we consider this title, according to our version, it well suits the church, who is Christ's love. 1. 'Objectively; She is the object of his love, was so from eternity, will be so throughout all time, and when time shall be no more; he has given the fullest proofs of it in his undertaking, as a Surety for her, in his assumption of her nature, in dying in her room and stead, and in making satisfaction for all her transgressions. The nature of this love has been shown already on ver. 2. 2. She is Christ's love subjectively; Christ's love is fixed upon her, and is shed abroad in her heart, by the Spirit, and this causes love in her soul to him; that so as Christ loves her, she loves him, with a real, hearty, sincere, and superlative love; she is therefore Christ's love, both because he loves her, and also because she loves him.

II. Here is made, by Christ, a comparison of her, " to a company of horses in Pharaoh's chariots: I have compared thee, O my love," &c., that is, I *thought* and *imagined thee to be like* unto them,[b] or *I have made thee like unto them;* which shows that she was not only like unto them, he having asserted her to be so, who must certainly know, but also that this was owing to him, that show as so: or to my mare, as some render it,[c] which being a present by Pharaoh to Solomon, he might have a particular regard for it; nor is such a comparison of a woman a disagreeable one; many women have had their names from this creature, from some celebrated excellence in them, as Hippo, Hippe, Hippia, &c., and the same figure is made use of by various writers.[d] Now the church is compared to a company of horses to set forth her greatness and excellency, and to Egyptian ones, which were esteemed the best, and to those in Pharaoh's chariots, which, no doubt, were best of all: all believers may very well be compared " to a company of horses in Pharaoh's chariots;" 1. Because the horses in Pharaoh's chariots were a choice and select company, picked and singled out from others, peculiarly for his service: so R. Sol. Jarchi interprets it, " a collection of horses," which, no doubt, was a choice and curious one; for if there were any more than others, it is very reasonable to suppose, that they were in Pharaoh's chariots. The church of Christ is a " chosen generation, a royal priest-hood, an holy nation, and a peculiar people;" they are distinguished and separated from others, by electing, redeeming, and calling grace; they are a collection from the rest of mankind, made by the free, sovereign, and distinguishing grace of God: they are " a remnant, according to the election of grace," chosen and singled out from others in Christ, before the foundation of the world; they are " redeemed from among men, and that out of every kindred, tongue, people, and nation;" whom God is pleased by his mighty, powerful, and efficacious grace to call, even one of a city, and two of a family, and bring to the participation of peculiar favours and privileges, through Christ, in the church on earth, and with Christ for ever in glory. 2. These horses in Pharaoh's chariots were, no doubt, bought at a very great price; Egyptian horses went at a very great price, in Solomon's time; a single one was valued at a hundred and fifty shekels of silver: see 1 Kings x. 29; and therefore those, which were bought for Pharaoh's service, who was king of Egypt, being the best, must be supposed to be bought at a very great price. The church and people of God are bought with a price, and that with a very great one indeed, such a one, that angels

---

[a] רעיתי amica mea, Pagninus, Montanus, Tig. Vers. Mercerus, Michaelis.   [b] דמיתיך similem te judico, Tig. Vers.   [c] לססתי τη ιππω μυ. Sept. equae meae, Pagninus, Montanus, Gussetius p. 581.

So Aben Ezra, Syr. and Ar. equabus, Piscator.
[d] Theocrit. Idyll. 18. v. 29. Theognis Sentent. v. 257. Plato in Hippias Major, p. 1250. Horat. Carmin. l. 3. ode. 11. v. 9.

and men could never have given; they are purchased, not with "corruptible things, as silver and gold;" no, all the riches in the world amassed together, could not have purchased a single soul, nor have given to God a ransom for it; "but they are bought with the precious blood" of the unblemished and unspotted Son of God; they are bought for the service of the King of kings, and at no less a rate, than at the expense of his own blood and life; the ransom which is given for them is himself; O how valuable must they be to Christ, and how much must they be esteemed by him! 3. These horses, being well fed, looked very beautiful and pleasant. Believers are fed with the finest of the wheat, with Christ and his fulness; Christ himself is the Bread of life, and the hidden manna, which being fed upon by faith, removes hunger, supports life, and preserves from the second death, his flesh is meat indeed, and his blood is drink indeed, which give spiritual and divine refreshment to believers; his grace is represented by wine, and milk, and honey, on which his people feeding plentifully, grow and look exceeding delightful and beautiful in his sight. 4. These horses, being the king's horses, as they were well fed, so, no doubt, they were well taken care of; they had proper persons appointed on purpose to attend upon them, and to supply them with what was necessary for them. Believers in Christ have a guard of angels to attend upon them, who encamp about them, and minister to them; for those "ministering spirits are sent forth to minister for them who shall be the heirs of salvation;" also the ministers of the gospel, being furnished with suitable grace and abilities, are appointed to feed them with the doctrines of the everlasting gospel, and to give to every one "their portion of meat in due season." Moreover, they are not left merely to the care of angels and ministers, but the Lord himself likewise concerns himself for them; when his church is represented as a vineyard, he is said to be the keeper of it, who "watches over it night and day lest any hurt it;" when it is compared to a city, he is the wall of fire round about it; and when to a flock of sheep, he is the Shepherd of it; and being here compared to a company of horses, it is owing to the food that he gives them, and the care he takes of them, that they appear "as his goodly horse in the battle," Zech. x. 3, 5. Horses have been and are much delighted in by princes; and there is no reason to question but that those which ran in Pharaoh's chariots were so by him; Solomon's fancy and inclinations ran so strongly this way, and he took so great a delight in those creatures, that he broke through a divine command, Deut. xvii. 16, compared with 1 Kings x. 29; to satisfy and indulge his carnal pleasure; and many other princes have run prodigious and excessive lengths this way. Julius Cæsar set up a marble effigy of his horse in the temple;* Antoninus Verus erected a golden image for his. Nero clothed his with a senator's robe, and told him out a weekly stipend; Poppea Sabina, Nero's wife, had golden shoes made for hers; Caligula used to invite his to supper, and held out his golden cups to him; he would have made him a consul, as he afterwards made himself a priest, and his horse his colleague; Alexander the great built a city in honour of his Bucephalus; Cimon the Athenian buried his mares by his own sepulchre; and Commodus the emperor buried his horse in the Vatican. These instances, though vain and sinful, and not to be imitated, yet show how much some princes have delighted in this sort of creatures. Now, as these creatures were the delight of princes, and, perhaps, of Pharaoh, so are believers the delight of Christ; he first makes them beautiful, and then delights in that beauty which he has put upon them; "the Lord taketh pleasure in his people, he will beautify the meek with salvation;" his heart is often ravished with his own grace in them, and his soul delights in that which he himself has given them; there is nothing in them of their own which can render them acceptable to him, and yet they are his jewels, the apple of his eye, and the delight of his heart. 6. Horses are stately and majestic creatures, especially a company of choice and well fed ones, that run in a chariot, as these were. There is a stateliness and majesty in believers, especially when they are united together in gospel-order, in a church-state; and the majesty, stateliness, and glory of a church of Christ, do not consist in the multitude of members, nor in their outward riches, pomp, and splendour; but in their being all clothed with Christ's righteousness, and possessed of his grace; in the enjoyment of his presence in ordinances; in their walking in love and unity with each other, and wisely towards them that are without; in having their conversation as becometh the gospel of Christ, and the profession which they make of it, and in showing a becoming zeal for the truths and ordinances thereof: being thus blessed with these things, they may be truly said to be as stately and majestic as "a company of horses in Pharaoh's chariots," which were well fed, and harnessed in a splendid manner. 7. Horses are very strong creatures, especially a company of them joined together, as these were; concerning the strength of the horse, the Lord says to Job, chap. xxxix. 19, "Hast thou given the horse strength; hast thou clothed his neck with thunder?" Believers are strong, not in themselves, but in Christ; their strength lies in their Head, and in their union to him; they can do nothing of themselves, but "can do all things through Christ, who strengtheneth them;" having strength communicated to them from him, they can endure all hardships, go through all difficulties, withstand all temptations, and perform all duties which he calls them to: and next to their

---

* Frantz. hist. Animal. sacr. par. 1. c. 12.

union to Christ, the strength of a society and company of believers, or a church of Christ, lies in their union and close adherence to each other; they are like the bundle of sticks in the fable, which, whilst kept bound together, could not easily be broken, but when separated from each other, were soon snapped asunder; which consideration should excite mutual love among believers, and an endeavour "to keep the unity of the Spirit in the bond of peace;" by doing which, they will not so easily fall a prey to their enemies, but will appear "terrible as an army with banners." 8. Horses are of an undaunted courage, especially such as are well fed, as these were; an elegant description of the majesty, and undaunted courage of the horse, as given by God himself, may be read in Job xxxix. 20—25. Believers in Christ "are bold as a lion; whilst the wicked flee, when no man pursueth;" they remain undaunted at all the reproaches, threatenings, and menaces of men, and cannot be deterred thereby, from the service of Christ; they fear not the wrath of kings and princes; neither can confiscation of goods, imprisonment of body, racks, tortures, or death itself, scare them from a profession of Christ and his gospel; but viewing all these with an undaunted courage, say, "Who shall separate us from the love of Christ?" instances of this we have in Daniel and his companions, the apostles of Christ, the believing Hebrews, whom Paul wrote to, and thousands of martyrs for, and confessors of, the truth in all ages. 9. These horses were not employed in ordinary service, in mere drudgery, but were selected for the service of Pharaoh, to run in his chariots. The elect of God being called by divine grace, are not, or at least, they should not be employed in the service and drudgery of sin and Satan; but being subjected to Christ, whom they acknowledged to be their Lord and King, are directed and guided by him, into those paths in which he would have them go, and so readily, cheerfully, and swiftly, "run the ways of his commandments." These are not common, servile horses, which the church is here compared to, but royal ones, such that were in the service of a king. 10. These horses were not wild, nor loose, running at random, but being fitted for service, were joined and coupled together, and so peaceably and orderly drew one way; and perhaps, were all of the same colour, and of an equal size and bigness, which is usual in the chariots of princes. The church is not a company of wild and unconverted sinners, running loose, and enjoying their carnal liberty; but of persons, who by divine grace, are put under the yoke of Christ, being joined together in Gospel-bonds, and "strive together for the faith of the Gospel, worshipping the Lord with one shoulder and one consent;" and when they are all of the same faith, of the same mind and judgment, speak the same things, and harmoniously agree together, without disorders, contentions, and divisions, then may they be said to be like " a company of horses in Pharaoh's chariots." But,

III. It may be inquired, why this comparison is made and mentioned here; which was, 1. To comfort and support her under the mean apprehensions she had of herself, and also to strengthen her against the reproach and scandal that was thrown upon her by others; therefore Christ lets her know, that though she was black in her own eyes, and slighted and despised by her mother's children, yet she was glorious in his, for he had compared her to a "company of horses," &c. 2. To inform her, that she was in a militant state, and that she must not expect much ease and rest, which she seemed to be seeking for in ver. 7; therefore he would have her know, that this was a time for fighting the Lord's battles against sin, Satan, and the world; and for that purpose he had "made her as his goodly horse in the battle," Zech. x. 3, 3. Christ having directed her to tread in the "footsteps of the flock, and to feed her kids beside the shepherds' tents," would have her consider, that she must expect trouble, persecution, and opposition from those other shepherds, whose flocks are mentioned as distinct from Christ's, in ver. 7; and therefore to support her under, and comfort her against these, he tells her, that he had "compared her, or made her like to a company of horses," stout, strong, courageous, warlike, and victorious; and therefore, seeing he had "not given her the spirit of fear, but of power, and of love, and of a sound mind," she should not be discouraged and dismayed at these troubles and afflictions that came upon her.

Verse 10. *Thy cheeks are comely with rows* of jewels, *thy neck with chains* of gold.

CHRIST in these words continues to give an account of the church's beauty and glory; and that either in opposition to what she had said in ver. 5, 6; and assures her, that her cheeks and neck were not so black as she imagined; but were like the blushing cheeks of a beautiful woman, adorned with jewels, and her fair neck adorned with bracelets, necklaces, and chains of gold or pearl; see Ezek. xvi. 11, 12; or else he continues the metaphor used in the preceding verse, where he compares her to a "company of horses in Pharaoh's chariots;" whose bridles being richly adorned, having chains of gold hung about their necks, as the camels of the kings of Midian had, Judges viii. 26; gloriously set forth the beauty of the church; and perhaps, the church's glory under the Old Testament dispensation is represented in this verse, and a further increase and display of it under the New Testament dispensation promised in the text. And here,

I. Her cheeks are said to be "comely, with rows of jewels."

II. Her "neck with chains of gold."

I. Her cheeks are said to "be comely with rows of jewels:" the word *jewels* is not in the Hebrew text, but supplied by our translators; and the word

Torim, translated *rows*, sometimes signifies *turtles*, which gave occasion to the Septuagint to render the words thus: "How beautiful are thy cheeks, as the turtledove's." R. Aben Ezra thinks that the bridles of those horses, to which she is compared, had the images of turtles upon them; others,[f] that these were some ornaments of women, as jewels and ear-rings, which had the figure of a lamb upon them, and therefore were called *turtles*, or *turturellas*, according to Drusius; even as those pieces of money, which had the figures of turtles upon them, are called *lambs*, Gen. xxxiii. 19, Job. xlii. 11. Now the cheeks of the church being said to be comely with these, show her innocency and harmlessness, her love, chastity, faithfulness, and beauty; all which appear in this creature. The Targum renders it *bridles*, and very well refers it to the law given on mount Sinai to the people of Israel; which is as a bridle, both to restrain persons from sin, who are by nature as the horse and mule, without understanding, and also to guide and direct them in the right way, that they may not depart from it; and on these bridles were rows of jewels or precious stones. The word *Tor*, which is the singular of this in our text, signifies an order, or disposition, and course of things;[g] see Esth. ii. 12, 15: and is not amiss rendered by our translators, *rows*, that is, of jewels, or precious stones; and by them are intended, either.

1st, The precepts of the moral law;[h] which 1. Are beautifully ranked and disposed in order; the precepts thereof are so strictly and closely joined together, that he that offends in one point, breaks the link, and so is guilty of all. 2. These are so many rows of jewels, valuable and excellent, and are "more to be desired than gold, yea, than much fine gold." Or else.

2ndly, The ordinances of the ceremonial law; which may be compared to rows of jewels, 1. For the variety of them; this law is "a law of commandments," of many commandments, "contained in ordinances," which, as they were carnal, so they were divers, see Eph. ii. 15, Heb. ix. 10. 2. For the excellency of them, as they prefigured the Lord Jesus Christ; it is true, after Christ the substance was come, they were "weak and beggarly elements," useless and insignificant; but before Christ's coming, they were lively representations of him, exceeding useful to the saints, and highly valued by them.

Now the church's cheeks, that is, the outward face and appearance of the church, were comely and desirable in the eyes of Christ, being adorned with these rows of jewels; her outward conversation being according to the laws of God, she appeared beautiful and delightful, "for holiness becomes the house of God" for ever: there was a beauty in ceremonial worship; the tabernacles of God were amiable to the saints, and the saints themselves were so to Christ, in their attendance on the service and ordinances of God; the statutes and ordinances with which the external face of the church was beautified, were such as were not given to other people during that dispensation; which manifestly showed that God had a peculiar regard for them.

II. Her neck is said to "be comely with chains of gold." The word *gold* is not in the Hebrew text, but supplied by our translators, and the word *Charuzim*, which is only found in this place, is generally interpreted by the Jewish doctors, *chains of gold*, or *jewels* and *precious stones*,[i] bored through and hung in a string, to be worn about the neck. A pearl necklace was in use with great personages; so the eldest daughter of Priamus had *collo monile baccatum*,[k] a pearl necklace, which Æneas made a present of to Dido; and such like was the chain of gold beset with amber, presented to Penelope by her suitors, which shone like the sun.[l] And 1st, I shall enquire what is meant by the church's neck. 2ndly, what by those *chains of gold, or precious stones*, with which it is adorned and made comely.

1st. By her *neck* may be meant, either the grace of faith, by which the church cleaves to Christ the Head, and exalts him; this is also accompanied with other graces, which are linked together as a chain, and is attended with good works: or else, by it is meant the ministers of the Gospel,[m] who, as the neck, are placed in the most eminent part of the body, the church, and are the means of conveying spiritual food from Christ the Head, to the members thereof. But of this, see more on ch. iv. 4.

2ndly. By those *chains of gold*, with which the church's neck is beautified and adorned, may be meant, 1. The laws and ordinances of God; which the ministers of the Gospel, and members of churches, should be careful to observe; and are, as Solomon says, Prov. i. 9, "an ornament of grace unto the head, and chains about the neck," of those who regard them. Or, 2. Those diversities of gifts which are bestowed on the ministers of Christ, by which they are made "able ministers of the New Testament;" and so become useful to many, and appear comely and beautiful, both in the eyes of Christ, and of such souls to whom they minister. Or, 3. The various graces of the Spirit, with which, not only ministers, but all believers are adorned; for sins and vices are so chained and linked together, that where there is one, there is all; so the graces of the Spirit are like chains of gold, which are so closely linked together, that they cannot be separated, but where there is one grace there is every grace, which very much beautify and adorn the believer. This

---

[f] Vide Mercer, Brightman, and Ainsworth in loc.
[g] Vide R. David Kimchium in lib. Shorash. rad. תור.
[h] These *rows* are interpreted by the Jews of their written and moral law, and of the laws of burnt sacrifices, meat offerings, &c. in Pesikta apud Yalkut in loc.
[i] R. Sol. Jarchi in loc. R. David Kimchi in lib. Shorash. rad. חרז.
[k] Virgil Æneid. l. v. 650. pendebant tereti gemmata monilia collo, Ovid. Metamorph. l. 10. fab. 3.
[l] Homer. Odyss. 18. v. 295.
[m] So Isidore in loc.

golden chain of grace which is put about the church's neck, consists of these ten links: the first is *faith*, that precious pearl and valuable jewel which is alike precious in all saints, as to its nature and object; the fruit of electing love, the Father's gift, the Son's grace, and the Spirit's work. The second is *hope* which is called, " good hope through grace;" this carries the soul cheerfully through all the difficulties of life, and makes not ashamed at death; it is both the Christian's anchor and his helmet; it is valuable in its nature, and useful in its actings. The third link in this golden chain is *love*, which is " the fulfilling of the law;" this is highly valued by Christ, see ch. iv. 10; and is of so great a price, that if a man " would give all the substance of his house for it, it would utterly be contemned," ch. viii. 7. The fourth is *humility*; which is, in " the sight of God, of great price;" and the believer, being clothed with it, appears very beautiful and comely; it is a sparkling gem in this necklace. The fifth is *patience*, which is of exceeding use in the believer's life, much recommends his character and profession, and is greatly taken notice of by Christ; see Rev. ii. 2, 3, 19. The sixth is *self-denial*, which is required of, and should be in exercise in all Christ's followers, but seldom appears in its lustre and splendour, being frequently sullied by carnal and selfish principles and actions. The seventh is *contentment* in every state of life; this is an exceeding great rarity; few persons are possessed of this jewel; the apostle Paul had it, as appears from what he says, " I have learned in whatsoever state I am, therewith to be content." The eighth is a *saving knowledge* of Jesus Christ; this is eternal life itself, and is by believers preferred to all the things of this life; who, with the apostle, " count all things but loss for the excellency of the knowledge of Jesus Christ, their Lord." The ninth is *long-suffering* and *forbearance*, whereby saints are not easily provoked, and do readily forgive those who have offended them; this gives great grace, and is exceeding ornamental to the believer. The tenth and last link in this golden chain is *sincerity*; this runs through all other graces, and makes them so glorious as they are; this was exceeding bright, and shone with a great deal of lustre in Nathaniel, of whom Christ said, " Behold an Israelite indeed, in whom is no guile." Or, 4. Those blessings of grace which are laid up in an everlasting covenant, come through the blood of Christ, and are communicated to all his people, may be meant by these chains; they go inseparably together; where a person is blessed with one, he is blessed with all: for though our interest in them may be gradually discovered to us, yet are we blessed at once, " with all spiritual blessings in heavenly places in Christ." Not one of these links can be broken; this golden chain of grace and salvation is excellently described by the apostle, when he says, Rom. viii. 30, " Whom he did predestinate, them he also called; and whom he called, them he also justified; and whom he justified them he also glorified:" where we may observe, how all the blessings of grace are inseparably linked together; and which being put about the believer's neck, must needs make him look very beautiful and comely.

Verse 11. *We will make thee borders of gold with studs of silver.*

CHRIST having described the church's comeliness in the former verse, as she was beautiful under the legal dispensation, with the precepts of the moral and ceremonial law, and with that measure of grace which was then bestowed on her, proceeds in this verse to promise in his own, and in the name of the other two persons, a greater glory, and a larger measure of that grace unto her, under the gospel dispensation. And,

1. The thing promised is, to " make her borders of gold, with studs of silver."

II. The persons by whom this is to be performed, who are more than one; " We will make thee," &c.

I. The thing promised is, that she shall have borders of gold, " with studs of silver" made her: some read it, " turtles of gold:" the Septuagint renders it " similitudes, or likenesses of gold,[a]" and it is probable they mean the images of some things, perhaps turtles, which might be wrought in silver studs, with pieces, or plates of gold, which also R. Aben Ezra seems to intimate; others translate it " rows of gold,"[b] as in the former verse, it being the same word which is used there; our translators render it *borders*, respecting the borders of garments, where the Jews wore their fringes, and which, in Christ's time, the Pharisees, who were ambitious of being esteemed more holy than others, wore very large. Now a promise of golden borders may here intend the glorious righteousness of Christ; that golden and silver studded work of his, that raiment and needlework and curious piece of embroidery, with which the church and all believers are beautified and adorned; in which the church, the queen, stands at the right hand of the king, the Lord Jesus Christ, as one clad in gold of Ophir. Moreover, by these " borders, or rows of gold, with studs of silver," may be meant, either, 1st. The ordinances of the Gospel, which are far preferable to those under the law; the church's cheeks and neck were comely with these rows and chains, under the legal dispensation; but these are not said to be rows or chains of gold: the words *jewels* and *gold* are not in the original, but supplied by our translators, as has been there observed; but when he speaks of gospel-ordi-

---

[a] Ὁμοιώματα χρυσίου, Sept. Murænulas aureas, Vulg. Lat.

[b] תוֹר ordines, Marckius, Michaelis.

nances, which he would appoint, and his church should enjoy under the gospel-dispensation, he makes mention of gold and silver; as the Lord does in the prophecy of Isaiah, when he is speaking of, and promising glory to the church in those times, saying, Isa. lx. 17. "For brass, I will bring gold, and for iron, I will bring silver; and for wood, brass; and for stone, iron." Gospel ordinances are preferable to the law: 1. They are more easy, pleasant, and delightful; the ceremonial law was a yoke of bondage, and some of the ordinances of it intolerable; but Christ's yoke, under the gospel dispensation, "is easy, and his burden is light;" those ways were ways of pleasantness," in which God would have his people walk under the law, much more are those which they are directed to under the gospel; if those statutes and carnal ordinances were more to be desired than gold, yea, that fine gold," much more are those which believers enjoy now; the ordinances of that legal dispensation were servile and slavish, and suited to persons who were under a spirit of bondage; but those of the gospel became Christ's freemen, to be found in obedience to, and are no ways an infringement of their spiritual liberty, but rather an advancement of it; these commandments are no ways grievous, but every way delightful and pleasant, and are suited to a free, ingenuous, and gospel-spirit. 2. They are more lasting and durable; the ordinances of the Mosaic dispensation were imposed upon the Jewish church until "the time of reformation," that is, until the coming of Christ in the flesh, and the oblation of his sacrifice: for when he, the substance of all those shadows, was come, they vanished and disappeared; " the middle wall of partition is now broken down; the law of commandments, contained in ordinances," is entirely abolished, and the whole economy is at an end; but the ordinances of the Gospel will last till time shall be no more; when there will be no more need of such helps as these to assist our sight, or such lights as these to direct us in our way; they will last till the coming of Christ, till the " Sun of righteousness arises with healing in his wings:" these are things which will remain, till then, unshaken and immoveable; the gospel-dispensation is a " kingdom which cannot be moved," in opposition to the legal one, which is already moved, and entirely abrogated. 3. They are more clear and perspicuous; there was a great deal of obscurity in the legal dispensation; the faith of God's children was led to Christ through dark representations and cloudy types and figures: but now, under the gospel dispensation, we all with open face beholding through those ordinances, which we now enjoy, " as in a glass, the glory of the. Lord, are changed into the same image from glory to glory." 4. They are more spiritual; the ordinances of the ceremonial law are called *carnal ordinances*, Heb. ix. 10. The external worship of the Jews was attended with a great deal of pomp and splendour, but not with so much spirituality and power of godliness as that of believers under the gospel, who " worship God in the Spirit, rejoice in Christ Jesus, and have no confidence in the flesh." 5. The obedience which was performed under the legal dispensation, was not so free and ingenuous as this which is performed by believers under the gospel; that sprang from fear, and was performed under a spirit of bondage, but this from principles of love and grace. Believers, in their obedience to Christ, as under the constraints of love, are guided, influenced, and assisted by the Spirit of God, who is a free Spirit, or a Spirit of liberty: for " where the Spirit of the Lord is, there is liberty." Or else 2udly. The doctrines of the gospel may be here intended; which being " words fitly spoken, are like apples of gold in pictures of silver:" these may be called " rows, or borders of gold studded with silver;" for the doctrines of grace are by the apostle, in 1 Cor. iii. 12, compared to gold, silver, and precious stones, as are the doctrines of man's invention to wood, hay, and stubble. Now these may be very well called " borders of gold studded with silver." 1. For their valuableness; they are valued by souls who have tasted the sweetness, and felt the power of them, more than " thousands of gold and silver," yea, more than their necessary food, nay, more than life itself; they contain riches of grace and glory, yea, " the unsearchable riches of Christ." 2. For the glory and splendour of them; they give a glorious display of the divine perfections, and in a resplendent manner represent the glory of Christ's person, office, and grace; and therefore the gospel is called the " glorious gospel of God and Christ," 1 Tim. i. 11, 2 Cor. iv. 4. 3. For their being tried ones; " The words of the Lord," says the Psalmist, xii. 6, " are pure words, as silver tried in a furnace of earth, purified seven times:" they have been tried by saints, and have never failed to support and comfort them, nor to guide and direct them in the right way; they have been tried by enemies, and have stood the brunt of all their rage, malice, and persecution. 4. For their durableness: they are as lasting as " borders of gold studded with silver." Attempts have been made to destroy the gospel, and remove it out of the world, but have all proved abortive; it is an everlasting gospel, it is immoveable, a burdensome stone to all those who endeavour to subvert or remove it: though all things in nature are fading and perishing, and subject to change and alteration, yet " the word of God liveth and abideth for ever." 5. They may be called " rows of gold," for their orderly disposition and connexion; there is an entire harmony and agreement between the truths of the gospel; one truth has an entire dependance upon another, and they have all close connection with each other; this is what the apostle calls the proportion or analogy of faith, Rom. xii. 6. 6. The gospel is full of the silver specks or studs of " exceeding great and precious promises ;" it abounds with them, and is delightfully studded by them; it is filled with such a variety of them as are both useful and pleasant to believers.

Now there being such a display of the doctrines of grace, under the Gospel dispensation, it appears to be far more glorious than a legal one; it is true, the law had a glory attending it, but the Gospel has an excelling one; the law was " the killing letter and the ministration of death," but the Gospel is the ministration of life, " the spirit that quickens;" the law is the " ministration of condemnation, but the Gospel is the ministration of righteousness;" the law is that " which is done away," but the Gospel is that " which remaineth," and will abide for ever. Or else, 3rdly. By these " borders of gold, with studs of silver," may be meant the rich and glorious graces of the blessed Spirit, and a larger increase of them under the Gospel-dispensation; which are, 1. Rich and enriching, excellent and valuable as gold and silver; nay, grace is " much more precious than gold than perisheth ;" it is rich in its own nature, and enriches all that are possessed of it; therefore, says Christ, Rev. iii. 18, " I counsel thee to buy of me gold tried in the fire, that thou mayest be rich." 2. The graces of the Spirit adorn and beautify a soul, as much, nay, more than " borders of gold studded with silver" do the body; on the account of these the church is said to be " all glorious within ;" and though believers in their nature-state were black, like those who " have been among the pots," yet being called by, and adorned with the grace of God, are like " the wings of a dove covered with silver, and her feathers with yellow gold." 3. The graces of the Spirit, are as lasting and durable as golden borders with silver studs ; nay, more so, they shall not perish, can never be lost; grace is an immortal and incorruptible seed, which remains in the believer, and shall do so for ever. 4. A larger measure of grace is dispensed under the Gospel dispensation than was under the legal one; it was neither so clearly revealed, nor so largely communicated before Christ appeared in the flesh, " full of grace and truth," as it was afterwards; and such a larger revelation and increase of grace must needs make the church look more glorious under the one than it did under the other. Or else, 4thly. These " borders of gold " intend the ground-work of believers' faith and which hope, is Christ, as " Jehovah our righteousness," who is the only sure foundation, and the " chief corner-stone;" and the " silver studs " the curious work of sanctification, with all the delightful fruits thereof, even those " beauties of holiness" which are so ornamental to, and do so much become the believer; Christ's righteousness, imputed to us, is the ground-work and foundation of faith and hope; and his grace imparted to and wrought in us, is the superstructure that is raised upon it; the one the golden " borders," the other the silver " studs." Or, 5thly, Souls called by Divine grace are meant, even the " precious sons of Zion, comparable to fine gold ;" and as a great number of these being called in enlarge the borders of the church, so they likewise increase the glory of it; this is one way by which Christ " beautifies the place of his sanctuary, and makes the place of his feet glorious." Or, 6thly, and lastly. The glories of heaven may be here intended; for as Christ gives his people grace here, so he will give them glory hereafter, which he and the other two persons are preparing and making ready for them ; and we need not wonder that these heavenly glories are represented by " borders of gold studded with silver," when the new Jerusalem is described; Rev. xxi. 18, 19, 21 ; as a " city of pure gold, like unto clear glass, and the street of it pure gold, as transparent glass, the wall of it of jasper, the foundations thereof garnished with all manner of precious stones, and the twelve gates, said to be twelve pearls." Can any thing appear more glorious and magnificent than this account of that city, which has " foundations whose builder and maker is God ?" and those, who are enriched by divine grace here, need not doubt of being partakers of the celestial glory hereafter. But let us now consider who they are that promise and will perform all this. For,

II. As the things promised are here mentioned, which are " borders of gold with studs of silver;" so the persons who promise to make these, are intimated in those words, " we will make thee," &c. It is not the chorus of virgins, or the daughters of Jerusalem, who here speak; nor angels, who are both incapable of and unfit for such an undertaking; nor is God introduced her speaking *regio more*, in the manner of kings, who sometimes used to speak in the plural number, when they only mean themselves: but a trinity of persons is no doubt here intended, even " the Father the Word, and the Holy Ghost, which three are one," and are jointly concerned in all the works of grace, as they were in the works of creation: it is a way of speaking much like that in Gen. i. 26. R. Solomon Jarchi paraphrases it thus, " I and my house of judgment," as he also does Gen. xix. 24. Now the ancient Jews by this speech meant a trinity of persons, though the modern unbelieving ones, as Ainsworth, observes, are ignorant of it; yet still retain the phrase, and use it as the forementioned Rabbi does in those places where a trinity of persons manifestly appears: for the house of judgment never consisted of less than three persons. Now this work may very well be ascribed to them; for 1st. The ordinances of the Gospel are the institutions of all the three persons ; divine adoration is given to them in all; and they are enjoined on believers, and are regarded by them, as being all equally concerned in authorizing them, and in sharing the glory which arises from them; thus for instance, baptism is required to be performed "in the name of the Father, and of the Son, and of the Holy Ghost," Matt. xxviii. 19; and accordingly is performed in this manner. 2ndly. The Gospel itself is the work of all the three persons; God the Father is the author of it, and therefore it is the "Gospel of God," Rom. i. 1; and so is Christ, hence it is also called his, ver. 16; and so is the Spirit, and therefore it is called "the ministration of the Spirit," 2 Cor. iii. 8. The grace of all the three persons is discovered by it, and the glory of them all concerned in it; the Father sends it, Christ is the sum and substance of it, and the Spirit powerfully applies it. 3rdly, The work of grace upon the soul is performed by all the three persons; thus the regeneration and quickening of a sinner, "dead in trespasses and sins," is ascribed to God the Father, 1 Peter i. 3; to the Son, John v. 21, and to the Spirit, John iii. 5. 4thly, The increase of grace, which seems to be the thing here intended, is owing to them all; thus grace and peace, that is, a larger measure of them, is wished and prayed for by John for the seven churches of Asia, from all the three persons, Rev. i. 4, 5. 5thly. All that glory which saints shall have hereafter, is procured and prepared by them all; the Father, he has prepared the kingdom for them from the foundation of the world, and it is his pleasure to give it to them; the Son he has opened the way to it with his blood, and is gone to prepare a place for them; and the Spirit, he is the earnest and pledge of it, he discovers the invisible glories of it to them, and will never leave them till he has made them meet for, and brought them into the enjoyment of them. So that all the three persons, in all these senses, may be very well understood as promising to make for the church these "borders of gold with studs of silver:" which shows,

1. That believers should have a great value for the Gospel, and the ordinances thereof; seeing they are not only so valuable in themselves, being preferable to gold and silver, and are so useful and ornamental to the church, but are also the work of all the three persons. 2. That the work of grace upon the heart of a sinner, and the carrying it on to perfection, is done by an Almighty power, and is the work of the eternal Three; the renewing of men requires the same power, and is effected by the same hands, as the first making of them did; those who said at the creation of man, "Let us make man," say at this new creation, and in the carrying on and perfecting of the work, "We will make thee borders of gold," &c., as they were all jointly concerned in the one, so they are in the other, which shows the greatness and glory of it.

3. That all these "borders of gold studded with silver," are made for the comfort, glory, and happiness of the church, "We will make thee, or for thee," &c., the whole Gospel, with all its doctrines and promises, are given for their instruction and consolation: all the ordinances thereof, for their comfort and improvement, as well as for God's glory; all the grace which is provided in Christ, wrought by the Spirit in their hearts, as well as the glory which is laid up in heaven; all, I say, is to make them "a glorious church, without spot or wrinkle, or any such thing."

Verse 12. *While the King sitteth at his table, my spikenard sendeth forth the smell thereof.*

CHRIST having given very large commendations of his church, and promised a great deal of grace and glory to her; she in this and the two following verses, declares what advantages she received by him, how lovely his person, and how delightful his company were to her. These words may be understood either,

First, Of the time of Christ's not being manifested in the flesh, after the promise of it, and of the exercise of the faith, hope, love, desire, expectation, &c., of the Old-Testament saints, respecting his coming in the flesh: and then the sense is this, Whilst he, who is constituted King of saints, is appointed to be the Mediator between God and man, the promised Messiah and Saviour of the world, is with God, as the only-begotten Son in the bosom of the Father," and not yet manifested in the flesh; "my spikenard sendeth forth the smell thereof;" that is, my grace is in exercise; my soul is breathing with earnest desires after him; I long for his coming, and am in earnest expectation of it; I live in the hope of enjoying this valuable blessing; I firmly believe that he will come according to the divine promise, though his stay is long, and therefore will patiently wait the appointed time. Christ did exist from eternity, as the Son of God; was set up as the Head and Mediator of God's elect, and was appointed and constituted King over God's holy hill of Zion." He bore this character throughout all the Old-Testament-dispensation; and being promised to be the Messiah and Saviour of sinners, from the time of the first declaration and publication of it, the Old-Testament-saints lived in the faith, hope, and earnest expectation of his coming in the flesh. Or else,

Secondly. They may be understood of the time of Christ's being in the temple, or in Jerusalem, or in the land of Judea; during which time the Gospel was preached, and the sweet odour of it diffused throughout all the parts thereof. Christ was promised to come into the world as the church's King; "behold thy King cometh," &c., Zech. ix. 9; and as such he did come; the wise men of the East sought him under the character of "the King of the Jews." He was accused of making himself King, and for it was put to death. Hence this superscription was written on the cross, "This is the King of the Jews;" though most were ignorant of the nature of his office and kingdom, which were "not of this world." Now whilst this great King was here on earth, the savour of the Gospel was spread abroad; it was preached by Christ himself in the temple, in the synagogues of the Jews, and in several parts of the land; for he was "not sent but to the lost sheep of the house of Israel." He sent out his disciples to preach it, but limited them to Judea's land, and forbade them to "go in the way of the Gentiles," or enter into any of the cities of the Samaritans. So that the sweet odour was then confined within that land; though after his resurrection he enlarged the commission of his disciples, and bid them go and preach the Gospel to every creature, beginning at Jerusalem; which they accordingly did, and their ministry was owned for the conversion of many, but afterwards being rejected by the Jews, they returned to the Gentiles; for it was proper and necessary, that the word should be first preached to them, that "out of Zion might go forth the law and the word of the Lord from Jerusalem." Or,

Thirdly. These words may be understood of Christ's being now in heaven, whither, after his resurrection, he ascended, where he now is, and he will continue till his second coming, "whom the heaven must receive, until the times of the restitution of all things;" it is from thence that saints expect him. Now these words, "while the King sitteth at his table," very well suit with Christ's exalted state in heaven; his kingly office and power appear more manifest, he is now declared to be "both Lord and Christ;" his posture there is, "sitting at the right hand of God," where he is "in his circuit,"[p] as the words may be read; it being the usual custom anciently among the Jews, to sit at table in a circular form, 1 Sam. xvi. 11. Christ being in heaven, is "in his circuit," encompassed about with angels and glorified saints; thus in Rev. v. 6—11, 12: a large number of angels and saints are said to be "round about the throne," (and Christ, the Lamb, in the *midst* of them) singing his praises and feasting with him on those joys which will never end.

Now, whilst Christ is thus solacing himself with saints above, at such a distance from his church below, he is not unmindful of her, but gives such large communications of his grace, as causes her "spikenard" to "send forth the smell thereof." Which may be meant, either,

1st. Of the graces of the church being in exercise on Christ: Christ, though now in heaven, and so invisible to the bodily eye, yet is the Object of faith, love, hope, and joy; "whom having not seen, ye love; in whom, though now ye see him not, yet believing, ye rejoice, with joy unspeakable and full of glory," 1 Pet. i. 8. The distance of place no way hinders either the communications of grace to us from Christ, or the exercise of our grace on him; but while he is there, he is giving it forth to us, and we are exercising it upon him;

it is the manifestation of Christ's love and grace to us that makes our *spikenard* send forth its smell. Or else,

2udly. The prayers of the saints may be intended by it; which are odorous, and of a sweet-smelling savour to God, being perfumed with Christ's mediation, and offered up with his "much incense;" and therefore says David, Psal. cxli. 2, "let my prayer be set forth before thee as incense." R. Aben Ezra thinks, that by the smell of the spikenard, is meant the smell of the incense, which burnt under the law. Now while Christ is in heaven, the saints put their prayers into his hands, who takes notice of them, and is always ready, with his *golden censer*, to offer them up to his Father on the *golden altar*, in which he smells a sweet savour; and therefore the prayers of the saints are called *odours*, Rev. v. 8. See also Rev. viii. 3, 4. Or rather,

3rdly. This may be expressive of the Gospel, and the sweet "savour of the knowledge" of Christ, which by it is made "manifest in every place," wherever it comes, 2 Cor. ii. 14. Now the Gospel may be compared to *spikenard*. 1. Spikenard is but a small, low plant or shrub;[q] the Gospel is mean and contemptible in the eyes of the world; it is accounted foolishness by them, and preachers of it are abject and despicable persons in their esteem. Yet, 2. It is very excellent; it is by Pliny[r] accounted the chief and principal ingredient in ointments; and therefore, John xii. 3, the "ointment of spikenard, which Mary took and anointed the feet of Christ with, is said to be "very precious and costly." The Gospel is valuable and excellent, both in its nature and effects; it is a rich and an enriching Gospel; and therefore called the unsearchable riches of Christ," an exceeding valuable treasure that is put in earthen vessels; it is a revelation and declaration of the riches of grace, which Christ bestows upon sinners here, and of those riches of glory which saints shall be made partakers of hereafter. 3. It of an exceeding sweet smell, so is the Gospel; there is such an efficacy in the odour of it, that enlivens dead sinners, and therefore is said to be the "savour of life unto life," and will revive the spirits of fainting believers: though it is reported of spikenard,[s] that by its being carried over sea it grows mouldy and rots, whereby it loses its sweet smell, and stinks exceedingly; so the Gospel, to those that perish, is not only of an ill smell, and abhorred by them, but is "the savour of death unto death." Many of the Jewish writers[t] understand the smell of the spikenard here as an ill one. 4. Spikenard is of a hot nature,[u] and digestive of cold humours; it is hot in the first, and dry in the second degree. The Gospel being powerfully applied by the Spirit of God, warms the hearts of God's children, makes them burn within, and drives away

---

[p] במסבו in circuitu suo, Montanus, Piscator, Michaelis. [q] Plin. l. 12. c. 12. [r] Plin. l. 12. c. 12. [s] Matthiolus in Dioscorid, l. 1. c. 6. [t] T. B. Sabbat, fol. 88. 2. and Gittin, fol. 36. 2. Targum and Sol. Jarchi in loc. and Zohar in Exod. fol. 7, 2, 3. [u] Fernel. method, med. l. 5. c. 22.

luke-warmness, deadness, and dulness, occasioned by indwelling sin. 5. It is of a very comforting and strengthening[w] nature to the stomach, it exhilarates the spirits: so are the doctrines and promises of the Gospel to the souls of believers; these strengthen and nourish, comfort and refresh them, they, like Jeremiah, find the word and eat it, and it is the joy and rejoicing of their hearts." For these reasons the Gospel may be compared to spikenard; which some of the Jewish[x] writers think is musk, other a kind of spice somewhat like saffron; but it is best to understand it of nard, of which there are many sorts; the best of which is that which grows up in spikes, and therefore is called spikenard, which is what is here intended. Again,

Fourthly. These words may be understood of Christ's feasting with his saints here below, during which time their grace is in exercise; there is a mutual feasting between Christ and believers, he sups with them, and they with him; Christ has furnished a table for his people in this wilderness, with plenty, and variety of suitable food; and though he is a King, constituted by his Father, and acknowledged by his church, yet he sits at this table, with poor, mean, and worthless creatures, and welcomes them to those sweet provisions, saying, "Eat, O friends; drink, yea, drink abundantly, O beloved." Moreover, Christ's presence with his people, and his grace manifested to them, have a mighty influence to draw forth their grace into exercise, even as the rising sun opens the flowers, and exhales the odour thereof, and agreeable breezes spread it abroad. Thus when the graces of believers are in exercise under the influences of Christ, and the enjoyment of his presence, they are exceeding odorous, both to Christ and others; their *spikenard* may then be said to "send forth the sweet smell thereof." On this table, which is sometimes called "the table of the Lord," are set the body and blood of Christ, whose "flesh is meat indeed, and whose blood is drink indeed;" on which believers, being encouraged by Christ's presence, and assisted by his Spirit, feed plentifully; and he sits there and delights himself by viewing the graces of his own Spirit in exercise; thus at this table they are both mutually feasted and delighted. Yet there seems to be an emphasis on the phrase *his table*, as if it was a table peculiar to himself; and it was usual with great personages, and at grand entertainments, for the master of the feast and each of his guests to have separate tables, though together in the same room; this was formerly a custom with the Jews though now disused,[y] and with the ancient Greeks,[z] and with the old Germans,[a] also it seems with the Romans,[b] but this did not hinder their mutual pleasure.

The conjecture of a certain Expositor,[c] that Christ himself is intended by the *spikenard*, is not to be slighted, he being called a "bundle of myrrh," and a "cluster of camphire," in the following verses: it was usually in feasts to anoint the head of hair as well as feet of persons invited thereunto; and ointment of spikenard, was often used,[d] as is manifest from Mark xiv. 3, John xii 3; to this custom the Psalmist alludes, Psal. xxiii. 5. At royal banquets in Syria, as this here was one, it was usual to go round the guests and sprinkle them with Babylonian ointment.[e] Now the church was at table with Christ as a guest, and was entertained with the most delicious fare; here was nothing wanting to render the entertainment delightful and pleasant; Christ himself, as he is both the Master of the feast, so he is the ointment of spikenard to his guests: and it is as if she should say, "I am now at a sweet and heavenly repast with my beloved, he sits at the table, and I with him; and as he is my food, so he is my spikenard;[f] he is my 'all in all;' as long as he is here I need no flowers to delight me, no spikenard, myrrh, cypress, or unguents made of these to refresh me, for he is all this, and much more unto me." Christ's person and grace, his sacrifice, blood, and righteousness, are, like spikenard, of an exceeding sweet smell; his person is "altogether lovely; the savour of his graces or ointments" attract the love of his people; his "sacrifice is of a sweet-smelling savour to God," and to all believers; his garments, or robe of righteousness, "smell of myrrh, aloes, and cassia," and in them believers are acceptable and well-pleasing to God.

Verse 13. *A bundle of myrrh* is *my well-beloved unto me; he shall lie all night betwixt my breasts.*

THE church in these words continues the account of that comfort, delight, and satisfaction which she had in Christ, expressing the greatest love and strongest affection for him: and therefore she compares him to the very best herbs and spices, and declares that if her *spikenard*, or the graces of the Spirit in her, sent forth an agreeable smell to him, whilst he was at his table, much more grateful and odorous was he, being as "a bundle of myrrh" unto her.

I. Here is a title or character which she gives him; "my well beloved."

---

[w] Ibid. and l. 4. c. 7. [x] *Vide* R. David Kimchium in lib. Shorash. rad. נרד. [y] Tosephot T. Bab. Beracot, fol. 42. 1. [z] Homer. Odyss. 8. v. 69. Athenæi Deipnosophist. l. 1. p. 4. [a] Tacit. de Mor. German. c. 22. [b] *Vide* Cuperi Observ. l. c. 2. p. 13. [c] Sanctius in loc. [d] Madidus nardo comas, Martial. l. 3. ep. 56. tinge caput nardi, folio ib. Assyrioque nardo potemus uncti, Horat. Carmin. l. 1. ode 11. v. 16, 17. *Vide* Tibull. eleg. l. 2. el. 2. v. 7. and l. 3. el 7. v. 31. and Ovid de Arte Amandi, l. 3. [e] Athenæi Deipnosophist. l. 15. c. 13. p. 692. [f] Tu mihi stacte, tu cinnamomum, &c. l'auti Curculio, act. 1. sc. 2. v. 6.

II. What Christ is unto her; "a bundle of myrrh."

III. The entertainment she is resolved to give him; "he shall lie all night betwixt my breasts."

I. Here is a title or character which she gives unto him, "my well beloved." Ainsworth observes, tnat the Hebrew word *Dodi*, which is thus translated, is written with the same letters as David is, a name which is frequently given to Christ in the Old Testament. See Jer. xxx. 9, Ezek. xxxiv. 23, 24, Hosea iii. 5. David was a type of Christ, and of him, according to the flesh, he came; for he is "the root and offspring of David;" as he is God, he is David's Lord; and as he is man, David's son, both words, Dodi and David, signify *beloved*, and both David and Christ are beloved of God. "David was a man after God's own heart," and Christ his "beloved Son, in whom he is well pleased," and both of them beloved of God's people. The Septuagint render it by a word which signifies *a nephew*,[g] a brother or sister's son. Christ is near akin to his church, he is partaker of the same flesh and blood as they are, is of the same nature with them; they are "members of his body, of his flesh, and of his bones;" the Hebrew word *Goel*, which is frequently rendered a *Redeemer*, signifies also a near kinsman; and being applied to Christ, as it is in Job xix. 25, shows, that he, who is our Redeemer, is also our near kinsman: but the word is very well rendered here, "my beloved, or well beloved," and is expressive, 1st. Of Christ's love to the church; he is her "well beloved," and has shown his love by undertaking her cause, espousing her person, assuming her nature, and dying in her room and stead; which love of his is eternal, free, sovereign, unchangeable and unparalleled, and is the strongest motive to, and has the greatest influence upon her love to him; therefore she may well call him her "well beloved." 2ndly. It is expressive of her love to Christ, which springs and arises from the manifestations of his love to her, for "we love him, because he first loved us;" which love was now in exercise in her soul, he being present with her; and therefore she gives him this affectionate title as an evidence of it. 3rdly. It shows that she had a sense of her interest in him, and his love; a greater blessing, a soul cannot be possessed of, than an interest in Christ and his love, whose person is "the chiefest among ten thousand, and whose loving-kindness is better than life," and all the comforts and blessings of it; and next to this is a knowledge and sense of it; a soul may have an interest in Christ, and yet not have the sense of it; the former renders this state safe and secure, the latter makes his life comfortable and pleasant, and is an additional blessing and favour; for a person is then able to say, he "hath loved me, and hath given himself for me."

II. She declares that Christ her "well beloved was a bundle of myrrh unto her." By a "bundle of myrrh," we are not, I think, to understand the twigs or branches of the myrrh-tree bound up in faggots, which the Arabians used to make fires with, the fumes whereof were very noxious and pernicious, as the historian[h] tells us, and unless they burnt the gum, called *storax*, would produce incurable diseases; but either the little sprigs or flowers thereof bound up together, and put in the bosom as a pleasant nosegay to smell to, may be meant; for Christ is exceeding sweet and delightful to the believer, being "the rose of Sharon, and lily of the vallies;" or else the gum *stacte*, which springs from the myrrh-tree, and so the Septuagint read it, "a bundle of stacte;" or liquid myrrh, which sweats from the tree of its own accord, without incision, and is accounted the best: and then by *a bundle* of it is meant a *bag*,[i] or bottle of it, the same word which is used is translated *a bag*, in Hag. i. 6, Job xiv. 17; and is an allusion to persons who carry bag of perfumes, and sweet powders, or smelling-bottles in their bosoms, for the reviving of their spirits; now what these are to such persons, that and much more is Christ to his church. R. David Kimchi[k] relates out of Midrash Chazith, that Abraham, the father of the faithful, is there compared to myrrh; but Christ, who was the object of Abraham's faith and joy, may be much better and more aptly compared thereunto,[l] which I shall now consider. And,

1st. Christ may be compared to myrrh, if we regard the nature and properties of it; it being,

1. An excellent spice, and one of the most precious and principal spices; it is reckoned among the chief spices, chap. iv. 14, and as such Moses is ordered to use it in the anointing oil, Exod. xxx. 23. Christ is "the chiefest among ten thousands," and exceeding precious to every believer, in his person, office, and grace; there is none among the angels in heaven, or saints on earth, so desirable to them as he is; nor none who deserves to have the pre-eminence in, and over all things, as he does; seeing he is "the image of the invisible God, and the first-born of every creature." 2. It is very odorous, it is called "sweet smelling myrrh," chap. v. 5; and the church is said to be perfumed with it, chap. iii. 6. Christ, in his person, sacrifice, and righteousness, is of a sweet-smelling savour, both to God and believers, as has been shown on ver. 12. Believers smell a sweet smell in all his offices, characters, and relations: he is in all these as a bundle of myrrh, exceeding delightful to them. 3. Yet it is somewhat bitter in taste, it is *gustu leniter amara*, as Pliny[m] observes; which may be ex-

---

g Ἀδελφιδός, nepos ex fratre vel sorore.
h Solin. polyhist. c. 46. i צְרוֹר folliculus, Coccejus; sacculum, Marckius; fasciculus vel sacculus, Michaelis. k In lib. Shorash. rad. מר.
l So the Cabalistic Doctors interpret it of Tiphereth, the bridegroom, Lexic. Cabal. p. 669.
m Lib. 12. c. 16.

pressive, (1.) Of the sufferings of Christ; which, though they were grateful, and of a sweet-smelling savour to God, for it pleased the Lord "to bruise him;" here was not only *voluntas Dei*, the will of God, but here was also *voluptis Dei*, the pleasure of God; yet they were bitter to Christ, witness his agonies in the garden, his sorrows on the cross, and the spittings, buffettings, scourgings, and revilings of his enemies; his head being crowned with thorns, and his hands and feet pierced with nails; being forsaken by his God and by his friends, could not be grateful and pleasant to him: but though these were so bitter to Christ, yet, like myrrh, how sweet and odorous is a crucified Christ to believers! they desire to know none but Christ, and him crucified; the bitter cup which he drank, is the ground of their joy and triumph; his death and sufferings are the foundation of their comfort, and which only can secure them against the fears of hell and wrath; it is this which embitters sin unto them; sin never appears more odious than in the glass of Christ's sufferings; and they never mourn for it in a better or truer sense, than when they "look upon him whom they have pierced;" repentance is a tear that drops from faith's eye, and is never more evangelic than when faith views a sin-bearing and sin-atoning Saviour; now from the sufferings of Christ, or from a crucified Christ, distil and drop down the sweet-smelling myrrh of spiritual blessings, as justification, sanctification, adoption, pardon of sin, peace, reconciliation, and a right to eternal glory; all which come to us through the blood, sufferings, and death of a crucified Jesus. (2.) The myrrh, being bitter in taste, though sweet in smell, may show, that the cross goes along with Christ: for as Luther says, *Christianus est crucianus*, a Christian is a crossbearer; it is required of every one that will follow Christ, that he take up the cross; for he that would wear the crown, must bear the cross; and he who would have the sweet, must have the bitter; indeed the Christian generally has his share of afflictions, crosses, and trials in this life. The passover-lamb was eaten with bitter herbs, to show, that he that "will live godly in Christ Jesus, must suffer persecution;" yet so sweet is Christ, this bundle of myrrh, to believers, and communion with him, under all afflictions, so delightful, that they would not be without him, though they might be freed from them; this tree of life sweetens these bitter waters of Marah; they have peace in him, when in the world they have tribulation: they are contented with, and rejoice in their portion, and are willing to have the bitters, so they may have but the sweet; for these bitter afflictions and tribulations which they endure for Christ's sake, distil and drop down some precious gums of faith, patience, experience, and hope; see Romans v. 3—5.

2ndly. Christ may be compared to myrrh, for the use that has been made of it. 1. It being very valuable, and highly esteemed of, was used in gifts and presents to great persons; thus we find it in the present that Jacob made to his son unknown, then governor of Egypt, Gen. xliii. 11, and it was part of that which the wise men of the East brought to Christ at his incarnation, Matt. ii. 11. Christ is the great gift of God's grace to sinners, and an *unspeakable* one he is, which does not go alone, for "with him he freely gives all things."[a] When God gave Christ, he gave a manifest proof of his greatness and goodness; he gave like himself, and what was suitable to us sinners; a favour which we neither deserved, desired, nor expected. O boundless grace! amazing love! 2. It was used, and was a principal ingredient in the anointing oil; see Exod. xxx. 23; and may signify that "oil of gladness which Christ is anointed with above his fellows," which being poured upon his head, in its fulness, ran down to all his members, like the oil on Aaron's head, which ran down to the skirts of his garments; for it is from him that we receive that "anointing which teacheth all things." 3. The *stacte*, which is the gum that drops from the myrrh-tree, was used in the sweet incense; see Exod. xxx. 34, and may represent the intercession of Christ, who stands at the golden altar, with a golden censer in his hand, to offer up the prayers of all his people, which he perfumes with his much incense; which is exceeding grateful and odorous, like sweet-smelling myrrh unto the saints. 4. It was used to render persons comely and acceptable in the eyes of others; thus Esther, and the rest of the maidens, were purified with oil of myrrh, for their admission into the presence of king Ahasuerus, Esther ii. 12; it is in Christ the beloved, that saints only are accepted with God, being clothed with those garments of his, which "smell of myrrh, aloes, and cassia." Thus they have liberty of access into God's presence now, and shall have a ready admittance into his kingdom and glory hereafter. 5. It was used in the embalming of dead bodies, being useful to keep them from putrefaction and corruption; for this purpose Nicodemus brought a mixture of myrrh and aloes to preserve the body of Jesus, John xix. 39, 40; an interest in Christ, this "bundle of myrrh," and an application of him to our souls, will secure us from going down into the "pit of corruption," and will eternally save us from perishing; nothing safer and better than to have this in our bosoms, without which sinners, "dead in trespasses and sins," will rot and putrify. 6. It is very useful in healing[a] wounds and ulcers. Christ is the great Physician that heals all the diseases of his people, freely, perfectly, and infallibly, which he does in an uncommon and unusual way; he performs his cures by his blood and stripes; his blood is a *panacea*,

---
[a] Fernel. method. med. l. 6. c. 14, 15.

a sovereign medicine for all diseases, and " by his stripes we are healed," Isaiah liii. 5.

3rdly. Christ may be compared to " a bundle of myrrh." 1. To denote the abundance of the spiritual odours of divine grace in him, he is full of grace and truth," as a man and Mediator; " for it hath pleased the Father, that all fulness should dwell in him;" which is communicated to believers, as they stand in need of it; who sometimes receive such large measures of it, that they can say, " the grace of our Lord is exceeding abundant" in them; Christ is " a bundle of myrrh" unto them; they have large views of his love, and sweet communications of his grace. 2. To show the security of this grace in Christ; our life is sure in Christ's hands, being bound up in the bundle of life with the Lord our God, with all the mercies and blessings of it, both for time and eternity; therefore they are called " the sure mercies of David," being hid with Christ in God, so that they can never be taken away from us. 3. To show the inseparableness of Christ and his grace; Christ and the blessings of his grace never go separate; where God gives his Son, he gives all things with him; and where a soul enjoys Christ, he possesses all things; peace, pardon, and righteousness, and life are all in Christ: and the believer is blessed with all spiritual blessings in heavenly places in him.

Now Christ is not so to all persons, only to them that " believe he is precious," and to none but them; Christ is a " bundle of myrrh" to none but his church; " my beloved is unto me," &c., which shows not only the strength of her affection to Christ, the value that she had for him, and the delight she took in him; but also a particular application of him by faith, to her own soul; which is also expressed in the following verse, " my beloved is unto me as a cluster of camphire, " &c.

III. In these words we have also the entertainment which she resolves to give him; " he shall lie all night betwixt my breasts:" Wherein is to be considered, 1st. The place she appoints him, " betwixt her breasts." 2ndly. How long we would have him lie there, " all night. " And, 3rdly. For what ends and purposes.

1st. The place allotted Christ by the church is, " betwixt her breasts." R. Aben Ezra understands by them the two cherubim, or the midst of the camp of Israel; R. Solomon Jarchi, the two bars of the ark;[*] but it would be much better to understand them either of the two Testaments, the Old and New, which are both full of Christ where he is to be found, and does abide, or else of the two ordinances of the Gospel, baptism, and the Lord's supper, which may be called the church's " breasts of consolation;" see chap. iv. 5; in these ordinances Christ shows himself, and grants his presence to his people: or rather by Christ's lying " betwixt her breasts," is meant his dwelling in her heart by faith, than which nothing is more desirable to the saints: they have no better room than their own hearts, and therefore are desirous that he would lodge there; as Christ lays them in his bosom to testify his love to them, so they would have him dwell in their hearts to testify their love to him; and a wonderful condescension it is in Christ, who is " the High and lofty One that inhabiteth eternity," to take up with such a residence as this. So R. Alshech explains the phrase " betwixt her breasts," of being " in her heart."

2ndly. The time she mentions, is *all night*; by which may be meant the night of affliction, temptation, &c., it being in Christ alone that she could meet with any relief or comfort, under such dispensations; or else it means that she would have him with her, not as a stranger, sojourner, or guest, for a short time, but would have him dwell in her heart, lie in her bosom, and grant her intimate communion with himself, all the night of this life, until the everlasting day of glory breaks. Communion with Christ here is frequently interrupted, which the church had a long experience of, to her grief and sorrow: and therefore she desires to enjoy it without interruption.

3rdly. The ends and purposes for which she was desirous that he should lie all night betwixt her breasts, were, 1. For ornament; sweet flowers in the bosom are ornamental, and are placed there often for that purpose. Christ "the rose of Sharon, and the lily of the vallies," being carried in the hand of faith, or in the bosom of love, exceedingly adorns the believer. 2. For delight, pleasure, and refreshment; nosegays are carried in the bosom, to delight the eye and refresh the spirits. Nothing more delightful to the eye of faith than Christ; and nothing more savoury and of a sweeter smell to a believer, than his person, blood, and righteousness; the most delightful and sweet-smelling flowers fall short of expressing Christ's beauty and savour. 3. That she might always have him in her eye, mind, and memory; persons out of sight are too apt to be forgotten, even our dearest friends and best enjoyments. The church had no doubt, some experience of this, and therefore to remedy it, she would have Christ, this bundle of myrrh, always in her bosom, and in her sight, to contemplate upon and wonder at; as the Psalmist did, who says, Psalm. xvi. 8. " I have set the Lord always before me." 4. That she might keep him safe; thus persons often put things into their bosoms; which they would not lose; she had often lost a sight of Christ, and been without an enjoyment of his presence, which had given her a great deal of uneasiness; and for the future was therefore resolved to be more careful in keeping him, and for that reason would have him lie in her bosom. 5. To show her singular value for Christ, and her invaluable chastity to him : she sets him

---

[*] *Vide* Yalcut in loc.

in the highest place, and gives him the best entertainment: she gives him admittance where she would allow none else; he, and none but he "shall lie all night between my breasts;" these were inaccessible to any but to Christ.

Verse 14. *My beloved is unto me as a cluster of camphire, in the vineyards of Engedi.*

THE church having had such sweet communion with Christ at his table, ver. 12; which excited and drew forth her grace into exercise, enters into a commendation of him, ver. 13; and finding so much sweetness in him, she scarcely knew what was excellent enough to compare him to, that thereby she might express his excellency in himself, his usefulness to her, and that delight and pleasure which she took in him; having declared that he was "a bundle of myrrh" to her, which she desired might always have a place in her bosom, she does, in these words, compare him to "a cluster of camphire."

I. She gives him the same title or character as before; "my beloved."

II. Says that he was, to her, "as a cluster of camphire in the vineyards of Engedi."

I. She gives the same title or character to Christ here, which she had in the former verse, "my beloved;" which teaches us, 1. That Christ being once the believer's beloved, is always so; he has always an interest in Christ, and can never lose it; it is true, he may not always have the manifestations of Christ's love, but he has always an interest in him, as his beloved; for nothing can "separate him from the love of Christ." 2. This shows, that her faith in him, and her love towards him, still continued; these two graces are never separate; they are implanted in the heart at one and the same time; they grow up and increase together, "faith works by love;" they continue together, and can never be lost; they are not indeed always alike in exercise, but they are always in being; but here they were in exercise as before, and rather increased, while she was contemplating and commending her beloved's excellencies. 3. From hence it appears that she was not ashamed of Christ under this character, and therefore she repeats it, and indeed she had no reason: for her Maker was her husband, "the Lord of hosts is his name, the God of the whole earth shall he be called;" he had more reason to be ashamed of her, she being a poor, sinful, and despicable creature in herself, and he the Creator of all things, and the holy One of Israel; and indeed, she was so far from being ashamed of Christ as her beloved, that she took a pleasure in looking on him, and conversing with him as such. 4. Her repeating it, shows not only the vehemence of her love to him, but also the singular esteem that she had for him; that he was her beloved, and none else; that she chose, approved of, and valued him above all others; he was to her "the chiefest among ten thousands," and preferable to all other beloveds.

II. She compares him to "a cluster of camphire in the vineyards of Engedi:" it is somewhat puzzling and perplexing to interpreters, to know what this *copher*, which is translated *camphire*, was.

First. It is, by the Septuagint, rendered, Cyprus, by which is meant either the island so called, of which we read, Acts xi. 19, 20, and xxvii. 4; and then we must understand, by "a cluster of Cyprus," a cluster of the grapes of those vines which grew in Cyprus, which were the best and largest vines, as[p] Pliny observes; and these being said to be in the vineyards of Engedi, mean either those vines that were brought from Cyprus, perhaps in Solomon's time, and planted in the vineyards of Engedi; or else, some of the best vines in the land of Canaan, which were much like those in Cyprus. The land of Canaan was very fruitful of vines, and some of the best sort, which bore very large clusters; such an one was that which was carried by two men upon a staff, who were sent by Moses to spy the land, Numb. xiii. 23, 24; in memory of which the place whence it was taken was called *Eshcol*, the same word that in this text is rendered *a cluster*; and it is highly probable, that those vines, which grew in the vineyards of Engedi, were the best of all: R. Solomon Jarchi relates, out of the Agadah,[q] that these vineyards brought forth fruit four or five times a year, and R. Alshech says seven times. Now Christ may be compared to a cluster of grapes, which grew in these vineyards; he compares himself to a vine, John xv. 1; and therefore may be very well compared to a cluster of grapes that grew upon the vine. And that,

1st. For the number of berries that there are in a cluster of them. 1. In Christ is a cluster of divine and human perfections: "in him dwelleth all the fulness of the Godhead bodily"; every divine perfection is to be found in him; eternity, immutability, omniscience, omnipresence, omnipotence, &c., are as it were in a cluster in him; and as all divine, so all human perfections are in him; for he is perfectly man, as well as perfectly God; he is "God manifest in the flesh;" he was made in all things like unto us, sin only excepted, which is the greatest imperfection of human nature. 2. In Christ is a cluster of all spiritual graces; he is "full of grace and truth;" he is full of grace to communicate to others, as Mediator; and has all grace habitually in his human nature, God having not given "the Spirit by measure" to him; for he is "anointed with the oil of gladness above his fellows;" a cluster of the graces of the Spirit, which are in the human nature of Christ, may be seen in Isa. xi. 1—3. The Jews used to call such men who had all excellencies and virtues in them,

[p] Nat. Hist. l. 14. c. 1.

[q] *Vide* Yalkut in loc.

אשכולות, *eshcoloth*, clusters; hence they have a saying,[r] that "after the death of Jose Ben Joezer, a man of Tzereda, and Jose Ben Jochanan, a men of Jerusalem, the clusters ceased, according to Micah vii. 1;" and they say,[s] "what is אשכול *eshcol*, a cluster?" why say they, "it is שהכל בו איש, *ish shehaccol bo*, a man that has all things in him," that is, that has all virtues, a perfect knowledge of the law, &c. Now Christ is such a cluster that has all moral and spiritual perfections in him; all virtues and every grace are clustered together in him. 3. In Christ is a cluster of all spiritual blessings; all the blessings of the everlasting covenant are in his hands, and at his dispose; and saints are "blessed with all spiritual blessings in heavenly places in him; he is the believer's "wisdom, righteousness, sanctification, and redemption;" there is not a mercy we want, but is in him; nor a blessing we enjoy, but what we have received from him; he is the believers' "all in all." 4. In Christ is a cluster of "exceeding great and precious promises," all suited to the various cases of God's children, and to advance his glory; for "in him are all the promises, yea, and in him, amen, to the glory of God by us:" and these look like "a cluster" of grapes growing "in the vineyards of Engedi."

2ndly. Christ may be compared to a cluster of grapes for the abundance of juice that is in them. 1. The cluster is squeezed and pressed, that the juice may be obtained; so Christ was "wounded for our transgressions, and bruised for our iniquities, under the severest strokes of justice, and pressure of his Father's wrath; for "it pleased the Lord to bruise him," and all this for our good, that our sins might be expiated, our souls comforted, and persons accepted with God. 2. The juice squeezed out of this cluster may denote the blood of Christ and efficacy of it; which being "shed for the remission of sin," perfectly procured it; it "cleanseth from all sin," and purgeth "the conscience from dead works," and has an influence in our justification, and in every other blessing of grace. 3. As the wine, which is the blood of the grape, is of a cheering and refreshing nature, so is a crucified Christ to a poor sinner; that there are salvation, righteousness, peace, and pardon through his blood, for the chief of sinners, is a reviving cordial to those that see themselves so, and the best and most acceptable news that they can hear of; this is more cheering and refreshing than the choicest wine. Or else,

By *Cyprus* is meant the Cyprus-tree[t] which grew upon the banks of the Nile, and at Ascalon in Judea, and very probably in the vineyards of Engedi, here mentioned, as it did also in the island of Cyprus, from whence, perhaps, it had its name. The word Copher is used in the Misnah[u] and translated Cyprus; and Maimon and Bartenora[w] say, it is the same which in the Arabic is called אלהנא, the Alhenna, and refer to this place; and observe, that there are some that say it is the spice called the clove. Of the Alhenna Dr Shaw[x] says, "this beautiful and odoriferous plant, if it is not annually cut and kept low, grows ten or twelve feet high, putting out its little flowers in clusters, which yield a most grateful smell, like camphire." There seems to have been a likeness between the Cyprus-tree and the vine, especially in their flowering; and it is said to bear a flowery fruit like a grape in flower; and hence as vines when they flower are said to Cyprize, as the Greek version of chap. ii. 15, so a bunch of Cyprus-flowers in likeness to the vine, is called here a cluster;[y] and with propriety is the flower of the Cyprus referred to, since it induces sleep;[z] see ver. 13. And, 1. The[a] seed of the Cyprus-tree is much like a coriander seed, which the manna also resembled, Numb. xi. 7; which was typical of Christ, who is called "the hidden manna," Rev. ii. 17; being exceeding sweet, delightful, pleasant, and nourishing to believers. 2. The[b] flower of the Cyprus-tree which may be chiefly designed, is of a white colour, and a sweet smell; and may denote the purity of Christ's nature, and the innocence and holiness of his life, who in both appeared to be "holy, harmless, and undefiled;" as also the sweet fragrancy of his person, blood, sacrifice, and righteousness. 3. The[c] leaves thereof are good for the healing of ulcers, &c. "So the leaves of the tree of life," which is Jesus Christ, are said to be "for the healing of the nations;" that is, for the healing of their spiritual maladies and diseases. 4. An excellent[d] oil was made out of it; and of this with other things was made an ointment which by Pliny, is called *the royal ointment*. Christ is by the holy Spirit anointed above measure with the "oil of gladness," and is possessed of those good ointments which are exceeding savoury; and from him do saints receive that "anointing, which teacheth all things."

Secondly. Some[e] think that the Cyprus or Cypirus, of which Pliny writes, lib. 21, c. 18, is here meant, which is a kind of rush or swordgrass, is of a sweet smell, and has bulbous roots, to which it is thought the allusion is here made. And, 1. The smell of it, as Pliny, in the place before cited, writes, is much like that of spikenard; and for the same reasons that Christ may be compared to the spikenard, in ver. 12, may he be compared to the cyperus here. 2. The smell of it, as the same naturalist observes, makes men *vegetiores et firmiores*, more lively and strong, active and robust: in Christ is all a believer's

---

[r] Misnah, Sotah, c. 9. s. 9. [s] Vide T. Bab. Temurah, fol. 15. 2. R. Sol. Jarchium and Ez. Chayim in Misnam, ibid. [t] Plin. l. 12. c. 24. [u] Sheviith, c. 7. s. 6. [w] In ibid. [x] Travels, p. 113, 114. ed. 2 [y] See Origen. in Cant. Homil. 2. fol. 87. E. F. and Comment. in Matt. p. 463, 464. and Huet. Not. in ibid. p. 79. [z] Plutarch. Sympos. l. 3. p. 647. [a] Plin. l. 12. c. 24. [b] Ibid. [c] Ibid. l. 23. c. 4. [d] Plin. l. 12. c. 24. and l. 13. c. 2. [e] Vid. Cocceium and Bishop Patrick in loc.

strength, and from him they receive fresh supplies of it; and the more they exercise faith on him, the stronger they are: so that though they are poor weak creatures in themselves, yet they " can do all things through Christ, which strengtheneth them." 3. The root of it, as is observed by the same author, is good against the bitings of serpents, especially scorpions. Christ, who is " the root of Jesse," was typified by the brasen serpent, which Moses, by a divine command, erected upon a pole, that every Israelite that was bitten by the fiery serpents, might look to it and have a cure. Christ was lifted up on the cross, and now is in the Gospel, that whosoever looks unto him may live and not perish; see John iii. 14, 15; he is a sovereign and infallible remedy against the bitings of those fiery serpents within, our own sins and corruptions, and of that old serpent without, the Devil.

Thirdly. Others have thought that a cluster of dates, the fruit of the palm-tree, is here intended, which is the opinion of R. Aben Ezra and other Jewish writers; and indeed Engedi, as is manifest from Pliny,[f] was famous for those sort of trees, as was Jericho, which is therefore called *the city of the palm-trees*. Dent. xxxiv. 3; and it is very probable that Engedi was called Hazzazon-tamar, as it is 2 Chron. xx. 2, for the same reason; also the[g] fruit of this tree grows in clusters, and is very sweet and luscious, and may be expressive of Christ, and the fruits of divine grace, which souls receive in clusters from him, and are exceeding sweet to their taste.

Fourthly. Others think, and particularly Sanctius, that the balsam-tree is here intended, which only[h] grew in the land of Judea: this place, Engedi,[i] was remarkably famous both for that and palm-trees; so Origen observes,[k] that Engaddi abounded not so much with vines, as with balsams; the *vinedressers* in Jer. lii. 16, are interpreted by R. Joseph,[l] of *the gatherers of balsam*, from Engedi to Ramatha; and places where those trees grew might with propriety be called vineyards, since the balsam-trees were like to vines,[m] and were cultivated after the manner of vines.[n] From this tree dropped the precious balsam, which was of a sweet smell, and of an healing nature; to which Christ may be very well compared, who is the great and only Physician of souls, whose blood is a balsam for every sore, and has virtue to cure every disease.

Fifthly. The word *Copher* is by our translators rendered *camphire*, and so it is by " Pagnine, David de Pomis," and others; which[o] is of a sweet smell, is a very good remedy against the pains and aches of the head, a reviver of the spirits, and a refresher of the brain; and, if intended here, may be expressive of that sweet consolation and Divine refreshment which believers enjoy, resulting from views of acceptance in Christ's person, pardon through his blood, and justification by his righteousness. Though what we call *camphire*, seems not to be known to the ancients, nor does it grow in clusters; but is the tear or gum, or something of a resinous nature, which drops from an Indian tree.

Sixthly. There is one thing more to be remarked, and that is, that the Hebrew word כפר copher signifies " an atonement or propitiation;" and so may very well be applied to Christ, who is " the propitiation for our sins," and has made full atonement for them by " the blood of his cross." Bishop Patrick[p] observes, that the ancient Hebrew doctors, by dividing the first word אשכל, " eshcol, a cluster," found out the mystery of the Messiah in these words, and considered them as if they were read us, איש כל כפר, *ish col copher*, " my beloved is unto me the man that propitiates or expiates all things," that is all sins and transgressions. In the Talmud[q] it is explained, " He whose all things are, has atoned for my iniquity." Both the Targum and R. Sol. Jarchi carry it in the sense of atonement, though not as made by the Messiah: but it is certain that the great atonement for sin was to be, and is completely made by the Lord Jesus Christ, the true Messiah; in which appeared a cluster of all the Divine perfections, shining in equal glory; here grace and mercy, justice and holiness, truth and faithfulness, sweetly joined and harmonised together; whereby also a cluster of Divine blessings was procured and eternally secured to all his redeemed ones, such as peace, pardon, justification, &c., all which are sweet and comfortable, and fill them with unspeakable joy and pleasure.

Verse 15. *Behold, thou art fair, my love: Behold, thou art fair; thou hast dove's eyes.*

THE church having spoken in the three former verses of the glory, excellency, and sweetness, which she saw and experienced in Christ; he reassumes his part in this verse, and sets off the fairness and beauty of the church. In which,

I. Is a general assertion that she is fair; " Behold, thou art fair, my love: Behold, thou art fair."

II. A particular instance of her beauty given; " Thou hast dove's eyes."

I. Here is a general assertion of her fairness: In which we have, 1st. the thing asserted, that she is fair. 2ndly. An " ecce, a behold," prefixed to it; " behold thou art fair." 3rdly. A loving character given, " my love." 4thly. The assertion repeated.

1st. The general assertion is, that she is " fair;" not on the account of her good works,

---

[f] Lib. 5. c. 17. [g] Plin. l. 13. c. 4. [h] Ibid. l. 12. c. 25. [i] Josephus Antiqu. l. 9. c. 1. s. 2. [k] Homil. 2. in Cant. fol. 87. B. [l] In T. Bab. Sabbat. fol. 26. 1. [m] Plin. l. 12. c. 25. [n] Justin. Hist. l. 36. c. 3. So Foliot in loc. Vide Jerom. de loc. Heb. in voce Engaddi. [o] Fernel. method. med. l. 5. c. 17. and l. 6. c. 1. [p] In loc. [q] T. Bab. Sabbat. fol. 88. 2. Yalkut in loc.

or any righteousness performed by her, which is as filthy rags and " an unclean thing," as the Targum and R. Sol. Jarchi interpret it; but on the account of her being clothed with Christ's righteousness, washed in his blood, and sanctified by his Spirit, as has been shown on ver. 5.

2ndly. To this general assertion is prefixed an *ecce*, a *behold;* which is sometimes, 1. A note of attention; and may be here designed to stir her up more seriously to consider her own beauty, which she had in and from him: believers are too apt to keep their eyes upon their blackness, sins, and imperfections which fills them with sorrow, weakens their faith, and inclines them to diffidence; and though a consideration of this is sometimes necessary for the humbling of our souls, and the magnifying of Divine grace; yet we should not have our eyes so fixed upon these things as to be unmindful of and not regard our perfection, completeness, beauty, and comeliness, we have in Christ, who is " both our sanctification and our righteousness." 2. It is sometimes a note of admiration. Christ here, setting forth the greatness and excellency of the church's beauty, is introduced wondering at that " comeliness" which he himself had put upon her, she being in his eyes " the fairest among women;" and much more reason have we to wonder at it, that we who are " by nature children of wrath," whose natures are corrupted and depraved, who are both by actual and original sin, black, uncomely, and deformed, yet are now fair and beautiful in Christ, through his blood and righteousness; that we, who were clothed with the rags of sin, are now arrayed with " the Sun of righteousness; that we who were cast out into the open field, to the loathing of our persons, in the day that we were born, yet now should be clothed with raiment of fine linen, silk, and broidered work," and be adorned with bracelets, chains, jewels, and ear-rings; O stupendous grace! astonishing love! 3. It is sometimes a note of asseveration; and may be so used here, to assure her of the truth of what he asserted concerning her. Believers are very apt to call in question their fairness and completeness in Christ; and to indulge themselves in fears, doubts, and unbelief about it, especially when they consider how full they are of imperfections, sins, and spots; in the view of which they are very hardly brought to believe, that they are " all fair, and there is no spot in them :" Christ therefore to remove his church's doubts and fears, banish her unbelief, and strengthen her faith, uses this way of speaking.

3rdly. Christ gives his church here a very affectionate title, " my love," which has been already considered and explained on ver. 9; and is here mentioned again to let her know, that she was still the object of his love, pleasure, and delight; that his love towards her was great, strong, lasting, and unchangeable; as also how much his heart was ravished with her.

4thly. This assertion of Christ's respecting the church's beauty, is repeated, " behold, thou art fair;" which repetition is, 1. To show the exceeding greatness of it: she was " fair, fair," that is, exceeding fair; no such beauty to be found in any as in Christ, he is " fairer than the children of men;" and next to him is the church; she is " the fairest among women :" it is a superlative, surpassing, and excelling beauty that she is possessed of. 2. It being repeated, shows the reality of it; this is inward and real, and not merely outward, nor painted: outward favour is deceitful, and natural beauty is vain: but such is not the church's, which is supernatural, spiritual, glorious, and perfect. 3. It manifests the great value and esteem which Christ has for her, and her beauty, and how much he desired it; none so beautiful in his sight as she is, nor any beauty so desirable to him as hers; his thoughts are fixed upon, his eyes are sweetly delighted, and his heart surprisingly and divinely ravished with it; therefore he repeats it here and elsewhere, again and again in this Song. 4. It is repeated to show that she was both inwardly and outwardly fair; she was fair, both with respect to justification and sanctification.

II. He gives a particular instance of her beauty, " thou hast dove's eyes," or eyes like doves :[a] her eyes are taken notice of, because much beauty lies in the eyes, either in the size or colour of them;[b] and the eyes of doves are observed, because of some distinguished properties in them: the dove is a creature which furnish out much matter for poets, which they apply to lovers.[c] By her eyes may be meant, either,

1st. The ministers of the Gospel; who are that to Christ's body, the church, as eyes are to a human body; and what Job says of himself, may, with as much justness, be applied to them: " I was," says he, Job. xxix. 15, " eyes to the blind, and feet was I to the lame;" and the apostle seems to intimate this in 1 Cor. xii. 16—21. Now these may be called the church's eyes. 1. Because as the eyes are placed in the eminent part of the body, so are ministers set in the highest post and place in the church; and therefore are said, 1 Thes. v. 12; to be over others in the Lord; and it is as necessary and proper that they should be so, as it is, that the eyes should be in the head. 2. As the eyes are set there to watch and observe lest any hurt comes to the body, so ministers of the Gospel are placed in the church for much the same purpose; for this reason they are frequently called *watchmen*, and their business represented to be a watching for or over the souls of men committed to their care, and to give them

---

[a] עיניך יונים oculi tui velut columbarum, Pagninus, Munster, so Ben Melech.   [b] So Juno, Minerva, and Chryseus, are described by their eyes in Homer, Iliad. l. ver. 99, 206, 551.   [c] Vid. Barthii animadv. in Claudian. in nupt. Honor, od. 4. v. 21.

warning and notice of any danger that might befal them; of which we have instances both in the Old and New Testament; see Isa. lii. 8, and lxii. 6, Ezek xxxiii. 7—9, Heb. xii. 17, 2 Tim. iv. 5. 3. They may be called the church's eyes, because they pry, search into, and make a discovery of Gospel-truths to others; for which reason they are called the "light of the world," and more especially are the lights of the church: they are the stars which Christ holds in his right hand, and makes use of to hold forth the "light of the word of life," and light to others; they shine not in their own, but in a borrowed light: they receive all from Christ; they would not be capable of looking into and discovering the precious truths of the Gospel, nor be able to show to others the way of salvation, did not the Spirit of truth, ὁδηλήσει, go before, lead the way, and guide into all truth. 4. As the eyes observe, order, and direct the members of the body in their several actions; so the ministers of the Gospel, being appointed inspectors and overseers, observe the life and conversations of the members of the church; and if any thing disorderly appears, in a proper way correct, admonish, and reprove them for it; they make it their business to teach the whole church all things which Christ has commanded; to guide, direct, and instruct them how to behave themselves in their whole walk and conversation, both in the church and towards them that are without.

Now these eyes of the church may be very fitly compared to doves. 1. For clearness and perspicuity; the eyes of doves[d] are clear and sharp-sighted, so are ministers to search and penetrate into Gospel-truths: it is with much more clearness they behold, and plainness they deliver Gospel-truths now, than they could under the legal dispensation; and there is a time coming, when they shall do it with much greater evidence and perspicuity, when "the watchmen shall see eye to eye;" though in this imperfect state we know but in part, and prophecy but in part, and see through a glass darkly, in comparison of that light and evidence, in which those glorious truths shall appear to all believers in another world. 2. For their sincerity and simplicity; when Christ sent forth his disciples to preach the Gospel, he bid them be "wise as serpents, and harmless as doves:" those who are his faithful ministers, act with all simplicity and godly sincerity, and dare not, "as many, corrupt the word of God; but as of sincerity, but as of God, in the sight of God, speak they in Christ:" they use no artful methods to conceal their principles, and bring off persons from the plain truths of the Gospel to a reception of erroneous doctrines; but they are such who have "renounced the hidden things of dishonesty, not walking in craftiness, nor handling the word of God deceitfully; but by manifestation of the truth, commending themselves to every man's conscience in the sight of God:" they are exceeding careful and jealous lest souls, who are under their care, and are made their charge, should by any means be "corrupted from the simplicity that is in Christ." 3. For bringing in the olive-leaf of the Gospel; Noah's dove brought an olive-leaf in its mouth, which was an indication that the waters of the flood were abated: the ministers of the Gospel bring the good tiding of good things; they publish salvation by Christ, and bring the news of peace and pardon by his blood, justification by his righteousness, life through his death, and acceptance in his person. 4. For those dove-like gifts of the Spirit, with which they are endowed, and by which they are qualified for that work which they are called unto; there are diversities of them, of which one and the same Spirit is the Author, and these being given unto them, make them able ministers of the New Testament; so that they become both useful and beautiful. The Jews[e] interpret those eyes of the Sanhedrim. Or else,

2udly. By the church's eye may be meant, the eyes of "her understanding being enlightened" by the Spirit of God; and more especially the eye of faith, by which a soul takes a view of Christ's glory, fulness, and suitableness, and looks unto him alone for life and salvation; which may be compared to dove's eyes: 1. For the clearness and perspicuity of it; the dove, as has been already observed, is a quick and sharp-sighted creature; the eye of faith penetrates into those things "within the vail," brings distant things near, and makes unseen things manifest unto the soul; for it is "the substance of things hoped for, and the evidence of things not seen;" the things which the eye of nature and carnal reason could never take cognisance of, are observed by faith; whose object is an unseen Christ, and the unvisible things of another world which "eye hath not seen, nor ear heard." 2. For its singleness and simplicity in looking only to Christ: the dove[f] is an exceeding chaste and loving creature to its mate; the eyes of doves look only to their mates, to whom they keep an inviolable chastity; faith looks only to Christ and nothing else; it looks only to his person for acceptance with God, and not either to its duties or its graces; it looks only to Christ's righteousness for justification, and not to its own works, whether they be moral or evangelical, works done before or after conversion; it looks only to his blood for pardon and cleansing, and not to its tears of humiliation and repentance; it looks not to its frames, nor grace received, for its supply and support, but to an all-sufficient and inexhaustible fulness of grace in Christ: now this is the pure, single, and chaste look of faith, which is so pleasant and delightful to Christ Jesus. 3. For finding out, and feeding

---

[d] Frantz. hist. animal. sacra. par. 2. c. 15.
[e] Yalkut in loc.
[f] Plin. l. 10. c. 34. Ælian Hist. animal. l. 3. c. 5. 44.

upon the pure and wholesome doctrines of the Gospel: the dove[s] singles out and feeds upon only pure seed and grain, and rejects all other, as not being agreeable and proper food; so a believing soul cannot feed and live upon any thing; he cannot live upon the husks which swine eat, but upon the "wholesome words of our Lord Jesus Christ;" any food will not do, none but the "bread of life and the hidden manna;" it is the earnest desire of such a soul, that the "life which he lives in the flesh, might be by the faith of the Son of God;" he would always live on Christ and with Christ, and cannot be satisfied with any thing short of him; for having once tasted "that the Lord is gracious," he evermore desires this bread. 4. For the exceeding beautifulness of it in Christ's eye; as the eyes of doves are beautiful and delightful, so is this eye of faith to Christ, his heart is even ravished with it; "thou hast ravished my heart," says he, in chap. iv. 9, "with one of thine eyes:" Christ's eyes, for the beauty and glory of them, are said to be, in chap. v. 12, "as the eyes of doves, by the rivers of water, washed with milk and fitly set;" and so are the church's here; nothing more beautiful than the eye of faith. 5. For the meekness and humility of it: dove's eyes are meek and humble, not fiery, fierce, and furious, as some creatures, nor proud and lofty as others. Faith is a low and humble grace, it takes nothing to itself, but ascribes all the glory to Christ; it renders the disposition of a soul possessed of it mild and meek, not fierce and cruel, for "faith works by love:" a fiery temper, and a furious disposition do not become a believer; nor is it either excited or encouraged by faith: which promotes a meek, humble, and lowly spirit, of which Christ, the object of faith, is the best example, who says, "learn of me, for I am meek and lowly in heart:" who checks the furious, and resists the proud, but takes delight and pleasure in the humble soul, whose eyes are up unto him alone.

Verse 16. *Behold, thou art fair, my beloved, yea, pleasant; also our bed is green.*

THE church having heard her own praises in the former verse, and being conscious to herself of her sins and infirmities, and that what beauty was in her came from her beloved; she, as it were, breaks in upon his discourse, and ascribes it all to him; and it is as if she should say, Dost thou say that I am fair? thou only art eminently, essentially, and originally so: for all the beauty which I am possessed of, as it is by way of eminency in thee, so it is derived from thee; therefore the praise of it is not due to me, but to thyself, to whom be all the glory. In these words.

I. The same thing is asserted by the church concerning Christ, which he had asserted concerning her in the former verse; "behold, thou art fair, my beloved."

II. An addition to it, "yea, pleasant."

III. That their bed, which belonged in common to them both, "was green."

The same thing is here asserted by the church concerning Christ, which he had asserted concerning her, and that much in the same manner. For,

1st. The title which he gave her is, "my love," and that which she here gives him is, "my beloved." They seem, not only in these two verses, but indeed throughout the whole Song, to be, as it were, striving to outdo each other in their mutual expressions of love; but this title has been already explained on ver. 13.

2ndly. She asserts of this beloved of her's in the very same words, that he is fair; she returns it to him, to whom she judged it more properly belonged; whose beauty is natural and essential, hers not so; his original and underived, but hers derived from him: his infinite, inconceivable, inexpressible, and transcending all others, but hers of an inferior nature. Now her returning the same commendation back to Christ, shows that she not only looked on her beauty as far inferior to Christ's, and not to be mentioned with it; as also that it was derived from him; and that if she was in any sense comely, it was through that comeliness which he had put upon her; but likewise it shows her modesty and humility, as well as the nature of true faith, which gives all the glory of what the soul is, or has, to Christ and his grace; its usual and common language is, "not I, but the grace of God which was with me, and it is by the grace of God I am what I am." Now Christ may be said to be fair.

1st. As he is man; and so he is, both in body and soul; that body which was prepared him by the Father, and which was in an unspeakable and surprising manner conceived in the Virgin's womb by the power of the Holy Ghost, as it was free from sin, so was no doubt free from all the blemishes and defects of nature; and in this sense, as well as in some other, may he be said to be "fairer than the children of Adam;" and more especially he was so at his transfiguration, when "his face did shine as the sun, and his raiment was white as the light:" though what with sorrows and sufferings, with tears, dust, sweat, and blood, "his visage was marred more than any man, and his form more than the sons of men;" yet now being raised from the dead, and exalted at his Father's right hand, is beautiful and glorious: for that same human nature, which here below was the ridicule of men, is now the wonder of angels; that head which was crowned with thorns, is now "crowned with glory and honour;" and that face which was spit upon, will be the delightful object of the saints' everlasting vision, after

[s] Frantz. Hist. animal. sacr. par. 2. c. 15.

the resurrection morn: when with their bodily eyes they shall gaze on the glory of Christ's human nature, whom they "shall see for themselves, and not another:" in short, Christ's glorious human body will then be the pattern and exemplar, to which our bodies shall then be fashioned and made like. Moreover, as he is fair in his human body, so likewise in his soul; the powers and faculties of which act in an agreeable order, nothing being misplaced, nor any disorder in the whole frame or contexture of it, being free from all sin, and full of every grace: holiness here appears in its beauty, and knowledge and wisdom in their perfection; all which were manifest and evident throughout the whole of his life. In short, the whole human nature had an immeasurable unction of the Holy Spirit, on the account of which he is said to be fairer than others; he was "anointed with the oil of gladness above his fellows; grace was poured plentifully into his lips, from whence it freely dropped like "sweet smelling myrrh."

2ndly. He may be said to be fair, as God-man and Mediator, which I suppose is chiefly designed here; for as such, this branch of the Lord is exceeding beautiful and glorious in the eyes of believers. For, 1. The glory of all the divine perfections is resplendent in him: as such, he is "the brightness of his Father's glory, and the express image of his person;" all God's creatures, works, and actions, show forth the glory of his perfections in some measure; but they are no where so clearly discerned, nor so gloriously displayed, as they are in the person and office of Christ as Mediator; for "the light of the knowledge of the glory of God" is given us in the face, or person of Jesus Christ: and a glorious, delightful, and ravishing sight it is to a believer. 2. There is a mediatorial glory which he is possessed of, which makes him look exceeding fair and beautiful; this is what was given him before the world began, when he first entered into covenant with his Father, became our Surety, and was set up as the Mediator of God's elect: which, when he had finished his work, he desired might be given to him, that is, might be more clearly manifested, and a greater display of it given to the world, and it is what shall feed the eyes of his saints with wonder and pleasure to all eternity. This is what Christ desires that they may be with him for, namely, "to behold his glory," for then indeed shall they "see him as he is:" now, in the glass of the Gospel, saints behold a great deal of the glory of Christ Jesus, which gives them much pleasure and delight; but this is but little in comparison of what they shall be everlastingly indulged with. 3. Christ appears with much fairness and beauty to believers, as he is possessed of all grace; this was the glorious and soul ravishing sight, which the evangelist John, together with others, had of him, which he takes notice of, saying, John i. 14, "we beheld his glory, the glory as of the only-begotten of the Father, full of grace and truth;" and what makes it still more delightful is, that all this grace is treasured up in him for them, that they from "his fulness may receive, and grace for grace:" there is every thing in him that souls want, and every thing they want they may have from him, for "he is of God made unto us wisdom, righteousness, sanctification, and redemption," which consideration must needs render him fair, beautiful, and delightful in the believer's eye. 4. Christ is fair in believer's eyes, in all he is unto them, or has done and suffered for them; their souls are delighted in the views of him, as their prophet, to teach and instruct them, whose "lips are like lilies, dropping sweet smelling myrrh" of Gospel doctrines, counsels, and promises; as their priest, who, by his active and passive obedience, has made full satisfaction to the righteous law, an atonement for their sins by his blood, and is now interceding for them in heaven, and therefore, his "hands are as gold rings set with the beryl, and his legs as pillars of marble set upon sockets of fine gold;" and as their king, to rule, govern, protect, and defend them, whose head "is as the most fine gold, his locks are bushy, and black as a raven." Moreover, he is exceeding fair and beautiful in their eyes, considered in all the relations he bears to them; as he is their indulgent Father, their tender Husband, loving Brother, and faithful Friend: and so he is to them, in all that he has done and suffered for them; it is an exceeding delightful sight to view him undertaking their cause, espousing their persons, assuming their name, bleeding and dying in their room and stead, arising again as a victorious conqueror, sitting at God's right hand, where he ever lives to make intercession for transgressors.

3rdly. The same word *behold*, is prefixed by the church to this commendation, as was to the other by Christ, as wondering at that beauty she saw in him, and that one so fair should take any notice of her; and being affected with his glory herself, she stirs up others to a contemplation of it; for all have reason, upon a view thereof, to say, "how great is his goodness, and how great is his beauty," Zech. ix. 17.

II. She not only asserts the same of him as he had done of her, but also makes an addition to his character, saying, "behold, thou art fair, yea, pleasant." This shows the exceeding great value and esteem that she had for him, and that she found it difficult to find words fully expressive of his excellency; and indeed all words fall short of expressing his worth. She was not contented with the former commendation of him, and therefore adds another word, striving as it were, to exceed him in her commendations. They were not mere words of compliment she used, for her heart and affections went along with them; nay, she laboured under a difficulty of finding out words, apt, strong, and full enough to express the real and just sentiments of her mind concerning him, and therefore, as she thought one word was not enough, she adds another, "yea, pleasant." 1. The person of Christ is so to a believer; He looks pleasantly upon believers with an eye of love and grace, "his eyes are as the eyes of doves by the rivers of water, washed with milk, and fitly set" upon them. He does not look upon them in a frowning, furious, and angry manner, but as having the greatest respect for, and taking the greatest delight in them; and whilst they are enabled by faith to view him with love in his heart and smiles in his countenance, their souls are filled with an universal pleasure; for if it is "a pleasant thing for the eyes to behold the sun" in the firmament, it is much more pleasant to behold the "Sun of righteousness arising with healing in his wings;" to see our acceptance in his person, pardon through his blood, justification by his righteousness, reconciliation with God through his atoning sacrifice, and every needful supply of grace from his infinite fulness: O how pleasant must Christ be to a believer under all those sweet considerations! 2. Christ's covenant and promises are exceeding pleasant to them. What can be a more delightful sight, than to view Christ as the Mediator, Surety, and Messenger of the covenant of grace; to see all the blessings, and the "exceeding great and precious promises" of it, all secured in his hands; as also their interest in it, and in him as their covenant-head? so that they can say, as David did, 2 Sam. xxiii. 5, "although my house be not so with God; yet he hath made with me an everlasting covenant, ordered in all things and sure: for this is all my salvation and all my desire, although he make it not to grow;" it is this will give satisfaction and content, under all the troubles and exercises of life, and fortify against the fears of death. 3. The doctrines of Christ are pleasant to believers. "Pleasant words are as an honeycomb, sweet to the soul, and health to the bones;" such are the wholesome words of our Lord Jesus, the doctrines of the everlasting gospel; these are sweeter to a believer's taste than "the honey, or the honey-comb;" they are salutary and nourishing, and therefore valued by him more than his necessary food; he often, with Jeremiah, finds these words, and eats them, and they are to him "the joy and rejoicing of his heart." 4. The ordinances of Christ are pleasant to them. The commands of Christ are far from being grievous, his "yoke is easy and his burden light;" all his tabernacles are amiable and lovely, his "ways are ways of pleasantness, and his paths are paths of peace," especially when they enjoy his presence, have communion with him, and are assisted by his Spirit in an attendance on them. 5. Christ's company and conversation are exceeding pleasant and delectable: no fellowship like "fellowship with the Father, and with his Son Jesus Christ." This is the believer's peculiar privilege, his sole delight, and the matter of his glorying: no presence like the presence of Christ, "in whose presence is fulness of joy; and at whose right hand are pleasures for evermore." Communion with angels, and fellowship with saints, must needs be very pleasant and delightful to believers; but not to be compared with the enjoyment of his presence, who is the Head of angels, and the king of saints; this is the saints' comfort here, and will be their eternal happiness hereafter.

III. Having thus given this great and glorious commendation of her beloved, she asserts that their bed, which was common to them, and which made for the glory of them both, green; also our bed is green: where we are to consider, 1st. What this bed is. 2ndly. Whose it is. And, 3rdly. What is said of it.

1st. It will be proper to inquire what is meant by this bed. R. Solomon Jarchi observes; that the tabernacle and temple were called so; and for this purpose cites Cant. iii. 7, 2 Kings xi. 2, 3, and so it is explained in Yalkut. Theodoret[b] thinks that the scriptures are here intended, which are oftentimes the instrumental means of begetting souls to Christ; see James i. 18, 1 Peter i. 23. But it seems better to understand it of the church itself, and the seat of it; where Christ and believers comfortably rest together, enjoy sweet fellowship and communion with each other, and where many souls are begotten and born again; for "of Zion it shall be said, this and that man was born in her."

2ndly. Whose bed is this: she calls it our bed, which denotes a mutual property and interest that Christ and believers have in the church; it is what the Father has given him, which he has purchased with his blood, and is the Author and Maker of; "behold his bed, which is Solomon's:" this he has chosen for his rest, solace, and refreshment, saying, "this is my rest for ever, here will I dwell." Moreover, it is the bed which believers have a right to, and therefore are admitted to all the privileges of it; here they enjoy the presence and company of Christ their beloved, they have an interest in him; therefore the apostle says, "if Christ be yours, all things are yours."

3rdly. It is said of this bed, that it is green, that is, flourishing and fruitful; so the word is used in Dan. iv. 4, Psalm lii. 8, and xxxvii. 35, and intends either, 1. The fruitfulness of the saints in grace and holiness, who being "planted in the house of the Lord, flourish in the courts of our God," as trees of righteousness, which are filled and laden with the fruits thereof which is owing to the refreshing dews and influences of divine grace. Or else, 2. The numerous increase of converts in the church; and so

[b] In loc.

the Targum and R. Sol. Jarchi explain it: and it may be an allusion to a custom used in the eastern nations, in strewing the nuptial bed with green leaves and flowers; and with the Latins, *torus*, a bed, is so called from *tortis herbis*,[1] from herbs writhed and twisted together, and put under the shoulders of those that lay on them; and it was usual to strew them with green herbs, grass, and leaves of trees.[k] A numerous increase of converts, which makes the bed, the church, look so green and flourishing, was frequently promised and prophesied of in the Old-Testament; and had a glorious fulfilment in the first dawn of the gospel, when three thousand souls were converted under one sermon; and will be gloriously and completely fulfilled in the latter day, when the church shall say, "the place is too strait for me, give place to me that I may dwell."

Verse 17. *The beams of our house are cedar, and our rafters of fir.*

THESE are either the words of Christ, inviting the church into their house, which was so firmly and delightfully built; or else the words of the church, continuing the praise of Christ, and all that were about him, or belonging unto him; or rather, they are the words of the bride and bridegroom, and the virgins her companions, all joining together in a chorus, to set forth the glory and excellency of the church: in which may be considered,

I. What is meant by this house, which they seem to have a common interest in, and therefore call it "our house."

II. What those beams are which are said to be cedar.

III. What those rafters are which are said to be of fir.

I. I shall consider what is meant by the "house, whose beams are cedar," and whose *rafters* are *of fir*. R. Sol. Jarchi understands it of the tabernacle, the glory and praise of which, he thinks, is here set forth; and so the Targum refers it to the temple built by Solomon, but yet acknowledges that that which shall be built in the days of the king Messiah, shall be much more glorious and beautiful. But it is much better to understand it, either,

1st, Of "our house, which is from heaven,"[l] which saints know that after their dissolution they shall enter into. The word in the Hebrew is in the plural number "our houses,"[m] and so may intend those many mansions which are in Christ's Father's house, preparing by him for all his people for their everlasting entertainment; and the *beams* and *rafters* of these houses being of cedar and fir, which are trees of a sweet smell and durable nature, may represent that fulness of joy, and those delightful pleasures which are in "Christ's presence, and at his right hand for evermore;" it shows that this "house is not made with hands, but eternal in the heavens;" that these habitations which Christ has prepared for them, and will bring them into, are everlasting; and that that inheritance which they are born heirs unto, and shall certainly enjoy, is "incorruptible, undefiled, and fadeth not away."

Now if we suppose these to be the words of Christ, his design then seems to be, by commending the endless joys and never-ceasing pleasures of the saints above, to raise the affections and quicken the desires of his church after the enjoyment of the same, that they with him may enter the nuptial chamber, and spend an eternity in everlasting communion with each other; but if they are the words of the church, then they seem to intimate the comfortable views she had of the heavenly joys, and her interest in them; she knew that when this "earthly house was dissolved, she had an house not made with hands," firmly built and delightfully furnished, which she should have admittance into, and which is "eternal in the heavens;" as also, the earnest desires of her soul to be there; she saw this house afar off, what a goodly structure it was, what soul-ravishing delights it was filled with, therefore longed to be within the walls of it, and "groaned earnestly, being burdened with a body of sin and death, desiring to be clothed upon with her house, which is from heaven;" likewise she seems to speak of this house with the utmost thankfulness to her Lord and spouse, and adoration of his grace, that had provided so convenient and delightful an habitation for her. Or else,

2ndly. By this house may be meant the church of God here below, which seems most agreeable; for so it is called in 1 Tim. iii. 15, where the apostle promises Timothy to instruct him how he should "behave himself in the house of God, which, says he, is the church of the living God, the pillar and ground of the truth;"[t] so believers are said to be Christ's house, in Heb. iii. 6; "but Christ, as a son over his own house whose house are we, if we hold fast the confidence, and the rejoicing of the hope firm unto the end." Now the church may be said to be Christ's house, 1. Because it is of his building: the ministers of the Gospel are instruments in building up his church; but he is the great Master-builder: the materials of this building are "lively stones," which are the saints; but he himself is both the "foundation and the corner-stone; it is upon this rock he builds his church, and the gates of hell shall not be able to

---

[1] Isidor. Originum, l. 20. c. 1. [k] Vid. Alstorph. de lectis veterum, c. 1. p. 2, 8—10. Graminei tori, Val. Flac. l. 8. v. 255. Viridante toro confederat herbæ, Virgil. Æneid, 5. v. 388. In medio torus est de mollibus ulvis impositus lecto, Ovid. Metamorph. 8. v. 685. [l] So Cocceius in loc. [m] בתינו domorum nostrarum, V. L. Pagninus, Montanus, &c. ædium nostrarum, Marckius.

prevail against it." 2. Having built it, he dwells in it, and makes it the place of his residence: the church is the habitation of all the Three Persons, and particularly of Jesus Christ; saints are built up " for an habitation of God through the Spirit ;" they are the temples of the Holy Ghost, and in their hearts Christ dwells by faith : the church is the habitation of his holiness, and the place where his honour dwelleth; here he delights to be, and condescends to show himself; here souls may expect to find him, and enjoy his presence; for he has promised to be here until the end of time. 3. Here he eats, feeds, and feasts with his people; it is not an empty house he keeps, but having built it, he furnishes it with suitable provisions, which are called " the goodness and fatness of his house: here he makes a feast of fat things, a feast of wines on the lees, of fat things full of marrow, of wines on the lees well refined: this is his banqueting house," into which he brings his people, and sups with them, and they with him. 4. Here he takes his rest with the church, his bride: " this, says he, is my rest for ever: here will I dwell, for I have desired it ;" here he solaces himself, and takes the utmost delight and pleasure : as houses are not only to feed in, but to rest in, so this use does Christ make of his church. 5. Here he lays up his treasure, and what he esteems his portion, and the chief part of his riches; for " the Lord's portion is his people, Jacob is the lot of his inheritance ;" the saints are his jewels and peculiar treasure, and these he brings into and preserves safe in his house below, until he removes them into his house above. 6. As his house, he fills, repairs, and beautifies it at pleasure; he fills it with members, and these he fills with gifts and grace suitable to their places in this house, for he is "ascended to fill all things ;" when any breaches are made, he makes them up; when it is fallen to decay, he repairs it, by bringing in a large number of converts, and beautifies this house of his glory with his own presence. 7. He is the Master of it, and manages all the affairs of it; the key of it is in his hands, and the government of it upon his shoulders; he is sole King and Ruler here; he enacts laws, demands obedience to them, and places officers here to see them put in execution; he is " the high Priest over this house of God," and transacts all affairs between God and his people: he is the great Prophet that teaches and instructs them ; the careful Husband and indulgent Father that provides all for them ; in short, " of him the whole family in heaven and earth is named ;" so that the church may be very well called Christ's house.

But then this house is said to be the church's also; " the beams of our house," &c. Saints are the materials of this house ; Christ is the builder, the foundation, and the Corner-stone: but they are the lively stones which are laid on this foundation, and so " are built up a spiritual house, an holy priesthood, to offer up spiritual sacrifices, acceptable to God by Jesus Christ ; they have a right to, and are in the enjoyment of all the privileges of this house ; they are " fellow-citizens with the saints, and of the household of God ;" here they are born and brought up, have their food and education ; " thy daughters shall be nursed at thy side," Isa. lx. 4 : here they dwell, rest, feed, feast, and enjoy sweet communion with Christ Jesus ; and therefore they may say, as David did, Psalm lxxxiv. 4 ; " blessed are they that dwell in the house, they will be still praising thee ;" as they have a great deal of reason so to do.

Also the word being in the plural number, and rendered, our houses, may intend the particular churches of Christ, which are all his houses, where he dwells; his golden candlesticks, among whom he walks, which hold forth the word of light and life to others ; and his gardens where he delights to be, eating those pleasant fruits, and feeding among those lilies, which grow there ; for there is but one " general assembly and church of the first-born, which are written in heaven," yet there are many particular churches and congregations of saints here on earth.

II. The beams of this house are said to be of cedar. By cedar beams we are not to understand angels, who encamp about, protect and bear up the saints, and are ministering spirits to them, which is the opinion of some ;[n] but rather, the ministers of the Gospel,[o] who may be called pillars in Christ's house, as James, Cephas, and John were ; who by their exemplary lives, savoury doctrines, and undaunted courage, add much strength and glory to the church of Christ ; as by rafters afterwards may be meant weaker believers, who have all their proper places, work, and usefulness in the house of God: or else, by cedar beams may be meant in general, the saints and people of God, which are all beams and pillars in this house, and serve to support it; for being " fitly framed together, they grow up unto an holy temple in the Lord ;" and being joined and cemented to each other in faith and love, they worship the Lord " with one shoulder, or with one consent ;" and these are compared to cedars in scripture ; see Psal. xcii. 12, Numb. xxiv. 5, 6 ; and may be very well compared unto them, 1. For the height and tallness of them; the cedar-tree is a very tall tree, as may be learnt from 2 Kings xix. 23, Amos. ii. 9. The saints, though they are mean, abject, poor, and low by nature, even beggars on the dunghill, yet by divine grace they are raised on high, set among princes, and made to inherit the throne of glory; they are higher than others in their gifts and graces, faith, knowledge, and experience, as well as in their privileges and attainments ; they are growing up higher still in their head Christ Jesus, and are reaching forwards and upwards in their affections and desires, in hope of enjoying " the prize

[n] Foliot. in loc.   [o] So Isidore, Alcuin, and others in loc.

of the high calling of God in Christ Jesus." 2. For their straightness and uprightness; for which reason perhaps the righteous are said to grow not only like the palm-tree, but also the cedar in Lebanon: the saints are upright, both in heart and conversation; they both speak and walk uprightly. 3. For its durableness; Pliny[p] ascribes even eternity unto it; it is used for immortality;[q] it will not rot, nor admit any worm into it; the saints will endure for ever; for though they have much corruption in them, yet they themselves shall never corrupt; they have that grace in them which will keep them from putrefaction, and which will never decay itself: for it is incorruptible, immortal, and never-dying seed. 4. For the sweet odour which it sends forth;[r] it is of an excellent smell; so are the persons of the saints to God the Father, being clothed with the garments of salvation, and robe of Christ's righteousness, which "smell of myrrh, aloes, and cassia;" so are the graces which are wrought in them by the Spirit to Christ himself; see chap. iv. 10; and so are all their sacrifices of a sweet-smelling savour, being offered up in Christ's name, and perfumed with the sweet incense of his mediation. 5. The cedar-tree is well rooted, always green, and the older the more fruitful: believers are rooted in Christ Jesus, so as all the winds and storms of sin and temptation cannot tear them up: they are always green, and their leaf doth not wither, because they are "planted by rivers of water;" where, being refreshed with continued supplies of divine grace, they bring forth fruit in old age, because the Lord, he is upright, he is their rock, and there is no unrighteousness in him.

III. The rafters of this house are said to be of fir. By rafters may be meant the ordinances of the Gospel, which are administered in the church, and are for the comfort and edification of it. The Hebrew word here, translated rafters, is in Gen. xxx. 38—41, and Exod. ii. 16, rendered gutters and troughs of water, where sheep used to be watered; and some of the Jewish writers[t] would have it understood in this sense here. R. Aben Ezra observes, that if it is taken in this sense, then the word rendered fir, should signify marble stone, and be read thus, "our canals are of marble stone."[u] Now these canals or gutters of water are called רהטים, *rahatim*,[w] from the Chaldee word רהט *rehat*, which signifies *to run*, because waters run in them. The grace of the Spirit is frequently, both in the Old and New Testament, represented by water; which, for its purity and purifying nature, is called *clean water*; for its quickening virtue and efficacy, water of life and living water: and for its plenty and abundance, "rivers of water:" this grace is commonly conveyed and communicated to us in the use of ordinances; these are the canals or conduit-pipes in which this water runs, and is brought unto us; the first conveyance is usually this way: faith, conversion, and every grace that attends it, come by hearing, and hearing by the word of God; and as this, so other ordinances are the means of increasing faith, joy, and comfort, and of conveying fresh supplies of grace and strength. Christ's fulness is the fountain from whence all grace springs; and his ordinances are the golden pipes, through which the golden oil and grace of divine love run and empty themselves into our souls. Also the same word is translated *galleries*, in ch. vii. 5, "the king is held in the galleries." R. David Kimchi says,[x] that they were buildings in high houses, in which they walked from house to house, or from one part of the house to the other; they were such as our balconies; and they may be called by this name, because they run along the sides of houses; agreeable to this, Junius and Tremellius translate it, *ambulachra nostra, our walking places*. Now the ordinances are the galleries, or walking-places, where Christ and believers walk and converse together; here he grants them fellowship with himself, tells them all his mind, and discloses the secrets of his heart unto them; in these galleries they behold "the king in his beauty;" here he shows them his covenant-love and grace, and from hence they take a prospect of the good "land that is very far off." But the word may be very well translated *rafters*, which are joined together, and run in each other; and so the Targum renders it; and in this sense is the word used both in the Misnah[y] and in the Midrash.[z] Now as rafters are for the strength and support of buildings so are the ordinances to the church of Christ; by them oftentimes saints are supported and refreshed; and whilst they are waiting on Christ in them, they renew their strength, they mount up with wings as eagles, they run and are not weary, they walk and faint not, as it is promised to them in Isa. xl. 31.

Now these rafters are said to be of fir. The word is only used in this place, and is so rendered by Arias Montanus, Pagnine, and others, and is so understood by many of the Jewish writers;[a] the word being by the change of a single letter to wit, שׁ into ת, which is used in the Chaldee and Syriac languages, the same with that which

---

[p] Lib. 13. c. 5, 13. and l. 16. c. 40. [q] Et cedro digna locutus, Pers. satyr. 1. v. 42.
[r] Plin. l. 13. c. 5. Odoratam stabulis accendere cedrum, Virgil. Georgic. l. 3. v. 414. [s] Plin. l. 16. c. 21. [t] R. Aben Ezra in loc. R. Jonah in R. David Kimchi, lib. shorash. rad. רהט Vid. David de Pomis Lex. Heb. rad. רהט and so the Tigurine version renders it. [u] ורהטינו canales nostri, Tigurine version, so some in Vatablus; impluvium nostrum, Hiller. de Keri and Kethib. p. 48, [w] Vid. Elias Levit. Methurgeman, rad. רחט.
[x] In lib shorash rad. רהט. [y] As quoted by R. Sol. Jarchi in loc. [z] In R. David Kimchi, lib. shorash. rad. רהט. [a] Vid. R. Aben Ezram in loc. R. David Kimchium in lib. shorash. rad. ברת and Elias Levit. Methurgeman.

is commonly used for the fir; and this, Pliny says,[b] is the best and strongest wood for roofing and raftering: now these rafters, the ordinances of the Gospel, may be said to be of this, because, 1. The fir-tree is, *hilaris aspectu*,[c] of a pleasant, cheerful, and delightful look; the ordinances of the Gospel are exceeding delightful to believers, when they have the presence of Christ with them, and the communications of his love unto them; then are those tabernacles amiable and lovely; wisdom's ways are then ways of pleasantness; their souls are filled with joy and pleasure; nothing so desirable to them as these, neither does any thing give them such satisfaction and contentment; and therefore with the disciples they think it is good for them to be here, and would always abide under such a roof as this, whose rafters are of fir. 2. It is a very shady tree, *folio pinato dansa, ut umbres non transmittat*,[d] it is so thick with leaves, that it will not let through showers of rain; the ordinances of Christ are a delightful shade, under which saints oftentimes sit with pleasure, have much spiritual consolation and refreshment; in which being protected from the enemies of their souls, they serve the Lord with liberty and enlargement of heart. 3. It is always green,[e] and never casts its leaf, and therefore is called the "green fir-tree," in Hos. xiv. 8. Ordinances are those green pastures, into which the great Shepherd leads his sheep, and in which he causes them to lie down; which being blessed and owned by the Spirit of grace unto believers, make them fat and flourishing, fruitful in every good work, even in old age; so that their leaf does not wither in the winter season.

Others think that the cypress-tree is here intended, and so read the words, and our rafters or galleries of cypress; so the Septuagint, Vulgate Latin, and Tigurine versions, David de Pomis, and others. Now these rafters may be said to be of this wood, because the cypress-wood[f] is very lasting and durable; it admits of no worms, it will not rot, nor is it sensible of old age; which may be expressive of the durableness and continuance of Gospel-ordinances, until the second coming of Christ; for as long as Christ has an house on earth, these cypress-rafters will last; it will never need new roofing; as long as there is a church, there will be those ordinances, which are now in force, and will continue so to the end of time, without any change or alteration in them. This wood is also of a very pleasant smell;[g] which may signify the delight and pleasure which believers take in ordinances, and how grateful they are to them.

Others think that the brutine-tree is meant; so Ainsworth, Brightman, Junius, Cocceis, and Michaelis; and it may be that which Pliny[h] calls *bruta*, which some take to be the tree of Paradise; and its name is near in sound to the Hebrew word *brotim* here used, the singular of which is *brot*; which, Pliny says, is much like the cypress, and of a smell like cedar; and being applied to the ordinances of the Gospel, may signify, as before, the durableness and delightfulness of them; and now who but would desire to dwell in such a house, and under such a roof as this? What encouragement is here, and what an inducement should this be, to souls to come into the house of the Lord, and wait upon him there, the beams of whose house are cedar, and the rafters of fir?

CHAPTER II.

Here begins a new colloquy between Christ and his church; in which they alternately set forth the excellencies of each other, and express their mutual affection for, and the delight and pleasure they take in each other's company. Christ seems to begin, in an account of himself and his own excellencies, and of the church in her present state, ver. 1, 2. Then in her turn praises him, and commends him above all others; relates some clear proofs she had of his love to her, and communion with him in his house and ordinances, to such a degree as to overcome her, ver. 3—6; and then either he or she gives a charge to the daughters of Jerusalem, not to disturb either the one or the other in their sweet repose, ver. 7. Next the church relates how she heard the voice of Christ, and had a sight of him on the hills and mountains at some distance; then more nearly behind her wall, and through the lattices; ver. 8, 9; and expresses the very words in which he spake to her, and gave her a call to come away with him; making use of arguments from the season of the year, the signs of which are beautifully described, ver. 10—13; and requests that she would come out of her solitude, that he might enjoy her company, whose countenance and voice were so delightful to him; and gives a charge to her and her friends, to seize on such as were hurtful and prejudicial to their mutual property, ver. 14, 15; and she closes the chapter with expressing her faith of interest in Christ; and with a petition for his speedy approach to her, and continued presence with her, ver. 16, 17.

Verse 1. *I am the rose of Sharon, and the lily of the vallies.*

HERE begins a new colloquy between Christ and his church, in which they alternately set forth the praises and excellencies of each other, discover the strength of their mutual affection, and express the delight and pleasure they take in each other's company: but who begins this colloquy is not so easily determined. What is here said, may be applied either to Christ or to the church; and therefore I shall consider the words in both senses.

First. The words may be considered, as the words of the church expressing the excellency of her grace, loveliness, and beauty, which she had received from Christ; and at the same time in-

---

[b] Lib. 16. c. 42.   [c] Plin. l. 16. c. 10.   [d] Ibid.
[e] Plin. l. 16. c. 21.   [f] Ibid. c. 40, 42. Hence monuments to perpetuate the memory of things were made of it, Plato de leg. l. 5. p. 848.   [g] Plin. l. 16. c. 33. Ευωδει κυπαρισσω, Theocrit. spigram. 4. v. 7.   [h] Lib. 12. c. 17.

tinating her being exposed in the open field and low vallies to many dangers and enemies; and therefore tacitly desires his protection over her, which he seems to promise in ver. 2. That these are the words of the church, seems to be the general opinion of the Jewish doctors,[a] and is also embraced by some Christian interpreters.[b] And

1st, The church may be compared to " the rose," 1. For beauty ; it is called the beautiful flower ;[c] its colour is beautiful and delightful : the figure is exceeding just; nothing is more common in poems of this kind, than to set forth the beauty of women by the rose ; such as Hero,[d] Aspasia,[e] and others; some have had the name of Rhoda from hence ; and Helena for her beauty was called Ροδοχρως.[f] The church may be fitly compared to it; no " rose of Sharon" can be more beautiful in colour, and delightful to the eye, than the church is in the eyes of Christ; as she is clothed with his pure and spotless righteousness, adorned with the graces of his Spirit, and standing at his right-hand in cloth of gold, bespangled with the sparkling gems of divine grace; her beauty is desirable to him, she being in his eye " the fairest among women."

2. For its sweet odour ;[g] the church and all believers are as the fragrant and sweet-smelling rose; their persons are so as considered in Christ, and all their graces, especially when in exercise ; and all their duties and services, when performed in faith, and perfumed with Christ's mediation ; see chap. iv. 10, Phil. iv. 18, Rev. v. 8, and viii. 3, 4. 3. For its delight in sunny places ;[h] it thrives and flourishes the best there, and has the most fragrant smell : Christ is " the Sun of righteousness," under whose warming, comforting, and refreshing beams, believers delight to be, and under which their souls grow, thrive, blossom exceedingly, and bring forth much fruit. 4. For its blossoming and flourishing, " the desert shall rejoice and blossom as the rose;" the church may be said to do so, when there is a large increase of members, and these much in the exercise of grace, and " fruitful in every good work :" then may the church be said to be as the blossoming rose.

2ndly. She may be compared to the " lily of the vallies :" some women have their name from the lily, as Susanna ; and so Sysigambis is the name of the mother of Darius,[i] which signifies the *white lily* ;[k] to which for beauty women are sometimes compared : and with propriety enough may the church be called a lily.[l] She is compared to the " lily among thorns " in the next verse, and saints are frequently compared to lilies in this Song. And, 1. She may be likened to a lily for the glory, beauty, and sweet odour of it. Christ says, Mat. vi. 29, of the lilies of the field, that " Solomon in all his glory was not arrayed like one of these ;" and for the same reasons that she is compared to the beautiful and sweet-smelling rose, is she likewise to the lily ; which Pliny[m] says, *rosæ nobilitate proximum est*, " is next in nobleness and excellency to the rose." 2. For its whiteness ; there are various sorts of lilies, and they are of different colours ; some are of red and purple colours, others are white ; and it seems to be the white lily which is intended here, for this seems best to express her beauty ; for the red rose and the white lily make her look somewhat like her beloved, " white and ruddy," a perfect beauty ; and of the white lily, Pliny[n] says, *candor ejus eximius*, that its whiteness is singularly excellent ; the church, and all believers in Christ, are very aptly resembled by the white lily, who are clothed with " fine linen, clean and white, which is the righteousness of the saints " wrought out by Christ, imputed by God the Father, and laid hold on by faith ; this is so exceeding white, that being arrayed with it, they are all fair, and there is no spot in them." 3. For its fruitfulness ; Pliny[o] says, *nihil est fœcundius, una radice quinquagenos sæpe emittente bulbos*: " nothing is more fruitful, for oftentimes one root sends forth fifty bulbs :" and as fruitful are believers when the Sun of righteousness shines upon them, and Christ is as the dew unto them ; for then " they grow as the lily, and cast forth their roots as Lebanon ; their branches spread, and their beauty is as the olive tree." The church brings forth many souls to Christ ; and these bring forth much fruit, to the glory both of him and his Father. 4. For its height, for which it is commended : the lily grows very high ; Pliny[p] says, *nec ulli florum excelsitas major, interdiu cubitorum trium ;* " no flower exceeds it in height ; for in the day-time," (that is, when it erects itself,) " it is three cubits high." Believers are trees of righteousness, and plants of Christ's Father's planting, which do not run along the ground, and cleave to earthly things,

---

[a] Targum, R. Aben Ezra, and Yalkut in loc. so it is interpreted of malcuth, or the bride, by the Cabalistic Doctors, in Lexic. Cab. p. 333. and in Zohar. in Lev. fol. 46. 2. [b] Tres Patres, Lyra, Ainsworth, Brightman, Vatablus, Cocceius, Michaelis.
[c] Το ροδον καλον εστι, Theocrit. Idyll. 24. Ροδης τε καλον ανθος, Antilochus apud Athen. De pnosophist. 1. 2. c. 12. Vid. l. 15. c. 3. p. 670. [d] Museus de Hero. v. 59. Vid. Barth. Animadv. ad Claudian. de nupt. Honor. v. 247. [e] Ælian. Var. Hist. l. 12. c. 1. [f] Theocrit. Idyll. 18. [g] The rose by the Arcadians was called ευοςφαλον, that is, sweet-smelling, Timach, ides apud Athenæi Deipnosophist,

l. 15. c. 8. p. 682. [h] Rosa locis apricis gaudet, estque odoratior, Junius in loc. [i] Curtius, Hist. l. 3. c. 3. Hiller. Onomastic. p. 632. [k] Lilia non domina suit magis alba mea, Propertius, l. 2. so Venus is compared to a lily by Anecreon.
[l] So the lily is interpreted of Malcuth, the bride, the church, by the Cabalists, Lexic. Cab. p. 708, 709.
[m] Lib. xxi. c. 5 [n] Lib. xxi. c. 5. Toto candidior puella cycno, argento nive, lilio, ligustro, Martial. l. i. Lilia tu vincis. l. 8. c 28. [o] Lib. 21. c. 5. [p] Ibid. Lilia summa metit, Ovid. Fasti, l. 2. prope finem.

but lift up their heads heaven-wards, and grow up on high in their desires and affections, having their hearts above, where their treasure is: believers are like the flowers of the lily, open towards heaven, but shut towards the earth. 5. For the weakness of its body, and largeness of its head: Pliny*q* says of the lily, *languido semper collo et non sufficiente capitis oneri*; that it has " a weak neck, or body, which is not sufficient to bear the weight of the head." Christ is the Head of the body, the church, and far greater than that; he is not supported by it, but he supports it: the church's strength lies in her head, as Samson's did in his locks; she is weak in herself, but strong in Christ her Head, and therefore says, " surely in the Lord have I righteousness and strength." 6. The church may be compared, not only to a lily, but to " a lily of the vallies:" there is a lily which is called *lilium convallium*, " the lily of the vallies:" but this seems not so much to intend the distinguishing name of some particular lily, as it does the place where it grows. And, 1. Vallies are low places; and, when the church is called " the lily of the vallies," it may be expressive of the low estate and condition which he is sometimes in: believers are Christ's myrtle-trees, and these are sometimes in the bottom, in a low condition; but he grants his presence with them, and the discoveries of his love to them; they are his doves, and they are often " like doves of the vallies, mourning every one for their iniquity, being humbled and pressed down in their souls under a sense of sin and unworthiness; they are not only humble in themselves, and low in their own eyes, but are often in the deeps of affliction, sorrow, and distress, and out of these depths cry unto the Lord; see Psal. cxxx. 1. 2. Lilies that grow in the vallies are exposed to danger; they are liable to be plucked up by every one that passes by, to be trodden upon, and eaten by the beasts that feed there, and also to be washed away, and destroyed by hasty showers of rain, that run from the hills and mountains down into the vallies with force and violence; so the church of Christ here on earth, in her low estate, is exposed to the rage of her adversaries, to be trodden under the feet, and torn in pieces by the teeth of those bulls of Bashan, that beset her around, and to be carried away by the flood of persecution, which " Satan the old serpent casts out of his mouth after her." Now it is a glorious instance of God's mighty grace and power in protecting and defending his church, that this lily grows and abides in the vallies, notwithstanding all this danger. 3. Lilies of the vallies have more moisture, verdure, and greenness in them, than those upon the hills and mountains; because the sun has not that power over them, as R. Sol. Jarchi observes, to scorch and dry them up, and therefore are much more beautiful and excellent; so believers, being planted by " rivers of water," are green, flourishing, and fruitful; whilst others look like " the heath in the desert," dried and parched up. Christ is to the saints as " rivers of water in a dry place, and as the shadow of a great rock in a weary land:" by the one he refreshes them, and makes them fruitful; and by being the other he shades from that which would scorch them, and make them barren and unfruitful: and thus is the church the " lily of the vallies," as well as " the rose of Sharon." And the Targum here renders it, " the rose in the plain of the garden of Eden:" and some interpreters think the rose is meant; and we sometimes read of roses in vallies,*r* and certain it is there were roses in the vale of Sharon. But,

Secondly, the more commonly received opinion is, that these words are the words of Christ, owning all the glory and praises the church had given him in the former chapter, and setting forth more largely the beauties and excellencies of his person the more to effect, enamour, and ravish her soul, and make her seek and long for him: and indeed it seems best to understand them of Christ, for self-commendation does not so well agree with the church as with him. What Solomon says, Prov. xxvii. 2, is worth regarding, " let another praise thee, and not thine own mouth: a stranger, and not thine own lips;" though it is lawful for the saints to speak of their glory, beauty, and excellency, as considered in Christ, in order to magnify the riches of his grace, for the instruction and encouragement of others, and in vindication of themselves against the calumnies of the world, and to obviate their mistakes concerning them, as in chap. i. 5, she says, " I am black but comely;" but her chief province and design in this Song appears to be, to set forth his praises, and not her own; and indeed the majesty and agreeableness of the style with Christ's language in the New Testament, such as, " I am the door, I am the good shepherd, I am the vine, I am the way, the truth, and the life," &c., as well as the connection of the words with the following verse, as one well observes,*s* manifestly bespeak them to be the words of Christ, who may very well be called,

1st, " The rose of Sharon." Christ fitly compares himself to a rose, which, as Bishop Patrick observes, is still one of the goodliest things to which a great prince can be likened in those Eastern countries; and gives an instance of it in the great Mogul complimenting one of our kings, as being like a rose in a garden; in the Misnah*t* mention is made of the king's lily, or the king's rose, being the king of flowers, and fit for a king, and an emblem of one; so the men of the great congregation of Ezra are compared to roses in the Targum of Cant. vii. 2; and the ances-

---

q Ut supra.   *r* Roscis convallibus Ætnæ, Claudian. de rapt. Proserp. l. 3. v. 85.   *s* Durham in loc.   *t* Misn. Kilaim, c. 5. s. 8. and Maimon. in ib.

tors of Melissus the Theban, after many calamities, are compared to the flourishing rose, for the height of honour and power they arrived unto." Nor is this simile unfitly used by the bridegroom of himself, since it is sometimes given to men by their lovers;"ʷ and is very properly used in a Song of love, as this is, seeing the rose, as Philostratus calls it, is ερωτος φυτον, *the plant of love*; and Anacreon calls it το ροδον των ερωτων, *the rose of loves*; it was sacred to love; the graces are represented, one of them as having a rose, another a myrtle-branch;ˣ and a crown of roses, was consecrated to the muses;ʸ all this because of the beauty and loveliness of the plant. And to it Christ may be compared, 1. Because of its red colour; which may be expressive of the truth of his humanity, and signify that he is really and truly man, having taken part of the same flesh and blood, that his people are partakers of; as also of his bloody sufferings in the same nature, on the account of which he is said to be "red in his apparel:" likewise both these together, the red rose and the white lily, make up that character which is given him, chap. v. 10: that he is "white and ruddy," a complete beauty, like the charming lily and blushing rose, "fairer than the children of men." 2. He may be compared to the rose for its sweet smell, as for the same reason he is in the former chapter to spikenard, myrrh, and camphire: his person, sacrifice, grace, and righteousness, have a delightful odour in them; no rose smells so sweet, as Christ does to believers: this Sharon-rose refreshes them, quickens their spiritual senses, and ravishes and delights their souls. 3. The rose is of a cooling nature,ᶻ and therefore useful in burning fevers, inflammations, &c., Christ, by the effusion of his blood, by the oblation of himself, and by his dying in the room and stead of sinners, has appeased and removed his Father's fierce and burning wrath from them; and it is only an application of this Sharon rose, the person, blood, and righteousness of Christ, which can cool and comfort the conscience of a sinner set on fire, and terrified by the law of God; the discoveries of his love and grace can only remove those dreadful terrors, and fire of divine wrath, which is kindled by a "fiery law," and cure those inflammations raised thereby. 4. He is called "the Rose of Sharon," for the excellency of it; the roses which grew there perhaps were the best of any. Sharon is the name of a fruitful plain or country, where herds and flocks were kept, as appears from 1 Chron. xxvii. 29, Isa. xxxv. 2, and lxv. 10; this plain or country lay between Cæsarea and Joppa, beginning at Lydda; hence they are joined together, Acts ix. 35, and reaching to the Mediterranean sea: hence the Jews in their writings say,ᵃ from Lydda to the sea in the vale; and this was so very fruitful, that the Targumist on this place renders it, "by the garden of Eden:" and Sharon is described in the Jewish map,ᵇ as fat and fertile, having in it very desirable fields, fruitful vines, and abounding with flowers and roses. There are various sorts of roses in different places, some better than others; those of the first class with the Greeks,ᶜ were those of Olenum, and next those of Megara Nisea, and then those of Phaselis, and then of others; with the Romans, the best were those of Præneste and Campania, and then others :ᵈ but of the roses in Judea, the rose of Sharon seems to have been the best, and therefore to that the comparison is made; there was a garden of roses in Jerusalem,ᵉ but not to them, but to those in Sharon, is the allusion. The word for a rose is only used in this place and in Isa. xxxv. 1, and is so called, either from the collection and compression of leaves in it, or from the shadow of it; for the word seems to be compounded of one, that signifies to *hide* and *cover*, and another that signifies *a shadow*; so Gussetius,ᶠ and so may be rendered, "the covering shadow:" but why a rose should be so called is not easy to say; unless it can be thought to have the figure of an umbrella, or that the rose of Sharon was so large as to be remarkable for its shadow, like that Montfauconᵍ saw in a garden at Ravenna, under the shadow of the branches of which more than forty men could stand. Christ is sometimes compared to trees for their shadow, which is pleasant and reviving, as in ver. 3, Hosea xiv. 7; but he here seems to be compared to the rose of Sharon on another account, even the excellency and fragrancy of it; for, Pliny says,ʰ that the rose does not delight in fat soils, rich clays, or well-watered grounds, but thrives the best in poor lean ground; and that those are of the sweetest smell which grow in dry places, for *ruderatum agrum amat*, "it loves rubbish earth." Now such dry and rubbish earth was that which was about the city of Sharon; for we read of such a place as inhabited, Acts ix. 35, as the Talmudic doctors assert; who also tell us,ⁱ that those who built a brick house in Sharon, had no benefit of the law, mentioned in Deut. xx. 5, because the earth thereabout was not fit to make bricks of, nor would houses made of them continue long. Hence they also say,ᵏ that the high priest, on the day of atonement, prayed particularly for the Sharonites, that

---

ᵛ Pindar Isthm. ode 4.   ʷ Mea rosa, Plauti Asinari, act. 3. sc. 3. v. 74. Bacchides, sc. 1. v. 50. Tu rosa, Circulio, act. 1. sc. 2. v. 6.
ˣ Pausan. Eliac. 2. sive l. 6. p. 391.
ʸ Sappho apud Plutarch. sympos. l. 3. p. 641. Theocrit. epigr. 1. v. 1, 2.   ᶻ Fernel. method. med. l. 5. c. 3. and l. 6. c. 2.   ᵃ T. Hieros. Shevi.ith, fol. 38. 4.   ᵇ Apud De Dieu in Act. ix. 35.

ᶜ Nicander apud Athen. Deipnosoph. l. 15. c. 9. p. 683.   ᵈ Plin. nat. hist. l. 21. c. 4.   ᵉ Misn. Masserot, c. 2. s. 5.   ᶠ Comment. Ebr. p. 239.
ᵍ Diar. Ital. c. 7. p. 100.   ʰ Lib. 21. c. 4.
ⁱ In Misna Sotah, c. 8. §. 3. and R. Sol. Jarchi, Maimon, and Bartenora in idem.   ᵏ T. Sol. Soth, fol. 23. 1.

their houses might not become their graves. Now these being the best and sweetest roses which grew in this soil, and Christ being compared to one of them, denotes the excellency and preferableness of Christ to all others.

Some[l] think that some other plant or flower is here intended; as the Targum renders it, "the narcissus:" of which some are white, having white leaves surrounding a yellow flower,[m] and some of a purple colour;[n] and which Pliny[o] calls purple lilies: he says,[p] there are two sorts of them, one that has a purple flower, and the other is of the grass kind; some, he says,[q] have a white flower and a purple cup. The Heathens used to call the narcissus the ancient crown of their superior deities;[r] and it was reckoned a beautiful flower, and of a sweet smell;[s] and for beauty Christ may be compared unto it: its white colour may denote the purity of Christ; and the purple, his royalty, or rather his purple blood and sufferings of death. The Septuagint translates the words thus, "I am the flower of the field;" as do also the Vulgate Latin and Pagnine. Now Christ may be called so, 1. Κατ' ἐξοχην by way of eminency, as being the chiefest and most excellent flower in the field; there is no such flower in the heavenly paradise as he is; among all the holy angels and glorified saints, there are none to be compared with him; and in his garden here below, no such flower grows as this: he is "the flower," the choicest, the best, and the most excellent in the whole field or garden. 2. The flower of the field is liable to be plucked up or trodden under feet by beasts; Christ was exposed to the rage and fury of his enemies, those "strong bulls of Bashan" of which he complains, Psal. xxii. 13, 14. The sweet flower was laid hold on by "wicked hands," and cropped; and still his precious person, blood, and righteousness, are slighted, contemned, and "trodden under foot" by Christless and unconverted sinners. 3. This may be expressive of the meanness of Christ in the esteem of the world; a field-flower is little regarded; Christ is as "a root out of a dry ground," and therefore they say, "he hath no form nor comeliness, and when we shall see him, there is no beauty that we should desire him: hence he is despised and rejected of men," they not knowing the real worth and value of this precious flower; see Isa. liii. 2, 3. 4. The flower of the field is not of man's planting, nor is it raised by his care and industry: Christ was conceived in the womb of a virgin, and born of her without the help of man: as the flower of the field, he had no father but his Father in heaven, and no mother but the virgin on earth; and so was Melchisedeck's antitype, "without father as man, and without mother as God." 5. The flower of the field is open to all; whoever will may come to Christ for life and salvation; there is liberty of access to all sorts of sinners, to come to him and partake of his sweetness and benefits; he is not a flower in an inclosed garden, that cannot be come at, but stands in the open field; every sinner that labours under a sense of sin, and is heavy laden with the weight and burden of it, may come to him, and not fear a rejection from him; he is not "a fountain sealed, but opened to the house of David, and inhabitants of Jerusalem, for sin and for uncleanness."

2ndly. Christ may be very well compared to "the lily of the vallies," 1. For its whiteness; the lily, as has been already observed, is exceeding white, which may intend the purity and holiness of Christ, who both in nature and life is "holy, harmless, undefiled, and separate from sinners; he is the Lamb without blemish and without spot," without the blemish of original or spot of actual sin; for he never knew it in his nature, nor did he ever commit it in his life, either in thought, word, or deed: or else the whiteness of the lily may signify his eternity, for so his head and his hairs are described by John, Rev. i. 14, to be "white like wool, as white as snow;" which represents him as the Ancient of Days, and as existing from everlasting to everlasting. 2. For its tallness; the lily grows up very high, as has been taken notice of. Christ, as Mediator, is "the rock that is higher than we are;" from whence the waters of divine grace flow, to the refreshment of our souls when overwhelmed; "he is higher than the kings of the earth; nay, he is higher than the heavens," and all the angels there; for he is "set far above all principality, and power, and might, and dominion, and every name that is named, not only in this world, but also in that that is to come," Eph. i. 21. 2. For its fruitfulness; the lily is very fruitful, as has been before observed. Christ is "filled with all the fruits of righteousness," and is possessed of all the blessings of grace; he is like a tree richly laden with fruit, and therefore is compared to an apple tree, in ver. 3; all the church's fruit and fruitfulness come from him; he is the green fir-tree, from whom all her fruit is found." 4. He may be compared to the lily for its excellency and glory; it being the next flower to the rose, and which is preferred by Christ to the glory of Solomon. Christ is the brightness of his Father's glory; is now, in our nature, "crowned with glory and honour;" and will shortly appear in his own glory and in the glory of his Father, and of the holy angels. 5. He may be said to be the lily of the vallies, because of his wonderful humility and condescension, in assuming our nature, suffering in our stead, and in humbling himself unto the death of the cross for us; his whole life was one continued series of humility, as was his death an

---

[l] *Vide* R. Aben Ezram in loc.
[m] Croceum florem—foliis medium cingentibus albis Ovid. Metamorph. l. 3. fab. 6.   [n] Pro purpureo narcisso, Virgil. Bucolic. ecl. 5. v. 28. Aut suave rubens narcissus, ibid. Cyris.   [o] Nat. hist. l. 21. c. 5.   [p] Ibid. c. 19.   [q] Ibid. c. 5.   [r] Sophocles apud Plutarch. sympos. l. 3. p. 641.   [s] Καλα ναρκισσος, Theocrit. Idyll. 1. ναρκισσον ευπνοον, Idyll. 19.

undeniable instance of it: Christ here on earth did not appear as the lofty cedar, but as the lowly lily, and that not of the mountains, but of the vallies; it is with humble souls he delights to dwell; for though he is the high and lofty One, in his divine nature, yet he condescends to dwell with such who are of an humble and contrite spirit.

Verse 2. *As the lily among thorns, so is my love among the daughters.*

THOUGH it may not be so evident whose are the former words, whether Christ's or the church's, yet these manifestly appear to be his; and if we take the preceding verse as the words of the church, then we may consider this as the words of Christ, either owning and confirming what she had said of herself in it; as that she was indeed the most beautiful of all the roses and lilies which grew in fields and vallies, and that all others were but like thorns and briars when compared to her; and also, at the same time that he owns and commends her beauty, puts her in mind of her present state and condition in this life, as being attended with afflictions, sorrows, and sufferings: or else the words may be regarded as the answer[t] of Christ to her complaint in the former verse, where she says, that she was indeed the blushing rose and charming lily, but then she was the rose and lily in the open fields and vallies, liable to be plucked up by every one that passed by, and to be devoured or trodden under feet by the beasts of the field; to this Christ replies here, by owning it all to be true, and promising that he will keep and preserve her safe in the midst of her enemies, "as the lily among thorns;" nay, that her very enemies should be her protection, these thorns should be as an hedge about her. But if we take the former verse to be the words of Christ, which seems most agreeable, then we are to consider these as his also; who, having in the former verse set forth his own beauties and excellencies, which was proper to be done in the first place, does in this set forth his church's, in which may be observed,

I. What he compares her to; "a lily among thorns."

II. The title which he gives her, "my love;" which discovers his regard unto her, and affection for her.

III. Her excellency and preferableness to all others in his esteem.

1. The church is here compared by Christ to "a lily among thorns." The Targum renders it, *the rose;* and so it is in Zohar;[u] and that this is intended, some strenuously contend, for which, and not the lily, they say, grows among thorns: Ainsworth would have what we call the *woodbind* or *honey-suckle* here meant, which grows in hedges; and indeed this is sometimes called *lilium inter spinas,* "the lily among thorns,"[w] to which the church may be compared, because of its sweet smell; the flower of it gives an exceeding sweet smell; and makes those fields where it grows in abundance very delightful: believers in their persons, grace, and conversation, are like the "smell of a field which the Lord hath blessed;" being clothed with the sweet-smelling garments of Christ's righteousness, and anointed with the savoury ointments of the Spirit's grace. Also the woodbind or honeysuckle cannot bear up itself, but has its dependence on others; it does not grow up erect, but for its support wraps itself about the body, branches, and twigs of other trees, *convolvens se adminiculis quibuscunque,* as Pliny[x] observes; therefore we call it *woodbind,* from its *binding* about other trees; and for the same reason it is in Greek called *periclymenon,* which is also used by Latin writers: believers are weak, and cannot support themselves, and therefore by faith lean on Christ, who is their beloved; and are upheld by him with the right-hand of his righteousness; they cleave close unto him, and depend upon him for all grace here, and for glory hereafter. But the word will very well bear to be translated *a lily,* being the same that is so in the former verse; where it has been shown in what sense the church may be compared to one; and therefore I shall only observe, 1. That Christ and the church bear the same names. Is he a lily? so is she; the church being married to Christ, and they two becoming one flesh, have one and the same name, hence the church is called *Christ,* 1 Cor. xix. 12; so the same name *Jehovah our righteousness,* which Christ is called by, Jer. xxiii. 6, is given to her in chap. xxxiii. 16. Again, Christ is called *Israel,* Isa. xlix. 3, which is the name of his church and people: for being espoused together, and having partaken of each others natures, they also bear each others names. 2. That there is a very great likeness and near resemblance between Christ and his church; for when he says, she is "as the lily," he means, she is as himself, who is, "the lily of the vallies," ver. 1; and therefore, as one well observes,[y] he does not say she is the lily, but as or like the lily; for as he is, so are we, that is, believers, in this world. Christ and the church are both lilies in God's eye, and are loved by him with the same love: believers bear the image of Christ, wear his righteousness, have the same spirit, though in measure, and are exposed to the same hatred, malice, and persecution of the world, being wounded with those thorns even as he was: and they shall be much more like him in another world; for they shall then be like him, and see him as he is: they shall then have everlasting and transforming views of him, which will change

---

[t] Vide R. Aben Ezram and Brightman in loc.
[u] In Gen. fol. 82 2, 3. and in Exod. fol. 74. 3. but in Lev. fol. 16. 2. it is explained of the pome citron-tree. [w] Vide Mercer. in v. 1. [x] Lib. 27. c. 12.
[y] Durham in loc.

them into the same image, from glory to glory; for as they will then have more communion with him, so they will then have a greater conformity to him, who is "the first-born among brethren." 3. That all the church's beauty and loveliness come from Christ: it is because he is the lily, that she looks like one; her beauty is not natural to her, but is derived from him, who is her Head and Husband; she is indeed a perfect beauty, but then it arises from that comeliness which he has put upon her.

Moreover she is not only said to be as the lily, but "as the lily among thorns." By thorns may be meant, 1. Wicked and ungodly men, sons of Belial which are "as thorns thrust away, because they cannot be taken with hands," 2 Sam. xxiii. 6; these, like thorns and briars, are the curse of the earth, are worthless and unfruitful in themselves, and hurtful and grieving to the saints: David, Isaiah, and others have complained of them; righteous Lot was pricked with these thorns; his soul was vexed, and grieved from day to day with their unlawful deeds: also like thorns, their end is to be burned, and that by the fierceness and fury of God's wrath, who says, Isa. xxvii. 4: "Who would set the briars and thorns against me in battle? I would go through them, I would burn them together;" which he will do at the last day, when he will bind up those thorns in bundles, and cast them into "the lake which burneth with fire and brimstone;" where "the people shall be as the burnings of lime; as thorns cut up, shall they be burnt in the fire;" the terror of which sometimes surprises the sinners in Zion, who therefore say, "who among us shall dwell with the devouring fire? who among us shall dwell with everlasting burnings?" Isa. xxxiii. 12—14. 2. By thorns may be meant the reproaches, revilings, and persecutions of wicked men, whereby they afflict and disturb the saints; the Targum explains these thorns, of the wicked edicts and decrees of princes, by which the congregation of Israel was oppressed in captivity: the prophet Ezekiel is encouraged by the Lord faithfully to deliver his message to the people of Israel, though briars and thorns were with him, and though he had his dwelling among scorpions, that is, though he was reproached, reviled, and persecuted by them for it. Christ's lily in all ages has more or less been attended with, and has grown up, among such thorns as these; for every one that will live godly in Christ Jesus, shall suffer persecution of one kind or another; and yet they abide like "the lily among thorns," in their faith, purity, and holiness; so that neither the frowns nor flatteries of the world can prevail upon them to desert the Redeemer's interest, forsake the Gospel, nor turn aside from the true worship of God; to which agrees R. Sol. Jarchi's gloss on the text, which is this: "As the lily among thorns, which prick it, yet stands continually in its beauty and redness; so is my love among the daughters, who entice her to follow after them, and go a whoring after other gods, but yet continues in her religion." 8. By thorns may be meant heretics and heretical doctrines, which pierce, prick, and grieve the children of God: now these false teachers, these wolves in sheep's clothing, may be known by their fruits, which are none at all, that are good for any thing; for, "do men gather grapes off thorns, or figs off thistles!" there is no fruit of faith, sound doctrine, or a gospel-conversation to be found upon them; but are like unfruitful thorns, whom God suffers to grow up in his churches, that those which are filled with the fruits of righteousness might be made manifest; and in all ages, more or less, Christ's lily, the church, has grown up among, and been pricked by, and pestered with such thorns as these. 4. The corruptions of our nature may be called so: these Canaanites remaining in the land, dwelling in our hearts, are pricks in our eyes, and thorns in our sides; these grieve and disturb us, and they make us groan with the anguish our souls are filled with by them. Perhaps the breaking forth of some corruption is intended by the thorn in the flesh, and messenger of Satan, that the apostle speaks of, 2 Cor. xii. 7; though the temptations of Satan may also be called by these names, which often give the saints a great deal of uneasiness, and throw them into much heaviness; and it may be that both the corruption of nature, and the temptations of Satan, which the apostle might labour under, are intended; and the thorn in the flesh may be expressive of the breaking out of some corruption; and the messenger of Satan may intend his temptations, by which it was stirred up and encouraged: though I rather think that both phrases are only expressive of the corruption of nature, which was wont to be called by the Jews, *the messenger of hell;* a phrase much like this used by the apostle. So in Midrash Hanneelam,[*] we read that R. Hona, in his sermons, used to advise persons thus, "O ye children of men, take care of the messenger of hell: but who is this? The evil imagination, (by which the Jews always intend the vitiosity of nature) is the messenger of hell. Now this being a phrase that was well known, the apostle adds it by way of opposition to the thorn in the flesh, as explanative of it. Moreover, worldly cares are compared to thorns which choke the word; they are pernicious to saints, and make them barren and unfruitful, as well as grieve and disturb them, Matt. xiii. 22; but though Christ's lilies here on earth grow up among, and are annoyed by those thorns of sin and corruption; yet when they are transplanted into Christ's garden above, "there shall be no more a pricking briar, nor a grieving thorn," to give them the least disturbance.

II. Whilst Christ is comparing his church to

---

* In Zohar in Gen. fol. 67. 4.

a "lily among thorns," he gives her a loving and affectionate title, *my love*, which has been already explained in chap. i. 9; and his mentioning it here shows, that even in her present state and condition she was a beauty in his eye; and that her being among thorns, was so far from detracting from it, that it rather served as a foil to set it off the more; as also, that she was still the object of his love, though in the midst of wicked and ungodly men, men of unclean lips and lives, haters of peace, religion, and godliness; though she was reviled, reproached, and persecuted by them, yet she was loved, valued, and esteemed by him; nay, though she was attended with many infirmities, sins, and corruptions, that were grieving to her, and dishonouring to him, yet neither these, nor any thing else, should ever separate her from his love: she was Christ's love and lily still, though among thorns. The lily is often made use of in this love-song, to set forth the beauty of the church and of the saints in the eye of Christ: and his great love to them, and delight in them, and very justly.^a

III. He sets forth her excellency and preferableness to all the daughters. By whom we are to understand the nations and men of the world; for it is usual in the Hebrew tongue to call the inhabitants of countries the daughters thereof; thus we read of the daughters of Tyre, Edom, Babylon, &c., none of which are to be compared with the church; these are like thorns to Christ's lily: or else carnal, hypocritical, and formal professors may be intended, whom she calls in chap. i. 6, *mother's children*; who made an external profession of religion, but wanted that real and internal beauty which she was possessed of, and differed only in name from the rest of the sons and daughters of fallen Adam; but she, being distinguished by divine grace from them all, was preferable to them, 1. In beauty; these looked like thorns, she like a lily; they were black and uncomely, she the perfection of beauty, and the fairest among women. 2. In harmlessness; though there are thorns about, yet none upon the lily; ungodly persons are not only uncomely in themselves, but like thorns, pricking and hurtful to others; but as for the saints, they are "blameless and harmless, in the midst of a crooked and perverse generation," like lilies among thorns. 3. In fruitfulness: no fruit grows on thorns, but on Christ's lilies grow all sorts of precious fruit; they are laden with them. 4. In their last end Christ's lilies will be gathered by himself and his angels, and be put in his garden above; but the wicked, which are Satan's tares and thorns, shall be bundled together, and cast into everlasting burnings; the one being highly valued and prized by Christ, the other hated and rejected by him; for as much as the lily exceeds the thorns which grow about it, so much does the church of Christ excel the men of the world among whom it is here on earth; and as there is a difference now between them, though growing up together, so there will be one, and that far greater and more visible, when separated; the one, will be everlastingly glorified, the other everlastingly punished.

Verse 3. *As the apple-tree among the trees of the wood, so is my beloved among the sons: I sat down under his shadow with great delight, and his fruit was sweet to my taste.*

CHRIST having commended the church in the former verse, and declared that she was as preferable to all others, as the lily was to the thorns; she in this verse returns the commendation to him, and asserts that he as much excelled all the sons, as the fruitful apple-tree did the wild and barren trees of the wood;^b and at the same time gives an account of that sweet experience she had of his excellency, preciousness, and usefulness to her. Now in the words may be observed,

I. A comparison which she makes of him to an apple-tree; in which she sets forth his excellency and preferableness to all others.

II. She instances in two particular things; in which, by good experience, she found him to be so to her own soul. First, The shadow of this apple-tree was delightful to her; "I sat down under his shadow with great delight." Secondly, The fruit thereof was exceeding sweet to her; "his fruit was sweet to my taste."

I. She compares him to an apple-tree, and that no doubt of the best sort. The Targum renders it, a *pome-citron*, or *citron-apple-tree*: which, 1. Is a very large tree;^c and somay be fitly used to express the greatness and excellency of Christ, who is posssesed of all divine perfections, and is "over all, God blessed for ever." He is a Saviour, and a great One; who has, as an instance of his great love, condescension, and power, wrought out a great salvation for great sinners. He is a High Priest, and he is a great one, both in the glory of his person, and in the virtue and efficacy of his sacrifice and intercession. He is the King of saints, and as such is higher than the kings of the earth: He is equal with God, therefore greater than angels, and more excellent than all the sons of men. 2. It is a very fruitful tree; it is sometimes so full of fruit, that it is even pressed down with the weight thereof,^d and is, as Pliny says,^e *omnibus horis pomifera*, "always bearing fruit:" it has at one and the same time flowers, ripe and unripe fruit; whilst some are putting forth, others are dropping off; so Christ abounds with the fruits of divine grace; he is not the barren fig-tree, but the green fir-tree, from

---

^a The lily is called ambrosia; and is said to be the delight of Venus, because of its pleasing colour. Nicander apud Athenæum, l. 15. c. 8. p. 683. and of Juno, Clement Alex. pædagog. l. 2. p. 181.

^b Quantum lenta solent inter viburna cupressi, Virgil. Bucolic. eclog. 1. v. 26. Lenta salix, &c. eclog. 5. v. 16.   ^c Solin. Polyhist. c. 59.
^d Ibid.   ^e Lib. 12. c. 3.

whom our fruit is found, and that at all times; for he is that "tree of life which bare twelve manner of fruits, and yielded her fruit every month; and the leaves of the tree were for the healing of the nations," Rev. xxii. 2. Here may believers come at all times, and pluck and eat; for here is not any deficiency of fruit, it is always growing, always plucking, and yet never lessened. 3. The fruit of this tree [f] is of a bitter taste, but of an exceeding sweet smell, as are the leaves; which being put among garments, not only give them a delightful odour, but also drive away noxious creatures from them; for the same reason is Christ compared to myrrh in chap. i. 13; for though his sacrifice, death, and sufferings, are sweet and savoury, both to his Father and to his people, yet they were bitter unto him, who not only tasted of, but drank up the whole cup of his Father's wrath: and though the blessings which spring from hence are of a sweet smell, exceeding grateful and delightful to believers, yet are they enjoyed in this life with a variety of crosses, afflictions, and tribulations; this passover-lamb is eaten with bitter herbs. 4. It is an excellent remedy against poison.[g] Sin is that poison of asps which has infected all human nature, and spread itself over all the powers and faculties of the souls of men, as well as over all the members of their bodies: now the Christ is the sovereign antidote against it; this fruit of the citron-apple-tree is the most proper remedy for it; his righteousness justifies, his blood cleanses, and his grace will eternally clear his people from their sins. 5. It is very good for shortness of breath, and to remove a stinking one;[h] hence the Parthian nobles used to boil the kernels of it in their food for that purpose; it is the presence of Christ, and communion with him, that only can cure our panting souls when we are wearied, and almost out of breath in seeking him; and it is the sweet incense of his mediation that perfumes our prayers, which are the breath of our souls, and which otherwise would be so far from being grateful to God, that it would be strange unto him. And thus may Christ be compared to a citron-apple-tree; though perhaps the common apple-tree is here intended, which the Talmud[i] interprets of the Israelites, but R. Aben Ezra understands it of the Shecinah, as do the Targum and R. Sol. Jarchi, of the holy and blessed God, and Lord of the world; as also does R. Chaya, in the book Zohar,[k] who says, that the congregation of Israel set forth the praises of the holy and blessed God by an apple, because of its colours, smell, and taste; so the Cabalistic doctors interpret of *tiphereth*, or the bridegroom, because of the same.[l] Christ is this Shecinah, the holy and blessed God, and Lord of the world, who may be compared to an apple-tree, (1.) Because it is a very fruitful tree. There are various sorts of fruit which it bears; Christ is full of fruit: he is Joseph's Antitype, who is called "a fruitful bough, even a fruitful bough by a well, whose branches run over the wall:" all the fruits of righteousness grow on him, every grace is in him; he is that "tree of life which bears twelve manner of fruits;" there are justifying and pardoning grace, sanctifying and adopting grace in him; all that a believer can want here, and all that can make him happy hereafter: and as fruitful boughs bend downwards, being laden with fruit, and may be easily reached, so Christ, being full of grace and truth, gives to sinners the utmost liberty of access to him for grace from him; for though as God, he is "the high and lofty One," yet as man and Mediator, he is meek and lowly, and condescends to take notice of, and admits into familiarity, poor, mean, and abject creatures; he gives them a gracious allowance to approach near unto him; that apple-tree, whose fruitful boughs of divine grace hang so low, that the hand of faith may easily reach them, where the poor sinner is heartily welcome to pluck and eat at pleasure. (2.) It is of a very beautiful aspect when laden with fruit, and especially as growing among the trees of the forest. Some have thought that the fruit of this tree is what was forbidden our first parents; which being so "pleasant to the eyes," was a temptation to the woman to eat thereof; therefore is in Latin called *malum, evil*, because sin entered into the world hereby: though others think it was another sort of fruit. The Jewish writers differ much about it; some say it was the fig-tree, so R. Sol. Jarchi, and some others in R. Aben Ezra on Gen. iii. 6; which they gather from Adam and Eve's immediate sewing of fig-leaves together, as soon as they had sinned, to cover themselves with: others, that it was the pome-citron, or citron-apple tree, so Baal Hatturim in Gen. i. 29, but the same author on Numb. v. 3, seems to intimate as if it was the grape, the fruit of the vine; which is also the opinion of the Jews in Zohar,[m] who think that it is particularly the black grape; though others have thought it to be the apple, as the author of the old Nizzachon;[n] which was either his own and the opinion of some other Jews, or else he took it from the common notion of Christians. But whether it was the apple-tree or no, which was so pleasant and desirable to the eyes of the woman, yet it is certain that this is very pleasant and delightful to the sight, when laden with fruit. Christ as Mediator is a beautiful sight to believers, as he stands in all his endearing characters and relations; as he may be viewed undertaking their cause, assuming their nature, suffering, bleeding, and dying in their stead, rising again for their justification, ascending into heaven, and entering there with their names and

---

[f] Solin and Plin. in locis citatis.
[g] Solin. and Plin. l. ibid. and Fernel. method. med. l. 5. c. 21. [h] Plin. l. 11. 'c. 53, and l 12. c. 3. Athen. Deipnosophist. l. 3. c. 7. p. 83.
[i] T. Bab. Sabbat, fol. 88. 1. [k] In Lev. fol. 30. 4. [l] Lexic. Cabal. p. 738. [m] In Exod. fol. 59. v. and in Numb fol. 53. 3.
[n] P. 147. apud egenseil. Tela Ignea.

persons upon his heart, and there ever living to make intercession for them: Christ, as possessed of all the blessings of the everlasting covenant, being the Surety, Mediator, and Messenger of it, is exceeding delightful to the eye of faith; "his glory is as the glory of the only begotten of the Father, when he appears to souls full of grace and truth. (3.) The fruit which grows upon the apple-tree, as it is of various sorts and of a beautiful aspect to the eye, so it is of a cooling and comforting nature. Christ has cooled, turned away, and appeased the fierceness of his Father's fiery wrath, by his death and blood; and does by his mighty grace sweetly cool and refresh the heart of a poor sinner, inflamed by a fiery law, and commands serenity and peace in its conscience filled with wrath and terror; and when his people are ready to faint and sink, he comforts them with his apples, the sweet discoveries of his love and grace, of which the church having had some experience, and desiring some renewed instances thereof, says, in ver. 5, "comfort me with apples;" where I shall more largely take notice of this, as well as of their pleasant and delightful smell. (4.) The apple-tree has been accounted an hieroglyphic of love,[o] under it lovers used to meet, with the fruit thereof they entertained each other, under its delightful shade they sat; to which perhaps an allusion is not only made in this verse, but also in chap. viii. 5. "I raised thee up under the apple-tree." Christ and his church are throughout this song introduced as lovers, and the subject of their whole conversation is love: He, who if the apple-tree is the church's beloved, whom she loves and prefers before all others; it is his love her soul is ravished with; his fruit she feeds upon; his shade that she with so much content and pleasure sits under, where she is delighted with his love and grace, and sensibly feels her soul all enamoured with him. Some other things might have been taken notice of, particularly the fruit and shadow of this tree, which are both mentioned in the text; but these will be considered under another head.

Now Christ, whom the church here compares to an apple-tree, is by her preferred to all others; and she signifies, that as much as the apple-tree excels the wild and unfruitful trees of the wood, so much does Christ excel all the sons: by whom may be meant either the angels, so the Targum, who are by creation the sons of God; but not in so high and eminent a sense as Christ is: he has a more excellent name and nature than they; as God, he is their Lord and Creator, and the object of their highest worship and adoration; and as Mediator, they are obliged unto him, being upheld and secured by his grace in that state wherein they are; and though in his human nature he was made a little lower than they, yet now in the very same nature he is exalted above them; for "to which of the angels said he at any time, Sit thou at my right-hand?" Or else by them may be meant the saints, who are the sons of God by adopting grace: Christ, the eternal Son of God has the pre-eminence in, and over these; he is their Creator and Redeemer, their Lord and King, their Head and Husband, their everlasting Father and glorious Mediator, to whom they are infinitely obliged for all the needful supplies of grace here, and for all the glory they expect hereafter. Or else by them may be meant the men of the world, the sons of Adam; and these Christ infinitely excels, as much as the apple-tree does the trees of the wood; for he is "fairer than the children of men;" there is none like him in all the armies of heaven, nor any to be compared with him among all the inhabitants of the earth; if both worlds were to be searched with the utmost scrutiny, not one single individual person could be found comparable to him: and perhaps particularly by these may be meant the great princes and monarchs of the world, who are sometimes in scripture compared to large and lofty trees; see Ezek. xxxi. 3, 5, 6, 8, Dan. iv. 20—22. But Christ is far preferable to these in beauty, glory, and majesty; he is "higher than the kings of the earth, they receive their crowns and kingdoms from him;" they are at his command, and under his dominion; he sets them up, and puts them down at pleasure; these must all submit to his awful judgment, even as the poorest peasant; and will be equally as fearful of "the great day of his wrath," which when come, they will call to the rocks and mountains to fall on them, and hide them from the face of this omnipotent Judge. Moreover, with respect to the saints, the fruits of Christ's grace are to them far preferable to the kingdoms, crowns, and sceptres of the greatest monarchs, nay, reproach, for Christ's sake, is more highly esteemed of by them, and accounted greater riches than all the treasures of this world. Though it seems as well as to be understood in general of all wicked, Christless, and unconverted sinners, who are like to the trees of the wood, wild, barren, and unfruitful; and what fruit they do bring forth, is sour, wild, and unprofitable; and though like the trees of the wood, they may run up a great height, yet they shall be cut down and thrown into everlasting burnings: for, "the ax is laid to the root of the trees; therefore every tree which bringeth not forth good fruit, is hewn down and cast into the fire," Matt. iii. 10. Thus the church, by this comparison, sets forth the excellency and preferableness of Christ to all others. But,

II. She instances in two excellent properties of this apple-tree, of which she had had some comfortable experience.

First. The shade of it was delightful to her, "I sat down under his shadow with great de-

---

[o] The apple was sacred to love, Scholiast. in Aristoph. Nubes p. 180. the statue of Venus had an apple in one hand, and a poppy in the other. Pausan. Corinth. sive l. 2. p. 103.

light." Secondly. The fruit of it was sweet unto her; "his fruit was sweet to my taste."

First. The shade of this apple tree was very delightful to her: "I sat down under his shadow with great delight:" in which may be inquired, 1st. What is meant by the shadow under which she sat. 2ndly. What her sitting there intends or supposes. 3rdly. What she desired to sit there for. 4thly. From whence that pleasure and delight arose, which she was filled with.

1st. It will be proper to inquire what is meant by the shadow of Christ, under which she sat. Some[p] have thought that the ceremonial law, with its festivals, is here intended, which was a shadow of good things to come, of which Christ was the sum and substance; under this shadow the Old Testament saints sat during the legal dispensation, where their souls were much delighted and sweetly refreshed by viewing Christ represented in the types and sacrifices of that law. The Targum understands it of the shadow of God's Shechinah, or Divine Majesty, under which the congregation of Israel desired to sit, when God gave the law on mount Sinai: but that dispensation was not so desirable; the law which was then given, was a fiery one; and the words which were then spoke were such, that they that heard them, intreated that they should not be spoken to them any more: therefore it may be better understood of the Gospel and the ordinances of it, than either of the moral or ceremonial law; under this refreshing shadow saints delight to sit; here they enjoy sweet communion and fellowship with Christ; the sound of the Gospel is joyful to them; the truths and doctrines of it are nourishing; the ordinances of it are comfortable and delightful; these tabernacles are amiable and lovely; and all wisdom's ways are ways of pleasantness; and therefore it is no wonder that souls desire to sit under this shadow, and when they do, it is with delight.

Moreover, some[q] think that an allusion is here made to the nuptial ceremony of spreading the skirt, used by the Jews at the time of marriage; of which see Ruth iii. 9; and to which an allusion is made in Ezek. xvi. 8; or to that veil, which being borne up with four rods or staves, was carried over the heads of the new-married couple, at the time that the bridegroom brought home the bride into his own house, where the whole solemnity was finished; this nuptial ceremony perhaps may give the best light to Luke i. 35, "the Holy Ghost shall come upon thee, and the power of the Highest shall over-shadow thee:" so that this phrase of sitting under Christ's shadow, may be expressive of the church's being married to Christ, and of that delightful communion which she enjoys with him as her husband, when brought home to his own house; of which we have an account in the next verse, where she is entertained after a noble manner: and has as much of his love manifested to her, as she is capable of bearing, nay so much, that she is overcome with it. But I rather think that the metaphor is continued from the former part of the verse; and that the allusion is made to the shadow of an apple-tree, such an one as Christ was; whose shadow arises from his person, blood, and righteousness; which shadow is, 1. A protecting one from heat; such as Jonah's gourd was to him, or as the pillar of cloud was to the Israelites in the wilderness, or as a great rock to a weary traveller in a hot country. Christ and his righteousness are a shadow, which protect souls from the heat of his Father's wrath; he, by making atonement for sin, and satisfaction to divine justice, hath delivered his own people from the wrath to come, and will eternally screen them from it; for though showers of divine wrath will fall on Christless sinners, yet those that are under this shadow of Christ's righteousness, shall not have one drop of it fall on them; for being justified by his blood, they shall be saved from wrath through him; also it is this, laid hold on by faith, which screens from the curses of a fiery law, and from the heat of that wrath which it sometimes works in the conscience; which is only rightly removed by the sprinklings of that blood which speaks peace and pardon, and by the application of that righteousness which justifies from all sin, and produces a peace which passeth all understanding: likewise Christ is the shadow which protects and shelters from the fiery darts of Satan; he is as a shadow from the heat, when the blast of the terrible ones, those fiends of hell, is as a storm against the wall; his blood and righteousness keep off Satan's fiery darts, preserve from his suggestions, and protect from the violence of his temptations; and the soul is still more secured by the prevalent mediation and intercession of Christ in heaven, which is founded upon his blood and righteousness; so that what faith makes use of on earth to oppose to Satan's temptations, Christ does in heaven to secure his people from his false charges and accusations: to this might also be added, that he is the shadow which protects from the heat of persecution, under which he causes his flock to rest at noon; when this sun smites them with the greatest violence, he is then their shade on their right hand, so that the sun shall not smite them by day; and this is their comfort and support under all their fiery trials, that they have such a shadow to have recourse to. 2. It is also a refreshing one; for if it is a shadow from the heat of God's wrath, the terrors of the law, the temptations of Satan, and the persecutions of the world, it must needs be so; what can be more refreshing to a weary traveller, that is almost scorched, and ready to faint with heat, than a cooling and delightful shade? so refreshing is Christ to poor sinners,

---

[p] Ambrose in Psal cxviii. octon. 5. col. 908.
[q] Sanct. in loc. and so R. Simeon Ben Joachi seems to understand it in Exod. vol. 43. 1.

who is as "the shadow of a great rock in a weary land;" nay, is a large spreading apple-tree, that at once furnishes them with an agreeable shelter and suitable provisions. 3. It is a fructifying one: the shadows of some trees, as Pliny[r] informs us, are very hurtful and noxious to some plants that grow under them, and others are very nonrishing and fructifying: Christ's shadow is such an one; for "they that dwell under this shadow shall return; they shall revive as the corn, and grow as the vine; the scent thereof shall be as the wine of Lebanon," Hos. xiv. 7; and indeed all the fruitfulness of those who are the Lord's planting comes from Christ: for, unless they abide in and under him, they can bring forth no fruit. The shadows of some trees are injurious to men that lie under them;[s] not so Christ's shadow; but there are others[t] very delightful and wholesome, to which he may be compared.

2ndly. It may also be inquired what her sitting under this shadow is expressive of, or does suppose. And, 1. It shows the sense she had of herself, and present condition, and the need she stood in of Christ as a shadow; she was not only scorched with the sun of persecution, with afflictions, temptations, &c., but she was likewise sensible thereof, and therefore, betook herself to a proper shade. 2. It manifestly appears from her sitting under this shadow, that she looked upon Christ to be a suitable one for her in such cases; and that as the idolaters in Hos. iv. 13, sacrificed on mountains, and burnt incense under oaks, poplars, and elms, "because the shadow thereof was good;" so the church here sat under this shadow of Christ's, because she looked upon it to be a good one, and preferable to all others. 3. It is expressive of her faith and confidence in Christ; the vain confidence of the Israelites in an arm of flesh, is called their "trust in the shadow of Egypt," Isa. xxx. 2, 3; and the holy confidence and faith of God's children in him, is frequently called a "trusting in the shadow of his wings;" see Psalm xxxvi. 7, and lvii. 1; which seems to be the same with sitting under it here: the church did not sit idle under Christ, but her faith was in exercise upon him; and she was rejoicing alone in him, having "no confidence in the flesh." 4. It seems to intimate that security, peace, quietness, and satisfaction of soul, she enjoyed; here she sat as under her own vine and fig-tree, and none to make her afraid; where being safe and secure from all her enemies, she solaced herself under this delightful shade, enjoying much peace of conscience, and satisfaction of mind: for she did not sit here with any manner of uneasiness, but with the utmost delight and pleasure. 5. It denotes her continuance here; faith takes up its dwelling in Christ; it will not move from hence, and is desirous of always enjoying sensible communion with him; "he that dwelleth in the secret of the Most High, shall abide under the shadow of the Almighty," Psal. xci. 1. But

3rdly. What was it she desired to sit here for? For thus may the words be rendered, "I desired, and I sat down;"[u] that is, I desired to sit down, and I did sit down, I had what I wished for; and what was that? no doubt, protection from heat, rest, and refreshment for her weary and fainting soul; that she might be comforted with those apples which grew on this tree, and be revived by tasting of and feeding upon the sweet fruit thereof, as well as be comforted with its delightful shade.

4thly. She sat here with delight; and indeed it could not be otherwise when its shade was so agreeable, and the fruit so sweet: this pleasure and delight of hers arose from the enjoyment of Christ's presence, "in whose presence is fulness of joy, and at whose right-hand are pleasures for evermore;" from the discoveries of his love to her soul, which is better than life, and all the comforts of it; and were had in the exercise of faith upon him, in the actings of which grace the soul is filled with "joy unspeakable and full of glory."

Secondly. The fruit of this apple-tree was sweet unto her taste: by this fruit are either meant the fruit of his doings, what his hands have wrought out, and his blood has procured for sinners, even all the blessings of grace, such as peace and reconciliation, justification, sanctification, pardon of sin, adoption, nearness of access to God, &c. or else, the fruit of his lips; such as his word and Gospel, preached by himself, which is sweet to a believer's taste, and is preferred to his necessary food; his promises, which are exceeding great and precious, and are highly valued by believers, for his mouth is most sweet, from whence they proceed; and his ordinances and commands, in which they enjoy sweet communion with him, and have the discoveries of his love to their souls; and therefore "are more to be desired than gold, yea, than much fine gold; sweeter also than the honey or the honey comb."

These are called his fruits; they are his in a covenant-way; all the blessings of grace, which make up the everlasting covenant, are in Christ's hands, and at his dispose, being placed there for that purpose by God the Father; and they are also his, being procured by him; for though they are all the gifts of free grace, yet are they all obtained by Christ, and come to us through his blood: likewise they may be said to be his, because in his possession; every grace in its fulness is in him, he is full of grace and truth, and

---

[r] Lib. 17. c. 12. Juniperi gravis umbra, nocent et frugibus umbræ. Virgil. Bucol. eclog. 10. in fine.

[s] Arboribus certis gravis umbra tributa est, Lucret. l. 6. v. 783. [t] ——Ubi mollis amaracus illum floribus et dulci aspirans complectitur umbre, Virg. Æneid. l. 1. prope finem. Oportuna sua blanditur populus umbra, Ovid. Metam. l. 10-

[u] המדתי וישבתי et neupivi et sedi, Pagninus, Montanus, Mercerus, Munckius.

is communicated to us from him, for from him all our fruit is found; remission of sin, justifying righteousness, adopting grace, &c., come to us through and by him; and we are indulged with the gospel-promises and ordinances, as instances of his grace to us.

Now these are all sweet to the taste of a believer, though not to a natural man, who hath a vitiated taste, and calls evil good and good evil: puts bitter for sweet, and sweet for bitter; he savours the things of the flesh; sin is his food, from whence he receives an imaginary pleasure; and therefore disrelishes all spiritual things, looks upon them as poor and insipid, and finds no more taste in them than in the white of an egg; which arises from the predominancy of sin, that hinders from tasting any sweetness in divine things, and will do so whilst their taste remains in them, and their scent is not changed; but as for a spiritual man, he savours the things of the Spirit, and disrelishes others; sin is rendered odious, bitter, and unpleasant to him; it is in some measure expelled, so that he can taste that the Lord is gracious: and therefore every thing he says or does is sweet unto him; for as his state can discern perverse things, so it can relish spiritual ones: such as the fruit before-mentioned is, which grows upon and drops from the apple-tree, Christ Jesus: this delightful shade and excellent fruit, which believers find in Christ, render him very acceptable to them, and preferable to all others. Now when souls at any time have some experience of Christ's love and grace, in such a way and manner, it is very proper to speak of it, for the glory of Christ, and the encouragement of other souls, as the church does here; which she also continues to do in the following verse, where she meets with a larger display of it.

Verse 4. He brought me to the banqueting-house, and his banner over me was love.

THE church here goes on to give an account of some larger experiences of Christ's love, which she had met with from him; for she is not only indulged with his shadow, and refreshed with his fruit, as in the former verse, but is also brought into his banqueting-house, where she is entertained by him, of which she gives an account in this: where may be observed,

I. What is meant by the banqueting-house.
II. What by being brought into it.
III. The manner in which she was brought; "his banner over me was love."

I. I shall inquire what is meant by the banqueting-house, into which the church was brought: it is in the Hebrew text, a house of wine:[w] by which may be meant, either the wine-cellar,[x] the place where wine is kept under-ground; or else the place[y] where wine is poured out, and where it is drank, according to R. Aben Ezra; and so may very well be rendered a banqueting-house. Thus we read of a banquet of wine which Esther invited king Ahasuerus and Haman to; and wine, being much used at feasts, may be put synechdochically, for all the other accommodations thereof; by which we may understand either,

1st. The covenant of grace; this is built for a banqueting-house for souls; it is a superstructure of grace and mercy, whose foundation is the person of Christ; it is well stored with all needful provisions for a nobler entertainment; it is ordered in all things, and sure;" it is full of Christ, his love and grace; it is well stored with spiritual blessings, and precious promises, which will serve as an everlasting banquet for those who are interested in it. Or else,

2ndly. The Sacred Scripture, which is a true banqueting-house: here is a variety of food, and plenty of it; here is milk for babes; and meat for strong men; which is exceeding pleasant and delicious, sweeter to the taste than the honey or honey-comb; revives and refreshes those who participate thereof, and is also exceeding wholesome to the souls of men: though there are vast numbers daily feasted here, yet there is no want; it abounds with the bread of Gospel-truths, with the wine of Gospel-promises, and is full of Christ, the hidden Manna, who is also the Bread of Life; he is the Alpha and Omega of the scriptures, the sum and substance of them, on whom faith lives, and by whom, from time to time, it is sweetly refreshed. Or else,

3rdly. The church is this banqueting-house. The Targum refers it to the house of the school, where the Israelites learnt the law at mount Sinai from the mouth of Moses; R. Alshech understands by it Sinai itself, and so it is interpreted in Yalkut; R. Sol. Jarchi thinks the tabernacle of the congregation is intended, where the sense and explanations of the law were given; but it may much better be understood of the church of Christ, which is a house built by widsom, and furnished with all the necessary provisions of grace; here is " a feast of fat things prepared, of wines on the lees well refined. Christ is the Master and Provider of the feast, and he himself is the chief entertainment; his flesh is meat indeed, and his blood is drink indeed; to all which he gives his people an hearty welcome; meets them himself at his well-furnished table, and feasts with them; gives them spiritual appetites, and blesses all the provisions of his grace to them; hence those are the blessed persons who have admittance into, and a dwelling-place in this house, for these shall be continually " satisfied with the goodness and fatness thereof;" hence it is that souls are so desirous of being here, and are so well-pleased with their habitation, because it is a banqueting-

---

[w] בית היין domum vini, Pagninus, Montanus, &c.
[x] Cellam vinariam, V. L. Tigurine version; εἰς τον οινωνα, Symmachus.
[y] Locum convivii, Junius and Tremellius.

house unto them; and no wonder then is it, that those who are "Planted in the house of the Lord, flourish in the courts of our God."

II. What it is to be "brought into" this banqueting-house;" which may be considered according to the several senses before given. And

1st. Seeing by the banqueting-house may be meant the covenant of grace, it may be proper to inquire, What it is to be brought into that, and by what means? And now here observe, that water-baptism, and a submission to it under the New-Testament, give a person no right unto, nor interest him in the covenant of grace, even as circumcision did not, nor could under the Old; instances of both might be given of persons, where there is no reason to believe they have any share or lot in this matter; neither does church-fellowship bring a person into it, nor a mere submission to any or all the ordinances of the Gospel, for "they are not all Israel which are of Israel;" nor are they all instances of covenant-grace, who are church-members; for there are tares as well as wheat grow in Christ's field below; and goats as well as sheep are folded in his fold on earth, the church; there are foolish as well as wise virgins, and there are "sinners in Zion," as well as the "living in Jerusalem;" neither are faith and repentance terms and conditions of a man's entering into this covenant; for they are some of the blessings of grace contained in it; they do not bring a person into it, but are evidences of his being there before; but what brings a person into it, is an act of sovereign and unchangeable grace before all time; all, interested in the everlasting covenant, before the world began, did by electing grace "pass under the rod of him that telleth them;" for when God made a covenant of grace with his Son on the account of these chosen ones, he brought them all into the bond of it, and put all grace and blessings into the hands of his Son for them. Now the Spirit of God in time does in conversion take and apply this covenant grace to those persons, for the quickening, pardoning, justifying, and sanctifying them; he shows them the covenant, and their interest in it, and enables them to lay hold upon it; and every time he does do so, he may be said to bring a soul into the covenant, as an effect and fruit of that original, ancient act, made before the world began; which is what the church might experience here, to wit, a fresh manifestation of her covenant-interest; for "the secret of the Lord is with them that fear him, and he will show them his covenant;" Christ led her into his banqueting-house, and there feasted her with his royal dainties; for to bring, is to lead one to an entertainment.*

2ndly. If we understand the scripture by the banqueting-house; then to be brought into it is to have the understanding opened, so as to behold wondrous things out of it; the heart affected with the glorious truths thereof, so as to taste the sweetness of the "sincere milk of the word;" and distinguish the doctrines of the Gospel from those which are not so, and be capable of appropriating the promises of it to the comfort and satisfaction of our souls; and when we are enabled thus to do, we shall find the scripture to be a delightful banqueting-house indeed! Now all this Christ does by his Spirit; who is the Spirit of truth, who guides and leads his people into all truth. But

3rdly. If by the banqueting-house we understand the church of Christ: then to be brought into it, is to be made a partaker of all the privileges of it, as those who are no more strangers and foreigners, but fellow-citizens of the saints and of the household of God. Christ first calls men by his grace, then by his ministers invites them to come in, that this house may be filled; and by his Spirit powerfully works upon their souls, sweetly inclining them not only to give up themselves to him, but likewise to one another by the will of God; he, as an instance of his distinguishing grace, takes one of a city, and two of a family, and brings them to Zion, where he invests them with all the privileges and immunities thereof; here he grants them his gracious presence, sheds abroad his love in their hearts, and often entertains them with a delightful banquet. Now Christ's thus bringing his church into his banqueting-house, shows, 1. Inability on her part; we cannot bring ourselves into the covenant of grace, nor can we take views of our interest in it at pleasure; but he who of his own grace placed us there, must show it us; nor can we of ourselves know the depths and mysteries of the sacred writings; they will remain a sealed book to us, unless the Spirit of Christ open the book, and our understandings to look into it: nor will his church, with all the ordinances of it, be a banqueting-house unto us, unless he himself be present with us. 2. Wonderful grace and condescension on his side; that he, who is the King of kings, and Lord of lords, should take one thus mean into his own apartments, and there entertain her with the best his house could afford. But this will still appear more manifestly, if we consider,

III. The manner in which she was brought; "his banner over me was love." It was in a very stately and majestic manner, as well as a loving one, that she was brought; and for the illustration of this, it will be proper to consider the use of banners, and how they may be applied here. And

1st. The use of banners, standards, or ensigns, is to gather and keep persons together: thus Christ himself was lifted up on the cross, and is now lifted up in the Gospel, as an ensign to gather souls unto him: and so his love, being displayed in the preaching of the Gospel, has a power and efficacy in it to draw souls after him; for as a fruit and

---

* אל in, Pagninus, Junius and Tremellius, Piscator, Marckius, Michaelis.

* Ad prandium me adduxit, Plautus.

effect of everlasting love, " with loving kindness " he draws them : and in the same way and manner Christ here drew the church unto himself, and held her fast; and constrained her to keep close to him, and follow hard after him; see 2 Cor. v. 14.

2ndly. A banner displayed, or a standard set up, is an indication of war; it is to prepare for it, and to animate to it,[b] see Jer. li. 12, 27. This may serve to inform us, that the church of Christ here on earth is militant, and therefore in chap. vi. 4, is represented as formidable and terrible as an army with banners: she has many enemies to engage with, as sin, Satan, and the world, and yet has the greatest encouragement to fight, for she is bannered under the Lord of hosts; Christ is Commander-in-chief; he is given to be a Leader and Commander of the people, and is every way fit for it; he has courage enough to appear at the head of his armies, and conduct enough to lead them on, and bring them off at pleasure; those that are under him are well provided for; their bread is given them in due season, and their water is sure: they are furnished with the πανοπλία, or whole armour of God; they may be assured of a crown and kingdom as soon as the battle is over, and even of victory beforehand, for they are more than conquerors through him that hath loved them; likewise the motto, which is written upon the banner, under which they are, is *love*: and if all this will not encourage them to fight, what will?

3rdly. A banner displayed is also a sign of victory; sometimes when a town, city, or castle is taken, the flag is hung out as an indication of it; see Jer. l. 2. Christ has gotten the victory over all his and our enemies; he has conquered sin, Satan, and the world; and given his church and people a share in all his conquests; and as an evidence of it, has set up his banner over them. Or this may principally intend the conquest, which he, by love, had gotten over her heart; she surrendered herself into the victor's hands; and now, as an instance of his mighty grace, he introduces her into his own house, under the banner of love, by which she was conquered.

4thly. A banner is for protection and defence; hence Moses built an altar, and called it *Jehovah nissi*, that is, *the Lord is my banner*; because the Lord had been on the side of him and the people of Israel, and defended them from the Amalekites. The church was now enjoying sweet communion with Christ in his banqueting-house: and that she might be safe and secure from her enemies, and abide there during his pleasure, without any molestation or disturbance, he sets up his banner over her: thus " when the enemy comes in like a flood," to disturb our peace, joy, and comfort, " the Spirit of the Lord lifts up a standard against him," Isa. lix. 19.

5thly. It is to direct soldiers where to stand, when to march, and whom to follow; see Numb. i. 52, and ii. 2, which may teach us, who are enlisted in Christ's service, not to fly from our colours, but adhere closely to Christ and his Gospel, his cause and interest, his church and people, and to follow him, the Standard-bearer, wherever he goes; and nothing can more strongly engage us to do so than love, which is the motto of his banner; this first drew us to him, this animates us in his service, and keeps us close to his person and interest.

6thly. It is to distinguish one band from another; see Numb. ii. 2. As one band has one motto upon its banner or ensign, by which it is distinguished from another; so the motto on Christ's banner is *love*, by which his band or company is distinguished from all others: it is this which has made them to differ from others; has distinguished them in electing, redeeming, and calling grace; and will keep them a distinct and peculiar people to all eternity; it is not any works which they have done, but Christ's boundless love and grace alone, that make the difference between them and others. The allusion may be to the names of generals being inscribed on the banners of their armies; so Vespasian's name was inscribed on the banners throughout his armies.[c]

Verse 5. *Stay me with flagons, comfort me with apples, for I am sick of love.*

THE church being brought into Christ's banqueting-house or house of wine, and having there such large discoveries of his love, she falls into a deliquium or fainting fit, not being able to bear up under the present enjoyment; and therefore calls to her friends and acquaintance that were about her, to give her their assistance in her present circumstances. In these words may be considered,

I. The church's case and condition in which she was; " sick of love."

II. What relief she asks for. 1st. To be " stayed with flagons." 2ndly. To be " comforted with apples."

III. Who the persons are to whom she makes application.

I. We have in these words the present case and condition in which the church was; she was *sick of love*; this was a sickness of the soul, and not of the body; though the one has oftentimes an influence upon the other; for as there are various bodily sicknesses and diseases, so there are various spiritual ones. 1. There is the sickness of sin, which, if mighty grace prevent not, is a sickness unto death; it is in its own nature mortal, and can only be cured by Christ, the great Physician, who heals diseases by forgiving iniquity: this is what is natural and hereditary to us; we bring it into the world with us; for we are all " shapen in iniquity, and in sin did our mothers conceive

---

[b] Vexillum proponendum, quod erat insigne quum ad arma concurri oporteret, Cæsar.. de Bello Gallic.   [1]. 2. c. 20.   [c] Sueton. Vita Vespasian. c. 6.

us:" it is an epidemical distemper, which has infected all human nature; all are diseased with it, though all are not sensible of it; and it has overspread all the powers and faculties of the souls of men, as well as all the members of the body; so that there is no part nor place exempted from it; for the whole head is sick, and the whole heart faint: but this is not the sickness intended here. 2. There is a sickness which souls are incident to, that arises from a sense of sin, want of the fresh manifestations of pardoning grace, absence of Christ Jesus, and a longing after the enjoyment of his person, and the discoveries of his love; which though it is not a sickness unto death, yet it is very painful and afflicting, and can only be cured by the enjoyment of the object loved; this discovers itself by a violent panting after Christ; a carefulness and activity in the use of means, to enjoy his presence and company; a resolution to go through all difficulties for the sake of him, and an uneasiness until it receives some instances of favour from him: with such souls, Christ is the subject of all their discourse; they love to hear his name mentioned, especially with commendation, their thoughts are continually upon him, and their minds are not easy till they enjoy him: this is the sickness which the church was attended with in chap. v. 8; where see more of it. 3. There is a sickness which springs from views of Christ's person, discoveries of his love, and manifestations of his grace; which sometimes overpower the soul, and throw it into the utmost amazement, at the consideration of the greatness of Christ's person and grace, and its unworthiness to be interested in it; so that it becomes like the queen of Sheba: who, when she saw the riches, glory, and wisdom of Solomon, it is said of her, that "there was no more spirit in her." And this I take to be the case of the church here; it did not arise from the want of Christ's presence, or discoveries of his love, but from the enjoyment of them both; he had introduced her in a most stately manner into his banqueting-house, and gave her a noble entertainment; yea, he had plentifully shed abroad his love in her heart, which occasioned her to speak after this manner; his person appeared so glorious and lovely, the entertainment was so large and sumptuous, the motto of love upon the banner so bright and glittering, and what she felt in her own soul so powerful and inconceivable, that she was quite overcome therewith; she was "sick through love:" or, as the Septuagint[d] renders it, she was "wounded with love:" not that this arises from the nature of love itself, which is not painful and grievous, but is owing to our weakness and imperfection, who cannot bear large views, nor support up under the mighty power of boundless love; we are but poor narrow earthen vessels, that can receive and retain but little of it: this was that pressure under which she now laboured, and for which she seeks relief; which brings me,

II. To consider what it is she calls for to relieve her at this time. 1st. She desires to be "stayed with flagons." 2nd. To be "comforted with apples."

1st. Her request is, that some person or other would stay her with flagons. The word translated *flagons* is differently rendered by interpreters; some render it flowers, as Jerom and the Vulgate Latin; and so she may be considered as having reference to sweet flowers bound up in nosegays, the odour of which is very refreshing and reviving; or, "make me to lie down in flowers," so Symmachus; according to Plato,[e] love delights to be in odoriferous places; where there are sweet-smelling flowers, there is its habitation, and there it abides. Now the church being in love, says, stay me, revive, or support me with flowers; perhaps chiefly regarding Christ, who is the only strength and support of believers, who only can keep them both from falling and fainting; for having heard him speak of himself under the names of those delightful flowers, the rose and lily, in ver. 1, she is desirous that she might be stayed by, and supported with them: the Septuagint renders the words thus, "strengthen me with ointments,"[f] by which may be meant the graces of Christ, which are called so in chap. i. 3, ointments were used at feasts, and are of a cheering, reviving, and strengthening nature; and may very well express the grace of Christ, by which souls are cheered, revived, established, strengthened, and settled; our translators have rendered it flagons, and that very well; for according to the best Jewish writers,[g] it signifies vessels in which either wine or fine flower are put; and perhaps may be comprehensive of all the entertainments of a banquet, which are proper to satisfy, delight, and exhilarate; and wine being a principal one, may chiefly intend flagons of that; see 1 Chron. xvi. 3, Hos. iii. 1; flagons are, by a metonymy, put for wine contained in them, as the cup is, Luke xxii. 20; for the church was desirous of those that were full and not empty; such as were full of the wine of Christ's love, which is as reviving, cheering, and refreshing as the best wine: and which greatly strengthens and supports the animal spirits.[h] In what sense Christ's love may be compared to wine, and is preferable to it, has been shown on chap. i. 2: and by flagons of it may be meant the doctrines of grace, in which Christ's love is displayed; or the ordinances of the Gospel, by which it is communicated to the

---

[d] Τετρωμένη ἀγάπης, Sept. amore langueo, V. L. so Michaelis; ægrotus is used in this sense in Terent. Heautont.-l. 1. The Tigurine version renders the words thus, Quia infirma sum dilectione, because I am weak in love; and understands it in the same sense as when persons are said to be weak in faith,

and therefore need support.
[e] Symposium, 1189.   [f] Στερίσατέ με ἐν μύροις, Sept.   [g] R. Sol. Jarchi, and R. Aben Ezra in loc. R. David Kimchi in lib. shorash. rad. אשׁשׁ.
[h] Vino fulcire venas cadentes, Seneca, ep. 95.

saints; and may also intimate, that though the love and grace of Christ are given forth in measure to them, yet that they are large measures, which believers are desirous of receiving; those who have most grace, would have still more; and those who have the greatest sense of Christ's love, would have a larger experience of it, and are not content without it; they are like "the two daughters of the horse-leech, crying, give, give:" and it may be also, that the church may have in view the glories and joys of another world; where she should have her fill of love, drink freely and plentifully of this wine new with Christ in his Father's kingdom, and continue in the uninterrupted enjoyment of his presence. Now it ought to be observed, that she is desirous of more of that which had brought her into this condition: Christ's love had wounded her, and that only could heal her; what had brought her into this sick and fainting condition, could only bring her out of it: this wounds and heals, kills and makes alive: and is the only reviving cordial.

2ndly. She desires that she might be "comforted with apples;" as in the former request, she had a regard to the banqueting-house, where she now was; so in this to the apple-tree, whose delicious fruit she had lately tasted. Apples are of a cooling and comforting nature,[i] and are good against a syncope and palpitation of the heart, and the smell of them is very reviving: Solinus[k] tells us of a certain people who eat no food, but *odore vivunt pomorum sylvestrium*, live by the smell of apples that grow in woods; and that when they go long journeys, carry them with them, *ut olfactu alantur*, that by the smell of them they may be nourished and sustained. The words may be rendered, "strew me with apples";[l] strew them about me, and strew them under me: the apple was an emblem of love, as before observed; to send or throw an apple to another, was a sign of love;[m] and must be still more so, to strew them about in quantities. By these apples may be meant, either the blessings of grace procured by the blood of Christ, which remove the fierceness of divine wrath, and being powerfully applied by the Spirit of God, do abundantly comfort and refresh the soul: or else the doctrines of the gospel, when fitly spoken, and fitly applied, are like "apples of gold in pictures of silver;" how comfortable and reviving are the doctrines of justification, pardon, perseverance, &c.; the church had found them so by good experience, and therefore desires them. The Targum, by flagons, understands the words of the law; and by apples, the interpretations of them; which, it says, are sweet to the taste as the apples of the garden of Eden: but it is much better to understand them, as we have done, of the doctrines of the gospel, which have often been experienced to have relieved persons in a fainting condition, such as the church was now in; and who knowing the virtue and efficacy thereof, calls for them. And,

III. The persons she makes application to, the word being in the plural number, are either the chorus of virgins, or daughters of Jerusalem, her dear friends and acquaintance, to whom she often told her case, especially when in distress, and desired their assistance, who seem to be near to her, by that solemn adjuration given unto them in ver. 7; or else, any other Christian friends that might be standing by her; for they that fear the Lord, speak often one to another, converse together, and comfort each other: or rather the ministers of the Gospel, who, by preaching the glorious doctrines of it, are instrumental in the hand of the Spirit for comforting the distressed, and reviving the fainting souls of God's children; though perhaps she principally intended Christ, who we find immediately came to her relief, as appears from the following verse.

Verse 6. *His left hand is under my head, and his right hand doth embrace me.*

THESE are still the words of the church, declaring what experience she had of Christ's grace and presence; who immediately upon the notice she gave of her distress, came to her assistance, and with both hands supported her in her fainting fit, and brought her out of it. And it may be observed, that she called to others for relief in the former verse, but it was Christ only that could help her: the flagons and apples of a gospel-ministry and gospel-ordinances will not be effectual to comfort and sustain the saints in such circumstances, unless Christ himself appears in them, and gives a blessing to them; which is what the church comfortably experienced here, and therefore speaks of it. And,

I. I shall consider what these words are expressive of.

II. In what manner they are delivered by her.

III. To whom they are directed, and for what reasons.

I. It may be proper to consider what Christ's left hand being under her head, and his right hand being said to embrace her, are expressive of. And,

1st. They are expressive of Christ's tender love unto, care of, and regard for his church and people; he acts the part of a loving husband, who, seeing his bride and spouse ready to sink and faint, hastens to her relief, embraces her in his arms, lays her in his bosom, and discovers the strongest and most endeared affection to her: Christ had a love for his church from all eternity; his heart was then ravished with her, and he took the

---

[i] Fernel. method. medend. l. 5. c. 6, 21.
[k] Polyhist. c. 65. [l] רסדוני sternite ante me, so some in Vatablus; substernite mihi, Tigurine version, Piscator. [m] Melo Galatea petit. Virgil Bucol. eclog. 3. ver. 64. Vid. Theocrit. Idyll. 3. v. 10, 40, 41. and Idyll. 6. v. 6, 7. and Suidam in voce. Μηλον.

utmost delight in her, viewing her in all the glory his Father meant to bring her to; and therefore requested of his Father that she might be his spouse and bride, which was accordingly granted to him; who has ever since remained a faithful and loving husband, and has given her the fullest and most incontestible proofs of it; he has assumed her nature, died in her room and stead, paid all her debts, procured every needful blessing for her, has given her right unto, and will put her into the possession of all that he has; he has raised her from the dunghill, the depths of sin and misery, taken off her filthy garments, clothed her in rich attire and royal apparel, and set her at his own right hand, in gold of Ophir.

This love of his remains the same as ever it was, and will do so for ever, notwithstanding all her failings and infirmities, her revoltings from him, and unkindness to him; for he is "Jesus, the same yesterday, to-day, and for ever:" though it is true, he does not alway manifest his love to his people, but sometimes hides his face from them, and kindly chides them for their good, and his own glory; yet he cannot always withhold his love in the manifestations of it to their souls; for though he seems to treat them severely for a while, yet his heart is full of love, pity, and concern; his bowels yearn, and, Joseph-like, cannot refrain himself, but must make himself known unto his brethren. Christ now has various ways of showing his love to his people, which he does the most suitably and seasonably; when tempted, he succours them; when disconsolate, he comforts them; and when afflicted, he sympathizes with them; when hungry, he feeds them; when naked, he clothes them; when sick, he, as the great Physician, heals them; when weak, he supports and upholds them with the right hand of his righteousness; and when fainting, he cheers and revives them; "he giveth power to the faint, and to them who have no might, he increases strength;" and this he does by putting his left hand under their head, and by embracing them with his right hand; the doing of which is an amazing and surprising instance of his grace.

2ndly. These phrases are expressive of that near fellowship and communion the church has with Christ; which is variously expressed in scripture, as by supping, and walking with him, and leaning on his bosom, and here by lying in his arms; which is an indication of very near and intimate communion indeed: to be admitted into Christ's banqueting-house, and there sit with him at his table, or into his privy chambers, and there have converse and communion with him, argue great nearness to him, and intimacy with him; but to lie in his arms, and have a place in his bosom, what can be nearer? This is the effect of that near and indissoluble union souls have with Christ; and what by divine grace, they are called to the enjoyment of; are frequently indulged with in their attendance on ordinances; and is that one thing they are desirous of, and uneasy without; but which, when obtained, gives them the greatest pleasure and highest satisfaction.

3rdly. They are expressive of the enjoyment of blessings from Christ, in whose right hand is length of days, and in whose left hand are riches and honour. Temporal mercies are Christ's left-hand blessings;[n] and such a measure of them Christ hands forth to his people in a covenant way, as will be needful for them to support them whilst in, and comfortably carry them through this wilderness; but Christ's right-hand blessings are of a spiritual nature, such as a justifying righteousness, pardon of sin, peace, and reconciliation by his blood, and adoption; all which being, by Christ's hand, applied unto his saints, cheer, revive, and comfort, when ready to faint; and which sustain, uphold, and strengthen them, when ready to sink and die away.

4thly. They are expressive of the safety and security of the church: they must needs be safe from all enemies, and secure from falling, who are encircled in the arms of Almighty grace, sustained by Christ's left hand, and embraced by his right hand, for out of his hands none can pluck them: such are, and will be preserved in Christ Jesus, until they are safely brought to glory. The Targum and R. Sol. Jarchi expound these words of the divine care and protection which the Israelites enjoyed in the wilderness; whereby they were not only provided with every thing that was useful and necessary, but also defended from every thing that was noxious and hurtful.

II. We may now consider the manner in which these words were delivered; and that they may be considered, either, 1. As a[o] prayer, and be read thus, "O that his left hand was under my head, and that his right hand would embrace me!" and suppose her still in the same case in which she was in the former verse; and seem to intimate, that she had a sense of her present state and condition, and a desire to be out of it; also, that she was without Christ's presence and communion with him, though she had a value for it, and an earnest desire after it, and did firmly believe that the enjoyment of it would relieve her. Or, 2. They may be considered as spoken in the strength of faith, that it would be so; and then the words may be read thus, "his left hand will be under my head, and his right hand will embrace me;"[p] and the sense of them is, as if she should say, It is true I am now in a very weak, feeble, and fainting condition; yet I know I shall not totally sink, fall and perish; for he will hold me up and support me, so that I shall not be moved: the words seem then to be spoken much in the same manner, and to argue the same strength of faith, as those spoken by the church in Mic. vii. 7, 8.

---

[n] So Isidore in loc.   [o] Tigurine version, some in Mercer. Ainsworth, Marckius.   [p] V. L. Pagninus, Montanus.

Or else, 3. As expressing her present experience that it was so; and then the words may be read as they are rendered by our translators, "his left hand is under my head," &c., which experience of hers she mentions with thankfulness, as she ought to do, to the glory of his love and grace, who had so kindly and graciously appeared for her in a time of distress; and this she does also in an exulting manner, and with a kind of boasting; for though we are not allowed to glory in ourselves, nor have any reason to boast of any thing which we have done, yet we may glory in Christ, and boast of what he is unto us, and has done for us.

III. The person to whom she speaks, are either the ministers of the Gospel, whose assistance she had desired; and having enjoyed the comforting and supporting presence of Christ, in the ordinances, and under the ministry of the word, she lets them know of it, to encourage them in their work, and that they, with her, might bless the Lord for it: or else, the daughters of Jerusalem, whom she adjures in the following verse; who are persons newly converted, to whom she directs her discourse, and gives them this account of her experience, that she might allure them to the ordinances, and encourage them to walk in the ways of Christ, as well as engage them to join with her in giving thanks to him for the reception of so great a mercy; which is very agreeable to David's practice, in Psal. xxxiv. 2, 3, "My soul shall make her boast in the Lord: the humble shall hear thereof, and be glad. O magnify the Lord with me, and let us exalt his name together."

Verse 7. *I charge you, O ye daughters of Jerusalem, by the roes and by the hinds of the field, that ye stir not up, nor awake my love, till he please.*

There is some difficulty in these words concerning the person speaking, who it is, whether Christ or the church: interpreters are divided about it; and there are reasons, not to be despised, given on both sides.

Some think that they are the words of the church, charging the daughters of Jerusalem to give no disturbance to Christ, her love, and cause him to depart from her, with whom she now was, enjoying sweet communion with him; which seems to be the sense of our translators: and this sense of the words bids fair, if we consider, 1. The person to whom these words are spoken, "the daughters of Jerusalem;" who were the friends of the church, "the virgins, her companions;" who attended and waited upon her: Christ is represented in this Song as having his friends with him; and the church, as having hers with her, and that in allusion to a nuptial entertainment; and therefore it seems most reasonable that she should speak to her friends, and not his.

2. In all other places, where these words are used, they seem to be the words of the church, and not of Christ; see chap. iii. 5, and viii. 4. 3. The manner of speech shows it, which is not by way of command, which is proper to Christ; but by way of adjuration, or giving a charge with an oath, which is usual with the church of these persons; for which, besides the places before-mentioned, see chap. v. 8. 4. If we also consider the matter, it suits well with the church's language; the character, "my love," is very applicable to Christ, he being the Person whom her soul loved; the charge that this love should not be stirred up, but at pleasure, agrees with Christ, who is endued with sovereignty, and ought to be at his own liberty to stay with, or remove from his people when he pleases. 5. It suits with the context and scope of the place: the church was now in Christ's arms, where she lay with a great deal of pleasure and satisfaction; and being willing to have communion with Christ continued, and not interrupted by these persons, she solemnly adjures them after this manner; which carefulness and solicitude of her's seems also to be the scope and design of those other places, chap. iii. 5, and viii. 4.

But there are others who think that they are the words of Christ, and not without some reason; for, 1. It was the church, who having solace and ease in Christ's arms, was fallen asleep there, and not he in hers; and therefore, that she might have no disturbance, he charges the daughters of Jerusalem by no means to awake her, till she herself thought meet. 2. The church in this Song, when she gives Christ a character, which is expressive of her love, does not use this word אהבה, *ahabah*, love, which is of the feminine gender; but another, דודי, *dodi*, my beloved, or well-beloved, which is of the masculine; but Christ makes use of this same word in giving a loving title to his church, as in chap. vii. 6; and therefore they seem to be the words of Christ speaking concerning and in behalf of his church. 3. Both the word אהבה, *ahabah*, love, and תחפץ, *techphatz*, which is in construction with, and is rendered *he please*, are both of the feminine gender, and so best agree with her,[q] and may be rendered, "that ye stir not up nor awake my love till she please." 4. The following words seem to confirm this sense, "the voice of my beloved!" What voice was this she heard? Why, the charge he gave to the daughters of Jerusalem not to disturb her; which discovered so much love and goodness in him, and her heart was so much affected with it, that she breaks out into this pathetic exclamation, "the voice of my beloved!"

And now though the former sense is not to be despised, yet I must confess I chiefly incline to the latter, and having thus considered whose words they are, I shall now consider the words

---

[q] So the Cabalistic doctors interpret the word of malcuth, or the bride Lexic. Cabal. p. 43, 44.

themselves; in which may be observed,

I. The charge given; not to "stir up nor awake *the* love till he or she please."

II. The persons to whom this charge is given; "the daughters of Jerusalem."

III. The manner in which it is delivered; "I charge you by the roes and by the hinds of the field."

I. Here is a solemn charge given not to "stir up nor awake the love," or "this love," the well-known love,[r] "till he, or she please;" which I have observed may be understood, either as the church's charge to these persons not to disturb Christ, in whose company she now was; or else, as Christ's charge to them not to awake the church, who was now sleeping in his arms; and both these senses being pressed with such reasons as have been before observed, I shall consider the words both ways: and then if we consider them as the church's charge, not to disturb Christ her love, they will lead us to observe, 1. That Christ is the object of the church's love, and of all true believers; there is none in heaven or on earth, that has so great a share in their love as he has; they love him with all their hearts and souls, and above all things else whatever; and that so sincerely and unfeignedly, that they can appeal, with Peter, to the Searcher of hearts, and say, "Lord, thou knowest all things, thou knowest that I love thee;" which arises from the discoveries of Christ's love to them, and the views which they have of his loveliness; and is still more and more increased, by having nearer communion, and more intimacy and acquaintance with him. 2. That Christ sleeps and takes his rest among his church and people; this is manifest from her carefulness not to have him stirred up and awaked; the Lord is sometimes said to sleep, and not to awake, when he does not arise to deliver his people from danger, or out of the hands of their enemies; see Psal. xxxv. 22, 23, and xliv. 22, 23, and sometimes when he grants his presence to them and communion with them, as here: the church is Christ's resting-place, where he "rests in his love," towards his people, grants his presence to them, converses with them, and "lies all night betwixt their breasts." 3. That Christ may be disturbed, and raised up from hence by the sins of his people; their vexatious contentions one with another, their unfriendly and ungrateful carriage to him, often provoke him to remove from them; they grieve his Spirit, and cause him to hide his face, which is no ways for their honour or comfort.

4. That believers should be very careful that they do not provoke Christ to depart from them; and therefore should watch against the very first motions of sin, and "abstain from all appearance of it;" for sinful thoughts, as well as sinful actions, are an abomination to him, and lead on to the commission of them; and it is the desire of believers under the influences and by the assistance of the Spirit of grace, so to do; which shows that communion with Christ is highly valued by them, and what they would not have by any means interrupted. 5. That communion which souls have with Christ, is entirely at his pleasure; they cannot have it, when and as long as they please, but when and as long as he pleases; for "when he giveth quietness, who then can make trouble? so when he hideth his face, who then can behold him?" as Elihu says, Job xxxiv. 29. The discoveries of Christ's love and grace to his people; the grants of his presence to them, and communion with them, as much depend upon his sovereign will and pleasure, as the first actings of his grace towards and upon sinners do: he may withdraw from his people without any provocation, as he sometimes does; for he is a God that "hideth his face from the house of Jacob;" and is not obliged to give any reason for it, but his own sovereign well; though he always designs their good, and his own glory by it; yet he is oftener caused to arise, and remove from them, through their carnality, lukewarmness, ingratitude, and unbelief.

But if we consider the words as the charge of Christ to the daughters of Jerusalem, not to disturb the church, then we may observe, 1. That the church is Christ's love; she is frequently called so by him in this Song, as in chap. i. 9, 15, and ii. 10, and in other places: she has the greatest share in his affections, as he has in hers, and has given the fullest proofs of his love of her; which put it beyond all dispute, that she is the object of it, and will always continue so, notwithstanding all her failings and infirmities. 2. That the church sleeps and takes her rest in Christ's arms; there is a sleepiness or drowsiness which attends God's children, that is a sinful one; when they fold their own arms together, and do not lie in Christ's; in this frame was the church, chap. iii. 1, and v. 2; but this here is a rest which Christ gives, a sleep which he brings his into, when he puts under his everlasting arms, and embraces them in his bosom; for "so he giveth his beloved sleep," Psal. cxxvii. 2, 3. That Christ values the company and conversation of his children: these are "the excellent in the earth, in whom is all his delight;" he loves to see their persons, and hear their voice; the actings of their grace upon him are exceeding delightful to him, and therefore would not have them be disturbed, hence it can never be a work well-pleasing to Christ, for any to sadden the hearts, lessen the joys, and weaken the faith of God's children. 4. That Christ would not have his church's peace disturbed; though it often-

---

[r] So lovers are frequently called amor and amores, love and loves; vid. Theocrit. Idyll. 2. and Ovid. Briseis Achilli, v. 12. Plauti Curculio, act. 2. sc. 3. v. 78. Miles, act. 4. sc. 8. v. 67. Mostel. Arg. v. 1. Persa, Arg. v. 4. Poenulus, act. 5. sc. 3. v. 42.

times is by " quarrelsome and contentious persons," who are always uneasy themselves, and endeavour to make others so; by " carnal professors, whose lives and conversations are wounding and grieving to pious souls;" by " errors and heresies," which, " springing up" in churches, trouble some, and defile others; and often by " inward corruptions," those domestic enemies, which are of all the worst and most afflicting; as well as by Satan, that unwearied enemy, who, though he cannot devour, yet will disturb; but whether this be done one way or other, it is no ways pleasing and grateful to Christ. 5. Though believers, when under the gracious influences of the blessed Spirit, are desirous of communion with Christ; and if they might have it as long as they please, they would have it always, and say, as the disciples did, " Lord, it is good for us to be here;" yet when they begin to be sleepy and drowsy, they grow careless and indifferent about it; which justly provokes Christ to deprive them of it. So much for the charge itself.

II. The persons to whom this charge is given, are the " daughters of Jerusalem;" by whom we are to understand young converts, as has been observed in chap. i. 5. Now these are very apt to disturb Christ by their impatience; who, like new-born babes, are unwilling to wait till their food is prepared for them; till Christ's own time is come, when he will more fully reveal himself unto them, and give them large discoveries of his love: and also by their frowardness, who, when their food is prepared for them, grow sullen and will not eat it; and, like Rachel of old, " refuse to be comforted;" or else, through " the weakness of their faith, and living upon their frames," which young converts are very apt to do; for no longer than they have the discoveries of Christ's love, and sensible communion with him, can they believe their interest in him; and therefore, like froward and impatient children, or poor weaklings, give him a great deal of disturbance: and so taking them as the words of the church, she seems here to act the part of a mother; and charges these her children to be still and quiet, and give her loving Husband no disturbance, whilst she enjoyed his delightful company.

Moreover, these daughters of Jerusalem, or young converts, are very apt to give the church disturbance; and therefore Christ may be represented as charging them not to do it: this they sometimes do through weakness, not being able to bear the doctrines of the Gospel; such some of the Corinthians were, who were " babes in Christ," and therefore the apostle fed them with milk, and not with meat, for they " were not able to bear it;" by reason of which, many contentions, divisions, and disturbances, were raised in that church: as also, sometimes through "ignorance of Gospel-order," not being so well versed in, and acquainted with the rules, laws, and ordinances of Christ's house; so that oftentimes, for want of knowledge in Gospel-discipline, as well as in Gospel-doctrine, they give disturbance to the church of Christ; all which, Christ knowing full well, gives them this solemn charge.

III. The manner in which this charge is given, which is very solemn and awful; it is with an oath, " I adjure you, or I cause you to swear by the roes and by the hinds of the field, that ye give no disturbance to my love; creatures which ran in fields, forests, and woods, and were their native places.' The meaning is, not as if either Christ or his church swore by those creatures; for swearing by heaven or earth, or by any creature in them, is condemned by Christ, Matt. v. 34—37; an oath ought not to be taken in trifling cases, nor in any other name than in the name of God; which perhaps is the reason why the Targum thus paraphrases the words here: " I adjure you, O ye congregation of Israel, by the Lord of hosts," or Tzebaoth, which same word is used for *roes* here, " and by the strengths or fortresses of the land of Israel," &c. And either, 1. The words may be paraphrased thus, I charge you, who are among the roes and hinds of the fields, you daughters of Jerusalem, who are shepherdesses, and keep your flocks where roes and hinds skip and play; or who love to hunt them, and delight in such exercises;† I charge you, that you give my love no disturbance. Or else, 2. Thus I charge you, O ye daughters of Jerusalem, that ye remain or abide with the roes and hinds of the field, so Junius; mind your own business, keep your flocks, stand without whilst I and my love enjoy each other's delightful conversation, without any interruption or molestation from you. Or, 3. Those creatures, the roes and hinds, it may be, are called in as witnesses to this solemn charge, and to be produced against them, if ever they should break it; as to which sometimes heaven and earth, animate and inanimate creatures, are called in scripture; see Deut. xxx. 19, Josh. xxiv. 27. Or, 4. This adjuration or charge is made by all that is dear, the roes and hinds being pleasant and lovely creatures, as in Prov. v. 19; as if he or she should say, I charge you, O ye lovely daughters of Jerusalem, by the hinds and roes, which for beauty and loveliness are like to you, as R. Aben Ezra observes; if, O ye lovely ones, ye have any love for me, I beg, I earnestly intreat of you, that you will cause neither me nor my love any interruption. Or, 5. It may be considered as a severe threatening to those persons, if they should be unmindful of the charge given; and it is as if he should say, I swear, that if you stir up, or awake my love, that you shall be food as common to all, as the roes and hinds are; to which purpose as R. Sol. Jarchi's gloss: and

---

* Cerva silvicultrix. Catullus, v. 64, 72. † Virginibus Tyriis mos est gestare pharetram, Virgil. Æneid. l. 1.

these creatures being very swift ones, may note the suddenness and swiftness of those judgments which should come upon them in case of disobedience. Or, 6. The sense may be this: that as ye would, O ye daughters of Jerusalem, be cautious how you start those timorous creatures,ᵃ the roes and hinds; so would I have you be as cautious how you stir up and awake my love, which is as easily and as quickly done. Or, 7, and lastly, I charge you, for the sake of these roes and hinds, the Gentiles and nations of the world, that ye do not disturb the peace of my church, by fomenting and increasing divisions in it; and so cause my name to be dishonoured, my ways to be spoken evil of, and me to depart from you; but rather keep peace within, and " walk in wisdom towards them that are without;" and by so doing, you will gratify me, and allure these Gentiles to your society and fellowship; who otherwise, like timorous roes and hinds, will be frighted and scared from it.

Verse 8. *The voice of my beloved! behold! he cometh leaping upon the mountains, skipping upon the hills.*

THOUGH there was some difficulty in understanding the former words, whose they were, whether Christ's or the church's; yet it is certain that these are spoken by the church, who hearing Christ, her beloved, give such a solemn charge to the daughters of Jerusalem, not to awake her, is so affected with his love to her, and care of her, that she could not forbear breaking out into this pathetic exclamation upon it; and not only takes notice of this, but also of some other instances of his love and regard unto her; or else it may be supposed, that the sweet and comfortable communion which she had before enjoyed with Christ, mentioned in the preceding verses, had been for some time interrupted, he having withdrawn himself, and she being fallen into a spiritual drowsiness; but he returning again to her, and calling her out of this state, as in ver. 10, she awakes, and takes notice of the several steps and procedures of his grace, and records several instances of his love unto her; two of which are mentioned in these words.

I. He calls unto her, and she hears and knows his voice, and says, It is " the voice of my beloved."

II. He not only calls, but comes, and she spies him coming; the manner of which she describes to be, " leaping upon the mountains, skipping upon the hills."

I. The first thing she remarks is his voice, with which she seems to be wonderfully affected, " the voice of my beloved!" Some Jewish writersʷ interpret this of the voice of the Messiah; by which may be meant, the Gospel of Christ, in which he speaks both to saints and sinners; and which has a virtue and efficacy in it to quicken dead sinners, and comfort living saints; for though it is powerful, yet alluring; though full of majesty, yet soft and charming, and makes delightful music in the ears of believers; concerning which may be observed,

1st. That the voice of Christ is known and distinguished by believers from the voice of others: the church was capable of doing this, and therefore says, " the voice of my beloved!" she could know it to be his voice, and distinguish it from another's, even though but just raised out of her sleep; nay, she could do this when she was as it were between sleeping and waking; when indulging herself in drowsiness and security, as in chap. v. 2, and thus Christ says, John x. 4, 5, of all his sheep, that they not only heard his voice, but knew it, and therefore followed him and not strangers; for, says he, " the voice of strangers they know not." Now if any one should ask how Christ's voice can be known and distinguished from others; I answer, 1. By the majesty of it; by this we know the scriptures to be the word of God, there appearing such a shine of majesty in them, as does not in any other writings; and hereby we know the Gospel to be the voice of Christ, and can distinguish it from that which was not so: Christ speaks in the Gospel, " as one having authority, and not as the scribes;" there is a vast difference between " the words which man's wisdom teacheth," and those " which the Holy Ghost teacheth;" the one are low, mean, dead, and lifeless; the other not only come with evidence, and " the demonstration of the Spirit and of power" to believers, but even fasten convictions of the original and authority of them upon the minds of wicked men; see 1 Cor. xiv. 24, 25. 2. By the power and efficacy of it; the Gospel which is Christ's voice, comes " not in word only, but also in power, and in the Holy Ghost;" and so not only reaches the ear, but also the heart; it opens blind eyes, unstops deaf ears, quickens dead sinners, awakes sleepy, and comforts distressed saints, and is in fine, " the power of God unto salvation, to every one that believes." 3. By the spiritual food and divine refreshment it affords to believers; who find Christ's word and eat it, and it becomes " the joy and rejoicing " of their hearts; that which is not Christ's word and Gospel, is like the chaff to this wheat; and that which is opposite to those " wholesome words of our Lord Jesus," instead of nourishing and refreshing, as these do, " eat as doth a canker." 4. Believers know this voice of Christ, and can distinguish it from others, by its bringing them to him, and not sending them from him; that voice which sends

---

ᵃ —Pavidos formidine cervos terret, Ovid. Fasti, l. 5. v. 173. Formidantes cervos, Ovid. Metamorph. l. 15. fab 43. Timidi damæ, Virgil. Bucol. eclog. 8. v. 28. and Georgic. l. 3. prope finem. Pavidæ damæ, Horat. Carmin. l. 1. ode 2. v. 11. hence κραδιη ελαφοιο, cor cervi, Homer. Iliad. l. 1. v. 225. ʷ Pesikta in Yalkcut in loc.

me to my own righteousness, and not to Christ's, for acceptance with God, and justification before him; which sends me to my tears of repentance, and not to Christ's blood, for pardon and cleansing, can never be the voice of Christ; that voice which bids me keep off from Christ, till I have prepared and qualified myself for him, by my own acts of humiliation and obedience, is contrary to that voice of Christ which bids me come to him as a poor, vile, filthy, and perishing sinner in myself, without him, and venture on him for life and salvation; and therefore that cannot be the voice of Christ: thus may it be known from the voice of a stranger. 5. Believers have the Spirit of Christ, who is "the Spirit of truth," whose work and office it is to "guide them into all truth," and to enable them to distinguish truth from error; and this he accordingly does, for he "searches the deep things of God," and reveals them to the saints, and abides in them as a "spirit of wisdom and revelation, in the knowledge of Christ." 6. They know it by the scriptures of truth, which they diligently search, and by which they examine every doctrine: and whatsoever sound or language is disagreeable thereunto, they reject, as not being the voice of Christ; "to the law and to the testimony" they appeal; and whosoever does not "speak according to this word," they judge "it is because there is no light in them," Isa. viii. 20

2ndly. It may be observed that this voice of Christ, as it may be known and distinguished by believers from the voice of others, so it is exceeding pleasant and delightful to them. The church seems to speak of it as being so to her; and no wonder it was, for it is, 1. A voice of love, grace, and mercy to poor sinners; it is not like the law, a voice of terror, wrath, and fury; no, it speaks peace and pardon to rebellious creatures, and publishes life and salvation to lost sinners. Christ came leaping and skipping like a roe or a young hart; or, as it is said of Naphtali, like "a hind let loose, who giveth goodly words;" and no wonder then that his voice was so delightful. 2. It was also the voice of her beloved one, who dearly loved her, and had given incontestible proofs of it, and whom she loved with all her heart and soul; and therefore his voice, as well as his countenance and person, was sweet unto her; it was the voice of the bridegroom, and therefore need not be thought strange that the bride, as well as her friends, should rejoice at it.

3rdly. We may learn from hence, that Christ's voice may be heard before he is seen: the church first heard his voice, and then she saw him come leaping and skipping over the mountains and hills; and this indeed is one way by which souls are brought to a sight of Christ, viz., by the preaching of the gospel; nay, believers, even when they are without sights of Christ, and sensible communion with him; yet, in hearing the word, can distinguish Christ's voice, and can set to their seals that it is his, though perhaps they cannot immediately take in the comfort of it.

4thly. Believers would have others know Christ's voice as well as they; the church knew this to be the voice of Christ; but she is not content with the knowledge of it herself, and therefore speaks of it for the information of the daughters of Jerusalem. But,

II. She not only heard his voice, but also spied him coming to her, though at some distance; and perhaps as soon as ever she had heard his voice, or the noise of his feet, as R. Aben Ezra explains it, she lifted up her eyes, or turned herself, and saw him upon the march towards her. Here must be considered, 1st. What is meant by his coming. 2ndly. The manner of it, "leaping upon the mountains, and skipping upon the hills." 3rdly. Why she prefixes an *ecce*, or a *behold* unto it; behold he cometh," &c.

1st. It will be proper to consider what is here meant by Christ's coming: which must be understood either of his coming in the flesh, which the church had then a distant sight of, and is since accomplished: this coming of Christ from heaven, and out of his Father's bosom, into this sinful world, was not by a change of place, but by assumption of nature; whose great end in it was to save sinners, which is entirely answered: now, as this had been long promised, frequently prophesied of, and nothing was more earnestly expected, and passionately wished and prayed for, so nothing was more delightful to the Old-Testament saints, than the near approach of it, nor more welcome than when it was accomplished. Or else by his coming here, may be meant his spiritual coming; for though he withdraws and absents himself from his people for a time, yet he will not leave them altogether, and always comfortless, but will come unto them; and the church's spying him as coming, supposes that he was at some distance from her, with respect to sensible communion or enjoyment of his presence, though not with respect, either to union or affection; for in this sense she is always near unto him: and also that he was upon the return to her, whom faith spied, though at a distance, which is agreeable enough to the nature of it; this filled her soul with joy and pleasure: for even distant sights of Christ are pleasant, though his nearer approaches give a greater satisfaction; his presence is always welcome to a believer, and there is a great deal of reason for it: for he always brings something along with him, and never comes empty handed; yea, never visits without leaving something behind him.

2ndly. The manner of his coming is expressed by "leaping upon the mountains, skipping upon the hills:" the allusion is to the leaping of a roe or a young hart, as in the next verse, remarkable for leaping, even one just yeaned;[x] so a young hart is described as leaping to its dam;[y] the leap of one of these creatures is very extraordinary:[z] which, if understood of Christ's coming in the flesh, shows, 1. That there were many difficulties in the way, and such that were comparable to hills and mountains: the greatness of his person was no inconsiderable one; nay, such an one, that it could never have been thought that it should have been got over, had not God himself declared it should be; and we have undeniable evidence that it has been; for God to become man, the Creator a creature, and the Word to be made flesh, and dwell among us, is such an amazing stoop of Deity, and surprising instance of divine condescension, that it is even the wonder of men and angels: also the greatness of the work he was to do, when come, was no small difficulty; here was a broken law to fulfil, angry justice to satisfy, sin to atone for, the wrath of God to bear, many enemies to grapple with, and a cursed death to undergo; and all this for the vilest of miscreants, the worst of creatures, whose characters are sinners, ungodly persons, and such who were enemies to him in their minds by wicked works. Yet, 2. These difficulties which seem insuperable to us, were easily surmounted by him: he leaped and skipped over those mountains and hills, which all became a plain before our great Zerubbabel; what appear mountains to us, were mole-hills to him; therefore he readily engaged, and voluntarily undertook before time to assume human nature, which in time he did with the utmost cheerfulness; and showed his eager desires after it, long before his incarnation, in often appearing in a human form; and when he was actually become incarnate, how eager was he for the accomplishment of the work he came about! how easily did he break through all difficulties, discouragements, and impediments, that lay in his way! and nothing could stop him till he could say the work was finished which he undertook; and thus, with the utmost swiftness and celerity, he came " leaping upon the mountains, and skipping upon the hills." If we understand it of his spiritual coming, it shows, 1. That there are impediments in the way of Christ's visiting his people; such as their unbelief, carnality, and lukewarmness, their want of faith in him, and affection to him, their backslidings from him, and ingratitude towards him: yet all these mountains and hills he leaps and skips over, resolving that nothing shall separate him and them. 2. That Christ's coming to his people in a way of grace, is very conspicuous to them; the eye of faith spies him at a distance, as it were, upon the mountains; and also, that it is very glorious and beautiful; for if " beautiful upon the mountains are the feet of him that bringeth glad tidings," much more beautiful must

the feet of Christ, or Christ himself be, when he comes and grants his gracious presence to his people. 3. It denotes the speediness, swiftness, and readiness of Christ, to help his people; he makes haste and delays not, and therefore is said to leap and skip; his heart is set upon it; and nothing shall prevent him, though mountains and hills are between them.

3rdly. She prefixes an *ecce*, a *behold*, to this coming of Christ unto her; which, if applied to his coming in the flesh, may be considered, either, 1. As a note of admiration; as in Isa. vii. 14, " Behold a virgin shall conceive and bear a Son:" the incarnation of Christ, though it was confirmed to the church by promises, types, and prophecies, yet was so strange and stupendous a thing, that nothing but faith could receive it, and that with the most profound admiration. 2. As a note of attention or asseveration; and so is used by her to stir up the daughters of Jerusalem to an observation of his near approach, and to encourage them in their faith and expectation of it, as well as that they might participate of her joy in the views thereof; see Zech. ix. 9.

Again, if we understand it of Christ's spiritual coming; this is, (1). Matter of admiration, and therefore may well have an *ecce*, a *behold*, prefixed to it; we have all, who know any thing of this, reason to say with Judas, not Iscariot, in John xiv. 22, " Lord, how is it that thou wilt manifest thyself to us, and not unto the world?" (2). It is also worthy of observation : Christ's special grace and favour in this regard ought not to be carelessly overlooked; but we should take notice of it with thankfulness, and wonder at it ourselves, and remark it to others, that they may join with us in magnifying the Lord on such an occasion, as the Psalmist did, in Psal. xxxiv. 1—3; who, as the church here, was so affected with the loving-kindness of the Lord, in this instance of it, that he tells it to others for this purpose.

Verse 9. *My beloved is like a roe, or a young hart: behold he standeth behind our wall, he looketh forth at the windows, shewing himself through the lattice.*

THE church continues her discourse concerning Christ, and takes notice of the several steps he took in manifesting himself unto her.

1. She compares him to " a roe or a young hart."

2. Declares the several gradual discoveries of himself unto her.

I. She compares him to " a roe or a young hart;" which seems to be occasioned by his swift and speedy approach unto her, mentioned in the former verse; for these are creatures remarkable for their swiftness;[a] see 2 Sam. ii. 18. and many have reference to Christ's celerity in

---

[x] Vid. Dionys. Prieg. p. 843, 844. [y] Νεβρος αλοιτο, &c. Theocrit. Idyll. 8. prope finem. [z] The hart is said to leap sixty feet at a leap, Bochart. Hierozoic. par. 1. 1. 5. v. 17. col. 882.

[a] Cervi veloces, Virgil Æneid. l. 4. v. 253. Cerva æripes, swift as the air, Ibid. l. 6. prope finem.

his coming in the flesh; who as soon as ever "the fulness of time" was come, made no delay, but immediately clothed himself with human nature, in order to dispatch, with the utmost speed, the work which he had agreed to do; and with no less speed does he haste to the assistance of his people, when under trials, desertions, temptations, and afflictions, and shows himself to be "a very present help in trouble:" likewise his second coming to raise the dead, judge the world, reward his saints, and punish his enemies, will be equally as swift and sudden; for which reason it is compared, Matt. xxiv. 29, to "the lightning which cometh out of the east," and in a moment, in the twinkling of an eye, shineth even unto the west: but besides the swiftness of these creatures, Christ may be compared to them, or be said to be like to them on some other accounts; as, 1. For their pleasantness and lovingness; they are pleasant and loving creatures, as appears from Prov. v. 19. Christ is pleasant and desirable in his person to his people, being "white and ruddy, and the chiefest among ten thousand;" he is loving in his carriage and deportment to them, and has given the most undeniable proofs of the reality, sincerity, strength, and immutability of his love, in shedding his blood, and by giving his life for them. 2. For their choiceness and excellency, as R. Sol. Jarchi observes; young roes and harts being the most choice and excellent: Christ is so in his nature, Person, office, people, and ordinances; he is so in the esteem of his Father, and in the esteem of men and angels; for though he is disallowed by some, yet he is highly valued by others. 3. For the antipathy there is between these creatures and serpents: historians[b] report of them, that they search out the lurking-places of serpents, and not being able to come at them in their holes, do, by the very breath of their nostrils, draw them out from thence,[c] and then trample upon them, tear them in pieces, and eat them: this may in some measure represent that enmity there is between that old serpent Satan, and Christ Jesus, the seed of the woman, who was manifested in human nature, to break his head, and destroy his works, which he has accordingly done. It is also farther reported of the hart,[d] that after eating serpents, it grows prodigiously thirsty, which occasions dreadful cries and lamentations, and violent pantings after the water-brooks; to which an allusion is made in Psalm xlii. 1; and yet knowing, by an instinct in nature, that it is dangerous to drink until it has digested them, forbears a while. Thus Christ, when he destroyed that old serpent the Devil, sustained the weight of his Father's wrath, which occasioned a bloody sweat in the garden, piteous moans upon the cross, a violent consumption of the radical moisture; so that his "strength was dried up like a potsherd," and his tongue cleaved to his jaws," with the violent thirst that was upon him; such an one he had, as is manifest from those words of his, when suffering upon the cross, *I thirst*. Moreover, it is reported in Lybia,[e] where there is a great number of serpents, that when they see a hart lying alone, will, in great numbers at once, attack him; some wrapping themselves about his feet, others about his horns, his neck, and belly, and bite him dreadfully: upon which he gets up and runs about, here and there in great distress, but at length throws himself upon his back; some he rubs to death, and others he devours, and then hastens to the water-brooks to cleanse and refresh himself: thus Christ was beset by all the infernal powers, yet spoiled them all, got an entire victory over them, and now enjoys the glories of it. These were creatures fit for food, and were allowed to be so by the Levitical law; naturalists say,[f] that by their being hunted, their flesh becomes softer: Christ is the Bread of Life," and the "hidden manna;" he is very agreeable food for souls; his "flesh is meat indeed," and his "blood is drink indeed;" and by reason of the sufferings which he underwent in our nature, is become very suitable food for faith. 5. These creatures are long-lived ones: it is reported,[g] that Alexander the Great, having taken some of them, put golden chains about them, with which they were found, covered with fat, a hundred years afterwards, and scarce any appearance of old age in them. Christ lives and will live for ever; he died once for the sins of men, but will never die more; "I am he," says he, "that liveth and was dead, and behold, I am alive for evermore," Rev. i. 18; for such reasons as these, and perhaps some others, Christ may be said to be "like a roe or a young hart." The Septuagint here adds, "upon the mountains of Bethel," which is not in the Hebrew text.

II. She declares the several gradual discoveries of himself unto her. In the former verse, she tells us, that she first heard his voice, and then saw him come "leaping upon the mountains," and "skipping upon the hills;" and here she observes some nearer approaches of him to her. 1st. She says, that he stood behind their *wall*. 2ndly. Looked forth at the *windows*. 3rdly. Showed himself through the *lattice*.

1st, She says, that he stood behind their wall; by which is meant, either. 1. The incarnation of Christ, whose glorious Deity was covered and hid under the wall of our humanity;[h] which is called our wall, because he was made partaker of the same flesh and blood with us. Or, 2. The walls

---

[b] Plin. l. 8. c. 32. Ælian. de animal. l. 2. c. 9. Solin. Polyhist. c. 31. So Theodoret. in loc. [c] Hence the hart has the name of ελαφος, according to Plutarch. de Solert. Animal. p. 976. [d] Frantz. Hist. animal. sacr. par. l. c. 15. [e] Frantz. ibid. [f] Ibid. [g] Plin. l. 3. c. 32. Solin. c. 31. Vid. Pausan. Arcad. sive l. 8. p. 472. Hence cervina senectus, Juvenal, satyr. 14. v. 251. [h] So Isidore in loc.

of our hearts, of which we read, Jer. iv. 19, "I am pained at my very heart;" in the Hebrew it is, "I am pained at the walls of my heart;" such are our sins and transgressions,[l] which are as so many walls of separation between Christ and us, particularly unbelief, lukewarmness, carnal reasonings, &c., behind which Christ stands; and which, by the mighty power of his grace and Spirit, he batters down and demands an entrance. Or else, 3. The ceremonial law, which the apostle calls, Eph. ii. 14, "the middle wall of partition:" this separated between Jew and Gentile, and was made up of many hard and difficult precepts; behind this wall Christ stood under the Old Testament dispensation, and showed himself to his people in types and figures, though but darkly and obscurely in comparison of the Gospel revelation. Or else, 4. By it may be meant the church's defence and protection: the church is a city, and a walled one; God himself is a wall of fire round about it; and has also appointed salvation for walls and bulwarks: his ministering servants, he has not only set upon Zion's walls, but has made them as walls of brass unto them; he has set them both for the defence of the church of the Gospel; now Christ's standing behind her wall, may show that he is ready to protect his people, redress their grievances, and revenge himself upon their enemies. Or rather, 5. In general it shows, that Christ was nearer unto her than he had been before; she then saw him, but at some distance, upon the hills and mountains afar off; but now he was come nearer, even to her very home, and stands behind her wall, being desirous to enter in; but still there was some distance of communion, a wall between them, and a wall of her own building; it was owing to her own infidelity, carnality, and sleepiness, that Christ stood at a distance, and drew no nearer than he was; and yet notwithstanding this, he stands waiting as it were for an invitation to enter in.

2udly. She takes notice of a farther discovery of himself: he comes from behind her wall and looks in at the windows, to see in what posture his church was, and how things were managed in his house. The allusion is to the quicksighted roe or young hart; which, as it is remarkable for its swiftness, as in ver. 8; so for the sharpness of its sight; Pliny says,[k] it is never dim sighted; it has its name *dorcas* in Greek, from its sharp sight.[l] By *windows*, we are not to understand the windows of the heavens, through which the Lord looks down upon his people, and beholds them under all their afflictions, and in their several cases and circumstances, as some of the Jewish writers[m] do; but rather, the ordinances of the Gospel, which are that to the church, as windows are to a house, they let in light to souls; which windows, for the glory and excellency of them, are said, Isa. liv. 12, to be as gates. Christ looks forth at these, and shows himself in his glory and beauty to his saints; even as kings and great men look forth at the windows to be seen in their majesty and splendour by their people; also in at these windows Christ looks, and takes notice how his children behave themselves under the ordinances: with what reverence and attention, faith and affection, they hear the word: and in what becoming manner they carry themselves at the table of the Lord; and there is not the least motion of the heart that escapes his notice.

3rdly. She takes notice of his showing himself through the lattices; which seems to attend a more clear and glorious discovery of himself in the means and ordinances of the Gospel; though indeed, our clearest sights of Christ here, are but as through a glass darkly, through windows and lattices, and not face to face, as they will be in another world: and it may be observed from hence, that unless Christ shows himself unto us, we can get no sight of him; for "when he hideth his face, who then can behold him?" as also, that Christ usually discovers himself in the use of means through the ordinances; and therefore these are to be observed carefully, and attended on constantly. Moreover, a behold is prefixed to all these gradual manifestations of himself; which shows us, that Christ's discoveries of himself to his people are exceeding wonderful and ravishing: a glimpse of him behind the wall, is a surprising instance of his grace, much more his looking forth at the windows; and his showing or flourishing[n] himself, in all his beauty and glory, through the lattices, as the word signifies; this is enough to throw us into the greatest raptures and eestacies of mind, and fill us with a joy unspeakable and full of glory.

Verse 10. *My beloved spake, and said unto me, Rise up, my love, my fair one, and come away.*

CHRIST having made so near an approach to his church, as to come to her very wall, nay, to look in at the windows, and show himself to her through the lattice, calls aloud to her to arise from her sleep, and come away with him; which she distinctly heard and understood, and therefore relates the very words he said to her which she might be capable of; for if she could say it was the voice of her beloved, when he was a great way off, at a distance from her upon the hills and mountains: she must needs know and understand distinctly what he said now when he was so near her. These then are the words of the church, giving an account of what her beloved said to her, when he made her this

---

[i] So R. Alshech in loc. c. 11. [l] Απο τη οξυ δορκειν, Origen in loc. so Theodoret in loc. [m] R. Sol. Jarchi, and R. Aben Ezra in loc. and so Lyra. [k] Nat. Hist. l. 28. [n] Efflorescens, Junius; so Ainsworth, Piscator, and Michaelis. מציץ proprie de plantis dicitur, quum id proferunt, quod florem præcedit, Mercer. in loc.

kind and indulgent visit: in which may be considered,

I. The preface to the following discourse; "my beloved spake, and said unto me."

II. The exhortation which he presses a compliance to rise up, and come away."

III. Some affectionate titles which he gives her: "my love, my fair one."

I. The preface which she makes to this discourse of Christ to her, of which she gives an account in this and the following verses, is, "my beloved spake, and said unto me:" in which may be considered, 1. The person speaking, "my beloved;" which title has been frequently met with and explained, particularly in chap. i. 13. 2. The mode of expression in this preface, which in the Hebrew text is thus, "my beloved answered, and said unto me;"º which mode of speaking is frequently made use of by Christ in the New Testament; and perhaps is an hebraism in all those places where it is there used; but here it seems to be expressive of an answer to a secret petition of hers. There is undoubtedly such a thing as mental, as well as vocal prayer, in which the desires of the soul are put up to God; and that under the influences of the Spirit, who maketh intercession for the saints, with groanings which cannot be uttered: and such mental petitions and desires are heard, regarded, and answered by Christ Jesus, who is privy to the secret motions of our souls God-ward, and understands full well the language of a sigh and groan; which shows him to be the omniscient God; gives a manifest proof of his Deity; as well as evidences his tender regard to his people, and his readiness to help them under all their distresses. 3. The notice which she takes of it. As Christ is not always mute, but opens his mouth, and returns suitable answers, gives proper directions and instruction, and speaks peace and consolation to his people; so they are not always deaf, but have ears to hear, they listen to what he says; and as they can distinguish his voice from another's, so they regard it above all others: what he speaks unto them, is received with much pleasure and delight; his words are not harsh and austere, but full of love, grace, pity, and compassion. Now it may be observed from hence that there is such a thing as souls being satisfied when Christ speaks to them, and that it is not a delusion; the church knew that it was her beloved that spake, and not another; and that he spake, to her in particular, "my beloved spake, and said unto me:" and so every believer may, in some measure, know when Christ speaks unto him, and that it is not a delusion; as when it make us love Christ more, and quickens us to our duty; or when it discovers Christ's love to us, and our interest in him; when it excites our faith, our hope, and joy, has a tendency to promote holiness of heart and life, puts us upon glorifying Christ, and makes us more active and vigorous in his service; all which seem to be the effect of Christ's speaking to the church here. But,

II. What Christ says unto her is by way of exhortation; which consists of two parts. 1st. To rise up. 2ndly. To come away.

1st. He exhorts her to rise up, and that in the most tender and affectionate manner, as will be observed hereafter; which supposes, either that she was asleep upon a bed of carnal security, indulging herself in ease and sloth; or else, that she was cast down in her soul under a sense of sin, and for want of his presence, sitting in darkness, without the light of his countenance, bemoaning her sorrowful and disconsolate condition: as also, that walking in the path of faith, and running in the ways of Christ's commandments, better became her, than sitting still and being indolent; and likewise, that to lift up the head, and to be of a cheerful spirit, better suited with the spouse of Christ, than a sad and dejected countenance; who had no need to sit in the dust, and clothe herself with sackcloth and ashes, when she is the king's daughter, nay, the queen herself, whose clothing is the gold of Ophir: so that neither an indolent and inactive, nor a sorrowful and dejected spirit, become the people of God and spouse of Christ.

2ndly. He exhorts her also to come away; from whence? why, from off her sluggish bed, or from out of her prison of darkness and unbelief, or from the company and conversation of wicked and ungodly men; and, in short, from every thing that might bring a dishonour to him, or be prejudicial to herself; which shows the great regard that Christ had for her. But whither would he have her come? why, to himself, where she might have peace and comfort, enjoy sweet communion with him, be out of the reach of enemies, and free from danger by them; he would have her quit her former companions, her former ease and pleasures, and go with him, where she should enjoy ease, pleasure, and conversation superior to these; he would have her be up and about her duty, following him, the Lamb, whithersoever he went: in giving which advice, he sought her own good and comfort, as well as his own glory. The Jewish writersᵖ understand it as God's call to the people of Israel to come out of Egypt.

III. The loving and affectionate titles which he gives her, are, 1. "My love," which has been already explained in chap. i. 9. 2. "My fair one;" in what sense the church is fair and comely, has been shown in chap. i. 5; the church is Christ's fair one; not upon the account of her works of righteousness, as the Targum explains it; but upon the account of the imputation of Christ's righteousness, the pardon of her sins through his

---

º ענה respondit, Montanus, Vatablus, Marckius, Michaelis.

ᵖ Targum, R. Sol. Jarchi, and R. Aben Ezra in loc.

blood, and the sanctification of his Spirit. The Septuagint adds a third character, "my dove;" but this is not in the Hebrew text. Now he uses these titles, (1.) To show her his ardent love and tender affections to her; that though she was in a carnal and secure frame, and negligent in her duty, yet she was his love and fair one still. (2.) To remove all discouragements from her that might arise from the consideration of her present state and condition. (3.) To prevail upon her to arise and go with him; and indeed an exhortation, expressed in such moving language, delivered in such an affectionate manner, none would think, could not fail of succeeding, especially when pressed with a claim of interest in her, my love, and my fair one; as also when designed for her own good, for so the words may be read, "rise up for thyself, and come away for thyself;"[q] it will turn to thy advantage, if thou dost do so; if not, it will be detrimental to thee. What other arguments he makes use of to enforce this upon her, will be seen in the following verses.

Verse 11. *For lo, the winter is past, the rain is over and gone.*

CHRIST here presses upon and encourages his church to rise up from her present state of sleep and sloth, and come away with him, where she might enjoy peace and pleasure! and this he does by informing her, that it was now spring-time; that the winter was past, and the spring was come, in which every thing looked gay, pleasant, and delightful; the rain was over and gone, which made journeys difficult, and rivers impassable, and in the room of it, fair and sunshine weather; that that time of the year was over which was bad to travel in, as Christ says, "pray ye that your flight be not in the winter;" and therefore she might without fear, and with the utmost safety as well as pleasure, venture abroad with him. Winter and rain are very properly put together, since rain is frequent in the winter-season; and hence it has the name of *imbrifer*[r] from it. Now by this winter, which is said to be past, and the rain that is said to be over and gone, may be meant, either,

First. The state and condition both of the Jews and Gentiles, before the coming of Christ in the flesh, when it was a winter, a rainy and stormy dispensation with both of them. Winter is used by some writers, not for the season of the year, but for a storm and tempest;[s] and figuratively, for some calamity, as war,[t] &c. And,

1st. It may be expressive of the state of the Jews before Christ's coming.[u] It is true, they were a people peculiarly chosen by God, and were indulged by him with special favours above the Gentiles; they had the knowledge of the true God, and were instructed in his mind and will; for he gave them his law to direct them, and sent his prophets time after time to inform, teach, rebuke, warn, and admonish them; whilst the Gentiles lived without the law, and had only the dim light of nature to guide them: and yet the dispensation which the Jews were under, before Christ's coming, when compared with the gospel-dispensation, may be said to be a winter, a rainy and stormy one; which began when the law was given on mount Sinai, which was attended with blackness, darkness, and tempest. These people were all along treated by God, as if they had been under a covenant of works; for whilst they lived in obedience to the divine will, they enjoyed without disturbance their civil and religious privileges; but when they broke and transgressed the divine laws, the clouds of God's wrath gathered thick and black about them, and stormy judgments descended on them, which begat in them a spirit of bondage; so that their services which they performed to God, were not attended with that spirit of liberty and ingenuity, with that faith and cheerfulness, as now appeared in the saints in this spring-time of the gospel: it was a time of coldness and barrenness, the Sun of righteousness not having as yet risen in their horizon, with his warming and fructifying influences as he has done since: it was a time of much darkness and obscurity; for though there were some discoveries of Christ and his grace to believers then, yet these were made through dark shadows, cloudy and smoaky sacrifices: a little before Christ's coming in the flesh, and appearing in his public ministry, there was a violent rain, nay, a flood of error, infidelity, and profaneness, came pouring in among them; the law of God was corrupted with false glosses, his institutions and ordinances changed and altered, and his temple profaned; one sort set up the traditions of the elders, against the positive commands of God; another denied the resurrection of the dead, and a future judgment; and both obstinately persisted in their infidelity concerning the Messiah, when he appeared among them. This was the face of things when Christ was manifested in the flesh; who, by his ministry, checked the infidelity and profaneness of the age; and, by his death, put a period to the Mosaic dispensation: so that now those cloudy and shadowish ceremonies are gone; the night of Jewish darkness is ended, and the old covenant is waxen old, and vanished away.

2ndly. It may also point out the state and condition of the Gentiles before Christ's coming. The times before the Gospel came among them, were times of ignorance; they were strangers to the knowledge of the true God, to his mind, will,

---

[q] קוּמִי לָךְ וּלְכִי לָךְ surge tibi and abi tibi, Montanus, Cocceius, Ainsworth, Vatablus, Marckius.
[r] Hyems imbrifera, Sil. Ital. l. 31. v. 197. Pluviosa hyems, Plin. Nat. Hist. l. 18. c. 25.
[s] Emissamque hyemem sensit, Neptunus, Virgil Æneid. l. 1. v. 129. Miseranda rogabo unam hyemem, Statii Achill. l. 1. v. 50, 51. Vid. Val. Flacc. l. 1. v. 197. [t] Νίφας πολεμοιοχειμεριον ζοφον, Pindar. Isthm. ode 4. [u] Ante adventum Christi hyems erat, venit Christus, fecit æstatem, Ambros. Enarrat. in Psal. cxviii. octon. 7. p. 921. Vid. Isidor. in loc.

and worship; darkness covered them, yea, gross darkness was all around them; storms of divine wrath hang over their heads; they were under the manifest tokens of God's displeasure, being given up to judicial blindness and hardness of heart, and were shut up in sin and unbelief; their hearts were frozen up; and seemed scarce capable of having any impressions made upon them; the Gentile world looked like a heath, a desert, or a wilderness, all barren and unfruitful, like the earth in winter time; an impetuous rain and flood of profaneness, error, and seduction, overflowed it: God suffered them to walk in their own ways, and to follow the imaginations of their own hearts; they were left to worship birds, four-footed beasts, and creeping things; to fall down to stocks and stones, and graven images, and pray to a god that could not save: but when the gospel was sent among them by Christ, the face of the Gentile world was quite altered, and appeared like the earth after a winter season, upon the returning spring; gospel light diffused itself through all the parts thereof, and dispelled the shades of darkness, blindness, ignorance, profaneness, and infidelity; gospel grace, with its warming influences, thawed their frozen hearts, and left some deep and lasting impressions on them; that which looked like a wilderness, is become a fruitful field; and that which was as a desert, now appears as the garden of the Lord: such a mighty change has the spring-time of the gospel made in the Gentile world! Or else,

Secondly. This winter and rain, which Christ says were past and gone, may be understood of the spiritual state of souls; and that either before or after conversion. The state of believers before conversion, may be represented by it, which is a time of darkness, deadness, coldness, barrenness, and unfruitfulness, and is only removed by the powerful and efficious grace of Christ; and often after conversion, is a winter season with them; they are frequently annoyed with the blustering winds and rains of Satan's temptations, which beat upon them like a storm against a wall: this enemy of their souls often comes in like a flood upon them, and would bear them away, were it not for the power and grace of the Spirit of God, which are opposed unto it; they are often under the fearful apprehensions of storms of impending wrath for their sins and transgressions against God; they are seldom free from sharp crosses and afflictions, and are often under the nipping blasts of persecution; which may be compared to the winter season for its sharpness and severity, though exceeding wholesome.

Moreover, they are sometimes in a great deal of darkness of soul; the clouds interpose between Christ and them, so as they cannot behold him, and their interest in him; their hearts are often hard and frozen up, so as no impressions are made either by the preaching of the word, or by the providences of God; a great deal of coldness frequently attends them; there is a chill upon their love to God, to Christ, to his people, ordinances, cause, and interest, which is occasioned by the prevailings of sin and corruption in them: sometimes they look like trees in winter, barren and unfruitful, with no appearance of the fruit of grace, nor leaves of profession, but as if they were entirely dead and lifeless; and when this is their case, it may be said to be a winter-season with them; but though this is sometimes their case, it is not always: they have their returning seasons of peace, joy and comfort when it may be said, "the winter is past, and the rain is over and gone;" then light breaks in upon their souls, and there hearts are melted with a sense of divine love; they become lively in their frames, and in the exercise of their grace, and fruitful in every good word and work; calmness and serenity of mind, peace of conscience, and joy in the Holy Ghost, are the delightful blessings which the soul now enjoys; all these, and much more, does the Sun of righteousness bring along with him, and produce in us, when he arises with healing in his wings, and turns a cold and nipping winter into a pleasant and delightful spring. But when it is a winter-season with believers, they have a little or no communion with Christ, which was the church's case here; the rains that fall, and the floods occasioned thereby, interrupt their fellowship; and the clouds of darkness, and doubts and fears, which hang over their heads, hinder them from beholding Christ, and their interest in him; now this must needs be a very melancholy and uncomfortable time unto them; and therefore to hear that the winter is past, and the spring is come; that the rain is over and gone, that the clouds are dispersed, and the air is clear, bright, and serene, must needs be good news and glad tidings to them. Moreover, souls, whilst in such a state, are usually indolent and inactive; they have neither hearts nor hands to work, but both are sealed up; they are neither diligent in the way of their duty, nor active in the exercise of grace, as the church appears to be here; also they are ready to think that the winter is not over when it is, but fear that there are more storms behind; not only of crosses, afflictions, persecutions, and temptations; but which are worse than all the rest, that there are storms of divine wrath and anger behind, which will fall upon them; though these have been all borne by Christ, and are effectually and eternally removed by him; and believers may be assured of this, whatever their fears are, that not a drop of wrath shall fall upon them for Christ has satisfied law and justice, and so hath delivered them from the wrath which is to come; and he that has done this, says, the winter is past, and the rain is over and gone: this is the voice of the Gospel, and a joyful sound it is. The Jewish writers[w] interpret this of the bondage of the people of Israel in Egypt, and their deliver-

---

[w] Targum, R. Sol. Jarchi, and R. Aben Ezra in loc. and so Lyra.

aance out of it; as do some Christian interpreters,[x] of the Babylonish captivity, and the Jewish deliverance from thence; it being a Chaldee word[y] that is here used to express the season of the year by: but the sense before given, seems to be much preferable to either of them; though it is true, that the two former deliverances did produce a spring-time of joy and rejoicing, after a cold and nipping winter of trouble and sorrow; and were indeed wrought in the spring of the year, as was also our redemption by Christ Jesus, they were typical of.

Verse 12. *The flowers appear on the earth, the time of the singing* of birds *is come, and the voice of the turtle is heard in our land.*

THE church goes on to give an account of the pressing instances that Christ made unto her, to arise and come away; which he had done in the former verse, by assuring her that the winter was past, and therefore she need not be afraid of nipping blasts and blustering storms, nor of heavy rains, which would make travelling difficult, as well as unpleasant; and here he encourages her to arise and come with him, from the pleasantness of the spring, of which he gives the following account, in this and the next verse, enough to tempt her to a compliance, and which is very pleasant and inviting to lovers.[z] In this verse he says,

I. That "the flowers appear on the earth."
II. That "the time of the singing of birds was come."
III. That "the voice of the turtle was heard in their land."

All which are so many evident demonstrations of the spring-time of the year, which of all others is the most pleasant.

I. The first sign of the spring, and which he mentions to prevail upon her to quit her present place and posture, and go with him, is, that "the flowers appear on the earth;"[a] in the winter-season the earth appears barren and unfruitful, being nipped with cold winds, frost, and rain; but when the sun returns with its warming influences, it quickens those herbs and plants which before lay hid, and causes them to spring forth and flourish; so that the fields and meadows, as well as gardens, are covered with a variety of herbs, plants, and beautiful flowers, which are very pleasant to the eye, and cause walking in the fields to be very delightful. Some Jewish writers, as Jarchi and Alshech, interpret them of the two Messiah's, the Jews dream of, and vainly expect; it is much better to interpret them of the one and only true Messiah, who appeared on earth in the spring of the acceptable year of the Lord; and who is compared to various flowers in this book, particularly to the rose and lily, ver. 1, which are both spring-flowers:[b] but rather, by these flowers may be meant, either "the graces of the Spirit" in the saints, which, when it is a winter-season with them, lie dormant, and are as it were dead and lifeless, and are scarcely discernible either to themselves or others; but upon the return of "the Sun of righteousness," they revive and show themselves in all their glory, send forth a grateful odour, and give a delightful prospect to all beholders; such are those flowers of faith, hope, love, humility, self-denial, patience, long-suffering, forbearance with and forgiveness of each other: or else, by these flowers may be meant the saints themselves. The Targum interprets them of Moses and Aaron; but R. Aben Ezra thinks that all the righteous men of Israel are intended; and it is best to understand them of all the saints, especially when in a flourishing condition, and in the exercise of grace; who may be compared to the flowers of the field, 1. For the production of them; the covering of the earth with grass, herbs, plants, and beautiful flowers, in the spring-season, is a great instance of God's mighty power; it is no other than a kind of re-creation; this strange, though common change that is made in the earth by the returning spring, is elegantly described, as well as entirely referred to the divine Spirit by the royal Psalmist, thus, Psalm civ. 30, "Thou sendest forth thy Spirit, they are created; and thou renewest the face of the earth;" saints are flowers, not of man's, but of God's raising; they are "not born of the will of man, nor of the will of the flesh, but of God;" their grace, and all the flourishings of it, are not owing to their own care, diligence, and industry, but to the power and Spirit of God, who "worketh in them both to will and to do of his good pleasure;" for this work of grace upon their souls, is a work of Almighty power, and is no less than a new creation; and whether we consider it in its first beginning, or in its after-growth and increase, it must be referred to a power superior to ours. 2. For their fra-

---

[x] Brightman and Cotton in loc. [y] כתר quod legitur quasi סתיו scriberetur, alibi in scriptura non invenitur, est autem vox Chaldaica סתוא pro Hebræa חרף hyems, Mercer in loc. Vid. Vitringam in Jes. 4. 6.

[z] Vere gaudet Venus, Ovid. • Vere florifero, Senecæ Oedipus, v. 649. Ver præbet flores. Ovid. de Remed. Amor. 1. 1. v. 188. Omnia tum florent. Ovid. Metamorph. 1. 15. fab. 3. Vernus sequitur color, omnis in herbas turget humus, Claudian. de Rapt. Proserp. 1. 2. v. 90. So flowers are called τεκνα εαρος, the children of the spring, in Athenæi Deipnosophist. 1. 13. c. 9. p. 608. Whatever was flowery, used to be called spring, because of the nature of it, Orpheus

[b] Cum rosam viderit, tunc incipere ver arbitrabatur, Cicero. in Verrem, orat. 7. Rosa verna, Propert. l. 3. eleg. 5. v. 22. So it is represented by Anacreon as a spring flower; and by Pancrates, apud Athen. Deipnos. l. 15. c. 6 p. 677. So Seneca calls the lily, florem vernum, a spring-flower, epist. 122. Spring-flowers are various; some grow in fields, meadows, vales, hills, and banks of rivers; some in gardens, as the violet, crocus, hyacinth, narcissus, rose and lily, vide Athen. Deipnosophist. l. 15. c. 8. p. 681, 682. of which the violet, rose and lily, were preferred for their beauty and smell, Theocrit. Idyll. 24. v. 29—31.

grancy: the persons of believers are of a sweet-smelling savour, being perfumed with Christ's mediation, and covered with the sweet smelling garments of Christ's righteousness; and so are their services, their prayers, and praises, put up and performed in the faith of Jesus. 3. For their beauty and ornament: how beautiful and glorious must those fields look, where roses are, and lilies grow: which in glory are equal with, nay, superior to the greatest of princes; for "Solomon in all his glory was not arrayed like one of these;" such as Sharon's field and the roses and lilies there, which are here alluded to: saints are exceeding beautiful in Christ, and ornamental to him, being sanctified by his Spirit, and clothed with his righteousness. 4. Saints may be compared to flowers which appear on the earth in the spring-season with an air of gaiety and cheerfulness, on the account of that joy and consolation which their souls are possessed of when their grace is revived and in exercise; particularly when faith is, and when Christ returns to them, and they enjoy his presence; thus the blossoming and flourishing estate of the church is joined with joy and rejoicing, in Isa. xxxv. 1, 2. Now all this fragrancy, beauty, and flourishing condition of the saints, are owing to the arising of the Sun of righteousness upon them, to the dews of divine grace, showers of boundless love, frequent waterings of heaven, and to their being planted and growing in a fruitful soil, Christ Jesus: and perhaps it may not be amiss to interpret this of that large production and conversion of souls to Christ, and of that appearance of many beautiful flowers in the church of Christ in the first ages of Christianity; when saints appeared " in the beauties of holiness," and Christ had " the dew of his youth;" and which time was a delightful spring-season, after a long winter of Jewish and Gentile darkness.

II. Another indication of the spring's being come, and which Christ makes use of as an argument to induce the church to arise and come away, is, that " the time of the singing of birds was come;" the spring, when birds begin to chirp and sing, to couple and build their nests: hence the spring is called *ver nidificum*.[c] Some[d] understand this of the time of cutting and pruning vines, or lopping trees: and to this purpose the Septuagint reads the words thus, *the time of cutting is come;*[e] which agrees well enough with the first times of the Gospel, when Christ's Father acted the part of an husbandman, and lopped of the unfruitful branches, the Jews, engrafted the Gentiles, caused them to bring forth fruit, and pruned them, that they might bring forth more; which seems well enough to agree with the season of the year,[f] the spring, at which time, especially at the beginning of it, vines were usually cut and pruned; some object to this as unseasonable: by the Targum, it is referred to the " time of cutting, or gathering in the first fruits;" as it is also by some,[g] to the gathering of flowers, making of garlands, &c., as well as applied by others,[h] to the time of making incisures in the Balsam or Cyprus-trees in the vineyards of Engedi; but nothing is more agreeable than our version, and which is the sense that is given of the word by several Jewish writers;[i] and exactly suits with the Gospel-dispensation, in which, " from the uttermost parts of the earth, songs are heard," sung in warbling notes and tuneful lays, by souls called by divine grace; whose usual themes are, the grace and mercy of God the Father, the redeeming love of God the Son, the spiritual blessings in him; the glory of his righteousness to justify them, and the fulness of his grace and power to keep and preserve them; like little birds, they sit and chirp and sing the praises of the Lord, " in psalms, and hymns, and spiritual songs, making melody in their hearts unto him;" and this they do as well as they can in this imperfect life, though their hearts are often out of tune, and they sing with faint and feeble notes; but the time is coming, when they shall be clothed in white, have harps in their hands, hallelujahs in their mouths, and be employed in this delightful service for evermore. But however, this present gospel-dispensation may well be called a " time of the singing of birds," a time of joy and rejoicing, in comparison of the legal one, in which was heard, not the chirping and singing of birds, but " the sound of a trumpet," and " the voice of words," which were awful and terrible. This may not be unfitly applied to the singing of the angelic host, those heavenly choristers, at the birth of Christ, Luke ii. 13, 14.

III. As a farther evidence of the spring's being come, and the more to allure her to arise and go with him,[k] he says, that " the voice of the turtle was heard in their land;" which is a kind of dove, that, as naturalists[l] tell us, lies hid in the winter-time, and appears in the spring; its voice is never heard in winter, unless on a fine day.[m] By which may be meant, either the church, which is compared to a turtle dove, Psalm lxxiv. 19, whose voice is heard in prayer to Christ; and who, in the preaching of the Gospel, speaks of him, and in the public profession of his cause and interest, speaks for him; which voice, in ver. 14, is very

---

[a] Senecæ Medea, v. 713. [d] Plerique in Sanct. in loc. Vide R. Aben Ezra in loc. [e] Καιρός τῆς τομῆς ἔφθακε, Sept. Tempus putationis advenit, V. L. Pagninus, so the Syriac, Arabic and Ethiopic versions. [f] Plin. l. 17. c. 22. Hence says the poet, ἔαρος νέον ἱσταμένοιο, τὴν φθάμενος, οἶνας περιταμνέμεν, ὥς γαρ ἀμεινον, Hesiod Opera and Dies, l. 2.
[g] Greg. Nyssen. and Psellus in Sanct. in loc.
[h] Sanct. in loc. [i] R. Sol. Jarchi, R. Aben Ezra, and R. Sol. Ben Melech in loc. Zohar. in Gen. fol. 29. 2. and 65. 2. and 121. 3. though the other sense of cutting or pruning seems to be intended, in Zohar in Gen. fol. 3. 4. and in Lev. fol. 2. 1. [k] Thus one part of rural pleasure is described by the poet, "εἰδὸν κύρυδοικαι ἀκανθίδες ἔστενε ταρνιγῶν Theocrit. Idyll. 7. [l] Plin. l. 10. c 24. and 18. 28.
[m] Myndius apud Athen. Deipnosophist. l. 9. c. 11. p. 394. So Pliny, Hyeme mutis, vere vocalibus, l. 10. c. 35. The turtle appears in summer, in winter it disappears, Aristot. Hist. Animal. l. 8. c. 3.

pleasant to him; or else, the voice of the Holy Ghost, according to the Targum, who once appeared in the form of a dove, and whose voice in the hearts of believers is very comfortable; for he speaks peace and pardon through Christ's blood, bears witness to our sonship, and is the pledge of our future inheritance: or the voice of God the Father, declaring his well-pleasedness in Christ, which was heard in Judea, both at his baptism and at his transfiguration upon the mount: or the voice of John the Baptist," who was the forerunner of Christ, and declared him to be at hand; and so R. Alshech interprets it, of Elijah, that was to come before the Messiah, and cites the passage in Mal. iv. 5; and others° understand it of the Messiah himself: or else, the voice of Christ himself, preaching the everlasting Gospel;[p] R. Simeon Ben Jochai[q] understands it of the voice of the law in the days of the Messiah; but rather the Gospel itself, that joyful sound of peace, pardon, righteousness, life, and salvation by Christ, is meant; which was heard for a while only in Judea, which perhaps is the land here intended, called, by way of eminency and speciality, "our land;" though afterwards this voice was heard throughout the Gentile world; for Christ gave his disciples a commission to go into all the world, and preach the Gospel to every creature: who accordingly did, and their sound went into all the earth, and their words unto the ends of the world; and a joyful season it was, and still is to the poor Gentiles, where this voice is heard; and blessed be God, it is heard in our land.

Verse 13. *The fig-tree putteth forth her green figs, and the vines with the tender grape give a good smell. Arise, my love, my fair one, and come away.*

To the three former evidences of the spring, here are added two more.

I. " The fig-tree putteth forth her green figs."
II. " The vines with the tender grape give a good smell." As also
III. The former call is repeated, " Arise my love, my fair one, and come away."

I. As a fourth evidence of the winter being over, and the spring being come, Christ tells his church, that the fig-tree was putting forth her green figs; which is a full confirmation of its being come, nay, of its being pretty well advanced; for Christ, in Matt. xxiv. 32, makes it a sign of the summer's being at hand, when the fig-tree shoots out its tender branches, and puts forth its leaves: Theopompus[r] speaks of figs in the middle of the spring; and Plutarch, of the vernal leaves of the fig-tree.[s] R. Aben Ezra thinks, that the word translated, " putteth forth," signifies the sweetening of the figs, and so points out the time when the green or unripe figs begin to grow sweet and eatable: so that as the flowery fields would be delightful to her eye, and the chirping birds affect her ear; there were also figs ripening apace to please her taste; as the vines with the tender grape in the following instance, would give a refreshing odour to her smell; all which would be very entertaining to her, and one would think enough to invite her to arise and go with him. By the fig-tree, both the Targum and R. Aben Ezra understand the congregation of Israel; who they say, is here compared unto it; as indeed Israel is to the first ripe fruit of this tree, Hos. ix. 10; and the godly among the captive Jews are, in Jer. xxiv. 2—5; and therefore by it may be meant the saints, putting forth their grace in exercise on Christ; who may be compared to fig-trees for the following reasons.

1. The fig-tree is a tree full of large leaves, so large, that our first parents, after their fall, by sewing them together, made themselves aprons to cover their nakedness; which may be an emblem of a profession of religion, and of a conversation agreeable to it; which, though they ought to be found in us, yet are not sufficient to cover us; for we must also have Christ's righteousness put upon us, and his grace wrought in us, otherwise we shall be like the fig tree to which Christ came, Matt. xxi. 19, " and found nothing thereon but leaves only." And therefore, as the saints are like fig-trees that have the large ever-green and flourishing leaves of a Christian profession and gospel-conversation upon them; so, 2, They may be compared to them for their fruitfulness: the fig-tree is a tree that bears fruit as well as leaves, and that which is very wholesome, pleasant, and delightful; and if the Egyptian fig-tree is meant, that is said[t] to bear fruit seven times a year, and as soon as you gather one fig, immediately there is another; it is true, there are barren fig-trees, that have no fruit upon them; such an one is mentioned in Luke xiii. 6, 7; as there are also barren professors; but such are not the saints, who are filled and laden with the fruits of righteousness, and graces of the Spirit, which they receive from Christ Jesus, from whom all their fruit is found: now as this is to be found from none but him, so neither is it found in any but in them; for, do men gather grapes of thorns, or figs of thistles?" it is impossible; this fruit appears upon no other tree but the fig-tree, and therefore by their fruit ye may know them. 3. It is a tree that puts forth its fruit before its leaves;" which shows us, that though we ought to have the leaves of profession upon us, yet the fruit of grace ought to precede it; and therefore when persons take upon them a profession of religion, and submit to the ordinances of Christ, care should be taken that they, as John says, Matt. iii. 7, both have and bring forth fruits meet for repentance, there must be faith in the heart, as well as a con-

" Psellus and Tres Patres in loc. ° Pesikta in Yalkut in loc. [p] So Isidore in loc.
[q] In Zohar in Gen. fol. 121. 3. [r] Apud Athen. [s] Plin. Nat. Hist. l. 16. c. 26.
ut supra, l. 3. c. 4. p. 77. [t] Θρίοις εαρινοίς, de Defectu Oracul. p. 410. [u] Solin. Polyhistor. c. 45.

fession of it in the mouth; and the one ought to go before the other; and both these make souls to appear honourable believers and professors; and such Christ's fig-trees are. 4. It may not be amiss to observe, that the Egyptian fig-tree, which is no other than the sycamore, into which Zaccheus climbed to see Christ, Luke xix. 4, may be here intended, seeing that there was great plenty of them in Judea, as is manifest from 1 Kings x. 27; though it is true another word is used here, than what is there. Now of this tree, Pliny says,[w] that when it is cut down and cast into the water, it sinks, being dry; but when it is thoroughly wet, it will swim; so saints, when they first enter the waters of affliction, like Peter, they sink; but when they have been more used to them, they lift up their heads above the waters of tribulation; and as good soldiers, with courage and magnanimity of mind, endure hardness: and do not sink in their spirits under the weight of reproaches, persecutions, and afflictions, laid upon them, being supported and borne up by Christ and his grace. 5. The same author[x] says, that this kind of fig-trees will not ripen any other way than by scratching it with iron hooks: men do not begin to grow in grace, or become fruitful in good works, until their hearts are pricked with the goads and nails of God's word, or till the fallow ground of their hearts is thrown up by the Spirit of God; nor will they grow afterwards to any purpose, unless Christ's Father, who is the Husbandman, takes his pruning-knife in his hand, and uses it; and indeed some saints never grow better than when they are attended with tribulations and afflictions, like the people of Israel, in Egypt, or like Christ's lilies among thorns.

Moreover, the green figs which the fig-tree is said to put forth may intend, 1. The beginnings of grace in the soul, which are like the young, green, and unripe figs, that the fig-tree first puts forth; such as stirrings of affection to Christ, desires after a saving knowledge of him, and interest in him, pantings and breathings after the ordinances of Christ, and love to his people; all which appear very soon in the soul, and discover the work of grace begun, though as yet it is but very imperfect. For, 2. These green and unripe figs show the imperfection of grace in the saints; grace in the best is very imperfect in this state of life, much more must it be when it is first put forth; the work of grace in us, though it will be performed, yet at present is but a begun one, and not a finished one; saints are not arrived to the perfection they shall; they are but like green figs, and especially young converts. 3. These beginning of grace in the soul, being compared to green figs, show, that grace is liable to be lost, and would be so, were it not for the almighty power which pre-

serves it and increases it; for of all fruit, none is more easily shaken off by the wind and lost, than green and unripe figs are; see Nahum iii. 12; it is no less than a miracle of grace, that these first impressions are not wholly erased by the impetuous force of corruptions within; or that these precious blossoms are not entirely blown off by the blustering winds of Satan's temptations; or that our naughty hearts do not of themselves, as the fig-tree, cast off this unripe fruit: this is all owing to mighty, powerful, and efficacious grace. 4. It may also be observed that grace, though imperfect, is taken notice of by Christ; yea, in the very infancy of it, as soon as ever it begins to appear, even when in its bud and blossom: so far is he from despising the day of small things; where there is but little grace and little strength, as in the church of Philadelphia, he observes it, and does not crush it, but increases it; for " a bruised reed shall he not break, and the smoking flax shall he not quench," Isa. xlii. 3. 5. It may be remarked from hence, that grace being in exercise in others, though weak, should be an argument and motive to excite and stir up ours; and indeed it is disgraceful and dishonourable to old professors, for young converts to be more active and lively in the exercise of grace than they. Christ seems to press this argument here upon the church.

Again, the putting forth these green figs, signifies the exercise of grace on Christ, which saints put forth unto him, not by virtue of a power of their own, but by virtue of his grace, which enables them to do it; for the putting forth of these green figs, is owing to the warming and quickening influences of the Sun of righteousness: the beginning, increase, and perfection of grace, are all from Christ; the implantation of it in the soul, and the exercise of it, depend upon him. But,

II. As a fifth and last evidence of the spring's being come, and which puts it beyond all doubt is, the flourishing of the vines, " the vines, with the tender grape, give a good smell." Fig-trees and vines are frequently mentioned together in scripture, as in Psal. cv. 33, Mic. iv. 4; and in many other places; and one reason is, because they grow together; for fig-trees were planted in vineyards, as is manifest from Luke xiii. 6; nay, it is judged by naturalists,[y] to be very proper they should grow together: one sort of figs, the black fig, is called the sister of the vine.[z]

By *vines* may be meant, the several distinct congregated churches of Christ, or else particular believers, see Psal. lxxx. 14, 15, Isa. v. 7, and xxvii. 3: who may be called so, 1. Because of their fruitfulness: the vine is a fruit-bearing tree, it produces very fine and excellent fruit; especially the vines in the land of Canaan did, of which there is a famous instance in Num. xiii. 23; saints being

[w] Lib. 13. c. 7. Vid. Solin ib.   [x] Plin. Ibid.
[y] Vid. Plin. l. 17. c. 23.   [z] Hipponax apud Athen. Deipnosophist. l. 3 c. 4. p 78.

engrafted in Christ Jesus, the true vine, and receiving life and nourishment from him, do, by abiding in him, bring forth much fruit, and such as is not to be found in others; not wild and sour grapes, such as Christ's Father takes no delight in, but such as he is pleased with, and glorified by. 2. Because of their dependence on Christ; the vine-tree does not grow up erect of itself; for if it is not fixed to a wall with nails,[a] or supported by something else which it lays hold on, it creeps along the ground: saints do not grow up erect of themselves, but lean upon Christ, are supported by him, and so grow up in him. 3. For their tallness in Christ: vines being propped, will run up a great height; saints being engrafted in, and upheld by Christ, who is himself higher than the heavens, grow up from shrubs to taller trees; from babes in Christ, to " the measure of the stature of the fulness of Christ;" and, by virtue of grace and strength, received from him, arise from a low and mean state and condition unto a much higher one, until at length they arrive unto the full possession of the " prize of the high calling of God in Christ Jesus." 4. For their weakness and unusefulness in themselves: the vine is a weak tree, and, as has been observed, cannot bear up itself: saints, they are weak in themselves, though strong in Christ; they can do nothing of themselves; neither perform duties, subdue corruptions, nor withstand temptations; but they " can do all things through Christ strengthening them." The wood of the vine is of very little worth or use, as appears from Ezek. xv. 2, 3; and is obvious enough to every one's observation: saints are but poor, worthless, and unprofitable creatures of themselves; their best works and most excellent performances, are neither profitable to God, nor can they procure salvation to themselves; but are all as an unclean thing, and as filthy rags; they are unworthy of the least mercy they enjoy, and therefore it is a wonder of grace that God should in any respect be mindful of them. 5. For their durableness; though the wood of the vine is but weak and worthless, yet it is said to be very lasting and durable; Pliny ascribes eternity to it, and says of it,[b] *nec est ligno ulli æternior natura, no wood is of a more eternal or durable nature than this is;* saints, however weak and worthless in themselves, yet shall continue and abide for ever in Christ; they are born of an incorruptible seed; they are built upon a rock, and secured by almighty power, so as they shall never perish, but shall for ever enjoy the incorruptible inheritance that is reserved for them.

Also these vines are said to have the tender grape upon them. The word translated *the tender grape,* is only used in this song, and that but in two other places besides this, viz., ver. 15 of this chapter, and chap. vii. 12, but is used both in the Targum[c] and Misnah,[d] in the same sense. Most of the Jewish writers[e] think, that by it is meant the small and tender grape, which appears as soon as ever the flower is fallen off, when the vines begin to knot, and one grape can be known and may be distinguished from another; which sense our version expresses. But I am rather inclined to think that it means the flower itself; for in the Targum on Is. xviii. 5, this word סמדר, *smadar,* is used to express the Hebrew word נצה, *nitzah,* which signifies a flower: and not only Pliny[f] and others, but the scriptures also testify that vines do blossom and flower, as in the aforementioned place, Is. xviii. 5, and in Gen. xl. 10; and the good smell which these vines are said to give, seems best to be understood of their time of flowering, than of any other time; for it is reported of some vines,[g] and perhaps may be true of the vines which grew in Judea, seeing that the wine of Lebanon is commended for its agreeable odour, Hos. xiv. 7. I say, it is reported of some vines, that in the time of their flowering they send forth so sweet a smell, that not only the vineyards themselves, but the country round about is refreshed with the sweet savour thereof; so that walking or sitting among them is both wholesome and delightful; nay, that the smell of them is so great, that serpents and other venomous creatures are driven away by it: so then the words may be rendered thus, " the vines, being in flower, give a good smell."[h] Now by these tender grapes, flowers, or blossoms of the vines, may be meant, either the graces of the Spirit in their first appearance, as before; or else young converts, to which I rather incline, who are the fruit of Christ's vine, the church; and though very weak and tender, yet are very dear unto, and are much regarded by Christ; and when there is a large appearance of them, it is a great encouragement to the church, and promises a glorious vintage: so the Targum interprets it of young men and babes praising the Lord at the Red Sea, for their deliverance out of the hands of the Egyptians: and R. Sol. Jarchi says, it is explained of repenting sinners, in an ancient book of theirs, called *Pesikta;* and so I find it is also in another book of theirs, called *Raya Mehimna.*[i]

Moreover, these vines having their tender grapes upon them, or being in flower, are said to give a good smell; which must be understood of the fragrance of the persons of believers, being

---

[a] Vites claviculis adminicula tanquam manibus apprehendunt, atque ita se erigunt ut ánimantes, Cicero de Natura Deorum, l. 2. c. 47.   [b] Plin. l. 14. c. 1.   [e] In Isa. xviii. 5.   [d] Tract. Orlah, ch. 1. §. 7.   [e] R. Aben Ezra, R. Sol. Jarchi, and R. Sol. Ben Melech in loc. R. David Kimchi in lib. shorash. rad. סמדר David de Pomis in Lexic. p. 111. col. 3. and Ez. Chayim in Tract. Orlah, 1.7. Misnah, Gittin, c. 3. §. 8. T. Hieros. Nazir, fol. 55. 1. T. Bab. Kiddushin, fol. 54. 2.   [f] Lib. 16. c. 25. and 17. 22. Si bene floruerit vinea, &c. Ovid. Fasti. l. 5. so Horat. Epod. ode 16. v. 44.   [g] Danæus in Herb. xiv. 7. Levin. Lemnii Herb. Bibl. Explic. c. 2.   [h] סמדר οιναυθη, Symmachus; in flore constitutæ vites, Mercerus, Michaelis; vitis pars florens, Munster; vineæ florentes, Tigurine version; nihil gratius florentis odoe vitis, Ambros. Hexaemeron, l. 3. c. 12.   [i] In Zohar in Exod. fol. 50. 1.

clothed with the sweet-smelling garments of Christ's righteousness, and the delightful odour of their graces being exercised on his person; as well as of their sweet savour, which their pious and godly conversations send forth to all that know them, or are about them.

III. Christ having given such full demonstrations of the spring being come, renews his call to the church, and says again, "Arise, my love, my fair one, and come away;" which repetition shows 1. Our backwardness and sluggishness: we need one call after another, one exhortation upon another, and all will not do, unless the power of divine grace is exerted: for after repeated calls, we shall sleep on and take no notice, as the disciples did, being overborne with a body of sin and death. 2. It manifests the exceeding greatness of his love to us, and care of us; that though we have backslidden from him, yet he calls us back again; and though backward to his calls, yet he persists in them, and all along uses the most endearing and tender language to work upon us: he gives no other words but such as these, "my love, and my fair one." 3. It is a plain indication that he is unwilling that we should be without him, or he without us: and therefore having taken the most winning methods, and used the most prevailing arguments, he repeats the call. 4. It shows his importunity, and that he will have no denial;[k] and indeed one would think there could be none given, when both our pleasure and profit are so much concerned in it; and what he calls us to, tends so much to advance both; and there will be none, and can be none, when he exerts the mighty power of his grace.

Verse 14. *O my dove! that art in the clefts of the rock, in the secret places of the stairs: let me see thy countenance, let me hear thy voice; for sweet is thy voice and thy countenance is comely.*

THESE are the words of Christ to his church; and may be considered either as coming immediately out of his own mouth; or else, as recorded and related by her, as the former were: in which may be considered,

I. The title or character which Christ gives to his church; "my dove."

II. Her then present place of residence; "in the clefts of the rock, in the secret places of the stairs."

III. A request which he makes, which consists of two parts. 1st. That he might see her countenance. 2ndly, Hear her voice.

IV. The motives or arguments that he makes use of to prevail with her; which are also of two sorts, suited to both parts of the request. 1st, Because her voice was sweet. 2ndly, Her countenance was comely.

I. Here we meet with a new title or character given by Christ to his church, "my dove;" an epithet sometimes used by lovers:[l] he had called her his love and his fair one before, but not his dove, till now; though it is true, he had compared her eyes to dove's eyes, in chap. i. 15. Now the church may be compared to the dove, for the following reasons: 1. The dove is a very beautiful creature; so is the church, as she is washed in Christ's blood, justified by his righteousness, and sanctified by his grace; for though, while in a state of nature, she lay among the pots, and so looked black and uncomely; yet now being called by, and made a partaker of divine grace, she looks like "the wings of a dove covered with silver, and her feathers with yellow gold." 2. It is a very cleanly creature;[m] it loves cleanliness; it keeps its own body clean, and teaches its young to carry their dung out of their nests; it feeds only upon pure grain, and delights in clean water: the church, or believers in Christ, are not only clean through the word which Christ has spoken, but also have their hearts purified by faith in his blood, and delight in purity of life and conversation.

3. It is a very innocent and harmless creature; and therefore Christ says to his disciples, Matt. x. 16; "Be ye wise as serpents, and harmless as doves:" believers are, or at least should be, "blameless, harmless, the sons of God, without rebuke in the midst of a crooked and perverse nation;" they should live not only inoffensive to the world, but also peaceably and quietly among themselves; not biting and devouring one another; nor acting the part of wolves and tigers; but behaving themselves as Christ's innocent sheep and harmless doves. 4. It is an exceeding loving and chaste creature to its mate;[n] it inviolably keeps its conjugal faith; adultery is rarely known among these creatures, and, whenever committed, is punished with death; for males will tear a male to pieces, and a female a female that is found guilty of it: it is also reported of the turtle-dove,[o] that upon the loss of its mate, it remains inconsolable; does not couple again, but continues a widow, and lives a mournful and sorrowful life, avoiding every thing that might tend to remove it, and create pleasure; and that whereas before it delighted in pure and clean water, it now will not drink until it has first bemudded it; nor will it sit upon green and flourishing, but upon dry and withered branches of trees: all which is a lively emblem of the church, who is presented as a chaste virgin to Christ, who bears an exceeding great love and affection to him, and whose absence is what she cannot bear. 5. It is a very fruitful

---

[k] Odit verus amor, nec patitur moras, Senecæ Hercul. Fur. v. 587. [l] Mea columba, Plauti Casina, act. 1. sc. 1. v. 10. Doves being loving creatures, the chariots of Venus were drawn by them, Charter. de Imag. Deorum, p. 218. vid. Apulei Metamorph. 1. 6. and were sacred to Venus, Plutarch. de Isid. et Osir. p. 379. Ælian. de Animal. l. 4. c. 2. [m] Frantz. Hist. Sacr. Animal. par. 2. c. 15. num. 3. [n] Plin. l. 10. c. 34. Ælian. de Animal. l. 3. c. 48. [o] Grapaldus in Sanct. in loc.

creature; though it has not many young ones at a time,ᵖ yet has them very often; *Ælianus* says,ᑫ that it has young ones ten times in a year; nay, in Egypt, twelve times: the church, who is married to Christ, is not only fruitful in grace and good works, but also brings forth many souls unto him, which has been and will be still more eminently seen in the Gentile church; see Isa. liv. 1. 6. It is a sociable creature; doves flock together as birds of a feather usually do: so saints delight to be in each other's company; they join in fellowship one with another, and carry on a social worship together; and do not forsake the assembling of themselves together, as the manner of some too often is. 7. It is a weak and impotent creature, and is often oppressed by birds of prey: the church is often distressed and persecuted by the men of the world, and forced to fly into holes and corners, as the dove does. 8. It is a very fearful and timorous creature; hence Ephraim is compared to the trembling dove,ʳ in Hos. xi. 11; saints are often in trembling fits, at the word of God, and in the exercise of their faith on Christ; under a sense of their own vileness, and in the apprehension of their weakness and want of power to keep and preserve themselves. 9. It has a mournful voice: saints are like doves of the valleys, mourning every one for their iniquities; and often for the loss of Christ's presence, which they are frequently deprived of, through their unbecoming carriage to him. 10. It feeds only upon pure grain: the church feeds only on Christ, and on the wholesome words or comfortable doctrines of the everlasting gospel; she cannot live upon husks that swine eat, nor will she be fed with the chaff of man's inventions. 11. It is also very swift in flying; and therefore David wished for the wings of a dove, that he might flee away, and be at rest: souls, in their first fleeing to Christ for life and salvation, move as swift as the manslayer did from the avenger of blood to the city of refuge; and afterwards, under all their trials and afflictions, he is the Strong Tower, whither they run and are safe: and then more especially, may they be said to be as doves, when they are upon the wing of faith, and mount up as eagles do, run and are not weary, and walk and faint not.

Lastly. It is reported of the dove,ˢ that it will allure wild doves by its familiar converses into the dove-house with it: those who are called by grace, will use all proper ways and methods to allure and gain others to Christ, and to a compliance with his ways and ordinances, as the church does the daughters of Jerusalem in this Song; she being a great lover of the society of saints, and of the glory of Christ therein; as the dove is of its own country, particularly of its own dove-house, and especially when near the habitations of men.

Now Christ's calling the church by this name, " my dove," not only shows his interest in her, but also his affection to her; and perhaps the principal thing he had in view, was to assure her of it, and to encourage her in her present condition; though she was in the cleft of the rock, in a poor, desolate, and forlorn condition, yet she was his dove still; which is the next thing to be considered. For,

II. She is said to be " in the clefts of the rock, in the secret places of the stairs;" which may be understood, either in allusion to the usual place where the dove makes her nest, which is in the rock,ᵗ and " in the sides of the hole's mouth," see Jer. xlviii. 28, and Adrichomiusᵘ tells us, that there was a stone tower near Jerusalem, southward of the mount of Olives, called *Petra Columbarum*, " the rock of the doves," where often five thousand doves were kept at one time; and perhaps here may be an allusion to it: or else, it may be understood of the place where doves are forced to fly when pursued by the hawk, even into a hollow rock, as described by Homer:ʷ and so may be expressive of the state of the church under persecution, when saints are forced to flee into holes and corners, and cannot openly and publicly, worship God, as they used to do, according to his mind and will; but even then God has his hiding-places for them, where he protects and preserves them until the heat of the persecution is over; for at such a time God will have a church, it shall never be entirely rooted out: neither shall his people be without his presence, and some visible manifestations of himself unto them; for he has as great a love for them as ever; the church is his dove then, and her countenance is as comely, and her voice as sweet as ever; nor would he have her be disconsolate and disheartened in her present condition. Most of the Jewish writersˣ refer the words to the condition that the people of Israel were in, when they were pursued by Pharaoh at the Red Sea: which seems, in some measure, to agree with the former sense which has been given. Or else, by the clefts of the rock, may be meant, either, 1. The eternal decree of election, in which, as in an immoveable and inaccessible rock, the church dwelt from all eternity, and will do so until all eternity; which is the sense that Junius gives of these words; God's eternal decree of election is as immoveable as a rock; it is a foundation that stands sure, being laid, not upon the conditions of faith and holiness in the creature, but upon the sovereign will and pleasure of that God, who, " will have mercy on whom he will have mercy," and " will

---

ᵖ Arist. de Gener. Animal. l. 3. c. 1. ᑫ Var. Hist. l. 1. c. 15. ʳ Accipiter trepidas agitat columbas, Ovid. Metamorph. l. 5. ˢ Frantz. Hist. Sacr. animal. par. 2. c. 14. ᵗ Qualis spelunca subito commota columba, cui domus et dulces latebroso in pumice nidi, Virgil. Æneid. 5. v. 213. ᵘ Theatrum Terræ Sanctæ, p. 171. a. ʷ Iliad. 21. v. 493, 494. ˣ Targum, Yalkut, R. Sol. Jarchi, and R. Aben Ezra in loc.

be gracious to whom he will be gracious;" whose purposes cannot be disannulled, nor his counsel made void, nor he ever be frustrated of his end, for the thoughts of his heart shall stand to all generations; and as the degree of election is immoveable, irrevocable, and cannot be altered, so the doctrine of it will stand, maugre all opposition, and will prove a burdensome stone to all those that set themselves against it. Now in the clefts of this rock, the people of God dwell as in a hidden and secret place before conversion; it being neither known to themselves nor others, that they are the objects of it, until called by divine grace: and here they dwell secure, and are safely preserved, notwithstanding the fall of Adam, and their own actual sins and transgressions, until the grace that is laid up for them is actually bestowed upon them; for every one that dwells here, shall be called and sanctified, and at last eternally glorified; not one shall be lost, nor any one link in the golden chain of salvation ever be broken: of which we have an account in Rom. viii. 30, " whom he did predestinate, them he also called; and whom he called, them he also justified; and whom he justified, them he also glorified:" moreover, these persons are and ever were the objects of Christ's love, and so they ever shall be; his love was set upon them, and his delights were with him before the world began; these are his doves, and this the place of their habitation. Or else, 2. By this rock may be meant Christ, who frequently bears this character in scripture, and particularly is said, 1 Cor. x. 4, to be that spiritual rock, of which the Jews drank in the wilderness; and by the clefts thereof, may be meant the wounds of Christ,[y] which were opened for the salvation of sinners, and in which believers dwell by faith, and perhaps to this the allusion is made in Exod. xxxiii. 22, where it is said, that God put Moses into the cleft of the rock, and made his glory to pass before him; for the glory of all the divine perfections is no where so manifestly seen as in a crucified Christ. Now saints are the inhabitants of this rock; here Christ's church dwells, and that safely, being built upon a rock, against which the gates of hell cannot prevail; this is her fortress and strong-hold, where she need not be afraid of any enemy whatever, for her place of defence is the munition of rocks; and therefore, whenever under any apprehension of danger, she betakes herself to her stronghold, to Christ, the Rock that is higher than she. Moreover, the church being said to dwell here, not only shows the safety of her state, but also her majesty and greatness, and her exaltation above others: see Jer. xlix. 16; for dwelling in a rock, she dwells on high; she is not now in the miry clay, but her feet are set upon a rock and her goings are established; she is not now upon the dunghill, but upon the throne; not in a mean cottage, but in a well-built, strong, and fortified castle. Indeed the other phrase, the secret of the stairs, seems to denote abasement and humiliation; though it may be better understood of Christ, as the former expression seems to be; for Christ is the stairs or ladder which Jacob saw in a vision, which reached from earth to heaven; he being God and man in one person, has, by his mediation, blood, and sacrifice, made peace between God and sinful man, reconciled those two contending parties, brought heaven and earth as it were together, and filled up that vast distance that there was between them; he is the ladder or those stairs also, on which the angels of God ascended and descended; see Gen. xxviii. 12, compared with John i. 51: he is likewise our way of access to God, by whom, as by steps, we ascend to him, have admittance into his presence, and are indulged with communion with him: now in the secret of these stairs or steps, did the church lie, as the dove is said to do in some hidden place during the winter season; which was the case of Christ's dove here, see ver 11, for Christ is the " hiding place from the wind, and a covert from the tempest;" and if any thing is particularly intended by the secret of the stairs, Christ's justifying righteousness seems not unlikely; which is secret and hidden to the men of the world, and is only revealed in the Gospel from faith to faith: hither souls betake themselves in times of distress, and, by it they are screened and sheltered from sin, law, hell, and death; and dwelling here, they are in safety; for " he that dwelleth in the secret place of the Most High, shall abide under the shadow of the Almighty." The Ethiopic version renders it, in the shadow of the rock; to which Christ is compared, Isa. xxxii. 2, and so the Septuagint version, in the covering of the rock:[z] which is the shade of it; which seems to be a better sense than what some Jewish writers[a] give of the words, who interpret them of the sanctuary or temple, and of the holy of holies, which was in it. But,

III. I shall now consider the request which he makes unto her, which consists of two parts.
1st. That he might " see her countenance."
2ndly. " Hear her voice."

1st. He desires that she would show him her countenance; which supposes that she had either covered her face, as mourners do, and was bemoaning her present state and condition, bewailing her inward corruptions, as well as her outward afflictions: or else, that she was filled with shame, under a sense of sin, and blushed, as Ezra did, and could not lift up her head and eyes to Christ; but smiting upon her breast, like the poor publican, discovered the inward confusion of her mind: or else, that she was attended with fear, and that not so much with a fear of her enemies,

---

[y] So Foliot, Alcuin, and not. Tigur. in loc.
[z] In tegimento petræ, i. e. tuta præsidio passionis meæ and fidei munimento, Ambros. de Isaac, c. 4. p. 281. in vulneribus quæ pro salute sponsæ sponsus accepit, Isidor. in loc.
[a] In Zohar. in Gen. fol. 59. 1.

as of his displeasure; being conscious to herself that she had acted an unbecoming part towards him: or rather, that she was filled with shamefacedness and bashfulness, and could not, with an holy boldness and an allowed freedom, approach his presence: unless we understand it of the state of the church under the Old Testament, in opposition to this under the New; when the face of the church was veiled, and she only saw Christ through dark shadows and typical ordinances; whereas we now, " with open face, behold, as in a glass, the glory of the Lord." And now, what Christ would have her do in opposition to all this is, to lift up her head with joy, exercise faith upon him, use freedom with him, come with boldness to him, and look him full in the face, and keep always looking to him for every fresh supply of grace, and whatever she might stand in need of he would not have her be shy and bashful, fearful and faithless, but free and familiar with him, with whom he would assure her she might. Unless we would rather understand it of his desire, that she would appear more publicly in his worship, and not lurk in holes and corners, in the clefts of rocks, and under dusty stairs; but show herself in his house, and in the courts of it, and " present herself a living sacrifice, holy, acceptable unto God, which was but her reasonable service;" and especially seeing there was now no danger, for the storms were over, " the winter was past, and the rain was over and gone."

2ndly. He desires that he might hear her voice. Believers should not be dumb when Christ would have them speak: there is a dumbness or silence which is laudable, and that is, either when they are under the afflicting hand of God, or are vilified and reproached for the sake of Christ and his Gospel; but then there is a dumbness which is not so: for as there is " a time to keep silence," so there is " a time to speak." 1. Believers should speak of Christ, of what he is in himself, of the glory of his person, the excellency of his righteousness, the efficacy of his blood, and the sufficiency of his grace; they should also speak of what he is unto them, being of God made unto them, " wisdom, righteousness, sanctification, and redemption;" of what characters he bears, and of what relations he stands in to them, as well as of what he has done for them, in redeeming them, and calling them by his grace. 2. They should speak for Christ, as well as of him; and he is as a person that is much spoken against by the men of the world, therefore believers should speak for him, in vindication of his person, cause, and interest; boldly assert the truths of his Gospel; bravely bear a testimony against all errors, both in doctrine and worship; and not be afraid of men or their revilings. 3. They should speak to Christ; and this perhaps is the voice which Christ more especially desired to hear; they should speak to him in prayer, in praises and thanksgivings,

and ascribe all the glory of their salvation to him; which is but just and reasonable in itself, becoming them, and makes for the advancement of Christ's glory.

IV. The motives or arguments he makes use of to prevail upon her, to grant him what he desired her, 'are these two; 1st. The sweetness of her voice. 2ndly. The comeliness of her countenance: which he mentions, not only to show what induced him to make the request, but also to encourage her to grant it.

1st. He says, that her " voice was sweet;" that is, grateful, acceptable, and exceeding well-pleasing, and therefore he desired to hear it; which she had no reason to be ashamed of. Herodotus[b] makes mention of a dove that spoke with a human voice; such a voice Christ's dove speaks with, and is very grateful to him; the voice as well as the countenance of lovers, is very pleasing;[c] and such was the voice of the church, 1. In speaking of Christ, of what he is in himself and what he is to her, and has done for her, is sweet unto him; he loves to hear his people speak of these things; we are told, Mal. iii. 16, that " they that feared the Lord," spake often one to another;" and what did they speak of? no doubt of the excellency of Christ, of what he had done for, shown unto, and wrought in them: now what acceptance did this meet with from him? why, " he hearkened and heard it, and a book of remembrance was written before him," of all they spake of one to another. 2. Her voice in speaking for him, confessing his name, and bearing a testimony to his truths, is sweet unto him; for he says, Matt. x. 32, that " whosoever shall confess him before men, him will he confess before his Father which is in heaven;" but as for those who are " ashamed of him and of his words " here on earth, he highly resents, and will be ashamed of them another day, and in another world. 3. Her voice in speaking to Christ is sweet; whether it be in prayer or in praise; her voice in prayer is so; and thus the Targum paraphrases the words, " let me hear thy voice, for thy voice is sweet in 'prayer, in the house of the little sanctuary." The prayer of a poor believer makes sweet music in Christ's ears; nothing is so delightful to him; so little reason have souls to be discouraged, or fear a kind reception of their petitions with him: and so her voice in praise and thanksgiving is sweet unto him; praise is not only pleasant in itself, and comely in us, but is also exceeding delightful, to him; this " pleases the Lord better than an ox or bullock that has horns and hoofs," Psal. lxix. 30, 31.

2ndly. He tells her, that her " countenance was comely:" that is, beautiful, and much to be desired; and this Christ says, not only in opposition to what she was in the esteem of the world, who counted her as the offscouring of it, but also to what he was in her esteem, who looked upon

---

[b] Euterpe, sive l. 2. c. 55.   [c] Ω καλλιπροσωπε, χαριτοφωνε, vid. Athen. Deipnosoph. l. 13. c. 2. p. 564.

herself as black and uncomely, and therefore was ashamed to lift up her head, or to have her countenance seen by him; therefore, in order to remove her unbelief, bashfulness, and misgivings of heart, he declares what she was in his esteem, whose judgment is preferable to her own, and to all others beside; for in his opinion, she was "the fairest among women," of a beautiful aspect and comely countenance, being made perfectly comely through that comeliness which he had put upon her: he saw no iniquity in her, nor any spot upon her, as clothed with his righteousness; she was in his eye a "perfection of beauty;" having the most just symmetry and proportion of parts, the most agreeable shape, and the most lovely features in her face; her cheeks, being "comely with rows of jewels, and her neck with chains of gold," as in chap. i. 10. Faith is most properly the believer's face or countenance, by which he looks on Christ, and views a fulness and suitableness in him, and expects all needful supplies from him; which look of faith on Christ, for life and salvation, is exceeding pleasant, nay, ravishing to him; and therefore he would have his church behold him again and again; for saints never appear more comely in Christ's eye, than when they take a full view of him.

Verse 15. *Take us the foxes, the little foxes that spoil the vines; for our vines have tender grapes.*

WHETHER these words are the words of Christ or of the church, is not so manifest. Some think that they are the words of the church, to whom the care of the vineyard was committed: which, though she had in some measure neglected, as appears from chap. i. 6, yet now is heartily concerned for the flourishing of it; and therefore calls upon her attendants and companions to assist in destroying those noxious creatures the foxes, which did so much mischief to the vines that grew in it; though they rather seem to be the words of Christ, who is the owner of the vineyard, and has an authoritative power over the officers of the church, and ministers of the gospel, to stir them up to be sedulous and careful in the discharge of their work; for the words seem to be directed, not to angels, nor to his bride, the church, nor to the civil magistrate, but to ministers, who are more particularly employed in the care of Christ's vineyard: and if we take them to be the words of Christ, it not only shows the power and authority of Christ over those he speaks to, and lays his commands on in so strict a manner; but also his love to, and care of his vines, the several churches, which his own right-hand has planted: though perhaps they may be words of them both jointly together; for the church, with Christ, and under him, has a right to stir up her officers to perform their work, and fulfil their ministry, which they have received of the Lord Jesus; the doing of which will redound to his glory, and her good; they both having an interest in the vines here mentioned; also the foxes, which they are ordered to take, were common enemies, both to Christ and his church; and therefore it is not said, "take for me or thee, but take for us the foxes." In these words may be observed,

I. A command that is laid upon the ministers of the Gospel, "to take the foxes, even the little foxes."

II. Some arguments or motives proposed to stir them up to an observance of it."

I. The thing enjoined them, is, to "take the foxes."

By foxes we are to understand, either,

1st. The sins and corruptions of our nature, which may be compared unto them for the following reasons: 1. As foxes have their lurking-holes in the earth, so have these in the hearts of men, where they lie a long time undiscovered; and that not only in the hearts of wicked men, but also in the hearts of God's own people; and therefore, says David, Psal. xix. 12, "Who can understand his errors? cleanse thou me from secret faults;" now it is only the Spirit of God, who "searcheth the deep things of God," that can search the inmost recesses of our hearts, discover our vile corruptions, bring them out of their lurking-holes, and slay them by the mighty power of his grace. 2. The sins and corruptions of our nature may be compared to foxes for their deceitfulness, therefore are they called "deceitful lusts;" and well they may, for we are often imposed upon by them, and deceived with them, and that under the notion either of pleasure, profit, or honour, which they promise to us, but leave us entirely short of: there is a deceitfulness in sin, which makes our hearts so deceitful, and desperately wicked as they be. 3. For the crooked ways which they take: the fox[d] does not walk straight forward, but with several windings and turnings; the ways of sin are all crooked ways; they are so many distortions from the ways of God and godliness, which are straight and even; and are so many aberrations from the divine law, which is the rule of our obedience unto God. 4. For making places barren and desert,[e] wherever they come: sin makes persons barren and unfruitful, both in the knowledge of Christ, and in the performance of duty; so that they look like "the heath in the desert," and like "parched places in the wilderness." 5. For their friendship with serpents:[f] there is a secret correspondence held between Satan, that old serpent, and the corruptions of our nature; by virtue of which he often compasses his end, and gains his purpose, which he could not do on Christ, there being no such matter for him to work upon; he had none of his old friends there to let him in, as he has in our hearts.

---

[d] Frant. Hist. Sacr. Animal. par. 1. c. 17.
[e] Ibid.   [f] Ibid Aristot. Hist. Animal. l. 9. c.
1. Plutarch de Solert. Animal. p. 981.

Now the ministers of the Gospel may be said to take these foxes, when they lift up their voices like a trumpet, and exclaim against them, expose the wickedness and deceitfulness of them, and show souls the danger they are in by them, when they are made useful to bring persons under a conviction of them, and, as it were, to ferret them out of their lurking holes: moreover, by the power of the Spirit of God attending the ministry, the "strong-holds of sin" are pulled down, and the vain imaginations of men's hearts subdued, and every vile thought brought "into captivity, to the obedience of Christ," and a revenge taken upon all disobedience. Not but that private Christians, as well as ministers, should watch and pray against them; fight in order to take them, and, when taken, should bring them to Christ, as his and their enemies, to be slain by the mighty power of his grace; and not only gross sins, but even "little foxes," the very first motions of sin, are to be watched against and struck at; we should abstain from all appearance of it, knowing that lesser sins will bring us into the commission of greater, and insensibly grow upon us; so R. Alshech interprets these little foxes of little sins. Or else,

2ndly. By these foxes may be meant false teachers or heretics; so the false prophets in Ezekiel's time were called by him, Ezek. xiii. 3, 4. "O Israel, thy prophets are like the foxes in the deserts;" and so may false apostles and false teachers now, and that for the following reasons; 1. For their craftiness, and subtlety. The fox is remarkable for its cunning and craftiness, of which some writers give us many instances: sometimes he feigns himself dead, lies upon his back, with his mouth open, and his tongue out, so that he looks every way as a dead carcase: by which means he invites the fowls of the air to feed upon him, but when come, devours them with open mouth;[g] for the same purpose, at other times, he rolls himself in the red earth, that he might appear as bloody, and then, as before, lays himself down upon the ground as dead, and thereby lays a bait for the unwary birds: so when he is taken in a snare, and finds that there is no escaping, he prostrates himself upon the ground, holds his breath, and in all appearance seems dead, which the snare-setter supposing to be real, looses the snare, without any suspicion of his escaping: but finding himself free, gets upon his legs, and away he runs; also when hunted, he will run among a flock of sheep or goats, and leap upon the back of some one of them, which puts the whole flock into a fright, and causes them to run one after another, and, for fear of damage, the huntsman is obliged to call in his dogs: these, with many other instances of his subtlety, as his artful method of catching crabs and lobsters with his tail, destroying of wasps, clearing himself of fleas, tricking the hedge-hog, revenging himself upon the badger, and catching of hares, are recorded by several writers.[h] Hence false teachers may be very fitly compared unto them, who act in disguise, lie in wait to deceive, walk in craftiness, and handle the word of God deceitfully, speak lies in hypocrisy, use good words and fair speeches, and thereby deceive the hearts of the simple. 2. For their malignity: foxes are cruel as well as cunning; they are very noxious and hurtful creatures; and so are false teachers, they are wolves though in sheep's clothing; their heresies are damnable, their doctrines are pernicious, and their words eat as doth a canker; they subvert the faith of some, and bring ruin and destruction upon themselves and others. 3. For their hunger and voraciousness: all the cunning and cruelty that the fox uses, is to satisfy his greedy appetite; and so the principal end of false teachers, is not to serve Christ, but their own bellies, to devour widows' houses, and making merchandise of others, to enrich themselves, and indulge their own pride and vanity. 4. For their feigning themselves to be domestics: it is reported of the fox,[i] that when it draws nigh to a farm-house, it will mimic the barking of a dog, which the hens and geese being used to, walk about with less guard, and with more confidence approach to him, and so are surprised and devoured by him; so false teachers put on sheep's clothing, transform themselves into angels of light, as their master before them has done; mimic the voice of Christ's ministers; use some phrases and expressions which they do, which serve as a blind to the people; and so craftily do they put their words together, that it is not an easy thing to discover them. 5. As foxes are filthy, abominable, and stinking creatures, so are these, not only to God, but to his people; and therefore are also compared to wolves and dogs; and are not so much as to be received into the houses of good people, nor to be bid God-speed by them.

Now the ministers of the Gospel are to take these foxes; they being overseers of the flock, and keepers of Christ's vineyard, are to watch against them, and make a discovery of them, they are to oppose and refute their erroneous doctrines; and being detected, and convicted of heresies, they are with the church after proper admonitions given, to reject and cut them off from the church, and communion with it: it is true, they are not to take away their lives, but they are to exclude them from fellowship with them, and not suffer them to continue with them either as members or officers; nay, even the little foxes are to be taken. Heresy is compared to leaven: the erroneous doctrines of the Scribes and pharisees are called so, and "a little leaven leaveneth the whole lump." Heresies and heretics are to be nipped in the bud, otherwise they will increase to more

---

[g] Vid. Isidor. Origin. l. 12. c. 2. [h] Ælian. de Animal. l. 4. c. 39. and l. 6. c. 24, 64, and l. 13. c. 11. Olaus Magnus, Hist. Septent. l. 18. c. 31. and Frantz. Hist. Sacr. Animal. par. 1. c. 17. [i] Olaus Magnus in loc. supracit.

ungodliness; great things have risen from small beginnings: these things should be taken in time; for errors, seemingly small at first, have grown larger, have spread themselves, and have been very fatal to the churches of Christ; therefore no error or heresy should be connived at, under a notion of its being a small or a harmless one; for even little foxes are to be taken. Some[d] connect the word little with the vines next mentioned; and so it strengthens the reason, why care should be taken to preserve them from the foxes, since they are small and tender.

3rdly. Here the motives and arguments proposed to induce a compliance to this command of Christ's. 1. The mischief which these foxes do to the vines, is made use of as one, which spoil the vines; it has been observed by many,[1] that these kind of creatures do hurt to the vines; and that by destroying the fences, gnawing the branches, biting the bark, making bare the roots of the vines, devouring the ripe grapes thereof, and infecting all with their noxious teeth and vicious breath: so heretics and false teachers break down the church's fence, by making schisms and divisions, make bare her roots, sap the very foundation of religion, by corrupting the word of God, and denying the great doctrines of the Gospel; and hurt her fruit, by disturbing the peace of her members, unsettling some, and subverting others. 2. Another argument that is made use of to stir them up to diligence in taking the foxes, is because the vines have tender grapes; by vines are meant the several distinct congregated churches of Christ; by the tender grapes or flowers thereof, we are to understand young converts, whom Christ is very tender of, and has a particular regard unto; see Isa. xl. 11, and xlii. 3, and these having but a small degree of faith, knowledge, and experience, like children, are more easily "tossed to and fro, and carried about with every wind of doctrine, by the sleight of men, and cunning craftiness of these foxes, whereby they lie in wait to deceive: now generally they make their onset upon these, as being more easily wrought upon, and by whom they can with more facility compass their end; and this being then the case, the ministers of Christ ought to be more sedulous and diligent in the discovering of those foxes, from whom so much mischief may be expected, and more bold, vigorous, and courageous in opposing and rejecting them; seeing the churches of Christ are like to sustain so considerable a loss by them, and in danger of having a promising vintage spoiled. It is true, the foxes love the ripe grapes and devour them, and not when they are blossoming and knotting; which shows Christ's care of his vines to be the greater, that he would have little foxes taken while the vines were blowing; for by such time as the grapes were ripe, these little foxes would be great ones, and would be capable of doing more damage, and not so easy to be taken neither; so that the consideration also of there being less difficulty now, than there would be hereafter, might animate them to set about the work immediately. 3. Christ seems to intimate as if they had some interest in these vines; for which reason they ought to be the more heartily and vigorously concerned for the welfare of them; therefore they are called our vines: it is true, Christ has a sole right unto, and property in the vineyard; the vines are all of his planting, and the fruit of them belongs to him; yet those to whom the vineyard is let out, who are intrusted with the care of the vines, and who must give an account of them to the chief and principal owner, have also an interest therein; for though our great Solomon must have a thousand, whose the vineyard is; yet "those that keep the fruit thereof must have two hundred," Cant. viii. 11, 12; so that if they should be negligent in their work, and suffer the foxes to overrun the vineyard, and spoil the vines, they would not only incur the displeasure of the owner of them, but sustain a loss themselves, by coming short of the fruit which otherwise would be distributed to them. Now such arguments as these, which have interest and profit contained in them, usually have the greatest influence upon persons; Christ knew this, and therefore uses such an one here.

Verse 16. *My beloved is mine and I am his: he feedeth among the lilies.*

CHRIST having given such evidences of his love, and instances of his care and kindness to the church in the preceding verses; she, in this, declares her faith in him, and signifies the obligation which she lay under to observe his commands. "My beloved is mine;" he hath given himself to me, his heart is set upon me, and is always careful of me, and concerned for me; of which he has given the fullest proof, I could wish for: "and I am his;" I give up myself to him, and am at his disposal, and think myself obliged to observe whatever he enjoins me, and to follow him whithersoever he calls me; especially seeing it is for my good; it makes both for my pleasure and profit, as well as for his glory; for "he feedeth among the liles." I need not fear his leading me into danger, or any desolate places, but where lilies grow, where is all delight and pleasure; he will lead me into green pastures, where I may have food, and fulness of it. And,

First. These words are expressive of the mutual interest and property which Christ and the church have in each other; "my beloved is mine, and I am his;" he has interest in me, and I have the same in him.

1st. She says, "my beloved is mine." She first asserts her interest in Christ, and then his

---

[k] Vid. Theodoret. in loc.   [l] Vid. Theocrit. Idyll. 1. v. 48, 49. and Iydll. 5. v. 112, 113. So Soldiers are compared to foxes, because they eat the grapes in the countries they come into, Aristoph. Equites, act. 3. sc. 1. p. 350.

interest in her; for Christ is first ours, and then we are his because he is ours; he loves us before we love him; he first gives himself to us, and then we give ourselves to him. But how comes Christ to be ours? I answer, 1. By the Father's gift; he gave him for us, and he gave him to us; therefore Christ is called, John iv. 10, "the gift of God," and that by way of eminence, he being the first and best gift, the most comprehensive one, that includes all others in it, and brings them with it; for he that gives the greater gift, will give the lesser; if he gives his own Son, "he will give all things with him;" him he has given to be a Husband to his church, and a Head over her; he has given him to be a Priest to offer up sacrifice, and to make intercession for her; to be a Prophet to teach, and a King to rule her; and surely such a gift as this deserves the utmost thanks: so that there is reason to say with the apostle, 2 Cor. ix. 15, "thanks be to God for his unspeakable gift;" and thus Christ becomes ours. 2. By his own gift; he has given himself to us as well as for us; he gave himself a sacrifice for us, and that as an instance of his love to us, as well as a fruit of his having given himself in covenant to us before. 3. By marriage: Christ has not only espoused our cause, but has also espoused our persons, and betrothed us to himself "in righteousness, and in judgment, and in lovingkindness, and in mercies, and in faithfulness," and that for ever; so that, O astonishing grace! he that is our Maker is become our Husband. 4. By possession: we have him and all things pertaining to life and salvation with him; we have him in us as the hope of glory, dwelling in our hearts by faith, living there as in his own house and temple, and reigning there by his grace and Spirit, as in his own palace; and those souls who can experience this, may say with the church, my beloved is mine; I have an interest in him, for I am in possession of him. Thus Christ is the church's. But

2ndly. She says also, that she was his; I am his; and that because he is mine. Now how come souls to be Christ's? I answer, 1. By the Father's gift: he that gives Christ to us, gives us also to Christ; and this he did in the everlasting covenant, to be his bride and wife, to be his portion and inheritance, and to be kept and preserved by him safe to glory. Christ having pitched his love upon us, chose us for his own, and asked us of his Father, who granted his request; "thine they were," says Christ, John xvii. 6, "and thou gavest them me." 2. By purchase: he has bought us with a price, and that not with corruptible things, as silver and gold, but with his own most precious blood; so that he does, as he justly may, claim an interest in us upon this account. 3. By the conquest of his grace upon our hearts: he pulls down the strong-holds of our hearts; enters in with his glorious train and retinue of grace, dispossesses Satan, dethrones sin, sets up a throne for himself, and places his own Spirit in the midst of us, which is the grand evidence of our being his; "for if any man have not the Spirit of Christ, he is none of his;" from whence it may be inferred, that he that has the Spirit of Christ, is one of his. 4. By a voluntary surrender of ourselves unto him; which cannot be better expressed than it is in Isa. xliv. 5, "One shall say, I am the Lord's;" which is the language of the church here: "another shall call himself by the name of Jacob;" which is the name of Christ's church; "and another shall subscribe with his hand unto the Lord, and surname himself by the name of Israel;" and this in New-Testament-language, is called a giving themselves to the Lord, and to the church by the will of God; so that as Christ is ours by his own consent, we are Christ's by our consent, being made a willing people in the day of his power.

Now from Christ's being ours, it follows, 1. That all he has is ours; all his perfections are ours; not that they are communicated to us, for that would be to deify us; but they are all engaged for our eternal good and welfare; we have the comfort of them. Is he the Almighty? then he is able to save us from law, sin, hell, and death, and to keep and preserve us safe to his kingdom and glory. Is he omnipresent? hence saints enjoy his gracious presence, in all places, in all his ordinances; he can be with them, when and where he pleases. Is he omniscient? he knows their persons, their wants, their enemies, &c., and is both able and willing to help them. Is he immutable? Is he Jesus, "the same yesterday, to-day, and for ever?" they need not then fear any variation of his mind, any alteration in his love, nor change in their state; and thus all other of his divine perfections serve to advance their comfort and happiness. 2. That all he has is theirs; his Person is theirs, to render them acceptable to God; his blood theirs, to cleanse and pardon them; his righteousness theirs, to justify and acquit them before God; his fulness theirs, to supply their wants; and all covenant-blessings and promises which he has in his hands, are theirs. Therefore, 3. It follows, that they can want no good thing; for as he has ability to help them, he has a heart to do it, and will not withhold any thing that may be needful and proper for them, especially seeing they have an indisputable right to and interest in them.

Moreover, from our being Christ's it follows, that we are not our own; our persons, our time, and talents, our gifts and graces, are not our own, but his, and therefore we should give up all unto him, and glorify him with all: nor are we any others; we are not Satan's, for Christ has delivered us as lawful captives out of his hands: nor sin's, for Christ has redeemed us from it; nor the world's, for Christ has both chosen and called us out of it; and therefore we should serve none but him, who has an incontestible right to us, and a sovereign power over us.

Secondly, These words are expressive of a near union, that there is between Christ and his church; these two are one in a conjugal relation, as husband and wife are one; my beloved is my Husband

and I am his wife, and we are both one flesh. Which union is, 1. Personal: it is an union of persons, that is to say, the whole person of Christ as God-man, is united to a believer; and the whole person of a believer, body and soul, is united to Christ; and by virtue of this union, as the souls of the saints shall be received into everlasting habitations till the resurrection-morn, so the bodies of the saints shall be raised from their dusty beds, and shall then live with Christ for evermore. 2. It is a spiritual union; "he that is joined to the Lord, is one spirit:" Christ and his church being one, they have one and the same Spirit; Christ has it without measure, and the church in measure; and this she has as the fruit of her union to Christ, and also as the evidence of it. 3. It is a vital union; such an one as is between the vine and branches: where the Spirit of Christ is given, a principle of life is implanted; when souls are ingrafted into Christ, they receive life from Christ; nay, he lives in them, and maintains this spiritual life by fresh communications of life from himself, who is the Fountain of it; and because he lives, they shall live also; as long as there is life in the Head, there shall be life in the members; and because there is life in the root, the branches shall not wither. 4. It is very mysterious: the union of the three Persons in one divine essence, and that of two natures in Christ's person, are very mysterious; these, without controversy, are the great mysteries of godliness: and next to them is this union of souls to Christ, which the apostle having spoken of, thus says, Eph. v. 32, "This is a great mystery, but I speak of Christ and the church;" that is, of the union there is between Christ and the church: that it is an ineffable and inconceivable one, appears from its being compared to the union of the divine Persons in the Godhead, John xvii. 11—23. 5. It is an indissoluble one: Christ and the church can never be separated; the union-bond can never be broken; and what is that? The generality of divines say, that it is the Spirit on Christ's side, and faith on ours; but neither the Spirit nor faith are the bond of union, but the fruits and effects of it: the reason why the Spirit is given, or faith, or any other graces are wrought, is, because the soul is already united to Christ. What then is the bond of union? I answer, Christ's everlasting love; it is this which is the cement that knits and joints souls unto him. What was it that knit and united the souls of David and Jonathan together, and made them as if they had been but one soul, but love? What is it that knits the saints together? so as they appear to be of one heart and one soul, but love? This is the bond of union between them; and so it is between Christ and his church; and now who or what can separate from this love? This betrothment, which was done in loving-kindness and in mercies, can never be made void; this marriage-knot can never be loosed; this union-bond can never be broken; Christ's love is everlasting, unchangeable, and inseparable.

Now from this union flow, 1. An interest in all he has; he being ours, and we his by marriage; all his goods are ours, all the aforementioned things are ours. 2. A communication of names: the church is called by the name of Christ, 1 Cor. xii. 12, Jer. xxiii. 16, compared with Jer. xxxiii. 6; and Christ is called by the church's name, Isa. xlix. 3; which is somewhat remarkable; for though it is usual for the wife to take the name of the husband, yet not the husband the name of the wife. 3. Conformity to Christ: by virtue of this union, the soul receives the same Spirit that Christ has, and has grace daily communicated from, is indulged with transforming views of, and therefore cannot but bear some resemblance to him; which will more fully appear in the other world, when saints shall be like him, and shall see him as he is. 4. Communion and fellowship with him: communion with Christ follows upon union to him; because his saints and he are both one, he is not ashamed to call them brethren; but takes them into his bosom, indulges them with his presence, grants them nearness to and familiarity with him.

Thirdly. These words are also expressive of the mutual affection, delight, and complacency, which Christ and his church have in each other: it is as if she should say, He is a beloved to me, and I am the same to him; he loves me and I love him; yea, there is no love lost between us. He says, that the lines are fallen to him in pleasant places, and that he has a goodly heritage: he is well pleased with his portion, and I am well pleased with mine: for, "whom have I in heaven but him? and there is none upon earth that I desire besides him." He says, that I am in his eye "the fairest among women," the greatest beauty in the world, and so is he in mine; he is white and ruddy, a complete beauty, "the chiefest among ten thousand."

Fourthly. There is in them a manifest declaration of the assurance of that knowledge and faith which she had of her interest in Christ; it shows us, that such a thing is attainable; and, sure I am, next to the enjoyment of the heavenly glory, nothing is more desirable; it is a mercy not only to have an interest in Christ, but also to know it, to be capable of saying with Thomas, "My Lord and my God;" or with Job, "I know that my Redeemer liveth;" or with the apostle Paul, "I know whom I have believed;" for this makes much for the comfort of souls. The church seems to speak this in the triumph of faith, rejoicing in the comfortable views of Christ as her own; and as it were boasting of it, excluding all other beloveds, as not worthy of her notice, and as not to be mentioned with her beloved.

Lastly. She tells us, that this beloved of hers was feeding among the lilies; "he feedeth among the lilies:" which may be regarded either as an apostrophe to him, and may be read thus, "O thou that feedest among the lilies!" thou, and thou only, art mine, and I am thine: or else, these words may be descriptive of his person, and prevent a question that might be asked, viz., who her beloved was, that she thus claimed an interest in? To which she answers, My beloved is that yonder person you see feeding among the lilies; and at the same time also points out to us the place where he was, and what he was about: his employment was feeding, that is, either feeding himself; which Christ does, when he delights and recreates himself in his gardens, the churches, and among his lilies, the saints; observing how their faith grows, and how that all o'her graces are exercised upon himself: or else, feeding his flock, as R. Sol. Jarchi observes; for as he bears the character of a Shepherd, so he performs the work of one; "he feeds his flock like a shepherd;" see chap. i. 7. The place where he is here said to feed, is among the lilies; by which may be meant, either a good, quiet, and delightful pasture, as R. Sol. Jarchi glosses it. Christ leads and feeds his people in "green pastures, beside the still or quiet waters;" and what can be more delightful than to lie down among, or to sit and feed where lilies grow? or else, by these lilies may be meant the scriptures of truth, the precious promises and comfortable doctrines of the gospel, and the ordinances thereof, with which Christ feeds his church: or rather, by them may be meant the saints, who are compared thereunto, in verse 2, of this chapter. Now it is among these that Christ feeds; and therefore do any want to know where Christ feeds, as the church did, in chap. i. 7? he feeds among his saints, where they are congregated in gospel order, where his lilies grow. It may be observed, it is not said, he feedeth on, or feeds his flock with lilies, but among them; for it is remarked,[m] that sheep will not eat them: or the sense may be, Christ feeds himself, and feeds his people, and feeds among them, as if he was crowned with lilies, and anointed with the oil of them; as was the custom of the ancients at festivals,[n] thought to be here alluded to by some, who read the words,, "that feeds;" that is, feeds, sups in, or with lilies, being crowned with them, and anointed with the oil of them. The lily is a summer flower;[o] the winter was now past, verse 11; and so agrees with the time when those words were spoken.

Verse 17. *Until the day break, and the shadows flee away; turn, my beloved, and be thou like a roe, or a young hart, upon the mountains of Bether.*

THE former part of these words, "until the day break, and the shadows flee away," may stand connected with either part of the preceding verse, either with those words, my beloved is mine, and I am his,[p] which are expressive, as has been observed, of that mutual interest, union, communion, satisfaction, and delight, which Christ and his church have in and with each other; and then the sense is, as long as day and night continue, and God's covenant with both stands sure, so long will my covenant-interest in, and union to Christ, who is my beloved, abide solid and unshaken; I can no more be separated from his person, and from his love, than day and night can cease; and when they do, I shall be taken up into everlasting and uninterrupted communion with him, which is now subject to the same vicissitudes as these returning seasons are: or else, they may stand connected with the latter part of the preceding verse, " he feedeth among the lilies, until the day break,"[q] &c., and so are expressive of the continual presence of Christ in his church, until his second coming, when the everlasting day shall break, and all shadows of darkness flee away; till then, as in chap. iv. 6, he will be on his mountain of myrrh, and hill of frankincense; where he will delight himself with, and feed among his saints, until all his elect ones are called by grace, and till all his lilies are grown up to their full maturity, when he will gather them to himself; though the words may be also considered as connected with the latter part of this verse, "turn my beloved," &c., and so they contain a prayer of the church's for Christ's speedy access unto her, and continued presence with her, until the day should break, and the shadows flee away. In which may be considered,

I. The favour which she requests of him, which is, 1st, To turn, that is, unto her; and this she desires that he would do speedily, and therefore says, " be thou like a roe or a young hart upon the mountains of Bether."

II. The time unto which she desires this favour might be continued to her: and that is, until the day break, upon which the shadows would flee away.

I. The favour which she desires of him is, that he would turn unto her; which seems to intimate as though he was about to leave her; which, upon some account or other, she had a suspicion of, therefore importunes him to stay with her; and seeing him upon the motion, upon the turn, ready to depart, she desires that he would turn again, and continue with her: or else, it supposes that he was entirely gone, and that she was sensible of it: and having a great value for Christ's person and presence, desires that he would turn again to her: such a petition as this, under a sense of desertion, is frequently put up by the psalmist, particularly in Psalm lx. 1, and lxix. 16, 17, and lxxxvi. 16; though the word may be rendered, *turn about* or *surround*,[r] that is, with thy favour and loving-kindness; let me always be under thy care and protection; be thou a wall of fire round about me; so shall I be safe and secure from all enemies, until the glorious and wished-for-day breaks, when I shall be out of fear, as well as out of dan-

---

[m] Tuccius apud Soto Major in loc. [n] Fortunat. Schuc. Eleochrysm. Sacr l. 1. c. 28. p. 137.
[o] Theophrast. apud Athen. Deipnosophist l. 15. c.
[p] So R. Sol. Jarchi in loc. [q] Vid. Sanct. in loc. [r] סבי *circui*, Montanus, Sanctius; *circumito*, some in Michaelis.
7. p. 679.

ger: and this favour she desires might be speedily granted to her, and therefore says, "be thou like a roe or young hart;" which are not only loving and pleasant, but also swift and nimble creatures. She had experienced Christ to be so before, and therefore might the more comfortably hope that he would be so to her now: she adds, "upon the mountains of Bether;" by which perhaps may be meant Bithron, of which we read in 1 Sam. ii. 29, and was so called, because it was parted or separated from Judea by the river Jordan; though some think it should be read *Bethel*, by a change of a letter: and so the Septuagint reads it in ver. 9; which is there an addition to the Hebrew text; though they here render it, ὄρη κοιλωμάτων, *the mountains of cavities*, that is, such that were full of clefts and hollow places; but be they what they will, it is certain that they were such places where roes and fawns used to skip and run. The words may be very well rendered, *the mountains of division*,* which, if referred to Christ's first coming in the days of his flesh, may regard the ceremonial law, which made and kept up the division between Jew and Gentile, was the partition wall between them, which was broken down by Christ Jesus: or else, the two people divided by it, to whom Christ came, for whom he made peace, to whom he preached it, and thereby made both one. But if we refer the words to Christ's spiritual coming in a way of special grace to visit his people; then these mountains of division, upon which Christ comes, and over which he leaps as a roe or a young hart, may be our sins and corruptions, which often separate between him and our souls; though, when he is pleased to come, they are no obstacles in his way, but are easily surmounted or removed by him; but if they be applied to Christ's second coming at the day of judgment; these mountains of division may intend the spacious heavens, in which Christ shall then appear, which at present interpose between him and us, and separate us from the enjoyment of his bodily presence; one part or branch of whose awful work then will be, to separate the sheep from the goats. But,

11. How long does she desire to be indulged with this favour of enjoying his gracious presence, in the discoveries of himself, and of his love unto her, without which she could not live, and therefore desires it might be speedily granted to her? and that is, "until the day break, and the shadows flee away;" which may be understood, either,

1st. Of Christ's coming in the flesh, which was the break and dawn of the Gospel day, until the day break; or, according to the Hebrew text, "until the day breathe or blow,"† and naturalists" have observed, that upon the sun's rising, an air or wind has been excited: so upon the rising of "the Sun of righteousness with healing in his wings," were raised some fine, cool, gentle, and refreshing breezes of divine grace and consolation. Before Christ's coming in the flesh, it was night, not only in the Gentile, but in the Jewish world; there was a great deal of darkness, blindness, and ignorance, infidelity, sleepiness, and security; but upon the arising of this Sun, and breaking or breathing of this day, all this was in a great measure dispelled, and light, nay a great light, was introduced; for Christ's coming was "as the light of the morning, when the sun riseth, even a morning without clouds;" he came as the light of the world, and made that day, that Gospel-day, which, by way of eminency, is so often spoken of in the Old Testament, when the shadows of the old law fled and disappeared: so the law is called "a shadow of good things to come," and that because it was a representation of them; which were so sooner come, but this was gone, and, like a shadow, appeared fleeting and transitory; and whilst it continued, was dark and obscure; though there was some glimmering of light in it, which led the faith of the Old Testament saints to Christ, who was represented by it; but now these shadows are gone, Christ the body and substance being come; this middle wall of partition is broken down; this hand-writing of ordinances is taken away, and the whole Mosaic dispensation and economy is waxen old and vanished; there being a disannulling of it because of the weakness and unprofitableness thereof; and a glorious dispensation and bright day of Gospel grace introduced in the room of it, and all by the appearance of Christ in our nature; which was the great thing promised, prophesied of, long expected, and earnestly wished for by the Old Testament saints, as it was perhaps by the church here. Or else,

2ndly. This may be understood of Christ's second coming to judgment: which, as the former is called that day in the Old Testament by way of eminency, as being that great, glorious, and notable day of the Lord, so is this in the New; for the former, see Isa. xi. 10, and xxv. 9, and xxvi. 1, and xxvii. 1, 2, 13, and for this, see Phil. i. 6, 2 Tim. i. 12, 1 Thess. v. 2, 4; and this as well suits both with the Hebrew text, and with the natural philosophy of it, as the former: Christ's second coming will be at the evening, both of the world and of the Gospel dispensation, when "the shadows of the evening are stretched out upon us; at a time when there will be a great deal of darkness and ignorance, much want of faith, and a very great sleepiness and security, which will seize upon professors, as well as upon profane; but upon Christ's

---

* על הרי בתר, in montibus divisionis, Vatablus, Piscator; scissionis, Cocceius; dissectionis, Marckius; sectionis vel separationis, Michaelis.

† עד שיפוח ἕως οὗ διανεύσῃ, Sept. donec vel dum spiret, Mercerus, Cocceius; aspiret, Marckius, spiraverit, Michaelis.   " Plin. Nat. Hist. l. 7. c. 47. Senecæ Nat. Quæst. l. 5. c. 8.

appearance, a glorious and everlasting day will break, the shadows of darkness and ignorance will flee away; we shall know as we are known, and see him as he is; not as now, "through a glass darkly, but face to face;" all infidelity, doubts and fears, will be removed; everlasting joy will be upon our heads; no interposing clouds will be between Christ and our souls; but we shall have the everlasting enjoyment of him, and uninterrupted communion with him: there will then be no need of the sun and moon, of gospel-ordinances; for the glory of God will lighten both our persons and the place of our residence, and the Lamb himself will be the light thereof; so shall we ever be in his presence, see his face clearly, without any mixture of darkness and unbelief, and without any fear of the shadows of the evening returning upon us; there will be no more night, but one pure, bright, and everlasting day. Moreover, naturalists[w] have observed, that the wind often blows fresh, and fine breezes of air are raised at the sun-setting, as well as at the sun-rising; so that the words, until the day blow or breathe, that is, at the cool of the day, when the wind blows fresher, and there are gentle breezes of air, which often are in the evening; at which time it may be very well supposed that God appeared to Adam in the garden after his fall; I say, these words may be very well applied to the evening of the world, or second coming of Christ; which, though it will be with flames of fire, to take vengeance on the wicked, yet to the saints it will be "a time of refreshing from the presence of the Lord;" which time is earnestly wished for by them; their desire is, that Christ would be as a roe or young hart to hasten it; for, as he says, "I surely come quickly," they return and say, "Amen, even so, come Lord Jesus." So some Jewish[x] writers interpret these words of the day of judgment, and compare them with Mal. iv. 1.

CHAPTER III.

In this chapter an account is given of an adventure of the church in quest of her beloved; of the time when, and places where, and the persons of whom she sought him: and of her success upon the whole; with a charge she gave to the daughters of Jerusalem, verse 1—5, by whom she is commended, verse 6; and then Christ her beloved is described by her; by his bed, and the guard about it, verse 7, 8; by the chariot he rode in, verse 9, 10; and by the crown he wore on his coronation-day; to which sight the daughters of Zion are invited, verse 11.

Verse 1. *By night on my bed I sought him whom my soul loveth; I sought him, but I found him not.*

FROM hence it appears, that the day was not as yet broken, which the church had mentioned in the last verse of the preceding chapter; but that the night was still upon her, even the night of Jewish darkness, when the shadows of the ceremonial law were stretched out upon her; yet having some small knowledge of Christ by types and prophecies, which had raised in her a desire of knowing more of him, as well as filled her with love to him, she sought after him; which at present was not attended with success, it not being his will as yet to appear to her in that manner she was desirous of: though indeed the words may be taken in a more large and comprehensive sense; and may represent the state and condition of the church of Christ, and all true believers, in all ages of the world, at one time or another; and in them may be observed,

I. The church's case, which was the absence of her beloved.

II. How she behaved herself under it, or what she did in order to remove it; "she sought him." And, 1st. The person whom she sought is described; "him whom my soul loveth." 2ndly. The place where she sought him is mentioned; "on my bed." 3rdly. The time when; "by night." 4thly. The success she had in seeking; "but I found him not."

I. The church's case here appears to be, absence of her beloved; which is not only manifest from her seeking of him, though that clearly shows that he was absent from her, but also from the time in which she sought him, which was by night; for as Christ's presence makes the believer's day, so his absence makes it night with them; as well as from the place where she sought him, and that is, upon her bed; which shows that she was in a sleepy, slothful, and secure frame of spirit, which is never attended with a lively sense and feeling of Christ's gracious presence. Now from this being the church's case, we may observe, 1. That the change of a believer's frame is often very sudden; not only their frames are changeable, but they are often changed: it was not long since that the church was in the banqueting-house with Christ, and there had her fill of love, and was sweetly refreshed with his gracious presence: and though she fell into a relapse of dulness and sleepiness, yet he in love visits her again, and recovers her out of it; insomuch that she became so lively in the exercise of her faith, that she could claim her interest in him, and relation to him, and say, "My beloved is mine, and I am his;" and yet now she is at a loss for him, and knows not where he is; she is grown dull and sleepy, carnal and secure, and he withdraws himself from her; so that a believer can sometimes say, as the Psalmist did, Psalm xxx. 7, "Lord, by thy favour thou hast made my mountain to stand strong;" and perhaps immediately, nay, almost at the very same time complain, "thou didst hide thy face,

---

[w] Plin. l. 2. c. 47. Aristot. Problems. 25. c. 4. Adspirant auræ in noctem. Virg. Æneid. 7. v. 8.

[x] Tanchuma in Yalkut in loc.

and I was troubled." 2. That Christ absents himself from his own church and people; he "hides his face from the house of Jacob," from his own flesh and blood, from his love, his bride, and spouse; which he does both for her good, and for the advancement of his glory: though Christ's absence is very uncomfortable and disquieting to his people, they cannot tell how to bear it, especially when they are sensible of it; for sometimes they are not, but are attended with sleepiness, carelessness, and security; he is gone from them, and they are not aware of it, and therefore are unconcerned about it, until such time as they are awakened by him, and then they are made sensible that he is withdrawn from them: not but that Christ is always present with his church in some sense, though they have not always the comfortable sense of it upon their souls. 3. That Christ's absence does not dissolve that covenant-interest and union which his people have in him with him; though there may be a distance as to communion, yet there is a nearness as to union; she was his, and he was hers, now as much as ever, though absent from her; neither did it destroy that love and affection which she had in her heart towards him; for still it is "him whom her soul loveth," though she could not see him nor hear of him.

II. What the church did in this case, comes next to be considered: she sought him; which shows that she was sensible that he was gone from her. Believers are sometimes like Samson, they wist or know "not that the Lord is departed from" them; but it seems that the church was apprised of it: perhaps she had slept quietly for some time, imagining that her beloved was with her, but finding herself mistaken, seeks for him: and from hence it also appears, that she saw her need of Christ's presence, had a value for it, and was in hopes of enjoying it again, otherwise she would never have sought for him. Now Christ's presence, when lost, should be sought after. 1. Timely, or "while he may be found," as Isaiah says, chap. lv. 6; for otherwise, by missing an opportunity, as Thomas did, he may be gone, as he was in chap. v. 6, when the church opened to him. 2. With our whole hearts; not feignedly or hypocritically, as some did, of whom complaint is made in Isa. lviii. 2; nor with worldly ends and views; not for loaves, as some of Christ's followers did. 3. Fervently, and not in a careless and negligent manner; as it may be the church did here, and therefore did not immediately succeed. 4. With care, diligence, and constancy, until he is found, as the church did afterwards, in ver. 2, 3, 4. 5. In proper places, as well as at proper times; as in the church of Christ, and in the public ordinances of the gospel, as well as privately in the closet, by prayer, meditation, and reading; and such seekers as these are most likely to meet with success. But it will be proper to consider more particularly the seeking of Christ here; where may be observed,

1st. The description of the person whom she sought; "him whom her soul loved;" which shows not only the reality and sincerity of her love to Christ, whom she loved "with all her heart and soul, as appears from her retaining an affection for him, even when in the worst of frames, and when he was departed from her; for nothing could separate her from the love of Christ; all the waters of afflictions, temptations, desertions, &c., could not extinguish that flame of love that was kindled in her soul: I say, it not only shows the heartiness and reality of her love to Christ, but also that she sought him from a principle of love, and not with sinister ends and views; she sought him because she loved him, and she loved him "because he first loved her;" and this is an indication that she was not wholly forsaken by him; seeing this grace of love was in her soul, and maintained there by a secret and invisible hand, nay, brought into act and exercise in some measure.

2udly, The place where she sought him is also mentioned, and that is, on her bed: by which we are not to understand the temple, nor the church of Christ, and the public ordinances thereof; for had she sought there, she had sought aright; besides, these seem to be intended in the following verse, by "the streets and broad places" of the city; this bed is distinguished both from that mentioned in chap. i. 16, and also from that in chap. iii. 7; in the former of which places it is called "our bed," Christ having a joint property in it; and in the latter it is said to be his bed. Christ being the only maker and principal owner of it: but this bed is said to be hers, "by night on my bed;" which was purely her own, and where she was without the presence of Christ, who was justly displeased with her for being there: moreover a different word is here used than what is in either of those places. Some[*] by it understand the bed of contemplation; the bed being a proper place, as the night is a proper time, to have the thoughts composed in meditation; see Psalm iv. 4; but it seems rather to intend a bed of affliction, sorrow, and tribulation, which she was cast into, in which she sought the Lord, as it is usual with persons in such a condition; see Rev. ii. 22, Hos. v. 15. Though I should choose to understand it of a bed of carnal ease and security, upon which she was fallen; and seems to be expressive of the manner in which she sought him, which was in a cold, lazy, lukewarm, and formal way, rather than of the place where.

3rdly. The time when she sought him, and that is, "by night;" which shows, that it was either a time of great affliction with her; or else, of darkness and desertion; this is manifest enough; as also, that she was very uneasy and restless in her present condition, being brought in some mea-

---

[*] Greg. Nyssen. in Cant. Homil. 6.

sure to a sense of it; and that she had an exceeding great love for Christ, seeing, that at a time when others were taking their rest, she was seeking for him. In the Hebrew text the word is in the plural number, and may be rendered, *by nights*;[b] that it is one night after another successively, "I sought him;" but to no purpose; and so it may be expressive of her diligence and constancy in seeking, as well as of her condition when she sought.

4thly. The success she met with is here related, "I found him not;" either, because she did not seek him aright, as James says, chap. iv. 3, "Ye ask and receive not, because ye ask amiss;" so she sought and found not, because she sought amiss, in a cold and lifeless way and manner; Christ would not be found in such a way of seeking: or else it was the will of Christ to be absent for a time, and not manifest himself upon first seeking; not for want of love to her, nor because he was regardless of her, but to exercise her grace, try her faith and patience, and to make her more earnest and diligent in her search: as also that she might prize him the more when she had him, as well as be more careful to retain him; which had the desired effect upon her, as appears from ver. 4.

Verse 2. *I will rise now, and go about the city, in the streets, and in the broad ways; I will seek him whom my soul loveth: I sought him, but I found him not.*

THE church, finding that the former methods she had taken were not attended with success, consults others, being sensible that she was wrong before, which she resolves to pursue without any more delay. In these words we have,

1. The church's resolution, which consists of three parts: 1st. To "rise now," immediately. 2ndly. To "go about the city." 3rdly. To "seek Christ in the streets and broad ways "thereof."

II. Her performance of this resolution; "I sought him."

III. Her success in it, which was as before; "but I found him not."

I. Here is the resolution of the church, to take other methods than what she had done before, in order to find her absent beloved; which shows, not only that she was sensible that she had taken some wrong ones before; and that no good was to be obtained that way, for Christ would not be found in such a way of seeking him, as upon the bed; but also, that her former disappointment had not discouraged her from pursuing her search of him; nay, it had made her more lively and active, zealous and vigorous in it, as appears from this new resolution of hers, and her putting it into practice; which consists of the three following things.

1st. She resolves now to rise, that is, from her bed of sloth and carnal ease, and to appear more vigorous; and that now, without any more delay; for resolutions are not to be breathed upon: no time should be allowed them but the present; we should immediately proceed to the performance of them, otherwise flesh and blood, which are too often consulted in such cases, will find many ways to elude them; but these, as they are not to be made in our own strength, so neither are we to expect the performance of them by it; but, however, the church resolving to quit her bed, and forego her own carnal ease and pleasure in search of Christ, and that she might enjoy his presence and company, not only shows the exceeding greatness of her love to him, and the reality and sincerity of it, but also the uneasiness of her soul, and the distress of mind she was in; she could not be easy and contented without him, and therefore resolves to seek until she found him.

2ndly. She not only resolves to rise, and that directly, but also to "go about the city." Her design in rising, was not to seek him in a superficial manner, but search the city, the streets thereof, and thus seek him whom her soul loved. By *city* is here meant the church of God, which is frequently called so in scripture; see Psalm lxxxvii. 3, Heb. xii. 22, 23; and no doubt but here is a regard had to the city of Jerusalem, by which name the church often goes, and to which it is frequently compared in scripture; but why it is so, will be shown on chap. vi. 4, and therefore I shall only at present show in what sense and for what reasons the church may be said to be a city, which are as follows: 1. Cities being large and populous, and having in them great and spacious buildings, are generally built where there is good foundation: the church of God is a city that is well founded; for "the Lord himself hath founded Zion," and the foundation which he has laid there is a sure one; and that is Christ himself, who is able to support the whole building, and will never fail; for he is that Rock upon which his church being built, "the gates of hell cannot prevail against it." 2. Cities are commonly delightfully situated, upon an eminence, in a good air, and by a pleasant river: the church of God is "beautiful for situation;" it stands upon rising ground; this "mountain of the Lord's house is established upon the top of the mountains;" it is in a good air, and is comfortably fanned with the gentle and refreshing breezes of the blessed Spirit; it is situated by a pleasant river, even the river of God's boundless love and grace, "the streams whereof make glad this city of our God." 3. In cities are usually fine, large, and magnificent buildings: the church is God's architecture; it is not of this building, and therefore must needs be well built; every believer is a temple, and that a temple of the Holy Ghost's; there is a great deal of glory, beauty, and excellency in these buildings, as well as strength and firmness; see Isa. liv. 11, 12, Rev. xxi. 10,

---

[b] בלילות *ev νυξὶν*, Sept. per noctes, V. L. Junius and Tremellius, Piscator; in noctibus, Pagninus, Montanus, Tigurine version, Marckius, Michaelis.

11, 12, 18, 21. 4. Cities are very populous and numerous; there are a great many inhabitants in them; so is the church of God: it is true, it is called but a little flock, when compared with the world, but yet considered by itself, it is very large and numerous; John saw at once, after he had beheld the forty and four thousand, "a great multitude, which no man could number," and that of such who belonged to Christ, and were saved by him; and so will the church, even on earth, appear very numerous; when those prophecies are fulfilled, which you may read in Isa. xlix. 19, 20, and lx. 4—8. 5. In cities, as there are large numbers of inhabitants, so there is a diversity of them, as rich and poor, good and bad; in Christ's church here on earth, there is a very great difference of its members; some have greater gifts, and more grace than others have; some are more public-spirited than others, and so of greater usefulness; some are real and hearty believers, others are only painted hypocrites; for there has been always tares among Christ's wheat, wolves and goats among his sheep, and some who have had a name and place in this city, whose names were never "written among the living in Jerusalem." 6. In well regulated cities there is a good order and decorum kept; there are good laws made, and proper officers appointed to put them in execution; as well as a good watch and guard provided for the security of the inhabitants: in the church of God, there are good and wholesome laws enacted by the great Legislator, which concern the admission of persons into this city, their behaviour whilst in it, and their removal from it if disagreeable; and these are preferable to all others, not only because God is the author of them, but also, because they are written upon the hearts of all those who are true citizens, according to that promise, Jer. xxxi. 33, "I will put my law in their inward parts, and write it in their hearts;" moreover, here are proper officers appointed, such as ministers of the gospel, who are to see that these laws are carefully observed and exactly complied with; who also bear the character of watchmen in the next verse, being set as well for the defence of the church, as to give direction and instruction to her. 7. In cities there are peculiar privileges which belong to the citizens thereof; and so there are in the church of God: all, who are Christ's freemen, and are "fellow citizens of the saints," have a right to all the ordinances of the gospel, to all the privileges and immunities of Christ's house: they shall never be arrested by justice, nor be brought into a state of condemnation; nor is it possible for them ever to lose their freedom.

Now her "going about the city, " is, 1. Expressive of her diligence and industry in seeking Christ; she lost no opportunity; she sought in all other places, as well as in the open streets, wherever she thought he might be found, or there was any probability of hearing of him. (2.) It shows the pains she took, as well as the diligence she used in seeking; for it must be very painful and laborious to go round about or all over a city, especially a large one, such an one as Jerusalem was, to which the allusion is here made; her search was as sorrowful and as fatiguing, as that of Joseph and Mary, who, after three days search, in their company, among their kindred, and about the city, at length found Christ in the temple: but all this toil and labour she regarded not, so she could but find him whom her soul loved. (3.) This being done in the night, which was an unseasonable time to walk about the city in, especially for women, is a farther indication of the strength of her affection to him, in that she did not value the reproach that might attend her. (4.) She not only ran the risk of reproach and scandal, but also of danger and mischief, which the night-season exposed her to, and which she experienced in chap. v. 7; but being fired with love and fearless of danger,[c] she puts all to the hazard, regarding no inconveniences that might ensue; for her heart was so set upon finding Christ, that she was resolved to try all ways, whatever she suffered in the experiment.

3rdly. She resolves to seek "him in the streets and broad ways;" where we have, 1. The person whom she was resolved to seek described, him "whom my soul loveth;" which is the character she gives of him in the former verse; and shows that her love to him was still the same, was not abated, though she had been disappointed of finding him; nay, that it was rather increased, and therefore she repeats this over and over, as not knowing how to speak of him any other way. 2. The particular places in the city, where she resolved to seek him, "in the streets and in the broad ways;" by which we are not to understand places[d] where worldly business is transacted, and to which crowds of people flock for the same purpose, as the court, the market-place, or the exchange; for Christ is not found there; worldly employments, especially when immoderately pursued, rather draw souls from him than bring them near to him: nor are the books, writings, and tenets[e] of the Gentile philosophers here intended; for she could not expect to find him there, where he was never known or heard of: but by them we are to understand, either the Jewish synagogues, where prayer was wont to be made, and the word of God preached, there being a probability of finding him there; or rather, the public ordinances of the gospel, which are the "streets and broad ways of this city," the church, in which Christ walks, and often shows himself to his people; and in seeking him here, she sought aright; though, for reasons hereafter to be mentioned, she did not meet with immediate success. But these phrases may in general intend the diligence and

---

[c] Audacem faciebat amor, Ovid. Metamorph. l. 4. fab. 4.   [d] Vid. Sanct. in loc. and Ambros. in ibid.

[e] Alcuin in loc.

exquisiteness of her search, as in Jer. v. 1. So some cities are described as having broad ways in them, as Troy[f] and Athens.[g]

II. She gives an account of her performance of this resolution; I sought him, says she; she not only resolved upon it; but also did it; nay, she no sooner said it but likewise did it. Resolutions, without putting them in practice, avail little; and unless they are made in the strength of Christ, and are performed by the same, are never performed, neither aright, nor to any good purpose; but this of hers was quickly performed; she was soon enabled to set about it, being assisted by divine grace, and not left to consult with "flesh and blood."

III. Her success is also mentioned by her; "but I found him not:" which she seems to take notice of with much sorrow and concern; that though she had such an earnest desire after, so strong an affection for, and had been so diligent in her search of him, had spared no pains, and had run all risks of losing her good name, and of being exposed to danger, and yet he would not show himself to her; she could not get sight of, nor hear any tidings concerning him; and this still shows that strong was her love; for had she not dearly loved him, she would not have been so much concerned at her disappointment in not finding him. And now this was, 1. To chastise her for her former negligence in duty, and for her indulging herself in carnal ease and security; for he seems resolved, that as she had lost him through her ease, she should not find him without trouble; for we are not to suppose that he resented her present way of seeking, nor her present behaviour to him, which seems very agreeable; but this he does to show how much he was affronted with her former carriage. 2. To exercise her faith, and try her patience: thus when the apostle Paul, 2 Cor. xii. 8, 9, was sorely buffeted by Satan, he "besought the Lord thrice that he might depart from him;" but all the answer he could for the present obtain, was, "my grace is sufficient for thee." 3. To show that even means themselves, though they are to be used, are not to be depended on; these cannot help souls to a sight of Christ, unless he is pleased in them to reveal himself; for "when he hideth his face, who then can behold him?" yet nevertheless, they are to be carefully observed and diligently used by us.

Verse 3. *The watchmen that go about the city found me:* to whom I said, *Saw ye him whom my soul loveth?*

THE church continues to give an account of her adventure, and what befel her when in the streets and broad ways of the city; as how she was found by the watchmen, whose business is to take up and examine persons that they meet with in the night; of whom she inquires after her lost spouse, but for the present can have no tidings of him. In these words we shall,

I. Inquire who are meant by "the watchmen."
II. What by their "finding" of her.
III. Consider the question proposed by her to them; "Saw ye him whom my soul loveth?"
IV. Show why no answer is mentioned, as returned to this question.

I. It will be proper to inquire who are meant by the watchmen here; and by them we are not to understand angels, as some;[h] though these are thought to be called watchers, in Dan. iv. 13, 17; and are the saints' life-guards, attend upon their persons, watch over them, and encamp about them: nor the princes and great men of the world, who have the care and government of kingdoms, provinces, and cities; but are ignorant of Christ, and know not the "Lord of glory," as others:[i] nor false teachers,[k] who are called, Isa. lvi. 10, "blind watchmen, dumb dogs that cannot bark;" but rather, the true ministers of the Gospel; the prophets under the Old Testament, and the apostles and faithful teachers under the New, who frequently bear the title of watchmen in scripture; see Isa. lii. 8, and lxii. 6, Ezek. xxxiii. 7. The Jewish writers[l] interpret these words of Moses and Aaron with the Levites, who kept the watch of the tabernacle. The ministers of the Gospel are called watchmen, either in allusion to shepherds, who watch over their flock by night, Luke ii. 8; or else, to watchmen in cities, as here; and their work may be considered,

1. With regard to themselves; they are to watch over themselves as well as others; they are to watch over their conversations, that they be as become the Gospel they preach, and so that they may give no ill examples to others, nor cause the ways and doctrines of Christ to be evil spoken of, and render their ministry useless; they are to watch over their doctrines, and take heed that they be agreeable to the oracles of God; and they delivered nothing but the "wholesome words of Christ Jesus," and such as may be for the edifying of their hearers, and suitable to the cases of souls; they are to watch all opportunities to preach this gospel, as the apostle says, 2 Tim. iv. 2, to "be instant in season and out of season;" and then they are to watch and observe the success of it, and how it is blessed and made useful to souls: moreover they ought to have a very great guard upon themselves; for if the enemy can but surprise, decoy, or corrupt them, it turns much to his advantage. Now ministers of the Gospel should take heed to themselves, lest they fall asleep, or grow careless and indifferent in the work of the Lord; or are diverted from it through the frowns or flatteries of the world; or be corrupted with errors and false doctrines; for these things

---

[f] Πολις ευρυαγυια, Homer, Iliad. 2. v. 29, 66, 141, 329. and 14. v. 88. Odyss. 22. v. 230. [g] Ibid. Odyss. 7. v. 80. [h] Foliot and Sanct. in loc.
[i] Diodat. in loc. [k] Mercer. in ver. 4. [l] Targum, R. Sol. Jarchi, and R. Aben Ezra in loc. So Lyra.

tend much to the ruin of Christ's kingdom and interest.

2. With regard to others, their work is, 1. To give the time of night, as in Isa. xxi. 11, 12; the question is put, "Watchman, what of the night? Watchman, what of the night?" the answer is, "the morning cometh, and also the night." Sometimes it is night with the church; she is fallen asleep upon a bed of security: the wise virgins sleep as well as the foolish; it is then the work of ministers to give the time of the night, to apprize the church what a condition she is in, and to endeavour to awake her out of it: though sometimes the ministers, the watchmen, are asleep, as well as the churches, and know not what time of the night it is, which is a dreadful case; and then are the churches of Christ in a poor plight and condition indeed. 3. Their work is to give notice of approaching danger; they are to give notice of the danger that sinners are in, who are walking in the broad road to destruction; and also the danger that churches may be in through errors and heresies springing up among them, as well as by indulging themselves in any vicious practices, which they are severely to check and reprehend. Now this work requires vigilance, prudence, courage, and faithfulness; and also shows the necessity and usefulness of the public ministry, which can no more be dispensed with than watchmen in a city; and likewise what care the Lord has of his churches, in placing such officers in them, as well as the awfulness of the work they are concerned in; for if the watchman does not discharge his duty, the blood of those he has to do with will be required of him. These watchmen are farther described by their "going about the city:" by the city, we are to understand the church of God, as in the former verse: and their "going about" it, is mentioned to distinguish them from those that were upon the walls, who kept their stands, and did not stir from their places; and also to show their proper work and business, which, as it appears from hence, they are diligent in; and so it proves them to be true watchmen and faithful ministers of the Gospel, who, in imitation of Christ their Lord and Master, go about doing good to the souls of men.

II. Being thus in the discharge of their duty and using diligence therein, they found the church; which is the next thing to be inquired into: they found me; that is, they fell upon the subject of my case and condition in their sermons, and exactly took notice of and spoke to my case, as if somebody had told them of it beforehand, and as if they had particularly designed me above all the rest of their audience; which shows the power of the word, and its piercing and penetrating nature; it often finds out particular sinners in a congregation, and points out their particular sins unto them; it searches into the inward recesses of their hearts, brings secret sins to light, sets them in order before them, and brings them to an open and ingenuous confession of them; likewise it finds and points out the particular cases of believers, oftentimes unknown to the minister, and unlooked for by the believer, which seems to be the church's case here. It is amazing how this is sometimes effected; insomuch that some have thought that some friend or other, to whom they have communicated their cases, have told the minister, and he has purposely treated on such a subject to meet with them; though when they have more narrowly inquired into it, have found it otherwise, to their great surprise; nay, sometimes a minister, by stepping out of the way, going off from his subject, and making a digression, has met with souls, and hit their case, as Austin did with the Manichee. God has given many instances of the secret energy of the word, and the mighty power and grace of the Spirit, in applying it to the different cases of persons. But,

III. Having met with something under the ministry of the word suitable to her case, she is encouraged to take her opportunity, after public worship was over, to speak privately to the ministers, and propose this question to them: "Saw ye him whom my soul loveth?" in which may be observed, 1. The person concerning whom she enquires, and that is, him whom her soul loveth. Christ is still the subject of her discourse and enquiry; whether she talks with ministers or private Christians, she is upon the search after him; and though she cannot as yet find him, she is not discouraged from seeking; nor is her love and affection towards him abated, though she cannot see him. 2. The manner in which she proposes this question, and that is very abrupt; for without giving them an opportunity to speak to her first, or using any preface to excuse her freedom with them, she immediately puts the question, as soon as she came up to them, "Saw ye him," &c., where it may be also observed, as has been already on chap. i. 2, that she uses the relative *him* without an antecedent, and does not express the person's name whom she inquires about; which shows the singular excellency of Christ, that he was to her the only him in the world; and likewise the singular esteem she had for him, the strength of her affection to him, how much her thoughts were upon him, and her desires after him; insomuch that she thought everybody must know whom she meant, and whom she loved, without mentioning his name; and more especially it supposes, that she concluded that these ministers knew whom she meant. 3. Her putting this question to them, shows, (1.) That she had a value for them, had entertained a good opinion of them, and judged them proper persons to apply to; which might arise from what she had met with under their public ministry. (2.) That she was unwilling to let any opportunity slip, in which there was any likelihood of finding Christ; therefore she will not only hear the ministers publicly, but converse with them privately; and such a practice is highly commendable in, and to be imitated by all the saints; oftentimes much is lost by missing an opportunity. What did Thomas lose by not being with the rest of the disciples when Christ appeared to them? Why, a sight of Christ; and not only so, but also fell into a fit of unbelief. (3.) That when persons apply to ministers, they should keep close to their own soul's cases, as the church does here, and not trouble them with long and tedious discourses, filled up with invectives against their fellow Christians, and animadversions upon their weaknesses and imperfections; but their chief concern should be, the case of their own souls; and the subject of their discourse, Christ, and his grace. (4.) That ministers had need to be well acquainted with the various cases of souls, that they may know how to speak aptly to them, and communicate a word in season to their refreshment; which, when fitly spoken, is like apples of gold in pictures of silver. But,

IV. Here is no answer returned to this question, that is here recorded; the reason of which is, not because they could not give one; nor were those blind watchmen, which were without the light of faith and experience themselves; those dumb dogs which cannot bark, and know not how to speak to the cases of souls, being unacquainted with them, of which we read in Isa. lvi. 10; nor it may be, was it because they did not return an answer, though she has not recorded it; and if they did not, it might be owing to her overhaste in not waiting for one; or if they did, yet she not being able to apply it with comfort to her own soul, takes no notice of it; and this might be, to let her see the need of a divine blessing upon means, and the power and grace of the blessed Spirit to attend them: but yet though she did not find immediate comfort and relief, she might get something from them, which was afterwards useful to her, as seems to appear from the following verse; for oftentimes the Spirit of God brings to our remembrance, and sets home, with power upon our souls, things which have been dropped in the ministry of the word, or in private conversation, which were of no use in the hearing of them.

Verse 4. *It was but a little that I passed from them, but I found him whom my soul loveth; I held him, and would not let him go, until I had brought him unto my mother's house, and into the chamber of her that conceived me.*

THE church having sought about the city, in the streets and broad ways of it, for her beloved, and made inquiry of the watchmen concerning him, though attended with little success; yet is not discouraged, but keeps on seeking, till at length she finds him; which not only filled her with a transport of joy, but also puts her upon using all the means she could to continue him with her, and secure his presence and company for the future. In these words are,

I. An account of the church's finding Christ; "I found him whom my soul loveth."

II. The place or time, where or when she found him; "It was but a little that I passed from them, but I found," &c.

III. Her behaviour towards him; "I held him," &c.

I. The church gives an account of her finding Christ; "I found him," &c. She had sought, but not in vain; that promise was made good to her, "seek, and ye shall find:" which was also when all means failed: she had sought him privately, by prayer and meditation; and publicly, by an attendance upon the ordinances of the gospel: she had heard the ministers of Christ preach, and had conferred with them alone, and yet could not find her beloved; which may inform us, 1. That means, though they are to be used, yet not to be depended on: they will not avail without a divine blessing; Bethesda's pool must be moved by an angel, or no cure can be performed; the Spirit of God must move upon the waters, the ordinances, or they will not convey light and life to souls; Paul may plant, and Apollos may water, but it is God only that giveth the increase; the most comfortable doctrines and precious promises of the Gospel, opened and delivered in the most powerful manner, will not be useful without the special energy of the Spirit. 2. That we should not be discouraged when all means fail; because he is found sometimes when they do so, as he was by the church here; therefore when, with Job, chap. xxiii. 8—10; we have gone backward and forward, on the right hand and on the left, and yet cannot behold him; we should with him rest contented, and say, he knoweth the way that I take, though I do not know which way he has taken; and when he hath tried me, I shall come forth as gold. 3. This shows us, that unless Christ show himself, there is no finding him; for, "when he hideth his face, who can behold him?" 4. Finding Christ, when all means fail, gives the greatest discovery of Christ's love and grace, the freeness and sovereignty of it; and makes it appear, that it does not depend upon our will or works, but upon his sovereign good will and pleasure. 5. Finding Christ after so many disappointments, must needs be joyful and welcome; she seems to speak it with an air of pleasure, and in an exulting manner, as those disciples did, who said, John i. 41, "we have found the Messiah, which is, being interpreted, the Christ;" for his long absence from her, and the fatigue she had endured in seeking of him, did but serve the more to endear and sweeten his presence to her.

2. She declares where or when she found him; "it was but a little that I had passed from them:" that is, either it was but a little space of time, as R. Aben Ezra observes; or, I had gotten but a very little way ere I found him. She is said to pass from the ministers, not out of disrespect unto them, for she had an entire value for them; nor because she had received no benefit

from them, for they had hit her case, though she had not present enjoyment of Christ; nor was it because she was above ministers and ordinances, for these will continue in the church, and are to be used by believers until the second coming of Christ: but this passing from them shows, that she did not rest here; that though she applied herself to ministers, and made use of ordinances, yet she did not forget Christ, but looked beyond all these to him; and went a little farther than she had done before, in the lively exercise of her faith upon him: also her meeting with Christ, when she had a little passed them, shows, that Christ is not far from his ministers and ordinances: for he has promised to be with them unto the end of the world: and therefore there is a very great encouragement for souls to attend unto from the church's experience, here recorded by them, not only from that promise, but also her.

III. Her behaviour to him is next mentioned. 1st. She "held him *fast*, and would not let him go." 2ndly. "Brought him into *her* mother's house, and into the chamber of her that conceived her."

1st. As soon as she saw him, she laid hold on him, and cleaved so close to him, that he could not stir a step from her; which, on her part, is expressive, 1. Of her faith in him: it is the nature of faith to lay hold on Christ; the actings of it are frequently expressed by it; see Prov. iii. 18, Heb. vi. 18; the believer lays hold on Christ as his Saviour; on his righteousness, and pleads it as his justifying righteousness before God; on Christ, as God's strength, to do all for him, and in him; and on the covenant which is in Christ's hands, with all the blessings and promises of it, and appropriates them to himself, Isa. xxvii. 5, and lvi. 4. 2. Of her love and affection to him; and therefore she grasps him in her arms, will not let go her hold on him, nor suffer him to stir from her; but, could she have her will, would have him always in her sight; and, as Ruth said, chap. i. 16, to Naomi, where he goes, she is resolved to go; where he lodges, she will lodge; his people shall be her people, and his God her God; so pleased was she with him, so dearly did she love him. 3. Of her fears and jealousies lest he should remove from her: she knew the bitterness of Christ's absence, as well as had had experience of the sweetness of his presence, and therefore dreaded parting again; was afraid of every thing that had a tendency to it, and therefore gives that solemn charge she does in the following verse. 4. Of her steadiness and resolution to hold him, whatever was the consequence; though she might be reproached and persecuted for it, suffer the loss of her good name, and everything else that was valuable in this world; yet Christ to her was worth more than ten thousand worlds; nothing could tempt her to part with him.

Moreover, on his part, these words are expressive, (1.) Of a seeming offer or desire to depart; such an one as the angel who wrestled with Jacob made, when he said, "let me go, for the day breaketh," Gen. xxxii. 26, which, as it made him, so it made her cleave the closer to him, wrestle the more with him, and keep faster hold of him. (2.) Of a gracious allowance which he had granted her to lay hold on him: it is a surprising instance of his grace, that such vile, sinful creatures as we, should be suffered to come so near his person. O astonishing grace! that such should be invited to come, and should be welcome to lay hold on Christ and his righteousness, and not incur the crime of rudeness nor presumption. (3.) Of his wonderful condescension, to be held by a creature, and that a sinful one: it was not because she was stronger than Christ, that she held him: and would not let him go, but because he condescended to let it be so; for she received the strength from him, by which she held him: it shows indeed the great power and strength of faith, thus to hold Christ; but then she had it all from him, who is the Object of it. (4.) Of that delight and pleasure he took in the exercise of her faith upon him: as it does not argue weakness in him to be held by her, so neither does it unwillingness; he was no more held against his will, than he was by a superior force; he was held by her because it was both his will, and well-pleasing to him; "without faith it is impossible to please God," or Christ; in the exercise of it they are much delighted, and are well pleased to be held as it were by it.

2ndly. The other part of her behaviour towards him, is, that she brought him into her mother's house, and into the most private and retired part of it, even into the chamber of her that conceived her; and this is indeed what she principally had in view in holding of him. The allusion is to the tents and apartments women had in former times, distinct from their husbands, Gen. xxiv. 67, and xxxi. 33. By her mother's house and chamber, the Targum understands the school that was kept in the chambers of Moses and Joshua, where the children of Israel studied the law; R. Sol. Jarchi interprets them of the tabernacle in Shiloh: as does R. Aben Ezra of the ark of the testimony. Some [m] think that by her mother's house, is meant the temple; and by the chamber the holy of holies, which was accessible to none but the high-priest: though Brightman thinks that both these phrases are expressive of Christ's incarnation, which the church was importunately desirous of, which may be expressed by her mother's house, and the chamber of her that conceived her; because in becoming incarnate, he was a partaker of the same flesh and blood with her; and she may be said to bring him into it, because it was for her sake that he assumed human nature. But I think it should rather be under-

---

[m] Bishop Patrick in loc.

stood either of the visible church, which is the mother of all believers; see Gal. iv. 26; in which many souls are born again through the ministry of the word, and are nursed and nourished up with the words of faith and good doctrine, with the sincere milk of gospel truths, and the refreshing breasts of gospel ordinances; and Christ may be said to be brought in here, when his name is publicly professed in the congregation of his saints, his gospel asserted and vindicated, and his ordinances submitted to; when the mighty instances of his grace to his people are made known, and united praises upon that account are offered up unto him: and this no doubt the church had in view in introducing him here, that she, and others with her, might magnify the Lord together, for all the special instances of his kindness to her, and that they might in having fellowship one with another, in the house of God, have intimate fellowship with the Father and with the Son: or else, by her mother's house, may be meant her heart, where the incorruptible seed of divine grace was cast, and where the new creature was conceived, born, and brought up; and where it grows until it becomes a perfect man, and arrives to the measure of the stature of the fulness of Christ: and by the chamber of her that conceived her, the inmost recesses thereof; there she desired to bring him, that he might dwell there by faith; that he might live in her, and she in him, and so have intimate and uninterrupted communion with him; which is the purport and design of the solemn charge which is given to the daughters of Jerusalem in the following verse.

Verse 5. *I charge you, O ye daughters of Jerusalem, by the roes and by the hinds of the field, that ye stir not up, nor awake my love, till he please.*

These are either the words of Christ,[n] adjuring the daughters of Jerusalem, young converts, who were the virgins, the companions of his bride, to give his church no disturbance, nor awake her, who was his love, before she pleased; for the church was now taking sweet repose, being weary and fatigued with running after and searching for him till she found him; it is therefore the will of Christ, that now she be not disturbed: or else, they are the words of the church, which is the more commonly received sense; who knew how to prize Christ's presence, having experienced a long absence, and had been in a great deal of pains and trouble to find him, and now having obtained her much wished for and long desired end, she is not willing to part with him; but as she had had much trouble to find him, is willing to use some care and diligence to keep him: and being fearful lest these young converts should by any unbecoming word or action provoke him to depart, she gives this solemn charge, which is the same with that in chap. ii. 7, where it is more largely explained. The Targum understands it as the charge of Moses to the people of Israel, not to go up into the land of Canaan, until the term of forty years was expired.

Verse 6. *Who is this that cometh out of the wilderness, like pillars of smoke, perfumed with myrrh and frankincense, with all powders of the merchant?*

Some of the Jewish writers[o] think, that these are the words of the nations of the earth, wondering at the coming of the Israelites out of the wilderness, before whom the Lord went in a pillar of cloud by day, and in a pillar of fire by night, which appearance was very surprising to them. Though they are rather, as some[p] think, the words of the Jews, wondering at John the Baptist and his ministry, of whom all men mused in their hearts whether he was the Christ or not; and therefore the Jews dispatched messengers to him, to know the truth of it: his first appearance was in the wilderness of Judea, which fulfilled an ancient prophecy concerning him, "the voice of him that crieth in the wilderness;" hither great numbers, like pillars of smoke, flocked to him, to attend upon his ministry and baptism: he was a burning and shining light in his day; there was a great deal of zeal, warmth, and fervency in his preaching; for which work he was extraordinarily fitted, being richly perfumed with those gifts and graces of the Spirit, which are comparable to myrrh, frankincense, and all powders of the merchant. Others[q] take them to be the words of the Jewish church, wondering at the large number of converts appearing in the beauties of holiness, in the Gentile world, which before was like to a dry heath or a barren wilderness; see Isa. xlix. 21, and lx. 8, though others[r] think Christ himself is here introduced, admiring the beauty of his church, and the graces of his own Spirit in her. But I am rather of opinion, that they are the words of the daughters of Jerusalem, who, upon this happy meeting of Christ and his church, saw a greater glory and a more excellent beauty in her, than ever they had done before: and especially, it must not be supposed, that the angels[s] are here speaking and admiring the church's beauty, seeing these bear no part in this song; much less the church herself,[t] for this no way suits with that modesty and humility which always appear in her: but it very well agrees with the daughters of Jerusalem, to whom so solemn a charge is given in the former verse, which excited and stirred them up to take a fuller view of her; and the more they looked upon her,

---

[n] Alcuin and Diodat, in loc.   [o] Targum and R. Sol Jarchi in loc, and Zohar. in Gen. fol. 100. 4. and 101. 1.   [p] Cotton in loc.   [q] Isidore and Alcuin in loc.   [r] Mercer in loc.   [s] Diodat in loc.   [t] Jun. in loc.

the more they wondered at her; and in expressing it, thus highly commend her, which they do.

I. By describing her as "coming out of the wilderness."

II. By comparing her ascent from thence to "pillars of smoke."

III. By saying that she was "perfumed with myrrh and frankincense, with all powders of the merchant."

I. They commend her, by describing her as coming out of the wilderness. By the wilderness, out of which she is said to come, may be meant, either,

1st. A state of nature, which all the elect of God are in before conversion; out of which, by mighty and efficacious grace, they are brought. Now this may be called a wilderness. 1. Because of the barrenness and unfruitfulness of persons in such an estate: a wilderness is a dry and barren place; see Psal. cvii. 35, Zeph. ii. 13; and so are the hearts even of God's own people before conversion; and therefore are called "dry, parched, and thirsty ground," Isa. xxxv. 7, and xliv. 3, which is only moistened, watered, and made fruitful by the effusion of God's Spirit, and the flows of his love and grace; whilst in a state of nature, they are like the barren heath or fallow ground, until they become God's husbandry, being broken up, manured, and made good ground, so as to bring forth fruit to his glory. 2. Because a wilderness is full of perplexed ways; a man that is in it is often at a loss, and knows not which way to take: and as bewildered is a man in a state of nature; he is a stranger to the way of peace, life, and salvation, by Jesus Christ; there are many by-ways present themselves to him, which he is ready to imagine are the right; as his civility, morality, legal righteousness, and external profession of religion; which tracks he follows, if religiously inclined; if not, he pursues the paths of open sin and profaneness; and so he goes on, not knowing whither he goeth, because that darkness hath blinded his eyes; he is in a wilderness, and so he continues, until the Spirit of God guides his feet into the way of peace. 3. Because of the want of provisions therein; see Psal. lxxviii. 19; a man that is in a state of nature, has no spiritual provisions, no heavenly food, no divine refreshments; there is no bread of life here, only husks, which swine do eat; therefore souls that are in such an estate, are in a starving and famishing condition; hence it is called a "pit, wherein is no water," Zech. ix. 11. 4. Because of the danger thereof; in a wilderness, there is not only danger of losing one's way; and falling into holes and pits, but also of being devoured by wild beasts; a state of nature is certainly a dangerous one; the wrath of God abides upon such that are in it; destruction and misery are written upon all the ways of sin; these have a tendency to bring souls thereunto, which they inevitably will, if grace prevents not. Now, in this state and condition God finds his people, when he calls them by his grace, as he did Israel of old; of whom it is said, Deut. xxxii. 10, "he found him in a desert land, and in the waste howling wilderness;" but he does not leave his people here, he brings them out of it which is an instance of his distinguishing and surprising grace, of which the church here was made a partaker; and therefore the daughters, in a way of admiration in it, say, "Who is this that cometh out of the wilderness?" which is expressed in the present tense, because of the incompleteness and imperfection of the work of grace in this life; which, though it is at present unfinished, yet is continued and carried on, and will be performed unto the day of Jesus Christ. Or else,

2ndly. By the wilderness, out of which the church is said to come, may be meant this world; so the nations of the world may be, and particularly the land of Babylon, into which the Jews were carried captive, is called the wilderness of the people, in Ezek. xx. 35. And now this world may very well be so called; and especially the passage of God's children through it, may be compared to the passage of the Israelites through the wilderness of Egypt. 1. Because of the roughness of the way; the children of God, in their passage through it, as the Israelites did, meet with many difficulties, trials, and afflictions; in this world they must have tribulation, and through a variety of it "must enter into the kingdom of God;" for the way to heaven is, ὁδὸς τεθλιμμένη, an afflicted way, or a way strewed with afflictions. 2. Because of the many pits, traps, and snares, that are in it; this world is full of them, every thing in it is of an ensnaring nature to God's children; therefore "let him that thinks he stands, take heed lest he fall." 3. Because of the many venomous creatures and beasts of prey which are in it; and therefore the wilderness, through which the Israelites travelled, is called, Deut. viii. 15, "the great and terrible wilderness, wherein were fiery serpents and scorpions; to which the ungodly men of this world may be compared, for their poisonous and infectious practices, their serpentine cunning, spite, venom, and cruel malice, among whom the saints are obliged to be whilst in this wilderness. 4. Because of the frequent want of provision, and the method of supplies in it: the Israelites, whilst in the wilderness, were often in want of food, and sometimes reduced to such extremity, that they thought it almost impossible to have relief, and therefore said, Psalm lxxviii. 19, "Can God furnish a table in the wilderness?" but yet, notwithstanding these seeming impossibilities, and their frequent murmurings and complaints against him, he was pleased to give them meat to the full; so in this wilderness of the world, which yields of itself no suitable provision to God's children, they are supplied with food, and that in such a way, as the world knows nothing of; God feeds them with the Bread of Life, and gives them to eat of the hidden manna, the food of the wilderness; he refreshes their souls with his grace and presence, affords them spiritual nourishment from Gospel doctrines, promises, and ordinances, and withholds no good thing that is proper for them. 5. As the Israelites, through a great many windings and turnings came safe to Canaan's land, and were led by a right way, though not a direct one, but often backwards and forwards, to the city of their habitation; so the people of God, through various turns of providence, and many trials and afflictions, are led through the wilderness of this world, but yet always in a right way; in a way that makes most for God's glory, and their own good; and shall all be brought safe to the city of habitation and place of rest, which God has prepared for them. Now the church is said to be coming out of this wilderness. Saints though they are in the world, yet they are not of it, being chosen and called out of it; and then may they be said to be coming out of it, when they not only profess not to belong to it, but do openly withdraw from, and quit the company and conversation of the men of it; when their affections are so weaned from it, as that they can readily forsake, and cheerfully suffer the loss of all things in it, for the sake of Christ. Moreover, when neither the frowns nor flatteries of the world can draw them aside from Christ and his Gospel; but regardless of either, are breathing and longing after another and better world than this: and when this is the case of souls, as perhaps it was of the church here, they have made a good progress towards coming out of this wilderness. Or else

3rdly. By it may be meant a state of sorrow and distress, which the people of God were often in, in this life, but are sooner or later brought out of it. God sometimes brings them into the wilderness, into a distressed and disconsolate condition, being without his presence, and the discoveries of his love and grace; where having no views of Christ, and their interest in him, they are bewildered in their souls, and scarce know where they are, nor whither they are going; but he will not leave them so long, but will bring them out of it, and speak comfortably to them. Now in such a bewildered state and condition the church had been, not knowing where her beloved was, which caused her to run up and down, here and there, like a person in a wood, seeking for him, and calling after him; but now she is represented as coming out of this state, having gotten some glimpse of him, and enjoying some communion with him. But,

II. She is not only described by her coming out of the wilderness, but also this ascent of hers from thence is said to be like pillars of smoke; which seems to be expressive of the motions of her desires and affections towards Christ; and shows, 1. That her affections towards Christ were afresh kindled; either by the fire of the Spirit, which was applied unto her; see Matt. iii. 11; or of the divine word, which is compared thereunto, Jer. xxiii. 29; which powerfully wrought upon her; or else, by the presence of Christ, which sometimes causes the hearts of his people to burn within them: this she now enjoyed, which stirred up her affections the more unto him: now these being said to be "like pillars of smoke," intend the first appearances of them; for as soon as ever the fire takes, there will be smoke, and often in great abundance; for which reason the first appearance of grace in young converts is compared to "smoking flax," Isa. xlii. 3. 2. That her affections were heavenly, and rising upwards, "like pillars of smoke;" they were not set upon things on earth, but upon things in heaven, and especially upon Christ, who is there; and particularly upon her person, blood, and righteousness; all which take much with the believer's affections, and are exceeding precious to him. 3. Her affections towards Christ, being compared to pillars of smoke, shows the uprightness of them; that they went up to Him like pillars in a strait line, and did not bend either this way or that: and it may be observed, that the word translated *pillars*, signifies *palm-trees*,⁰ or pillars arising up in the form of palm-trees; which grow very upright, even though very great pressures and weights be laid upon them; and therefore the righteous are compared unto, and said to grow up like them, in Psal. xcii. 12. 4. The steadiness and constancy of her affections to Christ may be represented hereby; which can by no means be diverted from him; neither by the winds of temptation, nor by the tempests of afflictions, nor by the blasts of persecutions; though it is true, pillars of smoke are by every wind easily turned this way or that: but perhaps the allusion is here made unto the smoke, which ascended daily from the altar of burnt-offering; and, if we will believe the Jews, this smoke could never be dispersed, nor bent by any wind; for, among the ten wonders which were seen in the temple, these are mentioned,ʷ viz., that the rain never extinguished the fire of the wood, which was laid in order upon the altar; nor did the wind ever conquer the pillar of smoke, so as to disperse it, nor bend it in this way or that. 5. This may also represent the offering up of herself as a whole burnt-offering to the Lord, as a living sacrifice, holy and acceptable unto God, which was but her reasonable service; see Rom. xii. 1. Or, 6. It may set forth the obscure state and condition of the church in this world, by reason of outward crosses and afflictions; which are such as hide her inward glory and beauty from the men of the world; for though she is separated from the world, and is coming out of it, yet she looks like pillars of smoke, dark, and cloudy, but little brightness or glory appearing in her to them.

III. She is also said to be "perfumed with

ᵘ היכרות elationes, columnæ, ad formam palmæ assurgentes, Buxtorf. ut palmæ, Mercerus, Cocceius; sintur palmarum, Tigurine version, Michaelis. Vid. R. Aben Ezram and Sol. Jarchium in loc. and R. David Kimchium in lib. shorash. rad. חמר.
ʷ In Pirke Abot, c. 5. s. 5.

myrrh and frankincense, with all powders of the merchant."

1st. She is said to be "perfumed with myrrh;" which may be understood, either of Christ himself, who is as "a bundle of myrrh" unto his people, exceeding grateful to them; and which renders them acceptable to God, being held in the hand, or carried in the bosom of faith: or else, of his death, which though like myrrh, exceeding bitter to himself, yet is of a sweet-smelling savour to his Father, and a delightful perfume to believers: or else, of his righteousness, which is that garment of Christ's, which, whether considered as in himself, or as put upon his people, "smells of myrrh, aloes, and cassia;" and with which they being clothed, their "smell is as the smell of a field which the Lord hath blessed."

2ndly. She is said to be also "perfumed with frankincense;" by which may be meant the mediation and intercession of Christ, which is that much incense, with which Christ offers up the prayers of all saints to his Father; and with which their persons and their prayers being perfumed, they meet with acceptance with God, which otherwise would be a stink in his nostrils; see Rev. viii. 3, 4, Psalm cxli. 2.

3rdly. She is said to be "perfumed, or to be possessed with all powders of the merchant." Christ is this merchant-man; the graces of the Spirit are those powders which Christ, as Mediator, is full of; all which are sweet and savoury, rich and costly; "the merchandise of them is better than the merchandise of silver, and the gain thereof than fine gold." Some read this last part of the words thus,[x] "which is above or more excellent than all powders of the merchant, druggist, or apothecary;[y] for no spice in the merchant's warehouse, no precious drug or aromatic powder in the apothecary's shop, is to be compared with those graces of the Spirit, which Christ bestows upon his own people.

Verse 7. *Behold his bed, which is Solomon's: threescore valiant men are about it, of the valiant of Israel.*

These are either the words of the daughters of Jerusalem continued, as some[z] think; who having begun, go on to commend the church from that communion and fellowship she enjoys with Christ, and from that safety and security which she has in him: or rather, according to others,[a] they are the words of the church; who perceiving that the daughters of Jerusalem were much taken with her beauty; and fearing, lest they should ascribe too much to her, to the prejudice of her beloved; she breaks in upon them, and proposes a far more glorious object to them to gaze upon and wonder at, even Christ, from whom she received all her beauty and glory; him she describes by his bed,

and the guard about it, in this and the following verse; by the chariot he rides in, in ver. 9, 10; and by the royal crown he wore on his coronation-day, in ver. 11. In these words we have,

I. To consider who is meant by *Solomon*.
II. What by his *bed*.
III. The *guard* that is about it, which is here described.
IV. Why a *behold* is prefixed to all this.

I. It will be proper to consider who is meant by Solomon; and I apprehend we are not to understand this literally of Solomon, the son of David, and king of Israel; but mystically, of Christ, who was typified by him; it may be said of this place, what our Lord said in another case, that a "greater than Solomon is here." Solomon was undoubtedly an eminent type of Christ; the whole seventy-second psalm, which is entitled, "a Psalm for Solomon," is generally expounded, not only by Christian, but also by Jewish interpreters,[b] of the Messiah, whom Solomon prefigured; and there is an agreement and likeness between them in the following things: 1. They were both the sons of David: Christ, as well as Solomon, was so according to the flesh; God promised that he would raise up the Messiah from his seed, which promise he accordingly made good: the Jews lived in the expectation of him, as being to spring from him; and therefore when Christ put that question to them, "What think ye of Christ? whose Son is he?" they readily answer, The son of David:" hence he is called both "the root and offspring of David;" as he is God, he is the *root* of David; and as he is man, he is *his offspring*. 2. They were both the sons of God; see 2 Sam. vii. 14, compared with Heb i. 5, only with this difference; Solomon was the Son of God by adopting grace, Christ by nature and eternal generation. 3. They were both Jedidiah's, beloved of God: that Solomon was so, is manifest from 2 Sam. xii. 24, 25, and therefore had that name given unto him; that Christ is the dear Son of God's love, was testified by a voice from heaven more than once, particularly at his baptism, and at his transfiguration upon the mount; see Matt. iii. 17, and xvii. 5. 4. They were both kings and preachers in Jerusalem; for Solomon, see Eccl. i. 1, 12, and of Christ it is manifest that here he exercised great part of his public ministry; and here also did he sit upon the throne of his father David, though in a spiritual way. 5. He was a type of Christ in his wisdom. It is said of him, 1 Kings iv. 30, 31, that his "wisdom excelled the wisdom of all the children of the east-country, and all the wisdom of Egypt; for he was wiser than all men:" and of Christ it is said, Col. ii. 3, that "in him are hid all the treasures of wisdom and knowledge," he as much,

---

[x] So Junius and Tremellius, Piscator, Schmidt.
[y] רוכל negotiator, mercator, aromatarius, Buxtorf. μυρεψῶν, Sept. pigmentarii, V. L. Montanus; pharmacopolæ, Tigurine version; institoris, seu seplasiarii, Mercerus, Cocceius; aromatarii, Junius and Tremel-lius, Marckius.   [z] Foliot, Sanctius, and Soto Major in loc.   [a] Junius, Durham, &c.
[b] Targum, R. Aben Ezra, R. David Kimchi, R. Sol. Jarchi, Miclol Yophi, and R. Abendana in not. in Miclol Yolphi in loc.

nay, infinitely more, exceeded Solomon in wisdom, than he did all other men; for never man spake such words of wisdom, his enemies themselves being witnesses, as he did. 6. He was also a type of Christ in the largeness of his kingdom: as God gave him "largeness of heart, even as the sand that is on the sea-shore;" so he likewise gave him a kingdom suitable to it, and made him to reign "over all kingdoms, from the river unto the land of the Philistines." Christ's kingdom, however small it may appear now, shall in the latter day be very large; for "he shall have dominion from sea to sea, and from the river unto the ends of the earth; for when he takes to himself his great power, and reigns, "the kingdoms of this world shall become the kingdoms of our Lord and of his Christ;" see Psal. lxxii. 8, Rev. xi. 15, 17. 7. He prefigured him in the peaceableness, as well as in the largeness of his kingdom: "Solomon's kingdom was a peaceable one, as well as a large one;" "he had peace on all sides round about him;" and his subjects "dwelt safely, every man under his vine and under his fig-tree, all his days;" which was all typical of Christ and his kingdom; one of whose titles is, "the Prince of peace;" whose sceptre is "the gospel of peace;" whose kingdom is not "meat and drink, but righteousness and peace, and joy in the Holy Ghost;" and whose subjects are "the sons of peace;" on whom he bestows peace of conscience now, and will introduce them into an everlasting peace hereafter. 8. He was also a type of him in the riches of his kingdom: there was such plenty of gold in the days of Solomon, "that silver was nothing accounted of," but was as common "in Jerusalem as stones;" Christ's "riches, are unsearchable;" he has riches of grace, and riches of glory, which he bestows upon his subjects, so that they are all as kings and princes: it may be much more truly said of all Christ's subjects, what the king of Assyria in a boasting manner said of his princes, "Are not my princes altogether kings?" all the subjects of Christ's kingdom are princes, and all these princes kings; and therefore it must needs be a very rich and opulent one. 9. Solomon was a type of Christ likewise in his marriage of Pharaoh's daughter, an Egyptian woman; one that was an "alien from the commonwealth of Israel, and a stranger from the covenant of promise;" which is not more surprising, nor indeed so much, as that "the Holy One of Israel, the God of the whole earth," should espouse to himself such poor, mean, vile, and sinful creatures, as we by nature are; so that he who is our Maker, is also our Husband; astonishing! stupendous grace! 10. He was a type of him in his building the temple, which prefigured the church of Christ, which is built on Christ, "the Rock, the Foundation, and Corner-stone; in whom all the building, fitly framed together, groweth unto an holy temple in the Lord:" nay, it is not only built upon him, but it is also built by him, therefore to him all the glory should be ascribed; for "he shall build the temple of the Lord, and he shall bear the glory," Zech. vi. 13. And now seeing that Solomon was a type of Christ in so many instances, it need not be wondered at, that he should bear his name in this, and in some other parts of this Song. But,

II. The next thing to be enquired into, is, what is meant by his bed: and there is a variety of opinions concerning it.

The Targum understands by it, the temple; R. Sol. Jarchi, the tabernacle of the congregation; in both which the priests and Levites watched and kept guard; R. Alshech, the congregation of Israel. Some[c] think that the temple of Christ's body is here intended, in which "the fulness of the Godhead dwells;" and which was guarded and protected from the fury and malice of Herod and others, by angels, who were continually ascending and descending on him: others,[d] the hearts of believers, in which Christ condescends to dwell; which are kept by his power, and guarded by that "peace of his which passeth all understanding." Some[e] have been of opinion, that Christ himself is this bed: others,[f] that it is his cross: and others,[g] that the happiness of the saints in glory is here meant; who, dying in the Lord, "enter into peace, and rest in their beds;" which are those mansions that are prepared and reserved for them in heaven. Though others[h] think that the scriptures are this bed; in hearing and reading of which, souls are often begotten again; they are written for the comfort of God's children, being opened, are made very useful to them, where they frequently meet with Christ, and have communion with him; these, notwithstanding the cunning and malice of wicked men, have been safely kept and strangely preserved by the providence of God; as the doctrines of them have been strenuously maintained and defended against heretics by the ministers of the Gospel. But I am rather inclined to think, that by this bed, we are to understand the church of Christ:[i] it is here Christ dwells; this is his resting-place: here souls are begotten and born again; and here he grants to his people nearness of access unto him, sweet familiarity, and delightful fellowship with him. Now this may be said to be his bed, because the Father has given it to him, and he has purchased it with his own blood; as also, because it is of his own making. But,

III. We now proceed to consider the guard about this bed; which are either the angels of God,[k] who are ministering spirits to the church, and "encamp round about them that fear the Lord;" who, as they are always ready, so they

---

[c] Cotton and Brightman in loc. [d] Greg. Nyssen. in Cant. Homil. 6. and Ainsworth in loc.
[e] Ambros. de Isaac, c. 5. [f] Apponius in Sanct. in loc. [g] Beda in Sanc. in loc. and Foliot. in loc. [h] Theodoret in loc. [i] So the Cabalistic doctors interpret it of malcuth, the congregation of Israel, the bride, the church, Lexie. Cab. p. 527. [k] So R. Alshech in loc.

are able and mighty to do the pleasure of Christ, and to defend his church; who are as valiant and courageous in doing their Master's work and will, as they are faithful and trusty: or rather, by this guard about the church, we are to understand the ministers of the Gospel;[1] who, "by night stand in the house of the Lord," and act the part of watchmen there; defend the truths of the Gospel, and vindicate the cause of Christ against all opposers. These are described,

1st. By their number, threescore; which perhaps was just the number of guards which Solomon had every night about his bed; and that not only for the safety and security of his royal person, but as an indication of his majesty and greatness: and it may be observed, that these are just double the number of David's worthies, Solomon excelling his father in glory and majesty; though perhaps here is a certain number mentioned for an uncertain, which may be particularly mentioned, because it is a competent and sufficient one.

2ndly. By their qualifications, "valiant or mighty men:" they are such who are strong in Christ, in his grace, and in the power of his might; and so indeed they had need to be, to discharge the work they are called unto: they are capable of digesting the word of God themselves, and of dividing it to others; they have courage enough to defend the gospel against all its enemies, and are "valiant for the truth upon earth;" they quit themselves like men, being strong; and "stand fast in one spirit, striving together for the faith of the gospel."

3rdly. By their original, or descent; they are "the valiant of Israel:" the Israelites were noted for valiant men, and were a terror to their enemies; and these were the choicest, the very flower of them; these were Israelites indeed, who had something of the spirit of old Israel in them; who, as a prince, had power both with God and men, and prevailed,

4thly. By their posture; they stood round about the bed, on all sides: which shows not only their diligence in their work, and how careful they were that nothing might prejudice the church, nor disturb its rest and repose; but also the safety and security of it: not that this is all the security the church has; for besides the angels, and these ministers of the gospel, who attend it, the Lord himself is round about; "for as the mountains are round about Jerusalem, so is the Lord round about his people:" but yet it is a great mercy and blessing that the Lord is pleased to set such a guard as this about his bed, or set such watchmen as these upon the walls of his Jerusalem.

IV. To all this a behold is prefixed; which may be considered, either as a note of attention, to stir up the minds of the daughters of Jerusalem to consider this great person, whose bed this is which is guarded after such a manner as is here represented; from whence they might conclude, that if his bed was so stately, his person must be much more so: or else, as a note of admiration, which she takes up, not only to show how much she was affected with the glory and greatness of Christ's person, and with those privileges which she enjoyed through, and by him; as that she should be in his bed, where he condescended to grant her communion with himself, about which so strong a guard is set as is here described: but likewise, she does it to stir up the affections of these daughters towards Christ, that they might be filled with desires after him, and not be at rest until they also had some enjoyment of him, in whose presence she had found so much sweetness.

Verse 8. *They all hold swords, being expert in war: every man hath his sword upon his thigh, because of fear in the night.*

IN these words is a farther description of the guard about Christ's bed: and that

I. By their armour; they "all hold swords."

II. By their skilfulness in using them; being "expert in war."

III. By their readiness to engage upon any occasion; "every man hath his sword upon his thigh."

IV. The reason of this guard, and their being thus armed, and standing in this posture, is also assigned; because of fear in the night."

I. Here is a farther description of the guard about Christ's bed, by the armour which they appeared with; they "all hold swords:" they are not only mighty and valiant men, men of courage "but also armed men;" and therefore are more capable to act both defensively and offensively. Now by the sword, which they hold in their hands, or have girt upon their thighs, is meant the word of God, which in scripture is called, 1. "The sword of the Spirit," Ephes. vi. 17; and that because it is a spiritual one; for as none of "the weapons of our warfare are carnal," but spiritual; so likewise is this, which is no small part of our Christian armour; and which none but "the spiritual man" does, or can use to any good purpose against "spiritual wickednesses in high places;" as also because it is made by the Spirit of God; he is the Author of it; it is he that furnishes us with it, and makes it powerful and efficacious to answer the ends for which it is both made and used. 2. It is called a sharp one, nay, said to be, Heb. iv. 12, "sharper than any two edged sword;" which sinners have found to be true, by those sharp threatenings and severe reproofs it has given for sin; and those cutting convictions, which, in the Spirit's hand, it has laid them under for it; for then it pricks the very

---

[1] Isidore in loc.

heart and conscience, and pierces, "even to the dividing asunder of soul and spirit;" it cuts and hews persons down, that are either going on in a course of profaneness, or are vainly boasting of their own righteousness; nay it not only cuts, but kills, according to Hosea vi. 5, compared with ver. 4, "therefore have I hewed them by the prophets, I have slain them by the words of my mouth." Satan has often felt the keenness of this sword, especially as it was in the hand of Christ, and managed by him against him in the wilderness; who repelled every temptation of his, with a "for it is written:" neither is there any weapon more powerful and successful in the hand of faith, when strengthened by the Spirit of God, to resist that enemy of our souls, than this is; nor is there any that is more formidable to him, nor more dreaded by him. Moreover it has appeared, and has been sufficiently tried, to be a sharp sword in the refutation of errors and heresies; it has at once cut the nerves and sinews of sophistic arguments, and laid open naked truth to public view; and will still appear more evidently so in the destruction of Antichrist, that man of sin, "whom the Lord will consume with the spirit of his mouth, and destroy with the brightness of his coming." 3. It is also called a *two-edged one;* Christ is represented, Rev. i. 16, as having such an one proceeding out of his mouth; and the saints, in Psalm cxlix. 6, as having the like in their hands; in both which places I am inclined to think, that the word of God is intended, whose two edges are the law and gospel. The law is one of those sharp edges of the word of God, which in the hands of the Spirit, makes piercing and cutting work in the heart of a poor sinner; it lays open not only the gross enormities of life, but also the vile corruptions of nature, and discovers the wrath of God, which is the due desert thereof; it not only accuses and convicts, but also curses and condemns; nay, becomes a *killing letter*, so that the poor sinner, under the powerful workings of it, is in his own apprehension a dead man: this sharp and cutting work of the law, the apostle Paul went under; this keen and sharp edge of the word of God he sufficiently felt, as is manifest from Rom. vii. 9—11. Moreover, the gospel is the other edge of this sword; and a sharp one it is, in the Spirit's hand, to cut down both the best and worst in man; it cuts down the best in man, his goodness and goodliness, his strength and wisdom, his righteousness and best performances, and lays them all aside in the business of his justification before God, and acceptance with him: it also cuts down the worst of man; it gives the greatest blow at his sins and corruptions of any thing else, and teaches him the most powerfully to deny ungodliness and worldly lusts; it puts him upon an abasing of himself, and a magnifying of the grace of God. Now this sword, the guard about Christ's bed had in their hands, and upon their thighs, to defend it from all the dangers it was liable to: and though in our bibles it is rendered swords, in the plural number; yet in the Hebrew text it is in the singular number, *the sword;*[m] for it is but one sword, which is the word of God, that these persons were acquainted with, and firmly held for the safety and protection of the church.

And now, by their holding this sword, is meant, not only their acquaintance with the word of God, and their apprehension of it, but also their retention of, and firm adherence to it: they not only held it forth to others, but also held it fast themselves; which is a necessary qualification in the ministers of the gospel, or in those who are about Christ's bed: for having this sword always in their hands, they are in a readiness to "war a good warfare;" which they are not strangers to, as appears from the following character of them. For,

II. They are farther described by their skilfulness in military affairs, "being expert in war:" these had been in God's γυμνάσιον, or school of exercise, where they had been in some good measure taught, and versed in the art of war, and had their spiritual "senses exercised to discern between good and evil." The ministers of the Gospel are, in common with other Christians, engaged in a war with sin, Satan, and the world; but being endowed with greater light and knowledge, faith, and experience, as they must be supposed to have a greater degree of courage to oppose; so they must be allowed to have a greater expertness in managing a war with those spiritual enemies, than usually private believers have; having a large knowledge of, and acquaintance with the many windings and turnings of a deceitful and treacherous heart, as well as the depths of Satan, and the cunning and crafty wiles and methods he takes to deceive souls; as also the various, charming, and alluring baits of an ensnaring world: and besides all this, being set in a higher post and place in the church, it is highly necessary that they should be more expert in fighting the good fight of faith," against all opposers of the doctrines of the Gospel; for it is not only proper that they should be mighty men, men of courage, who are concerned in such a work; but also men of skilfulness, who know how to use those spiritual weapons which they are accoutered with : so as both the truth of the gospel shall be defended and established, and error and heresy be refuted and overthrown.

III. They are also described by the posture of readiness which they are to engage upon any occa-

---

[m] אחזי חרב κατέχοτες ρομφάιαν, Sept. tenentes gladium, Coccieus; stringentes gladium, Junius and Tremellius; prehensi gladio, Mercerus; apprehensi gladio Montanus; capti sunt gladio, Tigurine version.

sion; "every man hath his sword upon his thigh:" to have the sword upon the thigh, is a preparation for war, and an indication of readiness to engage in it; see Psalm xlv. 3; for being there, it is near unto them; they can come at it on all proper occasions, and are hereby in a posture of defence. All this may be expressive of that familiar acquaintance which ministers of the gospel have with the word of God, and how near it is unto them? it is in their *mouths* and in their *hearts*; it dwells richly in their hearts, with which they meditate upon it; and it is in their mouths in the preaching of it; they can quickly and easily come at it, and furnish themselves with sufficient proofs of gospel-truths, and with proper arguments for the refutation of erroneous doctrines; so that as they are "set for the defence of the gospel," they are always in a posture of readiness to act for it.

IV. The reason of this guard about Christ's bed, and of their being thus armed and standing in this posture, is here assigned; which is, "because of fear in the night;" which some understand of that dread and terror which is injected into the minds of men by evil spirits; and so the Targum explains this, as it does also the terror by night, in Psal. xci. 5, of apparitions and evil spirits which walk in the night; which those who have the seal of circumcision in the flesh, which the paraphrast supposes is meant by the "sword upon the thigh," have no reason to be afraid of: but it is much better in the Talmud," understood of the fear of hell, which is comparable to the night; though that fear, which believers are apt to be possessed of in their times of darkness, seems rather to be intended: and from hence may be observed, I. That believers have their nights of affliction, temptation, desertion, darkness, sleepiness, and carnal security. 2. That they are often possessed with fears in such seasons; as "without are fightings," so "within are fears;" as that Christ is not theirs; that they shall never get to heaven, nor hold out to the end; and are frequently terrified with the formidable posse their enemies bring against them, to which they find their own power and strength unequal; and therefore are ready to faint, and be discouraged; and their peace, rest, and quietness in Christ, are much disturbed. 3. That Christ has provided a guard for his church, to remove those fears, support them under those discouragements, and defend them from those who would make inroads upon their faith and comfort; and these are the ministers of the Gospel, whom he has set upon the walls of Zion, and placed about his bed, the church; that so the out-works and fortifications of Gospel doctrines may be kept firm against all opposition without, and the precious promises of the Gospel may be open and dispensed within; that so her peace and comfort may not be broken in upon; which, as it shows the safety and security of the church, so it does likewise the tender care and concern of Christ for her.

Verse 9. *King Solomon made himself a chariot of the wood of Lebanon.*

THE church having described Christ's bed, proceeds to give some account of his chariot, which he had made for himself and spouse. The word here translated *chariot*, is to be found in no other part of the scripture, and is differently rendered. Some translate it a throne, which Solomon had prepared for himself; so Junius and Tremellius: others, a stately palace or bride chamber, which he had built on purpose for the more honourable reception of his bride; so David de Pomis, R. Sol. Jarchi, and Arias Montanus: others, a bed; which is so called from the fruitfulness thereof, which in chap. i. 16, is said to be green; but then it must mean such a bed, in which the bride used to be carried, as R. David Kimchi° observes. So that it seems to signify the nuptial bed, or an open chariot, or some such like thing, in which the bride was carried in pomp to the bridegroom's house: and in this sense is the word used in the Misnah;ᵖ where mention is made of a decree "that the bride should not go out into the city, באפריון, beappirion, the word here used, "in the nuptial bed, or open chariot;" in which as R. Sol. Jarchi says, in his gloss upon the words, "they carried her from the house of her father to the house of her husband." And so the Septuagint here renders the word by φορεῖον, which signifies something in which persons or things are carried, and is very much like in sound to the Hebrew word; and someᑫ have thought that it is this very Greek word which is here made use of, which might not be unknown to the Hebrews; and לבנות אפריון is a usual phrase with the Rabbins, to express the celebration of marriage.ʳ It seems to be the nuptial chariot: in which, according to Pausanias,ˢ three only were carried; the bride, who sat in the middle, the bridegroom on one hand, and the friend of the bridegroom on the other: something of this kind is the Palki or Palanquin of the Indians; in which the bridegroom are carried on the day of marriage on four men's shoulders.ᵗ By this chariot, R. Sol. Jarchi and Alshech would have the tabernacle of the congregation understood; though the Targum and R. Aben Ezra understand it of the temple, which was made of the cedars of Lebanon: but by it rather is meant, either,

First. The human nature of Christ, in which, as in a chariot, Christ made himself visible and

---

ⁿ Gemara, Bab. Sanhed. cap. 1. fol 7. 2. Yebamot, fol. 109. 2. and Yalkut in loc. ° In lib. shorash. rad. מרה. ᵖ Massech. Sotah. c. 9. s. 14.
ᑫ Cocceius and Heunischius in loc. Vid. Cohen De Lara, Ir. David, p. 19. ʳ Vid. Buxtorf. Epist. Heb. l. 2. ep. 7. p. 235, 237. ˢ Vid. Suidam in voce Ζευγος. ᵗ Agreement of Customs between the East-Indians and Jews, art. 17. p. 68.

conspicuous to men, and gave a glorious display of his greatness and majesty; "for in him dwelleth all the fulness of the Godhead bodily;" it was in this he descended from and ascended up to heaven; and by which saints have access to God, and a communication of grace from him; for our way of access to God, and of acceptance with him, as well as of conveyance of all covenant-grace and blessings from him, is "consecrated for us through the vail, that is to say, Christ's flesh." Concerning which chariot of Christ's human nature, we may observe, 1. The author, king Solomon, Christ himself: and this serves to set forth the magnificence of it; for if it is the work of so great a person, it must needs be curiously wrought; and at the same time it shows his wonderful humility and condescension, in that one who was possessed of royal dignity, should be employed in such a work; and in nothing did he give a greater instance of it, than in the assumption of human nature, in his being found in fashion as a man; which work purely ascribed to himself; it was *sine virili opere*, without the help of man that Christ became man; his human nature is the "stone cut out of the mountain without hands," and the tabernacle which God pitched, and not man; and because of this, it is wondrous and surprising: when it was first prophesied of, it is ushered in with a "behold, a virgin shall conceive," &c., and when the news was brought to the virgin herself, it was startling and astonishing to her, and made her say, "How shall this be, seeing I know not a man?" but this being a work of God, with whom nothing is impossible, was effected by him: but though Christ assumed our nature, and became man without the help of man; yet not exclusive of the help and assistance of his Father, who prepared a body for him; nor of the Holy Ghost, who formed and sanctified it in the virgin's womb. 2. The matter of it, and that is of the wood of Lebanon: Christ was conceived and born of the virgin Mary, who dwelt at Nazareth, a city of Galilee, at the foot of mount Lebanon; and the wood of that mountain, which was cedar, being of an incorruptible nature, may very well express the incorruption of Christ's human nature; for though he died and was buried, yet he never saw corruption: moreover this being very excellent and valuable wood, may denote the excellency and glory of Christ's human nature; whose countenance is as Lebanon, excellent as the cedars; for though, by his sorrows and sufferings, his visage was more marred than any man, and his form than the sons of men; yet he was fairer than any of the sons of Adam. 3. The end for which this chariot was made; it was for himself: for though all the three persons had a hand in making it, yet none but the second person appeared in it; it was the Son only, and not the Father, nor the Spirit, who was made flesh, and dwelt among us; which was done for the showing forth of his own glory, as well as for the sake of his body, the church. Or else,

Secondly. By this chariot, may be meant the church of Christ;[u] where he shows himself openly to his people in his ordinances, and they behold his power and his glory, in the sanctuary; here he rides in triumph over his enemies; from hence he sends forth the rod of his strength, and makes mighty conquests by his grace over the hearts of men; here his Gospel is preached, his ordinances administered, his name borne up, his cause and interest carried on, and his person alone exalted. Concerning which chariot we may also observe, 1. The author of it, Christ himself; it is he that builds this temple, and bears the glory; he is the Rock, the Foundation, and Corner-stone on which, and the chief architect by whom, it is built; there are indeed many workmen and under-builders whom he employs herein, but he himself is the principal; his own hands have laid the foundation, and reared up the super-structure; it is he that has knit all together; and bears, supports, and maintains the whole fabric; and will bring in the head-stone, with the joyful acclamations of grace, grace unto it. 2. The matter; of the wood of Lebanon: the temple which was built by Solomon, was an eminent figure of the church of Christ; now this was built of cedars fetched from Lebanon, which, though it was upon the borders of the land of Israel, yet was not in it; for Solomon sent to Hiram king of Tyre for them, whose servants cut them down, hewed them, and made them fit for the building: Christ's true church is made up only of believers, such who are comparable to the cedars in Lebanon; who, though whilst in their state of nature are aliens from the commonwealth of Israel, and therefore are invited to come with Christ from Lebanon, in chap. iv. 8, yet are cut down from off their old stock, and being hewn and fitly framed for the building by the grace and Spirit of God, are laid in it, and so grow up unto an holy temple in the Lord: and this wood of Lebanon being lasting and durable, may denote the final perseverance of the saints, and the continuance of the church of Christ; which being built upon him, the Rock, the gates of hell cannot prevail against it; it is as immoveable as mount Zion, and as incorruptible as the cedars. 3. The end for which it is made, and that is, for himself: Christ has made all things for himself; and more especially his church he has made for his own use; it is his house to dwell in, his garden to walk in, his bed to rest in, and his chariot to ride in; he has also made it for his own glory, and indeed much arises from it; his manifestative glory is much increased by it; this people he has formed for himself, and they shall show forth his praise. Or else,

3rdly. By this chariot, may be meant the Gospel, and the preaching of it; which may be also

---

* The Cabalistic doctors interpret it of malcuth, or the bride, the congregation of Israel, Lexic. Cabal. p. 144.

represented by the white horse, in Rev. vi. 2, on which Christ rides and goes forth, conquering and to conquer; the ministers also of which may be compared to chariots, as Elijah, in 2 Kings ii. 12, is called "the chariot of Israel, and the horsemen thereof;" so Theodoret interprets it of the holy apostles. In this chariot Christ shows himself in all the glory of his love and grace; here, as in a glass, saints behold the glory of the Lord, and are changed into it; in this he is carried up and down the world, and by it is conveyed to the souls of men; this is that vehicle in which he is brought home unto them, and in which he triumphs over all his enemies, and makes his ministers to do so likewise: so that this is a triumphal chariot which he has made, and in which he shows himself to the world. And, 1. He is the alone author, as well as the subject, sum, and substance of it; and therefore it is called "the Gospel of Christ." It is not the contrivance of human wisdom, the device of man's brain, nor the produce of carnal reason; it was neither projected, formed, nor delivered by man, but by the revelation of Jesus Christ; it is he that has given it to men, and given men a commission to preach it, and furnished them with all necessary qualifications for it. 2. The matter of it is said to be "the wood of Lebanon;" which being incorruptible and durable, as has been before observed, as well as of a sweet-smelling savour, may very well be applied to the Gospel of Christ, which is preached by his faithful ministers; who are not as some, who corrupt the word of God; but in doctrine, and also in life, show incorruptness, gravity, and sincerity, and deliver sound speech which cannot be condemned; which will abide and continue, notwithstanding all the efforts of men and devils; and is of an exceeding grateful smell to believers, to whom it is the savour of life unto life. 3. This he has made also for himself: that is, for his own glory; which end is answered, when the riches of his grace and love are displayed, his person and offices magnified and exalted, and he declared to be the only way of salvation to lost sinners; as also when sinners are converted, and saints are edified under the ministry of the word, and the success of all ministerial labours is ascribed unto him. Or else,

4thly. By this chariot, may be meant the covenant of grace; in which, as in a chariot, Christ shows his royal person, and the glorious sovereignty and freeness of his love; by this, as in a chariot, many poor souls are borne up and supported under, and are comfortably carried through a great many trials and exercises in this life, and in which they are brought triumphantly to glory; the same blood of the everlasting covenant, which fetched Christ out of his grave, brings souls out of the pit wherein is no water, and introduces them into the kingdom of Jesus Christ. And, 1. Of this chariot, Christ, who is here meant by king Solomon, is the author: man is not in a capacity to make a covenant with God; he has nothing of his own, but what God, before all articles, agreements, conditions, grants, and promises, has a prior right unto; but Christ, as the Representative of the elect, has made a covenant with his Father on their account; his wisdom drew the plan and model of it, he then acting as the Counsellor, or as the Angel of the great council;[w] his power effected it, being the mighty God, and his grace filled it, as the Mediator of it; he had so great a hand and concern in it, as that he is called the Surety, Mediator, and Messenger of it, nay, the covenant itself. 2. The matter of it, or of what it was made, is the wood of Lebanon; which may intend the durableness and inviolableness of the covenant of grace: for God will not break it, nor alter the thing that is gone out of his lips; it is as lasting as the wood, and as immoveable as the mountain of Lebanon itself; its promises are yea and amen, and its blessings are irreversible; it is of an everlasting nature in itself, and can never be disannulled by men or devils; and contains things in it both for time and eternity. 3. His end in making this is his own glory, as well as the good of his people; he had both in view: the former is mentioned here, he made it for himself; the latter in the next verse, where it is also said to be for the daughters of Jerusalem. Christ's glory and his church's good are inseparable; his glory is great in their salvation; which shows with what wisdom, and in what a beautiful and excellent order, the covenant of grace is made. It is interpreted of the everlasting covenant by some Jewish writers.[x]

Verse 10. *He made the pillars thereof of silver, the bottom thereof of gold, the covering of it of purple; the midst thereof being paved with love, for the daughters of Jerusalem.*

THE church goes on to give some further account of this chariot, which Christ, the true Solomon, had made for himself; and says,

I. That "the pillars of it were of silver."

II. The "bottom of gold."

III. The "covering of purple." And

IV. That "the midst of it was paved with love; and that either by or for the daughters of Jerusalem." Now the explanation of these several parts must be according to the several senses which have been given of the chariot in the former verse. And

I. If by the chariot we understand the human nature of Christ, then

1st. By the pillars of it, are meant the several graces of the Spirit, which both adorned and supported it; for besides the habitual holiness of his nature, and the innocence of his life, there appeared in him a strong faith in God; and that not only throughout the whole of his life, but in the midst of his dolorous sufferings, nay, when deserted by his Father; as also great courage and mag-

---

[w] Μεγάλης βουλῆς ἄγγελος. Sept. in Isa. ix. 6.   [x] Vid. Yalkut in loc.

nanimity of mind, as well as much patience and humility in doing and suffering all he did; and these may be called pillars, both for the mighty strength that was in them; for grace was not weak in Christ, as it is in us; and also for the support they were of unto him; in the exercise of which the chariot of the human nature was kept, as it were, upon its wheels; and these are said to be of silver, to denote the excellency, brightness, and solidity of those graces; and which appeared to be so, even when as silver they were tried in the furnace of affliction. And

2ndly. By the "bottom of gold," may be meant his Deity; and so denotes, that the subsistence of the human nature is in the Divine Person; the human nature never did, nor never will subsist without it; as soon as ever it was conceived in the virgin's womb, it was united to the divine person of Christ, and has ever been since supported by it, both in its state of humiliation and exaltation; it is this which lies at the bottom of, and puts an efficacy into all Christ's mediatorial actions, and makes them powerful to answer the ends for which they are performed; the effusion of his blood, the oblation of his sacrifice, and the bringing in of a righteousness, would not have been sufficient to have expiated sin, satisfied justice, answered the demands of a righteous law, and discharged the sinner, had they not been the blood, sacrifice, and righteousness of God; it is the impress of Deity upon them, which makes them efficacious to answer all the purposes. Now this being called a *bottom*, is no way a lessening or a diminution of the glory of Christ's Deity, any more than his being called a *foundation* is; but rather serves to set forth the glory and greatness of it, as its being said to be of gold manifestly shows. And then also,

3rdly. By the purple covering of the chariot, which seems to be an allusion to the curtains of the tabernacle, Exod. xxvi. 1, may be meant, either the passion and sufferings of Christ in the human nature, by which his garments were as though they had been dyed; and he appeared red in his apparel; nay clothed with a vesture dipped in blood; so that the covering of the human nature of Christ may well be said to be of purple; or else, it means his royal dignity, and his exaltation after sufferings; this being a colour used by kings and great persons; he was clothed with a purple robe before his sufferings, by way of derision; but now he is really made Lord and Christ; he was then, in a way of mockery, crowned with thorns: but now, in the same nature, is crowned with glory and honour. And then,

4thly. By the midst of it, which is paved with love for the daughters of Jerusalem, may be meant the heart of Christ, which is filled with, and as it were, paved with love for poor sinners; or as the word[y] may be rendered, *inflamed*, or set on fire with love. It was this that moved him to espouse their cause, take upon him the care and charge of their persons, assume their nature, and die in their room and stead; which love of his, as to its quality, is the best; as to its degree, the greatest; as to its duration, for ever; from whence there is no separation, to which there is no parallel; and at present, to us finite creatures, incomprehensible; and all this is for the daughters of Jerusalem, the elect of God, or young converts; that is, it is all for their sakes, and out of love to them he made this chariot, or assumed human nature, according to what is said, Heb. ii. 14, "forasmuch then as the children are partakers of flesh and blood, he also himself likewise took part of the same:" or else the meaning is, that such is the love of Christ towards these daughters, that if any one could but look into his heart, they would find the very images and pictures of them drawn there; who are not only engraven upon the palms of his hands, but are also set as a seal upon his heart; which was prefigured by the high-priest's bearing the names of the children of Israel in the breast-plate of judgment upon his heart, before the Lord continually; all which is expressive of that strong affection which he has unto them. But then,

II. If by the chariot we understand the church of Christ, then,

1st. By the pillars thereof are meant the ministers of the gospel; so of James, Cephas, and John, the apostle Paul says, that they seemed to be pillars, and such as these are intended by the seven pillars, which wisdom had hewn out, and built her house upon, in Prov. ix. 1; who, for their strength, stability, and support to the church of Christ, may be compared to those two pillars in the porch of the temple, which are called, the one *Jachin*, and the other *Boaz*: for these are of great strength to the building; there is a very great weight rests upon them; these are the legs in Christ's body, which, like pillars of marble, stand firm and immoveable, notwithstanding the several pressures of reproaches, afflictions, persecutions, &c., which fall very hard and heavy upon them; for none of these things move them; but with an unshaken courage and magnanimity of mind they stand up under them; and in so doing, are very great supports to the cause, interest, and church of Christ; for though Christ is the Foundation and the chief Corner-stone, yet these are pillars, and have their usefulness. Now these are said to be of silver, because of their valuableness, both in the esteem of Christ, who has placed them in his church, and from whom they have all their strength and usefulness; and likewise in the esteem of saints, to whom they are made useful; for the tongue of the just, and especially of a gospel-minister, is as choice silver: these are the silver trumpets,

---

[y] רָצוּף succensum, Montanus, Marckius; accensum, sive exustum, some in Vatablus, so Aben Ezra. רִצְפָּה is used to signify a live coal, in Isa. vi. 6. vid. Mercer. in loc. so inflammatus amore conjugis, is used by Virgil, Æneid. l. 3. v. 330.

which sound forth and proclaim peace and pardon, life and salvation to poor, lost, and rebellious sinners; their words, when fitly spoken, and adapted to the cases of souls, either of afflicted saints, or distressed sinners, are like apples of gold in pictures of silver. Moreover, this may be expressive of their shine and lustre, both in doctrine and life; who preach the gospel in its power and purity, hold the mystery of the faith in a pure conscience; and who, the more they are vilified, reproached, afflicted, and persecuted for the sake of the gospel, the brighter they are, like silver purified seven times. And then,

2ndly. By the "golden bottom," may be meant Christ; who is the foundation of his church and people, on which they are laid and firmly built; and is the only foundation of their everlasting salvation, of all their faith, hope, joy, and comfort here, and of their eternal happiness hereafter: and a good bottom this is; happy is every one that is upon it; it may well be said to be "of gold," because of the glory and splendour of it; it is the "foundation of the apostles and prophets," which they ministerially laid, and on which their persons are secured equally with others; hence the foundations of the new Jerusalem are said to be twelve, and each of them compared to a precious stone, to set forth the excellency thereof: nay, this foundation is a super-excellent one; "for other foundation can no man lay," which is in any respect valuable, or upon any account to be compared to this "which is laid, which is Christ Jesus." Moreover, for the durableness of it, it may be said to be of gold; for "the righteous is an everlasting foundation;" that is, the righteous man's foundation is such an one; or he is built upon one that will last for ever; and such an one is Christ; a foundation that will never decay; but will always abide firm and strong: and is sufficient to bear the whole weight of the building to all eternity. And then,

3rdly. The "purple covering" may intend either, 1. The suffering state of the church; being attended with a variety of afflictions, tribulations, and persecutions, and sometimes as it were covered with blood, as the histories of several ages testify. Or else, 2. Her regal dignity, to which she and all believers are advanced by Christ, who has made them "kings and priests to God and his Father:" purple being a colour in use among great persons, may very well represent this. Or, 3. Her being clothed with the robe of Christ's righteousness; which may be said to be of a purple colour, because it is the produce and effect of Christ's blood, and is as it were dipped into it; hence believers are said to be "justified by his blood," in Rom. v. 9. Or, 4. It may signify her being washed in Christ's blood, together with the outward garments of her conversation, and so appear to be of this dye. And then,

4thly. By the midst thereof, which is "paved with love," may be meant, either the hearts of believers, or of the church, filled with a sense of Christ's love shed abroad in them, or inflamed with love to Christ,[a] which, though it is sometimes in a decaying and declining condition, yet is never entirely moved; for who "can separate from the love of Christ?" that is, either from Christ's love to his people, or from their love to him: or else, by this pavement of love in the midst of the church, may be meant the ordinances of Christ; which he has instituted for the sake of the daughters of Jerusalem, or young converts; through which he discovers his love unto them, and by an attendance on which they discover their love, both to Christ and to his church; and the church again discovers her love to them, by a cheerful admission of them to these ordinances. But then,

III. If by the chariot we understand the gospel and the preaching of it, then,

1st. By the "silver pillars thereof," are meant the truths and doctrines of it; which, like pillars, are solid and substantial, and continue firm and immoveable, and not like chaff, which is driven away with every wind; nor like such combustible and perishing things, as wood, hay, and stubble; but like gold, silver, and precious stones; and are of very great use to support God's children under the several trials and exercises which they are attended with, and that either in adversity or prosperity, life, or in death: and therefore for their value, utility, and duration, may be compared to pillars of silver: and ought to be as diligently and carefully sought for and into as silver is, and to be received and preferred before it: for to get wisdom in Gospel truths, "is better than gold;" and to get understanding in Gospel-doctrines, "is rather to be chosen than silver," Prov. xvi. 16. And then,

2ndly. By the "golden bottom," may be meant Christ himself, who is the sum and substance of the Gospel: to preach Christ, and him only, as God's way of salvation to sinners, was the old, primitive, and apostolical way of preaching: and which God blessed and owned, and continues so to do, for the conversion of sinners, and the comfort of saints. that gospel, of which Christ is not the sum and substance, is like a chariot without a bottom; and such an one is good for nothing; for who would venture to ride in it? but where Christ is the main and principal subject insisted on, there is a good bottom, nay, a golden one: or a good seat, ἀνακλιτον, "a reclining place," as the Septuagint render it, to sit and rest in, or lean upon. And also,

3rdly. By the "purple covering," may be meant particularly those doctrines of the Gospel, which concern our redemption from the law, and the curses of it; the pardon of our sins, and our justification through Christ's precious blood;

---

[a] Cujus media pars strata fuit amore fœminarum Jerusalem, Tigurine version; amore filiarum, Vatablus, Mercerus.

for which reason they may be said to be of this colour. And

4thly. This pavement of love may signify that the whole Gospel is full of love; wherein, in a very lively manner, is set forth the love of God the Father, in contriving and drawing the scheme and the model of our salvation before all time; and in sending his Son in the fulness of time, to accomplish what was agreed on before, that he should do; as also the love of Christ in becoming man, sustaining all the sorrows of life; and sufferings of death; and all for the sake, and in the room and stead of vile, sinful, and rebellious sinners; it gives us such instances of love as never were heard of before, which never were, nor never will be paralleled; its whole language is love; it is nothing else but a free promise and declaration of God's love and grace to sinful man; so that it may well be said to be paved with it; and how delightful must such a pavement be to the daughters of Jerusalem, to all young converts, either to behold or sit upon, where nothing but the love that is between Christ and his church is beautifully described? But then,

IV. If by the chariot we understand the covenant of grace, then,

1st. By the silver pillars, may be meant the promises thereof; which, like pillars, are firm and immoveable, solid and substantial; they are all yea and amen in Christ; not one of them shall ever fail, being free, absolute, and unconditional; and therefore are called better promises, as being preferable to those in the covenant of works, which required conditions to be fulfilled before the enjoyment of the things promised. These, like pillars, are the support of God's children, under the variety of troubles they are exercised with; these yield them relief, are reviving cordials, and fill them with joy and comfort when nothing else can. O! of what profit and advantage has a promise been to a sinking believer, when it has been seasonably brought, and suitably applied by the Spirit! there are some promises which the saints would not have out of their Bibles for millions of worlds: and these may be said to be of silver, because of their preciousness, richness, and durableness; they are "exceeding great and precious," are of more worth than "thousands of gold and silver;" and will last for ever, being the sure "mercies of David;" nay, the more they are tried, used, and handled by faith, the brighter and more glorious will they look. And then,

2ndly. By the golden bottom of this covenant, must be meant Christ; who is the covenant itself, not only materially, but fundamentally; he is not only the matter and substance of it, all the blessings and promises of it being comprised in him, but also the Foundation of it; he bears the whole weight of the covenant, and is, as has been obser-ved, the Surety, Mediator, and Messenger of it. Now this bottom, for its richness, firmness, and duration, may be said to be of gold; souls who are in this chariot, the covenant of grace, need never fear falling through; it can never be unbottomed: once in covenant, and always so; and therefore it is said to be "ordered in all things, and sure;" because it has such a bottom, it can never be broken, nor will it ever be removed. And then.

3rdly. Its purple covering may intend the blood of Christ, which is called "the blood of the everlasting covenant;" by which, not only the covenant is ratified and confirmed; but all that are in it and are under this cover,[a] have their sins blotted out, hidden and covered; so that when they are sought for, and the most diligent scrutiny made for them by justice, they shall not be found. Moreover, their persons are hereby eternally screened from the wrath of God; so that though showers of wrath shall fall upon the heads of Christless sinners, yet all under this purple covering shall be safe, and not have the least drop fall upon them; but shall, in this chariot of rich and glorious grace, be safely preserved, protected, and conveyed to eternal glory.

4thly. The midst of it being paved with love shows that this covenant is full of love. It was love that set Christ on work to make it, and engaged him to be the Surety, Mediator, and Messenger of it; it is made up of nothing but love; love has filled it with precious promises and spiritual blessings; and all for the daughters of Jerusalem, to whom love in time communicates them. O! what a delightful and easy chariot must this be to ride in, which is lined with love! love is the hangings of it all around, and the velvet cushions and pillows on which faith leans; with what splendour, stateliness, and majesty, as well as ease and pleasure then, does the believer go to glory?

The Jewish writers, as I have already observed, by the chariot, understand the tabernacle or temple; and by its pillars, bottom, covering, and middle, the ark of the testimony, with the two tables of stone, which are more precious than gold and silver; the golden mercy-seat, the vail of blue and purple, and the seat of the shechinah between the two cherubims, which are upon the mercy-seat. To this purpose are the Targum, and the gloss of R. Solomon Jarchi upon the place.

Moreover, besides the several senses which have been already given of these words, it may not be amiss to observe, that by this bride-chamber, as some render the word in ver. 9, may be meant the royal palace: and how well the description of it in this verse agrees with what is given of the new Jerusalem, in Rev. xxi., will best appear by comparing both together: which bridal palace

---

[a] Purpura, sanguis Christi, ut autum operimentum, sive cœlum lecti tegit eos qui in lecto sunt, ita and sanguis Christi nos tegit, Not. Tig. in loc.

Christ is now preparing for his spouse, and when that is ready for her, and she for that, being "perfumed with myrrh and frankincense," she shall be kindly welcomed and cheerfully received; where the nuptial feast will be kept, and Christ shall be seen by all the daughters of Zion in all his glory, and with his royal diadem upon his head, as he is described in the following verse.

Verse 11. *Go forth, O ye daughters of Zion, and behold Solomon with the crown wherewith his mother crowned him, in the day of his espousals, and in the day of the gladness of his heart.*

These are not the words of Christ, for he is the person spoken of and represented in this glorious manner; nor are they the speech of the daughters of Jerusalem, young converts, for they are the persons spoken to, who are here called the daughters of Zion; nor are they to be considered as the angels' exhortation to all the elect to forsake the world, and contemplate Christ by faith in the glory of his kingdom after his resurrection, as some think: but they are the words of the church, who, observing that the daughters of Jerusalem were first struck with admiration at the sight of her, as coming up out of the wilderness, in ver. 6, and that their eyes were now intently fixed upon the bed and chariot she had been describing in the former verses, calls them off from these things, and proposes a far more glorious object to them, to whom her own glory was not to be compared; nay, king Solomon, in all his glory, either on his coronation or marriage-day, to which the allusion seems to be, cannot equal him; and if his bed and chariot were so acceptable to them, and gave them so much pleasure to behold, she might well conclude that a sight of his person, especially in all his regal glory, could not but be grateful to them; and therefore bids them go forth and behold him, to which no doubt they would be forward enough; for the sight of a crowned king, as he passes along the streets, especially on his coronation day, is very desirable to people, who come forth out of their houses, or look out of their windows to behold the sight.

There is a very great variety in the opinion of interpreters about the time to which these words should be referred. The ancient Jewish writers[c] refer them to the time of Solomon's finishing the temple, and his dedication of it, and to the joy and gladness which appeared on that solemn occasion; but that was neither his coronation nor his marriage-day. R. Solomon Jarchi[d] applies them to the time of the giving of the law, when the Israelites acknowledged God as their king, by subjecting themselves to it; for though Moses was legislator, yet God was king in Jeshurun; as also to the erection and dedication of the temple in the wilderness. Others refer them to the time of Solomon's being crowned king of Israel, which may be ascribed to his mother Bathsheba, as the moral cause of it;[e] who, by her entreaties and supplications, procured it for him; and which was "the day of his espousals" to the people of Israel, and no doubt "the day of the gladness of his heart." Others[f] refer to the time of his marriage to Pharaoh's daughter; at which time it was the custom, not only of other nations,[g] but of the Jews, to crown married persons, to which perhaps the allusion is made in Ezek. xvi. 12, and of those nuptial crowns mention is made in the Misnah:[h] others refer them to the incarnation of Christ;[i] and think that by the crown, is meant his humanity, which he received from his mother, the virgin Mary; at which time he espoused our nature, and was no less a day of gladness to him than to us; it being what he gladly performed, and had been long desirous of, as is manifest from the several preludiums of it in the Old Testament: though others[k] have been of opinion, that the words regard the passion and sufferings of Christ; at which time he was crowned with a crown of thorns, and by his blood purchased and espoused the church to himself; which bloody baptism of his was so desirable to him, that he was even straitened until it was accomplished: but though the allusion, as I have already hinted, is to the coronation and marriage-day of king Solomon; yet I should rather think that the words have reference to Christ, as the glorious Mediator, when first discovered to a poor sinner in all the fulness of his grace, as sitting and riding in the chariot of the everlasting gospel; concerning which we may observe.

First. The persons who are spoken to and exhorted to go forth and behold Christ, and they are the daughters of Zion: Zion was a mount, situate on the north side of Jerusalem, and is sometimes used for the city itself; and was a figure of the church of Christ, which sometimes bears this name in scripture: by the daughters of it, we are to understand the same who are in this song often called the daughters of Jerusalem, by which we have all along understood young converts; who may be called the daughters of Zion, because Christ, who is here thus gloriously

---

[c] T. Bab. Taanith, fol. 26. 2. Targum in loc. Zohar Gen. fol. 15. 3. and in Exod. fol. 24. 3. [d] So Lyra, who frequently follows Jarchi. [e] Dicitur vero a matre coronatus, quia ipsa precibus obtinuit, ut filius regnaret, quod moraliter coronare est, Sanct. in loc. [f] Vid. Sanct. and Bishop Patrick in loc. [g] Vid. Paschal. de Coronis, l. 2. c. 16, 17. p. 126. Barthii and Animadv. ad Claudian. de Rapt. Proserp. l. 2. v. 140. Magnisque coronis conjugium sit. Claudian, laus Serenæ, v. 189. 190. such a crown is called στεφος γαμηλιον. Bion. Idyll. prope finem. Vid. Plauti Casin. act. 4, 2. sc. 2. v. 17. Coronant and nuptiæ sponsos, ideo non nubimus Ethenicis, &c. Tertull. de Corona Militis, c. 13. [h] Misnah sotah, c. 9. s. 14. and Wagenseil. in ibid. [i] Isidore in loc. Beda, S. Thom. and Bernard in Sanct. in loc. and not. Tigur. in loc. [k] Theodoret and Tres Patres apud Ibid.

described, is king thereof; see Psalm cxlix. 2, Zech. ix. 9.

Secondly. The object which is proposed to them to behold, is king Solomon, or the Lord Jesus Christ, who is greater than Solomon, and was typified by him, and in what respects has been shown on ver. 7. And it may not be amiss to remark, what one[1] well observes, that there is a manifest gradation in these verses: in ver. 7 he is only called Solomon; in ver. 9 king Solomon; and here in this verse, "king Solomon with a crown;" for, as the same author observes, "the longer she speaks of Christ, and insists in mentioning his excellency, her thoughts draw the deeper, she sets him up the higher, and becomes warmer in her apprehensions, affections, and expressions concerning him." And therefore I shall now,

Thirdly. Consider this circumstance of Christ's glory, he being represented with a "crown, wherewith his mother crowned him in the day of his espousals," &c., and here it will be proper to inquire, 1st. Who we are to understand by his mother. 2ndly. Who by the crown wherewith she crowned him. 3rdly. The time of his coronation, which is here expressed, "in the day of his espousals," &c.

1st. By his mother, we are not to understand Bathsheba, the mother of Solomon; nor the Virgin Mary, the natural mother of Christ: but either, the church of Christ, the Jerusalem above, which is the mother of us all, who being the mother of Christ mystical, may be said to be the mother of Christ also; or else, every particular believer may be intended, who stands related to Christ as his brother, and as one who has sucked the breasts of one and the same mother; see chap. viii. 1; who not only is called Christ's brother and sister, but also his mother, Matt. xii. 50; in whose heart Christ is formed, by whom he is affectionately loved, even as an only child is by a tender mother; and for whose honour, glory, and interest there is a very great concern. But,

2ndly. What is meant by this *crown*, wherewith he is crowned by his mother. Christ has a crown and kingdom, as he is God, equal with the Father, but this is not put upon him, nor given to him by any; he has a natural right unto it which none can give nor take away from him; he being "in the form of God," and in all respects equal to him, "thought it no robbery" to assume this crown and kingdom to himself: he has also one as he is Mediator; and this is put upon him, not by his mother, but by his Father; who has "anointed him with the oil of gladness above his fellows," and placed him as "king over his holy hill of Zion," and set "a crown of pure gold upon his head." And thus now, by faith, believers see him, "crowned with glory and honour;" all which will more manifestly appear at the last day, when there will be a more open and visible coronation of Christ than has hitherto been; though he has very often now a "crown given to him," as the triumphant conqueror over the hearts of men; by the mighty power of his grace displayed in the everlasting gospel, in which he goes forth "conquering and to conquer." But it seems to me that the crown which is here meant, is that which every true believer puts on Christ, when their souls are brought to venture on him, and believe in him; every act of faith is a putting the crown on Christ's head; and every submission to his commands and ordinances, is an acknowledging of him as King of saints; and the giving up of their souls unto him, and owning him as their Head and Husband, is "a crown of glory, and a royal diadem" in his hand; even as converts are a "crown of rejoicing" to ministers, and "a virtuous woman is a crown to her husband:" and in nothing more do believers do this, than when they ascribe all they have and are, to his grace, and say, with the apostle, It is "by the grace of Christ I am what I am;" for by so doing, they not only cast their crowns at Christ's feet, but set another upon his head; whereas, on the contrary, they take the crown from off Christ's head, who do not believe on him, despise his commands, neglect his ordinances, and ascribe their salvation, either in whole or in part, unto themselves, their own works and duties. Moreover, this honour Christ justly deserves from us; and it is an incumbent duty to give it to him; for he, in creation, crowned man, and set him over all the works of his hands, and made him but little inferior to the angels themselves; and by his incarnation, has crowned the human nature with such glory and honour, as it never had in a state of innocence itself; it being united to a divine person, and is now exalted at the Father's right hand, which is an honour none of the angelic race ever enjoyed; for, "to which of the angels said he at any time, Sit at my right-hand?" who also, in the redemption of us from the curse of the law, the slavery and servitude of sin, Satan, and the world, in the remission of our sins by his blood, the justification of our persons by his righteousness, and sanctification of our hearts and natures by his grace and Spirit, has "crowned us with loving-kindness and tender mercies." In short, he has laid up for us a "crown of righteousness, life, and glory," which he, the righteous judge, will give unto and put upon the heads of all his people; so that there is a great deal of reason to crown Christ, and acknowledge him alone as our Lord and King, our Head and Husband, our Saviour and Redeemer, who was crowned with thorns for us, and has crowned us with his grace now, and will ere long crown us with glory. But,

3rdly. The time of his coronation is next to be enquired into; and that is said to be "in the day of his espousals," that is, on his marriage-day; for Christ's coronation and marriage-day are one and the same day. Now, by this "day of his espousals," we are to understand the time

---

[1] Durham on ver. 9.

of a poor sinner's being enabled, by mighty grace, to give up itself to the Lord, when it consents to be his for ever: this marriage was made and agreed upon in the everlasting council and covenant of grace and peace; Christ made it his request to his Father, and he granted him it; he gave his full consent unto it, so that there remained only the actual consent of the persons themselves, for whom Christ had such a strong love and affection; which is obtained by the powerful workings of his grace and Spirit in time upon their hearts; and that often under the ministry of the word, where they are "espoused as a chaste virgin to Christ;" at which time there is a large breaking forth, not only of Christ's love to and upon their hearts, but also of theirs to Christ; which is called the love of their espousals, and which Christ afterwards remembers, when it has grown cold and chill towards him: thus every time that a particular soul is brought to Christ, it is both a coronation, and an espousal-day; but the great coronation and espousal-day is yet to come, when all the elect shall be brought in, and it shall be said, "The marriage of the lamb is come, and the bride is ready;" then shall the king, with her, enter into the marriage-chamber, where the nuptials will be solemnized, and he openly and publicly crowned king of saints, where he will reign with them in all his glory. Some of the Jewish writers interpret this "day of espousals," of the days of the Messiah.[m]

Now this "day of his espousals," with particular believers, as well as the more glorious one that is to come, is called "the day of the gladness of his heart:" which shows how welcome poor sinners are to Christ, and how gladly and cheerfully he receives them; it is not only the joy of angels, but the joy and gladness of his heart, when sinners are converted to him, and believe on him; the bridegroom cannot more rejoice over his bride on his marriage-day, than Christ does over poor coming sinners; and when all his saints are together with him in heaven to behold his glory, what joy and gladness will then fill his heart? But,

Fourthly. We may observe the duty which is enjoined those daughters of Zion; and that is, 1. To go forth, i. e. out of themselves; for a man can never see any glory and excellency in Christ, until he looks out of himself alone to him, the church would have these daughters turn away their eyes from every thing else, and view this glorious object only for every thing else though never so valuable, is to be forsaken and left for the sake him, who is preferable to all enjoyments whatever. 2. To behold him: the former is in order to this; for as persons sitting within doors, cannot behold an object that is passing by, unless they arise, get up, and go forth or look out; so neither can believers discern this glorious object without going forth. The church would have these daughters behold Christ with attention, affection, faith, and admiration; she would have them fix their eyes upon him, look upon him, and love him; look upon him, and believe in him; look upon him, and wonder at him; for there are astonishing beauties, incomparable excellencies, transcendent glories in him, which deserve such looks as these.

CHAPTER IV.

In this chapter is contained a large commendation of the church's beauty by Christ: first more particularly, by an enumeration of several parts, as her eyes, hair, teeth, lips, temples, neck, and breasts, verse 1—5, and more generally, ver. 7, and having observed where he himself was determined to go, he invites her to go with him; which he enforces, partly from the danger she was exposed unto where she was, verse 6, 8, and partly from the comeliness of her person and graces in his esteem; with which he was ravished, and therefore was extremely desirous of her company, ver. 9—11; and then enters into some new description of her, as a garden and an orchard, as a spring and fountain, verse 12—14. All which she makes to be owing to him, verse 15. And the chapter is closed with an order from Christ to the winds, to blow on his garden, and cause the spices of it to flow out; and with an invitation of the church to Christ, to come into his garden, and recreate himself there, verse 16.

Verse. 1. *Behold thou art fair, my love, behold thou art fair; thou hast dove's eyes within thy locks; thy hair is as a flock of goats, that appear from mount Gilead.*

IN these words Christ reassumes his part in this Song, and enters upon a commendation of his church's beauty: which he does.

First. More generally by asserting it, when he says, "Behold thou art fair," &c., in which general commendation of her beauty, we have, 1st. An affectionate character given to her, "my love." 2ndly. Something asserted of her, that she was fair. 3rdly. This assertion repeated. 4thly. To this assertion the word *behold* prefixed. This commendation we have already met with, expressed in the same words, in chap. i. 15, where this kind and loving character has been opened: in what sense the church may be said to be fair, shown; as also the reasons of Christ's repeating this assertion, and prefixing to it the word behold, are given. The reasons why these words are again mentioned by him, perhaps may be to show how much his heart was taken with her beauty; that his love to her was the same as ever it was, notwithstanding her sleepy frames and unbecoming carriage to him; as also, because she might stand in need of the fresh discoveries of his love.

Secondly. He gives some particular instances of her beauty in this and the four following verses.

---

[m] Vid. Yalkut in loc.

1st. He describes the beauty of her eyes, and asserts, that she has dove's eyes within her locks; in which words we are to consider. 1. What we are to understand by her eyes. 2. Why they are called dove's eyes. 3. Why they are said to be within her locks.

1. By the church's eyes we may understand, either the ministers of the Gospel, who are to the church what eyes are to a human body; they are placed in the more eminent part of Christ's body, the church, to watch, overlook, guide, and direct the other members of the body: or else, by them may be intended the eyes of the understanding, being illuminated by the divine Spirit; and more especially the eye of faith, by which a soul, enlightened by divine grace, beholds the glory, fulness, and suitableness of Christ, and looks to him alone for life and salvation.

2. These eyes are called doves. Why ministers of the Gospel are compared to doves, and the eye of faith said to be a dove's eye, have been already shown on chap. i. 15.

3. These eyes are said to be within her locks; which, if applied to the ministers of the Gospel, may denote, 1. The imperfection of their light and knowledge, and that a great deal of darkness and obscurity attends them: they know but in part, and prophecy but in part; as eyes under the locks, being covered with them, cannot see so clearly, as when they are removed from them; so the ministers of the Gospel cannot see so clearly into Gospel-truths in this state of imperfection, as they shall, when these locks of darkness are removed; for then they shall see eye to eye; their knowledge of Christ is imperfect now; their light into Gospel-truths is weak and dim; and proportionate to their light and knowledge do they preach; the apostle Paul, who had the greatest light into the Gospel, and the largest share of the knowledge of Christ Jesus, that perhaps, ever any man had, yet desired to know more of Christ, and the power of his resurrection, Phil. iii. 10. 2. It may be expressive of their modesty and humility; locks being decently tied up, as this word signifies,[a] is an evidence of modesty, as the contrary is of wantonness; the ministers of the Gospel, though they have the greatest gifts bestowed upon them; yet reckon themselves less than the least of all saints; for notwithstanding all their parts, gifts, and graces, they do not think themselves sufficient, either to think or speak anything as of themselves; but acknowledge that their sufficiency is of God, who only hath made them able ministers of the New Testament; and whenever their labours are blest and owned, either for the comfort and edification of God's people, or for the conversion of sinners, they ascribe it not to themselves, but to the grace of God that is with them. 3. This phrase may be added, to set forth their beauty; eyes, from under or within the locks decently and modestly bound up, look very beautiful; or under locks of hair, plaited and curled about the face, so that the eyes are but just seen, which add to the beauty of them: the ministers of the Gospel appear beautiful, not only to Christ, who has counted them faithful, and put them into the ministry; but also to those to whom they are made useful, either for comfort and establishment, or for conviction and conversion; to these, even the very "feet of him that bringeth good tidings, that publisheth peace, that bringeth good tidings of good, that publisheth salvation, are beautiful," Isa. lii. 7.

But if by these dove's eyes we understand the enlightened eyes of the understanding, and particularly the eye of faith; then this phrase perhaps is used to denote, 1. The imperfection of faith: the greatest believer has need to pray, with the apostle, "Lord, increase our faith;" there are some, τά ὑστερήματα, some things lacking, some deficiencies in faith which need perfecting; it is true, "faith is the evidence of things not seen," yet oftentimes it is very dark and obscure: indeed, when compared with Old Testament saints, believers under the New may be said with open face to behold, as in a glass, the glory of the Lord; but when compared with saints, possessed of the beatific vision, they see but through a glass darkly; their eyes are within their locks. 2. To show us what a modest grace faith is: it looks alone on Christ, it lives only on him; it receives all from him, and gives all the glory to him; it ascribes nothing in man's salvation to itself, nor to any thing done by the creature, but all to Christ and his grace; and so excludes boasting, as the apostle says, Rom. iii. 27, "Where is boasting then? it is excluded. By what law? of works? nay; but by the law of faith." Had works any thing to do in man's salvation, boasting would have been encouraged and established; but God of his infinite wisdom has ordered it, that it should be of and through faith; that it might appear to be of grace, and not of works, lest any man should boast. 3. To set forth how beautiful faith is in Christ's eye, and how much his heart is taken with it; as appears from the ninth verse of this chapter, where he says, "Thou hast ravished my heart, my sister, my spouse; thou hast ravished my heart with one of thine eyes," that is, with the eye of faith.

2ndly. He describes her beauty by her hair, which he says, "is as a flock of goats that appear from mount Gilead;" that is, like the hair of such a flock of goats, so Ben Melech; which in some countries, hangs down like the locks of women's hair plaited; and is thought to be most like human hair, 1 Sam. xix. 13; in the hair of women their comeliness greatly lies, and without which they are not pleasing, as Apuleius' ob-

---

[a] לצמתך intra ligamina tua, some in Vatablus; vittam tuam, Cocceius; constrictam comam tuam. Michaelis, so Jarchi; vid. Horat. Carmin. l. 2. ode 11.

[b] v. 23, 24. Crines connexi. Propert, l. 2. eleg. 5. v. 23.

[b] Ælian. de Animal. l. 16. c. 30.

[c] Metamorph. l. 2.

serves: It is compared not to such hair for length and sleekness, as for the colour of it, being yellowish, which with women formerly was in esteem, and reckoned graceful; and great care was taken to make it look so, even as yellow as gold;[d] nor was it unusual to compare the hair of women, and represent it as superior to a fleece of the choicest flock;[e] women in former times had their perukes made of goat's hair.[f] This may be understood, 1st. Of the outward conversation of the saints; which may be compared to hair, for the following reasons.

1. Because as the hair is for covering, 1 Cor. xi. 15, so is a well-ordered and gospel-conversation a covering to the saints. A believer has many coverings; he has more garments than one; he is clothed with " the garments of salvation, and covered with the robe of Christ's righteousness; this is his justification, and what gives him a title to glory: he has also the garment of sanctification, which is curiously wrought by the Spirit of God; and this makes him meet for the King's presence: and he has, besides these, his conversation-garments, which he is to watch and keep from being spotted with the flesh, and to wash them and make them white in the blood of the Lamb; but these cannot cover sins, nor skreen him from divine justice; this only the righteousness of Christ can do, by which his sins are so covered, that when they are sought for they shall not be found; but his outward conversation is " a covering narrower than that he can wrap himself in," so as to be hid and secured from divine justice; if he was only to appear herein before justice, these very clothes would both abhor and condemn him: nor can they make him meet for the King's presence; this only the garment of sanctification can do: but then the outward conversation of the saints is a cover and a fence against the reproaches of the world; for though they have not whereof to glory before God, yet at some times and in some cases they may lawfully do it before men, and say, as Samuel did, " Whose ox have I taken? whom have I defrauded? whom have I oppressed, or of whose hand have I received any bribe?" thus their conversation is a cover and fence unto them; and is of service to make those " ashamed who falsely accuse their good conversation in Christ, and to put to silence the ignorance of foolish men. 2. As hair is very ornamental to the believer: as garments, though they do not make, as yet they adorn the man; so a good conversation, though it does not make, yet it adorns the Christian. It is decent and becoming the Gospel of Christ Jesus; it adorns the doctrine of God our Saviour, and recommends religion to others. 3. As hair that is ordered aright, and well taken care of, so is a well-ordered conversation; that is, such an one as is ordered, according to the rule of God's word, and by God himself; for the steps of a good man are ordered by the Lord;" David knew this full well that God did so, and that he himself was insufficient for it; and therefore he thus prays, " order my steps in thy word," that is, according to thy word, which is the rule of faith and practice: and such a conversation as this being like a well-set and ordered head of hair, is very grateful and well-pleasing to Christ; therefore he says, " to him that ordereth his conversation aright, will I show the salvation of God," Psalm l. 23. 4. As the hair upon the head is conspicuous and manifest to all, so is the conversation of the saints: that they are justified by Christ's righteousness, and sanctified by his Spirit, are not seen and known of all men; but their outward conversation is manifest, and so it should be; " let your light so shine before men, that they may see your good works, and glorify your Father which is in heaven," Matt. v. 16. 5. As hair has its dependence upon, and influence from the head; so has the outward conversation of the saints its dependence on, and influence from the grace of the Spirit: a graceless professor, though he may keep up a moral conversation for a time; yet it will drop off from him like leaves from the trees in autumn, or like hair that is shed from the head after a violent distemper; the " root of the matter " not being in him: the difference between a man of grace and a graceless professor, is elegantly given by Jeremy, chap. xvii. 5—8, the one is like the " heath in the desert," dry and barren; the other is like a " tree planted by the waters," moist and flourishing; " his leaf is green," and " he ceaseth not from yielding fruit." Thus the outward conversation of the saints may be compared to hair: and what may farther confirm this sense of the words, is that the apostle Paul, in 1 Tim. ii. 9, 10, instead of broidered hair, recommends shamefacedness, sobriety, and good works, as more becoming godliness; and the apostle Peter, in 1 Pet. iii. 3, 4, instead of plaiting the hair, exhorts to an adorning with the " ornament of a meek and quiet spirit."

Now this hair of the church's, or the outward conversation of the saints, may also be compared to a "flock of goats which appear from mount Gilead;" or, on mount Gilead, as Noldius. Gilead was a very proper place for cattle, Numb. xxxii. 1: and no doubt the goats which were fed there, as were usual on mountains,[g] were fat and fruitful: and being in large numbers, and kept in good order, might appear from this mount, to distant spectators, beautiful and magnificent; their hair particularly might be long, smooth, sleek, and glistering, and look very beautiful and lovely; especially in the morning at sunrising,

---

[d] Virgil. Æneid. 4. prope finem, aurea cæsaries Æneid. 8. v. 659. Vid. Barthii Animadv. ad Claudian. de rapt Proserp. l. 3. c. 86. [e] Quæ crine vincit Boetiei gregis vellus, Martial. l. 5. ep. 38. [f] Hoedina tibi pelle, Ibid, l. 12. ep. 38. [g] Theocrit. Idyll. 3. v. 1, 2.

that glancing on them, with its bright and glittering rays, they were very delightful to behold; so R. Jonah, from the use of the word in the Arabic language, which signifies the morning, interprets it, "which rise early in the morning:" and which, as Schultens[h] observes, some render, "leading to water early in the morning:" the Vulgate Latin version is, "that ascend from mount Gilead;" from a lower to a higher part of it; which Bochart approves of it.[i] So saints, being fruitful in every good word and work, and orderly in their lives and conversations, appear even to the world amiable and lovely; they are like to the he-goat, "comely in going," Prov. xxx. 29—31; nay, to a flock of them on mount Gilead. Or else,

2ndly. By her hair, we may understand the inward thoughts of her heart.[k] For, 1. As hair arises from and has its dependence upon the head, so do thoughts from the heart; it is out of the heart all evil thoughts proceed; Matt. xv. 19, "out of the heart proceed evil thoughts," &c., and so all good thoughts, which are likewise formed and cherished there by the Spirit of God. 2. As the hairs of the head are numerous, so are the thoughts of the heart: a believer has many thoughts of heart; there is a multitude of thoughts within him, Psal. xciv. 19; concerning the corruption of his nature, the sinfulness of his actions, and his frequent backslidings from God; a multitude of thoughts concerning Christ and his grace, and the glories of another world. 3. As the hair of the head is weak, and easily moved and tossed about by the wind; so are the thoughts of a believer's heart, sometimes this way and sometimes another; and are like the eyes of fools in the ends of the earth, unless fixed and established by the Spirit of God upon proper objects. 4. Being rightly ordered by the Spirit of God, as a well-managed and well-ordered head of hair, they are exceedingly admired and valued by Christ Jesus; for he has a "book of remembrance written," not only for them who speak of him and fear him, but also for those who think upon his name, Mal. iii. 16.

And as the thoughts of a believer's heart, thus fixed, managed, and ordered by the Spirit of God, may be compared to hair, so likewise to a flock of goats on mount Gilead; and then may they be so, when they ascend on high, and dwell upon the everlasting, unchangeable, and boundless love of God in Christ; which love has its heights and depths, its lengths and breadths; when they soar aloft, and dwell upon the everlasting covenant of grace; which covenant "is ordered in all things and sure," filled with all spiritual blessings and precious promises; when their thoughts are composed and settled upon the consideration of Christ's person, fulness, blood, and righteousness; when they are employed about and concerned in the contemplation of the sublime doctrines of the gospel, and the invisible realities of another world; all which are things that are above; then may they be said to be like a flock of goats which appear from mount Gilead. But,

3rdly. I rather choose to understand, by the hair, believers themselves. Thus the people of Israel and inhabitants of Jerusalem are represented by hair, Ezek. v. 1—5. Now believers may be called so, 1. For their number; the hairs of a man's head are numerous; therefore when the Psalmist declares the large number of his sins and transgressions, he makes use of this metaphor, saying, "they are more than the hairs of my head:" indeed believers, when compared with the world, are but few, a small number, a remnant, and a little flock; yet considered and viewed by themselves, and when all together, they are a great multitude which no man can number, Rev. vii. 9. 2. For their growing upon, and receiving nourishment from Christ, the head: the hair grows upon the head, receives its nourishment from it; Christ is the Head of his body, the church; believers are the hair which grow upon, and grow up into this head: and from thence do they receive all their grace and strength, their life and liveliness, their food and nourishment, and so increase with "the increase of God," Eph. iv. 15, 16, Col. ii. 12. 3. For their weakness in themselves, and dependence on Christ, the Head: hair is a weak thing of itself, and has its dependence on the Head; believers are weak in themselves, and can do nothing of themselves without him; their dependence is on him for strength, as well as for righteousness; and it is only through him strengthening them, that they do the things they do. 4. For their being an ornament to Christ, the Head; hair is an ornament to the head; "the beauty of old men is the grey head:" Saints are the ornament, beauty, and glory of Christ: they are a crown of glory and a royal diadem in his hand, and upon his head. 5. For their valuableness to him, and the care he takes of them: a well-set head of hair is highly esteemed, and is taken much care of among men; but this cannot be more valued, and taken more care of, than believers are by Christ: he values them as his jewels and peculiar treasure, he will not lose one of them; the hairs of our head are all numbered, and so are all the hairs of Christ's head, and not one of them shall be lost; it is true, those who are only nominal professors, and only by an external profession hold to the head, not being rooted in him, shall be shed from thence; but so shall not one of those who are one Spirit with him, and grow upon him.

Now saints may be compared to a flock of goats on mount Gilead. (1). They may be compared to goats; it is true, this word is used of carnal and Christless sinners; who are called so in opposi-

---

[h] Animadv. in loc.
[i] Hierozoic. par. 1. l. 2. c. 5. col. 628.

[k] So Tres Patres apud Theodoret in loc.

tion to, and contradistinction from Christ's sheep; but these creatures being offered up in sacrifice under the old law, prefigured Christ, Exod. xii. 5, and therefore we need not wonder that saints bear this character, who are enabled to present themselves to God, holy, living, and acceptable sacrifices; as also, perhaps they may be so called, on the account of the remainder of sin and corruption; for in them, that is, in their "flesh, dwells no good thing;" and are stinking and abominable in the esteem of the world, reckoned by them the offscouring and refuse of all things, as well as mean and vile in their own eyes. 2. May be compared to a flock of them, because they belong unto and are under the care of one and the same shepherd, folded in the one and the same fold, and fed together in one and the same pasture; as also, on the account of their social worship, their assembling and walking together in the faith and order of the Gospel. 3. To a flock of them on mount Gilead; they have a good pasture upon a goodly mount; they live and feed upon the Lord Jesus Christ, that great mountain, which shall ere long fill the whole earth; here they find the best of pasture, and become fat and flourishing, like the goats on mount Gilead; here they live and dwell safely, secure from danger, and out of the reach of enemies; their "place of defence is a munition of rocks, their bread is given them, and their waters sure," Isa. xxxiii. 16.

Verse 2. *Thy teeth are like a flock of sheep that are even shorn, which came up from the washing: whereof every one bear twins, and none is barren among them.*

THESE words contain the third particular instance of the church's beauty, viz., her teeth. Which were like the teeth of sheep, as their eyes were like the eyes of doves, and her hair like the hair of goats; and Galen long ago observed,[l] that human teeth are much like the teeth of sheep, in figure, order, and structure, as well as are small and white, neatly set, innocent and harmless; not ravenous and voracious, cropping only herbs and grass, the whiteness of the teeth is chiefly intended, in which the beauty of them lies;[m] and for which they are sometimes compared to Parian marble or whiteness,[n] These are compared.

I. To a "flock of sheep."
II. To a flock of sheep "even shorn."
III. To a flock of sheep that are just "come up from the washing."
IV. To a flock of sheep that are fruitful "whereof every one bear twins," &c.

By her teeth we may understand.

1st. The ministers of the Gospel;[o] the Targum interprets it of the priests and Levites; and other Jewish writers[p] of the disciples of the wise men. Ministers may be called the church's teeth, 1. For strength; teeth are strong, being of a bony nature; and indeed the work that is allotted to them requires strength; the ministers of the Gospel are Christ's strong men; who are, or at least need to be, "strong in the grace that is in Christ Jesus;" they have need to be "strong in the Lord, and in the power of his might;" for their work is great, and requires it, which is to labour in the word and doctrine; a work so great, arduous, and difficult, that the great apostle Paul, notwithstanding all his gifts and grace, said, "Who is sufficient for these things?" they have need of strength to quit themselves like men in the defence of the Gospel, for which they are set, against all opposers and gainsayers; they have need of strength to withstand Satan's temptations; for he generally bends his bow, shoots his arrows, and casts his fiery darts most at them; they have need of strength to bear the world's reproaches and persecution, of which they generally have the greatest share, and to sustain the infirmities of weaker saints, which are not few. 2. For their sharpness; teeth are sharp, and they ought to be so upon many accounts; the ministers of the Gospel, though they are not to be like that generation, "whose teeth are as swords, and their jaw-teeth as knives," to devour the flock; nor like ravenous wolves, who will not spare it, but prey upon it, for they are to use meekness and tenderness; yet in some cases, they are to use sharpness also, according to the power that Christ has given them, and lodged in them; as when persons are unsound in the faith, and corrupt in their morals; also as sharpness is necessary to teeth, that they may penetrate into, chew, and prepare the food for the stomach; so is it necessary to ministers of the Gospel, that they have abilities to penetrate into Gospel-truths, in order to feed souls with the Bread of Life. 3. In nothing can they more fitly be compared to teeth, than in their preparing food for souls; as the teeth break the food, chew it, and prepare it for the stomach; so ministers of the Gospel break the bread of life, make hard things plain, easy, and intelligible; for not only in Paul's epistles, but in many other places of scripture there are some δυσνόητα, "things hard to be understood." Now it is the work of the Gospel to open and explain those difficult passages, remove the hard shell that is over them, that souls may eat the kernel; nay, they not only break the bread of life, but chew it, i. e., meditate upon the word, and digest the doctrines of grace themselves, that so they may not propose unto, or set before persons crude, raw, and undigested food: but having chewed, digested, and well prepared it, they then present it to them; for these are the church's teeth, which cut[q] and rightly divide the word of truth, and give to every one their "portion of meat in due season." Now these teeth of the church,

---

[l] In Salazer apud Marckium in loc.
[m] Candidati dentes, venustis oculis, color suavis, Cicer. Tuscul. Quæst l. 5. c. 16.   [n] Theocrit.
Idyll. 6. v. 37, 38.   [o] So Psellus and Isidore in loc.   [p] Vid Yalcut in loc.
[q] Ορθοτομυντα, 2 Tim. ii. 15.

the ministers of the Gospel, may be compared,

I. To a flock of sheep, and to their teeth, for their harmlessness and innocence. They are sent forth by Christ as " sheep among wolves ;" and so they live like sheep, useful to many, but hurtful to none ; live harmless and inoffensive lives, though exposed to a variety of evils, for the sake of Christ and his Gospel : " they are counted as sheep for the slaughter;" and yet like sheep, they patiently bear all without murmuring, in imitation of their dear Lord, who was led like a lamb to the slaughter, and like the sheep before her shearers is dumb, so he opened not his mouth, Isa. liii. 7.

II. To a flock of sheep even shorn. There is no word in the original text for any animal, neither sheep nor goats ; it is only " to a flock of shorn ones ;" and may be supplied from the preceding verse, " a flock of goats even shorn :" for in some countries, particularly in Cilicia, goats were shorn, as sheep in other places ;[r] and so in Lycia :[s] but inasmuch as the word *sheep* is in a parallel text, chap. vi. 6, it seems best to supply it so here : and the comparison is to their teeth, that are equally alike in bigness and size ; do not stand out nor rise up one above another ; but are as if they had been cut, and planed, and made alike, as some[t] render the word ; which is a better rendering, since sheep are not shorn before washing, but after it ; nor is the word ever used of shearing wool ; which may denote the equality of the ministers of the word, having such an agreement with each other, as the cherubim in Solomon's temple, which were of " one measure and one size," 1 Kings vi. 25. Now the ministers of the Gospel may be compared to such teeth, 1. Because they are equal in power and authority; though one may be superior to another in gifts and grace, in parts and learning, yet one has not a superior power and jurisdiction over another ; for, as Christ says to his disciples, Matt. xx. 25, 26, " the princes of the Gentiles exercise dominion over them ; and they that are great exercise authority upon them ; but it shall not be so among you ; but whosoever shall be great among you, let him be your minister ;" no such dominion and authority are allowed by Christ to be exercised by one minister, pastor, or bishop, over another ; they are like to the teeth of sheep that are even ; one is not higher than another, nor superior to another in power ; Peter was not above the rest of the apostles. 2. They have all the same commission, and are sent about the same work : the disciples of Christ were equally sent to preach the Gospel to every creature ; and the commission now is of the same and of as large extent as ever ; and the same commission that is given to one minister, is given to another; for they are all sent to preach one and the same Gospel, in the full extent of it ; not one part of it is assigned to one, and another part to another, but the whole is assigned to them all ; for a different Gospel is not given in commission to one to preach than what is given to another ; though their manner of preaching, and their success in their ministry, may not be alike. 3. They may be said to be as the teeth of sheep even, on the account of the harmony and agreement there is between the doctrines which they preach : though there may be a diversity of gifts, and one minister may have more Gospel-light and knowledge than another, yet the doctrine of grace, preached by them, is one and the same ; it is one and the same Jesus whom they preach ; one and the same way of salvation which they show ; and one and the same heavenly inheritance which they are pointing at ; which harmony and agreement of doctrine will more manifestly appear, when the " watchmen shall see eye to eye," even at the time " when the Lord shall bring again Zion," Isa. lii. 8. 4. These teeth of the church may be said to be like to the teeth of sheep even, to denote their mildness, meekness, harmlessness, and innocence; sheep not having teeth or tusks, standing out more, or rising up higher than the rest, as ravenous beasts, such as lions, bears, &c., but are all equal and even ; so such ministers do not devour, but feed the flock ! do not assume a lordly and domineering power over them ; but, behaving themselves quietly and peaceably among them, seek their good and welfare, and not their hurt.

III. To a flock of sheep just " come up from the washing ;" and so are white and clean ; which is another thing in which the beauty of teeth consists ; for it is not only requisite that they should be even, so as one does not grow out from, nor rise higher than the other; but likewise that they should be white and clean, like sheep that are just come out of the washing-pit : which some[u] think intends baptism ; though it may be better understood " of the washing of regeneration, and renewing of the Holy Ghost," which the ministers of the gospel ought not to be strangers to; for he that is not " born again of water, and of the Spirit," as he shall neither " see nor enter into the kingdom of heaven " himself; so he is not fit to preach the gospel of the kingdom of heaven to others : though I rather think it intends the pure and unspotted lives and conversations of Christ's ministers; who, being persons that hate the garment spotted with the flesh," and who " have washed their robes, and made them white in the blood of the lamb," become examples to the flock, not only in faith, but in purity of conversation.

IV. To a flock, of which " every one bears twins, and there is none barren among them." The figures are just and beautiful; it is common with sheep to bear twins or more in the eastern countries, as the philosopher[w] observes : these may answer to the two rows of teeth, and the word

---

[r] Aristot. Hist. Animal. l. 8. c. 28. Plin. l. 3. c. 50.   [s] Ælian de Animal. l. 16. c. 30.

[t] קצובות cæsæ, vel dedolatæ, Bochart. Hierozoic par. 1. l. 2. c. 45. col. 483, æquarum, Junius and Tremellus; statura æqualium Cocceius; vid. Aben Ezram in loc. and K'mchium in lib. shorash. rad. קצב.

[u] Isidore, Foliot, Alcuin, and Cottin in loc.

[w] Aristot. de animal. l. 6. c. 19.

for teeth is in the dual number; and when these are white, clean, and equal, are well set, and not one is wanting, none is rotten, nor shed, nor fallen out, look very beautiful. This is to be understood of the fruitfulness and successfulness of their ministry, in begetting and bringing forth many souls to Christ; which was more especially verified in the apostles and first preachers of the gospel, whose ministry, after an extraordinary manner, was blessed and owned for the conversion of many sinners; three thousand were converted under one sermon; the savour of Christ's "knowledge was made manifest by them in every place;" they bore twins to Christ, and were instrumental in the conversion of many, both of Jews and Gentiles; they went forth bearing and sowing the precious seed of the gospel; and returned, "bringing their sheaves with them," having reaped a glorious harvest: they travailed in birth, till Christ "was formed in souls;" and they did not travail in vain, for he that brought to the birth, caused to bring forth.

2ndly. Or else by teeth, if applied to particular believers, we may understand meditation and faith, by which they feed on divine and spiritual things. 1. By meditation a soul feeds on Christ, on his person, blood, and righteousness; and finds a pleasure, a sweetness, and delight therein: it is sometimes, as in Psalm lxiii. 5, 6, satisfied as with marrow and fatness, when it remembers Christ upon its bed, and meditates on his love and grace in the night-watches; by it a believing soul feeds upon the gospel, its truths, and promises, and receives much refreshment from thence; like Jeremy, chap. xv. 16; it finds the word by meditation, and eats it, and it is the joy and rejoicing of its heart. Now meditating souls may be very well compared to a flock of sheep, which are clean creatures, and chew the cud; for these chew the word of grace, and ruminate upon it; and to a flock of sheep even shorn, being in some measure rid of the old fleece of vain, carnal, and worldly thoughts; and are come up from the washing; being cleansed in some measure from their former filthiness and uncleanness of their minds, they ascend heavenwards in their thoughts, desires, and affections, which they employ by meditating upon pure, spiritual, and heavenly things; and such souls are usually fruitful; they are not barren and unfruitful in the knowledge of Christ and his gospel; but generally bring forth the twins of prayer and praise: meditation fits a man for prayer, and fills him with praise; meditating souls are commonly praying and praising ones; for whilst they are musing, the fire burns, and then speak they with their tongues, either in prayer or praise; it puts them either upon praying to God for a mercy, or upon praising him for one. 2. By faith a soul feeds on Christ and his grace: faith serves a great many purposes; it is the soul's eye, by which it sees Christ; and its feet, by which it goes to him; and the hand, by which it receives him and lays hold on him; and likewise the teeth, by which it feeds upon him: faith is expressed by eating his flesh, and drinking his blood, in John vi. 56, "he that eateth my flesh, and drinketh my blood, dwelleth in me, and I in him." An oral, corporal manducation, is not here intended, but a spiritual one, which is by faith: faith feeds on Christ, the Bread of Life, and eats that hidden manna, the food of the wilderness, lives wholly and entirely on him; which grace is peculiar to Christ's sheep, and therefore is called the "faith of God's elect;" and the reason why others do not believe and live upon him, is, because they are not of Christ's sheep; and though in some persons it is strong, and in others weak, yet it is in all alike precious faith in its own nature, and to Christ Jesus: these teeth are even, and so fit for eating; faith is alike as to quality in all believers, though not as to degree; and, like Judah's teeth, is white with the milk of the word, is pure, unfeigned, and sincere; and is always fruitful, attended with good works; and more especially bears and brings forth those twins, love to Christ, and love to the saints; for "faith works by love," Gal. v. 6.

Verse 3. *Thy lips are like a thread of scarlet, and thy speech is comely; thy temples are like a piece of pomegranate within thy locks.*

In these words Christ proceeds to give the fourth and fifth instances of the church's beauty; and says,

I. That her "lips are like a thread of scarlet," &c.

II. That her "temples are like a piece of pomegranate."

I. Her lips are compared to a thread of scarlet. The Targum on this place, by eyes, understands the princes and wise men of Israel, who sat in the sanhedrim, and enlightened the world; by the hair, the rest of the people of the land, in verse 1; by teeth, in verse 2, the priests and Levites, who offered the sacrifices, and eat the holy flesh; and by lips here, the lips of the high priest, who (as the Targum expresses it) by his prayer on the day of atonement, changed the transgressions of the people of Israel, which were like to a thread of scarlet, and made them white as wool. It is a received tradition among the Jews,[x] that when the scape goat was sent into the wilderness, a scarlet thread was tied to the temple-door, and when the goat was come to the wilderness, the scarlet thread turned white; which was not only a sign of the goat's arrival thither, but also a token to them of the remission of their sins, according to Isa. i. 18, "though your sins be as scarlet, they shall be as white as snow;" and they tell us,[y] that this scarlet thread ceased turning white forty years before the destruction of

---

[x] Yoma, c. 6. s. 8. in Misnah. [y] Talmud Yoma, fol. 39. 2.

the temple; which was about the time that Christ, the great sacrifice for sin, was offered up. R. Aben Ezra thinks, by the eyes are meant the prophets, who in scripture are called seers; by the hair, the Nazarites; by the teeth, the strong and mighty men; and by the lips here, the singers who sung the high praises of God. R. Solomon Jarchi expounds it, of the beauty and comeliness of the lips, in making and keeping promises; as the spies did to Rahab the harlot, whose token to know her house by, was a line of scarlet.

Lips are the instruments of speech; and by the church's lips here, are meant her words, which the following expression, " and thy speech is comely," manifests and confirms; which are compared to a thread of scarlet; to a thread for thinness, and to a thread of scarlet for colour, for these two things, thinness in substance and redness of colour, are the beauty of the lips: thin, red lips being beautiful, as well as white teeth; so the beautiful Aspasia had red lips,[a] and teeth whiter than snow: hence we sometimes read of red and purple lips:[a] and which were not only expressive of beauty, but of health, and of a sound constitution. Now by the church's lips, or words, are meant, either,

1st. Her prayers: Christ's prayers are, in Psal. xxi. 2, called the request of his lips; and so may the church's prayers, and every believer's, be called the request of their lips; which may be compared to a thread of scarlet, 1. For thinness. The prayers of believers are not filled with great swelling words of vanity, but with humble confessions of sin; bewailing the corruption and depravity of their natures; earnestly imploring views of pardoning grace, and the discoveries of God's love to their souls: acknowledging that they are unworthy to receive the least mercy and favour at the hand of God, but deserve the severest strokes of his justice, and the highest instances of his displeasure; they do not address the throne of grace with vanity and pride, but with an humble boldness, and oftentimes under a great deal of brokenness of soul; being conscious of their own guilt, and filled with a sense of God's majesty and greatness; was it not for the Mediator Christ Jesus, and his precious blood, which is carried within the vail, and his spotless righteousness, which they are allowed to plead, they durst not presume to approach the Divine Presence; they do not exalt themselves, and magnify their works of righteousness, nor extenuate their sins and transgressions, but are silent in the one, and frankly acknowledge the other, with all their aggravating circumstances; they do not act like the proud Pharisee,' Luke xviii. 11—13, who " stood and prayed thus with himself; God, I thank thee, that I am not as other men are, extortioners, unjust, adulterers, or even as this publican; I fast twice in the week, I give tythes of all that I possess;" but like the poor publican, who stood afar off, and " would not so much as lift up his eyes to heaven, but smote upon his breast, saying, God be merciful to me a sinner;" the lips of the publican, in this prayer, were like to a thread of scarlet. 2. For their constancy and continuance in them: the prayers of believers are like one continued thread of scarlet; no sooner are souls born again, but behold they pray; and they continue, or at least ought to continue praying souls all their days. Christ spoke a parable to this end, that " men ought always to pray, and not to faint;" and the apostle, Col. iv. 2, exhorts believers to " continue in prayer, and watch in the same with thanksgiving;" not that it is intended, in these places, that persons should always be actually engaged in this duty; but that believers should be often at the throne of grace; and when they are there, be importunate for the blessing they stand in need of; watch for a return of their prayers, and then be as diligent to attend the throne of grace with thankfulness; and when this is the common and constant course of a believer's life, his lips may be said to be like to a thread of scarlet. 3. For the fervency of them; the scarlet colour may denote the ardency, warmth, and fervour of a believer's spirit in prayer; such a warm, fervent, praying soul was Jacob, who wrestled with God, and would not stir without the blessing, but, " as a prince, had power with God, and prevailed;" and such an one was the Syrophœnician woman, who would take no denial from Christ; and such an one was Elias, James v. 16—18, who prayed earnestly that it might not rain, and it rained not; and again he prayed that it might rain, and the heavens gave rain; for the " effectual fervent prayer of a righteous man availeth much;" now when believers are thus fervent and importunate in prayer for the mercy or blessing they want, then may their lips be said to be like a thread of scarlet. 4. Because a believer's prayers are all tinctured with the blood of Christ, and so become like a thread of scarlet; they are all presented through Christ's mediation, being perfumed with his much incense; a believer does not put them up in his own name, but in the name of Christ; he pleads not his own worthiness, but the precious blood of Christ, and expects that they will meet with acceptance only through his mediation. 5. For their acceptableness with God; the scarlet colour is the best of colours, and most highly esteemed of; the prayers of the saints being offered up in faith, and in the name of Christ, being presented through his mediation, are very acceptable to God; they are pleasant music in his ears, and sweet fragrant odours in his nostrils; he is so far from despising the prayer of the destitute, that he delights and takes pleasure in it; it is like a thread of scarlet to him. Or else, by the church's lips, we may understand,

---

[a] Ælian. Var. Hist. l. 12. c. 1.   [a] Χείλεα πυρρα, Theocrit. Idyll. 15. Purpureis labellis, Ovid. Amor. l. 3. eleg. 13. Labiasque modicas purpurantes, Apul. Metamorph. l. 10. Labella rosea, Catullus.

2ndly. Her praises: as prayer is called the request of the lips, so praise is called the fruit of the lips, Heb. xiii. 15; as with our lips we pray to God, so with our lips we praise him: and the lips of believers in praising, as well as in praying, may be compared to a thread of scarlet. 1. They are thin, like a thread of scarlet; they are not filled with big swollen praises of themselves, and of what they have done; a believer takes the advice the wise man gives, Prov. xxvii. 2, "Let another praise thee and not thine own mouth; a stranger, and not thine own lips;" he does not speak in the commendation of himself, but of the goodness and grace of God; he praises him for all temporal mercies, for his being, the preservation of it, and for all the mercies of life, which make it comfortable; acknowledging that he is not worthy of the least of the mercies which God has shown him; and then his praises and thanksgivings rise higher for spiritual ones, for those all spiritual blessings, with which he is blessed in heavenly places in Christ Jesus; how does he adore, admire, and praise distinguishing love and grace, that such a poor, blind, ignorant creature as he, should be called out of darkness into marvellous light! that such a guilty wretch should be justified by Christ's righteousness from all his sins! that such a filthy creature should be washed and cleansed in Christ's blood, and have all his iniquities pardoned through the same! that he should be adopted into God's family, and be made an heir of God, and a joint heir with Christ Jesus! how thankful is he for the Gospel and the ministers of it, which have brought him the news of, and showed him the way unto life and salvation by Jesus Christ! and, above all, how thankful is he for Christ, that unspeakable gift of God's love. Now when the lips of believers, in praising, move in such a strain as this, then may they be said to be like a thread of scarlet. 2. The praises of believers are compared to a thread of scarlet, for the heartiness, sincerity, and affection that go along with them; as they draw nigh to God with their mouths, and honour him with their lips, so their hearts are not far from him, all the while they are praising, the fire of love burns within them; their souls are inflamed with it, and their lips look like scarlet, being touched with a live coal from off God's altar. 3. For the acceptableness of them through Christ's mediation; our praises, as well as our prayers, must be tinctured with Christ's blood; they must be offered up by him; for no other way are these sacrifices well pleasing to God, or accepted with him. Or,

3rdly. By her lips may be meant the doctrines of the gospel, delivered by her ministers; which are the church's lips, that "drop as an honeycomb," and publish the glad tidings of peace, life, and salvation to poor souls. Now these doctrines of grace, delivered by them, may be compared to "a thread of scarlet," 1. Because they are spun out of the scriptures: all scripture being divinely inspired, θεόπνευστος, breathed by God, "is profitable for doctrine," as well as for other things; it is the fountain from whence all the doctrines of grace spring; and the Lydian stone, by which they are all tried; for whatever is not according to this "law and testimony," is not to be received: hence Christ advises to "search the scriptures," and the noble Bereans are commended for doing so. 2. This scarlet thread of the gospel, being spun out of the scriptures, is smooth and even; there is an harmony and agreement in truths of the gospel; there is no jar and discord among them: this great trumpet does not give an uncertain sound; the doctrines of it are not yea and nay, contradictory to one another and truth itself, but are all of a piece, like one single "scarlet thread;" there is a close connection between them; they are linked and chained together, and cannot be separated; they look like, and are answerable to one another; there is a proportion or analogy of faith, according to which they are all measured. 3. The great subjects of the gospel are the blood, death, and sufferings of a crucified Christ; *we* says the apostle, 1 Cor. i. 23, "preach Christ crucified;" a crucified Christ was the sum and substance of their ministry; therefore the gospel, and the doctrines of it, may well be compared to a "scarlet thread:" the chief doctrines of the gospel are that the pardon of sin is procured by Christ's blood; that he has made peace and reconciliation for sinners by the blood of his cross; that sinners are justified by his blood, and so shall be saved from wrath to come; that Christ sanctifies his people with his blood, and has by it opened the gates of heaven for them; that it is by that he himself has entered into the holy of holies, and by which saints have a right so to do. Now these are the scarlet-coloured doctrines of the gospel; which, 4. Are valuable, precious, and highly to be esteemed of as scarlet; they are comparable to gold, silver, and precious stones; which angels desire to look into, and are by saints preferred to their necessary food; yea, are dearer to them than their lives, or any thing in life; witness the fines, imprisonments, loss of goods, racks, tortures, and death itself, which they have voluntarily and cheerfully undergone for the sake of it: thus her lips are like "a thread of scarlet."

It is further added, "and thy speech is comely:" which words are exegetical of the former; and manifestly show what is intended by her lips, namely, her speech; which is said to be *comely*, that is, graceful, amiable, and to be desired. And so is, 1. A believer's speech concerning Christ. When believers speak to others of what Christ is unto them; how he is "of God made unto them wisdom, righteousness, sanctification, and redemption;" and of what he has done for them, in atoning for their sins, bringing in an everlasting righteousness, and saving them from sin, law, death, and hell; when they speak of the glories of his person, the preciousness and efficacy of his blood, the excellency of his righteousness, and completeness of his sacrifice: when believers speak "often one to another" of these, "he hearkens and hears," listens as it were to hear what they talk of, and puts it down in the "book of his remembrance," as being well pleased with it. 2. The speech of a believer is graceful and comely to Christ, when they speak for him, in vindication of his person, people, truths, and ordinances; for he says, Matt. x. 32, "whosoever shall confess me before men, him will I confess also before my Father in heaven." 3. The speech of a believer to Christ is exceeding grateful and well-pleasing, whether it be in prayer or in praise, as has been already shown; hence Christ says, chap. ii. 14, "let me see thy countenance, let me hear thy voice; for sweet is thy voice, and thy countenance is comely." 4. It may intend the gracefulness of a believer's speech in his common conversation: it being attended "with grace," "and seasoned with salt, ministers grace unto the hearers;" is not infectious, pernicious, and destructive, as the corrupt and unsavoury communication of the wicked is; but tends to the pleasure, profit, and edification of others.

II. Her temples are next commended in these words which is the fifth particular instanced in the church's beauty; "thy temples are like a piece of a pomegranate within thy locks." R. Aben Ezra interprets these words of the priests, who had pomegranates of blue, purple, and scarlet, round about the hem of the *ephod* which they wore: but the Targum, on the place, understands by *the temples*, the king who was the head of the people of Israel, and was full of good works, as the pomegranate is of kernels; and by *the locks*, the governors and princes, who were next to him: but it seems more agreeable, that ecclesiastical officers are here intended, whom Christ has placed in his church, to take care of the discipline of his house, as well as to maintain and defend the gospel.

That there is, and ought to be, such officers in churches, who have the presiding, ruling, governing power therein, not only the nature of societies, but the scripture also does abundantly confirm, more especially the following ones; "Let the elders that rule well be counted worthy of double honour, &c., Obey them that have rule over you, &c., He that ruleth with diligence," 1 Tim. v. 17, Heb. xiii. 17, Rom. xii. 8. Their work is not only to preach the gospel, and feed the flock with wholesome food; but to admonish, warn, and rebuke those who stand in need thereof; to lay on and take off censures, to open and shut the doors of the church, that is, in admission and excommunication of members. Now this power is originally in the church, and only derivately in them; they are but the administrators of it, in the church's name: they have no despotic, arbitrary, and tyrannical power, lodged in their hands, to rule at pleasure; but are limited by the laws of Christ, which he has provided for the orderly government of his house, which they are to see put into execution. Now these may be called,

First. The church's *temples*.

1st. The *temples* are called, in the Hebrew tongue, by a word[b] which signifies thinness and tenderness; because the temples have but little flesh upon them, and are covered only with a thin skin; which may teach us. 1. That those persons who are called to such a work and office in Christ's house, though it cannot otherwise be but they must have flesh as well as spirit in them, being men of like passions and affections with others; yet these more especially ought not to live in and walk after the flesh; there should be a less appearance of carnality in them, and a greater discovery of spiritual-mindedness, and of the life and power of godliness in their conversations; therefore the apostle is very particular in giving their characters, 1 Tim. iii. 1—7, Titus i. 6—9. 2. It may also teach us, that there ought to be a great deal of tenderness in them, and used by them in the discharge of their work; for in so doing, they are like to be most successful: admonitions and reproofs for sin, mildly and tenderly given, are often kindly taken; they are like "an excellent oil, which does not break the head," but wins the heart: tender-heartedness is requisite in all Christians, but more especially in officers of churches, who are to deal as tenderly with persons, as surgeons do in dressing wounds, or in setting broken or dislocated bones; hence the apostle, in Gal. vi. 1, uses a metaphor taken from them, "you that are spiritual restore," καταρτίζετε, joint in, or set in joint again, "such an one in the spirit of meekness;" though it is true, in some cases sharpness is to be used; as when there is a gangrene in a member, which endangers the body, there must be a cutting off, an amputation of the member; so persons, when all means have been tried for their recovery and restoration, and there is no reclaiming them from an error in doctrine or practice; they are not only to be rebuked sharply, but to be cut off from the body, the church.

2ndly. The *temples* are called in Greek, κρόταφοι,[c] from the evident beating of the pulse there: now as a person's constitution may be judged of by the beating of his pulse; so may the constitution of a church by her temples, the officers, in their administration of affairs; if church discipline is neglected, and Christ's laws are not put in execution against delinquents, the church is in a bad state, and in an unhealthful and declining condition; and on the contrary, when officers are lively, zealous, and diligent in their work, and all things are kept in a just order and decorum,

---

[b] רַקָּה tenuis faciei pars, Marckius; tenuior, Michaelis; vid. R. David Kimchium, in lib. shorash. rad. רקק. [c] Παρὰ τὸ κροτεῖν τῇ ἁφῇν.

the church is then in an healthful and flourishing condition.

3rdly. The *temples* are placed between the eyes and the ears; and church officers being called so, teaches us that they have need of both in managing the affairs of Christ's house. Christ indeed, being God omniscient, "shall not judge after the sight of his eyes, neither reprove after the hearing of his ears;" but we have no other way of judging than by the sight of our eyes, and by the hearing of our ears, and therefore both are to be employed: the ears of the church-officers are to be open, without respect of persons, to rich and poor, high and low; they are to hear complaints and charges exhibited, if introduced in a regular manner, and then the evidence to support these complaints and charges; they must also hear the answers of the person or persons accused and complained of, and must not shut their eyes against clear light and plain evidence.

Secondly. These temples are said to be "within the locks;" under locks of hair plaited and curled about them; expressive both of secrecy and beauty: which may teach us. 1. That admonitions, in case of private offences, ought to be given privately, according to that golden rule given by our Lord, Matt. xviii. 15—17, "If thy brother shall trespass against thee, go and tell him his fault between thee and him alone;" let no one know it before thou hast told him, and let none be with thee when thou dost; "if he shall hear thee, thou hast gained thy brother;" therefore for ever after never speak of it to others, nor upbraid him with it; "but if he will not hear thee, then take with thee one or two more, that in the mouth of two or three witnesses, every word may be established; and if he shall neglect to hear them," matters being thus prepared, "tell it unto the church;" and then thou shalt have witnesses to support and make good thy allegations. This rule is so plain and easy, that one would think, none could mistake or go aside from it; and was it but closely adhered to, would prevent a great deal of scandal and reproach that is cast upon religion, as well as a great many disturbances, occasioned in churches by the neglect of it: and in so doing, the church's temples, in this branch of the administration of discipline, may be said to be within her locks; though it is true, in case of public offences, admonitions and rebukes are to be given publicly, that "others may fear," 1 Tim. v. 20. 2. It may also teach us, that all the affairs and concerns of churches ought to be kept private, and not blazed about in the world; their debates and determinations ought not to be told to other churches, unless there is a necessity for it; much less told in Gath, and published in the "streets of Askelon;" for every particular church should be as a "garden inclosed, a spring shut up, a fountain sealed," Cant. iv. 12. 3. The temples being within the locks, may denote the humility of church-officers in their work; they lie hid under the hair, the rest of the believers; they do not rise up above them, though they are taller and higher than they are in gifts and grace, as well as by virtue of their office and station in the church; yet they are, in their own esteem, "less than the least of all saints:" they do not assume to themselves a domination and lordly power "over God's heritage;" they do not impose their sentiments upon churches for final determinations in cases; but humbly submit themselves, preferring the judgment of the church to their own private ones; they become "all things to all, that they may save some." 4. May be expressive of the beauty of church-discipline: that church appears very beautiful, like the "temples within the locks," where the gospel is faithfully preached, the ordinances purely administered, and the laws of Christ's house strictly regarded. Believers, who walk together in the order, as well as in the faith of the gospel, appear very beautiful, stately, and magnificent to spectators; they are "like a company of horses in Pharaoh's chariot;" or like a garden, with a variety of flowers, well weeded and taken care of; or an "orchard of pomegranates," well dressed and managed: on the contrary, a church, in which no regard is had to order and discipline, is like "the field of the slothful, and the vineyard of the man void of understanding," which is all overrun "with thorns and nettles," its fence and "stone-wall being broken down."

Thirdly. These temples are said to be "like a piece of a pomegranate; not of the tree, but of the fruit, the shell or rind being broken; so the Septuagint render it.d The land of Canaan was a land of pomegranates; they grew there in great plenty, and therefore are frequently mentioned in this Song.

1st. The fruit, when the shell or rind is broken, appears to be full of grains or kernels, and therefore is a *pomegranate*; and it is the nature of this fruit, that if it hangs longer on the tree after it is fully ripe, it will burst and open of itself,e and its kernels will become visible: one of the mansions of the Israelites is called by them Rimmon-parez, Numb. xxxiii. 19; the pomegranate of rupture, or the burstened pomegranate, where probably they found such. And the church's temples are said to be like to such a burstened and broken piece of pomegranate, that is full of kernels, and visible; because those who are called to such work and office in the church, as has been mentioned, should be men "full of the Holy Ghost," as Stephen was; they should be as full of the gifts and graces of the Spirit, as the pomegranate is of kernels, that they may be capable of discharging the work aright; Christ knows full well that they stand in need of such,

---

d כפלח הרמון, ὡς λέπυρον ῥοᾶς, Sept. sicut fragmen mali punici, Vulg. Lat. and Montanus.   e T Bab. Zebachim, fol. 88. 2. and Gloss. in ibid.

and therefore, as he has "received gifts for men," so he "gives them to men," to qualify them for the work of the ministry, and for the well-ordering and governing of his churches; and yet, notwithstanding all that they receive, they are obliged to say, with the apostle, "Who is sufficient for these things?" And as they should be men full of the Spirit, so likewise full of good works; and these visible to men, even as the kernels of a burstened pomegranate;[f] their "light should shine before men;" they should have a good report of them that are without, and be examples to those that are within; and when they are so, then may the church's *temples* be said to be "like a piece of a pomegranate within her locks." Also the pomegranate, when broken, appearing to be full of kernels, all set in a beautiful order, and joined to each other, may be expressive of that union, harmony, and consent of church-members, with their officers, in acts of discipline; censures are laid and taken off, members are received or rejected, not by some single person or persons, but by the joint consent and unanimous voice of the whole church.

2ndly. As this fruit is full of kernels, so, when broken, there springs from it a redish, purple, sweet, and delightful juice: hence we read of the "juice of the pomegranate," chap. viii. 2, which the church would cause Christ to drink of; and nothing is more delightful in Christ's eye, odorous to his smell, and sweet to his taste, than this juice of the pomegranate is; namely, a pure administration of his ordinances, and a strict regard and close adherence to the laws of his house: nay, even to believers themselves, result from hence pleasure, delight, and satisfaction.

3rdly. The fruit of the pomegranate is very useful in medicine. 1. For repressing the heat of choler, and malignity of fevers.[g] God's children too often fall out by the way; there are frequently differences and divisions among them: many of them are of hot, fiery, and choleric dispositions: do not know "what spirits they are of," and at every turn are, like the disciples, for calling "for fire from heaven" upon those who have disobliged them. Now officers in churches are like a piece of a pomegranate; they allay and repress these heats, by wholesome advice and proper admonitions; they are instruments in making peace, and reconciling differing brethren; and either remove the causes of contention, or else, with the consent of the church, remove those who are the cause of these divisions and contentions. 2. For stopping the fluxes of the belly:[h] the pomegranate is of an astringent nature, the kernels bind more than the juice, and the shell or rind more than either, the officers of churches are useful in putting a stop to loose and disorderly practices, by warning, admonishing, rebuking, or withdrawing from those who walk disorderly. 3. For comforting the stomach and bowels:[i] so these officers comfort the children of God; for as they warn "the unruly, so they comfort the feeble-minded, and support the weak," by directing them to the person, blood, righteousness, and fulness of Christ Jesus; by delivering the sweet doctrines, and opening the precious promises of the Gospel.

Thus church-officers, in managing the affairs of Christ's house, in conjunction with his church, may be called her temples, which are "like a piece of a pomegranate within her locks;" or her veil,[k] as some render it; so Symmachus covered with a veil, as her eyes were, ver. 1; and here her cheeks; and so the Septuagint renders the word in Isa. xlvii. 2; such veils, covering those parts, were worn by women in the eastern countries, expressive of their modesty; and what was latent and much out of sight, seemed more beautiful. Likewise the temples, taken in a large signification, not only intend that part of the face, between the ears and eyes, and upwards, but include the cheeks also; and so the Septuagint[l] translate the word here: the purple juice of the pomegranate well expresses the colour of them, which is their beauty; hence we often read of purple cheeks as beautiful,[m] and of rosy ones blushing through shamefacedness and modesty:[n] a pomegranate cut affords a very agreeable resemblance of a beautiful cheek; and in Talmudic language, as Jarchi observes, the cheeks are called רומני דאפי, the pomegranates of the face. And these being compared to a "piece of pomegranate within her locks," may denote her modesty, shamefacedness, and beauty. 1. Her modesty: the cheeks are the seat thereof, and being within her locks, give the greater evidence of it. The church of Christ, or believers, are very humble and modest; they think the worst of themselves and the best of others, and so take the apostle's advice, Phil. ii. 3, "Let each esteem others better than themselves:" they are apt to think every saint has more grace and less sin and corruption in them than they have, and esteem themselves the least of saints and the chief of sinners: they frankly acknowledge that all they have, and all they are, is owing to the grace of God; that whatsoever they have, either of nature or grace, whether temporal or spiritual, they have received from him: and whatever they are, they say it is by the grace of God they are what they are; they do not envy the gifts and grace of God, which are bestowed on others, but could wish, with Moses, Numb. xi. 29, that "all the Lord's people were prophets;" yet they could be glad of

---

[f] So the Jewish writers interpret the words of the Israelites, as full of good works, as the pomegranate is of kernels. T. Bab. Eruvin, fol. 19. 1 and T. Bab. Chagigah. fol. 26. 1. Targum and R. Sol. Jarchi in loc. [g] Fernel. Method. Medend. 1. 5 c. 3. [h] Plin. Nat. Hist. l. 23. c. 6.
[i] Plin. Nat. Hist. l. 23. c. 6. [k] Vid. Mich-aelis Not. in Lowth. Prælection. 31. p. 165.
[l] Μῆλόν ση, Sept. gena tua, Pagninus; genæ tuæ, Vulg Lat. and Cocceius. [m] Purpureas genas, Ovid. Amor. l. 1. eleg. 4. Statii Thebaid. l. 1. v. 538. Ausonii Parental 23. v. 16. Purpurissatas genas, Apuleii Apolog. p. 239. [n] Ροδέην παρειην, &c. Musœus de Hero, &c. v. 194, 195.

more themselves, and are not puffed up with what they have, and therefore are far from despising others who are inferior to them; they are willing to be instructed by, and receive admonition from the meanest saint: they are very sparing in speaking of themselves; like their dear Lord, their "voice is not heard in the street;" and, when they do open their mouths, it is not in commendation of themselves and their own righteousness; but in lamenting the depravity and pollution of their nature, in acknowledging the imperfection of their obedience, and that when they have done all they can, they are but unprofitable servants. 2. Her shamefacedness and blushing; which is elegantly set forth by the broken piece of the shell or rind of the pomegranate, tinctured with the red and purple juice thereof: a believer oftentimes blushes before God under a sense of sin, and especially when committed against love, grace, and mercy; thus we read of Ezra, chap. ix. 6, that he was "ashamed, and blushed to lift up his face to God, because that grace had been showed them from him; and he had left them a remnant to escape, and had given them a nail in his holy place, and had extended mercy to them in the sight of the kings of Persia;" and yet, after all this, they had forsaken his commandment: it is this which cuts and grieves a believer's heart, and fills his face with shame and confusion; and never more is he put to the blush, than when he views sin in the glass of pardoning grace, and pacifying love, according to Ezek. xvi. 63, "That thou mayest remember, and be confounded, and never open thy mouth any more, because of thy shame, when I am pacified towards thee;" then are their cheeks like a piece of a pomegranate within their locks, or under a veil; they blush when no eye sees them, and for that which none ever saw or could charge them with: and whenever they are charged with or reproved for sin, they have not a brow of brass to outface the charge, but soon discover their consciousness of guilt by the blushing of their countenance. Moreover, whenever they cast their eyes upon their own righteousness, they are ashamed of it, it being nothing but filthy rags, and "as an unclean thing;" and oftentimes, when they come into Christ's presence, not having that holy boldness and confidence of faith in him, they hang their heads, and dare not so much as lift up their eyes to him; wherefore he says to them, as in chap. ii. 14, "Let me see thy countenance, let me hear thy voice, for sweet is thy voice, and thy countenance is comely;" and that in order to remove their fears, cheer their souls, and encourage their faith. 3. Her beauty: when a pomegranate is broken, there appears a reddish juice, like blood, as Pausanius * remarks: interspread between the white kernels, which gives a lively idea of her beauty; she being, as she says of her beloved "white and ruddy," and so a perfection of beauty: her modest dress and blushing looks: her temples or cheeks being within her locks, or under a veil; and these like a piece of a pomegranate, made her extremely beautiful in Christ's eyes; modest and humble souls he fixes his eye on, and delights to dwell with; to these he will give more grace, and will beautify them yet more with his salvation.

Verse 4. *Thy neck is like the tower of David, builded for an armoury; whereon there hang a thousand bucklers, all shields of mighty men.*

IN this verse Christ proceeds to give a sixth instance of the church's beauty, and compares her neck to the tower of David, &c. The Targum, by her neck, understands "the chief of the session or great council," who, for his works and worthiness, was like David king of Israel: R. Aben Ezra expounds it of the king, and the bucklers and shields of the princes: R. Solomon Jarchi interprets the neck of the chambers of hewn stone, where the great council sat, which, he says, was the strength and fortress of Israel; the bucklers or shields, the law, which is a shield or buckler to Israel, which God hath commanded to a thousand generations: and others of the Jewish writers p think, that by the neck, the house of the sanctuary or temple is intended. Though rather, by the church's neck are meant, either,

First. The ministers of the Gospel; who, 1. As the neck, are placed next the head, in the more eminent part of the body, they are set above the rest of the members; but yet in subjection to Christ, the Head; they are fixed between the head and the body, and are ruled by the one, and govern the other; but with no other laws but what are given forth by the head. 2. As the neck, they are adorned with chains of gold, which are the gifts and graces of the Spirit; which, in a variety, are given to them, to make them both beautiful and useful in the place wherein they are set. 3. As the neck joins to the head, so they hold to the Head, Christ Jesus, and nothing can separate them from him; the flatteries and allurements of the world cannot draw them; nor its terrors, reproaches, and persecutions, drive them from Christ; but they still espouse his cause, vindicate his person, preach his Gospel, and hold fast their profession, though it be with the peril of their lives. 4. As the neck, they bear up and support the Head, that is, the name, cause, and interest of Christ Jesus; so the apostle Paul is said to be "a chosen vessel, to bear Christ's name among the Gentiles," Acts ix. 15; and Psellus, an ancient writer, thinks that he is here particularly meant. 5. As the neck joins the body to the head, so they bring souls near to Christ who are afar off; and that by preaching "peace to them that were afar off, and to lead them that are nigh;" they show souls the way of salvation, and direct them to a crucified Christ;

* Bœotica, sive l. 9. p. 578.

p Vid. Zohar. in Gen. fol. 114, 3. and Yalkut in loc.

L

they woo and beseech them, and are the instruments of espousing them to him. 6. As the neck is the means of conveying food to the body; so they are the means of conveying spiritual food to souls from Christ; all spiritual food and nourishment is derived to the members from Christ the Head; and very frequently, through the ministry of the word: Christ gives his ministering servants light, knowledge, and understanding in Gospel truths, that they may feed others therewith; he breaks the bread of life, and gives it to them, that they may give to every one their portion; as he took the loaves, and distributed to his disciples, and they to the multitude. Now this neck of the church may be compared to the tower of David.

The tower of David[q] was either the stronghold of Zion, which he took from the Jebusites, and rebuilt; or some other tower, erected by him for an armoury, wherein his worthies or mighty men hung up their shields; such an one as the house of the forest of Lebanon, afterwards built by Solomon, was, where he put two hundred targets, and three hundred shields, all made of beaten gold: and therefore mention is made in Isa. xxii. 8, of the armour of the house of the forest." Now the ministers of the Gospel may be compared to David's tower: the Lord says of Jeremy, chap. vi. 27, "I have set thee for a tower and for a fortress among my people." I. They may be compared to the tower of David for its height; towers are usually built very high, and, no doubt, this tower of David's was built so; Mr. Sandys' says it stood aloft in the utmost angle of a mountain, whose ruins are yet extant: ministers are set in the highest post and place in Christ's house; are called with the high calling of God, to the greatest work therein, and are endowed with the largest measures of gifts and graces for it, and ought to be highly esteemed of for their works' sake. 2. For its erectness: towers are built erect, and for this reason the neck is compared to one: the beauty of the neck consisting in its straightness and uprightness; which may set forth the integrity and uprightness of ministers, both in doctrine and conversation: as Christ has counted them faithful, and put them into the ministry, and has put the word of reconciliation into their hands, so they will not let it go; but will hold fast the faithful word whatever it cost them, or whatever be the consequence of it: moreover, they are as careful to hold it forth in their lives, and to exercise a good conscience void of offence, both towards God and man. 3. For its strength: towers, as they are built high and upright, so they are usually built strong; and no doubt but this tower of David's was: the ministers of the Gospel, like towers, are strong and immoveable, cannot be easily moved away from the hope of the Gospel; bonds and imprisonment will not move them, nor death itself scare them from it; but, like strong towers and walls of brass, they stand the batteries of Satan and the world. 4. Towers were built for defence, and so perhaps was this of David's: ministers of the Gospel are set for the defence of it; and they have been enabled so well to do it, that it has not been in the power of the enemy hitherto to take and destroy it. 5. Sometimes they are built to watch in; thus we read of a watch-tower, in Hab. ii. 1; ministers of the Gospel are represented as watchmen, whose work is to give warning of, and to prevent approaching danger, and to watch over and for the souls of men. 6. This tower of David was built for an armoury,[r] on which were hung a thousand bucklers, &c.; this may intend that furniture which ministers have for their work; and that πανοπλία, or whole armour of God, which they are supplied with out of the scriptures, to defend the Gospel against all opposers. And so,

Secondly. By the church's neck, which is compared to "the tower of David," may be understood also the scriptures of truth; which, 1. As the neck is joined to the head, and being erect, discovers and makes it conspicuous; so the scriptures being near to Christ, point him out, lead and direct souls unto him; they hold him forth, and discover him to them; and therefore Christ exhorts us, John v. 39, to "search the scriptures," and for our encouragement declares, that they testify of him. 2. They are the means of conveying spiritual breath to souls: the words which Christ speaks, and when he speaks them to

---

[q] Turris David. Munita and excelsa valde, quæ in duarum voraginum angulo, in præruptæ rupis colle ex quadris lapidibus, ferro and plumbo indissolubiliter compaginatis, a Davide rege edificata erat. Cujus singularis fortitudo and egregia pulchritudo ad commendationem sponsæ Christi, quæ est ecclesia, a Solomone producitur, cum ait, Sicut turris David, collum tuum, &c. Adrichom. Theatrum Terræ Sanctæ, p. 168. b. [r] Travels, p. 139. * The Hebrew word הלפיות is only used in this place, and is left untranslated by the Septuagint. Jewish writers differ about the sense and derivation of it. Some, as R. Aben Ezra observes, take it to be a compound word, of תלה to hang, and פיות mouths or edges, that is, of swords; and so suppose this tower to be built to hang up swords in; which agrees well enough with our translation, and with Junius and Tremellius's version, who read the word, ad armaria. Others think, that it is compounded of תל an heap, and פיות mouths, edges, or corners; and so intends an heap of stones, built up very high and strong, cut in various forms and corners; so Kimchi, in lib. Shorash. rad תלל which are no other than the pinacles or battlements of towers; accordingly Arias Montanus renders the words, celsa acumina; and Cocceius translates it, in molem pinnarum. Others derive it from אלף to teach; and suppose it to intend some very beautiful structure, which might serve as a pattern, and be very instructive to artificers, so Jarchi in loc. though R. Jonah in Kimchi, lib. Shorash. rad עלף thinks, that it was designed to show travellers their way: accordingly Pagnine reads it, ad docendum transeuntes: and the Tigurine version, ad usum dirigendi homines; in which sense it may easily be applied to the ministers of the Gospel, whose business is to show men the way of salvation; and to the word of God, which is a light to our feet, and a lanthorn to our paths.

the soul, "they are spirit, and they are life;" and when attended with an almighty power, they make "dry bones live," and become the "savour of life unto life" to dead sinners. 3. They are the means of conveying spiritual food, as well as spiritual breath; as through the neck our breath is drawn, and food communicated to us, so through the scriptures we have spiritual breath and spiritual food; they supply us with that which is nourishing and satisfying, delightful, and pleasant, sweeter than the "honey or the honey-comb." 4. As the neck is beautified with chains of gold; so are the scriptures bespangled with glorious truths and precious promises, where every truth is a golden link, and every promise a pearl, to a believing soul.

Now this neck of the church, the sacred scriptures, may very justly be represented by "the tower of David." I. For height: the scriptures are an high tower; the truths and doctrines contained therein are sublime; they are out of sight, beyond the reach, and above the capacity of a natural man; they are things which the carnal eye hath not seen, the carnal heart cannot conceive of, and which are only known, judged, valued, and esteemed by the spiritual man, to whom the Spirit of God has revealed these deep things; for there are heights and depths in the sacred volumes, which require an eagle's eye and an angel's heart. 2. For strength, firmness, and immoveableness: Satan and his emissaries have used all their art and cunning, and employed all their power and might to remove the scripture out of the world; but they have found it "a burdensome stone" unto them; "the gates of hell" and earth have not been able to "prevail against it;" it has stood, and ever will, immoveable as a rock, and impregnable as a tower. 3. It is like David's tower, "built for an armoury, whereon hang a thousand bucklers, all shields of mighty men." From hence are saints furnished with spiritual armour, 1. To repel Satan's temptations: when that enemy of souls set upon Christ in the wilderness, and threw his fiery darts and poisoned arrows at him; he defended himself, and vanquished the enemy with bucklers and shields, and the like pieces of armour taken out of his armoury; he repelled and weakened the force of his temptations, by saying, at every assault of the tempter, "It is written," so or so: and thus likewise believers are enabled to do more or less; there is no better weapon to engage with that enemy than "the sword of the Spirit, which is the word of God;" neither is there a better storehouse, and magazine of spiritual armour, than the scriptures be; the reason why those young men, in 1 John ii. 14, are said to "overcome the wicked one" is, because the word of God abode in them. 2. To defend the gospel, and refute erroneous doctrines: thus Christ refuted the errors of the Pharisees concerning the law, and of the Sadducees concerning the resurrection from the dead, and proved the spirituality of the one, and confirmed the truth of the other by scripture testimonies: so Paul and Apollos mightily convinced the Jews, and proved from the scriptures, that Jesus was the Christ, the true Messiah; for, as in 2 Tim. iii. 16, 17, "all scripture is given by inspiration of God, and is profitable for doctrine, for reproof, for correction, for instruction in righteousness, that the man of God," every believer, and more especially a minister of Christ, "may be perfect, thoroughly furnished to every good work;" and particularly to defend truth, and refute error, for which he may be abundantly supplied out of this armoury; for here "hang a thousand bucklers," and these are "all shields of mighty men;" which mighty men may use, and by which they may perform mighty actions, and do great exploits.

Thirdly, By the church's neck, which is compared to "the tower of David," we may also understand the grace of faith; and 1. As the neck is united to the head and members, so believers, being united to Christ, lay hold upon him by faith, and closely adhere to him; by faith Christ dwells in our hearts, and by faith we dwell in him, being one with him. 2. It bears up and exalts the head; there is no grace which brings that glory to Christ, and honours him, as this does; it is a soul-emptying, self-abasing, and Christ-exulting grace. 3. Through it is conveyed, and by it are derived from Christ, the Head, all life, food, and nourishment to our souls: it is by faith we live on Christ, and receive life, and the comfortable supplies of it; all food and nourishment comes from Christ, the Head, which faith receives and conveys unto us. 4. It is adorned with other graces and good works: the other grace of the Spirit, such as hope, fear, love, humility, patience, self-denial, &c., are like chains of gold about this neck; besides there are also the fruits of righteousness which attend it, and make it look very beautiful and amiable. 5. It is like to the neck for erectness; it looks not downwards, but upwards to Christ, who is, "the Author and Finisher of it; it is attended with an humble boldness, an holy confidence, and a becoming cheerfulness.

This may now be compared to "the tower of David," 1. For its height: the author of this grace of faith is the Most High God: it has its original from above; its object is Christ, who is "made higher than the heavens;" and to him it looks, on him it lives, in him it dwells: and is still pressing on toward "the mark, for the prize of the high calling of God in Christ Jesus." 2. It is like a tower builded for an armoury; faith is the believer's defence, his buckler and shield, whereby he is enabled "to quench the fiery darts" of Satan: faith makes use of God as its shield, being encouraged so to do, by the declaration of grace made to Abraham, Gen. xv. 1, "Fear not, I am thy shield, and thy exceeding great reward." Faith improves and makes use of every perfection in God, as a shield, his love, grace, power, faithfulness, &c., faith makes use of all God's promises as such, there is never a promise in the gospel, but will serve for a buckler and shield for faith, which believers, at one time or another, have also used as such; but more especially, faith uses Christ as such, who is the believer's sun and shield, and will give grace and glory to them, and will withhold no good thing from them: Christ indeed rather than faith, is a storehouse and magazine of armour, whereon hang a thousand bucklers: in whom an inexhaustible, overflowing, and all-sufficient fulness of grace dwells: from whence faith is furnished with all sorts of grace, and every needful piece of spiritual armour.

Verse 5. *Thy two breasts are like two young roes that are twins, which feed among the lilies.*

THESE words contain the seventh and last particular instance of the church's beauty; in which her breasts are compared to "two young roes" very elegantly exposing the beauty of him; they are compared to "two young roes" for smallness, large breasts not being accounted handsome; "to young roes that are twins," because they are of equal size and bigness, not one larger and higher than the other, for that would be a deformity; and to "two young roes that feed among the lilies," which are fat and plump, and so well expresses the fulness of them, they being not dry and empty breasts: such are sometimes called *sororiantes*,[t] as if they were sisters, being alike; and full and distended with milk, reach and join to, and as it were kiss each other as such; or, "two fawns, the twins of a doe:" providence, as Plutarch[u] observes, has given to women two breasts, that, should they have twins, both might have a fountain of nourishment: and though the hind, for the most part, brings but one roe at a time; yet the philosopher observes,[w] there are some that bring twins. Now by the church's breasts, we may understand either,

First. The ministers of the Gospel. The Targum here makes mention of the Jews' two Messiahs: which is a Talmudic fiction, and shows the work, to be a later one than what is pretended: the words are thus paraphrased in it: "Thy two redeemers which shall redeem thee, Messiah son of David, and Messiah son of Ephraim, are like to Moses and Aaron, the sons of Jochebed, who are compared to two young roes that are twins; who, in their integrity, fed the people, the house of Israel, forty years in the wilderness, with manna and fatted fowls, and water of the well of Miriam." And agreeable to this paraphrase, other Jewish writers[x] would have Moses and Aaron here intended, who suckled and fed the people of Israel, and as twins, were very like one another. But I think they may be much better applied to the ministers of the Gospel; who impart the "sincere milk of the word" to persons; deliver the sweet, comfortable, and nourishing doctrines of grace: which may be compared to milk out of the breasts, with which they feed them, as the apostle says, 1 Cor. iii. 2, "I have fed you with milk;" which is nourishing to new-born souls, suitable to their natures, and easily digested by them. Now these breasts of the church, the ministers of the Gospel, may be compared,

1st. To two young roes, which are, 1. Loving and pleasant creatures; "let her be as the loving hind and pleasant roe;" &c., Prov. v. 19; ministers of the Gospel are loving and affectionate to such souls, more especially who are born again under their ministry, whom they feed with the milk of the word; they are as fond of them, and bear as great an affection to them, as the tender mother or nurse do to their sucking babes, according to what the apostle says, 1 Thess. ii. 7, 8, "But we were gentle among you, even as a nurse cherisheth her children; so being affectionately desirous of you, we were willing to have imparted unto you, not the Gospel of God only, but also our own souls, because ye were dear to us:" than which nothing can be more passionately spoken, nor in a more lively manner represent the strong affection and tender love and regard that ministers show to souls: moreover as they are as the loving hind unto souls, so they are as the pleasant roe in their esteem: they love them, and are loved by them; they appear exceeding beautiful and lovely in the eyes of those to whom God has made them useful; for the very feet of them that bring glad tidings are beautiful to them. 2. Those creatures are sharp-sighted ones; ministers of the Gospel, having their understandings opened, their judgments informed, and their souls led by the Spirit of God, into "the truth, as it is in Jesus," have light, knowledge, and penetration into the scriptures of truth, and are capable of directing and guiding the feet of, and showing the way of salvation unto others. 3. They are swift creatures; thus the apostles and first ministers of the Gospel, like young roes, ran, spread, and carried the Gospel all over the Gentile world; "their sound went into all the earth, and their words unto the end of the world:" and it may also denote in general, how expedite and quick of dispatch ministers are in doing of the Lord's work, notwithstanding a great many difficulties are in the way: yet, like young roes, they leap over these mountains, and skip over these hills, and are "not slothful in business, but fervent in Spirit, serving the Lord." 4. Here is only mention made of two young roes, and that to suit with the number of her breasts; and two breasts being sufficient for

---

[t] Papillæ sororiabant, Plauti Frivolari, Fragm. 1. 7. Mammas sororiantes, Plin. 1. 31. c. 6. [u] De Liberis Educand. vol. 2. p. 5. [w] Aristot. de Animal. 1. 6. c. 29. [x] R. Sol. Jarchi, Alshech, and Yalcut in loc.

one person, denotes the sufficient number of ministers which Christ provides for his church: when he had sent out the twelve apostles, he afterwards sent out other seventy disciples, and these he sent out "two and two;" and so in all ages of the world, as he has removed some, he has sent others, and when there has been want of such workmen in his vineyard, he has prayed "the Lord of the harvest" to send forth more labourers; and as the fruit of his ascension and intercession, sufficient gifts have been given to a competent number of men to fit them for the ministry, for the good of his body, the church.

2ndly. They are compared, not only to two young roes, but to young roes that are twins: which is expressive of their equal authority, joint commission, and harmony of doctrine, as has been already observed on ver. 2.

3rdly. They are compared to two young roes that "feed among the lilies; the lilies of the field," for such they were, Matt. vi. 28; and we sometimes read of harts and hinds being among lilies.[y] Now the lilies, among which the ministers of the Gospel feed, are either, 1. The scriptures, which they make their principal study, and the mean subject of their contemplation; here their own souls are delighted, comforted, and instructed, and so become useful in comforting and instructing others; from whence they gather food for themselves, and being nourished with the wholesome words of faith and sound doctrine, they are capable of feeding others also. Or, 2. The saints; in what respects the people of God may be compared to lilies, has been shown on chap. ii. 2, among these the ministers of the Gospel feed, and and to these they break and impart the bread of life. 3. It may be observed, that it is where Christ himself feeds, as in chap. ii. 16. The ministers of the Gospel feed where Christ feeds, and Christ feeds where they do; the great end of the Gospel-ministry is, not only that saints may have communion one with another, but also with their Head, Christ Jesus. Would any therefore enjoy communion with Christ? Are any desirous of knowing where Christ feeds? he feeds where his ministers do, and that is among the lilies, in the congregation of the saints; it may serve then as a direction to such, to sit under a Gospel-minister. Or,

Secondly. We may understand by the church's two breasts, the two Testaments, the Old and the New. A Jewish writer,[z] would have their two laws here intended, namely, the written law, and the oral law; the written law is that which was written on the two tables of stone; the oral law is what they imagine God gave to Moses by word of mouth, which he gave to Joshua, and so was handed down from one to another, and makes up the volume of their vain, unprofitable, and numerous traditions, called the Misnah: but it is much better applied by another of them,[a] to the two tables themselves, on which were written the ten commandments, five on one table, and five on the other; and so, like two young roes that are twins, answered one another: though the two Testaments, the Old and the New, seem to bid much fairer to be the sense of these words; which two breasts contain and impart the whole "sincere milk of the word," and afford everything that is nourishing and refreshing to believers; here is milk for babes, and meat for strong men; and, like "two young roes," are exceeding pleasant and delightful to believers; they rejoice the heart, cheer the spirits, and fill the soul with a universal pleasure; and as two young roes that are twins are alike, there is a harmony and agreement between them; they look to one another as the two cherubim over the mercy-seat did. They agree, 1. In the person, office, and grace of Christ: the Old-Testament has said nothing concerning the Messiah, what he should be, do, or suffer, but what the New-Testament has fully confirmed and more clearly discovered; and the New-Testament says nothing of Christ, his person, office, and grace, but what the Old bears a testimony to; and therefore, says Christ to the Jews, John v. 39, "search the scriptures," that is, of the Old Testament; "for they are they which testify of me." (2). They are alike in their doctrines; the doctrines concerning Christ's person, the remission of sins by his blood, justification by his righteousness, &c., are the same in both Testaments, notwithstanding they were spoken at "sundry times," and delivered in "divers manners;" though perhaps they are more clearly revealed in the one than in the other: the apostle Paul, that great asserter of the doctrines of grace under the New Testament, said no other things than what Moses and the prophets said under the Old. 3. The promises and prophecies of the Old-Testament have their completion in the New; there was nothing promised to be done, or prophesied that should be, but what has been exactly fulfilled and brought to pass; neither is there scarcely any thing in the New Testament, but what was promised and prophesied of under the Old. 4. The types and figures of the old law are exactly answered in the New-Testament: the law was nothing else but a "shadow of good things to come;" the passover lamb, the brazen serpent, the rock, and manna, the Jewish sabbaths, sacrifices, new moon, washings, and purifications, all prefigured and had their fulfilment in Christ Jesus: there is scarce any thing in the New-Testament, but what was typified under the Old; and nothing prefigured under the Old, but what has its completion in the New; and thus are they like two young roes that are twins: and they may also be said to be like roes that "feed among the lilies," because they abound with the lilies of gospel promises and gospel-doc-

---

[y] En aspicis illum, candida qui medius cubat inter lilia, cervum? Calphurnius apud Bochart. Hierozoic par. 1. 1. 3. c. 24. col. 924. [a] R. Aben Ezra in loc.
[z] R. Solom. Jarchi in loc. so in Yalkut in loc.

trines; these two fields are full of them; there are "exceeding great and precious promises," and heavenly and delightful truths, which make for the consolation, edification, and instruction of God's people. Or,

Thirdly. By the church's two breasts may be intended, the two ordinances of the gospel, baptism, and the Lord's supper; which are not dry breasts, but the breasts of consolation, out of which believers suck and are satisfied; in the Lord's supper, by faith they "eat the flesh," and "drink the blood" of the Son of God, and feed upon the bruised and *broken body* of a crucified Jesus, and in so doing, receive much strength and nourishment; in the ordinance of baptism, they look to a buried and risen Jesus, behold the place where their Lord lay, "who was delivered for their offences, and rose again for their justification;" and oftentimes go away, as the eunuch did, rejoicing: now these, like "two young roes," are exceeding pleasant and delightful to believers, when they have the presence and Spirit of God with them, and the discoveries of his love unto them; for then are wisdom's ways, "ways of pleasantness, and all her paths, paths of peace." Again, like two roes that are twins, they are both instituted by Christ, both lead the faith of God's children to him; they both require the same subjects, namely, believers, and ought to go inseparably together; he that has a right to the one, has an indubitable right to the other; and he that subjects to the one, should also to the other; for so did the first primitive Christians, who, as soon as converted, were baptized, and the same day joined themselves to the church, and stedfastly continued in holy fellowship and communion with it; a practice to be imitated and followed by us now. Moreover, these may be said to "feed among the lilies," because they are all acknowledged, received, and submitted to by the saints, who are compared to lilies; who not only entertain them, but maintain and vindicate them against all opposers.

There are some,[b] who think by the church's breasts are meant, love to God, and love to our neighbour, which are the two great commandments of the law; and therefore love is said to be the "fulfilling of the law." Now "we love God, because he first loved us," and we love the saints, because they are loved with the same love, redeemed by the same blood as we are, have the same grace wrought in their hearts, as we ourselves have, and all as the fruit and effect of divine grace; and being thus filled with a sense of God's love, they become very fruitful in good works, and, like "two young roes," are exceeding pleasant and delightful to Christ; and therefore he says, in ver. 10, "How fair is my love, my sister, my spouse," &c., both to me and to my saints: and like two young roes that are *twins*, are wrought at one and the same time in the soul; bear a very great resemblance to each other in their natures, properties, and usefulness, and do inseparably go together; for where there is love to God, there will be love to the saints: for to say we love God, and do not love our brother, is a manifest contradiction, as the apostle John says, 1 John iv. 20, "He that loveth not his brother whom he hath seen, how can he love God whom he hath not seen;" and these being fed by scripture-precepts and examples, grow and increase abundantly, like two young roes which are fat and plump, feeding among the lilies: but the other senses of the words before-mentioned seem better to agree with them.

Verse 6. *Until the day break, and the shadows flee away, I will get me to the mountain of myrrh, and to the hill of frankincense.*

Some[c] think these are the words of the church; who, not being able to bear any longer to hear herself so highly commended, as in the preceding verses, resolves to betake herself to some private place, where she might be out of the hearing of such praises and commendations: or else, being under great temptations and darkness of soul, resolves to go to the mountain of the Lord's house, the church of Christ, and there in reading, meditation, prayer, and other exercises, wait for his presence, and the manifestations of himself unto her: or rather, being in distressed circumstances, she is resolved to go to Christ himself, "the rock that is higher than" she; who, for the odour of his sacrifice, the fragrancy of his intercession, and sweet-smelling garment of his righteousness, may be called "the mountain of myrrh," and "hill of frankincense," as he is "a bundle of myrrh," in chap. i. 13. But I am rather inclined to think, that they are the words of Christ; in which we are told,

First. The place where he resolves to go to and abide; "the mountain of myrrh, and hill of frankincense;" which I apprehend intend one and the same place; though two places in Arabia were so called.[c] The allusion may be to mountains and hills, where those odoriferous plants grew; such as were in or near Judea. It is said of Pompey the Great, that when he passed over Lebanon, after-mentioned, ver. 8, he went through sweet-smelling groves, and woods of frankincense and balsam;[d] and Lebanon is thought by some,[e] to have its name from the frankincense that grew upon it; though rather, from the whiteness of the snow continually on it, and is, in the Targum of ver. 8, called "the mountain of snow;" see Jer. xviii. 14. Secondly. How long he proposes to continue here; "until the day break, and the shadows flee away."

---

[b] Bernard and Carpath. in Sanct. in loc.
[c] Vid. Ainsworth and Sanct. in loc.   [c] Shilte Hagihborim, c. 48. fol. 95. 4.   [d] Florus de Gest. Roman. l. 3. c. 5.   [e] Vid. Gabriel Sionit. de Orient. Urb. c. 6. p. 14.

Now by "the mountain of myrrh, and hill of frankincense," most of the Jewish writers[f] understand the temple, which was built on mount Moriah, 2 Chron. iii. 1, the place where Abraham offered up his son Isaac; in which mountain as the Lord then, so frequently in after-ages, especially when the temple was built, appeared unto his people. Now the *temple* may be called "the mountain of myrrh, and hill of frankincense," either in allusion to Moriah, the name of the mountain on which it was built; which perhaps might have its name originally from the abundance of myrrh which grew upon it; or else, because in it was the holy anointing oil, one ingredient in which was "pure myrrh;" and also the incense, which was made of "pure frankincense," together with other spices; which was likewise put upon their meat-offerings, which were there offered up unto the Lord: and this sense of the words is not altogether to be despised; for in the temple, the *shechinah* or Divine Majesty dwelt, until Christ came in the flesh, when the gospel-day broke, and the shadows of the ceremonial law vanished, fled, and disappeared, as has been shown in chap. ii. 17. Though I think rather, by "the mountain of myrrh, and hill of frankincense," is intended the church of Christ;[g] where he has taken up his residence, and resolves to dwell until his second coming; which may be compared to a hill or mountain. 1. For their height: hills and mountains are higher than any other parts of the earth; and so is the church of Christ than the rest of the world; saints are higher in Christ's esteem than all the world besides; and are exalted by his grace, and dignified with favours by him above all others; and however low and mean they may now appear in the eyes of the world, the time is coming when this "mountain of the Lord's house shall be established in the top of the mountains, and shall be exalted above the hills," Isa. ii. 2. 2. For their immoveableness: hills and mountains cannot be removed; no more can the church or believers in Christ, Psalm. cxxv. 1; for "they that trust in the Lord shall be as mount Zion, which cannot be removed, but abideth for ever:" they shall never be removed either from Christ's hands or Christ's heart; they shall never be removed from a state of justification to a state of condemnation; they are secured by electing love, and preserved in Christ Jesus; they are held fast by covenant-bands, and are built upon "a sure foundation, upon a rock," against which "the gates of hell can never prevail." 3. For being places where trees grow, as oaks, cedars, olives, &c., and famous for these were Bashan, Hermon, Lebanon, the "mount of Olives," &c., in the church of Christ are "trees of righteousness," which, being planted by Christ's Father, flourish like palm-trees, and grow like cedars in Lebanon. 4. For being places of pasture for cattle; such were Bashan, Carmel, and Gilead: in the church of Christ there is pasture for all his sheep; there plenteous provisions of grace are made; "a feast of fat things," wine mingled, bread prepared, and a table sufficiently furnished for all Christ's friends and guests, in this his *holy mountain*, the church. 5. In hills and mountains worship used to be given, and sacrifices offered up to God, as may be collected from the discourse of Christ with the woman of Samaria, John iv. 20, 21, as well as from other places of scripture: in the church of Christ the worship of God is maintained, the word of God is preached, his ordinances are administered, and the sacrifices of prayer and praise are offered up to him in the name and through the mediation of Christ Jesus. And as it may be compared to a mountain and hill, so likewise to "a mountain of myrrh, and hill of frankincense." (1.) Because of the fragrancy of those graces with which the church is perfumed: hence she is said, in chap. iii. 6, to be "perfumed with myrrh and frankincense, with all powders of the merchant;" and in this chapter, ver. 10, the smell of them is said to exceed all spices; and that more especially when they are in exercise; so grateful, well-pleasing, and sweet-smelling are they then to Christ Jesus. (2.) Because of sacrifices which are of "a sweet-smelling savour, that are offered up here, as the sacrifices of prayer, which, in Rev. v. 8, are called *odours*; and are more especially so to God the Father, when they are offered up through Christ's mediation, being perfumed with his *much incense*: here are also the sacrifices of praise, which are of an exceeding grateful and delightful odour to God; for being offered up to him through Christ, these spiritual sacrifices become acceptable to him. (3.) Because of that pleasure and delight which Christ takes in his people, and that sweet communion which they here enjoy with him; so that to them both it is "a mountain of myrrh and hill of frankincense;" where the one concludes, it is good to be, and the other resolves to stay "till the day break," &c. The saints are "the excellent in the earth," with whom Christ delights to converse, and to whom his "goodness extends;" he says, "the lines are fallen to him in pleasant places;" and that he has a goodly heritage assigned him by his Father; inasmuch as they are his to live and dwell with him for evermore: and to the saints, Christ's "tabernacles are amiable" and lovely; they count "a day spent in his courts, better than a thousand elsewhere;" because there they see him, and have fellowship with him, whom their souls love. Now in this "mountain of myrrh, and hill of frankincense," Christ, as he delights, so he resolves to

---

[f] Targum, R. Aben Ezra, and R. sol. Jarchi in loc. and Zohar in Gen. fol. 75. 1. Alshech interprets it of mount Sinai, and the day-break of the captivity of Egypt. [g] So the Cabalistic doctors by these understand malcuth, the congregation of Israel, or the church, Lexic, Cabal. p. 229. 277.

"dwell, until the day break," &c. Which is,

1st. Until the day of grace breaks in upon every elect soul. All that the Father hath loved with an everlasting love, and hath chosen in Christ before the world began, he put into his hands; who, upon the reception of them, laid himself under obligation to redeem them by his blood, and bring them safe to glory; and as he has already done the former, he is now doing the latter, through the ministry of the word; and therefore the preaching of the gospel, a standing ministry, and a church state, are continued on earth; in which he will stay, until every one of those other sheep are called by divine grace, whom he has laid himself under obligation to bring in: and now, when grace breaks in upon a poor sinner's heart, it is like the break of day unto him; light springs into his understanding, which before was darkened; he was darkness itself, is now made light in the Lord; and is no more reckoned among the children of the night, but among the children of the day; for now the shadows of ignorance and infidelity are fled away; the scales of darkness are fallen from his eyes, and in God's light he sees light: he now sees his lost and undone state without Christ, the corruption and depravity of his nature, and the plague of his own heart; he sees the impurity and imperfection of his own righteousness, and the glory and fulness of Christ's; he sees Christ as a proper, suitable, able, and willing Saviour; he sees things he never saw before, and which will ever remain invisible to a carnal eye. Now until the day of grace has thus broken in upon every elect soul; and the shadows of blindness, ignorance, and infidelity, are thus fled and gone: Christ has taken up his residence, and will dwell in his church, which, to him, is a mountain of myrrh and hill of frankincense. Or else,

2ndly. Until the day of glory breaks; that everlasting day, in which there will be no more night; when all shadows of darkness, infidelity, doubts, and fears, will flee away; when saints shall be attended no more with the long, tedious, and dark nights of afflictions and sorrows, and shall stand in no need of shadowy ordinances; but shall enjoy Christ, the sum and substance of all, and dwell and be delighted with him perpetually, upon the everlasting mountains of spices, as has been shown on ch. ii. 17.

Verse 7. *Thou art all fair, my love, there is no spot in thee.*

CHRIST having mentioned some particular parts of the church, wherein she appeared very beautiful; in describing of which his soul was so taken with her beauty, that he resolves to dwell with her till his second coming; and now, lest it should be thought that there was a defect of beauty in the parts not mentioned, he sums up all in this general commendation; " Thou art all fair, my love, there is no spot in thee:" which commendation may regard the church in some particular period of time; or, in general, be expressive of the fairness and beauty of the church, and every believer in any age of the world. A learned Jewish writer,[h] would have the words referred to the days of Solomon; in which, he affirms, all Israel were righteous: and another[i] to the time when Israel received the law from mount Sinai; when, it is said, there were none lame, blind, and dumb, among them: but they much better agree with the primitive and apostolic church, that was gathered by the ministry of the apostles after Christ's ascension, which is the mind of some Christian expositors;[k] and indeed the church then bid as fair for this character, as in any other period of time whatever. Therefore, it may not be amiss if we consider how well it agrees with it; which will appear, if we observe,

First. The pure doctrines of grace which were then preached; the doctrines of the gospel by the first ministers thereof, were fully preached; they kept back nothing that might be profitable to the church's upon any pretence whatever; they shunned not to declare all the counsel of God, whatever was the consequence of it; and this they did in all sincerity and godly simplicity: they used no artful methods to conceal their principles, but renounced those hidden things of dishonesty; they did not handle the word of God deceitfully, but by manifestation of the truth commended themselves to every man's conscience; they did not corrupt the word of God,[l] and blend it with their own inventions, but as of sincerity, but as of God, being sent by him, in the sight of God, so spake they in Christ; and were always jealous, lest the souls they ministered to should be seduced and drawn away, by cunning and artful men, from the simplicity of the gospel: they were careful to deliver those doctrines consistently; their trumpet did not give an uncertain sound; their word was not yea and nay, sometimes one thing, and sometimes another, to the dishonour of the gospel, and the confusion of souls, but was all of a piece; they preached agreeable to the analogy of faith, and were very solicitous to keep to that rule, and not swerve from it: and with a great deal of warmth and zeal they adhered to these truths; bravely withstood all opposers, feared the faces of none, and studied to please no man; but were bold in the name of God to speak the gospel of God, though with much contention; and however weak, mean, and contemptible their ministry might appear to the world, it was attended with a demonstration of the Spirit and of power, and was made useful for the conversion of thousands of souls: for these truths being received

---

[h] R. Aben Ezra in loc.   [i] Vid. Yalkut in loc.
[k] Brightman and Cotton in loc.   [l] Καπηλεύοντες, cauponantes sermonem Dei; metaphora sumpta est ab hospitibus and cauponantibus, quibus in more est vinum aqua corrumpere, Aretius in 2 Cor. ii. 17.

in the love thereof, wrought effectually in them that believed: and were constantly adhered to and retained by them, maugre all the opposition of men and devils.

Secondly. If we consider the nature of their worship, which was pure and spiritual: the ordinances were kept by them, as they were delivered to them: were not mixed with human inventions, and, to their eternal honour, were constantly attended on by them: they were very frequent and fervent in the duties of fasting and prayer, and did nothing of moment in the church without them: all the parts of religious worship were performed decently and in order by them; in all things they sought the glory of God, and the consolation and edification of each other.

Thirdly. If we take notice of their discipline, which was strict, and according to rule: proper officers were chosen by the joint suffrages of the church; ministers were by them set apart for the ministry; and deacons chosen by them to take care of the poor, and serve the tables: church censures and excommunications were administered by the whole body, and that with a great deal of success; in case of private offences, they gave private admonitions, and for public crimes, rebuked before all, that others might fear: those who were erroneous in principle, they sharply reproved: and such as were disorderly in practice, withdrew from; an heretic after the first and second admonition, they rejected; and such who were the authors of division, and causes of contention, they carefully marked, observed, and avoided.

Fourthly. If we take a view of their Christian communion and fellowship with each other; they lived in entire unity and harmony with each other; they were all of one heart and of one soul; one soul did, as it were, dwell in, and actuate all their bodies; they had a great deal of sympathy for each other in all distresses, whether inward or outward, and freely communicated to each other; they wept with those that wept, and rejoiced with those that rejoiced; they kept Christ's new commandment, and entirely loved one another; and in so doing, gave an evidence of their being the true disciples of Christ; so that the very heathens took notice of it, and could say, "See how they love one another!" ᵐ which, though they could not condemn, yet it was not very grateful to them.

Fifthly. Their conversation was as becometh the gospel of Christ Jesus: they held the mystery of the faith in a pure conscience; that grace, which was revealed unto them, and wrought in them, taught them to deny ungodliness and worldly lusts, and to live soberly, righteously, and godly in this present world; and in so doing, they adorned the gospel, honoured their profession, stopped the mouths of gainsayers, and recommended religion to others; and thus the primitive church much continued for the first three hundred years after Christ: but we are not to imagine, that there were no blemishes and imperfections in her during all this time; for there were many, and more especially towards the latter end; but, being compared with the state of the church in after ages, she might then be said to be all fair, and no spot in her. But I rather think the words are not to be limited to the church in any one period of time, but are applicable to her and to all believers in any age of the world; who are all fair, not upon the foot of their own works, as the Targum on the place intimates; for all their righteousnesses are as filthy rags, and so are far from making them appear fair and beautiful in Christ's sight; but they are so, being justified by his righteousness, washed in his blood, and sanctified by his Spirit; and so shall be at last presented to him "a glorious church, not having spot or wrinkle, or any such thing," Eph. v. 27.

The title and character which Christ here gives to his church, "my love," I have already met with and explained in chap. i. 9. It is here predicated of her,

1st. That she is all fair. She is said to be fair, and is called by Christ, his fair one, and the fairest among women, before; but here, all fair: To show, 1. That she was a perfection of beauty, being made perfect through that comeliness which Christ put upon her: believers are perfectly justified by Christ's righteousness from all sin; stand complete in him, and so are esteemed all fair by him; and in respect of sanctification, there is a perfection of parts, though not of degrees; there is a perfect new creature in all its parts, though it is not as yet grown up to be a perfect man in Christ; even as a new born babe, which has every part and limb in just proportion, may be said to be perfect, though it has not as yet grown up to the stature and bigness it will do, if life is continued. 2. That the whole church, and all the true members thereof are so; all of the church, every member, every individual believer, is fair in Christ's eye; the meanest and weakest believer, as well as the greatest and strongest, is made perfectly comely with Christ's comeliness, and equally accepted in the beloved. 3. He says so of the church, to manifest the exceeding greatness of her beauty, and how much his heart was taken with it, that he, the king, greatly desired it, and delighted to be in her company. 4. To comfort her, banish her doubts and fears, and strengthen her faith; who, seeing her own vileness and sinfulness, and spots and blemishes, might be ready to despond in her mind, and call in question her interest in Christ, and his righteousness; therefore he says; "Thou art all fair, my love:" I do love thee, thou art exceeding fair and beautiful in my eye; all of thee is fair and beautiful; thou art fairer than all others, being adorned with my grace, and clothed with my righteousness.

ᵐ Vide, inquiunt, ut invicem se diligant, Tertull. apolog. c. 39. Sic mutuo, quod doletes, amore diligimus, quoniam odisse non novimus. Sic. nos, quod invidetis, fratres vocamus, ut unius Dei parentis homines, ut consortes fidei, ut spei cohætredes. Minut. Felix Octav. p. (mihi) 35.

2ndly. He asserts that there was no spot in her; which is not to be understood, 1. As if there was no sin in believers; for this is contrary to all the experience of God's children, as well as to express texts of scripture; the humble confessions and ingenuous acknowledgments of saints in all ages, their frequent groans and complaints of the weight and burden of it, are plain proofs to the contrary; their ardent prayers at the throne of grace, for the manifestations of pardoning love, that God would cleanse them from secret, and keep them back from presumptuous sins, not only testify their commission of sinful actions, but also their sense of indwelling corruptions; and their daily slips and falls loudly proclaim the depravity of their natures; to imagine that we have no sin in us, is but to deceive ourselves, and to give an evidence to others, that the truth is not in us: therefore, when Christ says of his church, that there is no spot in her, we are not to understand it in this sense. Nor, 2. As if the sins of God's people were not sins; for, though they are justified by Christ's righteousness from all sin, and have all their sins pardoned through Christ's blood: yet their sins do not hereby cease to be sins: pardon of sin and justification by Christ's righteousness, free souls from an obligation to the punishment due to sin, but do not destroy the nature of sin: violations and breaches of God's righteous law, made by his own people, are equally esteemed sins by him, as those made by others; and though he never will inflict his vindictive wrath upon them for their sins; yet he does oftentimes, in a fatherly manner, chastise them for them, and brings them under a sense and acknowledgment of them before him. But, 3. The church and all believers are so in Christ's account; though they have sin in them, and have committed sin, and, through infirmity, continue to do so, yet sin is not reckoned and imputed to them; for, being clothed with his spotless righteousness, he looks upon them as if they had no spot in them; and they are so covered with it, that when their sins are sought for by divine justice, they shall not be found, nay, God himself having accepted of Christ's righteousness and imputed it to them, sees no iniquity in Jacob, nor perverseness in Israel: though all sin is seen by him, *in articulo providentiæ*, in the article of providence, and nothing escapes his all-seeing eye; yet, *in articulo justificationis*, in the article of justification, he sees no sin in his people, so as to reckon it to them, or condemn them for it; for they all stand unblameable and unreproveable in his sight; and Christ will ere long present them in open view to men and angels, not having spot or wrinkle, or any such thing.

Verse 8. *Come with me from Lebanon, (my spouse) with me from Lebanon: look from the top of Amana, from the top of Shenir and Hermon, from the lions' dens, from the mountains of the leopards.*

CHRIST having, in the verses going before, given a large and full commendation of his church's beauty, and having his heart exceedingly taken with it, so that he could not bear a distance from her: invites her, as his spouse and bride, to go along with him, and look off from the several places mentioned. In the words are,

I. A special title given her, expressive of the nearest relation to him; "my spouse."

II. A kind invitation to go along with him, enforced with the most powerful arguments.

I. A special title is given to her, "my spouse." This is a new one, which we never met with before: He had called her his love, his dove, and his fair one, but never, till now, his spouse; which is expressive of that near relation and strict union that is between Christ and his church, which union is represented by several things in scripture, as by the union of the head and members, vine and branches; but by none more strongly than by the conjugal union of husband and wife, by which they become one flesh; which the apostle, Eph. v. 32, taking notice of, applies to Christ and his church: This, says he, " is a great mystery, but I speak concerning Christ and his church:" Christ and his church being espoused together, become one spirit; hence it is that they are called by the same names: Christ is called by the name of *Israel*, which is the church's name, and the church is called by the name of *Christ*; hence all that Christ has is the church's, and all that the church has is Christ's; her debts become his, and his grace becomes hers; there is a mutual interest of persons and things; and that which crowns all, is, that this union is indissoluble: this band can never be broken, nor this marriage-knot be ever untied.

I shall now very briefly show you, 1st. How the church came to be the spouse of Christ. 2ndly. Why she is first called so here.

1st. How the church came to be Christ's spouse; a person so much beneath him, at such a distance from him, and so unlovely and unlikely in herself, it may justly seem strange and be wondered at, how she came to be so nearly related to him. And here now observe, that the Lord Jesus Christ from all eternity pitched his love upon her: that he loved her from thence, is manifest from his suretyship-engagements for her; he asked her of his Father, who had a right to dispose of her, and he gave him his heart's desire, and did not withhold the request of his lips from him; which request being made by the Son, and consent given by the Father, he then betrothed her to himself for ever, and that in righteousness, and in judgment, and in loving-kindness, and in mercies; and resolved to bestow that grace upon her, which should cause her to know, own, and acknowledge him to be her Lord and Husband: but notwithstanding this, at present here was an actual consent of her own wanting; wherefore he sends his ministering servants in the several ages of the world to obtain it: these are sent to display his greatness, discover the richness of his grace, and speak of all his glories; which, being impressed upon souls by the mighty power of his Spirit and grace, they are willing to give up themselves to him to be his for ever, to love, own, and acknowledge him as their Lord and Husband; which may be called "the day of their espousal[s]" to him: but all this will more visibly and gloriously appear, when all the elect are gathered in, and every soul of them made willing to be a holy spouse unto him: then shall the nuptials be solemnized, and that voice should be heard in heaven, "the marriage of the Lamb is come;" whose wife, being "as a bride adorned for her husband," shall be received by him, and enter with him into the marriage chamber, where they shall spend an endless eternity in the enjoyment of each other.

2ndly. Why she is first called so here; she is in the following verses, and in other parts of this song, frequently called so, but never before this time. (1). Being all fair, without any spot or blemish, being prepared by his grace for himself, and having a grant from him to be "arrayed in fine linen, clean and white," he calls her his spouse; for now she looked something like one, having on the wedding garment, Christ's spotless righteousness. (2). The marriage was now consummated, "the day of his espousals" was over, which is mentioned in chap. iii. 11, for all that comes between that and these words, is a commendation of his church's beauty, which his heart was wonderfully taken with on his marriage-day; and when he had finished the commendation, salutes her with this title, *my spouse.* (3). The mentioning of it here, may be also to prevail with her to go along with him. Where should a wife be? or with whom should she be, but with her husband? I am thy husband, and thou art my spouse and bride; and therefore both duty and affection to me should oblige thee to go along with me: so that the import of the words is much the same with those; "forget thine own people, and thy father's house, so shall the king greatly desire thy beauty; for he is thy Lord, and worship thou him," Psalm xlv. 10, 11. Which leads me to consider,

II. The invitation he gives her to go along with him, "Come with me, my spouse," &c., or, as the words may be read, "Thou shalt come with me,"[n] &c., for whatever Christ invites and exhorts us to, he must give us grace and strength to perform, and, blessed be his name, he does.

Lebanon, from whence she is exhorted and invited to remove, was a goodly mountain, on the borders of the land of Canaan, northward; it was famous for odoriferous trees, and especially for cedars, wherefore frequent mention is made of it in this song; this was that "goodly mountain and Lebanon," which Moses had such a desire to see before his death, Deut. iii. 25, the allusion may be to the bringing of Pharaoh's daughter, whom Solomon married, from the house of the forest of Lebanon, where she might be first placed, to the house he built for her, when it was prepared to receive her,[o] 1 Kings ix. 24. Some of the Jewish writers[p] think, that a mighty conflux of people to the temple, from all parts of Judea, and even from among the uncircumcised, who are compared to lions and leopards, is here intended: but rather, we are to understand the words as an exhortation, to remove from the temple and from Jerusalem; for perhaps by Lebanon here, may be meant the temple, as in Zech. xi. 1, "Open thy doors, O Lebanon, that the fire may devour thy cedars;" which, by some Jewish writers,[q] is expounded of the temple, and the destruction of it: for they tell us,[r] that forty years before the destruction of it, the gates of the temple opened of themselves; at which R. Jochanan Ben Zaccai, as if affrighted, rebuked them, and said, "Now know I that thy destruction is at hand, according to the prophecy of Zechariah, the son of Iddo, Open thy gates, O Lebanon," &c. The temple might be called so, because it was made of the wood of Lebanon, of cedars which were brought from thence, and because the frankincense which grew there, was daily burnt in it, and the glory of it was brought into it. Now in Christ's time the temple was become a den of thieves, as he calls it, in Matt. xxi. 13; and in the apostles time was a den of lions, and a mountain of leopards; was full of painted and spotted hypocrites, and cruel persecutors; wolves in sheep's clothing, who made havoc of the church, and persecuted the saints from place to place; wherefore Christ removed from them, broke up housekeeping with them, and left their house desolate unto them; he took his gospel from them, ordered his ministers to depart far hence to the Gentiles, and calls forth his people from among them, to go along with him thither, "Come with me from Lebanon, my spouse," &c. Also he bids her look from the top of Amana, from the top of Shenir and Hermon: Amana[s] was a mountain, which divided Cilicia from Syria; from whence perhaps the river at the foot of it took its name, which in 2 Kings v. 12, is called Abana, but in the *keri* or margin it is read Amana: and so the Targum here expounds it of the people which dwelt by the river Amana: R. Solomon Jarchi would have it to be a mountain in the northern border of Israel, and that it is the same with mount Hor;[t] and indeed, in every place where mention is made of mount Hor, the Targum of Jonathan always renders it, Taurus

---

[n] הבראי venies, Pagninus, Montanus, Mercerus, Junius and Tremellius. [o] See Lightfoot's Works, vol. 1. p. 76. and Bedford's Scripture Chronology, p. 607. [p] Targum and R. Aben Ezra in loc. [q] R. Abendanæ not. in Miclol Yophi, R. Sol. Jarchi in Zech. xi. 1. [r] Talmud Yoma, fol. 39. 2. [s] Plin. l. 5. c. 22. Pompon Mela, l. 1. c. 12, and solin. c. 51. [t] So Talmud. Hieros. Challah, fol. 60. 1. and Sheviith, fol. 37. 4. [u] In Numb. 20. 22, 25, 27. and xxxiv. 7, 8. Deut. xxxii 50.

Umanus; for Amanus, according to Ptolemy, was a part of mount Taurus; it is joined with Libanon by Josephus,ʷ and was a part of it, where the snow lay all the summer; as it is both with that and Carmel by Ælianus.ˣ Shenir and Hermon were one and the same mountain, called by different names: Hermon perhaps was the common name to the whole mountain; and that part of it which belonged to the Sidonians, they called Sirion; and the other part which belonged to the Amorites, they called Shenir, Deut. iii. 9. Now all these mountains may be called dens of lions, and mountains of leopards, not only because they were inhabited by those wild beasts,ʸ but because they were inhabited by cruel, savage, and tyrannical persons, and by thieves and robbers, and such like persons, and especially Amana, as Strabo,ᶻ Cicero,ᵃ and Plutarchᵇ relate; and which appears also from what Lucan says, in his Pharsalia, lib. 3, ver. 244.

——— Venere feroces,
Cappadoces duri populus nunc cultor Amani.

Shenir and Hermon were formerly, as Jarchi observes, the dens of those lions, Sihon and Og, kings of Bashan and of the Amorites; unless they should rather be thought to be the proper names of some places about Lebanon, for Adrichomiusᶜ says, "The mountain of the leopards, which was round and high, was two miles distant northwards from Tripolis, three from the city Arcas southward, and one from mount Lebanon." Now from the tops of these mountains Christ would have his church look, and take a prospect how the gospel was received, what numbers of souls were converted, and how churches were planted in Phœnicia, Cyprus, Cyrenia, Antioch, &c., though it was contemned, rejected, and persecuted by the Jewish nation; so that the words may be understood of Christ's carrying his gospel into the Gentile world, and succeeding in it, and calling his people to take notice of it. Or else,

This may intend in general Christ's call to his church and people, to leave the society of, and come out from among the wicked men of the world, comparable to lions and leopards, and to go along with him, as in 2 Cor. vi. 17, and Rev. xviii. 4. And here are two sorts of arguments, which he makes use of to enforce this upon them.

First. That the persons from whom he exhorts them to remove, were no better than lions and leopards; and to converse with them, was no better than to dwell in the dens and mountains of such. 1. Wicked and ungodly persons may be compared to lions, especially those who are of a cruel and persecuting nature: hence David, being among such, says, "my soul is among lions ;" he frequently represents the wicked as such, and desires deliverance from them: likewise the apostle Paul calls a persecuting Nero, "the lion," out of whose mouth it pleased the Lord to deliver him. 2. They may be compared to leopards, (1.) For their being full of spots; the leopard is not fuller of spots, than the sinner is of sin; as the one is natural, so is the other; and as the leopard cannot change one spot, nor make any alteration in his nature; no more can the sinner change his own heart, nor by any power of his own remove the spots and stains of sin; as Jeremy says, chap. xiii. 23, "Can the Ethiopian change his skin, or the leopard his spots? then may ye also do good, that are accustomed to do evil." (2.) For their craftiness and cruelty, as is manifest from Jer. v. 6, Hos. xiii. 7. Ælianus reports,ᵈ that when the leopard is in want of food, it hides itself among the thickets, so as it cannot be seen; and, by the sweetness of its odour, draws the fawns, does, wild goats, and such like animals to it; and when they are near, breaks out of its lurking-place, and makes them its prey: other artful methods it makes use of for the same purpose, as is recorded by others;ᵉ which is a just emblem of the craftiness and cruelty of wicked and ungodly men, who use all the stratagems to ensnare, and exercise all the cruelty they can devise upon those who are "quiet in the land." (3.) For their swiftness; so in Hab. i. 8, the horses of the Chaldeans are said to be swifter than leopards: wicked men, though slow and backward to that which is good, yet are swift to do mischief; no sooner do their hearts devise wickedness, but their feet run to accomplish it.

Secondly. The second argument he uses with her to quit the society of wicked men, is, the enjoyment of his own company, which is far preferable to theirs; "Come with me, my spouse." 1. Christ's company is much more pleasant than theirs; though the ways of sin may seem pleasant for a while, yet at length they will appear no other than the haunts of lions and leopards; though the company of sinners may seem now sweet and delightful, they will be found at last to be more bitter than death; but Christ's ways are always "ways of pleasantness ." it is good for the believer to be always in his company, where he finds solid pleasure, and inexpressible delight; more than ever he did in the tents of wickedness. 2. It is more profitable: the company and conversation of wicked men is hurtful and pernicious; "evil communications corrupt good manners;" but the company of Christ is always profitable: a believer always gets something by it; it has a mighty influence upon the inward frame of his soul, and upon his outward walk in the world; it makes him both comfortable in himself, and

---

ʷ Antiq. l. 1. c. 6. s. 1.   ˣ De Animal. l. 5. c. 56.
ʸ Vid. Aristot. Hist. Animal l. 6, c. 3. Plin l 8 c. 16. and Brocard in Cocceii Lexic. p. 123.
ᶻ Geograph. l. 14. p. 465. and l. 1. 16. p. 517.
ᵃ Ad. Attic. l. 5. ep. 20.   ᵇ In Vita Ciceron. p. 879.   ᶜ Mons leopardorum rotundus et altus est, qui contra aquilonem a Tripoli daubus, versus austrum a civitate Arcas tribus, a Libano autem uno miliario distat, Adrichomii Theatrum Terræ Sanctæ, p. 186. 1.   ᵈ De Animal. l. 5. c. 40.
ᵉ Solin. c. 27. Frantzii Hist. Animal. par. 1. c. 8.

useful to others; so that he sustains no loss, but undoubtedly is a gainer, who parts with the company of the men of the world for Christ's. 3. Christ's company is much more safe than theirs: the company of wicked men is always dangerous; there is danger not only of being infected with their sins, but also of partaking of their plagues; it tends to ruin here, and leads to everlasting destruction; but the believer is always safe in Christ's company, in what place or condition soever he be; though he walks through the waters of affliction, and fire of tribulation, nay, though through the valley of the shadow of death: yet he is always safe, being guided by his counsel, supported by his hand, and comforted by his presence.

Now Christ in all this discovers a great deal of care over, and affection to his church and people. One would think she cannot withstand a request, delivered in such an affectionate manner, where her own comfort, profit, and safety, are so much concerned. Who would dwell in lions' dens, and in the mountains of the leopards, when they might have such agreeable and delightful company as Christ's is? which is to be valued and preferred before this world, and all the things of it; though God's own children are too apt to be taken with them; and therefore have need, as here, to be called to look off from them to things that are spiritual and heavenly; and not take up their rest and satisfaction in those things and places, where lions dwell and leopards walk.

Verse 9. *Thou hast ravished my heart, my sister, my spouse: thou hast ravished my heart with one of thine eyes, with one chain of thy neck.*

CHRIST, having invited his church to go along with him, here discovers the reason of it, because his heart was ravished with her; he had such an affection for her, that he could not bear to be at a distance from her. In these words, consider,

I. The titles given to her; " my sister, my spouse."

II. What he declares to her; " thou hast ravished my heart;" which expression is doubled.

III. What it was his heart was so taken with, which had such a mighty influence upon him; " with one of thine eyes, with one chain of thy neck."

I. I shall consider the titles he gives unto her, and they are two, " my sister, my spouse;" one of which, namely, " my spouse," has been explained in the former verse, and is here repeated to show his affection to her, how much he delighted in her under this character; as also, to assure her of the truth of it, as well as to manifest his satisfaction in this relation, and that he was not ashamed to own and acknowledge her as such: the other title, " my sister," we have not met before. Now Christ may call the church his sister, 1. *More amatorio*, it being a love-strain;[f] and this being a love-song, where Christ and his church are expressing their love to each other; such a title as this cannot be looked upon as an improper one: it being an endearing expression, used by husbands to their wives; as by Raguel to Edna, Tobit vii. 8, and by Tobias to Sara, chap. viii. 4. 3. *More Hebræorum:* it being usual with the Jews to call those of their own kindred and country, brethren and sisters, and with none but such were they allowed to marry; and perhaps to this the apostle has a respect, 1 Cor. ix. 5, " Have we not power to lead about a sister, a wife?" &c., agreeable to this, Christ calls his church his sister, whom he had espoused to himself. 3. He may call her so on account of his incarnation; he assuming the same nature, and partaking of the same flesh and blood the children did; and so being of one and the same mass and lump with them, is not ashamed to call them brethren; which, it may be, is intended in that wish of the church's, chap. viii. 1, " O that thou wert as my brother!" &c., that is, O that thou wert incarnate! that we were of the same flesh and blood, and thereby thou appear to be my brother, and I thy sister. 4. On the account of her adoption: God has by his sovereign, free, and distinguishing grace, adopted all his elect into his family, and has in his covenant of grace declared himself to be their Father, and them to be his sons and daughters; and now, being the sons and daughters of the same Father as Christ is the Son of, they become his brethren and sisters, which he acknowledges, John xx. 17. 5. Being born again, not of blood, nor of the will of the flesh, nor of the will of man, but of God, they bear this character; and are so in Christ's esteem, according to what he says, Matt. xii. 50, " Whosoever shall do the will of my Father which is in heaven, the same is my brother and sister, and mother:" Christ bears all relations to his people, and is willing to own them in all relations to him. 6. Perhaps the church is here first called Christ's sister; because Christ having called his people out of Judea's land, and gathered a church among the Gentiles, that little sister spoken of in chap. viii. 8; it might hereby appear that he had a real affection for her, that she was valued by him, and nearly related to him.

II. What he declares unto her, is, that she had " ravished his heart." It is but one word in the Hebrew text, and is used in this form and sense no where else, but twice in this verse; for Christ's love being so unspeakable and inexpressible, he coins, as one[g] well observes, new words to discover it by; it is variously rendered, and perhaps by laying the several versions together, it will appear more fully what is intended by it. 1. The words may be rendered, " thou hast heartened me, or put heart into me," and caused me to be of good cheer; so Cocceius and Schmidt: the word is used in this sense, in the Syriac Testament, in Matt. ix. 2, and 1 Thess. v. 14, and

[f] Sive tibi conjux, sive futura soror. Tibullus. [g] Durham in Loc.

then the sense may be this; the love which I bear unto thee, the charming ideas of thee, which I always carry in my mind, and the "joy which was set before me," of having thy company and presence for ever in glory; have made my heavy sufferings easy, animated me as man and Mediator, and cheerfully carried me through them all for thy sake, Heb. xii. 2. 2. Others read them, "thou hast unhearted me;" thou hast taken away my heart, and stolen it from me, so that I have no heart left in me, so the Septuagint; which reading R. Aben Ezra confirms. Sometimes fear throws persons into such a condition, that they are as if they had no heart, spirit, life, or soul in them; as the Canaanites in Judg. v. 1; sometimes wonder and surprise; thus the queen of Sheba, when she had seen Solomon's wisdom and glory, it is said, "there was no more spirit in her;" and sometimes love has such an influence on the heart, and so it had here on Christ; it was so powerful, that it had taken away his heart; "thou hast ravished my heart," that is, thou hast taken it away from me, as it were, by force and violence, that it is no longer mine, but thine; thou art master over it, and hast the command of it,[h] having claimed it to thyself as thine own. 3. It is rendered by others, "thou hast drawn my heart unto thee," so R. Solomon Jarchi; or, "brought me near, "or "caused me to draw nigh;" that our hearts should be drawn to Christ, by views of his loveliness, and discoveries of his love to us, it is no wonder; but that Christ's heart should be drawn to us, in whom were neither love nor loveliness, is surprising; which shows the exceeding greatness, freeness, and richness of Christ's love. 4. It may be read, "thou hast coupled my heart with thine;" and in this sense the Talmudists use the word:[k] Christ's heart and a believer's are so knit, joined, and coupled together, that they are but one heart, one soul, and one spirit; " he that is joined to the Lord is one spirit;" all the powers of hell and earth, united together, are not able to disjoin and separate, either a believer's heart from Christ, or Christ's heart from a believer. 5. The Targum paraphrases it thus, "thy love is fixed upon the table of my heart;" it is written there in legible characters, which can never be erased; the church is not only engraven on the palms of Christ's hands, but also upon the table of his heart: and so the church has what she wished for, chap. viii. 6, "Set me as a seal upon thine heart:" Christ's love to the church is so rivetted and fixed in his heart, that there is no removing it; "Who shall separate us from the love of Christ?" 6. It is translated by others, "thou hast wounded my heart," so the Vulgate Latin; which reading is not to be despised; R. David Kimchi[l] owns it: Christ's heart was wounded with one of love's darts,[m] with an arrow shot from one of the church's eyes; which is expressive of the force and power of love, with what vehemence it dwelt in, and what influence it had upon the heart of Christ.

Now this expression is repeated, to show the vehemency and passionateness of his love, and the exceeding greatness of it; as also to assure her of the reality of it; that he was hearty and sincere in it; and did not say this by way of compliment to her as lovers too often do; nor was it a word which was rashly spoken by him, or that dropped from him at unawares; but as it proceeded from his heart, so it was spoken by him in a deliberate manner; therefore he repeats it, not to correct, but to confirm it.

Hence we may conclude what interest a believer has in Christ's heart. What may he not expect? what can he want? what need he fear, that has so great a share in Christ's heart? and what reason has he to give Christ his heart, who has so much of Christ's?.

III. I shall now take notice of the things with which Christ's heart was ravished. 1. "With one of the church's eyes;" the eye is an attractive of love;[n] and therefore it is said in Prov. vi. 25, "Neither let her take thee with her eyelids." By the eye, with which Christ was so taken, may be meant, the eye of faith; by which a soul looks on him, and loves him; beholds his fulness, and wishes for an interest in him; and looks to him, and expects from him alone life and salvation: He says, it was with *one* of her eyes; which shows that a believer has more eyes than one; and therefore we read of "the eyes of their understanding," Eph. i. 18; but it was with this eye of faith, by which she looked to him, and believed on him, that his heart was so ravished; and that but with one look from it, or glance of it, as both Junius and Ainsworth read it; nay, though but a very glimmering one; for faith, even in its lowest degree, is exceeding precious to Christ Jesus; which shows how easily and quickly a conquest is gained over Christ's heart by faith; his heart must needs be full of love to believers, since it is ravished and overcome even with a single glimmering look from faith's eye; and if so, how much will his heart be ravished, when we shall see him "face to face, just as he is;" take a full view of him, look at him, and feed our eyes for ever upon the unutterable glories of his person? 2. "With one chain of her neck:" the neck is a beautiful part of the body, and being agreeably adorned, is exceeding enamouring: the Vulgate Latin version is, "with one lock of hair of thy neck," so Aquila; which hung down in it, and

---

[h] לבבתני vendicasti tibi cor meum, Tigurine version; occupasti, Lutherus, Marckius. [i] Gloss. in T. Bab. Sabbat, fol. 53. 2. and 88. 2. [k] In Sabbat, fol. 5. 2. and Avoda Zara; fol. 2. 2. in Misnah. Vid. Buxtorf. Lex. Heb. in rad. לבב and Lex. Talmud. p. 116. Cor copulasti mihi. uxtorf. Hottinger, Smegma, p. 162. [l] In lib Shorash. rad. לבב. [m] Sagittiferi amores, Stattii Sylva, l. 3. ode 3. v. 131. [n] Τᾶς πάντες επ ὄμμασιν ἵμεροι εντι, Theocrit. Idyll. 18. Perque tuos oculos qui rapuere meos, Ovid. Amor. 1. 3. eleg. 10. Vid. Barthii not. ad Claudian. De Nupt. Honor. v. 6.

looked very beautiful, and with which lovers are sometimes taken.° By the *neck*, we may also understand faith, as we have observed on ver. 4, it being neither unusual nor improper to represent one and the same thing under different metaphors: and by the *chain*, may be meant the graces of the Spirit, which, being linked and chained, do inseparably go together: and being put about this neck of faith, makes it look very beautiful: every grace is as a golden link or precious pearl in Christ's esteem; who having beautified his people with them, takes the utmost delight in viewing them; and whilst he is observing how beautifully they are adorned there-with, his heart is ravished with them.

Verse 10. *How fair is thy love, my sister, my spouse! how much better is thy love than wine! and the smell of thine ointments than all spices!*

CHRIST having declared in the preceding verse, how much his heart was delighted in, and ravished with the faith of his church; now proceeds to show how well pleased he was with her love, and other graces of the Spirit, in these words; where,

I. The excellency of her love is set forth.
II. The sweet smell of her ointments is commended.

I. He gives some excellent characters of her love to him, Christ is the object of a believer's love; and he is well pleased with that love which they show to him: the nature of this love, its spring and actings, have been shown already, on chap. i. 3, where it has been observed, that it is superlative and universal; a believer loves Christ above all, and all of Christ; it is, or at least ought to be, constant and ardent, and is always hearty and unfeigned; it springs and arises from views of Christ's loveliness, and sights of his suitableness and fulness, from a sense of his love, and a discovery of union and relation to him; and is heightened and increased by enjoying communion and fellowship with them; it manifests itself by a regard to his commands and ordinances, his truths, his people, and his presence, and by parting with, and bearing all for him, as has there been more largely shown. Now of such a love as this he says, 1. That it is fair; "How fair is thy love, my sister, my spouse!" the titles and characters he gives her, have been already explained; it was proper to repeat them here, that, whilst he was commending her love, he might show his own; and assure her of the relation she stood in to him, and that he had an undoubted right to the affections of her heart: he here says, that her love to him was fair, that is lovely, delightful, grateful, and acceptable; and it appears to be exceeding well-pleasing to him; for those persons, he declares, are the objects of his love, to whom he manifests himself in a way of special grace and favour; he overrules all things here for their good; he gives them more grace, has prepared glory for them, and will preserve them safe unto it: not that their love is the meritorious and procuring cause of all this, nor the condition of their enjoying it; for his love to them has resolved all these things for them beforehand, and is the cause of theirs; but when it is wrought in their souls, and discovers itself to him, he is pleased to show by those instances of his grace, how fair and lovely it is in his sight. 2. He says, that it is "better than wine:" he here asserts the same of her love, which she had of his, in chap. i. 2. Christ and the church, in this Song, do frequently gather up each others words, striving, as it were, to outdo each other in their expressions of love; but Christ will in no wise come behind, and be outdone by his church and people; though it may well be wondered at, that Christ should have the same to say of our love, as we have of his; yet so it is: he here declares, it is "better than wine," that is, more grateful and pleasant, more refreshing and reviving; "wine makes glad the heart of man," Psalm civ. 15; but it cannot cheer, and make glad the heart of man, more than a sinner's love does the heart of Christ: wine was used in feasts, and counted a principal part thereof; therefore the "house of feasting" was called the "house of drinking," that is, wine, Eccles. vii. 2; the feast which the rich Pharisee made for Christ, was not, as one[p] well observes, thought so much of by him, nor half so entertaining to him, as the love which the poor woman showed him: wine was used in the legal sacrifices; but the wine of legal sacrifices, or any external performance, is not so valued by Christ as a sinner's love is; and indeed no duties or performances whatever are acceptable to him, unless love be the inward principle from whence they flow, and by which they are acted. 3. He sets off the greatness and excellency of it, by using a word of the plural number; "How fair are thy loves,[q] how much better are thy loves," &c., which may be expressive of the several actings of it towards him, for it discovers itself in various ways: and also of the several fruits which accompany or spring from it; all which serve for the greater commendation of it. 4. The manner of the expressions, which is by way of interrogation and admiration; "How fair! &c., how much better!" &c., as if it could not be well expressed, how fair and lovely it was; which is an evidence of the valuableness of it, or at least an indication how much Christ esteemed it; Christ's love has its heights and depths, and lengths and breadths: and to hear souls speak af-

---

° Λιπαρα παρ αυχενα σειετ εθειρα, Theocrit. Idyll. 5. Cæsariem effusa nitidam per candida colla, Virgil. Georgic. 1. 4. v. 337. Comæ per levia colla fluentes, propert. l. 2. eleg 3. v. 13. P Durham in loc. q דודיך amores tui, Pagninus, Montarus, &c.

ter such a manner, concerning that, need not to be wondered at; but to hear Christ express himself after this manner, concerning ours, is strange and surprising.

II. Her ointments are next commended, and the smell of them: in chap. i. 3, we read of Christ's ointments, here of the church's; in both places one and the same thing is intended, namely, the graces of the Spirit; why these are called ointments, have been there shown. These ointments, or graces of the Spirit, are first Christ's and then the church's: the head is first anointed with them, and then the members; he without measure, but they in measure; which being poured forth upon them, and they anointed with them, the smell of them is exceeding grateful to him: the smell of these ointments intends the actings and exercises of grace upon him; which are very delightful to him, and preferred by him to all spices, even to all that were used in the holy anointing oil, Exod. xxx. 23, 24; that was not so valuable as this "anointing which teacheth all things;" nor the smell of that so much esteemed by Christ, as this is.

Verse 11. *Thy lips, O my spouse! drop as the honey-comb: honey and milk are under thy tongue; and the smell of thy garments is like the smell of Lebanon.*

CHRIST having declared, in the two former verses, how much his heart was taken with the faith and love of his church, and delighted with the smell of her ointments, here, with pleasure, takes notice of her mellifluous language, and sweet-smelling dress. Two things are here commended in her;

I. The sweetness of her speech.
II. The smell of her garments.

I. The sweetness of her speech: Christ's heart was not only ravished with her sparkling eye and dazzling chain, but also with her charming lips and graceful language; "Thy lips, O my spouse! drop as the honey-comb," &c., her lips dropped things for matter like the honey-comb; and these things in such a manner as the honey-comb does: so the speech of persons, flowing from the mouth and tongue, is said to be sweeter than the honey-comb;[r] and lovers are said to be sweeter to one another than the sweet honey.[s]

First. Things for matter like the honey-comb; "Pleasant words," says Solomon, Prov. xviii. 24, "are as an honey-comb, sweet to the soul, and health to the bones." Such pleasant words, which are as the honey-comb, drop from the church's, and from every believer's lips. 1. In prayer; so the Targum expounds these words of the priest's lips, dropping as the honey-comb, when they prayed in the holy court. The believer oftentimes drops things in prayer; which, as they are profitable to himself and others, for the effectual, fervent, ἐνεργουμένη, the inwrought "prayer of a righteous man availeth much," James v. 16; so they are sweet, pleasant, delightful, and acceptable to Christ: "the prayer of the upright is his delight;" the prayers of the meanest believer are as delightful music in his ears, as sweet-smelling odours in his nostrils, and like the honey or honey-comb to his taste. 2. In praises: Christ has done great things for his church and people in the redemption and salvation of them; and therefore praise becomes them; it is their duty: and as this work is oftentimes pleasant to their own souls; so in discharging it, they often drop things in the praise of Christ's person and grace, which are exceeding grateful and well pleasing to him. 3. In confessing Christ's name, and owning his truths before men: this is a work exceeding necessary, and a duty highly incumbent on God's children; at every opportunity, and whenever they are called to it, they ought to do it; and as the omission of it is much resented by Christ, so the performance of it will be graciously rewarded, as appears from Matt. x. 32; thus Paul, both at Jerusalem and at Rome, and many other martyrs and confessors, have, in the behalf of Christ and his gospel, dropped words like the honey-comb. 4. In the ministry of the word: the church's lips are the ministers of the gospel, so Theodoret; whose business is to deliver, not so much "the senses of the law," which is Jarchi's note on the words, as the doctrines of the gospel: these lips drop "the wholesome words of our Lord Jesus Christ;" and not words which eat like a canker, but words, which, like the honey-comb, are "health to the bones." 5. In common conversation: the lips of the saints do frequently therein drop words pleasant and delightful; which tend to the edification of those with whom they converse, and "ministers grace to the hearers;" and so are like the honey-comb, both pleasant and profitable.

2ndly. Her lips dropped these things in such a manner as the honey comb does; 1. Freely, and without pressing or squeezing; a soul that has received the "grace of God in truth, cannot but speak of the things which he has heard and seen: being full of matter, his belly is as wine which hath no vent, and is ready to burst, like new bottles;" therefore he must speak, that he "may be refreshed:" there needs no other constraint to be laid on him, than what he feels in his own breast. 2. Gradually: the honey-comb does not pour out all at once, but by degrees; a man of grace, like the virtuous woman in Prov. xxxi. 26, opens his mouth with wisdom, and not like the fool who pours out his foolishness, and utters all his mind at once; but delivers his words with moderation and discretion, and observes proper seasons and opportunities to speak his mind: now a word fitly, prudently, and season-

---

[r] Vid. Theocrit. Idyll. 21. v. 26. 27. Homer. Iliad. l. v. 249. [s] Plauti Asinaria, act. 3. sc. 9. v. 24.

ably spoken, is like apples of gold in pictures of silver;" for as we are to walk, so are we to "talk in wisdom," both to those "that are without," and to those that are within. 3. Constantly: the honey-comb, though it drops gradually, yet it keeps constantly dropping; so a believers' speech should "be always with grace;" he should be always praying or praising, or dropping something which may tend to the magnifying of God's grace, and the good and edification of souls.

These words in general show the choiceness of a believer's discourse; that it is not any thing that is the subject of it; no common and ordinary things which he is speaking of, but what are choice and excellent; as the honey which drops from the honey-comb is esteemed the best, being what we call life-honey; as also, how much Christ's heart was taken with it, and his affections drawn by it; it had a mighty influence upon him, and strongly engaged his heart towards her; see Prov. v. 3. Now the reason why her lips dropped after this manner, was, because "honey and milk were under her tongue;" and therefore they could not well drop otherwise. The ancients had a sort of food of this mixture, called by the Greeks *meligala*,[t] and sometimes *candylos*,[u] which was the same composition: according to Galen,[w] it was not safe to take milk, particularly goat's milk, without honey; Jove is said[x] to be nursed with such a mixture: and this being very grateful to the taste, the speech of the church for pleasantness is compared to it; so Pindar[y] compares his hymn or ode to honey, mixed with milk, as being sweet and grateful; and in Plautus,[z] it is said, "your words are honey and milk:" and it may be farther observed, that such a mixture of milk and honey, with poppies in it, was given to the new married bride, when brought home to her husband;[a] which was now the case of the church. By "milk and honey," may be intended the aboundings and overflowings of grace in a believer's heart, which thereby is made like Canaan's land, "flowing with milk and honey;" now out of the abundance of this grace, received into the heart, the mouth speaks: or else, by them may be meant the doctrines of the Gospel; which may very well be compared thereunto, words sweeter than honey and milk.[b] 1st. To honey. 1. The Gospel is gathered out of the choice flowers of the scriptures: the ministers of it, "who labour in the word and doctrine;" are the bees, who come laden with the honey of the Gospel, into the hive of the church, by which souls are delighted and refreshed. 2. It is like to honey for its sweetness: thus David could say, Psalm cxix. 103, by experience, "How sweet are thy words unto my taste! yea, sweeter than honey to my mouth:" a gracious soul, who feeds on the Gospel, and tastes the sweetness of it, finds it, as Ezekiel did his roll, "like honey for sweetness" in his mouth; and so it is always thus grateful to a spiritual man, who has a proper gust and relish of it. 3. Like honey, it is of a nourishing nature: honey was not only the food of babes, but of grown persons, as appears from Isa. vii. 15, 22; the Gospel has in it food both for children and for strong men, and that which is exceeding nourishing to both. 4. Like the honey which Jonathan ate of, it enlightens the eyes: when the Spirit of God introduces it into a sinner's heart, it gives light there, as the psalmist says, Psalm cxix. 130, "the entrance of thy words giveth light;" it gives light into a man's self, into his lost and miserable state by nature; it gives light into the impurity of his heart, and the imperfection of his obedience; it gives light into the person, grace, and righteousness of Christ; and is an instrument, in the Spirit's hands, "to guide his feet in the way of peace." 5. It is like the honey the Israelites sucked out of the rock in the wilderness: the rock is Christ, from whence the honey of the Gospel flows; he is the Author, and he is the Subject of it, Or, 6. It is like the honey Samson found in the carcase of the lion: Christ is the "lion of the tribe of Judah;" in whose slain body and precious blood, the honey of Gospel-grace is to be found by poor sinners, who feed upon it.

2ndly. As the Gospel may be compared to honey, so likewise to milk; it is called the "sincere milk of the word:" which is not mixed and blended with human doctrines, but is free from such adulterations; and so is exceeding profitable, and no ways hurtful to the souls of men. 1. It may be compared to milk, because it is easy of digestion, and therefore proper food for new-born babes: hence the apostle fed the Corinthians with the milk of the word, and not with the strong meat thereof; because they were not as yet able to bear it, could not digest it; but the plainer and more easy truths of the Gospel are like milk, easy of digestion to souls that are born again; though even these to a natural man are hard sayings, which he cannot bear. 2. Like milk, it is very nourishing; Christ's new-born babes grow hereby, being "nourished up in the words of faith, and of good doctrine." 3. Milk is of a cooling nature, and useful in abating the violence of inflammations;[c] so the gospel, being applied by the Spirit to a poor sinner, who has been under a work of the law, represses the violence of those inflammations raised in his conscience, by a fiery law's working wrath there; which is wonderfully allayed by the milk of the Gospel,

---

[t] Vid. Cohen de Lara, Ir David, p. 52. the word is used in T. Hieros. Challah, fol. 57. 4.　[u] Athen. Deipnosophist. l. 1. c. 8. p. 9. and l. 14. c 13. p. 644. Suidas in voce Κανδυλοος. Aristoph. Pax. and Florent. Christian. in ib. p. 633.　[w] Lib. de Bono Sapore, c. 4.　[x] Lactant. de Fals. Relig. l. 1. c. 22.　[y] Nemea, ode 3. p. 10, 11.　[z] Truculent. act. 1. sc. 2. v. 75, 76.　[a] Nec pigeat tritum niveo cum lacte papaver, &c. Ovid. Fasti, l. 4. v. 149. 150.　[b] Vid. T. Bab. Chagigah. fol. 13. 1.　[c] Fernel. Method. Medend. l. 5. c. 27.

and the application of the exceeding great and precious promises of it, which lead the soul to the person, blood, and righteousness of Jesus Christ. 4. Milk is esteemed useful to persons in consumptions, and therefore a milky diet is usually recommended to them; sin is a wasting and consuming distemper, which is only cured by bringing the milk of the Gospel: which, when powerfully applied by the Spirit of God, is " the savour of life unto life;" and will not only recover a person that is far gone, and in the most declining condition, but also restore him from death itself.

Now when these are said to be under her tongue, it intends either, 1. That they were in her heart; so Psal lxvi. 17, " he was exalted with my tongue," or he was exalted under my tongue, that is, in my heart; it was in my heart to exalt him, I purposed and designed it: so here " honey and milk are under thy tongue," that is, they are in thy heart; it is one thing to have a notion of the Gospel in our heads, and another thing to have it in our hearts by a comfortable experience. 2. It supposes that she tasted the sweetness of those truths; she rolled them as a sweet morsel under her tongue, as Job xx. 12; resolving to have all the pleasure and satisfaction which might arise from thence. 3. That these were the constant subject of her meditation, Psal. x. 7; having tasted a sweetness in them, which drew her affections to them, her thoughts were always employed about them. 4. That she was always ready to speak of them at suitable times, and on proper occasions, having them under her tongue. 5. This shows the difference there is between a carnal, Christless sinner, and a true believer; the one has " the poison of asps under his lips," Rom. iii. 13, and the other " honey and milk under his tongue;" the speech of the one is poisonous and infectious, and the language of the other sweet and edifying; so that as by their words they shall be justified, by their words also they may be known; their speech bewrays them, and declares to what company they belong.

II. The second thing commended in her, is the smell of her garments; the ancients used to scent their garments; Calypso gave to Ulysses sweet-smelling garments;[d] " and the smell of thy garments is like the smell of Lebanon:" in Lebanon grew many odoriferous trees, which did emit a fragrant smell to passers by, hence called " sweet-smelling Lebanon;"[e] so the graces of God's people are said to smell as Lebanon, Hosea xiv. 6. By her garments here may be meant, 1. The garments of salvation, and the robe of Christ's righteousness. Christ's garments are said to " smell of myrrh, aloes, and cassia;" now these very garments are put upon the believer, so that it is no wonder his garments smell like Lebanon; in these believers appear before God, as Jacob did before his father, in the garments of his elder brother Esau, and are in his nostrils a sweet smelling savour; for the smell of their raiment to him is like " the smell of a field which the Lord hath blessed;" he is exceeding well pleased with it, and with them in it. Christ smells a sweet odour, even in those garments which he himself has wrought out, and clothed his people with. Or else, 2. By them we may understand the outward conversation-garments of the saints; which are wholesome and savoury, and not like the conversation of the wicked, filthy, of an ill-smell, nauseous and infectious; when works go along with words, and practice with profession; when with lips dropping like the honey-comb, the sweet-smelling garment of a Gospel conversation is joined, how does it adorn a Christian, and render him lovely and acceptable, and causes his smell to be as that of Lebanon? Some Jewish writers[f] refer these garments to the sacerdotal garments of the priests: which were certainly typical of those, which Christ, as our high-priest, wears, and with which he clothes his people.

Verse 12. *A garden inclosed is my sister*, my *spouse; a spring shut up, a fountain sealed.*

CHRIST, having admired his church's faith and love, her language, and her dress; proceeds to give farther commendations of her, and makes use of new metaphors to describe her by; in which he represents her as a well-watered and fruitful garden.

First. He says, she is " a garden enclosed:" the titles he gives her, " my sister, my spouse," have been explained in ver. 8, 9. I shall only here enquire why she is called a garden, and that an enclosed one. And she is said to be a garden, 1. Because a garden is a piece of ground distinguished and separated from others for the owner's use: the church of Christ is distinguished and separated from others by electing and redeeming grace; by efficacious calling grace saints are also made to differ from others, and do in their lives and conversation live separate from them; and being set apart for God's own use, service, and glory, are a peculiar people to himself. 2. In a garden is a variety of flowers, herbs, and plants: in Christ's church are many members, and those of different sorts; they have gifts differing from one another, and grace also; some have greater gifts, and larger measures of grace than others have; but in them all there are many of those sweet flowers and precious plants. 3. In a garden, flowers, herbs, and plants, do not grow up naturally of themselves, but are either set or sown; nothing but weeds grow up of themselves; so in Christ's garden, the church, and in the members of it, the graces of the Spirit do not grow up of themselves; they are sown, planted, and raised up by the Spirit of God;

---

[d] Ειματα θυωδεα, Homer. Odyss. 5. v. 264. and 21. v. 52. Ητε μυρων εμπνοι αμπεχουσι, Posidippus apud Athen. Deipnosophist. l. 13. c. 7. p. 596.

[e] Λιβανω θυοεντος, Museus de Hero. &c. v. 48.

[f] Vid. Targum and R. Sol. Jarchium in loc. and Midrash in Mercer. in loc.

for in their hearts naturally grow nothing but the weeds of sin and corruption. 4. The ground must be dug and prepared for the setting of plants and herbs therein: the hearts of God's people before conversion are like fallow-ground; God is the husbandman, and they are his husbandry, this ground must be dunged, as well as dug, before it becomes good ground, or ever these flowers, herbs, and plants will grow there, which method Christ takes with his garden, and the several parts thereof. 5. To keep a garden in order, requires a deal of labour and care; the stones must be gathered out, the plants must be watered, the trees pruned, the ground dunged, and the fences kept up: all this, and much more, does Christ to his garden, the church; he gathers out those things which offend and hinder the growth of his plants; he watches over them night and day, and waters them every moment; he lops off the fruitless branches, and prunes those that are fruitful, that they may bring forth more fruit, and keep up the fences thereof, that " the wild boar of the forest" may not enter in, and destroy his garden. 6. Gardens are places where persons delight to walk: Christ walks in his garden, the church; in the midst of his golden candlesticks; you frequently hear of him in this song, that " he is gone down into his garden, to feed" there, and " to gather lilies;" nay, he not only takes his walks, but takes up his residence in his church. 7. A garden is usually but a small piece of ground; and so is Christ's church, in comparison of the wilderness and waste places of the world; it is a little flock, a small remnant, a few that shall be saved. 8. A fruitful and pleasant place; and so is the church, when compared with the world, " which lieth in wickedness," and is overrun with the briars and thorns of sin.

Also the church is said to be a garden enclosed, 1. For distinction-sake: the church is by God distinguished from others; the fence with which it is enclosed, and by which it is made to differ from others, is the free, special, and distinguishing grace of God. 2. For protection: Christ's church, as it is distinguished by God's grace, so it is protected by his power; he is " a wall of fire round about it, and the glory in the midst of it;" a noble fence indeed! a glorious enclosure! Jerusalem with all its mountains, and Zion with all its bulwarks, were not so well fenced as this. 3. For secrecy: it is hidden from, and is not seen and known by the world; it is like a garden that is walled around, and closely locked and barred,[g] whose flowers emit a sweet and fragrant odour, but are not seen; the saints, though they are exceeding useful in the world, yet are not known by the world; but are hid and shut up till the resurrection-morn, when it shall appear what they really are, for at present it does not. 4. It is compared to a garden enclosed, or locked and barred; for so the word[h] properly signifies, because it is not pervious to every one, neither ought it to be; every one has not a right to enter there, it should remain enclosed, bolted, and barred, to all but those who believe in Christ; none ought to walk here but those who come in at the right door, Christ Jesus; and every one that climbs up, and gets into this garden any other way, is reckoned by Christ as a thief and a robber. 5. It is said to be a garden inclosed or locked up, because it is only for Christ's use; therefore, in ver. 16, she desires him to " come into his garden, and eat his pleasant fruit;" for this garden is only his, and the fruits of it for his use alone: in chap. v. 1, agreeable to her request, he tells her, that he was come into his garden, had gathered the fruits of it, and had eaten; it being his sole property, which others had no right unto, he keeps it enclosed, locked, and bolted. The allusion perhaps is to a garden near Jerusalem, which Adrichomius[i] calls *hortus regius*, the *king's garden*, which was shut up, and was only for his use and pleasure; which is much more likely than what Mr. Maundrel relates,[k] that at a little distance from Bethlehem, are pools of water; and below those runs a narrow, rocky valley, enclosed on both sides with high mountains; which the friars will have to be the enclosed garden alluded to.

Secondly. He says that she is " a spring shut up, and a fountain sealed;" I put these together, because they seem to intend much one and the same thing; though perhaps the one may be more strongly expressive of the church's fulness and excellency than the other; a fountain may intimate a larger qantity of water than a spring, and sealing signify a stronger security than bare shutting; but are both designed to inform us, that Christ's garden was well watered, and that there is no danger of the herbs, flowers, and plants withering and perishing,

The Septuagint render the first of these expressions as before, κῆπος κεκλεισμένος, " a garden enclosed," or shut up; and so do the Vulgate Latin and Tigurine Versions, reading גנ for גל; Cocceius translates, " a heap locked up:" and thinks the church is compared to a heap of spices or fruits, which are locked up in a private place, that they may not be spoiled nor stolen away from the owner: Christ's church congregated together is a heap, but not a confused one; it is like an heap of spice or fruit laid in order; nor is it a heap of anything, but of sweet-smelling spices and pleasant fruits, such as are mentioned in ver. 13, 14; to which add also, it is an heap that is valued and cared for, and therefore kept up safe under lock

---

[g] Vid. R. Aben Ezram in loc. [h] נעל clausit, obseravit, pessulurs, obdidit, buxtorf. [i] Hortus regius, qui hortus conclusus dicitur; hortus erat in suburbanis Jerusalem muris undique septus and obfirmatus; atque sicut paradisus arborum, fructicum, herbarum, aromatum, florum, fructuumque ub- ertate amœnus; mulcendisque ac fovendis sensibus conveniens, and ad scressus voluptuarios idoneus; in quo erat inclytus ille sons Rogel and lapis Zoeleth, &c. Adrichomii Theatrum Terræ Sanctæ, p. 170. l. Vid. 2 Sam. xvii. 17. 2 Kings xxv. 4. [k] Journey from Aleppo, &c. p. 89. edit. 7.

and key. The other version of "a spring shut up," is more usually received and acknowledged, both by Jewish[1] and Christian Expositors, which also our Translators follow.

Now the church is said to be a spring and a fountain from whence waters flow, to water all the plants in Christ's garden; which are either, 1. The graces of the Spirit, which are in her as "a well, and rivers of living water, springing up unto eternal life," John iv. 14, and vii. 38, 39; and are called waters, because they are of a fructifying and reviving nature; the plants in Christ's garden being watered with these, revive and lift up their heads, and become green, flourishing, and fruitful; the souls of God's children drinking them in, and being filled with them, become like a watered garden, whose springs fail not. Or else, 2. The doctrines of the Gospel: the Gospel is thought to be the fountain, spoken of in Joel iii. 18, which should "come forth of the house of the Lord, and water the valley of Shittim;" it is with its gracious truths that the faithful ministers of the Gospel water Christ's garden; the Spirit of grace does it efficaciously, they do it ministerially; Paul plants, and Apollos waters, but God gives the increase; the doctrines of grace oftentimes flow in the ministry of the word, like floods of water upon the dry and parched ground, which soften, moisten, and make it fruitful; souls are refreshed, grow, and flourish thereby; their graces are revived, quickened, and drawn forth into exercise, and every thing looks gay and beautiful, as in a fruitful and pleasant garden. Now we are not to suppose that the church is so properly this spring or fountain, as Christ and his Spirit are; she has not an indeficient supply in herself, she receives all from another; but because of the abundance of grace and the means of it, which Christ is pleased to grant unto his church, therefore he calls her a spring and fountain; though she has grace enough to ascribe all the glory to him, and own him to be the alone spring and fountain from whence she is supplied, as in ver. 15, will be made more manifestly to appear.

Moreover the church is said to be "a spring shut up, a fountain sealed;" springs and wells of water being highly esteemed, and much valued in those hot countries, were highly preserved; they used to roll a large stone at the mouth of them, and, for farther security, seal it; as that stone was which was laid at the mouth of the lions' den, in which Daniel was cast: and that at the sepulchre in which Christ was buried: now these fountains were shut up and sealed, not only that the waters might not be bemudded by beasts, but also that they might not be converted to the use of others; thus it is reported, that among the Persians,[m] were such fountains that only the king and his eldest son might drink of; it being a capital punishment for any others to do so: and perhaps Solomon might have such a spring and fountain in his garden, which was shut up and sealed, and kept for his own private use, to which the allusion is here made; either at Jerusalem, or at Ethan, where he had a pleasure-house; which, for the delicate gardens, walks, and fountains, and the fruitfulness of the place, he took great delight in:[n] and near the pools at some distance from Bethlehem, supposed to be his, is a fountain, which the friars will have to be the sealed fountain, here alluded to; and to confirm which, they pretend a tradition, that Solomon shut up these springs and kept the door of them sealed with his signet, to preserve the waters for his own drinking: and Mr. Maundrel,[o] who saw them, says, it was not difficult to secure them; they rising under ground, and having no avenue to them, but by a little hole, like to the mouth of a narrow well. And if we apply this to the doctrine of the Gospel, it intends, 1. The secrecy and hiddenness of them to the men of the world; "for if our Gospel be hid, it is hid to them that are lost, whom the god of this world hath blinded," says the apostle, in 2 Cor. iv. 3, 4: it is an hidden Gospel to some, a book sealed both to the learned and unlearned, who are in a carnal and unconverted state; from many it is hidden, as to the external ministry of it; and to others it remains a secret, in the midst of the clearest light, and most powerful ministrations of it; it is shut up in parables, and appears to be nothing else but dark sayings to a mere natural man. 2. That they are peculiarly intended and designed for the elect of God: it is for their sakes he has sent it into the world; and for their sakes he will continue to keep it there, maugre all opposition, until every one of them are called by powerful and efficacious grace; "I endure all things," says the apostle, 2 Tim. ii. 10, "for the elect's sake, that they may also obtain the salvation, which is in Christ Jesus, with eternal glory;" that is, I preach the Gospel; and in doing it, undergo all the sufferings I do, purely upon their account; that salvation may be brought unto them, and they brought at last into the eternal possession of it; and as it is sent into, and continued in the world for their sakes, so it is only blessed to them for conversion and consolation; though the Gospel is preached to others, as well as to them, yet it does not become profitable to them, because it is not mixed with faith by them; for whilst it is the "savour of life unto life" to some, it is the "savour of death unto death" to others; and though these waters of Gospel-doctrines flow to, and fall upon others; yet is but like water that falls upon a rock, that quickly glides away, and makes no impression; and not like streams of water which run about the plants, and soak to the very root. The elect of God are only savingly converted,

---

[1] R. Sol. Jarchi, R. Aben Ezra in loc. and R. David Kimchi in lib. Shorosh. rad. נצר. — [m] Athen. Deipnosophist. l. 12. c. 2. p. 515. — [n] Joseph. Antiquitat. l. 8. c. 8. 7. 3. — [o] Journey from Aleppo, p. 88, 89.

refreshed, and comforted by Gospel-doctrines; they are peculiarly designed for them, and eminently blessed to them; they are only for their use, and are to them "a spring shut up, and a fountain sealed."

And if we apply it to the grace of the Spirit, it denotes, 1. That it is hidden, unknown, and is not communicated to any but to the elect of God: the natural man knows not the things of the Spirit, namely, the grace of the Spirit in regeneration and effectual vocation; these things are mysteries to him; he is a stranger to them, and unacquainted with them; they are only communicated to, and wrought in those to whom God would make known the exceeding riches of his grace: thus things are said to be shut and sealed up, which are kept secret and hidden, and are not conveyed to the knowledge of persons, as in Esther viii. 16, Dan. xii. 4--9. 2. That it is safe and secure: the grace of God's people is shut up and sealed; it can never be taken away from them; their life, and all their grace, and the fulness of it, "are hid with Christ in God; and what is given forth unto them, and wrought in them, is an immortal seed, and that good part which cannot be taken away. 3. It may intend the confirmation of it to the saints; so things are said to be sealed, when they are ratified, confirmed, and made sure; grace and glory are both so to the saints; the Spirit is the author of their grace, and the earnest and pledge of their glory, by whom they are "sealed unto the day of redemption." 4. It may signify Christ's special property in his church, and her inviolable chastity to him; and this I take to be the most proper sense of all these expressions; she is "a garden enclosed, a spring shut up, a fountain sealed;" she is Christ's garden and none but his; Christ's spring and fountain, to which none has a right but himself; she is his spouse and bride, and no other's; and being espoused unto him, as a chaste virgin, by mighty grace is kept so. The Jewish writers[p] generally understand it of the modesty and chastity of the daughters of Israel; and this sense seems to be abundantly confirmed from Prov. v. 15—18. "Drink waters out of thine own cistern, and running waters out of thine own well," &c. Let thy fountain be blessed, and rejoice with the wife of thy youth.

Ver. 13, 14. *Thy plants are an orchard of pomegranates, with pleasant fruits, camphire with spikenard. Spikenard and saffron, calamus and cinnamon, with all trees of frankincense, myrrh and aloes, with all the chief spices.*

CHRIST having compared his church to a garden, and observed that it was well watered, having in it a spring and fountain; he proceeds to show the fruitfulness of it, that it abounded with the choicest trees, the most pleasant fruits, and the chief of spices. In explaining these words, it will be proper,

I. To inquire what are intended by the church's plants.

II. Why these plants are said to be "an orchard of pomegranates."

III. Take notice of the several trees, fruits, and spices here mentioned, and what may be meant by them.

I. Who are meant by the church's plants. The Targum and Jarchi expound of the young men in Israel; and it is not unusual in scripture to call children plants; see Psalm cxxviii. 3, and cxliv. 12; therefore, by her plants, may be intended the members of the church, her children, young converts, believers in Christ, who are "planted in the house of the Lord, and flourish in the courts of our God;" these are not mere education plants, who spring up in the churches, and join themselves to them, because their parents did; and espouse religion, because they were brought up in it: these are not mere outward profession-plants, who have a name to live, and are dead; have lamps, but no oil in their lamps; and have a form of godliness, but deny the power thereof: such plants as these are fruitless ones; they are like the barren fig-tree, from which three years successively fruit was sought, but none found; if ever there was any appearance of fruit on them, it never came to any thing, but withered away; and whatsoever fruit they do bring forth it is to themselves, and not to God: like Israel, of whom it is said, Hosea x. 1, that he is "an empty vine, and brings forth fruit to himself;" and the reason of this is because they have not the root of the matter in them; nor are they engrafted into, and rooted in Christ Jesus; and therefore are like the stony ground-hearers, who heard and received the word with joy, but did not last long, because they had no root in themselves; and such being none of the Father's planting, shall be plucked up, according to what Christ says, Matt. xv. 13, "Every plant which my heavenly Father hath not planted, shall be rooted up;" and shall be bundled together, as fit fuel for the fire, like the unfruitful and withered branches, or like the tares in the end of the world, but these plants in the text are such who, 1. Are by divine grace transplanted from the wilderness of the world; they are Christ's vines, which he brings out of Egypt; his fir and myrtle trees, which he causes to spring up instead of briars and thorns; these he either takes out of the wilderness, or else makes it a fruitful garden by planting them there; he calls them out of the world, and translates them into his own kingdom, whereby he enlarges his church, and of a garden makes it an orchard. 2. Who have the grace of the Spirit planted in their hearts; who works in them every sort of grace, which he raises, cherishes,

---

[p] Targum, R. Sol, Jarchi, and R. Aben Ezra in loc. T. B. Yoma, fol. 75. apud Wagenseil. Sotah, p. 240. Seder Tephillot, fol. 203. 1. ed Basil. Addison's present state of the Jews, c. 5. p. 50.

and at last brings to perfection. 3. Who are engrafted into Christ Jesus: by nature they belong to, and grow upon the wild olive: but are by grace broken off from that, and are engrafted into the true olive, Christ Jesus; they are planted into the likeness of his death, and into the likeness of his resurrection, and so receive the benefits of both; they abide in him, as the branch in the vine, and receiving sap and nourishment from him, become fruitful souls. 4. They are such who have received the ingrafted word; it has been planted in them, and powerfully impressed upon them; they have received it in the love of it; it has effectually wrought in them, and brought forth fruit in them from the very day they heard and received it. 5. Such as these who are transplanted from the wilderness of the world, and are planted in Christ, and have had his word and grace planted in their souls, have a right to be planted ministerially in his church; and being planted there, will grow and flourish. Now such plants as these are choice and select ones; they are plants of renown, and pleasant ones to God and Christ; they are planted in a fruitful soil, and by rivers of water, therefore their leaf is always green; neither do they cease from yielding fruit; hence they shall never be plucked up; neither sin, nor Satan, nor the world can do it; and Christ Jesus never will; for they are his Father's planting, in whom he is, and will be glorified, and then is he so, when they bring forth much fruit.

II. These plants are said to be an orchard, or like unto an orchard of pomegranates. The word for plants, is by the Cabalistic doctors,[q] rendered waterings or rivulets; which, being derived, make her a garden of pomegranates, as full as an orchard is of them: and it may be rendered gardens;[r] particular churches, which make an orchard, or are like one; even a paradise, as the word is rendered by the Septuagint, and in other versions;[s] it is generally thought to be a Persiac word; see Nehem. ii. 8, but Hillerus[t] derives it from פרד, to separate; it being a garden separate and enclosed, as before; one like Eden's garden, exceeding pleasant and delightful; and not like an orchard of any sort of trees, but of pomegranates; of which there was plenty in the land of Canaan; called "a land of pomegranates," Deut. viii. 8; many places in it had their names from thence, Josh. xv. 32, and xix. 13, and xxi. 24. And the church,[u] with her plants, may be called so, in allusion to the garden of Eden, the earthly paradise of our first parents; where the "Lord God made to grow every tree that was pleasant to the sight, and good for food;" in the midst of it stood the tree of life, and out of it went a river to water all the garden, and was on all accounts exceeding pleasant and delightful: in Christ's garden, the church, are planted all manner of trees of righteousness, which are both pleasant and profitable; in the midst of this paradise of God, stands the tree of life, Christ Jesus: but with this difference from the tree of life in Eden's garden; for Adam might not put forth his hand, and take of that; but of this, whosoever will, may pluck and eat, and happy is every one that does so: here runs a river of boundless love and grace, the streams whereof water and refresh all the plants herein, and upon all accounts is an Eden of pleasure, a paradise which Christ has made for his own pleasure and delight,[w] and for that reason bears this name: but these plants are not only said to be an orchard, but an orchard or paradise of pomegranates, that is, in which pomegranates grew in great plenty. The church, like the land of Canaan, is a land or orchard of pomegranates; and the church's plants, believers in Christ, who are planted and grow there, may be compared to pomegranates, that is, not to the fruit and shell, as in ver. 3, but to the trees, 1, Because there are various sorts of them,[x] which bear fruit differing from each other; which may denote the difference there is in saints, by reason of their gifts and graces; they have grace and gifts differing from each other; one has more grace and larger gifts than other's have; they are not all of an equal size and bigness; they have not all a like measure of the Spirit, and yet they are all pomegranates, trees of righteousness, of the right planting. 2. Pomegranate trees in some countries are very large; and so they were in the land of Canaan, as appears from 1 Sam. xiv. 2, and perhaps may here denote such who excel others in gifts and grace; who are officers in churches, and are set over others in and by the Lord; as by other trees, fruits, and spices, after mentioned, may be intended lesser saints, who are of a lower form in the church of Christ. 3. They are very fruitful trees: the fruit they bear, as it is full of a delightful juice, so of grains or kernels; which may denote the saints being full of grace, and all the fruits of righteousness and good works, as the Targum and Jarchi observes here. 4. They grow up straight and upright, and so denote the saints uprightness, both in heart and life; they are men of upright hearts, and of upright conversations; are looking upwards to, and growing up into their Head, Christ Jesus. 5. They do not grow any where, in any soil; the wilderness, through which

---

[q] Lexic. Cabal. p. 237. [r] Vid. Guisium in Misn. Shevilth, c. 2. s. 2. [s] פרדס παράδεισος, Sept. paradisus, Pagninus, Montanus, Tigurine version, Cocceius, Marckius, Michaelis. [t] Onomastic, Sacr. p. 291.
[u] Possunt hæc etiam in ecclesia intilligi, ut ea melius accipiamus tanquam prophetica indicia precedentia futurorum; paradisum scilicet ipsani ecclesiam. sicut de illa legitur in Cantico Canticorum; quatuor autem paradisi flumina, quatuor evangelia; ligna fructifera, Sanctos; fructus outem eorum, opera eorum; lignum vitæ, Sanctum Sanctorum, utique Christum: lignum scientiæ boni and mali, proprium voluntatis arbitrium. Aug. de Civit. Dei, l. 13. c. 21. [w] פרדס παράδεισος, paradisus, pomarium, voluptatis and amœnitatis causa consitum, Buxtorf. [x] Vid. Plin. l. 13. c. 19.

the Israelites travelled, could not furnish them with any, though the land of Canaan could when they came thither; these plants or trees of righteousness, do not grow anywhere; they are not to be found every where; they grow in Christ's garden; in his house they are planted, and in his courts they flourish.

III. Here are several other trees, fruits, and spices, which are said to be in this garden or orchard; for it is added, with all pleasant fruits; that is, whatsoever is valuable, precious, and desirable, such as those after mentioned; as camphire with spikenard; both these have been observed in chap. i. 12, 14, but are here mentioned in the plural number, *cypresses*, or *cyprusses with nards;*[y] the camphire, or cypress, on the account of its fruits or berries; and the spikenard, because there are various sorts of it, as *nardus Italica, nardus Celtica*, and *nardus Indica*, which last is the right spikenard; and it may be, because the leaves which grow out of the root, are like a bunch of ears of corn: saffron: it is no where else mentioned in scripture: we call it by this name from the *Arabic, zaffran;* it is called so on account of its yellow and golden colour; its nature and usefulness are well known among us; according to Schindler,[z] it seems to have been read *carcos*, the same with *crocus*, which has its name from *Corycus*,[a] a mountain in Cilicia; so Pliny, lib. 21, c. 6, where it grew, and was the best: it is properly joined with spikenard, since itself is a spice, and is called *spica Cilissa;*[b] it bears a blue flower, in the midst of which are three stylets, or little threads, of a fine red colour, which are what is called saffron: *calamus and cinnamon;* both these were ingredients in the holy anointing oil, Exod. xxx. 23; both grow in India, and in Arabia,[c] and in Ethiopia; *calamus* is the sweet cane, mentioned in Isa. xliii. 24; it grows in India and Arabia; and is said to scent the air, where and while it is growing, with a fragrant smell; and cinnamon is the middlemost bark of a tree that grows in Ceylon in the East Indies; it is mentioned in Prov. vii. 17, as the harlot's perfume, and in Rev. xviii. 13, as part of the wares or merchandise of the whore of Babylon: some say,[d] what we call cinnamon is the cassia of the ancients; Herodotus[e] fabulously relates, what, from the Phœnicians, is called cinnamon, are stalks or barks, which the Arabs say, are found in the nests of certain birds. "With all trees of frankincense, myrrh;" frankincense chiefly grew in one of the Arabias, hence called *thurifera;*[f] and is said to come out of Syria;[g] it was used in the holy perfume, as was myrrh in the anointing oil, Exod. xxx. 23—34, which is a gum, from a shrub in Arabia, of a bitter taste, but fragrant; and with both these the church is said to be perfumed, chap. iii. 6, and aloes; either the ling-aloes, so the Targum here, of which mention is made in Numb. xxiv. 6, called *agallochium*, an aromatic plant, which grows in India and Arabia, and is of a sweet odour, as Isidore[h] says; or the herb aloes, which is of a bitter taste, but of a sweet smell, and with which garments were perfumed, Psalm xlv. 8, Prov. vii. 17; together with all chief spices, or precious ones; Solomon's gardens might be furnished with these from Arabia Felix, where all sorts of spices grew, hence called *aromatifera*, the spice country:[i] and be they what they will, they are all to be found in Christ's garden, or what is answerable to them. Now by these may be meant, the several graces of the Spirit, which are to be found in all those who are plants or members in Christ's church; which are called by these names, and compared to these fruits, herbs, and spices. 1. Because the graces of the Spirit are many, and therefore many herbs and spices are mentioned; see Gal. v. 22. 2. They are various, of different sorts; for as it makes for the pleasantness of a garden or orchard to have many trees, plants, herbs, and flowers, so to have them of different sorts; for if there were never so many, and all of one sort, it would not be so delightful: the church of Christ, and believers in Christ, as they have many, so they have various graces; there are faith, hope, love, &c.; faith is a grace differing from hope, and hope differs from faith, and love from them both. 3. They are rare and excellent; the herbs and spices here mentioned, such as spikenard, saffron, camphire, cinnamon, &c., are not to be found everywhere: they do not grow in every garden; they are very rarely to be met with: the graces of the Spirit do not grow any where, in any heart; there are but few that have them; they are exceeding rare, valuable, and precious. 4. These herbs and spices are all of them of a sweet smell: and so are the graces of the Spirit to Christ; they are a sweet perfume to him; the smell of these ointments is preferred by him to all spices, in verse 10. 5. Some of these herbs and plants cheer the heart,[k] and revive the spirits, as saffron, cinnamon, and camphire: the Spirit of God, in his operations of grace, and in exciting and drawing forth grace into exercise, wonderfully cheers our hearts, revives our spirits, and keeps us from fainting and swooning fits: in the multitude of our thoughts within us, his comforts delight our souls. 6. Some of them preserve from putrefaction, as myrrh and aloes; and therefore were used in embalming dead bodies, John xix. 39, the grace of the Spirit is of such a nature;

---

[y] So Junius and Tremellius, Piscator. [z] Lexic. Pentaglott. col. 910. [a] Corycii pressura croci, Lucan. Pharsal. l. 9. v. 809. Hic Cilico crocus editus arvo, Virgil. Culex. [b] Ovid. Fast. l. 1. v. 76. in Ibim. v. 200. Propert. l. 4. eleg. 6. v. 74. [c] Plin. l. 12. c. 19, 22. Strabo, l. 15. p. 478. Herodot. Thalia, c. 107. Cinnamomi and multi pastor odoris Arabs, Propert. l. 4. eleg. 13. v. 8. Vet. Ling. Ind. s. 10. p. 216. c. 111. Vid. Plin. l. 12. c. 19. [d] Vid. Reland. de [e] Thalia, five l. 3. [f] Plin. l. 12. c. 14. [g] Hermippus apud Athen. Deipnosophist. l. 1. c. 21. p. 27. [h] Origin. l. 17. c. 8. [i] Strabo, l. 16. p. 538. vid. p. 535. [k] Fernel. Method. Medend. l. 6. c. 7. and l. 5. c. 17, 21.

it is by this our dead souls are quickened, by this they are kept in life, and are preserved from putrifying and rotting in sin. 7. Some of them are green in winter-time; as saffron and the aloe:[l] grace is always alive, and ever green, even in winter-storms and tempests, though it does not always appear so to us; it is an immortal seed which never dies. 8. Some of these grow up higher and taller than others; the calamus,[m] cinnamon, myrrh, and others, grow up taller than the spikenard and saffron: now these may intend the graces of the faith, hope, and love, which rise upwards in their actings on the Lord Jesus Christ; and the latter, the graces of humility, meekness, lowliness of mind, &c. 9. All these emit the most fragrant odour, when they are either cut, bruised, or burnt; so do the graces of the Spirit, when they are exercised and tried in the furnace of affliction. 10. They are all, one way or another, more or less medicinal, and are healthful to the bodies of men; and so are the graces of the Spirit to the souls of men. Solomon understood the nature of all sorts of herbs and plants, and no doubt these are aptly chosen to set forth the graces of the Spirit by; and had we but his wisdom, we should know better how to apply them.

Verse 15. *A fountain of gardens, a well of living waters, and streams from Lebanon.*

CHRIST having commended his church as a well watered garden, and declared her fruitfulness; she breaks forth in these words, and ascribes it all to him, saying, " O fountain of gardens, and well of living waters," &c., as the words are rendered by some:[a] though others[o] take them to be the words of Christ; but rather are the church's. It is true, as if she should say, I am a garden, and a garden enclosed by thy sovereign grace, where the streams and flows of thy grace run and water all my plants, and make them so fruitful as they are: but I am not the spring, the fountain from whence they flow; it is thou who art the fountain of gardens, from whence I am supplied, and am put into, and kept in the flourishing condition I am; it is not owing to myself, but it is by thy grace I am what I am; and therefore I will ascribe all the glory to thee. So that the church here acknowledges Christ,

I. To be " a fountain of gardens."

II. " A well of living waters." And,

III. His grace to be like " streams from Lebanon."

There seems to be a respect to several places, called by these names. There was one called, " the Fountain of Gardens," which flowed from Lebanon, six miles from Tripoli, and watered all the gardens about, whence it had its name, and all the country that lay between those two places:[p] and there was another, called " the Well of living waters," a little mile to the south of Tyre;" it had four fountains, from whence were cut various aqueducts and rivulets, which watered all the plain of Tyre, and all its gardens; which fountains were little more than a bow's cast from the main sea; and in which space six mills were employed:[q] and there is a rupture in mount Lebanon, as Mr Maundrel. says, which runs up in seven hours travelling; and which on both sides is steep and high, and clothed with fragrant greens from top to bottom; and every where refreshed with fountains, falling down from the rocks, in pleasant cascades, the ingenious work of nature: and Rauwolff,[s] who was on this mountain in 1575, relates, "We came, says he, into pleasant groves, by delightful rivulets that arose from springs, that made so sweet a noise as to be admired by king Solomon," Cant. iv. 15.

I. She acknowledges him to be " a fountain of gardens." By *gardens* may be intended, either particular believers, whose souls are made like watered gardens, whose springs fail not; or rather, particular churches; Christ has more gardens than one; every particular church is a garden; such were the churches at Rome, Corinth, Colosse, Philippi, Thessalonica, and the seven churches of Asia; but though there have been, and still are many gardens, yet there is but one fountain, from whence they are supplied, and by which they are all watered, and that is the Lord Jesus Christ, as the church here owns; in him all fulness of grace dwells, and from thence believers " receive grace for grace;" he is the fountain from whence it all flows : all justifying grace flows from this fountain; in him alone is our justifying righteousness before God; by him are all the elect justified, and that from all things from which they could not be justified by the law of Moses; in doing which abundance of grace is displayed, both in bringing it in and applying it to the ungodly sinner; all which grace flows from this fountain : all sanctifying grace flows from hence; a holy nature, as well as a justifying righteousness, we have from Christ; he is both our sanctification and our righteousness; to him we must look for, and from him we must receive the one as well as the other: all the streams of pardoning grace take their rise from hence; Christ shed his blood to obtain the pardon of sin, and he has obtained it thereby for all his people; so that now as forgiveness of sin is according to the riches of God's grace, it is also upon the foot of justice, being founded upon redemption through the blood of Jesus; hence God's justice and faithfulness are concerned in the pardon of sin, as well as his grace and mercy displayed; Christ is

---

[l] Plin. l. 21. c. 6.   [m] Ibid. l. 12. c. 19. and Solin. c. 43. and 46.   [n] So Ainsworth, Junius and Tremellius, Piscator, Marckius.   [o] Isidore, Cocceius, Schmidt, Heunischius; so the Cabalistic doctors interpret the well of living waters, of malcuth, or the bride, the church, Lexic. Cabal. p. 183.

[p] Adrichom. Theatrum Terræ Sanctæ. p. 107, 108. [q] Ibid. p. 6.   [r] Journey from Aleppo, &c. p. 1, 2, 143.   [s] Travels, part 2. ch. 12. p. 187, 188. edit. Ray.

"the fountain opened," to wash in "for sin and for uncleanness;" it is his blood alone which "cleanseth from all sin" whatever. He is the fountain of all the blessings and promises of the everlasting covenant; of all that light and life that we are made partakers of; of all that strength and wisdom that are given forth to us, to act for him in our several stations of life; and of all that joy, comfort, and peace in believing, which our souls are at any times possessed of. He is the fountain of all fructifying and persevering grace, by which the plants in his garden become fruitful, and continue to do so: in short, he is the fountain from whence all his churches are supplied not only with grace, but with the gifts of the Spirit; he is ascended on high, "that he might fill all things;" he is filled himself as Man and Mediator, with the Spirit, without measure; he has received "the promise of the Father," and plentifully sheds it abroad among his people; he fills his churches with members and officers, and all these with suitable gifts and graces for their respective places; all comes from this "fountain of gardens."

II. She declares him to be "a well of living waters:" we read, in Isa. xii. 3, of wells of salvation, in the plural number, which intend the same as here; and are so called to denote the fulness, completeness, and excellency of salvation in Christ. Christ is a well, 1. Large and deep; like that which Isaac called Rehoboth, either from the largeness of it, or the liberty he had then obtained in enjoying it; or like Jacob's well, which was very deep, at which Christ met the woman of Samaria: the fulness of grace in Christ has its heights and depths, its lengths and breadths; it is bottomless and unfathomable, it is immeasurable and incomprehensible. 2. Christ is a full well: we read, 2 Peter ii. 17, of some that are wells without water; but such an one is not Christ; he is a full well, and not full of any thing, of any sort of water, but of living water; he is full of grace and truth. 3. This well was dug by, and filled alone with sovereign grace; it pleased the Father; it was an act of his sovereign grace, that Christ should be the Mediator, and that all fulness of grace should dwell in him as such; when he treasured up in him before the world began: the Lord, says Wisdom, Prov. viii. 22, possessed me; with what? with all fulness of grace; and when did he do this? in the beginning of his way, before his works of old; O boundless, sovereign grace! 4. Faith is the grace with which we draw from hence: it may indeed be said to us, what the woman of Samaria said to Christ, John iv. 11, "Sir, thou hast nothing to draw with, and the well is deep:" we have nothing of our own to draw with; but Christ, who has opened our eyes, as the Lord did Hagar's, to behold himself, the well of living waters, gives us faith, whereby we draw out of the wells of salvation, and receive from this overflowing fountain grace for grace. 5. The waters we draw from hence are living ones; such Christ told the woman of Samaria he could, as undoubtedly he afterwards did give unto her, even living water. Christ is a well, and a well full of living waters; which are so called, (1.) Because grace given forth, from Christ's fulness to dead sinners, makes them alive; these waters are like the waters of the sanctuary, in Ezekiel's vision; which, whenever they come, not only keep alive those that are so, but quicken such who are dead in trespasses and sins, and in this respect excel them: we are told, Prov. x. 11, that the mouth of a righteous man is a well of life; certainly Christ's mouth is so, when he says to sinners, whilst in their blood, live; his grace may then be said to be living water. (2.) Grace given forth from Christ's fulness, revives and quickens saints when dull, lifeless, and fainting; it comforts their hearts, and makes them cheerful, lively, and active. (3.) Grace maintains and supports life in believers: we have our life alone from Christ; he is the Author of it, and with him it is hid, secured, and preserved; it is by his mighty grace that our souls are upheld in it; from his fulness we have all the communications of it; and because he lives, therefore we do, and shall live also. (4.) It is this grace of Christ's that gives saints a right to, prepares them for, and will end in eternal life; justifying grace gives them a right to eternal life; sanctifying grace makes them meet for it, which is in them "a well of water springing up into everlasting life," John iv. 14. (5.) These are called living waters, because they are ever running;[t] and so opposed to standing waters, which are dried up in the summer season: Christ's grace is perpetual, everlasting, and inexhaustible; like himself, it is "the same yesterday, to-day, and for ever;" the fulness of grace in Christ, and the communications of it, are like those living or ever-running waters, mentioned in Zech. xiv. 8, "And it shall be in that day, that living waters shall go out from Jerusalem; half of them towards the former sea, and half of them toward the hinder sea; in summer and in winter shall it be;" that is, at all times and seasons of the year shall these waters flow: the saints before and after the flood, the saints before and under the law; the saints under the Old Testament, and the saints under the New, have all received from this fountain and fulness of grace in Christ; all the grace that angels have, and all that men have or shall have, all comes from hence; and yet it is an over-running, overflowing, and inexhaustible fulness. And this I take to be the principal reason why it is called "living water."

III. The church here acknowledges the grace of Christ to be like streams from Lebanon: mount

---

[t] Flumine vivo, Virg. Æneid. l. 2. v. 715. semper fluenti, i. e. naturali, Servius ind. Ib

Lebanon gave rise to some rivers, as Jordan,[u] Eleutherus, &c., and as these took their rise and streamed from thence, so does grace from Christ, "whose countenance is as Lebanon," chap. v. 15, who is intended here; from this high, goodly, pleasant, fruitful, and fragrant mountain, flow all the streams of divine grace to our souls. Now by this expression are intended, 1. The discoveries and breakings forth of grace to those who are the objects of it: the river of God's love ran under ground from eternity; so that those who are interested in it, and are the objects of it, know nothing of it, till it breaks forth in effectual vocation; when it comes pouring in unto them, like streams from Lebanon. 2. This expression may denote the rapidity, force, and power of divine grace: as the streams from Lebanon fall with great rapidity:[w] grace comes like a mighty torrent, and carries all before it; throws down the strong-holds of Satan, and is a match for the corruptions of nature; for when this works, nothing can let; all mountains become a plain: all obstacles and impediments are removed out of the way; and nothing can stand before it, when the exceeding greatness of its power is exerted; it is irresistible, invincible, and always victorious. 3. This phrase may be expressive of the abundance of grace which flows from Christ: there are aboundings of sin in our nature; but grace, streaming from Christ, abounds over all; where sin abounded, says the apostle, Rom. v. 20, "grace did much more abound;" it flows into, and it overflows in a believer's heart; the grace of our Lord was exceeding abundant, ὑπερεπλεόνασε, it abounded; yea, it superabounded with faith and love which is in Christ Jesus: there is an abundance of grace given forth to a single believer; how much then must it be that is given forth to them all! and how large that fulness which is in Christ! 4. Though this grace flows in abundance to poor sinners, yet it is in measure; grace is in Christ without measure, but in us in measure; it is in him as in a fountain, but is given forth to us in streams; and these streams should lead us to the fountain from whence they flow; for though we should rejoice in, and adore grace for the streams, yet we should not rest contented, without often going to the fountain itself. 5. The communications of grace are called streams, and said to be as streams from Lebanon, because they are exceeding grateful and delightful to souls; even as streams of water were in those hot countries: the streams which flow in this river of divine grace make glad the city of God; a spring of water to a thirsty traveller in the Arabian deserts, cannot be more welcome and delightful than the discoveries of grace, those streams from Lebanon, are to a believing soul; and therefore Christ is said to be "as rivers of water in a dry place, and as the shadow of a great rock in a weary land," Isa. xxxii. 2. 6. It intends the continued supplies of grace to believers: grace is always running, streaming, flowing to them; could the communications of grace be stopped, were those streams from Lebanon to cease, they would soon be in an empty, miserable, and wretched state and condition: but this "river of the water of life is proceeding out of the throne of God and of the Lamb;" it ever did, and so it does still, and ever shall; "my God will supply all your need," &c., Phil. iv. 19. 7. It intimates unto us the freeness of it; it is like the streams from Lebanon; it runs freely; whosoever will, may come and take of this water of life freely. The first of these expressions in the text, denotes the fulness of grace in Christ; the second, the perpetuity and inexhaustibleness of it; and this third, the exceeding freeness of it.

Verse 16. Former part. *Awake, O north wind, and come thou south, blow upon my garden, that the spices thereof may flow out.*—

CHRIST having taken notice of the fruitfulness of his garden, the church, in verse 12—14, and she, in verse 15, having acknowledged that it was all owing to himself, who is the fountain of gardens; he, in this verse, that nothing may be wanting to continue and increase the fruitfulness thereof, calls to the north and south winds, the one to awake, and the other to "come and blow upon his garden, that the spices thereof may flow out." The reason why I take these words to be the words of Christ, and not of the church, as some,[x] are, 1. Because the language seems best to suit with him; who has created the winds, and gathered them in his fist, and holds them there; who opens his hand and lets them loose, and can and does recall them of at his pleasure; who has his storehouse and magazines of them, and when he pleases, brings them forth out of his treasures; who, in the days of his flesh, gave a surprising instance of his power over them, in rebuking the wind and sea, and commanding a calm, when the disciples, with others, were in imminent danger; which occasioned the men to say, "What manner of man is this, that even the wind and the sea obey him!" he can shut up and let loose the winds, when he thinks fit; he has them at his command, and uses them as he pleases; so that it may be truly said of him, what the Heathen poet[y] said of his Jove:

Protinus Æoliis aquilonem claudit in antris,
Emittitque notum; madidis notus evolat alis.

2. It does not appear so agreeable that the church should petition Christ to let loose the north wind upon her; especially, if by it we understand, as I think we must, some rough dispensation of providence, as afflictions, temptations, &c., which though Christ knows they are agreeable to the accounts before given of those streams.   [x] Cocceius, Marckius, Michaelis.

---

[u] Plin. l. 5. c. 20. and Joseph. Antiq. l. 5. c. 3. s. 1.
[w] Ῥοιζωντος απο τυ Λβιανυ, Sept. quæ fluunt impetu de Libano, V. L. Et impetus descendens a Libano, Ambros. in Psal. cxviii. octon. 17. col. 1041. All
[y] Ovid. Metamorph. l. 1. fab. 7.

wholesome and useful to his people, and he makes them so, and therefore in his wisdom and grace sends them; yet they are not desirable to the saints; they do not pray for them. 3. The person here speaking, claims a right and property in this garden, on which the south wind is to blow. Now the church is not her garden, but Christ's, as she in the following part of the verse acknowledges; therefore it appears to be Christ who here speaks, and says, " blow upon my garden." Taking them then to be his words, I shall now consider what he says. And,

I. He calls to the north wind to awake, " Awake, O north wind." Which some[a] understand as a command, to remove and be gone, and blow no longer upon his garden: in Psalm cvii. 25, we read that God commandeth, and raiseth the stormy wind; it is in the Hebrew text, ויעמד, " and causeth the stormy wind to stand:" so that the raising of the wind, and continuing of it, in that language was called a causing it to stand; and perhaps a recalling it was, as here, called an awaking or raising it up, in order to be gone: and there are some reasons which may be alleged why it may be supposed that it was not the design of Christ, that the north wind should blow, but rather that it should not. 1. Because it was now spring time; " the winter was past, the rain was over and gone; the flowers appeared in the earth, the fig-tree put forth her green figs, and the vines with the tender grapes gave a good smell," chap. ii. 11—13; and therefore it was time for the north wind to cease blowing. 2. It being a cold and nipping wind, would be hurtful and injurious to the plants in his garden, mentioned in ver. 13, 14, and therefore it may be supposed that he would not have it blow. 3. The verb עורי, blow, is in the singular number, and seems to be only in construction with the south wind; and therefore is alone ordered to blow, and not the north wind. 4. Winds diametrically opposite to each other,[a] as the north and south be, cannot blow together under one and the same horizon with a continued blast; for if they blow with equal force, they will hinder each other from blowing freely; and if one is more powerful than the other, the weaker will be obliged to join the other, or else subside; though winds contrary may blow together obliquely and side-way; but the more oblique they are, the greater tempest they raise, which cannot be supposed to be Christ's design here: and now, when he orders the north wind to awake, arise, and be gone, he intends every thing that may be noxious, hurtful, and injurious to his garden. Though others think the meaning of this phrase, " Awake, O north wind," is, arise, exert thyself, and blow, together with the south wind, upon my garden; and so the Jewish writers think,[b] that both winds are designed to blow. The north wind, though a cold and nipping wind, yet Pliny says,[c] that it is the most wholesome wind that blows: and the scripture informs us, that though out of the north comes forth the cold; yet also from it proceeds fair weather; Job xxxvii. 9—22; and Solomon tells us, that the north wind drives away rain, Prov. xxv. 23, and then by the north wind, as I hinted before, we may understand rough dispensations of providence, as temptations, afflictions, &c., which Christ is pleased to suffer to come upon his people, and which he brings them under, for their good and his glory: and this shows, (1.) That none of these things come upon the saints without Christ's knowledge, permission, or appointment; there is not a wind blows upon them without his will and order: afflictions do not come out of the dust, nor trouble spring out of the ground, but are sent from heaven to the saints as covenant mercies; no temptation comes upon them, what is common to man; and Christ takes care that they are not tempted above that they are able to bear, and in his own way and time gives them deliverance from it. (2.) These are all for their good; it is, if need be, they are in heaviness through manifold temptations; all adverse and rough dispensations of providence, all afflictions, work together for their good; they are all in mercy to them, otherwise he that holds the wind in his fist, would not suffer the blustering north wind to blow upon them. (3.) They serve to make the spices flow out; that is, they are useful for the trial, exercise, and increase of grace; tribulation works patience, and patience experience, and experience hope; that is, tribulation exercises and tries these graces, and makes them to appear more bright and glorious: the manifold temptations the saints are attended with, are suffered to come upon them " that the trial of their faith being much more precious than of gold that perisheth, though it be tried with fire, might be found unto praise, and honour, and glory, at the appearing of Jesus Christ," 1 Pet. i. 6, 7.

II. He calls to the south wind, to come and blow upon his garden. The church is compared to a garden, in verse 12; and why it is so, has been there shown. Here Christ claims a property in it; and it is his. 1. By choice; he chose this spot of ground, and preferred it to all others, for this purpose and use. 2. By gift he asked it of his Father, and he gave it to him: " thine they were, and thou gavest them me," John xvii. 6. 3. By purchase; he has bought it, and at a dear rate: not with corruptible things, as silver and gold, but with the invaluable price of his own precious blood. 4. By his powerful and efficacious grace, has dis-

---

[a] Foliot, Sanctius, and Tig. not. in loc. so Ambrose, in Psal. i. 5. p. 686. Theodoret. in loc. and Tres Patres apud Ibid. [a] Aristot. Meteorolog. l. 2. c. 6.
[b] R. Sol. Jarchi, and R. Aben Ezra, and Yalcut in loc. [c] Lib. 2. c. 47.

tinguished and separated it from the wilderness of this world. 5. He uses it as his own; he purchased and set it apart for his own use and recreation, and here delights to walk; he is frequently to be found, seen, and heard of here: and this being his own garden, which he himself chose, his Father gave him, which he has purchased with his own blood, distinguished by his grace, and where he delights to take his walks; he therefore calls upon the south wind to blow upon it. And by the south wind, and blowing of it, I apprehend, is intended the Spirit of God, in his powerful operations, and special influences of grace, in and upon the hearts of God's people; and shall now consider how he may be compared,

First. To the wind in general. The Spirit of God bears the same name, and several of the properties therefore are applicable to him. 1. The wind, as our Lord says, John iii. 8, bloweth where it listeth; the Spirit of God is a free agent; he works how and where he pleaseth; he acts freely in the first application of grace to a poor sinner; and so he does in all the after actings, operations, and influences of it, as well as in the donation of those gifts, which he bestows upon men for different purposes; for though there " are diversities of gifts, differences of administrations, and diversities of operations, yet all these worketh that one and the self-same spirit; dividing to every one severally as he will," 1 Cor. xii. 4—11. 2. The wind blows imperceptibly; thou hearest, as Christ says in the above-mentioned place, " the sound thereof, but canst not tell whence it cometh, and whither it goeth; and so is every one that is born of the Spirit:" the workings of the Spirit of God in regeneration are invisible and imperceptible to the natural man; he can no more discern the Spirit's grace, than he can see the wind when it blows; he can no more tell from whence this grace comes, and how it is acted, than he can point at the treasures of wind, and tell from whence they take their rise, and why they blow sometimes one way and sometimes another; why sometimes only in a gentle breeze, and at other times rises to violent storms; why sometimes they drive on in a direct line, and at other times have a circular motion; and as he cannot account for these things, no more can he for the operations of the Spirit; for he neither knows his person nor his grace. 3. It blows powerfully and irresistibly; there is no stopping of it; it blows when, where, and how it listeth, for any thing that man can do; none but he who has created the winds, and gathered them in his first, can rule them at pleasure; and, when he lets them loose, and gives them a command they carry all before them; throw down houses, pluck up trees by the roots, rend the mountains, and break the rocks in pieces; for which reason the Spirit of God is compared to a mighty rushing wind, Acts ii. 2, which filled the house in which the disciples were on the day of Pentecost, and filled them with extraordinary gifts: the Spirit of God, in his mighty operations of grace upon a sinner's heart, carries all before him; there is no withstanding his grace and power; he throws down Satan's strong-holds, and demolishes the fortifications of sin; all mountains become a plain before him; and the whole posse of hell, and the corruptions of a man's heart, are not a match for him; for when he works, none can let: he has conquered the hearts of the vilest and most notorious sinners, such as a Manasseh, a Mary Magdalene, and a persecuting Saul; there is no resisting his grace and the power of it, nor holding of his almighty arm. 4. The wind is of a purifying nature, therefore some call it nature's fan; it clears the air of infections and noxious vapours; we are scarce sensible how much our health is owing to it; for without this, the air would soon be stagnated, and quickly destroy the life both of man and beast: the Spirit of God purifies our hearts by faith: which he does by leading it to the blood of Jesus, which cleanseth from all sin: and by sprinkling it upon our consciences whereby they are purged from dead works; these dead weights and heavy clogs, which hinder us in serving the living God. 5. It is of a piercing and searching nature: it penetrates into every hole and cranny: the Spirit of God searches, not only the deep things of God, but the deep things of man also; what is said, Prov. xx. 27, of the spirit of man, may in a higher sense be said of the Spirit of God, that it is " the candle of the Lord, searching all the inward parts of the belly ;" it penetrates into the utmost recesses of a man's heart, and discovers those hidden swarms of corruptions, which before lay indiscernible; it pierces even to the dividing asunder of soul and spirit, and of the joints and marrow, and is both a discerner and revealer of the thoughts and intents of the heart. 6. It is of a cooling nature; so is the Spirit of God, in his operations of grace upon a sinner's heart; which is often enflamed with wrath, through the workings of a fiery law, and the injections of Satan's fiery darts; the heat of which he allays, by acting as a comforter, and as the Spirit of promise, bringing home and applying to the conscience of the distressed sinner, the exceeding great and precious promises of the Gospel, which cool and refresh, by removing wrath and terror from thence.

Secondly. He may be compared to the south-wind in particular, 1. Because it blows warmly, brings heat with it, breaks up frosts, and thaws the ice; " when ye see the south-wind blow," says Christ, Luke xii. 55, " ye say there will be heat, and it cometh to pass :" so the Spirit of God brings heat along with him to the cold heart of a sinner, " dead in trespasses and sins ;" and by the mighty influence of his grace, thaws and melts his hard and frozen soul; and with his soul-warming gales, and comfortable discoveries of love, warms, enlivens, comforts, and refreshes the saint, when in a cold, lifeless, and uncomfortable frame. 2. It brings serenity along with it: it is not a blustering and tempestuous wind, as the north-wind is; but is still, gentle, and quiet; blows softly, as Elihu said to Job, chap. xxxvii. 17, "Dost thou know—how thy garments are warm, when he quieteth the earth by the south-wind?" the Spirit of God brings peace unto, and commands quietness in the heart of a distressed sinner, where were nothing before but storms and tempests: the fruit of the Spirit is peace, a conscience peace, "a peace that passeth all understanding;" which he works in the sinner's heart, by leading him to the person, blood, and righteousness of Christ. 3. It is very fructifying; by its warmth, together with the sun, it loosens the trees, and causes the sap to flow, which was congealed by the cold, and clothes them with leaves, flowers, and fruit: the Spirit of God, by his mighty grace and special influence, makes souls fruitful in every good word and work. (4). The south-wind usually brings rain, hence it is called *nubilus auster;*[d] and therefore the poet represents it as flying, *cum madidis alis*, with wet and moistened wings. Pliny[e] says, it produces greater floods than others do; which suits well with Junius's version, who renders the next clause thus, "let the waters flow through the spices thereof:"[f] the Spirit of God blows, and causes the floods of grace to rise; which, running about the several plants in the garden, makes them fruitful.

Thirdly. According to the mind of some Expositors,[g] the Spirit of God is intended by both winds, the north and south; and that, 1. On the account of his different operations; for which reason we read of "the seven spirits" of God, Rev. i. 4; not that there are so many distinct spirits personally existing; but by them are intended the variety and perfection of the gifts and graces of the Holy Spirit of God, who works them in, and bestows them on whom he will. 2. If the Spirit is intended by both winds, it may be expressive of the usual order of the Spirit in his operations: h is first as the north-wind, sharp and nipping; and then as the south-wind, warm and refreshing; he first acts the part of a convincer, and then that of a comforter; he first kills, and then makes alive; wounds, and then he heals; he humbles souls, and makes them low in their own eyes, and then exalts them: he brings them "into the wilderness," and then "speaks comfortably to them." 3. It may show that Christ's garden stands in need of both winds: that the saints sometimes need the Spirit as a reprover, to bring them to a sense of themselves; as well as a comforter, to relieve them under their distresses: the cold and nipping north-wind, as well as the warm and comfortable south wind. 4. Both winds are called upon, and that to cause the spices to flow out, that the odour of them may be spread far and near, that it might be carried from pole to pole, even all the world over. Now when Christ is here represented, saying to the Spirit, "come and blow upon my garden;" it must be understood of him as Mediator, calling unto, and as it were demanding of the Spirit to do his work assigned him in the church; which does not suppose any inferiority in the Spirit to Christ; for all the three persons having jointly agreed in the everlasting council and covenant of peace, to take their several distinct parts in man's salvation; and the Father having distinguished this spot of ground, this garden, by his grace; and Christ having purchased it by his blood; and the Spirit having planted it with precious plants, herbs, and spices; Christ calls upon him, by virtue of this former agreement, to do the remaining part of his work; see John xiv. 16, and xvi. 7; to blow upon his garden, that it may grow and flourish, and the sweet smell of these spices be carried far and near. Which brings me to consider,

III. The reason why he would have the south wind blow upon his garden; and that is, "that the spices may flow out;" might emit a fragrant smell; though Virgil[h] represents the south-wind as hurtful to flowers; so it might be in Italy, where it dried them up, as Severius on the place observes; and yet be useful to them in Palestine, where it blew from the sea, by which the south is sometimes called, Psalm cvii. 3. Now by *spices*, we must understand the graces of believers; which like spices, are rare, excellent, precious, sweet, and odorous, especially to Christ Jesus, by whom they are preferred to all spices: and the "flowing out" of them intend, either, 1. The exercise of them: grace is not always in exercise, but is like flowers, shut up; or like plants, herbs, and fruits, which seem to be withering; or like coals covered with ashes, that want to be "stirred up,"[i] or blown upon, as in 2 Tim. i. 6; but this believers are not capable of doing themselves; for they can no more exercise grace, than they can work it of themselves: Christ knew full well, that this is the Spirit's work; therefore he calls upon him to blow, and thereby open these flowers, revive these plants, and blow off the ashes from these coals, and draw forth grace into exercise upon himself, the proper Object of it. Or, 2. The evidence and showing forth of it to others: Christ would not only have grace in the hearts of his people, but would have it exert and show itself in the life and conversation; he would have these "lights shine before men," and this grace appear, not only to himself, but to others. Or, 3. The increase of

---

[d] Ovid. Metamorph. l. 11. v. 663. Fluvioque madescit ab austro, Ibid. l. 1. fab. 2. Pluvialibus austris, Virgil. Georgic. l. 3. v. 429. [e] Lib. 2. c. 47. [f] Perfluant aquæ aromata ejus, Junius. [g] Diodat, and Durham in loc. [h] Floribus austrum perditus, Bucolic. eclog. 2. v. 58. Velut primos expiraturus ad austros—flos, Statii Sylv. l. 2. ode 1. v. 106. [i] Verbum ἀναζωπυρειν, significat ignem cineribus tectum excitare, sopitam favillam in flammam proferre, Aretius in 2 Tim. i. 6.

grace: that these herbs and plants might be fruitful, the spices smell, and the whole garden be in a flourishing condition; in short, that the Spirit would be ripening and bringing to maturity grace in the souls of believers, and finish what he had begun there. Or else, 4. The diffusive odour of them: that their graces might emit such a sweet odour, both to himself and others, as a garden does, when after a delightful shower of rain, the wind gently blows upon it. Which request, or rather demand of his, no doubt was answered, as appears from the following words.

Verse 16. Latter part——*Let my beloved come into his garden, and eat his pleasant fruits.*

THE north-wind being awakened, and the south-wind having blown upon Christ's garden, the church, according to his order, the spices did flow out, her graces were stirred up, and begin now to exercise themselves: which causes her, before he had well done speaking, and made a stop, to break forth in these words, and earnestly desire his presence and company in his garden; so that in this one verse we have both Christ and his church speaking. In these words are to be considered,

I. A title or character she gives him; "my beloved."

II. A request or invitation she makes him; to "come into his garden."

III. Her end in it; to "eat his pleasant fruits."

I. Here is a title or character which she gives him, "my beloved;" which, as it comes from her mouth, is expressive, 1. Of her love to him, he was the object of her love, him whom her soul loved; and indeed how could she do otherwise than love so lovely a person, one who loved her so dearly, and had given such undeniable demonstrations of it? love, we usually say, begets love; and no wonder that Christ's love should beget love in her, when we consider his person, the nature of his love, and how undeserving she was of it. 2. Of her faith as to her interest in him, she could point him out, and distinguish him from all others, and had strength of faith enough to claim him as hers; faith and love go together, they are twins; they were born together in a regenerate soul, and grow up together; when one is in exercise, usually the other is also; for "faith works by love." 3. She makes use of this title as an argument to obtain her request, or make her invitations the more forcible: she who in this manner earnestly desires that he would come into his garden, was one who dearly loved him, stood nearly related to him, and had an interest both in his person and affections: arguments taken by the saints from their union and relation to Christ, and their interest in him, have very great influence upon him, and are not disregarded by him: David knew this, and therefore uses this way of speaking at the throne of grace, "I am thine," says he, Psalm cxix. 94, "save me."

II. Here is a request made, or an invitation given, by the church to Christ, to "come into his garden." By the garden is meant the church; and why it is so called, has been shown on v. 12; and in what sense it is Christ's, and how he came to have a right to it, and property in it, has been observed in the former part of this verse, where Christ claims it, and the church here owns it; he calls to the south-wind, and says, "blow upon my garden;" she here says, "let my beloved come into his garden:" believers are willing to acknowledge that all they have, or are, belong to Christ; that they are not their own, but "are bought with a price;" and therefore all they have and are, are for his use, and at his service; which they openly declare, and would have others take notice of, and therefore say, Psalm c. 3, "Know ye, that the Lord he is God; it is he that hath made us, and not we ourselves;" that is, who hath re-made us: we are new creatures in Christ, and are his workmanship, and not our own; "we are his people," in a way of special and covenant-grace; "and the sheep of his pasture," whom he has taken the care and charge of, as the Great Shepherd; has laid down his life for, and feeds and leads into good pasture.

The next thing to be taken notice of, is, what is meant by Christ's "coming into his garden." There is a threefold coming of Christ mentioned in the scripture.

1st. His coming in the flesh. This was what the Old-Testament-saints earnestly desired, prayed, and longed for: it was not only the wish of David, but of the whole church; he spoke the language of all their hearts, when he said, Psalm xiv. 7, "O that the salvation of Israel were come out of Zion!" This being long promised, and long expected, the faith of the saints sometimes grew weak and languid concerning it; therefore the promises which respected it, were frequently renewed and repeated, and the prophets bidden to say, Isa. xxxv. 4, to them that were of a fearful heart, "Fear not, be strong, your God will come and save you;" and when they by faith saw the time near at hand, and him approaching, they were filled with joy and exultation; hence it is said, "Rejoice greatly, O daughter of Zion! behold thy king cometh unto thee," &c., Zech. ix. 9; but this, I apprehend, is not intended in these words of the church.

2ndly. There is his coming at the last day to judge the world, which is usually called his second coming; which is what the apostle intends, when he says, Heb. ix. 28, "Unto them that look for him, shall he appear the second time, without sin unto salvation." The first time of his appearing in the flesh, though it was without sin of his own, yet not without the sins of his people; which were imputed to him, charged upon him, and he answered for them; but when he appears the second time, it shall be without them, they being already expiated and atoned for. He came the first time to obtain salvation for sinners, and will come the second time to put them into the full possession of it; and as the first coming of Christ was desired by the Old-Testament-saints; so this is desired by the New-Testament-saints; who, upon Christ's saying, "Surely I come quickly," answer, "Amen, even so come, Lord Jesus:" it will fill the saints with wonder and joy; for he, when he comes, will be both glorified in them, and admired by them, though it will strike the wicked with dread and terror, and fill them with the utmost consternation; for his coming will be "in flaming fire, to take vengeance" on them. But neither is this, I think, the coming intended here. But,

3rdly. There is a spiritual coming of Christ; which is, when he comes and pays a visit, grants his presence, manifests his love, discloses the secrets of his heart unto his people, which was what he promised his sorrowing disciples, when he was about to remove from them, and they were no longer to enjoy his bodily presence; says he, John xiv. 18, "I will not leave you comfortless, ὀρφανους, orphans or fatherless, I will come to you;" which promise Christ made good unto them, as he does to all his people at one time or another; for, says he, John xiv. 23, "If any man love me, he will keep my words; and my Father will love him, and we will come unto him:" that is, Father, Son, and Spirit, "and make our abode with him;" which is what the church desires here, that Christ would grant her his spiritual, gracious, and comfortable presence, and that she might have more intimate communion with him. From whence we may observe,

1. That Christ is sometimes absent from his church and people; He does not always manifest himself unto them; he sometimes hides his face, withdraws his presence, and seems to stand at a distance from them, he is sometimes *Deus absconditus*, the hidden God; he was so to the Jews in the days of his flesh, and he is so sometimes to his own flesh; for "he hideth his face from the house of Jacob;" his own church and people, for whom he has the greatest love and regard: not that Christ is ever really and wholly absent from his church; he is always in his garden; he has promised to be always with his people and ministers unto the end of the world, and his faithfulness stands engaged to make it good; but he does not always alike manifest himself unto them; they have not always alike views of his person, discoveries of his love, and enjoyments of his presence; which sometimes makes them say, with Job, "O that I were as in months past!" &c.; nay, sometimes in their apprehensions he is entirely gone, which is the church's case, in chap. v. 9; and such is their infirmity, and the strength of unbelief in them, that they are ready to say, He is gone, and will never return more; and therefore, as David did, read all that in the affirmative, which you will find in Psalm lxxvii. 7—9; though I do not think this to be the case of the church here; she seems not to be without the manifestation of Christ's love, and enjoyments of his presence, being in such a fruitful state, the south-wind having blown upon her, her grace appearing to be in exercise, and she in a comfortable frame; though she wanted more nearness to him, more intimate communion and fellowship with him: believers never think themselves near enough to Christ, nor never will, till they are with him in glory: the highest enjoyment of Christ here below, though exceeding ravishing and delightful, falls short of giving full satisfaction; for still the soul desires more and greater: the apostle Paul, who had as much communion and fellowship with Christ, as perhaps ever any man had on earth; and yet, when he had in view that eternal being with Christ hereafter, speaks as if he had never been with him here; all his communion with him here was nothing, when compared with that which he expected in another world, and therefore he had "a desire to depart, that he might be with Christ."

2. From hence may be observed, that Christ's presence is exceeding desirable to believers; this is the one thing they seek after, and cannot be easy without; which when enjoyed, gives them the utmost pleasure, and fills them with inexpressible joy: and the reason why Christ's company and presence is so desirable to them, is because he is nearly related to them; he is their beloved, their Head and Husband; they are "members of his body, his flesh, and of his bones;" he is their "all in all;" and when he is in the garden,[k] all they want, and all they desire is there; for there is none in heaven nor in earth with them comparable to him; his coming revives the plants and herbs, and makes them fruitful; it causes the spices to flow, grace to appear in exercise; it is like "the rain, and as the latter and former rain unto the earth:" also it is doing the saints the greatest honour; they have reason to say, Whence is this to us, that not "the mother of our Lord," as Elizabeth said to Mary, but our Lord himself, should come to us? and yet this honour have all the saints. Moreover, Christ's coming is always beneficial to believers; he never comes empty-handed; he never pays a visit, but he brings something with him; he never sups with his people, but he is at the charge of the whole entertainment. Again, it is Christ's presence that makes his garden, the church, an Eden of pleasure, a heaven on earth; which makes it a Bethel, and the "gate of heaven:" it is this which makes Christ's tabernacles "amiable and and lovely, his ways, ways of pleasantness, and his paths, paths of peace;" it is this which makes his "yoke easy," and his "burden light," and

---

[k] Vid. R. Sol. Jarchium in loc.

all his commandments not to be grievous, but delightful; and when all this is considered, it is no wonder that believers are so desirous of Christ's presence and company in his garden. 8. Hence it appears, that Christ's granting his presence with his church, is an act of wonderful grace and condescension; and therefore she asks it as a favour of him; and a surprising instance of his grace it is, that he who is the high and lofty one, should vouchsafe his presence to such vile and unworthy creatures as we be. The Septuagint render it, "let him descend into his garden;"[1] and, agreeable hereunto in chap. vi. 2, he is said to be "gone down into his garden, intending his wonderful condescension. Solomon, at the dedication of the temple, said, "But will God indeed dwell on the earth?" We have reason to say with Judas, not Iscariot, "Lord, how is it that thou wilt manifest thyself to us, and not unto the world?" especially when, with the centurion, we consider, that we are not worthy that he should come under our roof.

III. The end of her making this request or invitation, is, that he might "eat his pleasant fruits;" in which may be considered, 1st. What these fruits are? 2ndly. Whose they are. 3dly. That they are pleasant ones. And 4thly. What is meant by eating them.

1st. What these fruits are. By fruits are meant, either the graces of the Spirit, which are called "the fruit of the Spirit," Gal. v. 22, or else, the duties and services of God's people, their good works, which are performed in the exercise of grace, believers are "trees of righteousness;" and the fruits which they bear are called "fruits of righteousness;" being by grace made good trees, they bring forth good fruit, and are said to be "fruitful in every good work;" now these Christ is here invited to eat. The Targum expounds it of the offerings of the people, which God graciously accepted.

2ndly. Whose fruit is this, is the next inquiry; and they are said to be his, that is, Christ's: the garden is his, and all the fruit of it: only, as one[m] well observes, the weeds are hers; every thing else in the garden, that is either for service or pleasure, belongs to him. The graces of the Spirit are his, 1. He is the procurer and possessor of them; he obtained all grace for his church and people in the everlasting covenant; he then asked for it, and it was granted him and given to us in him, on condition of his performing certain articles then agreed upon; so that, as the glorious Mediator of the covenant, he is "full of grace and truth, and from his fulness do saints receive grace for grace;" it is all lodged in his hands, and from thence given forth to us. 2. He is the Author of all grace; he is said to be the Author and Finisher of faith; and as he is the Author of that, so he is of all other grace; he gives it to us, and by his Spirit works it in us; he is the green fir-tree, from whom all our fruit is found, for otherwise we have none of ourselves. 3. He is the object of all grace, particularly faith, hope, and love; he is the person in whom we believe, trust, and depend on for life and salvation; on whom our hope of glory is fixed, and to whom our love and affections are drawn; so that these fruits may be truly said to be his; also our duties, services, and good works, performed in the exercise of grace, are his; for, (1.) They are performed by virtue of union to him; and therefore the fruits of righteousness are said to be by Jesus Christ; and "as the branch cannot bear fruit of itself, except it abide in the vine," no more can any bear fruit, or perform good works aright, except they are engrafted and abide in Christ; he is the root which bears the branches, and from whence they receive sap and nourishment, which causes them to abound with fruit; "the root of the righteous yieldeth fruit," says Solomon, Prov. xii. 12, now the righteous man's root is Christ. (2.) They are done, not in their own strength, but in his; for without him they can do nothing; it is he who works in them, both "to will and to do of his good pleasure;" therefore they ascribe all their works, duties, and services to him: and say, as the apostle did, when he had asserted that he had laboured more abundantly than the rest of the apostles, corrects himself thus, "yet not I, but the grace of God which was with me." (3.) They are designed for his honour and glory, when performed aright; they do not seek themselves, their own carnal interest, nor worldly applause, nor expect to merit any thing by them; but what they do, is in a way of obedience and gratitude to Christ, and that he in all things may be glorified; they are performed in his strength, and designed for his use; and so are properly his; which being considered, destroys that notion which advances the merit of good works.

3rdly. These fruits are said to be pleasant, that is, grateful, well-pleasing, and acceptable to Christ; so are the graces of the Spirit, especially when in exercise, as appears from ver. 9, 10; and so are the good works of his people, when performed in faith, from a principle of love to him, and are directed to his glory; the smallest services of his saints to him, and the least acts of charity to his, are acceptable to him, when performed in the exercise of grace; and he will take notice of them, and openly declare it one day before angels and men, how well pleased he is with them.

4thly. What is meant by eating them: and this intends Christ's acceptation of them, and delight in them, as also his enjoyment of them; the phrase of eating and drinking being, with the Jews, expressive of enjoyment: and it also farther declares, the church's acknowledgment of Christ being the owner of the garden; for who should eat of the fruits of it but he who has planted it, and takes care of it, and to whom all the fruit belongs? knowing it therefore to be so, she here

---

[1] Καταβήτω εἰς κῆπον αὐτῆ, Sept.

[m] Durham in loc.

invites him to his own; which invitation is not disregarded, but observed by him, as appears from the following words.

CHAPTER V.

This chapter begins with Christ's answer to the church's request, at the close of the preceding chapter; in which he informs her, that he was come into his garden, as she desired; and gives an account of what he had done there; and kindly invites her, and his dear friends, to feast with him there, ver. 1. Then she relates her case and circumstances, which followed upon her sleepy frame, and ungrateful carriage to her beloved; which he resenting, he withdrew from her, and this gave her sensible pain, ver. 2—6. Also what treatment she met with from the watchmen; her charge to the daughters of Jerusalem; and the questions they put to her about her beloved, ver. 7—9, which led her to give a large description of him, by his several parts, head, hair, &c. ver. 10—15. And the chapter is concluded with a general commendation of him and his loveliness, and a claim of interest in him, ver 16.

Verse 1. *I am come into my garden, my sister, my spouse: I have gathered my myrrh with my spice, I have eaten my honey-comb with my honey, I have drunk my wine with my milk: eat, friends, drink, yea, drink abundantly, O beloved.*

This verse properly belongs unto, and is a part of the preceding chapter. The bible, when first written, was not divided into chapters, as now it is: this is a work purely human and not divine, therefore liable to correction. And I much wonder that the authors of this work should begin this chapter with this verse, which ought to end the former, as both the words and sense of them manifestly show; for this chapter ought to begin at ver. 2, where the church begins a new account of her state and case, and of some other remarkable occurrences which befel her, not hitherto spoken of. In this verse may be observed,

I. Christ's reply to the church's request, in the latter end of the former chapter, where she desires and invites him to come into his garden.

II. An account of Christ's carriage and behaviour, or what he did when he came into his garden.

III. A kind invitation given by Christ to his friends to feast with him.

I. Here is a reply made by Christ to the church's request or invitation; "I am come into my garden, my sister, my spouse." The titles which he gives her, have been already taken notice of and explained, in chap. iv. 8, 9, and this reply of his unto her may be considered, either by way of denial to her, so some[a] interpret it; as though Christ did not answer the church's wishes and desires, but rather gives a reason why he does not; and wherefore she had no reason to expect his presence a long time; because, says he, I have been in my garden already, and there I have gathered my myrrh and the rest of my spices; I have got in my harvest or vintage, and I have eaten my honey and honey-comb, and drunk my wine and milk; and therefore to what purpose should I now come into my garden? thou canst not expect me, until more myrrh and other spices grow: or else, as a correction of her mistake, as if he should say, Dost thou invite me to come into my garden, as if I was absent from it? thou art mistaken, I am always in it, and never out of it; and am now there, gathering my myrrh and spice, eating my honey and honey-comb, and drinking my wine and milk. From hence may be observed, that Christ may be in his church, among his people, or with particular believers, and they not know it; so God was in the place where Jacob was, and he knew it not: and thus it was with Mary at the sepulchre; Christ was at her elbow, and she knew him not; he speaks to her, and yet she is ignorant, and takes him for the gardener, until he calls her by her name, Mary, and then she knew him, and turns herself, "and saith unto him, Rabboni, that is to say, master." Though I rather think the words are to be taken as a direct answer of Christ's to the church; she desires and invites him to come into his garden, and accordingly he does come, and lets her know of it: in which we may take notice, 1. Of the speediness of it; she no sooner asks, but it is granted; no sooner invites, but he comes; and before she had well done speaking, makes a reply; his answer was ready; he was as willing to come, as she was to desire him; which makes good what is said in Isa. lxv. 24, "And it shall come to pass, that before they call, I will answer," that is, will be ready to give an answer; "and while they are yet speaking, I will hear:" a famous instance of this kind we have in Daniel; who, "while he was speaking in prayer," and confessing to God his own sins, and the sins of his people, the angel Gabriel was caused to fly swiftly to him; who informed him, that at the beginning of his supplications, as soon as the good man was on his knees, and had opened his mouth in prayer to God, "the commandment came forth," orders were given, and he, as a messenger from heaven, dispatched to bring him an answer; but God does not always do so; "the vision is for an appointed time," and must be waited for till it comes. 2. The nature of this answer is worth observing, being exactly according to her request; Christ does not always do so: when the apostle Paul had "a thorn in the flesh, a messenger of Satan to buffet him," he besought the Lord thrice, that it might depart from him: but it does not appear by the answer which was given him, that his request was granted immediately; the answer, "My grace is sufficient for thee," was a very glorious one, enough to support him under his present exercise, but gives us no intimation that it immediately freed him from it; it being some-

---

[a] Brightman in loc

times most for our good and for God's glory, not to be immediately and exactly answered: but here, as she was answered speedily, so exactly; she desires him to "come into his garden, and eat his pleasant fruits;" he tells her, that he was come into his garden, and did eat his honey-comb with his honey: which shows, 3. That her request was according to his will, in that she was answered so speedily and exactly; for "if we ask any thing according to his will, he heareth us;" and therefore our great concern in prayer should be, that we might be under the directions and influences of the Spirit of God, and that he would make intercession for us, according to the will of God, who perfectly knows it; and when we ask a favour or entreat a blessing, it should be always with submission to the divine will, in imitation of our dear Lord, and so shall we be most likely to succeed. 4. It may be observed, that Christ not only answers her, but lets her know it; not only grants his presence, but gives her intimations of it; he himself acquaints her with it; for, as has been observed, Christ may be present with believers, and they not know it: so he was with the two disciples who were going to Emmaus; he walked with them, conversed with them, opened the scriptures to them, and their hearts burned within them while he did so; and yet they knew him not, till he was made known to them in breaking of bread: it is not only an instance of Christ's grace to be present with us, but also to assure us that he is so. I have shown in chap. iv. 16, what is intended by Christ's coming into his garden; and therefore,

II. Shall now proceed to take notice of his carriage and behaviour there, or what he declares he did, or was doing, being there.

1st. He says, "I have gathered my myrrh with my spice." Myrrh is one of the chief spices, was a principal ingredient in the holy anointing oil, and was used in other ointments. We read of the oil or ointment of myrrh, in Esth. ii. 12, with which Esther and the other maidens were purified, in order to be presented to king Ahasuerus: this, and other sorts of ointments, as spikenard, were used in feasts, and were poured upon the heads of those who were the guests, as appears from Mark xiv. 3, to which custom the Psalmist alludes, Psalm xxiii. 5. Christ being about to make a feast, not only for himself, but for others, gathers myrrh, with other spices, to make an ointment of, to entertain and refresh his guests with. By *myrrh*, with the rest of spices, may be meant either repentance and humiliation for sin, and mortification of it, according to some interpreters;[b] and indeed repentance and humiliation for sin, when evangelical, being the work of the blessed Spirit, springing from right principles, and κατα Θεὸν, according to God's mind; when it arises from an apprehension of sin, as committed against a God of love and grace; and when it springs from faith's viewing a crucified Christ; though, like myrrh, it is bitter to the soul, yet is odorous and well-pleasing to Christ; it is taken notice of by him, as Ephraim's bemoanings, repentance, and humiliation, were by God; he has a bottle to put such tears as these in, which drop from faith's eye: and so mortification of sin considered as the Spirit's grace, is regarded by him, according to Rom. viii. 13, "If ye, through the Spirit, do mortify the deeds of the body, ye shall live." Or else, according to others,[c] by myrrh with other spices, are intended the suffering saints and martyrs, who have undergone bitter afflictions and persecution for Christ and his gospel; whom he values, esteems, takes notice of, and gathers into his Father's house; where he clothes them whith white robes, put palms in their hands, and everlasting hallelujahs in their mouths; see Rev. vii. 9—14; or, rather, the sufferings of Christ himself, and the fruits thereof; which, though bitter to him, yet are of a sweet-smelling savour to God the Father, and to all the saints; the fruits of which, appearing in the everlasting salvation of his people, are very delightful to him, for he now sees of the "travail of his soul, and is satisfied;" he is now reaping with pleasure a glorious harvest of all his sweat, toil, and labour. Though I rather choose to understand hereby in general the graces of the Spirit, which Christ delights in, and which go under the name of myrrh and other spices, in chap. iv. 13, 14. Christ having got in his harvest, as the word signifies, and the Septuagint renders it, provides a feast for himself and others; as was the custom of those times and nations, as it is now with us. And therefore,

2ndly. He says, "I have eaten my honey-comb with my honey. Honey was the food, not only of infants, but of grown persons, as is manifest from Isa. vii. 22, but that he should eat the honey-comb with it, seems to have some difficulty in it. The Septuagint read it thus, I have eaten my bread with my honey,[e] that is, either bread dipped in honey, or honey being put upon it, or else bread made with it; which sense is favoured by those words in Ezek. xvi. 13, "Thou didst eat fine flower, and honey, and oil," that is, bread made thereof. R. Sol. Jarchi says, it is the honey which grows in canes; he means sugar, which, by Arrianus,[f] is called μέλι καλάμινον, and that for the exceeding love he had for it, he is said to eat it out of the cane; but it rather seems to be a piece of an honey-comb full of honey, just taken out of the hive; such an one as the disciples gave Christ; and this was had in no small esteem among the Jews. The word for honey-comb, signifies a wood or forest,[g] and may design such

---

[b] Sanctius in loc. [c] Foliot, Alcuin, Cocceius, and Bishop Patrick in loc. [d] Ἔφαγον ἄρτον μυ μετα μέλιτός μυ, Sept. [f] In Cocceius in loc.

[g] יערי τον δρυμον μυ, Symmachus; mel sylvestre, Michælis.

honey as was found in woods; though here, it should seem, in a garden, of which there was plenty in Judea, 1 Sam. xiv. 25, which of its own accord dropped from the comb, and ran down the tree from it, in which it was, and was reckoned the purest honey: and the other word for honey, may signify common honey, or honey made of the fruit of the palm-tree; which, the Jewish writers say, is the honey meant in Deut. viii. 8,[h] and so the words may be rendered, " I have eaten my wood-honey with my palm-honey;" for it cannot be thought that the honey and the comb were both eaten together. And by the honey and honeycomb, may be meant the doctrines of the gospel, or the words of Christ's mouth, which are said to be sweeter than the honey or the honey-comb; so that Christ delights, not only in the graces of the Spirit, but also in the doctrines of the gospel, and the preaching of them,

3rdly. He says, "I have drunk my wine with my milk." Having eaten, he drinks, to show that he had a complete feast, and nothing was wanting to give him satisfaction; not only wine, but milk was used for drink, by many nations, and no doubt by the Hebrews; we find that Jael gave Sisera milk to drink when he was thirsty, as being preferable to water; but that wine and milk should be drunk together, is not so usual; though it may be observed, that a mixture of wine and milk was used by the ancients,[i] and is by us, which, Clemens of Alexandria says,[k] is a very profitable and healthful mixture. Some of the Jewish writers think, that by wine, is meant red wine, and by milk, white wine; and so the Targum expounds the words of God's acceptation of the drink-offering of red and white wine, which the priests poured upon the altar: R. Aben Ezra gives it as the sense of some of their Rabbins, though he does not approve of it; that by milk, is meant the white which ascends upon the wine; I suppose he means the froth or head that is made by pouring it out. But to leave these empty conjectures, this seems in general to intend the plenty of provisions, and satisfaction therein, which Christ found in his church; by which may be meant the doctrines of the gospel. Gospel grace is represented hereby, in Isa. lv. 1, "By wine and milk without money and without price:" wine revives and cheers the spirits, makes a man to forget his poverty, and to remember his misery no more: so do the doctrines of the gospel, when they come with power to a poor sinner, sensible of his poverty, and misery; they make him to forget it, and fill him with an unspeakable joy: milk nourishes and strengthens; and so do the doctrines of the gospel; therefore says the apostle, "I have fed you with milk," meaning the wholesome and nourishing words of faith. Now from all this I would observe, 1. That here is a variety: as at a feast, there is a variety of dishes, different sorts, both for eating and drinking; so here are myrrh and spice, honey, and the honeycomb, wine, and milk. 2. That here is nothing but what is sweet, savoury, and wholesome; myrrh and spice are of a delightful odour; honey is sweet to the taste, and wine and milk are wholesome and nourishing. 3. That all these are Christ's own; it is his own he feasts and makes himself welcome with; he does not say, " I have gathered thy myrrh with thy spice," which grows in thy garden; " I have eaten thy honey-comb with thy honey; I have drunk thy wine with thy milk;" but it is my myrrh and my spice, my honey and my honey-comb, my wine and my milk; Christ would leave but a poor entertainment, if he had no other than what we can provide for him of our own. 4. Christ appears exceedingly delighted and well-pleased with all this; therefore he plucks and gathers, eats and drinks: the smallest degree of grace, and the weakest performances of his people, he takes notice of, and regards; he eats his honey-comb, as well as his honey, and drinks his milk, as well as his wine; for a "bruised reed shall he not break, and the smoking flax shall he not quench."

III. In these words is also an invitation of Christ to his friends to eat and drink; he is not willing to eat his morsel alone; as he feeds, feasts, and delights himself in the graces of his own Spirit in his people, so he will have them feed and feast upon his person and grace; into whatsoever heart Christ comes, he will not only sup with them, but will make them also sup with him. And here are to be considered, 1st. The persons whom he invites. 2ndly. What it is he invites them to.

1st. Who the persons are whom Christ invites; and they are here called friends and beloved; by whom are meant, not the angels, which is the mind of some;[l] though it is true, they are Christ's friends, and rejoice at the conversion of elect sinners, and in the prosperity of his church and people; yet I think they are not intended here: nor the priests, whose right it was to eat the remainder of the sacrifices, as many Jewish writers[m] expound the words: but rather believers in Christ, who of enemies are made friends; being first reconciled to God by the death of Christ, and then to himself by his Spirit and grace; whom he regards and treats as such, by granting them his presence, paying them visits, and disclosing the secrets of his heart unto them; and so he said to his disciples, John xv. 14, 15, "Henceforth I call you not servants, for the servant knoweth not what his Lord doeth; but I have called you friends, for all things that I have heard of my Father, I have made known unto you:" now these are enabled, through divine grace, to show themselves friendly to Christ again, by valuing his presence, delighting

---

[h] See my Exposition in loc. [i] Et nivei lactis pocula mista mero, Tibullus, l. 3. eleg. 5. v. 34. [k] Pœdagog. l. 1 c. 6. p. 107. [l] R. Aben Ezra, Sanctius, and Diodat. in loc. and R. Sol. Jarchi in loc. [m] Targum

in his company, regarding his ordinances, and observing his commands; for though these things do not make friends, yet they show them to be so; as Christ says, "Ye are my friends, if ye do whatsoever I command you." These are also the beloved of his soul; he has loved them with an everlasting love, and has given the fullest proofs and clearest demonstrations of it that possibly can be; which being manifested to their souls, begets love to him again; on the account of which he calls them friends and beloved. But,

2ndly. It will be proper to consider what he invites his friends and beloved to; to eat and drink, yea, to drink abundantly: but what is it they are to eat and drink of, or to feast upon? why, Christ himself, who is the bread of life, and the hidden manna, whose flesh is meat indeed, and whose blood is drink indeed; which if a man eats, and feeds upon by faith, he shall never hunger, nor die the second death, but live for ever: moreover, his love is what they are to drink of, and that largely; it being preferable to wine, may be drunk of, without danger, plentifully: they may drink, yea, be inebriated with loves,[n] as the words may be rendered; for here is enough of it, and no fear of receiving any danger by it; and all this together makes up that feast of fat things, of wines on the lees well refined, which the Lord's supper is a representation of. And this shows, 1. The plenteousness of the provisions which Christ makes in his house for his people: it is not an empty house that Christ keeps, a niggardly feast that he makes; but here is food, and that in plenty, and drink enough and to spare. 2. That a believer is heartily welcome to the entertainment which Christ makes: it is true, we are unworthy creatures of ourselves; but seeing Christ has made such entertainments for us, and has so kindly invited us, let us use freedom and eat; and the more heartily we feed on these royal dainties, the more welcome we are; and to assure believers that they are so, he, in his invitation to them, gives them the titles of friends and beloved: nay, the very manner of the invitation, not only declares the plenteousness of the feast, but also the largeness and sincerity of his heart in it. 3. It also lets us know, that Christ neither invites nor allows any to feed and feast with him, but those who are his friends, whom he accounts and makes so; this is a privilege peculiar to them, which indeed none can enjoy but they. And as for the external ordinance of the Lord's supper, that feast of love, none have a right to eat of it, but those who are Christ's friends; and to none but those is it profitable and edifying; for he does not manifest himself, nor discover his love to any other: these are his darlings and favourites; with these he grants his presence at his table, and satisfies their souls with the goodness of his house.

Verse 2. *I sleep, but my heart waketh;* it is *the voice of my beloved that knocketh,* saying, *Open to me, my sister, my love, my dove, my undefiled: for my head is filled with dew,* and *my locks with the drops of the night.*

THESE are the words of the church, who here begins to give an account of her present state and condition; how that after this spiritual banquet, which she had partaken of with Christ, she fell asleep, as the disciples did in the garden, after they had been with Christ, at his table: and also, what methods he made use of to awake her; how basely and ungratefully she treated him; which he resented, and showed by a departure from her; which then she was sensible of, was troubled at, and made enquiry after him, first of the watchmen, who abused her, and then of the daughters of Jerusalem, who questioned her about him; which gave her occasion to give that large and excellent account of him, which closes this chapter: and it may be observed, that as Christ speaks most in the preceding chapter, so she does in this. In these words are these two things,

I. The church's account of her present state and condition.

II. Christ's carriage and behaviour to her in this condition.

I. The account she gives of her present state and condition;

" I sleep, but my heart waketh:" like persons half awake and half asleep, whom Cicero[o] calls *semisomni;* the phrase is sometimes used to describe a sluggish, slothful man.[p] This case which the church was now in, is different from that recorded in chap. iii., there she was upon her bed indeed, but not asleep: there she was seeking after her beloved; but here he is seeking to her, and entreating her in the most kind and affectionate manner to arise, and let him in; there she of her own accord arose and sought him in the streets and broad ways; but here she continues in this sleepy and lazy condition, notwithstanding the pressing instances and powerful arguments which he made use of, until he exerted his mighty grace, which caused her to arise and open to him; but then he was gone: there she enquires of the watchmen, who though we do not read of any answer they gave her, yet they did not abuse her; but here they smite her, wound her, and take away her veil from her; there, a little after she had passed from them she found him; but here she appears to be even sick of love before she found him. In this account of hers, two things are asserted by her, First, That she was asleep. Yet, Secondly, Her heart was awake.

First. She acknowledges that she was asleep.

---

[n] שְׁתוּ דוֹדִים inebriamini amoribus, Mercerus, Schmidt; inebriamini amœnitatibus, Cocceius; be drunken (that is, be plenteously filled, with loves, Ainsworth. See Prov. vii. 18. l. 7. ep. 1, so Seneca, ep. 122. [o] Familiar. Epist. [p] Qui vigilans dormiat, Plauti Pseudolus, act. 1. sc. 3. v. 151.

"I sleep." This is not the dead sleep of sin, in whom all unconverted persons are; nor that judicial slumber, which God suffers to fall upon some; but such an one, which though displeasing to Christ and unbecoming the believer, yet is consistent with a principle of grace. The church here was not so fast asleep, but she could hear, know, and distinguish the voice of Christ; her sleep is much the same with that of the wise virgins, who all slumbered and slept, as well as the foolish, and yet had oil in their lamps, which they had not. And in taking notice of this part of the church's case, I will endeavour, 1st. To show wherein this sleepy frame, which sometimes attend believers, does consists, or wherein it shows itself. 2ndly. What are the springs and causes of it, or from whence it proceeds. 3rdly. The danger of such a frame.

1st. It will be proper to show wherein this sleepy frame of spirit does consist, or wherein it shows itself. 1. It consists in a non-exercise of grace; though there is grace in the heart, yet it is but very little exercised by persons in this condition, it lies dormant; faith is weak and languid, hope abates in its former liveliness, and love in its warmth and fervency; it grows cold; there is such a thing, as a leaving, though not a losing our first love. 2. It appears in a sluggishness and slothfulness to or in duty; for though persons have not wholly cast off the fear of God, and restrained prayer before him, as Eliphaz, Job xv. 4, wrongfully charged Job; yet there is a backwardness to it, and a laziness appears in the performance of it; there is a want of that fervency and spirit, which formerly discovered itself whilst they were serving the living God. 3. It manifests itself in a contentation in the external parts of religion. Internal religion is at a low ebb in their souls; they hear, and read, and pray, and attend on ordinances, contenting themselves with the bare performance of these things, without having their hearts engaged, their faith in exercise, and their affections raised; and so come short of answering the character of being worshippers of God in the Spirit; either under the influences of the eternal Spirit, or with their own spirits influenced thereby, which formerly was their great concern in religious worship. 4. It discovers itself in a carelessness, lukewarmness, and unconcernedness for the cause of Christ: persons in such a condition may be observed sensibly to abate in their zeal, both for the doctrines of the gospel, and the discipline of God's house; they seek their own things, and not the things which are Jesus Christ's; they mind their own ceiled houses, and let the house of God lie waste; they come far short of imitating Christ, their glorious Head, of whom it is said, Psalm lxix. 9, that the zeal of God's house ate him up: things may go how they will for ought they care, who have gotten into this frame of spirit. 5. It shows itself in an unconcernedness, as to omission of duty, and commission of sin; time was, when these persons could not omit a duty occasioned by the hurrying business of life, but it gave them great uneasiness; could not do those things which by some are not accounted sinful, but it burdened their consciences; but now they can neglect duties time after time, fall in with the customs and corruptions of the age, and be very little concerned about it. 6. In a willingness to continue so: they do not love to be jogged; grow peevish when any attempts are made to awaken them; their language is that of the sluggard, Prov. vi. 10, "yet a little sleep, a little slumber, a little folding of the hands to sleep." This seems to be the case of the church, who being asleep, did not care to be disturbed; and therefore made those idle excuses she did, when called upon in the most tender and affectionate manner to arise.

2ndly. What are the true springs and causes of this sleepy frame, or from whence it does proceed. 1. From a "body of sin" they carry about with them; which fleshly, gross, and earthly part in them, induces heaviness, and inclines to sleep: the cold humours of sin benumb the soul, and bring upon it a spiritual lethargy; "like the poison of asps," it operates this way: the deceitful charms of sin sometimes lull them asleep. 2. Worldly cares have sometimes this effect upon God's people; an immoderate thirst and pursuit after the things of this world; oftentimes makes persons grow indifferent about the things of another; it runs them into many temptations and snares; it frequently causes them to omit private and family duty, and "chokes the word" and ordinances, that they become unfruitful; being surfeited and overcharged with it, they fall into this drowsy and sleepy frame. 3. It arises sometimes from a cessation from spiritual exercises: idleness, or a want of exercise induces sleep; when believers grow weary of well-doing, and grow remiss in the duties of meditation, prayer, hearing and reading; grace, as to the exercise of it, declines, and their souls fall into a spiritual slumber. 4. It sometimes springs from, and is increased by an absenting from the ministry, especially an awaking one, which might be useful to rouse them; and from the company of lively Christians by conversing with whom, their souls, through the blessing of divine grace, might be kept awake; but instead of this, they neglect the ministry of the word, leave off the company of those warm and lively souls, and converse with cold and formal professors, which bring them into, and continues them in this sleepy frame. 5. Sometimes it follows upon an enjoyment of ease, peace, and liberty; therefore some[q] interpret these words of the state of the church in Constantine's time, when the church not only enjoyed freedom from persecution, but also abounded in riches and

---

[q] Brightman and Cotton in loc.

prosperity, and upon it grew careless, secure, and sleepy; by reason of which many errors, both in doctrine and discipline, crept into the church; and I am afraid, that the long enjoyment of peace and liberty which we have had, has brought us into much the same frame of spirit.

3rdly. The danger of being in such a state and condition. 1. When the church of Christ is in such a condition, it lies liable to be filled with hypocrites, and pestered with heretics: to be filled with hypocrites, because it has not then such a spirit of discerning; these may then more easily impose themselves upon it: to be pestered with heresies and heretics, of which there have been lamentable instances, that "while men slept, the enemy sowed tares;" which roots of bitterness have sprung up with the wheat of sound doctrine, and have troubled some, and defiled others: and I wish I could say, that this is not the case of the churches of Christ now, nor these the dreadful consequences of her being in such an one. 2. Particular believers, who are gotten into this sleepy and drowsy frame, are exposed to every sin and every temptation; therefore said Christ to his disciples, Matt. xxvi. 41, "watch and pray, that ye enter not into temptation;" knowing, that when asleep, they might easily be led into it. What may not the "devouring lion" be suffered to do to persons in such a condition? Into what sins and snares may he not be permitted to lead them, though he shall never destroy them? 3. They are liable to be deprived of Christ's presence, which was the case of the church here: she had had a glorious enjoyment of Christ's presence; he had been with her in his garden, and had made a noble entertainment for her and his friends, quickly after which she falls asleep; and after he had made some attempts to awake her, and had given some notices of his regard to her, withdraws himself from her, ver. 6. 4. Such may be robbed of what is valuable and dear unto them; a man that is asleep, any thing that he has, money, jewels, &c., may be taken from him: so a believer, though he cannot lose his grace, nor that treasure which he has in heaven, yet he may lose his comfort and liveliness; and the truths of the Gospel may be more easily wrung out of his hands. 5. Such a sleepy, lazy frame, tends to spiritual poverty; it brings leanness upon the soul: grace as to its exercise, is brought low thereby, and the soul into a declining condition. 6. Such persons are liable to be surprised with the midnight-cry; though it is true those who are real believers, shall never be found without oil in their lamps, but shall be always ready in Christ for his appearance: yet it will not be so startling and surprising to the waking, as to the sleepy virgins. 7. Such a frame is both displeasing to Christ and uncomfortable to themselves: a lukewarm frame Christ so resents, that he threatens to "spue such out of his mouth;" neither is it very comfortable to themselves; it is but broken sleep they have; they are disturbed with many startlings and joggings of conscience; like persons who know it is their duty to arise and be about their business, and yet have no power to do so, being overcome with sleep.

Secondly. She declares, that notwithstanding she slept, yet her heart was awake. R. Sol. Jarchi divides these words, and refers the former clause, "I sleep," to the bride; and this here, "my heart waketh," to the bridegroom; and so he says, it is expounded in an ancient book of theirs called Pesikta:[r] and then the sense is, Though I have been, and am, in a sleepy frame of spirit, yet he who is in my heart,[s] my life, my soul, my all; he whom I love with all my heart, and who is the rock, the strength of my heart, and my portion for ever; he, I say, never slumbers nor sleeps, but watches over me night and day, even when I am asleep, that nothing hurts me. But in another ancient book of theirs, called Zohar,[t] I find both clauses referred to the church, and so they are to be understood; "my heart waketh," that is, my regenerate part, which is sometimes called in scripture, "the spirit," and the "inward man;" that is to say, so far as my carnal and unregenerate heart prevails, "I sleep;" and so far as I am renewed and sanctified, "my heart waketh:" she was not so fast asleep, but that, 1. She had some thoughts of heart concerning Christ; he was not wholly out of her mind; though she was asleep, her thoughts were running upon, and employed about her beloved; his image was so impressed upon her mind, that she thought him present; and every thing that stirred, supposed it was he, and that she heard his voice; even as lovers in their sleep, have their thoughts running upon the person, who is the object of their love. 2. There were some stirrings of affections in her towards him; though she had got into this sleepy and lazy frame of soul, yet Christ was still the object of her love; and therefore she says, "it is the voice of my beloved;" she was not so fast asleep, but that she could not only know and distinguish the voice of Christ, but she could also call him "her beloved." 3. There were no doubt some convictions of sin upon her conscience: we must not suppose her to be in such a dead sleep, as to be "past feeling," or to have her "conscience seared with an hot iron;" she was sensible of her evil, in indulging such a frame; though being overcome with sleep she had no power to guard against it. 4. It is highly probable, that she was not without some desires after being in her duty, as being uneasy in her present case; it seems to be with her, as it was with the disciples when asleep, of whom Christ says, that the spirit is willing, but the flesh is weak;" they, with her here, had a will to duty, a will

---

[r] And so Tanchuma in Yalkut in loc.
[s] A phrase used by lovers, meum cor, Plauti Pœnulus, act 1. sc. 2. v. 154, 170, 173. meum corculum, Ib. Cafina, act 4. sc. 4. v. 14. [t] InDeut. fol. 122. 2.

to watch and pray with him; "but how to perform they know not," being overpowered with this fleshly and earthly part.

Now from this whole account which she gives of herself, as sleeping, and yet waking, we may observe the following things. 1. That a believer has two different principles in him; a principle of corruption, and a principle of grace; the one he brings into the world with him, the other is wrought by the Spirit of God; and these are represented as two different persons, both by the church here, who speaks of an *I* that sleeps, and an *heart* that wakes; and by the apostles, elsewhere, who speaks of a new man, and old man; of himself, as having no good things dwelling in him, and yet of an *I* that sinneth not; see Rom. vii. 18—20, Eph. iv. 22—24. 2. That these two different principles may exert themselves, at one and the same time, in a believer; "the flesh lusteth against the Spirit, and the Spirit against the flesh, and these are contrary the one to the other: the law in the members wars against the law in the mind, and the law in the mind opposes the law in the members;" and at the same time she sleeps, her heart wakes. 3. That corruption may seem to have the ascendant, in a believer's heart for a time; it seems to have had it in the church here: sleep overpowered her, though her heart was awake: this law in the members may carry captive for some time, and have such a power over the believer, as that he cannot do the good which he would. 4. Notwithstanding true grace cannot be lost in a believer; it is an immortal seed which remains and abides; grace is always alive, though not always alike lively; it is "a well of living water springing up into everlasting life." 5. The difference between a carnal and a spiritual heart; the one is in a dead sleep, the other, though asleep, yet his heart wakes; the one has spirit as well as flesh, the other is nothing but flesh. And, considering these are the words of the church, they inform us, 1. That believers have a discerning of their state and condition; when in the lowest, they know in some measure how it is with them, and can observe a difference in themselves, from themselves, and from what they have formerly been, which an unconverted person is a stranger to; he is not capable of making such a remark as this upon himself, which the church here does; though it is true, the believer may be left sometimes to make a wrong judgment of himself. 2. That believers are ingenuous in acknowledging their sins, failings, and infirmities: which is an evidence of the truth of grace, and that there are more or less some stirrings of it, where this Spirit is. 3. That it is the duty of believers to take notice of their grace, as well as of their sin; and therefore the church takes notice of her "waking heart," as well as of her "sleeping I;" we should be careful how we deny or lessen the work of the Spirit of God upon our souls, but speak of it to the glory of him who is the Author of it; who can, does, and will keep our hearts awake, grace alive there: though we, with the church, may be sometimes suffered to fall asleep; thus much for her state and condition. Now follows,

II. Christ's carriage and behaviour to her when in this state, as acknowledged by herself.

1st. He called unto her, and that so loud, that she, though asleep, could hear, and own it to be his voice, saying, "It is the voice of my beloved." By the voice of Christ, we must understand the gospel, as preached by his ministering servants; by whom he often calls to his drowsy and sleepy saints to awake, as he does here. In what sense the gospel is the voice of Christ, and how it may be and is distinguished by believers from the voice of strangers, have been shown on chap. ii. 8. I need only add here, that as it is a distinguishing character of believers to know Christ's voice; so they are capable of doing it, even when in a carnal and sleepy frame of soul: believers sometimes, under hearing the word, are very dull and heavy; there is but very little exercise of faith in them; yet they can then distinguish the gospel from what is not so; though they are little affected with it, and receive but very little advantage by it: nay, it may be further observed, that she could say, it was the voice of her beloved; for though her faith and love were very low, yet they were not lost; but then let it be carefully remarked, that though she was capable of making such observations on what she heard, yet she was not thoroughly awakened hereby, but sleeps on still: thus, notwithstanding Christ's passionate expostulation with his disciples in the garden, saying, "What, could ye not watch with me one hour?" I say, notwithstanding this, they fall asleep again. Christ's word without his power, will neither quicken dead sinners, nor awake sleepy saints; neither of these will be affected by it, unless he puts in the finger of his powerful and efficacious grace, "by the hole of the door," as he does in ver. 4. Well, Christ calling her by his ministers, and not awaking her, he takes another method: and therefore,

2ndly. Knocks, and calls again, saying, Open to me, &c. There is, (1). A knocking at sinners hearts at first conversion. The heart of an unconverted sinner is bolted and barred against Christ, with the strong bolts and bars of sin and unbelief: elect sinners, whilst in a state of nature, are stout-hearted, and far from righteousness; they are unwilling to submit to Christ and his righteousness, nor to open the doors of their hearts, and let the king of glory in: he stands and knocks there, by the preaching of the gospel; and, having the key of David in his hands, "he openeth and no man shutteth, and shutteth, and no man openeth;" with this key of almighty and efficacious grace, he openeth their hearts, as he did Lydia's; and, with the hammer of his word, breaks them in pieces, and causes all bolts and bars to fly before him; plucks down the strong holds which Satan had made; dispossesses the strong man of his armour, wherein he trusted, to keep his palace in peace and safety; and reduces all in obedience to himself; where entering with his glorious train of graces, and having dethroned sin, sets up grace to reign in his stead; and takes possession of the heart as his palace, from whence sin and Satan will never be able to eject him. Now in this mighty work of grace, in thus conquering and subduing a sinner's heart, we are not to suppose that here is a force upon the will; for though before they were unwilling, as well as unable to open and let him in, yet are now made willing in the day of his power, to submit unto him; they become voluntary subjects to him; and Christ meets with a kind reception and hearty welcome from them; so that they are as desirous of having him there, as he is of entering in, when this day of his power has passed upon them. But, (2). There is a knocking at churches, or at the hearts of particular believers; and of this we read in Rev. iii. 20, "Behold, I stand at the door and knock," &c., the church of Laodicea there appears to be in much the same case and condition as the church is here: the church here was asleep, though her heart was awake; and the church of Laodicea there was lukewarm, neither hot nor cold; which being highly displeasing to Christ, in order to bring her to a sense of her present condition, he comes and stands at the door, and knocks, as he does here. Now we are not to suppose that Christ is ever turned out of doors; that the key is turned upon him; or that he has not always a dwelling in his churches, or in the hearts of particular believers; for he is Christ in us, and in all believers, the hope of glory; he is there, and will continue there, till he has brought them to that glory which they are hoping for; though sometimes they are so shut up in their frames, that they can neither come forth themselves, in the enlargement of their desires and affections, and in the exercise of grace, nor let in Christ unto them; there is but very little communion between Christ and them; and though there is no distance or separation with respect to union, yet there is with regard to communion; there stands as it were a door, a wall, a middle wall of partition, between Christ and their souls; and oftentimes, which is still worse, they are secure, careless and unconcerned about it; therefore Christ, in order to bring them to a sense of themselves, and their present condition; that they may see their need of, and that desires may be stirred up in them, after communion with himself, comes and stands at the door, and knocks: which knocking I take to be, not by the ministry of the word, as before: but in a providential way, in a way of chastisement, by taking in his hand the rod of affliction or scourge of persecution, and lashing his children with them; with such severe raps and blows of persecution did he knock at the door of the church, in the times of Constantius, Valens, and Julian, emperors of Rome, after she was fallen asleep, through the peace and prosperity which she enjoyed in the times of Constantine: the two former of which persecuted the orthodox ministers and others, in favour of the Arians; and the latter entirely apostatised from the Christian religion, and became a bitter enemy and cruel persecutor of it: and this is thought by some interpreters,ⁿ to be particularly intended here: and in this sense we are to understand knocking, in that parallel text, Rev. iii. 20, as is manifest by comparing it with verse 19, "as many as I love, I rebuke and chasten; be zealous therefore, and repent; behold, I stand at the door and knock," &c. His knocking there, is no other than his rebukes and chastisements in a way of love, which were designed to bring her to a sense of herself, as appears from that exhortation, "be zealous therefore, and repent;" and that she might see her need of, and have her desires enlarged after communion with him, as is manifest from these words; "if any man open to me, I will come in to him, and will sup with him, and he with me;" which also is his end and design in knocking after this manner here; "it is the voice of my beloved that knocketh, saying, Open to me." There is an emphasis upon the word *me!* open to me, who am thy Lord, thy Head, thy Husband, and thy Friend: and by opening to him, he means an enlarging of their affections and desires to him, which were now very cold and chill; and an exercise of their faith upon him, which was very weak; which they of themselves were no more capable to do, than a sinner is to open his heart to Christ at first conversion; this can only be done by him, who has the key of David, who openeth and no man shutteth, &c., and therefore we find this knocking was also ineffectual, until he exerted his mighty grace, as in ver. 4; his saying to her, "open to me," is designed to convince her of her present condition, and what need she stood in of his presence and assistance.

3rdly. Christ not only calls by the ministry of the word, and knocks in a providential way by his rebukes and chastisements; but he also gives her good works, kind and endearing titles and characters: he calls to her, "saying, Open to me, my sister, my love, my dove, my undefiled." The three first of these titles and characters have been already considered and explained: the first title, my sister, is expressive of the near relation the church stands in to Christ, being "flesh of his flesh, and bone of his bone," and has been spoken to on chap. iv. 9; the second, "my love," shows the strong affection Christ had for her, she being the alone object of it, and has been opened on chap. i. 9; the third, "my dove," declares the church's harmlessness and simplicity, her cleanness, purity,

---
ⁿ Brightman, Cotton, and Cocceius in loc.

and chastity, as has been shown on chap. ii. 14; and the fourth, "my undefiled," or my perfect one,* as it in the Hebrew text, is what we have not yet met with, and therefore will deserve a little more consideration. And here it must be observed, that all the descendants of Adam, by ordinary generation, are polluted and defiled, both in their nature and actions; all the parts of their bodies, and powers, and faculties of their souls are so; their will and affections, understanding, and judgment, mind, and conscience, are all defiled: and indeed how can it otherwise be, for " who can bring a clean thing out of an unclean? not one:" nay, believers themselves are not free from pollution; but complain of the uncleanness of their hearts and lips: and frankly acknowledge that they are all as an unclean thing, and that all their righteousnesses are as filthy rags: it may then seem strange, that Christ should call his church, and that in her present circumstances, his undefiled one: and so she is not in herself, but as considered in him; believers are full of spots in themselves, but having on his spotless righteousness, he looks upon them as all fair, and as having no spot in them; they are the undefiled in the way, even whilst in the way to glory; and on this side the heavenly inheritance, which is incorruptible, undefiled, and that fadeth not away, reserved in the heavens for them. Or else, this character may regard her chastity to Christ; who, though she was guilty of many failings and infirmities, yet she had kept her bed undefiled: had not committed spiritual adultery, which is idolatry, but kept close to his ways and ordinances, as those we read of in Rev. xiv. 4; who, because they did not join with the whore of Rome in her abominations, are said not to be "defiled with women, for they are virgins; these are they which follow the lamb whithersoever he goeth." Now Christ calls his church by all those loving and endearing titles, 1. To show that she stood in the same relation to him she ever did, and was loved by him with the same love she ever was: though sleepy and lazy, careless and negligent of her duty, and regardless of him, yet she is his sister, his love, his dove, his undefiled: notwithstanding all this, there was a change in the frame of her soul, and in her carriage and behaviour towards him: but no alteration in her relation to him, nor in his love to her, which shows him indeed " Jesus, the same yesterday, to-day, and for ever." 2. That all these knocks, raps, and chastisements, were all in love; he meant it for her good, and would have her take it so: we are too apt to think, when chastised and under God's afflicting hand, that it is in a way of wrath, and that he deals not with us as children; but when he knocks, and gives such endearing characters as these, it plainly shows that it is all in love. 3. To manifest how desirous he was of communion with her, and therefore takes all ways to obtain it; he calls and knocks, and calls again, and that in the most tender, moving language that can be. And this is not all; but,

4thly. He expostulates with her, and uses very pressing instances and powerful arguments to persuade her to open and let him in; "for my head," says he, "is filled with dew, and my locks with the drops of the night:" here, because of the great love and affection which he has for his church, and the desire he has of enjoying communion with her; here he is represented as coming in the night-season to pay her a visit, and standing knocking at her door, and waiting so long there for an answer, until his head was filled with dew, and his locks with the drops of the night: which may be understood, either, 1. Of the doctrines and blessings of grace, which Christ came full fraught with; these being compared to dew in scripture, see Deut. xxxii. 2, Hos. xiv. 6; and then the sense is, "Behold, my love, I stand at thy door knocking, and waiting to be admitted in; I pray thee, rise and open to me, for I am come filled with the comfortable and refreshing doctrines of the Gospel, and with all the spiritual blessings of the everlasting covenant of grace, which I know are needful and proper for thee." So R. Sol. Jarchi, by dew, understands God's blessings for those who turn by repentance; though by drops of the night, he thinks are meant punishments for those who forsake and despise him. Or else, 2. These words may intend the sufferings of Christ, which I rather incline to. Thus Nebuchadnezzar's body being wet with the dew of heaven, is expressive of the forlorn and miserable condition he was in, when being driven from men, he ate grass as oxen, and was exposed to all the inclemency of the heavens: so when Christ's head is here said to be filled with dew, and his locks with the drops of the night, it may mean his sufferings in his state of humiliation, who had no where to lay his head; whose constant practice it was some time before his death, in the day time, to teach in the temple, and in the night continued praying in the mount of Olives; and that night in which he was taken, appears to be a very cold one, from Peter's warming himself: so that there seems to be an agreement between those outward sufferings of his, and those represented in these words; though no doubt far greater than those intended here, which he underwent in his own person, on the account of his church; which may be compared to dew and drops of the night, 1. Because of the multitude of them, the dew and drops of the night being many: Christ's sufferings were many and

---

* חמתי τελείαίμη, Sept. perfecta mea, Montanus, Tigurine version, Marckius; integra mea, Junius and Tremellius, Piscator, Cocceius, Michaelis, Galatinus, l. 3. c. 30. de Arcan. Cathol. Verit. from the Midrash, would have it, that it was formerly read, תאומתי gemella mea, my twin; and I find in Zohar, in Deut. fol. 126. 3. it is observed that it should be so read.

various; there are the sufferings of his body and of his soul, and many of both sorts; what tongue can express, what heart can conceive what he underwent, when he bore our sins and his Father's wrath? and because of the multitude of them, they are compared, not only to dew and drops of the night, but to floods, Psalm lxix. 1, 2. (2.) As the dew and drops of the night are uncomfortable and prejudicial to health, especially in those hot countries; so Christ's sufferings were uncomfortable to the human nature, as is manifest from what he said to his Father in the garden, and when upon the cross; and they would have been intolerable to any but himself. (3.) As the dew and drops of the night, though prejudicial to the health of persons, yet are very useful and fructifying to the earth; so the sufferings of Christ, though uncomfortable to the human nature, yet have produced many blessings of grace, and are the means of bringing many sons to glory; see John xii. 24. Now the sum of the argument then is this; seeing I have suffered so much and so largely on this account, how canst thou be so cruel, so hard-hearted, so base and disingenuous, as not to arise and let me in? so lovers sometimes represent their case in such circumstances as hardly dealt with;[x] and know not which to call most hard and cruel, the door shut against them, or the lover within: and yet, notwithstanding such a moving and melting argument, what idle excuses does the church make to put Christ off, in the following words?

Verse 3. *I have put off my coat, how shall I put it on? I have washed my feet, how shall I defile them?*

THE sleepy and lazy frame which the church had fallen into, together with Christ's carriage and behaviour towards her in that condition, has been considered in the preceding verse; and in this we have the effect which Christ's calls and knocks, his melting language, and moving expostulations had upon her; all the answer he obtains from her, are only some idle excuses and frivolous shifts to put him off. Some interpreters[y] indeed have attempted to vindicate the church from slothfulness and rudeness, and would have this ascribed to her modesty, which would not admit her to appear before so great a person in such a disagreeable dress; but if this had been the case, he would never have resented her behaviour to him, as he did by withdrawing from her; he would never have suffered her to wander about the city in quest of him, as she did; nor would he have permitted the watchman to abuse her, as they did, by smiting, wounding, and unveiling her; nor should she have gone so long, until she was sick of love, before she found him, had not all this been to chastise her for her former slothfulness and rudeness. Nor are we to consider these words as of one asking for information-sake, how she should do this and the other thing, as being willing to comply with the request made to her, if she knew but how; for she had no desire to do it; her chief design being to keep her bed, her ease and rest, if possible; therefore, though she is not so rude as to say, that she would not arise and let him in; yet her words and actions manifestly show that she had no design to do it, and therefore makes the excuses she does; which are to be looked upon as an absolute denial, and were so interpreted by Christ; and may be parallel with that answer which the man gave to his friend, who came at midnight to borrow loaves of him, which, in Luke xi. 7, you will find to be this, "Trouble me not, the door is now shut, and my children are with me in bed; I cannot rise and give thee." Having given you this general view of the words, I will now consider the parts of them, or the particular excuses that she makes.

First. She says, "I have put off my coat," and from thence argues, "how shall I put it on?" It will be proper to consider what is meant by her putting off her coat; and also what the argument she forms upon it, or the conclusion she draws from it intends. 1. The believer's coat is Christ and his righteousness: his clothing is the garments of salvation, and his covering the robe of righteousness; all which he has from Christ, who is Jehovah, our righteousness; whose righteousness is the saints wedding-garments; which being made of fine linen, clean, and white, and put upon them, they are clothed as with the sun; their own garments, whether of sin or righteousness, are filthy ones; in the room of which, is given to them change of raiment. Now this coat or garment of justifying righteousness, being wrought out by Christ, and brought to the soul by the Spirit of God, faith puts on, according to Rom. xxii. 14, "Put on the Lord Jesus Christ," that is, the righteousness of Christ; which faith puts on, as a man does his clothes; and for this reason we are said to be justified by faith; not that faith, by virtue of its own, has an influence in our justification, or is a part of it; for we are not otherwise justified by it, than as it apprehends, lays hold, and puts on Christ for righteousness. Now this coat or garment being once put on, the believer can never be disrobed of it; it is an everlasting righteousness; it will never wear out, nor can it be lost, nor will it ever be taken away from him; Adam lost the righteousness in which he was created, but the believer's can never be lost; for it is not the righteousness of a creature, but of God; those who once have on Christ's righteousness, always have; for being once justified by it, they will always be so; nor must it be imagined, that ever a true believer will be left to despise and reject this righteousness; there is nothing dearer to him, and more valued by him than this

---

[x] Janua vel domina, &c. Propert, eleg. 16. v. 17—19. me medias noctes, &c. . 22.

[y] Vid. Sanct. in loc.

is; he often thinks of it in himself, and frequently speaks of it to others; he desires to be always found in it, living and dying; but yet sometimes his faith may be remiss about it; may lie dormant, and be very little exercised on this glorious object; sometimes a believer is gotten into such a carnal, secure, and lazy frame of spirit, as the church here was, that he contents himself with the bare performance of external duties, without having his soul affected with, or his faith concerned, about Christ, as the Lord his righteousness; nay, sometimes when he is not in such a frame, he is too apt to dwell upon his own heart, his graces, his frames, his duties; there is a great deal of legality sometimes in believers, and their practice runs contrary to their light and judgment. Now so far as we rest in ourselves, in our duties, and performances, or dwell in our graces and our frames; so far we may be said to have put off our coat, or to have laid aside and neglected the righteousness of Christ; though it is certain believers cannot be really disrobed of it; and perhaps this may be the sense of these words.¹ Or else, 2. They may intend her leaving her first love; as her faith in Christ's righteousness was very low, so her love to Christ, his people, ways, and ordinances, was very cold; there is such a thing as leaving, though not losing our first love, for which the church at Ephesus was blamed, Rev. ii. 4; now when saints are in the exercise of this grace of love to Christ or his people, they may be said to put it on, as the apostle exhorts in Col. iii. 14, "And above all these things, put on charity, or love, which is the bond of perfectness," and when they grow remiss and cold in it, they may be said to put it off. 3. These words may also represent her neglect of her duty; for she had not only dropped in a great measure the exercise of grace, but likewise the performance of duty; she was grown slothful and inactive; she had put off her clothes, as having done working, and therefore takes to her bed, and composes herself to rest; thus, as a performance of duties may be called a putting of them on; see Col. iii. 12; so a neglect of them may be called a putting of them off; which Eliphaz, in Job xv. 4, calls a casting off fear before God; for he intends thereby a disregard to religious exercises, which he supposed Job chargeable with. 4. These words manifestly show that she was in a sleepy, drowsy frame: had put off her clothes, and was gone to bed; that she was now off her guard, and had dropped her spiritual watchfulness; thus, as putting and keeping on of clothes is a sign of watchfulness; see Neh. iv. 23, Rev. xvi. 15; so putting them off is an indication of the contrary; and she having done so, is not only exposed to danger, but to shame, disgrace, and scandal. 5. Being now free from troubles, afflictions, and persecutions, she puts off her coat, and betakes herself to a bed of ease; and though Christ calls, yet she is unwilling to arise and go along with him, lest she should meet with the same trials and sufferings as before, for the sake of him and his Gospel; so much does the love of worldly ease prevail over God's own children, that they are sometimes loth to arise and follow Christ in his own ways.

Now from hence she argues, and thus she concludes, that seeing she had put off her coat, how should she put it on? Which discovers, 1, That she was apprehensive of difficulty in doing it, "How shall I," &c., that is, how difficult will it be for me to do it? and indeed it is easier dropping the exercise of a grace, or the performance of a duty, than it is to take it up again after we have so done; and when grace is called to exert itself, or a duty is presented to be performed, carnal reason raises a thousand difficulties as insuperable, which faith only gets over. 2. This way of arguing shows her sluggishness, and her love of ease; a sluggard thinks there is danger if he arises and goes into the streets, saying, " There is a lion without, I shall be slain in the streets;" and he is so wretchedly slothful, that having " hid his hand in his bosom, it grieveth him to bring it again to his mouth;" so she, having put off her coat, was so exceeding slothful and sluggish, that she was loth, it grieved her, it went to her very heart, she did not know how to bring herself to it, to put it on again. 3. Nay there was not only a loathness, but an aversion to it; the carnal and fleshly part in the believer is entirely averse, either to the exercise of grace, or to the discharge of duty; it lusteth against the spirit; though there is a willingness in the regenerate part thereunto, for he delights in the law of God, after the inward man: but the former seems to have the ascendant in the church here, which makes her say, " How shall I," &c., I am averse unto it. 4. It intimates as though she thought it unreasonable in him to desire it, seeing her clothes were off, and she was now in bed; for him to desire her to arise and open, and let him in, was, what she thought, an unreasonable request, and therefore says, " How shall I put it on?" that is, How canst thou desire it of me? though this which Christ called her to, and indeed, had it been much more difficult than it was, but her reasonable service. 5. It supposes that she was apprehensive of danger by doing it; that it would be incommodious and detrimental to her, break her rest, disturb her ease, and be prejudicial to her health; there being danger of it, as she imagined, by rising out of her bed, and putting on her clothes to let him in. Now arguments taken from, and formed upon such selfish principles, are much made use of by carnal reason, and are pleaded with a great deal of force and vehemency by it, against the observance of an ordinance or performance of a duty: it was upon this footing that those who were bidden to the wedding, excused themselves;

---

¹ Vid Brightman in loc.

it was against their worldly profit and pleasure to comply with the invitation; one had bought a piece of ground, another, five yoke of oxen, and a third had married a wife, and therefore they could not come; and in so doing, declared that they valued their worldly interest before the blessings of grace in Christ; as the church here in saying, "How shall I put it on?" shows, that she preferred her worldly ease to Christ's company, and that she sought more her "own things, than the things which are Jesus Christ's." 6. It may also signify that she knew not how to do it, because of that shame and confusion which attended her on the account of her sins and transgressions against him; being conscious to herself of these things she blushed and was ashamed, not knowing how to show her face, and appear before him with any confidence, and therefore puts him off with these excuses; and so it oftentimes is with believers, who, when they have fallen into sin, neglect their duty through shame, and so add sin to sin, as the church did here: and this sense of the words the Targum gives after this manner: "The congregation of Israel answered and said before the prophets, Lo, now I have removed from me the yoke of his precepts, and have served the idols of the people; and how can I have the face to return unto him?" though it makes the latter part of the text to be, not the words of the church, but of the Lord; who makes answer to her, and lets her know, that as he had removed his divine presence from her, because of her sins, how should he return to her again? which other part of the words come now to be considered.

Secondly. She urges that she had washed her feet; and therefore how could she "defile them." Washing of feet was a custom much used in the eastern countries, where they wore not shoes, but sandals, and therefore contracted a great deal of soil, especially in travelling, after which it was usual to wash them; which not only removed the filth from them, but much comforted and refreshed them: instances of this we have in Abraham and Lot, who desired that water might be brought to wash the feet of the angels, whom they thought to be men, also in Abraham's servant, in Joseph's brethren, and in Christ's washing the feet of his disciples a little before his death: washing of feet was also used before going to bed,[a] which is what is here referred to. Now this is to be understood, not of the washing of regeneration, with which no doubt she was washed, being Christ's spouse and bride, as well as washed in his blood; for that is the work of the Spirit of God, in his mighty operations of his grace upon her; but this appears to be something of her own doing, "I have washed my feet," &c., nor is it meant of the purity of her outward conversation; though feet and walking, when applied to the saints, do in a spiritual sense, intend this oftentimes, but it does not intend it here; for her outward conversation does not appear to be so clean and pure, and so becoming the gospel, and her profession of it, as it should be. But, 1. It may be observed, that she had plucked off her shoes or sandles, which are the gospel, and a conversation agreeable to it, according to Ephes. vi. 15, "And your feet shod with the preparation of the gospel of peace." Now when the believer's feet are shod thus, that is, when he holds "the mystery of the faith in a pure conscience," then may it be said of him, as in chap. vii. 1, "How beautiful are thy feet with shoes, O princes'-daughter!" but now the church here had plucked off hers, in order to wash her feet; that is, she was grown very careless about the doctrines of the gospel, and very negligent in keeping up a conversation answerable to them. 2. This phrase shows that she was grown weary of spiritual exercises; so persons when they are weary of work or travelling, used to wash their feet, and go to rest. She was grown weary of well-doing, and was much like those in Mal. i. 13, who said, in regard to the performance of religious exercises, "Behold, what a weariness is it!" and therefore washes her feet, lays aside an observance of ordinances and duties, and betakes herself to her carnal ease and rest; and being called from thence, she argues, "I have washed my feet, how shall I defile them;" which intimates as before, a loathness, an aversion to it; and as though she thought it unreasonable in him to desire it, and criminal in her to comply with it. Where observe her wretched mistake, in imagining that hearkening to, and obeying Christ's command's would be a defiling her; and it also shows us what poor, little trifling excuses, persons in such a condition will make, to keep themselves in their carnal ease and peace, in a state of slothfulness and inactivity; nay, these excuses of hers were not only idle and frivolous, as the putting on of her coat, and defiling her feet, but likewise vile and sinful, as will appear from the following considerations. (1.) She had slighted the means which Christ had made use of to awake her; she had made them null and void, and of no effect; he had called to her by the ministry of the word, and had knocked in a providential way, and yet to no purpose; she withstands both his knocks and calls, which must needs be an aggravation of her sin. (2.) She sinned against light and knowledge; she knew that it was the voice of her beloved that called unto her, and acknowledges it to be so; and yet she sleeps on, and makes these idle excuses as she does, which must needs increase her guilt. (3.) She had invited him to come but a little before, as in chap. iv. 16, "Let my beloved come into his garden;" accordingly he did come; and as soon as he was come, she falls asleep, and treats him after this base and disingenuous manner. (4.) She had purposely composed herself to sleep; it does not seem to have fallen upon her

---

[a] Απονιψατε, καθετε δ' ευνην, Homer. Odyss. l. 19. v. 317. Vid. v. 343, 351, 376, 387.

at an unawares; but she as it were sought it, and for this reason put off her coat, and washed her feet, that she might be the more fit for rest, and take it more easily. (5.) Yet she endeavours to shift the blame from off herself, as if she was no ways in the fault, but that the thing was either difficult and unreasonable, or else unlawful to be done; and therefore she says, "How shall I," &c. (6.) She appears in all this to be guilty of the greatest ingratitude; she fell into this sleepy and lazy frame after this, and a noble entertainment and sumptuous feast that Christ had made for her; she continues herein, notwithstanding the most affectionate characters he gives her, and the most powerful arguments he uses with her; she sleeps on, though he lets her know that his "head was filled with dew, and his locks with the drops of the night:" though he had suffered and undergone so much on her account, yet, O vile ingratitude! she is unwilling to be at the trouble of putting on a coat on his account, or to run the risk of defiling her feet for his sake. (7.) She also discovers the highest folly, in that she prefers her present ease to Christ's company. Well, but how does Christ take this? how can he bear to be affronted after this rate? does he not highly resent it? Yes: but this will farther appear in the consideration of the following verses.

Verse 4. *My beloved put in his hand by the hole of the door, and my bowels were moved for him.*

THE church proceeds here to give an account of some farther steps which Christ took in order to awake her, and cause her to arise and open to him; which, though they are instances of his grace unto her, yet manifestly show how much he resented her unkindness and ingratitude to him! and she also takes notice what influence this carriage of his towards her had upon her. In these words we have,

I. The method which Christ took in order to have entrance; he "put in his hand by the hole of the door."

II. The effect it had upon her; "her bowels were moved for him."

I. The method which Christ took to let himself in. Seeing she was so loath and so unwilling to arise and open to him, he attempts it himself; not by breaking open the door, but by putting in his hand by the hole thereof, in order to remove the bolt or bar which kept him from entering in. Some read the words, "My beloved put down his hand from the hole of the door, or lock:"[b] that is, withdrew or removed his hand from thence: he put it in there for the aforesaid reason; but hearing such language from within, as in the preceding verse, "I have put off my coat," &c., he desisted from his attempt, and went his way; resolving to chastise her for her base usage of him, by a departure from her; which, when she understood, it threw her into that concern of mind, which appears in this verse; and also put her upon taking those methods to find him, which the following verses show she did. But I shall consider the words according to our version of them, "My beloved put in his hand by the hole of the door;" and then, not to take any notice of the character which she gives him, "My beloved," which has been often considered and explained; I shall inquire, 1st. What is meant by the door? 2ndly. What by the hole of the door? 3rdly. What the hand of Christ signifies? 4thly. What the putting of it in is expressive of?

1st. It will be proper to inquire what is meant by the door. There are several things in scripture which bear this name, in a figurative and metaphorical sense; as Christ, the church, an occasion or opportunity of preaching the gospel, John x. 9, Cant. viii. 9, 1 Cor. xvi. 9, &c., none of which can be intended here. A Jewish writer[c] thinks, that the firmament is here meant, and that God put forth his hand from thence; perhaps either in a threatening way, or by inflicting some chastisement on the people of Israel, for their slothfulness and neglect of building the second temple: but by the door here, I apprehend we are to understand, either the door of faith, of which we read in Acts xiv. 27, "And when they were come," that is, "Paul and Barnabas, to Antioch, and had gathered the church together, they rehearsed all that God had done with them, and how he had opened the door of faith unto the Gentiles;" which must be understood, either of the preaching of the doctrine of faith among them, or of the implantation of faith in them, and perhaps both are intended: all by nature, whether elect or non-elect, are shut and locked up fast in the prison of unbelief; and when God comes to convert a sinner, he opens the door of faith, and sets them at liberty; though sometimes this door of faith, even afterwards, is so closely shut up, as that there is only a little crevice, a small hole, through which a little love breaks forth from the soul to Christ, and a little light breaks in from Christ unto the soul; which seems to be the case of the church here, and is what Heman the Ezrahite complains of, in Psalm lxxxviii. 8, when he says, "I am shut up, and I cannot come forth." Or else, by the door, may be meant the door of her heart, which was in a great measure shut against Christ, through weakness, and the prevailings of corruptions in her: thus Lydia's heart is compared to a door, which was opened by the hand of powerful and efficacious grace; by the means of which, Christ, with his large train of grace, were let in, of whom it is said, Psalm xxiv. 7—10, "Lift up your heads, O ye gates, and be ye lift up, ye everlasting doors;" which are not to

---

[b] דודי שלח ידו מן החור ἀδελφός μου ἀπέστειλε χεῖρα αὐτοῦ ἀπὸ τῆς ὀπῆς, Sept. dilectus meus demiseret manum suam a foramine, Junius. [c] R. Aben Ezra in loc.

be understood of the doors and gates of the temple, though perhaps there may be an allusion to them, but of souls which are of an everlasting make; and the king of glory shall come in. Who is this king of glory? the Lord of hosts, he is the king of glory; even the Lord Jesus Christ, who is the King of kings, and Lord of lords; who is glorious in his person, in his offices, and in his saints; and who demands an entrance into, takes possession of, and dwells by faith in the hearts of his people. The door then is either the door of faith, or the door of her heart; or if we put them both together, and say, it is faith in her heart here meant, I cannot see that it will be amiss. But,

2ndly. What is meant by the hole of the door, is our next enquiry. The word *door* is not in the Hebrew text; therefore some interpret it the hole of the window or casement, others of the lock; but it seems rather to be of the door: this hole was either in the door, or hard by it, so R. Solomon Jarchi thinks; or else was between the two leaves or foldings of the door, according to R. Aben Ezra; but however, it is the mystical and spiritual sense which we are chiefly concerned about. And having interpreted the door, of her heart, or of faith in her heart; and there being but a small hole in this door, through which Christ put his hand, it lets us know that her heart was much narrowed and straitened; her faith was very low in its exercise on Christ, which sometimes is an open door to receive him; but now was but as a hole, through which but little light was let in from Christ, and but little love returned to him; her affections were chill and cold, which used to be enlarged with fervency unto him; her obedience to him was but very small, not attended with that cheerfulness and spirit of liberty, as heretofore; which seems to be the case of David, when he says, Psalm cxix. 32, "I will run the ways of thy commandments, when thou shalt enlarge my heart;" his heart was then narrowed, and he was shut up in his own soul; there were not that cheerfulness and liberty, that warmth and zeal, that liveliness and sprightliness, which he had sometimes experienced, in his obedience to the divine commands; and this no doubt was the church's case here: but there being a hole open, though perhaps but a small one, yet it shows, that her heart was not entirely closed and shut up; it cannot be said of her, that there were in her no faith in Christ, no love to him, no fear of him; for grace once implanted, can never be lost; though it is not always in exercise, in motion, yet it is always in being: and herein lies the difference between a regenerate and an unregenerate man; the one has his heart entirely closed and shut up against Christ; there is not a crevice, a cranny open to Christ; but the other, though his heart may be much closed and shut up, yet there is always an entrance, though sometimes but a small one, for him: but you will say,

Why then does Christ say, in verse 2, "Open to me, my sister, my love?" &c., I answer, Because he found the entrance into her heart was not so wide, so open and so free, as it had heretofore been; and though he knew she was no more able to widen and enlarge her heart, and to open it to him, than she was at first conversion; yet to bring her under a conviction of her present state, he thus calls to her: no, this work is his alone; he alone can enlarge the heart, and make it wide enough for himself to enter in at; he has a key that can open this door, when he pleases, even the key of David, with which he openeth, and no man shutteth, and shutteth, and no man openeth. But I proceed,

3rdly. To show what is meant by the hand of Christ, which he puts in by the hole of this door: and this I take to be his mighty, powerful, and efficacious grace; and so the word is used in Acts xi. 21, "And the hand of the Lord was with them; and a great number believed, and turned to the Lord." The reason why the ministry of the apostles was so much owned for the conversion of souls, was, because it was attended with the mighty and efficacious grace of Christ: it was the want of this Isaiah complained of, when he said, Isa. liii. 1, "Who hath believed our report, and to whom is the arm of the Lord revealed?" If the ministry of any is made useful for the good of souls, it is because this arm is revealed, and this hand is put forth; and the ministers of Christ are willing to ascribe it to that, and not to themselves; and can freely join with the apostle Paul, in saying, "Not I, but the grace of God which was with me;" and without this hand, all the means of grace are ineffectual; but this can turn the key and open the door of any heart, though never so closely shut, and strongly barred and bolted against Christ: now the same mighty and efficacious grace is equally exerted and put forth in the awaking of a drowsy saint, reclaiming a backsliding professor, and quickening him to his duty, as in the conversion of a sinner, dead in trespasses and sins. Which brings me to consider,

4thly. What is meant by Christ's putting in his hand of mighty and efficacious grace, by the hole of the door. Now this intends the exertion and application of grace to the hearts of believers, which influence and quicken, support and maintain, grace in them; this is an internal work, and differs from all the other methods which Christ took with her, and appears to be more powerful than any of them; he had called in the external ministry of the word, and knocked in a providential way, by inflicting some chastisement upon her; he had given her good words, expostulated with her, and used persuasive arguments, and yet to no purpose: but now he puts in his hand of mighty grace, and the work is done; which hand moves secretly and invisibly, and yet powerfully and irresistibly; for " none can stay his hand, or say unto him, What doest thou?" though it uses no force or compulsion, but works sweetly and kindly upon the heart; for how unwilling and loth soever the church was before to arise and open to Christ, now she is entirely willing to do it; and that not through force nor fear, but out of a real affection for him, and love to him. Christ now, in putting in his hand, and thus powerfully and sweetly working upon her heart, shows, 1. The exceeding greatness of his love and grace unto her: that though she had treated him in so rude a manner, and discovered so much disingenuity and ingratitude to him, which made him take up a resolution to depart from her; yet he would not leave her without giving some evidence of his love to her, without putting in his hand, and leaving some myrrh upon the lock, and sweet-smelling myrrh upon the handles thereof. 2. His faithfulness to her. Christ never wholly and entirely leaves his people; he has promised that he will not, and he is faithful to this promise; Christ may so withdraw himself from them, as that they may not have sensible communion with him: but their union to him remains firm, and indissoluble; they may think that he has totally and finally left them when he has not, nor never will: he departs here from the church, but it was not a total departure; for he put in his hand by the hole of the door, and left something there, which stirred up her affections to him, and put her upon a diligent search and inquiry after him. 3. His power: What is it that the hand of Christ cannot do? what the external calls of the ministry, knocks, and raps of persecution, what good words and moving arguments could not do, that is done in a moment by Christ's putting in his hand; she lay still before, and put him off with idle excuses, but now she arises and opens to him. Which leads me to consider.

II. The effect of this, or what influence this had upon her heart; her bowels, she says, were moved for him: which is expressive, either,

First. Of that sorrow and grief which then possessed her heart. The word is used in Jer. iv. 19, Lam. i. 20, to express grief and sorrow; and indeed, it is no wonder that it should be so with her, when she began to be capable of revolving things in her mind, and comparing her carriage and his together; observing the baseness and disingenuity there were in the one, and the exceeding greatness of love and tenderness in the other. The words have a double reading in the Hebrew text: some copies read, "my bowels were moved, צָלַי, in me, or for me;" and this reading the Jewish commentators follow, particularly R. Solomon Jarchi, and so do Junius and Tremellius, the Tigurine version, and that of Pagnine's: other copies read, "my bowels were moved, עָלָיו, for him;" which, by Mercer, is esteemed the best and most correct reading, and is followed by our and other translators. If we read the words in the first way, they will afford us these two observations: 1. That her grief and sorrow was inward, and so real and sincere; her bowels moved within her; and such a sorrow as this is what is required, regarded, and approved of by God; "Thou desirest truth in the inward parts, and in the hidden part thou wilt make me to know wisdom," says David, Psalm li. 6; for it is not a shedding of tears, nor rending of garments, but a heart broken under a sense of sin, and melted down with the discoveries of boundless love, that is an acceptable sacrifice with God through Christ. 2. That her own sin and unkindness to Christ was the cause of all this; my bowels were moved for me, or concerning myself; for what I had done, and had been guilty of, I have none to blame but myself; I am the sole author of all this trouble to myself; my own sin and wickedness has brought all this upon me. O! it pains me, it cuts me to the very heart, to think that I should use the best of husbands so unkindly, and treat him after so base a rate as I have done!

But then if we follow the second reading, it will lead us to make the remarks following: 1. That sin, as committed against Christ, was the chief and principal cause of her trouble and sorrow; "my bowels were moved for him," because I had sinned against him; had it been another, it would not have grieved me so much: but against thee, thee only have I sinned; which shows her repentance to be right, and her sorrow to be true and genuine. 2. That the sufferings of Christ, occasioned by her sins and transgressions, influenced her sorrow; my bowels were moved for him; it grieves me, I am pained at the very heart, to think that my beloved's head should be wet with dew, and his locks with the drops of the night, through me; that he should suffer so much upon my account, and for my sake; now when repentance springs from faith's viewing a crucified and suffering Christ, it appears to be evangelical; see Zech. xii. 10. 3. That her frustrating the means which Christ made use of, added to her grief. Did my beloved call and knock, and call again; and did I know that it was the voice of my beloved? Did he give me good words, expostulate and argue with me in the most moving and tender manner? and yet, vile and ungrateful wretch that I am, did I lie still, and not move to open and let him in? could he get nothing from me but mere shifts and evasions? O! how does the consideration of all this overwhelm me with grief and sorrow? 4. That the loss of his company was also an ingredient herein; for, as Christ's company and presence fill the believer with the greatest joy, so his absence and departure from him give him the greatest uneasiness: "Thou didst hide thy face," says David, Psalm xxx. 7, and I was troubled; so here, her bowels moved, her soul was grieved, not only for what she had done unto him; but also for the loss of him. Or else, these words, "my bowels were moved for him," are expressive,

Secondly. Of the moving and stirring of her

affections to him, in which sense the word is used in Isa. lxiii. 15, Philem. 12, for though her affections had been chill, and her love to Christ cold, yet they were not lost; Christ's putting in his hand, stirred up the coals of love, which "many waters cannot quench:" so that they began to kindle and appear in flames; for not only the grace was in her heart, but in exercise, in motion there, "my bowels moved," &c., so that she could say, after all her sleepiness, slothfulness, negligence in duty, and base carriage towards Christ, as Peter, after his backslidings, "Lord, thou knowest all things, thou knowest that I love thee;" this love of hers was real, hearty, and sincere; it was not the moving of her lips or tongue, but of her bowels within her; she loved "not in word, neither in tongue, but in deed and truth:" and this her actions testify, which are recorded in the following verses.

Verse 5. *I rose up to open to my beloved, and my hands dropped* with *myrrh, and my fingers* with *sweet-smelling myrrh, upon the handles of the lock.*

IN these words the church gives an account of a second and third effect of Christ's "putting in his hand by the hole of the door."

I. She "rose to open to him."

II. Having done so, she laid hold on the "handles of the lock," in order to draw it back; and before she proceeds to take notice of any other steps she took, with the success thereof, she stops to give an account of a sweet piece of experience she met with, when she put her hands "upon the handles of the lock. My hands, says she, dropped with myrrh, and my fingers with sweet-smelling myrrh."

I. She says, that she "rose to open to her beloved." This is opposed to her former slothfulness and sleepiness: before she lay still and slept on, notwithstanding Christ's calls and knocks, his melting words and moving language; but now being touched by his hand of mighty and powerful grace, she shakes off her sluggishness, and arises to open to him, which is more than a mere resolution to do it; such an one as she made in chap. iii. 2, and the prodigal in Luke xv. 13. Now these resolutions were made in the strength of grace; and being assisted by divine grace to perform them, were quickly put in execution; though otherwise, resolutions made in our own strength, are seldom or never made good: but this was more than a mere resolution, it was an actual performance of it; not but that she resolved no doubt in her mind, to do it before she did it; but the dispatch was so quick, and there being so little time between the making and the execution of it, she had neither leisure nor room to regard it; "I rose to open to my beloved:" which act of hers shows, 1. That her design and intention to open to Christ, was real and hearty: had she lain upon her bed, and made ever such fair promises, that she would arise and open to him, and yet have kept her bed and slept on: there would have been but very little proof that she really and heartily designed it; but her rising in order to it, is a full indication of it; even as Abraham's rising up early, saddling his asses, taking his own and only son Isaac with him, and going to the place which the Lord directed him to; his putting the wood in order, binding his son, and laying him upon it; his taking the knife, and stretching out his hand to slay his son, manifestly showed that he really intended to obey the divine command, though so disagreeable to flesh and blood. 2. That her concern at her base and unbecoming carriage to him was sincere and unfeigned; the effects show that her sorrow was of a godly sort; seeing it wrought in her carefulness to obey his will, zeal for his honour and glory, fear and reverence of his person, a vehement desire after the enjoyment of his presence and company, and an indignation at her own sin and folly; see 2 Cor. vii. 10, 11; her repentance appears to be true and genuine, because it brought forth "fruits meet for it." 3. That she did not stay to confer with flesh and blood, but immediately arose, as soon as touched by the hand of mighty grace: had she done so, she would have argued thus with herself, "yet a little sleep, a lttle slumber, a little folding of the hands to sleep," and then I will arise and open to him; no, for though she put him off before with idle excuses, having consulted her own carnal ease; yet now, being, under the influence of powerful grace, she cannot defer it any longer, but without delay, rises to open to him. 4. That when a soul, in such a case as hers, is made sensible of it, it cannot rest easy upon a bed of carnal security: it may, with David, for a time be senseless, stupid, and unconcerned; and with Jonah, lie fast asleep in the sides of the ship, careless, thoughtless, and unconcerned; yet when awaked from hence, anguish and distress seize it; and it cannot be easy without some returning visits of love, some views of Christ's person, and some enjoyment of his presence; and therefore will arise and go out in quest of him: and now no difficulties discourage such a soul as none did the church; when she was upon her bed of ease, every little thing was difficult to her; her language was that of the sluggard's, "There is a lion in the way, a lion is in the streets;" it was then a trouble to her to put on her coat, and an intolerable hardship to defile her feet; but now neither the one nor the other hinder her; but she rises, opens, and ventures herself alone in the streets, runs among the watchmen of the city, and keepers of the walls, and from thence to the daughters of Jerusalem, to inquire of her beloved. 5. It also supposes that she thought Christ still at the door; though no sooner had he put in his hand, but he was gone, being willing to let her know, though he loved her, yet he resented her carriage to him: and here we may observe that God's children may be mistaken sometimes about the presence of Christ; sometimes he is present with them, and they know it not, as Jacob said, Gen. xxviii. 16, "Surely the Lord is in this place, and I knew it not:" and at other times when they are got into such careless, secure, and unconcerned frames of soul, like Samson, the Lord is departed from them, and they wist not, that is, know not, that the Lord is departed from them. 6. This shows the power of mighty and efficacious grace, and that she was under the influence of it; though perhaps the Spirit was willing before, yet the flesh was weak: though she might have a will to open to Christ, yet how to perform it she knew not: though indeed her will seemed to be very indifferent about it; there appeared a loathness in her, and a kind of unwillingness to it; but now she is made both able and "willing in the day of his power," to arise and open to him.

II. Having risen to open to Christ, she puts her hand "upon the handles of the lock," to draw it back, and let him in; which in order, is the third effect of Christ's "putting in his hand by the hole of the door." Now though this is not in so many words expressed in the text, yet it is manifestly implied; for if her "hands dropped with myrrh, and her fingers with sweet-smelling myrrh upon the handles of the lock;" it then supposes, that her hands and fingers must first lay hold upon the lock-handles, which was also absolutely necessary to do, in order to open the door. It will be proper here to consider, 1st. What we are to understand by the lock, and the handles of it. 2ndly. What by her hands and fingers, which laid hold on these handles to draw back the lock, and in what sense they might do it.

1st. It is needful to enquire what may be meant by the lock, and the handles of it: and as by the door, I suppose is meant the heart of a believer, so by the lock, which fastens and keeps this door shut, may be meant unbelief; by which as all by nature are locked and shut up in the state they are; so believers sometimes by it are so straitened, confined, and shut up in their souls, that they cannot come forth in the free exercise of faith, in which they are at other times found: and the handles of this lock may be lukewarmness and indifference of soul with regard to duty, a sluggishness and loathness to come to it, which oftentimes brings the soul at last to a neglect of it; for, first, persons grow indifferent about the performance of duties, or attendance on ordinances; do not care whether they perform them, or attend on them, or no; then they begin to be "slothful in business, not serving the Lord," with that fervency of Spirit which they have heretofore done; and at last wholly neglect them; which brings them into a carnal, secure and unconcerned frame of spirit; and all this strengthens unbelief, and keeps the door the closer shut against Christ; which seems to have been the case of the church here, and of that of Laodicea, in Rev. iii., when Christ stood at her door and knocked.

2ndly. By her hands and fingers may be meant her faith in its exercise and operation, attended with the fruits thereof. Faith is usually represented in scripture as the hand of the soul by which it receives Christ, as the Father's free gift; embraces him as the only Saviour: lays hold upon, and retains him, as he stands in all the endearing characters and relations which he appears in to his own people. Now this faith is not idle and inactive, but "works by love" to Christ and his people, to his ways and ordinances; it has its fruits, and is attended with the performance of good works, and will put the person that is possessed of it, on the discharge of his duty; it put the church here upon attempting to draw back the lock of unbelief; faith laid its hands and fingers upon the handles of it, and used all its might, power, and diligence to do it: but it may be asked, How could the church be able, with all her faith, industry, and diligence, to draw back this lock? I answer, Faith cannot do this of itself; unbelief is a "sin which easily besets us," but it is not so easily got rid of; it is a weight, that the hand of faith of itself, cannot lift and lay aside; the believer must say even in the exercise of faith, with the poor man in the Gospel, Mark ix. 24, "Lord, I believe, help thou mine unbelief;" this lock grows too hard for faith to draw it back of itself; but yet faith's looking to, and dealing with Christ's person, blood, and righteousness, much weakens unbelief. When an unbelieving Thomas was indulged with a sight of Christ's pierced hands and feet, and was enabled to thrust his hand into his side; his unbelief immediately vanished and disappeared, and he could say, "My Lord, and my God:" it is certain, that the stronger faith grows, lukewarmness, indolence, and carnal security decay; and the soul is quickened, stirred up, and put upon the performance of duty: and what is it that a soul is not enabled to do in the exercise of faith? difficulties which are insuperable to carnal sense and reason, are got over by faith; read over the eleventh chapter of the epistle to the Hebrews, and you will see what heroic acts have been performed by faith, though the strength in which these things have been performed, did not arise from the grace itself, but from Christ, the object of it, whose "strength is made in faith's weakness;" for without him we can do nothing, but his "grace is sufficient to enable us to do all things."

Now before she proceeds to tell how she succeeded in this attempt: she gives an account of a piece of sweet experience she met with, whilst she was trying to draw back the lock; "my hands," says she, "dropped with myrrh, and my fingers with sweet-smelling myrrh, upon the handles of the lock." By myrrh, is meant grace, in its aboundings and overflowings: but it may be inquired, From whence this myrrh came, and by whom it was brought? If we understand it of the Church's myrrh or grace, as brought here by herself, as some think;[d] who may be represented as taking up a pot of myrrh, intending with it to anoint and refresh his head, which was wet with dew, which she either unawares or else designedly broke; or else, being in a panic fear, her hand shook, and the myrrh ran over her hands and fingers; or rather, not having time to perfume her garments with it, as usual, see Psalm xlv. 8, she dipped her fingers in a pot of myrrh, to ingratiate and render herself acceptable to her beloved; supposing that he might be full of resentment on the account of her carriage and behaviour towards him: and then taking it in this sense, it will teach us these things following; 1. That her grace was now in exercise, it was flowing; this oil of myrrh before was as it were congealed; but now it is become liquid; it is upon the flow, and flows in such abundance, that it ran off her hands and fingers upon the handles of the lock. 2. Her hands and fingers dropping with it, show that these actions and good works of hers, intended by her hands and fingers, being performed in faith, were odorous and grateful to Christ: so the prayers of the saints are called odours, in Rev. v. 8; and some mean and small services of the Philippians, are called an odour of a sweet smell, Phil. iv. 18. 3. That when grace is in exercise, duty is both easy and pleasant; Christ commands then are not grievous, but his "ways are ways of pleasantness, and his paths, paths of peace:" before, nothing more unpleasant than to arise and open to him; but now, nothing more easy and delightful; her " hands drop with myrrh," &c. But I rather think, that the myrrh or grace of Christ is here meant, which was brought and left here by him; when he " put in his hand by the hole of the door," he then put in this myrrh he had gathered, ver. 1; and left it in the lock-hole; which she found in such abundance when she came to open, that her hands and fingers dropped with it: the allusion seems to be to lovers shut out, who used to cover the threshhold of the doors with flowers, and anoint the door-posts with sweet smelling ointment.[e] Taking the words in this sense, we may observe that grace is called so, 1. For the preciousness of it; myrrh is a precious spice, and one of the principal spices; and this in the text is the best of myrrh, there was a sort of myrrh called *odoraria*, sweet-smelling :[f] the word translated "sweet-smelling myrrh," signifies "passing or current myrrh;"[g] it being vendible or saleable, not in the least damaged, but what will pass; and so is in the same sense current, as money is said to be, Gen. xxiii. 16; or else, it is called "passing myrrh," because it diffuses its odour on every side: so R. Solomon Jarchi thinks: or, rather because it is that myrrh which bleeds or weeps, or drops from the tree of itself, which is always esteemed the best myrrh: and this sets forth the exceeding preciousness of Christ's grace, which is more valuable than all things else. 2. It sets forth the abundance of it; if there was such an abundance of it brought by Christ, and left in the lock-hole, so that it ran in such plenty over her hands and fingers, as to drop from thence. What an abundance? what an overflow of it must there be in himself, who is "full of grace and truth?" if there is a superabounding of grace in those in whom sin has abounded. What an overflowing fulness of it must there be in him, in whom is no sin, and who is the Fountain from whence all grace flows, and is communicated to his people? (3.) It is expressive of the odorousness of it: there is such a sweet savour in the grace of Christ, as it is in himself, that the love of the virgins is drawn forth to him by it; and it emits so fragrant an odour, as it is in believers, that Christ himself is delighted with it; see Cant. i. 3, and iv. 10.

Moreover, seeing it appears that this myrrh was brought unto and left in the lock-hole by Christ; it may be asked, for what purpose it was brought and left there? which was, 1. To draw and allure her heart unto him: the same grace that draws a soul to Christ at first conversion, draws it to him when it has declined and backslidden from him; Christ uses the same methods, and puts forth the same grace at one time as at the other; he draws "with the cords of love, and bands of a man." 2. To supple and soften her hard heart, and make this rusty lock go easy; this oil of myrrh being left there, removed the hardness of her heart, the stiffness of her will, and the rustiness of her affections; this melted her hard heart, made her stubborn will pliable, set her affections on the flow, her faith in exercise, and made the lock of unbelief draw back more easy. 3. To exercise and stir up her grace; it is Christ's grace, manifested and applied unto us that excites ours; it is his love "shed abroad in our hearts by his Spirit," that raises ours: for "we love him, because he first loved us." Now all these ends were answered hereby; it was this grace, this myrrh, left in the handles of the lock, that fetched her off her bed, softened the hardness of her heart and affections to him, that removed the bars and bolts that kept him out, and drew forth her grace into exercise.

Again the church's hands and fingers being said to drop with myrrh, which Christ had put into the lock-hole, shows, 1. That all the grace, all

---

[d] Vid. Sanct. and Bishop Patrick in loc.
[e] At lachrymans exclusus amator—postemque superbos unguit amaricino, Lucret. l. 4. prope finem.
[f] Plin. Nat. Hist. l. 12. c. 16. [g] מור עבר myrrham transeuntem, Pagninus, Montanus, &c. lachrymantem, Bochart. vid. Mercer. and Bishop Patrick in loc.

the myrrh, that a believer has, comes from Christ; it is from "his fulness we receive grace for grace," that is, all sorts of grace. 2. That a believer has most reason to expect a larger measure of grace from Christ, when he is in the way of his duty; whilst the church was sluggish and slothful, negligent of her duty, and taking her ease upon her bed of security, there is no mention of the flowings of this myrrh into her or upon her; but now she is up, and in the way of her duty, her "hands drop with myrrh, and her fingers with sweet-smelling myrrh:" not that our duties are deserving of any thing at Christ's hands, much less such large measures and overflowings of grace as these; yet Christ has been graciously pleased, for an encouragement, to grant the promise of his presence, and the communications of his grace to us, when found in the way of our duty, though not for the performance of it. How the church succeeded in this attempt of hers, in opening the door, may be seen in the following words.

Verse 6. *I opened to my beloved, but my beloved had withdrawn himself, and was gone; my soul failed when he spake: I sought him, but I could not find him; I called him, but he gave me no answer.*

In these words are,

I. A fourth and last effect of Christ's "putting in his hand by the hole of the door;" she opened to him.

II. The wretched disappointment she had met with; he "had withdrawn himself, and was gone."

III. What effect this disappointment had upon her; her soul "failed when he spake."

IV. Her endeavours to find her lost spouse.

I. Here is a fourth and last effect of Christ's "putting in his hand by the hole of the door," which is the exertion of his mighty and efficacious grace, "I opened to my beloved." This was what her beloved desired of her, and called for, in ver. 2; and which was his principal end in exerting the power of his grace. Now this opening to him, is to be understood of the exercise of her faith, by which her heart was enlarged and dilated to receive Christ; faith is the eye, the ear, the mouth, and the hand of the soul; faith's eye being opened, sees the beauties and glories of Christ's person, and spies wondrous things in his gospel; its ear being open to discipline, listens to what Christ says in his promises and commands, and takes in the comfort of the one, and carefully observes the other; its mouth being opened, speaks of the promises of Christ, the glory of his person, office, and undertakings; and its hand being opened, receives and embraces him, opens the door, and lets him in. From this act of the church, in opening to her beloved, may be observed, 1. That Christ had not only wrought in her a will, but had also given her a power to open to him; once she seemed to have but little inclination; her will did not seem so very free, being overpowered with sleep and sloth; and if her spirit was willing, yet it appears manifest that the flesh was weak; if she had a will to open, how to do it she knew not; but now, as by her rising off her bed, coming to the door, and putting her hands and fingers upon the handles of the lock, in order to draw it back, she showed that Christ had wrought in her to will; so by her actual opening to him, she made it appear that he had also wrought in her "to do of his good pleasure." 2. That she being assisted in this act by the mighty grace of Christ, is said to do that which is sometimes ascribed to God himself; thus in Acts xvi. 14, the Lord is said to open the heart of Lydia: it is true, there is a great difference between the opening of a sinner's heart at conversion, which is entirely shut against Christ; and the opening of a believer's, which is in part only shut and closed through unbelief, negligence, and carnal security: in the one, there were no principles of grace, previous to the opening of it; but in the other there are, though they lie dormant, and are not in exercise; but yet a believer, without the grace and power of Christ, can no more open his heart to him, when in such a case, than he could at first conversion: this work is attended with difficulties insuperable without the strength of Christ; therefore, whilst on her bed, she thought it impossible for her to do it, and unreasonable in him to desire it; till he put in his hand, and left such an abundance of the sweet-smelling myrrh of his grace, by which being assisted, she is said to do it. 3. That the heart of a believer is only patent and open to the Lord Jesus Christ, "I opened to my beloved;" though it is sometimes, in a great measure, closed and shut unto him; yet, when it is opened, it is only opened to him; he is the only object of a believer's faith and love: the church here did not open to strangers, only to her beloved, being "espoused as a chaste virgin" to him; therefore, in chap. iv. 12, she is said to be "a garden enclosed, a spring shut up, a fountain sealed." 4. Her opening to Christ, supposes that she thought Christ still at the door; so she did when she got off her bed to open to him; and so she did when she put her hands upon the handles of the lock; and perhaps was more confirmed in her thoughts, that he was still there, when she found such an abundance of his sweet-smelling myrrh in the lock, and upon the handles of it; but she was very much mistaken, as she afterwards found. For,

II. Her "beloved had withdrawn himself, and was gone;" a very great disappointment indeed! she expected, that as soon as ever the door was open, she should have seen him, and that he would have received her in his arms, and embraced her in his bosom; but instead of that, he was gone, and she could neither have any sight, nor hear any tidings of him. Here it may be inquired, 1st. What is meant by Christ's withdrawing himself from his church and people?

2ndly. Why he did now withdraw himself from the church? And, 3rdly. Why she makes use of two words to express his departure from her, and what they import?

1st. It may be enquired what is meant by Christ's withdrawing himself from his church and people? And, 1. It is not to be understood of him as the omnipresent God, who is every where, and fills heaven and earth with his presence; for as there is no fleeing from it, so there is no withdrawing of it, as David says, Psalm cxxxix. 7, "Whither shall I go from thy Spirit, or whither shall I fly from thy presence?" there is no place exempted from it, nor can be; he does not move from place to place, nor from person to person; nor is he sometimes with a person, and sometimes not; for if so, he would not be the omnipresent God. Nor, 2. Is it to be understood of the dissolution of a believer's covenant-interest in Christ, and union to him; a believer may lose sight of Christ for a time, but he can never lose his interest in him; the relation between them can never cease; the marriage-knot can never be untied, nor the union-bonds be ever broken; for Christ has said, Hosea ii. 19, "I will betroth thee unto me for ever:" the union between Christ and believers is in some measure like to that between the Father and the Son; and I will venture to say, that the one may as soon be dissolved as the other; see John xvii. 22, 23. Nor, 3. Is it to be understood of a withdrawing of his love and affection from them; for though they may sometimes think he has, yet he never does, nor never will withdraw it; his love to them is as unchangeable as himself; it is the "same yesterday, to-day, and for ever;" for "having loved his own, which were in the world, he loved them to the end;" he has given his word, that though he, "for a small moment forsakes them, yet with everlasting kindness will he have mercy on them;" and as if this was not enough, he joins his oath to it, and swears, that he "would not be wroth with them, nor rebuke them;" and declares, that his kindness and his covenant are as immoveable as, nay, more than mountains and hills; which, one would think, is enough to banish all doubts and fears from believers, and fill them with as firm a persuasion as the apostle Paul was possessed of, when he says, "I am persuaded that neither life nor death," &c., "shall be able to separate us from the love of God, which is in Christ Jesus our Lord." But, 4. It is to be understood of the withdrawing of the sensible manifestations of his presence and love; and this is what the church has experienced in all ages; for he is a God that "hideth his face from the house of Jacob;" and what particular believers have met with, as is manifest from David, Heman, and others. And this was what the church wanted, even some sensible enjoyments of Christ's presence and grace; she had his strengthening and supporting presence, which enabled her to rise and open; but she wanted his comforting and soul-rejoicing presence, and sensible communion with him; Christ's love is always the same, but the sense of it in believers is variable; the one is sometimes withdrawing, the other never.

2ndly. It may seem a little strange, and almost unaccountable, that Christ at this instant should withdraw himself from his church; seeing he had so importunately desired her to arise and open to him; had used all methods to win upon her, and by his grace had enabled her to do it; and yet now it is done, he withdraws himself and is gone: and therefore it is proper to inquire why he should do so; which was perhaps, 1. To chastise her for her former carriage to him: had he, as soon as she had opened the door, shown himself to her, and received her with all tokens of love and joy; she would not have thought the offence so great; nor that he was so much provoked by it, and did so highly resent it as he did; therefore to bring her to a sense of it, and to correct her for it, by suffering the loss of his company, he withdraws himself. 2. To try the truth and strength of her grace: her grace was now in exercise, as appears by her rising and opening; and now, the more to exercise it, and prove the strength of it, he withdraws himself; thus all our afflictions, temptations, and desertions, are for the trial of our faith, and other graces; which being tried, appear "much more precious than of gold that perisheth." 3. To inflame her love, and sharpen her desires the more after him; which effect his withdrawing from her, in chap. iii. 1—3, had upon her; and so it had here: many such instances we have in Job, David, and others; who being without the presence of God, have the more earnestly wished for, vehemently thirsted, panted, and breathed after a re-enjoyment of it; see Job xxiii. 2, Psalm xliii. 1, 2, and lxiii. 1: and it is usually so, that the want of a blessing, not only brings us under a conviction of the worth of it, and so draws out our affections to it, but also enlarges and increases our desires after it. 4. To endear his presence the more, when she came to enjoy it: when a soul has been destitute of Christ's presence for a time, and come to enjoy it again, O how sweet, ravishing, and delightful is it to him! and how much it is valued by him; the disciples were without Christ's bodily presence but a few days; and when he appeared to them, we are told, John xx. 20, that "then were the disciples glad, when they saw the Lord;" and what expressions of joy, and intimations of esteem for Christ's presence, does the church give, in chap. iii. 4, when she had found her lost spouse? 5. To keep her humble: had she immediately enjoyed his presence upon her rising and opening to him, she might have thought that she had, by those actions of hers, deserved such a favour at his hands; therefore, to hide pride from her, and to let her know the nothingness of all her doings, and that they fell abundantly short of meriting such a blessing, he withdraws himself: our enjoyment of Christ's presence, and the communications of his love and grace to us, as much depend on his free and sovereign will, as the first display of his grace to us; he gives these favours at pleasure, and that to whom, when, and where he pleases. 6. To show her the odious nature of sin, which was the cause of this; and that she might, through grace, be more upon her guard against it, and be more cautious of provoking him to it again: it was sin that was the cause of the angels being turned out of heaven, the place of the divine abode; and of Adam's being driven out of Eden, from the presence of the Lord God; and though sin cannot dissolve the union that is between Christ and a believer, nor destroy his covenant-interest in him; yet it is often the cause of God's hiding his face, and Christ's withdrawing his presence from him; " Your iniquities have separated between you and your God, and your sins have hidden his face from you," says the prophet Isaiah, chap. lix. 2, to the people of Israel; and it was the church's unbecoming carriage to Christ, which was the cause of his withdrawing from her now; and therefore to bring her to a sense of it, and to see the odious nature thereof, he withdraws himself; that when she enjoyed it again, she might be more careful not to provoke him again, by such steps as these: and such an effect it had upon her, in chap. iii. 4, 5, where she not only held him fast herself, and would not let him go; but also charges the daughters of Jerusalem to give him no molestation or disturbance.

3rdly. The church makes use of two words here to express Christ's departure from her, "My beloved had withdrawn himself, and was gone;" which signify and import, 1. That this was done suddenly and secretly, unseen, at an unawares to her, and unexpected by her; so the word translated, "had withdrawn himself,"[h] signifies a doing it secretly; he "turned himself about, and was gone[i] in a moment; he withdrew himself privately from the door, and passed by the window, and was gone; so that she could not set eyes upon him, nor hear any tidings of him. 2. That he was gone at a very great distance in her apprehensions: so believers think sometimes, when Christ has withdrawn himself from them, that he is gone a great way off, is not within call, and will never return more: see Psalm x. 1, and this is thought by some,[k] to be the import of the first word; and the other, being added to it, heightens the sense. 3. That he was really gone: it was not a mere imagination of hers, but it was certainly so; which she found to her great grief and sorrow. 4. The doubling of the words, or her using those two words without a copulative, he "had withdrawn himself, was gone," which she seems to speak in the utmost haste and confusion, represent the strength of her passion, the greatness of her sorrow, what a wretched disappointment she met with; and as if she was wringing her hands, and crying out, "He is gone, he is gone, he is gone." Which brings us to consider,

III. What effect this disappointment had upon her; "my soul," says she, "failed when he spoke," or went out;[l] I was as one dead, I immediately fell into a swoon, and was as one whose life and soul departed. Some[m] think that the church in these words excuses herself from the blame of not rising and opening to him sooner; as if she should say, I am not so much to be blamed, nor has my beloved so much reason to be provoked at, nor so highly to resent my not rising and opening sooner; for as soon as ever I heard his voice, saying, "Open to me, my sister, my love, my dove," &c., it overcame my heart, my soul failed at these words of his; I immediately fell into a swoon, and lay as one lifeless and helpless, and was not able to rise and open to him; but as soon as ever I came to my senses, and was recovered a little out of this fit, I arose and opened to him; but it does not appear from the context, that she did fall into such a fit at his calling to her, or was rendered *non compos mentis*: for she was capable all the while of observing all his words and ways; how he carried himself to her, and proceeded with her; what steps he took, and methods he used, till he had brought her to arise and open. Therefore the words seem rather to be expressive of that confusion of mind she was thrown into, when she found he was gone; even as it is said of the queen of Sheba, that "there was no more spirit in her;" occasioned through wonder and surprise in beholding Solomon's wisdom, and the order and management of his house and servants, that she knew not what to think or what to say: so the church here being surprised at Christ's absence, her soul fails her, no spirit is left in her; she knew not what to think, say, or do: or else they are expressive of the exceeding grief and sorrow that she was overwhelmed with; "my soul failed when he spoke," or "at his word;"[n] that is, at the remembrance of it:" O! now I call to mind how lovingly, kindly, and tenderly he spoke to me, when he said, "Open to me, my sister, my love," &c., yet, vile, ungrateful wretch, as I am, I took no notice of it; I put him off with idle excuses, I kept my bed and indulged myself in sloth and ease; but now it cuts me to the heart, it grieves me, I cannot bear up under it; when I remember his love, and my

---

[h] Vid. R. Sol. Jarchium in loc. [i] Vid Cocceium in loc. R. David Kimchi in lib. Shorash. rad. חמק and to this purpose Montanus and Pagnine translate it; the one renders it, circuierat, the other, verteret se. [k] Vid. R. Aben Ezra and Brightman in loc. [l] יצאה ἐξῆλθεν, Sept. ἐξήρχετο, Symmachus; egressa est, Pagninus, Montanus, Marckius. [m] Vid. Sanct. in loc. [n] בדברו ἐν λογῳ αὐτου, Sept. λαλοῦντος αὐτοῦ Symmachus in loquela ejus, Marckius.

unkindness, I sink, I faint, I die; I cannot live without his presence; his absence is death unto me; my soul fails at his words of love and grace which he spoke to me, and at his word of command which he enjoined me; to which, being disobedient, I have now lost his company, which is intolerable to me. She seems to be much in the same case that the Psalmist was, when he said, Psalm cxliii. 7, "Hear me speedily, O Lord, my spirit faileth: hide not thy face from me, lest I be like unto them that go down into the pit."

IV. Being somewhat recovered out of her fainting fit, she rallied together all the spirit and strength she had, and out she goes in search of her lost spouse; the methods she took, and how she succeeded therein, are as follow:

1st. She sought him, namely, in the public ordinances, "in the streets and broad ways of the city," as she had done before, in chap. iii. 2, and that with the same success; "she sought him, but found him not." The nature of seeking a lost Christ, and how to be performed, as also why the church succeeded no better, have been there shown; which will equally serve to explain and illustrate this.

2ndly. She called him, to wit, by name, as she went along the streets and broad ways; that is, she prayed unto him, that he would manifest himself to her in his own ordinances; and no doubt but the method she took was right, and may serve to instruct us, that we should not only before we attended upon an ordinance, pray for the presence of Christ in it; but also, when we are attending, our souls should be breathing after, and secretly begging for it. But how did she succeed herein? she "called him, but he gave her no answer;" resolving still to chastise her for her former ingratitude; to try her faith, and exercise her patience; to inflame her love to him, and increase her desires after communion with him. But, 1. This seems contrary to those kind promises; "Ask, and it shall be given; seek, and ye shall find, &c., call upon me in the day of trouble, and I will deliver thee," &c.; but she asked, and it was not given to her what she asked for; she sought, but found not; she called, but no answer is returned: to which it may be replied, that God does, and certainly will make good his own promises, and fulfil the petitions of his people; yet he does not always answer immediately, nor just in that way which they are desirous of: the church had his upholding presence, though not sensible communion with him; she was so far answered, as to be "strengthened with strength in her soul," to continue in her search and inquiries after him; though she had not those manifestations of his grace and love, which she was desirous of. 2. It is a very great affliction to a believer, when he labours under such apprehensions, that his prayers are not heard and answered: the church mentions this among her sore afflictions, in Lam. iii. 8, 44, that God had "shut out her prayer," and had "covered himself with a cloud, that her prayer should not pass through;" unconverted men, hypocrites, and carnal professors, are not concerned about the answer of their prayers; it is enough to them to perform these duties but believers are concerned about the returns of prayer, and are grieved to the heart, as the church here was, when they cannot observe any. 3. Christ here treats her just in the same way in which she had treated him; she is paid in her own coin; he had called to her, but she disregarded him, and turned a deaf ear to him, and returned him no answer, that deserved the name of one; she now calls to him, but he disregards her, turns a deaf ear to her, and gives her no answer, he treats her here, not in a way of vindictive wrath and punishment, as he will do the wicked at the last day; see Prov. i. 24—28; but in a way of chastisement and correction. What success she afterwards met with, will be seen in the following verses.

Verse 7. *The watchmen, that went about the city, found me; they smote me, they wounded me; the keepers of the walls took away my veil from me.*

THE church in the former verse gives an account of the wretched disappointment she met with, when she opened the door to her beloved, who had withdrawn himself, and was gone; at which she fell into a fainting fit, out of which, when she was a little recovered, she resolved not to stay at the door, lamenting the loss of her spouse, but to go out in search of him, which she did, but with no success; and she does in these words give an account of what she met with in the adventure; how she was taken up by the watch, and evilly treated by them. Where we have to consider,

I. Her being found by "the watchmen that went about the city, and keepers of the walls."

II. Their treatment of her, and carriage to her.

I. In this search of her beloved, she falls into the hands of the watchmen that went about the city, and the keepers of the walls thereof; who were officers of the church, set for the defence of it, and for the administration of those ordinances, in which she sought her beloved; and the description of them, or these titles and characters which they bear, may lead us to observe,

1st. That the church is a city: and no doubt is called so, in allusion to the city of Jerusalem, which was builded as a city that is compact together; it was the metropolis of the land of Judea, where Solomon kept his court, was well fortified, and delightfully situated; and therefore the church militant, as well as the church triumphant, is called by the same name; which is the city of God; of which the psalmist says, Psalm lxxxvii. 3, "Glorious things are spoken;" it is the place of the residence of the King of kings where his honour dwells, where he keeps his court, and has his palace; and therefore is called the city of the great King, in whose palaces God is known for a refuge; here he shows himself, here he may be seen; therefore she was in the right of it to seek him here: in this city are all needful and delightful accommodations; it is beautiful for situation, a river of boundless love and grace runs through it, whose streams supply, refresh, and make glad the inhabitants of it; here are the best provisions to be had, which are called the goodness and fatness of God's house; here are the most delightful company, and agreeable conversation; here souls have fellowship with the Father, and with his Son Jesus Christ; those who are brought unto, and are made inhabitants of this city of the living God, have communion with an innumerable company of angels, and spirits of just men made perfect by Christ's righteousness; in this city are many special and peculiar privileges and immunities, which the inhabitants of it enjoy; for being Christ's freemen, and freemen of this city, they have a right to all the ordinances of the gospel, and share in all the promises which concern the grace and presence of Christ; they are under no obligation to any other laws but those of Christ's, and are freed from the curses and condemnation of the law of works; so that to be a citizen of this city, and a fellow-citizen of the saints, is no small privilege; see Eph. ii. 19, Rev. iii. 12; but of the church's being compared to a city, see more on chap. iii. 2.

2ndly. Mention being made of the keepers of the walls of this city, shows us, that this city of God is a walled one; it is a fortified place, even as Jerusalem was, to which the allusion is made, when the church of God is spoken of, as in Psalm li. 18, and cxxii. 7; and it may be proper to inquire what are the walls of the church, which render it strong and impregnable. And, 1. God himself is the wall of it, according to what he himself says, Zech. ii. 5, "For I, saith the Lord, will be a wall of fire round about it, and will be the glory in the midst of her;" he is not only a wall that keeps the enemy from entrance into the city, but a wall of fire that consumes and destroys all that make near approaches to it; all the divine perfections are as so many walls, which encompass and defend the church; especially that of Almighty power, by which saints are kept as in a garrison,° through faith unto salvation: Jerusalem was fortified, not only by art, but also by nature, not only with walls, but with mountains; and "as the mountains are round about Jerusalem, so the Lord is round about his people, from henceforth, even for ever," Psal. cxxv. 2. 2. Salvation by Christ is the church's wall, which render it strong and impregnable: hence we read, in Isa. xxvi. 1, In that day, that is, in the gospel day, when salvation is accomplished by Christ, "shall this song be sung in the land of Judah, We have a strong city." But what is it which makes it so? salvation will God appoint for walls and bulwarks: and this song will be sung more clearly in the latter day, when the church shall call her walls, salvation, and her gates, praise: salvation wrought out by Christ, is the church's protection from all enemies; hereby believers are screened and secured from sin and Satan, law, hell, and wrath to come; no enemy can destroy them, no condemnation reach them, nor any wrath fall on them; but they shall be "saved in the Lord with an everlasting salvation." 3. Ministers may be called so, who are set for the defence of the gospel: so the Lord told Jeremiah, chap. i. 18, that he had made him a defenced city, an iron pillar, and brazen walls against the whole land; though they seem not to be intended here, because they are called the keepers of the walls, and not the walls themselves. Now the city of God being thus walled and fortified, shows, (1.) That it would otherwise be in danger from enemies; for the church of Christ has many enemies, who are lively and strong, crafty and cunning, vigilant and active, seeking all opportunities to get within, and there make disturbance, and do mischief: but this city is so well walled and firmly built, that let Satan, with all his emissaries, use all their power and cunning, and lay the closest siege unto it, the gates of hell will never be able to prevail against it. (2.) The great care which God takes of his church and people; for as birds flying or fluttering over and about their nest, in order to preserve their young, when they are in danger of being taken away from them; "so will the Lord of hosts defend Jerusalem; defending also, he will deliver it; and passing over he will preserve it," as it is said in Isa. xxxi. 5; which care for their preservation, is manifestly seen in his placing such walls about it.

3rdly. In this city are proper officers appointed and set to watch over and guard it; and these go under two titles or characters in the text. 1. They are called "watchmen that went about the city:" these are the ministers of the church, who are called so both in the Old and New-Testament; because they ought to watch over themselves, their doctrine and conversation, and to watch over others, who are made their care and charge: the business of watchmen is also to give the time of night, to give notice of present or approaching danger, either by fire, or by thieves and robbers, and to take up disorderly persons, and bring them to correction: so the ministers of the gospel give notice what time of day or night it is with the churches of Christ; they give notice to sinners of the danger which they are in, whilst in a state of nature; and also what danger churches may be in, through contentious persons and heretics, who

° Τας εν δυναμει Θεου ϕρουρουμενους, præsidio Dei circumvallamur; metaphora a castris vallo et fossis undique munitis ut nulla hostium vi vel astutia expugnari possint, Paræus in 1 Pet. i. 5.

endeavour to sow the seeds of discord, error, and heresy among them; likewise their business is to awake and arouse sleepy professors, who are indulging themselves in carnal ease and security in the streets of Zion; and to admonish, reprove, and rebuke all that stand in need thereof, and so bring them under the notice and censure of the church. These are said to go about the city, 1. To distinguish them from those upon the walls: those that went about the city, were to take care of the peace and safety of the city within; the keepers of the walls were to descry an enemy without, observe his motions, repel him if able, and to give notice to those within of danger from him, the one was a running watch, the other a standing one. 2. To show the nature of their work, and their diligence in it: it was the business of the keepers of the walls, to keep their stands, and not stir from their places; but the work of these was to go from place to place, and see that all was in peace and safety; but of these watchmen, see more in chap. iii. 8. 3. These officers are called " keepers of the walls;" by which some[p] understand angels, who encamp about, and protect the people of God; others,[q] civil magistrates, who the apostle says, Rom. xiii. 3, 4, are not "terrors to good works, but to the evil;" and that " he is the minister of God for good, and beareth not the sword in vain:" but if these were civil magistrates, they terrified the church in the way of her duty, and discouraged her in it: nay, turned the point of their swords against her, as often the princes of this world do, being ignorant of Christ and his church: but I rather think church-officers are here intended, and that they are the same with the watchmen, who went about the city; only they may be expressive of different branches in the ministry, or of different talents which ministers have, and are to use in the discharge of their work: some, their work chiefly lies in comforting and establishing the church in answering cases of conscience, and keeping peace and order within; and they have gifts suitable thereunto; and these may be called watchmen that go about the city: others, their work lies chiefly in defending the gospel against the avowed enemies of it; these keep the outworks good, and repel the enemy, whenever he makes an attack upon any doctrine of the Gospel; and these may be called " the keepers or watchmen of the walls;" and so ministers are called in Isa. lxii. 6. The Jews in Shirashirim Rabba, and in Yalkut on the place, understand by these keepers, the tribe of Levi, the keepers of the walls of the law.

But it may now be inquired, whether these were the true ministers of Christ, or no: some[r] think that they were: they are called watchmen, and watchmen in the city, the church, though it is true, false teachers may bear the same name as true ones, and be in office in the church as well as they; but what seems most to strengthen this opinion, is, that they were about their work, and in the discharge of their office; the watchmen were going about the city, as they should do, and the keepers of the walls were upon their stands, as they ought to be: others[s] think that they were not the true and faithful ministers of the gospel; but such who are called " blind watchmen," &c., in Isa. lvi. 10, 11, and that, 1. Because the church makes no inquiry of them, nor any application to them, which she did in a like case to the watchmen, in chap. iii. 3, and therefore it seems to intimate, that she, not looking upon them as ministers of Christ, had nothing to say to them, but would have shunned them if she could. 2. Because of their cruelty to her: they are not so pitiful, compassionate, and tender, as becomes the ministers to be to souls in such cases; they seem rather to be ravenous wolves, than faithful shepherds or watchmen, and are most like those in Ezek. xxxiv. 2—21. Plato[t] says, keepers of cities should be mild and gentle towards their own, but to enemies rough and severe.

Now these found the church seeking and enquiring for her beloved: which shows, that she was in the city, in the streets and broad ways of it: she searched all over the city, where the watchmen that went about it, found her; and escaping from them with blows and wounds, finding that her beloved was not there, she makes to the outparts of the city, perhaps designing to go without the city in search of him, where she fell into the hands of the keepers of the walls. This finding of her, also appears to be accidental, and at an unawares; they were not seeking her, nor was she enquiring after them; it was on a sudden that they found her; and as soon as they did find her, they fell upon her, and took her up for a stroller or night-walker; and by their treatment of her manifestly showed that they found her, not as a friend, but as an enemy; and therefore did not let her go safe, but with blows, wounds, and the loss of her veil. Which brings us to consider,

II. Their treatment of her, and carriage to her. And,

1st. " The watchmen, that went about the city, smote and wounded her;" which, if we understand of the true ministers of the gospel (though I rather think that others are intended) must be meant, either of their upbraiding and reproaching her for her former unkindness to Christ, and negligence of her duty; when they told her and hit her in the teeth of her former sins and miscarriages, they smote and cut her to the heart, opened the wound, and made it bleed afresh; and so, like Job's friends, proved miserable comforters,

---

[p] Ambros. in Psal. cxviii. octon. 7. col. 933. Psellus, and Tres Patres apud Theodoret. in loc. Foliot and R. Sol Jarchi in loc.   [q] Theodoret. in Sanct. in loc. and Diodat. in loc.

[r] Greg. Beda, Bernard. Aquin. in Sanct in loc, Isidore, Foliot, Alcuin in loc.   [s] Ainsworth and Mercer. in loc.   [t] De Legibus, l. 2, p. 602.

who broke him in pieces with words both of reproof and reproach: they laid open her sins to her, and sharply reproved her for them, when they should have comforted her with the doctrines of justification by Christ's righteousness and pardon, by his blood; for Christ's own ministers may sometimes be mistaken in timing reproofs and corrections; or else, she being under the ministry of the word, and hearing some sweet discourses concerning Christ's person and grace, her heart was smitten and wounded therewith, which made her charge the daughters of Jerusalem, in the following verse, that when they found her beloved, they would tell him, that she was sick of, or wounded with love. But if we understand it of false teachers, which seems most agreeable; then by those smitings and woundings, are meant, the scandalous lives of such persons, the rents and divisions they make, the false doctrines which they preach; and those human traditions, which, with force, they impose upon the consciences of men, being assisted by civil magistrates, whom they stir up to make penal laws, and put them in execution against the saints; by all which means they make the hearts of the righteous sad, and wound the consciences of God's children. One of the Greek versions is, "they scourged me,"[u] whipped her till she was black and blue; as the Jews did the first Christians in their synagogues.

2ndly. "The keepers of the walls took away her veil from her:" veils were used by women in those countries, sometimes for ornament, Isa. iii. 23; sometimes as a token of modesty; thus Rebekah, when she found that Isaac was coming to meet her, covered herself with a veil, Gen. xxiv. 65; and sometimes as a token of subjection to the husband; for which the apostle argues, that women ought to be covered, 1 Cor. xi. 6—10; at marriage, it was customary with the Grecians,[w] to give a veil to the new-married bride; the bridegroom, with the Romans, used to give the bride a veil, called *flammeum*,[x] from its being of a flame-colour, either yellow or red, expressive of the blushing and modesty of the new bride;[y] and the like custom might obtain with the Jews. Now for the keepers to take away her veil from her, was to strip her of her ornaments, and expose her frailties and infirmities, which ought to be covered; it was to disown her as the spouse of Christ, and to represent her as a whorish and impudent woman; and, whereas she professed herself to be Christ's, to serve him in the way of his appointments; they endeavoured to "corrupt her from the simplicity that is in Christ," and to draw her aside to a reception of false doctrines, and to a compliance with human traditions: and then more especially, may they be said to take away her veil, when they oppose and endeavour to subvert or remove the doctrine of imputed righteousness by Christ; Christ's righteousness is the believer's veil or covering; this is "the wedding garment," περιβολαιον νυμφικον, the nuptial robe, as Gregory Nyssen[z] calls the veil here; and when persons attempt to take away this doctrine, they do as much as in them lies to take away the church's veil. And now all this cruelty was exercised by persons professing religion, under a mask of godliness; by those who were officers in the church, from whom she might have expected a quite different treatment; and indeed, who were more bitter enemies to Christ and his apostles, than the priests and Pharisees were? and who have more cruelly persecuted in after-ages, than those who have professed Christianity! The church thus escaping from the watchmen and keepers, with blows, wounds, and the loss of her veil, meets with the daughters of Jerusalem, to whom she speaks in the following manner.

Verse 8. *I charge you, O daughters of Jerusalem, if ye find my beloved, that ye tell him, that I am sick of love.*

THE church having met with a disappointment, as has been observed in ver. 6, by her beloved's withdrawing himself from her; but resolving to find him, if possible, she seeks for him in the public ordinances; where she is taken notice of by the officers of the church, "the watchmen of the city, and keepers of the walls;" who very much abuse her, "smite, wound" her, and take away her veil from her; by reason of which, she making a hideous outcry in the streets, the "daughters of Jerusalem," the wise virgins, who were then sleeping and slumbering on their beds, were awakened and alarmed, and rose up to know what was the matter; who being observed by the church, had the charge in the text given unto them by her. In which we have,

I. The persons whom she addresses, and in this solemn manner adjures, "the daughters of Jerusalem."

II. The charge itself, which she gives them; which is, to tell her beloved, when found by them, that she was "sick of love."

III. The condition of this charge; "if ye find my beloved."

IV. The manner in which this charge is given, which is very solemn and serious.

I. The persons to whom she gives this charge; "the daughters of Jerusalem:" by whom we are not to understand the prophets, as the Targum does; though these were proper persons for the church to make application to in her present condition; but having been so evilly treated by the watchmen and keepers of the walls, she had but

---

[u] Εμωλωπεσαν με, Aquila.   [w] Homer. Iliad. 22. v. 470.   [x] Lutea demissos velarunt flammea vultus, Lucan. Pharsal 1. 2. v. 361. Ubi tibi corycio glomerarem flammea luto, Virgil. Cyris. Vid. Barth. ad Claudian. Fescen. ode 4. v. 4. and Plin. l. 21. c. 8.   [y] Vid. Chartar. de Imag. Deorum, p. 84, 89. and Kipping. Antiq. Rom. l. 4. c. 2. p. 695, 696.   [z] Homil. in Cant. 21. p. 651.

little encouragement to go to them: nor are angels here meant, as some [a] think; though they are "ministering spirits, sent to the heirs of salvation," and are often useful to the saints on many accounts: yet it does not seem to be their business, nor are they capable of assisting and relieving souls in such a case as this of the church's: nor are "saints departed" meant, as some popish interpreters [b] imagine: as if the church desired their prayers for her, who are incapable of giving her any assistance; but by them we are to understand saints here on earth, the friends and companions of the church, which belong to that Jerusalem which "is free, and is the mother of us all;" these were "fellow-citizens with the saints, and of the household of God;" perhaps were young converts, as has been observed in other places of this Song; and it is certain, that they were believers of the weaker sort; their knowledge of Christ was but small, though they had a great respect for the church, and a desire of seeking Christ with her, ver. 9, and chap. vi. 1. The church now making application to these person in her disconsolate condition, shows, 1. Her humility: that she is willing to be assisted by mean Christians or weak believers, who were much inferior to her in faith and knowledge; it is the nature of grace, and the tendency of such trying dispensations as these, in which the church was, to make and keep souls humble; the more grace they have, the more humble they will be; the greatest believer reckoned himself the "least of saints, and the chief of sinners," and is willing to be instructed and admonished by the meanest saint; see Psal. cxli. 5; and is glad of the prayers and assistance of weak believers, when in distress. 2. Her resolution to use all means to find her beloved, as Job did, chap. xxiii. 8, 9, she will leave no stone unturned, nor let slip any opportunity, where there was any probability or possibility of finding him; she had sought him; in public ordinances, but with no success; nay, had met with ill treatment from church-officers; yet she is not discouraged, but is resolved to persist in her search of him: she had spread her case before Christ in prayer, and could get no answer; and now she betakes herself to the company of private Christians, that by conference with them, and through their prayers for her, she might be brought to the enjoyment of what she was seeking after. 3. That communion and conversation with saints is a very proper method to be taken by believers in such cases; conversing together about the things of God, is very acceptable and well-pleasing to him: it is said, Mal. iii. 16, of the saints, who "spake often one to another," that the Lord hearkened and heard, listened as it were unto it, and took such notice of it, that "a book of remembrance was written before him" for them; he did, as it were, take notes and minutes of what they said and thought, and laid them up: as we should spread our cases before God; so it is very proper, and often very useful, to spread our case before one another; and therefore there should not be a "forsaking the assembling of ourselves together, as the manner of some is;" but so much the more should we assemble together, as our various wants and cases require. 4. That when souls are in distress, it is their duty and interest to make application to others; they should not only pray for themselves, which should be done in the first place, but they should also desire the prayers of others for them; for "the effectual fervent prayer of a righteous man availeth much:" and it is no disgrace nor dishonour for a person superior in office, gifts, and graces to others, to desire their assistance by their prayers for him at the throne of grace; instances of this we have, not only in the church here, but in that great man of God, an instance of grace, the apostle Paul, who frequently desired the prayers of meaner saints for him; see Eph. vi. 19, 2 Thess. iii. 1, 2. 5. That it is the duty of saints to be assisting to each other in their distresses, as much as in them lies; by singing the praises of God together, by praying one with and for another, and by conferring with each other about divine things, and so building up one another on their most holy faith: there ought to be a sympathizing spirit in the saints; they should "bear one another's burdens, and should mutually help each other; they should "weep with those that weep, and rejoice with those that rejoice." But,

II. Let us consider the charge itself, which is given to them by her; and that is to tell her beloved, when they found him, that she was sick of love. This does not suppose that he was ignorant or unmindful of her present state; he heard her, though he would not answer; he knew that she was enquiring after him, and what hardships she underwent in doing it; and also, how much her soul was filled with love to him, and longed for the enjoyment of him: though he would not immediately show himself, intending a little longer to chastise her for her former carriage to him; but the word shows the ardency of her love to Christ, and that she would have them declare this to him, in their prayers for her, which she thought might be a means to induce him to manifest himself to her; as also they show what familiarity souls may use at the throne of grace, what freedom they may take with Christ, when they come into his presence, "tell him that I am sick of love." They may tell him their own cases and the cases of others, as one friend may tell another, or as a child may tell its father; they may go with boldness to him, and spread their own and others' cases before him, without fear of being chided or upbraided by him, and indeed it is their duty to bear upon their minds, at the throne of grace, not only their own cases, and the cases of the church in general, as the apostle Paul frequently did; but also the cases

---

[a] Foliot in loc. and Psellus apud Theodoret in loc. [b] Vid. Sanct. in loc.

of particular persons, whom they know to be in distress; therefore Christ taught his disciples to pray after this manner, " Our Father, &c., and forgive us our debts," &c., to show that they should be concerned for others in prayer, as well as for themselves. The words in the Hebrew text may be rendered thus, " What shall ye, or should ye tell him?"* as if she should say, Do not tell him the blows and wounds that I have received from the watchmen! nor desire him to revenge the injuries and affronts they have given me, I freely forgive them; nor am I so much concerned for the sufferings that I undergo, as I am for the loss of him: " What shall ye tell him?" Tell him that which lies most upon my heart, under which I shall sink and die, if he does not relieve me; " tell him that I am sick of love." Again, What shall ye tell him? Tell him that which will be the most acceptable and agreeable to him; tell him I love him so, that I cannot live without him : she knew that he valued her love, and that his heart would be ravished with it, from what he had said, chap. iv. 9, 10; and therefore would have this told him. Again, " What shall ye tell him?" What shall I say to you to tell him? I have a great many things to tell him of; but I will not overburden your memories, but I will give you my mind in a few words, in the most concise manner, " tell him that I am sick of love;" and when I meet with him myself, I will tell him all my mind; but for the present, only tell him this. But let us a little more particularly consider the matter of this charge, or what the church would have the daughters of Jerusalem tell Christ, when they found him; which is, that she was " sick of love." And it will be proper to enquire,

1st. The causes of this sickness; which sometimes are, 1. A want of the views of pardoning grace, under a sense of sin, which perhaps was the case of the church here; she had sinned against Christ, in neglecting to arise and open to him; and she was now sensible of it, but wanted the manifestations of pardon; and was therefore in a languishing and fainting condition on the account of it; and it is only this which will cure this sickness: " The inhabitant shall not say, I am sick." Why so? " the people that dwell therein shall be forgiven their iniquity;" that is, they shall have the manifestations of pardoning grace to their souls, which shall cure them of their sickness and maladies: which was what the church here wanted. 2. The absence of Christ is sometimes the cause of this sickness; and this also was the church's case: Christ had " withdrawn himself from her and was gone," as in v. 6, and though she had diligently sought him, yet she could not find him, nor hear anything of him; and this brought this sickness upon her. 3. An eager longing after Christ's presence, and the discoveries of his love, is another cause of it: when a soul has sought Christ a long time in ordinances, and cannot find him: has lived in the hope and expectation of enjoying his presence time after time, and yet is still at a loss for him, then comes this sickness upon it; for, as Solomon says, Prov. xiii. 12, " hope deferred maketh the heart sick." 4. Sometimes the large discoveries of love which believers have, cause a sickness, which may be called a love-sickness; and this is what the church speaks of, in chap. ii. 5, " stay me with flagons, comfort me with apples: for I am sick of love:" she had been with Christ in his wine-cellar or banqueting-house, and had as much of his love let into her soul, as she could hold, nay, more; she was overpowered with it; " his banner over " her had been love. But this was not the church's case here: her sickness here arises rather from the aforesaid causes, and chiefly from a want of that love which she had such large discoveries of there.

2ndly. It may not be amiss to consider the nature and properties of this sickness. And, 1. It is not a sickness unto death; none ever died of this sickness; Christ will never suffer any to die with love for him: for he " loves them that love him," and will cause them "to inherit substance;" to enjoy himself, the substance of all felicity; and to inherit eternal glory, which is the better and the " more enduring substance;" where they shall have sweet and uninterrupted communion with him. Yet, 2. It is a very sore and painful sickness; like Hezekiah's, it is a pining one; and oftentimes wastes the body, as well as affects the mind. The Septuagint render it, " for I am wounded with love;" which gave her a great deal of pain and uneasiness; for " love is as strong as death." 3. It is an immedicable sickness without the enjoyment of Christ, the object loved; bodily physicians cannot cure it; these are in this case, like Job's physicians, of no value; merry companions are of no service to remove it; the enjoyment of another beloved will not do; the language of a soul in such a case, is, None but Christ, none but Christ; give me Christ, or I die; I cannot live without him: this sickness can only be cured by the object loved, and this infallibly cures; for, " as hope deferred maketh the heart sick, so when the desire cometh it is a tree of life."

3rdly. We may now consider the evidences of this love-sickness, or how it manifests itself: and, 1. There is in souls that labour under it, a violent pulsation and panting of the heart after Christ, even " as the heart panteth after the water-brooks;" they are restless and uneasy without him; their thoughts are continually running upon him; the desire of their souls, night and day, " is to his name, and to the remembrance of him." 2. They are prodigiously jealous of him and his love; and this is exceeding afflicting to them; for " jealousy is as cruel as the grave:" they are exceedingly afraid that he does not love them, or

---

* מה תגידו לו τι ἀπαγγείλητε αυτω, Sept. Quid indicaretis ei? Junius; Quid, narrabitis ei? Pagninus, Michaelis; Quid. indicabitis. ei? Montanus, Mercerus, Marckius, so Ainsworth.

that he loves others better than them; for, as the poet[d] says, *Res est soliciti plena timoris amor*. 8. They are very active and diligent, careful and industrious to gain his love; they use all the methods and stratagems they can devise; are bold and resolute, are not discouraged at any difficulties, but are willing to run all risks for the enjoyment of him. 4. They love to hear his name mentioned, and especially to be spoken well of; his name to them is "as ointment poured forth," exceeding grateful; it attracts their love, "therefore do the virgins love" him; they love his ways, his ordinances and his doctrines, and cannot bear to hear them spoken against; they love to look upon and converse with his people, because they are like him, and bear a resemblance to him.

III. The condition of this charge is, "if ye find him;" which shows, 1. That at present these daughters of Jerusalem had not any sight of Christ, nor communion with him; and this appears also manifestly from the following verse, where they enquire of her concerning him. 2. That it was possible that they might find him before she did; for Christ is sometimes "found of them that sought him not," and is "made manifest unto them that asked not after" him; she was enquiring after Christ, but found him not; and yet it was possible that they might find him before her, who had not been seeking after him; also Christ may manifest himself to poor, mean, and weak believers, when he does not to some that are superior to them in faith, light, and knowledge; he showed himself after his resurrection to a poor woman, to Mary Magdalene, out of whom he cast seven devils, before he did to his disciples. 3. That when they did find Christ, and had liberty of access to his presence, that they would then spread her sorrowful case before him, and use their interest with him, to take pity and compassion on her, who was "sick of love" for him; she entreats them to do such a favour for her, as Joseph requested of the chief butler, when he should be restored to his place; says he, Gen. xl. 12, "But think on me, when it shall be well with thee; and show kindness, I pray thee, unto me; and make mention of me unto Pharaoh, and bring me out of this house." So the church would have these virgins, when it was well with them, when they enjoyed the presence of Christ, to think on her and her sorrowful case, and make mention of it to him.

IV. This charge is delivered in a very solemn manner: "I adjure you,"[e] or "I put you to your oath, I make you swear," as the word signifies, that when you find him, you will tell him what I have said to you; I have given you your oath to do it; and now as you will answer it before God, in whose name and presence you have taken it, that you will carefully observe what I say to you, and faithfully deliver the message; if you have any regard to this solemn oath you have taken, or any love to me, I beg you will tell him that I am sick of love. She delivers herself in this solemn manner, not only to show the strength of her love to him, and that she was hearty and sincere in her search and enquiries after him; but also that she was serious in what she said to them, and would have them be serious, diligent, and faithful in telling her case to Christ. The answer returned by them, is as follows.

Verse 9. *What is thy beloved more than another beloved, O thou fairest among women? What is thy beloved more than another beloved, that thou dost so charge us?*

THE church having solemnly adjured the daughters of Jerusalem, that when they found her beloved, they would tell him that she was sick of love. In these words we have their reply to her, which show what an opinion they had of her, and what effect her words had upon them; in which may be observed,

I. The title and character they give her; "O thou fairest among women."

II. A question they propose to her; "What is thy beloved more than another beloved?"

III. This question repeated; where the reason of it must be considered.

IV. What the occasion was of their putting this question to her; which was her solemn charge, "that thou dost so charge us?"

I. The title or character which they give her, the "fairest among women;" which is expressive of the exceeding greatness of her beauty; she was not only fair, but the fairest, and that among women, whose beauty is excelling; she was the fairest of any of her sex; not as she was in herself, but as she is in Christ, justified by his righteousness, washed in his blood, and sanctified by his Spirit; and being considered thus, she appeared to these daughters, as indeed she really is, a perfection of beauty: and they were not mistaken herein, for Christ, who knew her perfectly well, and from whom she received her comeliness, gives her the same character in the very same words, in chap. i. 8; but then this opinion, which they entertained of her, though it entirely corresponds with that which Christ has entertained of her, yet is extremely different from that which the world has embraced; which shows, that these persons were not of this world, but called by grace out of it, seeing they had different sentiments of the church; the saints are by the world esteemed the filth thereof, and the offscouring of all things; they are accounted by them the foolish, base, weak, and contemptible things of the world; nay, even things that are not, as if they were mere nonentities, and did not deserve the name of men or beings; and indeed, as they see no beauty nor comeliness in Christ, it is no wonder that they can see none in the church; but these daughters of

---

[d] Ovid. [e] הִשְׁבַּעְתִּי ὥρκισα, Sept. adjure, Vulg. Lat. Cocceius, Pagninus, Mercerus, Junius: obtestor, Tigurine version.

Jerusalem could, for they judged not according to the outward appearance; the world only sees the outside of the people of God, which is generally poor, mean, and abject; but these could penetrate into the inside of the church, and viewed her, who is the king's daughter, as all glorious within, and therefore called her the fairest among women; for outwardly she was now black with sins, infirmities, reproaches, and persecutions; yet, notwithstanding, she is highly esteemed of by them; for they had made Moses' choice, having thought it more eligible to suffer affliction with the people of God, than to enjoy the pleasures of sin for a season, esteeming the reproach of Christ greater riches than the treasures in Egypt. Young converts, as I suppose these daughters were, have generally a great respect for old professors, for such that were in Christ before them: these are the excellent in the earth, in whom is all their delight; they love to see them, and take pleasure in their company and conversation: and indeed, as love to the brethren is made an evidence of passing from death to life, by the apostle John, 1 John iii. 14, so it shows itself in young converts, as soon as any thing else; for oftentimes, where there is but a small knowledge of Christ, and acquaintance with him, there is a great deal of love to Christ's people, which was the case of these daughters here; also it may be supposed, that they give her this title to assure her of the high esteem which they had for her, and that opinion which they had of her, that she might not think that they designed her any hurt by asking the following question; but rather, seeing they had such a value for her, that their design was to do her all the service, and be as assisting to her in her search of her beloved as they were able; and no doubt also, but this opinion which they had of her, made them listen to, and regard the more what she afterwards says of her beloved; for they concluded, that he must be some great and extraordinary person, that she, who was the fairest among women, had made the object of her choice and love; they took it for granted that one so fair, so wise and prudent as she was, would not take notice of any person, nor lavish and throw away her love upon every object; and this made them the more forward and eager to put the question, which is now to be considered.

II. The question which they propose to her, is, "What is thy beloved more than another beloved?" which is not put in a scornful, disdainful, or profane way, as Pharaoh said to Moses, when he demanded the dismission of the people of Israel, "who is the Lord, that I should obey his voice?" or as Rabshakeh to the men of Judah, in that railing, profane speech of his, in 2 Kings xviii. 33—35; the design and sense of which was, What is the God of Israel more than the gods of the nations? but such was not this question here; these persons were not the profane people of the world; they had a great esteem for the church, and therefore it cannot be supposed that they would insinuate any thing in a scornful and reproachful way of her beloved: nor did they propose this question with a design to ensnare her, as the Scribes and Pharisees frequently did to Christ; nor with a design to shift off any trouble from themselves, which they might suppose would arise from an observance of her solemn charge, but rather are willing to be assisting to her all they could; and therefore desire to have some distinguishing characters of him, that they might not lose their labour in seeking, and, when they found him, might perfectly know him; which, when she had given, to their entire satisfaction, they then desired to know whither he was gone, which way he took when he left her, that they might seek him with her, as is manifest from chap. vi. 1; nor does this question suppose that they were altogether ignorant of her beloved; for though their knowledge of Christ was small, yet they were not entirely destitute of it; and therefore, as one[f] well observes, they do not say, who, but what is thy beloved, &c., and indeed it cannot be reasonably thought, that they should be entirely ignorant of him; for she had, in chap. i. 5, given some account of herself to them; that though she was black in herself, yet comely in another; which is the reason why they here call her the fairest among women; and there is no doubt but she also gave them some account of him, from whom she received all her comeliness; and in chap. ii. 7, and iii. 5, she charges them very strictly, to give him, her love, no molestation or disturbance; which could not very well be, without informing them who he was; and in chap. iii. 11, she invites them to come forth and see this glorious person who was her Lord and Husband, in all his glory, on his coronation and espousal-day; to which invitation, they no doubt complied, and therefore must have some knowledge of him. The design then of this question is, that they might know him more and better; which also is the desire of every gracious soul, even of those who have made the greatest proficiency in the knowledge of our Lord Jesus Christ; the apostle Paul perhaps knew as much of Christ as ever any mere man on earth did, and yet he desired to know more of him and the power of his resurrection; for he valued the knowledge of him above all things else: these daughters of Jerusalem, though they knew but little, were willing to know more of Christ; as they had begun to know, they desired to follow on to know him, and make a greater improvement in this kind of learning; and being sensible of the church's abilities, desire her assistance, and are willing to be instructed by her: also those who know the most of Christ, are frequently desirous of having his praises and excellencies set forth by others; for they can never hear him enough extolled; his name to

---

[f] Durham in loc.

them is as ointment poured forth; therefore they love him, as did the virgins here; who excited the church hereunto, by putting this question, and so had their ends answered: and perhaps likewise they might have in view the trial of her faith in Christ, her knowledge of him, and love to him in her present state; she was now under his resentments; he had withdrawn himself from her, and she was exposed to the scandal, reproach, and persecutions of her enemies; and they were willing to know how her faith stood now, whether she loved him now as well as ever, and whether by his absence she had not lost all just ideas of him; and in this she gives them full satisfaction in her answer to them; where she gives an exact account of him, describes him from head to foot, and shows the strength of her faith in him, and affections for him, particularly in the close of it, verse 16; also in this question they seem principally desirous of knowing what those excellencies were which were in him, that distinguished him from other beloveds, and made him preferable to them. Christ was the chiefest among ten thousands in her esteem; to all that believe he is precious; not only precious upon an equal footing with others, but far more precious than all other things or persons besides; for there is none in heaven, nor any upon earth, that saints desire besides him: there are indeed a great many beloveds, but Christ is preferable to them all; and in what he is so, the daughters of Jerusalem were willing to know.

1st. The world, with the riches and grandeur of it, is the beloved of some persons. There are too many, both in the world and in the church, that have their affections too much set on earthly things; who neglect their own souls, and the cause and interest of Christ Jesus; having Demas-like, loved this present world: but, alas! What is this world, or any thing in it, to be compared to Christ, the believer's beloved? every thing, even the best that is in the world, is fading, perishing, and transitory; many temptations and snares, foolish and hurtful lusts, does an immoderate care for, and sinful love of this world, run persons into; therefore, says the apostle John, 1 John ii. 15, " love not the world, neither the things that are in the world," for they are not to be mentioned with Christ; he is infinitely preferable to them; see Prov. iii. 13—15.

2ndly. The sinful lusts and pleasures of this life are the beloveds of others. Every natural man has his beloved lust or lusts; and these he idolizes and adores, falls down to, and worships; he makes gods of them, as the apostle says, Phil. iii. 19, of some, " whose god is their belly;" and it may be said of all by nature, that they are " serving divers lusts and pleasures," being lovers of them; who are never better pleased and more satisfied, than when they are " fulfilling the desires of the flesh and of the mind;" but these pleasures are but short-lived; they afford no real satisfaction now; and, if grace prevent not, will end in bitterness and death: wherefore the worst of a believer, even his afflictions, are better than these; and therefore he thinks it more eligible " to suffer affliction with the people of God, than to enjoy the pleasure of sin for a season;" and if so, much more preferable must Christ, an interest in him, union to him, and communion with him, be to all such beloveds as these.

3rdly. The praise and applause of men is another beloved of some persons. This was the beloved of the hypocritical Pharisees, who, in all the parts of their religion and devotion, sought the honour of men, and not of God: as also of those who, though they were convinced in their consciences that Christ was the Messiah, and believed him to be so, yet " did not confess him, for they loved the praise of men more than the praise of God:" they were afraid that their good names, characters, and reputations should be blasted, as too many are now: and therefore drop the doctrines of the gospel, and desert the cause and interest of Christ Jesus: but though " a good name is better than precious ointment," it is not better than a precious Jesus, whose " name is as ointment poured forth;" nor better than the precious doctrines of the gospel; it is much preferable to be nick-named, reproached, and vilified with Christ and his gospel, than to have the best name, character, and reputation in this world without them; for what will it avail a man, " though he hath gained all this, when God taketh away his soul ?"

4thly. Near and dear relations are the only beloveds of others, as parents, children, &c. They set their affections so much on these, that Christ has little or no share in them: now, says Christ, Matt. x. 37, " he that loveth father or mother more than me, is not worthy of me: and he that loveth son or daughter more than me, is not worthy of me:" Christ is preferable to all such beloveds, and indeed to any creature-enjoyment whatever.

5thly. And lastly, Self is the beloved of many; nay, may not I say, too much the dearly-beloved of us all? Self lies close to us, is near and dear unto us; and we too much deserve that character, " lovers of ourselves, more than lovers of God;" and yet Christ requires of us, that we should deny this beloved self, sinful self, and part with it for him; nay even righteous self, our beloved righteousness, which we are naturally so fond of, and which is so hard and difficult a work to do; and yet souls are enabled by divine grace to do this, seeing a super-excellency in Christ and his righteousness, as the apostle Paul did; who, though he had been so much in love with his own righteousness; it had been his darling, he valued himself much upon it, and thought to have gained much by it; yet threw it all away as " loss and dung," and desired to be found in Christ, and in his righteousness only; that being far preferable to his former beloved.

Thus Christ excels all other beloveds; and he

must needs do so, for, 1. He is fairer than all others; there is no such beauty to be found in any beloved whatever as is in him; he is the "brightness of his Father's glory, and the express image of his person." 2. He is wiser than all others; he is a perfection of wisdom, as well as beauty; "in him are hid all the treasures of wisdom and knowledge." 3. He is richer than all others; he is possessed of "unsearchable riches;" riches which can never be told over, in time, nor to all eternity; he has riches of grace and riches of glory; "yea, durable riches and righteousness." Now one, in whom all beauty, wisdom, and riches meet, must needs be an excellent person, and appear preferable to all beloveds: Christ is such an one; he has all the accomplishments and perfections of the divine and human nature to make him so.

Again, the daughters of Jerusalem putting such a question as this to the church, shows, 1. Their regard unto her, and compassion for her: the watchmen and keepers of the walls, as soon as ever they found her, without asking any question, who she was, where she came from, whither she was going or whom she was seeking; I say, as soon as ever they found her, they fall upon her, smite her, wound her, and take away her veil from her; but these persons showed more regard and compassion; for, being willing to assist her in her present case, if possible, they stand conferring with her. 2. It appears from hence, that these were enquiring souls, which discover a work of grace begun in them; for no sooner are souls awakened to see their lost state by nature, but they are enquiring the way of salvation; and having got some glimmering knowledge of Christ, and salvation by him, they enquire still more after him, concerning his person, office, and grace; and having some impressions of his love on their souls, enquire the nature of a church, and the ordinances of Christ therein; they ask their way to Zion with their faces thitherward. 3. It is evident, from the question they proposed, that they were docible and teachable: they were willing to be instructed; they were not haughty, scornful, and above instruction; they did not think that they knew enough of Christ, and needed to know no more, nor be instructed better: but being conscious of their own ignorance, and extremely desirous of being informed better, they put this question to her.

III. This question is repeated by them; which shows the surprise that they were in at her solemn charge, and the stir she made about her beloved: and concluded from thence, that there must be some peculiar excellencies in him, which they had not been made acquainted with yet, and therefore repeat the question; as also to manifest their seriousness in it, and that they were in good earnest desirous of knowing Christ more and better; and likewise it is expressive of their importunateness to have a speedy answer from her.

IV. Here is also that which gave occasion to them to put this question to her; and that was her strict and solemn charge in the former verse, "that thou dost so charge us;" that is, so awfully and solemnly, so seriously and strictly, with so much warmth and vehemence: they were eye and ear-witnesses to her sufferings at the hands of the watchmen, and to her courage, constancy, and undauntedness therein? they saw that she was no ways discouraged by what she met with from seeking her beloved; but seemed rather by her solemn charge to them to be more warm and zealous, serious, diligent, and resolved to go on in search of him; and seeing all this, it put them upon enquiring what he was, what peculiar excellencies were in him, and what distinguished characters he might be known by. Thus the warmth, zeal, and liveliness of some Christians, have been the means of stirring up and quickening others to their duty; nay, the sufferings of the saints, and their courage and boldness therein, have not only filled beholders with wonder, but have put their very enemies upon making enquiry into the religion they had suffered for; and to ask, who and what that Christ was, for whom they had undergone such severe tortures and punishments; and this has been the means of the conversion of thousands; which gave rise to that saying, "The blood of the martyrs is the seed of the church:" and this is the gloss of R. Solomon Jarchi on this text, namely: "Thus the nations asked the Israelites, What is your God more than all gods, that ye are burnt and hanged for him after this manner?" Next follows a glorious description of Christ, the church's beloved, in answer to this question of the daughters of Jerusalem.

Verse 10. *My beloved is white and ruddy, the chiefest among ten thousand.*

THE church having, in ver. 8, given the daughters of Jerusalem a strict and solemn charge, that when they found her beloved, they would tell him that she was sick of love, made them, in ver. 9, very inquisitive after him; being as it were uneasy till they knew what he was, and wherein he excelled others; and therefore put this question to her, "What is thy beloved more than another beloved?" to which an answer is returned by her, in this and the following verses; in which she first gives a more general description of him, and then descends to particulars. The general description of him is in the words now under consideration; in which she describes him.

I. Positively, in regard to what he was in himself, as to his favour and complexion: "my beloved is white and ruddy."

II. Comparatively, as he may be considered with regard to others; "the chiefest among ten thousand."

I. She describes him by his favour and complexion, "white and ruddy." Which some[e] understand of his two natures, human and divine; who may be said to be white, as to his divine nature; "the ancient of days," the everlasting God, is represented in Dan. vii. 9, as being clothed with a "garment white as snow, and the hair of his head like the pure wool:" the description which John, 1 John i. 5, gives of the Divine being, is, that he "is light, and in him is no darkness at all ;" which is thought[h] to be best represented by this colour, which is simple, and has no mixture and composition in it, Christ is "the light of the world ;" he was known by this character to the Old Testament saints; he was prophesied of as the great light which should lighten the Gentile world; this was owned by old Simeon, witnessed by John, and asserted by himself: and then it is thought by these interpreters, that he may be said to be red or ruddy, as to his human nature. The first man, who was a type of Christ, and "a figure of him that was to come," was called Adam, which signifies red; and perhaps he had his name from the Hebrew word אדמה, *adamah*, which signifies *red earth*,[i] out of which he was formed, Gen. ii. 7; so Christ is called "the last Adam," 1 Cor. xv. 45, because he "took part of the same flesh and blood, the children" whom he loved, "are partakers of." Now, according to this sense of the words, her answer is this: Would you know who and what my beloved is, and wherein he excels others ? I will tell you, and be it known unto you, that he is no mean, common, and ordinary person ; no, he is a glorious and an extraordinary one; his name is פלא, *pele*, *wonderful*, *a wonder*, *a miracle* : and so is his person; two natures meet in him; he is God and man in one person; he is "the great mystery of godliness, God manifest in the flesh ;" and when you hear this, you will cease to wonder why I so charge you, and why I love, value, and esteem him above all others.

Again, others[k] understand these words of Christ's human nature only; and that he may be said to be *white*, because of the innocence, purity, and holiness of his human nature; which was not tainted with original sin, as ours is, he is not descended from Adam by ordinary generation; but was miraculously conceived in the womb of a virgin by the power of the Holy Ghost, and therefore it is called "that holy thing :" neither was there any sinful action committed by him in all his life; but both in nature and practice he was " holy, harmless, undefiled, and separate from sinners ;" he never sinned in thought, word, or deed, though he " was made sin for us." Also, they suppose, he may be said to be *red* or *ruddy*, on the account of his sufferings in this nature ; by reason of which he may be represented, in Is.

xiii. 1, 2, as being " red in his apparel," and as being clothed with " dyed garments ;" for what with the buffetings and scourgings of his body, the crowning his head with thorns, and piercing his hands, feet, and side, with the nails and spear, the garment of the human nature was like " a vesture dipped in blood :" to this purpose is Alcuin's note on the text, which is not to be despised ; he is *white*, says he, because without sin ; *red*, with the blood of his sufferings ; " chosen out of ten thousand," because he is the only mediator of God and men. Now there cannot appear a more beautiful and delightful sight, to those who desire " to know nothing but Christ and him crucified," than to see the just Jesus suffering for unjust ones ; him that " knew no sin, made sin for them ;" and the holy, harmless, innocent, and unspotted lamb of God, shedding his blood for the vilest of sinners ; according to this sense, the church's answer is : Would you know what my beloved is, and wherein he excels others ? I will tell you, he is not black with original and actual sin, as you and I are : for though you see him *red* with sufferings ; yet he was " not cut off for himself, but was wounded for our transgressions, and bruised for our iniquities :" for in his nature and actions he is *white*, pure, and spotless : and such a mixture of white and red, of innocence and sufferings, render him extremely amiable and lovely to me. Or else,

As others[l] have observed, these words may be understood of the different administrations of mercy and justice. Thus when Christ pardons sinners, " though their sins be as scarlet," he makes them " as white as snow ; and though they be red like crimson, they become as wool ;" and when he justifies persons, he is said to clothe them in " fine linen, clean and white, which is the righteousness of the saints ;" and when he promises glorification to them, it is in such words as these, " they shall walk with me in white, for they are worthy ;" and so glorified saints are represented, " clothed with white robes, palms in their hands, and hallelujahs in their mouths ;" for all which see Isa. i. 18, Rev. iii. 4, 5, and vii. 9, 13, 14, and xix. 8 ; and then when he is represented as taking vengeance on his enemies, and executing wrath upon his foes, he is said to be " red in his apparel," and to be " clothed with a vesture dipped in blood ;" for so they understand Isa. lxiii. 1, 2, Rev. xix. 13 ; and it may be further observed, that the wrath which the Lord poureth forth upon the " wicked of the earth," is represented by a cup of red wine, expressing the fierceness and fury of it ; " for in the hand of the Lord there is a cup, and the wine is red," &c., Psalm lxxv. 8. And this agrees with the common notion of the Cabalistic doctors, that when God appears in mercy

---

[e] Follot and Ainsworth in loc. Ambros. in Psal. cxviii. octon. 5. col. 907. Theodoret. and Tres Petras apud Ibid. [h] Color albus præcipue decorus Deo est, Cicero de Legibus, l. 2. [i] Vid. Buxtorf. and David de Pomis in Lex, in rad, אדם and Joseph.
Antiq. l. 1. c. 1. s. 2. [k] Hieron. Greg. Psellus, S. Thom. Beda, and Rupert. in Sanct. in loc.
[l] Vid. R. Aben Ezra R. Alshech. and Ainsworth in loc. and R. Sol. Jarchi in ver. 16.

and kindness, then he may be said to be *white*; but when in wrath and anger, *red*; of this frequent mention is made in Zohar, and in other Cabalistic books:[m] according to this sense, it is as if she should say, My beloved has mercy and grace for his people, which he bestows in a sovereign manner upon them; and he has vengeance for his adversaries, which he executes upon them according to the strictest rules of justice; and this mixture of mercy and justice, of white and red, renders him an extraordinary person: it makes some to love him, and others to fear him. Or else,

These words may be interpreted of Christ's battles and victories, and may represent him as a mighty warrior, and a triumphant conqueror. Thus in Rev. vi. 4, the warrior, who had "power given him to take peace from the earth," is introduced as riding upon "a red horse;" and in ver. 2, he that "went forth conquering and to conquer," as riding upon "a white horse;" thus Christ, who is "the Lord of hosts, the man of war," considered as fighting the Lord's battles, may be said to be red or ruddy; and as returning from the field of battle, as a mighty conqueror, having "spoiled principalities and powers," and gotten an entire victory over all his and our enemies, may be said to be *white*. And now this great person, as if she should say, has done all this for me, and "made me also more than a conqueror;" and this person is my beloved.

But passing these several senses, which perhaps may be thought too nice and curious, though agreeable to the analogy of faith, yet it may be, will not bear so well here; though I choose rather to understand them of the beauty, glory, and excellency of Christ, as Mediator, without applying particularly these colours of "white and ruddy," to either nature, or to any particular actions performed in either: and I cannot but think that the church, in this description of Christ, has some reference to the account that is given of David, 1 Sam. xvi. 12, which is, that " he was ruddy, and withal of a beautiful countenance, and goodly to look at." David was an eminent type of Christ; of his line the Messiah came, who is sometimes called David in scripture; and is both his "root and offspring, the bright and the Morning Star;" and as described by David, is "fairer than the children of men," being "white and ruddy," which discovers the best temperature, the most healthful constitution, and the completest beauty: as Mediator, he is a perfection of beauty; all divine perfections are in him; the glory of them all shine resplendently in his face or person; and they are all glorified in him and by him, who is "the brightness of his Father's glory, and the express image of his person." There is also a mediatorial glory that he is possessed of, which is the result and consequence of his work; and which renders him exceeding fair and beautiful in the eyes of believers now, and is what they will, with wonder and pleasure, everlastingly gaze upon in another world: likewise as Mediator, all fulness of grace dwells in him; and as "full of grace and truth, his glory appears as the glory of the only begotten of the Father."

Again, Christ as Mediator, is " white and ruddy," a perfection of beauty in the eyes of believers, as considered in all his offices of Prophet, Priest, and King, and in all his relations, as Husband, Father, Brother, and Friend, which he bears and stands in to his people: moreover he is exceedingly beautiful in their esteem, in all that he has done and suffered for them; but of this beauty and fairness of Christ, see more on chap. i. 15.

II. Christ is here described by the church comparatively, as he may be considered with with regard to others; " the chiefest among ten thousand."

The Septuagint render the words thus, "chosen out of, or from ten thousand;"[a] so Christ is both by God and men; he is chosen of God from among ten thousand, as Man and Mediator: when that large number of all the individuals of human nature, which he resolved to create in time, came up in his vast and eternal mind; a certain number of them he singled out for himself whom he meant to make instances of his mighty grace and mercy, and therefore ordained them to life and salvation; and out of this select company, which he had in his eternal view, he chose the man Christ Jesus, and singled out that single *individuum* of human nature only, to be united to the eternal λογος, *logos*, the second person in the glorious Trinity; and therefore he is said to " exalt one chosen out of the people;" he chose this glorious person to be the Saviour, Head, and Mediator of his elect ones; that Living Stone, which is disallowed and rejected by some men, who would be accounted builders, is " chosen of God and precious;" he has laid him as the foundation, and "made him as the Head of the corner;" he knew that he was furnished with suitable abilities to be the sinner's Saviour, therefore he "laid help upon one that is mighty;" he called him to the work, invested him with the office of a Mediator, and appointed him his "salvation to the ends of the earth :" and now, had all human beings been summoned together to have chosen a saviour for themselves, they could never have made a better choice than God has made for them; with this choice every sensible sinner is well satisfied, and rejoices in it; and was it to be done again, would say, as the Psalmist did, " He shall choose our inheritance for us," Psalm xlvii. 4.

He is also chosen of men from among ten thousand; there is none among all the angels in heaven, the large number of inhabitants that fill

---

[m] Vid. Shirhashirim Rabba in loc. fol. 20. 1.
[a] Ἐκλελοχισμένος απο μυριαδων, Sept. electus ex millibus, Vulg. Lat. David de Pomis in Lexic. Heb. fol. 18. 3. renders it magnificatus, electus.

P

the upper world: nor any among the vast crowds of the sons of men, so desirable to sensible sinners as he is; they make choice of him only for their Saviour; for being sensible that in vain is salvation hoped for any where else, they say of all the works of their hands, even of the best their hands ever wrought, "ye shall not save us:" neither will we any more give you such honour, nor have such a dependance on you, as to say, "ye are our gods;" but Christ, and he only, shall be our salvation; and though he slay us, yet will we trust in him: they choose him for their Ruler and Governor, their Lord and King; and though they have formerly been under, and have submitted to the government of others; yet they now desire to be his subjects and servants only, and to be obedient to his laws and commands: they likewise fix on him as the alone object of their love, whom they have the strongest affection for, and desirous to keep the most inviolable chastity to; for though he is out of sight, he is not out of mind, "whom having not seen they love;" nor can he be outrivalled by any, being preferable in their esteem to all others.

Moreover the Hebrew word may be rendered, a "standard bearer,º or one standard among ten thousand." The church of Christ here below is in a militant state: she has many enemies to grapple with, which cause fightings without, and fears within; and though these enemies are mighty and powerful, crafty and cunning, yet in the name and strength of her Lord, she sets up her banners, and appears as terrible to them and as majestic to others, "as an army with banners;" and this banner or standard, which is both her covering and her comfort in the day of battle, is love, according to chap. ii. 4. It is the love of Christ, as a banner displayed, an ensign set up, and standard erected, which invites and engages so many to enlist themselves in Christ's service; and, when enlisted, animates them to fight the Lord's battles so courageously as they do: Christ, he is the standard-bearer, and the great "Captain of our salvation," being by God the Father given as a "Leader and Commander" to the people. Now Christ being said to be "the standard-bearer among ten thousand," may be understood of the multitude, either of ministering angels,ᵖ who are under him and at his command; or of saints, who are enlisted in his service, and ready to do his pleasure; he having set up his standard, and being himself "an ensign to the people," multitudes flock unto him, and fulfil the prophecy of him, as the great Shiloh, to whom "the gathering of the people should be;" herein lies the glory and excellency of Christ, that he has ten thousand, that is, a large number of choice and select ones under his standard, such as there are not the like in all the world besides; and how stately and majestic does Christ look, and what a noble sight is it to see him bearing the standard before such a company! such a sight as this John had of him, at the head of a vast multitude of those shining ones, who were "clothed with white robes," and had "palms in their hands," having just obtained a glorious victory over their enemies, Rev. vii. 9, 13, 14. Or else, the intent of the word is, that Christ is a more excellent standard-bearer than all others:ᑫ there may be ten thousand persons who carry a flag, but none of them all are to be compared with him, either for comeliness, strength, or courage; none have such a choice and select company under them as he has; neither do any carry such a banner as he does, whose motto is love; and herein was he, who is "the lion of the tribe of Judah," represented by that tribe, which of all the tribes of Israel pitched their standard first, and had the greatest number under it; see Numb. ii. 3, 4.

But these words by our translators are rendered, "the chiefest among ten thousand;" and the sense of them is no ways opposed by the former versions; for if he is "chosen out of," and is "the standard-bearer among ten thousand," then he must be the chiefest among them; he is the chiefest among all the angels in heaven: for to "which of the angels said he at any time, Thou art my son," &c. He is the Son of God in a higher sense than angels and men are; angels are the sons of God by creation, saints by adoption, but Christ is the Son of God by an ineffable generation; as he is God, he is the Creator of angels, and to him they pay homage and adoration; they are his servants and are at his command, whom he sends forth as ministering spirits, to do his pleasure; and though as man, in the state of his humiliation and abasement here on earth in the days of his flesh, he was "made a little lower than the angels;" yet now in the very same nature in which he was abased below them, he is now exalted above them at the Father's right hand; for "to which of the angels said he at any time, Sit on my right hand," &c.; as Mediator, he has "obtained a more excellent name than they;" for the name of saviour or mediator is given to none of them; and as such they are beholden to him, though not to make peace and reconciliation for them, they having never sinned and incurred the divine displeasure; yet they are obliged unto him for confirming grace, to secure them in that state in which they stand. He is also the chiefest of all on earth, as well as of all in heaven; in all things, and over all persons, he has the pre-eminence; he is the Head of saints, their "everlasting Father," and tender Husband; he is the great Master of the family, and "the

---

º רגול מרבבה vexillatus, ornatus vel elatus ut vex illarius, Buxtorf. vexillatus myriade, Mercerus; vexillatus a decem millibus, Montanus; vexillarius est e myriade Junius; sub signis habens exercitum decem millium Tigurine version.   ᵖ Vid. Targum, Aben Ezra, and Shirhashirim Rabba in loc.   ᑫ Intelliges insignem præ decem millibus, ut ם præ comparationem designet, Mercerus in loc. Insignitus præ myriade, Cocceius, Marckius; insignius præ decem millibus, Pagninus.

first-born among many brethren;" he is the King of saints, and Lord of the creation; and should be the chiefest, and have the chiefest place in the desires of our hearts, in the contemplations of our minds, the affections of our souls, and in our ascriptions of glory; for " he is the chiefest among ten thousand."

Verse 11. *His head* is *as the most fine gold; his locks* are *bushy,* and *black as a raven.*

THE church, having given a general description of her beloved in the former verse, pursuant to the request of the daughters of Jerusalem, does in this enter into a more particular commendation of him, and continues unto the end of the chapter: which commendation consists of ten particulars, two of which are in these words,

I. She describes him by his head; which, she says, " is as the most fine gold."

II. By his locks; which "are bushy, and black as a raven."

I. She describes " his head as the most fine gold." Some think, that some ornament of the head is meant, as a diadem or crown of gold: or else, the hair of the head; which though afterwards is said to be black, yet, being powdered with gold dust, looked of the colour of gold, especially with the rays of the sun upon it: as did the hair of Solomon's youths that attended him, being thus decorated, as Josephus' relates; and which custom of powdering the hair with gold, was used by some of the Roman emperors.[s] By Christ's head may be meant, either,

1st. God the Father who is in scripture called so: Thus the apostle says, in 1 Cor. xi. 3, " The head of every man is Christ, and the head of the woman is the man, and the head of Christ is God," that is, God the Father; which is to be understood of Christ as Man and Mediator; for as he is God, the Father is not his head; he is not above him, nor superior to him in nature, power, or glory; for " being in the form of God, he thought it no robbery to be equal with him." It is true, the Father is the first person in Trinity; but he is not first in order of time, dignity, nor causality; some of the fathers and schoolmen have indeed said, that the Father, with respect to the other two persons, is *fons deitatis, principium, causa, the fountain of the deity, beginning, and cause thereof;* these phrases are better let alone than used: but he may very properly be said to be the head of Christ, as Man and Mediator; for as he is man, he is God's creature, the work of his hands, " a body hast thou prepared me;" and so subject to him, and under his power and government; and in this sense are those words of Christ to be understood, where he says, John xiv. 28, " My Father is greater than I;" being his Creator, Lord, and Head. And, 1. Christ as Man and Mediator, has his life from his Father; as he is God, his life is original and underived; it is not communicated to him from another: but his life, as Man and Mediator, is given him; he asked life of his Father, in the everlasting covenant, both for himself and for his people, and it was granted to him; and in this sense is that text to be understood, John v. 26, " As the Father hath life in himself, so hath he given to the Son to have life in himself;" as we derive our life from Christ, and have it maintained and supported by him: so Christ, as Man and Mediator, has his life from his Father, by whom also it is supported, he lives by him; " as the living Father hath sent me," says Christ,'John vi. 57, " and I live by the Father, so he that eateth me shall live by me;" and in this sense is God the head of Christ; he communicates life unto him, as Man and Mediator, and continues it in him. 2. Christ, as Man and Mediator, is subject to his Father, as the members of the body are to the head: thus, as God's " righteous servants" he was sent by him about the great work of man's redemption, was obedient to him, and carefully observed all the commands which he enjoined him; he still is, and will be to all eternity subject to his Father, as Man and Mediator; for when all things shall be put under the feet of Christ, as King of saints, then he, " the Son, shall be subject to him that put all things under him, that God may be all in all," 1 Cor. xv. 28. 3. Christ, as Man and Mediator, was guided and directed, taught and instructed by his Father, what he should speak and what he should do, as the great prophet in Israel, and Saviour of the world; and this gives light to those scriptures, John v. 20, and viii. 28, and xii. 49, 50; and proves the Father to be the Head of Christ. 4. Christ, as Man and Mediator, was strengthened and supported in his work by his Father as his Head; this was promised him in the everlasting covenant; and was made good to him " in an acceptable," suitable, and seasonable " time, in the day of salvation;" in the day he wrought out the salvation of sinners; which animated and encouraged him in the view of all that he was to go through; see Isa. l. 8—10; and proved him to be the " Son of man," whom God made strong for himself. Now this head of Christ " is as the most fine gold;" here are two words used in the Hebrew text, which both signify gold;[t] the one signifies pure, fine, and shining; the other, strong and solid gold; and may also be rendered, *the gold of Fez;*[u] from whence either the city of Fez had its name;[w] or else, this gold had its name from the land where it was in abundance; and perhaps is the name with the gold of Uphaz, mentioned in Dan. x. 5, Jer. x. 9; and this being the best and finest gold, the church uses it to set off the glory and excellency of Christ's head: not

---

[r] Antiquit. 1, 8. c. 7. s. 3. Hierozoic. par. 1. l. 3. c. 9. col. 154. aurum insigne, aurum purgatissimum, פז aurum soli-
[s] Vid Bochart,
[t] כתם
[u] Vid. Ainsworth, Bishop Patrick, and Sanctius in loc. dum, Buxtorf. scriptio. Africæ, l. 3 p. 273.
[w] Leo African. De-

that we are to suppose, as the apostle observes, Acts xvii. 29, that "the God-head is like to gold and silver," &c., for no likeness and similitude can be formed of the Divine Being; and indeed the church seems to be almost at a loss what to compare this head to; but gold being the richest, most excellent, and durable metal, and the gold of Fez being the best of any, she uses this to set forth the glory of it by: and yet, as not being satisfied, she says, it is as "the most fine gold;" if there is any better, it is like that; or, as the words may also be rendered, "his head is as gold of gold;"[z] and it is as if she should say, I would compare it to gold, because I can think of nothing better, richer, and more glorious; but I cannot find gold good enough to compare to it: this is "the gold of gold;" there is none such elsewhere; the whole universe cannot furnish us with the like; he that is my beloved's head, is "more glorious and excellent than the mountains of prey," yea, than all the golden mountains of Peru. Or else,

2ndly. By Christ's head may be meant, the divine nature in him;[y] which is the head, the chief, and principal nature in Christ; in which his highest characters are written, and which puts a glory and efficacy in all that he has done and suffered as Mediator; and it is this which supported him, and enabled him to go through the great work of man's salvation: all divine perfections are in Christ, and these all shine resplendently in him, who is "the brightness of his Father's glory, and the express image of his person;" this head is a head of pure, fine, and shining gold; "all the fulness of the Godhead dwells bodily in him;" and the glory of it is very manifest and conspicuous. Or,

3rdly. By Christ's head may be meant, his headship over his church, or his regal power and government, which I rather incline to; thus he is represented, in Psalm xxi. 3, as having "a crown of pure gold" upon his head, denoting his royal dignity and authority: so Nebuchadnezzar, or the large and flourishing monarchy which he was ruler of, is set forth by an head of gold, in Dan. ii. 32—38. And now Christ, as Lord of the church, and King of saints, may be compared to "the most fine gold," because his kingdom and government is the most excellent and glorious; it is managed with the utmost wisdom and prudence, and according to the strictest rules of justice and equity; his head is a golden one, and fit for the work he is called to, for in it "are hid all the treasures of wisdom and knowledge;" and therefore he is the only wise and just, as well as the only rich and powerful potentate in the universe: he is "King of kings, and Lord of lords;" all others receive their crowns and kingdoms from him, and are set up and put down by him at pleasure; and therefore it is by him that "kings reign, and princes decree justice;" all the wisdom and prudence, justice and equity, which appear in any of the governments of this world, are but faint resemblances of what of this nature appear in Christ's government; he is the "head of gold," all the rest are but like "brass, iron, and clay." 2. He is compared to fine gold, because his kingdom is pure and spiritual; it is "not of this world;" it consists in nothing that is worldly, earthly, and carnal; it is "not meat and drink, but righteousness, peace, and joy in the Holy Ghost." 3. Because like gold, it is solid and substantial; it does not consist in external pomp and gaudy shows, as the kingdoms of this world, which yet are fading, transitory, and perishing; but this, though it does not come with observation, but looks mean and abject in its outward appearances: yet is all of pure and solid gold, and will appear bright and glorious, when the gilt of others is worn off and gone. 4. It is compared to the most fine gold for the richness of it; Christ is the richest prince in the world; his riches are lasting and durable; they are unsearchable and incomprehensible; his kingdom is the richest on earth, and the meanest subject in it is a prince, nay, a king; that may be much more truly said of Christ's subjects, what the proud Assyrian monarch said boastingly of his princes, "Are not my princes altogether kings?" Christ's meanest subjects are so; for he has made them "kings and priests unto God?" Rev. i. 6. 5. Christ's kingdom may be compared to gold, because it is lasting and durable: Christ's "throne is for ever and ever?" there will never be any end of his government; nor of the increase of it, and of the peace and prosperity thereof; when all other kingdoms are destroyed, and all other rule, power, and authority put down, Christ's kingdom will stand; it will be more visibly set up, and appear more glorious, and so continue for ever. Thus Christ, as Head of the church, and King of saints, may be compared to the most fine gold; which is the first particular she instances in, by which he may be known from others. The Jewish writers[a] by this head of fine gold, understand the law, which is more to be desired than gold; as they do by the locks in the following clause, the several letters, sections, doctrines, and senses of it.

II. She describes him by his *locks*, which, she says, "are bushy and black as a raven." By his *locks* may be meant, either,

1st. The thoughts,[a] counsels, and purposes of God, who is the Head of Christ; which, 1. Like the hairs of a man's head are innumerable: the purposes of his heart concerning man's salvation; his thoughts of love, grace, and mercy towards sinners, "cannot be reckoned up in order to him; they are more than can be numbered; the sum of them is so great," that they exceed the sand upon the sea-shore. 2. Like bushy and black

---

[z] Aurum auri, Mercerus. [y] Mercerus in loc. so Theodoret. in loc. and Thom. Beda in Sanct. in loc. Targum, Shirhashirim Rabba, Alshech, Yalku and Jarchi in loc. Vajikra Rabba, parash. 19. [a] Vid. Ainsworth and Sanctius in loc.

locks, are intricate, dark, and obscure, unsearchable and incomprehensible; God's thoughts and purposes of distinguishing graces are out of our reach, and beyond our comprehension; and therefore are said to be "higher than our thoughts, even as the heavens are higher than the earth:" when we seriously consider that the great and infinite Being should pitch his thoughts of love from all eternity upon poor, sinful creatures; and upon some, and not all; and resolve on their everlasting salvation, and not on others; it obliges us to say, with the apostle, "O the depth of the riches, both of the wisdom and knowledge of God! how unsearchable are his judgments, and his ways past finding out!" Rom. xi. 33. 3. Yet these thoughts and purposes of God's heart, so far as they are made known to us, are like bushy and black locks of hair, very beautiful and delightful: how glorious and beautiful is the draught, the model and scheme of salvation, which was drawn in the eternal mind? with what exactness is it managed? what wisdom and grace appear in that "fellowship of the mystery," which the gospel leads us into an acquaintance with? How precious are those thoughts of love which run through all, as well as "how great is the sum of them?" Or,

2ndly. By these *locks* may be meant, the multitude of believers,[b] which grow upon Christ, as the Head of the church; and these may be compared to hair for their number, their dependence on Christ, and their reception of life and nourishment from him, as has been observed on chap. iv. 1; and these being called locks of hair, may intend their being congregated in gospel-order, their being united in faith and love, and their walking together in all the ordinances of Christ; "endeavouring to keep the unity of the Spirit in the bond of peace." Now saints being thus joined together in holy fellowship, having a strict regard to Christ's truths and commands, do much adorn the Head, Christ Jesus; and are a lovely and delightful sight to spectators; see Col. ii. 5. And these locks are said to be, 1. Bushy; the word may signify heaps;[c] and so denotes the multitude of believers that spring from, and have their dependence on Christ, the Head: or it may be rendered, thick,[d] being well-set; or pendulous,[e] hanging down in a beautiful order: and this may intend the ornament that believers are to Christ; "children's children are the crown of old men;" believers are "a crown of glory to Christ;" they are "a royal diadem in his hand," and upon his head: or it may be translated, crisp or curled;[f] and so be expressive of the hardness and strength of believers; curled hair [g] being the strongest and hardest: believers though weak in themselves, yet are strong in Christ; not only to perform duty, but to withstand enemies, and endure hardness as good soldiers of Christ Jesus; they are "strengthened with all might in the inner man," to fight the Lord's battles, are undaunted in their spirits, and immoveable as a rock. 2. They are said to be "black as a raven;" saints are black with original and actual sin, as they are also with infirmities, reproaches, scandal, and persecution; they have mean thoughts of themselves; and though exalted on the Head, Christ, yet look upon themselves as the least of saints, and chief of sinners: though I rather think, this does not intend their blackness by sins, infirmities, &c., nor their humble thoughts of themselves; but rather, their real beauty, which they have from Christ, and that ornament and glory which they are unto him. Or else,

3rdly, By these locks may be meant, Christ's administrations in the discharge of his kingly office: and this seems to me to be the best sense; for, as by his head, is intended his regal power and government; so by his locks, the administrations of it; which though sometimes dark, intricate, and obscure, being attended with severity to his enemies, and so may be said to be bushy and black; yet being managed with the utmost wisdom and prudence, and according to the strictest rules of justice and equity, look very beautiful and comely, and are admired and wondered at by all the saints; see Rev. xv. 3, 4.

Moreover in general these bushy and black locks of Christ may denote, 1. The fulness of wisdom which is in Christ; curled hair is a sign of an hot and dry brain,[h] which produces acuteness and sharpness of wit: all wisdom is in Christ; he is the wisdom of God; who has not only fulness of it for himself, which is requisite to qualify him for, and carry him through the work he is engaged in; but has also a fulness of it for the saints, to whom "he is made of God wisdom as well as righteousness." 2. His youthful strength, vigour, and courage, of which his black hair is accounted a sign in Rev. i. 14. Christ's hair is to be as white as wool, as white as snow, to denote his senile gravity; that he is "the ancient of days," who exists from everlasting to everlasting: but here his locks are said to be black, to set forth his juvenile vigour and strength, which is always in its bloom, without any change or alteration: he is the mighty God in his highest nature, and "mighty to save," as Mediator; he gave the fullest proofs of his strength and courage in fulfill-

---

[b] Foliot and Alcuin in loc. Greg. S. Thom. Beda, and Carpath. in Sanct. in loc. So these locks are interpreted of the disciples of the wise men, by R. Judah. in Shirhashirim Rabba in loc. [c] תלתלים cumuli, tumuli, Schindler. Lex. Pentaglott. fol. 1972. so Targum, Aben Ezra, Mercer. and Ainsworth, in loc. [d] Mercer. [e] Jarchi, and Bochart. Hierozoic. par. 2. l. 2. c. 10. col. 199 and so the Syriac, Arabic, and Ethiopic versions; and according to Castell, this is the best sense of the word, vid. ejus Annot. in Ethiop. vers. [f] Crispaturæ capillorum, Buxtorf. Marckius; crispis discriminibus, Junius: crispi, Cocceius, Montanus. [g] Aristot. de Generat. Animal. l. 5. c. 3. [h] Aristot. de Generat. Animal. l. 5. c. 3.

ing all the law required, in bearing all that justice inflicted, and in conquering all his and our enemies. 3. These black locks set forth the beauty of Christ: black hair was accounted the most beautiful, not only by the Jews but by the Romans; as is manifest from what is said by many of of the poets,[1] concerning both men and women: it was very desirable to them; insomuch that those, whose hair was not naturally black, used various ways and methods to make it so, and among other things, both Pliny[k] and Ælianus[l] tell us, they used the eggs, brains, and blood of ravens for that purpose. Now when Christ's locks are said to be black as a raven, the meaning is, that he looks exceeding beautiful, being "fairer than Absalom," or any of the children of men; his black shining locks, hanging down in a beautiful order from his head of gold, make him look very stately and majestic: and as the blackness of the raven is a very fine black, and what is natural to it, and not made by art; so the beauty of Christ is exceeding great, it is natural to him; it is not derived from another, as ours is from him, but what is original, underived, and essential to him, and this proves him to be the most excellent beloved, and "the chiefest among ten thousand."

Verse 12. *His eyes are as the eyes of doves, by the rivers of water, washed with milk, and fitly set.*

THIS is the third instance of Christ's beauty, or distinguishing character of him, which the church gives to the daughters of Jerusalem, whereby they might know him from others; having described him by his head and hair, she here describes him by his eyes; the order and method in which she proceeds is very just and natural. By his eyes may be meant, either,

First. The gifts and graces of the Spirit which are in Christ, as Man and Mediator;[m] who is represented, in Rev. v. 6, as a lamb that had been slain for the sins of men, with seven eyes, which are said to be "the seven spirits of God;" not that there are seven personal, distinct, divine subsistencies, which are called so; but the phrase intends that variety, fulness, and perfection of the gifts and graces of that one Spirit of God, who is the third person in the blessed Trinity; which gifts and grace of his, being bestowed on Christ, as Man and Mediator, furnished and qualified him for his work; of which seven spirits or various gifts of the Spirit, which he received for this purpose, you may read in Isa. xi. 2—4. Now these may be said to be "as the eyes of doves by the rivers of water;" because the Spirit of God did in an eminent and public manner descend upon him, as a dove, at the time of his baptism in the river of Jordan: and they may also be said to be as doves, or as the eyes of doves "washed with milk," to express the purity and holiness of his nature, sanctified thereby; for, as Man and Mediator, he was holy, harmless, undefiled, and separate from sinners: likewise they may be said to be as the eyes of doves fitly set, or set in fulness, because the Spirit was not given to him by measure, but in fulness; the whole fulness of the gifts and grace of the Spirit is given to him; and therefore he appears "full of grace and truth," and from hence they are communicated unto men. Or else,

Secondly. By his eyes may be meant the church's teachers,[n] or ministers of the Gospel; who, as they are the mouth by whom Christ speaks, so they are his eyes, by whom he sees, provides for, and watches over his church and people; and therefore are called *watchmen*, whose business is to watch for, and over the souls of men: these are the eyes which give light unto, guide, and direct the members of Christ's body; who point out unto them the way of salvation, and guide their feet into the way of peace. Now these may be said to be as the eyes of doves, on the account of those dove-like gifts of the Spirit, by which they are fitted for their work, and made able ministers of the New Testament; also for their honesty, faithfulness, and simplicity in preaching the everlasting gospel; and likewise for that harmlessness and innocence, which do and ought to appear in their lives and conversations. These may also be said to be as doves, or as the eyes of doves by the rivers of water, which may intend the scriptures of truth;[o] for as doves delight to sit by rivers of water, so do the ministers of the gospel delight to be reading of, and meditating upon the scriptures, which is their work and business: and from hence they fetch the doctrines they preach to others; they speak according to the oracles of God; and that "not in the words which man's wisdom teacheth; but which the Holy Ghost teacheth, comparing spiritual things with spiritual," 1 Cor. ii. 13. Likewise they may be said to be as doves, or as the eyes of doves washed with milk, because of their light and knowledge in the gospel, which is the sincere milk of the word; whereby they are made capable of feeding others with the plain and wholesome truths of the Gospel; or else this phrase may intend that pure and spotless conversation, which they ought to lead as examples to others in faith and purity. They may also be said to be fitly set; "for God hath set some in the church, first apostles, secondarily prophets, thirdly teachers," &c., 1 Cor. xii. 28; this was the

---

[1] Spectandum nigris oculis nigroque capillo, Horat. de Arte Poet. v. 37. Et Lyceum nigris oculis nigroque crine decorum, ib. Sermon. 1. 1. ode 32. v. 11. Leda fuit nigra conspicienda coma, Ovid. Amor. 1. 2. eleg. 4. v. 42. [k] Lib. 29. c. 6. [l] De Animal. 1. 1. c. 48. [m] So Theodoret. and Tres Patres apud Ibid. Thom. Aquin. Beda, and Rupert. in Sanct in loc.

[n] Isidore, Foliot, and Alcuin in loc. and Greg. Nyssen. in Cant. Homil. 13. Ambros. in Ps. cxviii. octon. 15. col. 1009. and Psellus apud Theodoret. in loc. and Carpathius in Sanct. in loc. They are interpreted of the Sanhedrin, by the Targum and Shirhashirim Rabba in loc. [o] The Jews, in Shirhashirim Rabba and in Yalkut in loc. understand by them the waters of the law.

fit and beautiful order in which the first ministers of the Gospel were placed by God himself; and indeed all the ministers of it are fitly set in the more eminent part of the body, the church, to overlook, direct, and be useful to the several members of it. But these seem rather to be the eyes of the church, than the eyes of Christ, which also are compared to dove's eyes in chap. i. 15, and iv. 1, as has been there observed; and therefore I choose rather,

Thirdly. To understand by these eyes, the omniscience of Christ: R. Aben Ezra seems to understand them of God's omniscience; for his comment is that text in Prov. xvi. 3, " The eyes of the Lord are in every place." Christ is the omniscient God; every creature is made manifest in his sight, all things are naked and open unto the eyes of him with whom we have to do; who is the living Word; and a critical Discerner of the thoughts and intents of the heart: in the days of his flesh here on earth he needed not that any should testify of man; for he knew what was in man; and gave convincing proofs to the scribes and Pharisees, that he was well acquainted with the secret thoughts of their hearts: Peter bore a noble testimony to Christ's omniscience, when he appealed to him, saying, " Lord, thou knowest all things, thou knowest that I love thee." And indeed was he not the omniscient God, how could he be capable of acting as the Head of his church, or as the Mediator between God and man, or of judging the world at the last day? but then he will give an incontestible proof of this. Divine perfection being in him; he will let all the churches, and all the world know, that he it is which searcheth the reins and hearts. Now when these eyes of Christ's omniscience are fixed on persons in a way of wrath and anger, they are said to be as flames of fire; especially when fixed upon heretics, idolators, false worshippers, or any of his and his church's enemies; see Rev. i. 14, and ii. 18, 20—23, and xix. 11, 12, 15; but when they are fixed in a way of special love and grace upon his own people, they may be said to be,

1st. As the eyes of doves, which are loving, lovely, clear, and chaste. 1. Christ's eyes may be said to be as doves, because of the lovingness of them; the eyes of doves are not fierce and furious, as the eyes of some creatures are; there are no fury in Christ's eyes, as fixed upon his people: " The eye of the Lord is upon them that fear him, upon them that hope in his mercy;" that is, his eye is upon poor trembling sinners, who come to the throne of grace and prostrate themselves at his feet, humbly imploring his grace and mercy, and venturing on him as sinners ready to perish; his eye is upon them all the while; not to destroy them, and cut them off from his sight, but to deliver their soul from death, and to keep them alive in famine: his eyes are upon all his righteous ones; not to cut off the remembrance of them from the earth, which he threatens to the wicked, but to deliver them out of all their troubles: his eyes are upon all creatures, and all things, for they run to and fro throughout the whole earth; but then it is to show himself strong in the behalf of them, whose heart is perfect towards him; his eye of love is always upon his people, to succour, relieve, protect, and defend them: his eye is upon them under all their trials, temptations, desertions, sorrows, and afflictions; his eye is upon them when in the furnace, to observe the exercise of their grace upon him, their carriage to him; and when tried, to deliver out of it: for his eyes behold, and his eyelids try the children of men. 2. They may be compared to dove's eyes, because they are lovely, as well as loving; and it is for this reason he compares the church's eyes to doves, in chap. i. 15, and iv. 1. Every part of this description serves to set off the beauty and loveliness of Christ's eyes; they are said to be " as the eyes of doves by the rivers of water," because doves delight to sit there; where being pleased with the pure and purling streams, their eyes look more quick and lively, and so more beautiful and lovely. Also they are said to be as doves, washed with milk, either as milk-white doves, which look very pleasant and delightful; or as doves washing themselves in streams of water, look as clean as if they had been washed in milk: likewise they are said to be as the eyes of doves fitly set; that is, neither too much staring out,[p] nor too much sunk within; neither hollow-eyed or goggle-eyed, which are both extreme deformities in the eye. 3. They may be compared to dove's eyes, because of their clearness and perspicuity; Christ's eyes are so clear, he is so sharp-sighted, that he can see all persons, and things in all places, at one view; for " the eyes of the Lord are in every place, beholding the evil and the good :" more especially his eyes behold, and he takes cognisance of his own people; these he knows by name, and distinguishes them in his care and affections from all others; he sees and knows all their wants perfectly well, is able to supply them, and has a heart to do it; and seeing that " all things are naked and open unto him, with whom they have to do at the throne of grace," they are encouraged to come thither with the greater boldness: he sees and knows all the contrivances and designs of wicked men against his people, though formed in the dark; for the darkness and the light are both alike to him; his eyes are so clear, sharp, and penetrating, that there is no darkness, nor shadow of death, where the workers of iniquity may hide themselves; and this makes much for the comfort of his people, as well as serves to command and set off the loveliness and excellency of him. 4. They may be compared to dove's eyes for their faithfulness and chastity: Christ is faithful to God, who appointed him to be the Mediator and Saviour of his people; and to that covenant of grace which he made with him;

---

[p] Vid. Jarchi in loc.

in which he promised many things, which are fully performed by him; and he received many blessings of grace for his people, which he is faithful to distribute unto them and bestow upon them: he hath given meat to them that fear him, as an indication that his eye is upon, and that he will ever be mindful of his covenant; he has a respect unto it, and therefore calls those by his grace, and brings them to glory, who are interested in it: also as the eye of the dove is only upon its own mate, is faithful and chaste unto it, and has no regard to any other; so Christ's eye of love is only upon his church; as she is his dove, so she is his only one; hence he says, "my dove, my undefiled, is but one;" and as he loves her above all others, so he loves none but her with his special and peculiar love in which he always rests and continues.

2ndly. Christ's eyes of love, as fixed on his own people, are as the eyes of doves by the rivers of water. Now this sets forth the loveliness and beauty of Christ's eyes, as has been already observed; the eyes of doves being more brisk, quick, and lively, when sitting by rivers of water, where they are delighted in and pleased with the clear and running streams thereof: and may also lead us to observe these two things: 1. The fixedness and constancy of Christ's eye of love being set upon his own people: doves sitting by a river side, keep their eyes fixed upon the purling streams; and in drinking, as Pliny[q] observes, do not, *resupinare colla*, erect their necks, and lift up their heads, but keeping their eyes fixed upon the water, drink a large draught of it in the manner of beasts; Christ, being sweetly delighted with his own people, has fixed his eye upon them, and never removes it from them; he withdraweth not his eyes from the righteous; his eye was upon them before time, continues so in time, and will be so to all eternity; for having loved his own which were in the world, he loved them to the end. 2. It may intend the object of Christ's love: some of the Jewish writers,[r] by the rivers of water, would have their schools and synagogues intended; where the waters of the law flow, the difficulties of it are explained, and its proper senses given; but they may be much better understood of gospel-churches, made up of righteous persons; who are justified by Christ's righteousness, sanctified by his grace, sprinkled with the clean water of the everlasting covenant, and who have low, mean, and humble thoughts of themselves; on such as these Christ's eye is fixed, and to these he looks; see Isa. lxvi. 2; here the ordinances of the gospel are administered in their purity, the waters of the sanctuary flow, the doctrines of grace are powerfully preached, and souls hereby much delighted and refreshed.

3rdly. These eyes of Christ are said to be as the eyes of doves washed with milk; and this is expressive both of the beauty and clearness of them, as has been already observed: eyes, when washed, are clearest, and so most lovely; like milk-white doves, which look the most beautiful, especially when they have just washed themselves: respect may be had to the colour of doves; white doves were had in esteem in Palestine and Syria.[s] And this may also intend the purity of Christ's eyes, who is of purer eyes than to behold evil, with any pleasure or approbation; and likewise the meekness and mildness of them: his eyes are not red and furious, but look as if they had been washed with milk, being full of mercy, pity, and compassion to poor sinners; his heart is full of it, and his actions, as God-man and Mediator, give the strongest proofs of his being a merciful as well a faithful High-priest.

4thly. These eyes are said to be fitly set, or fitting by fulness;[t] that is, by full channels of water. Christ himself is as rivers of waters, which denote the fulness and abundance of grace that is in him; and by these full fountains of grace, life, and salvation, he sits, dwells, and abides; and thither he, "the Lamb in the midst of the throne," leads his people. Or the words may be rendered, " sitting in fulness ;"[u] and so it expresses the loveliness and beauty of Christ's eyes, as has been already observed; his eyes were neither sunk too low within, nor stood too much out, but exactly filled their holes; they were fitly set as diamonds in a ring, or as precious stones in the breast-plate of the high-priest, which exactly filled the cavities which were made for them, and therefore were called stones of fulness; see Exod. xxv. 7, and xxviii. 17, 20; so R. Solomon Jarchi and R. Aben Ezra understand the words; though they may be better translated, " sitting upon fulness."[w] Christ's eyes are set or sitting, 1. Upon the fulness of this world: "the earth is the Lord's, and the fulness of it:" as he has a right unto it, so his eyes are upon it; for " his eyes run to and fro throughout the whole earth ;" they are in every place at one and the same time, beholding at one view the evil and the good, all their persons, and all their actions; his eye is upon that vast number of persons and things that fill the whole universe, and upon the large variety of actions performed there: now this sets forth the extensiveness of Christ's omniscience, and that general and universal knowledge he is possessed of; which sense is much favoured by R. Sol. Jarchi's note on the words. 2. Christ's eyes were set, or sitting upon the fulness of time, in which he was to come into the world, and perform the great work of redemption: for as he was appointed to be the author of this work, and the persons were pitched upon whom he was to redeem, so the time was also fixed when he was to do it; and this is called " the fulness of

---

[q] Lib. 10. c. 34. [r] Targum and R. Sol. Jarchi in loc. [s] Alba Palestino Sancta columba Syro, Tibullus, 1. 4. eleg. 7. [t] על מלאת ad plenitudinem, Tigurine version, Bochart juxta, Vatablus, so some in Brightman; juxta fluenta plenissima, Vulgate Latin, so the Septuagint, Syriac, and Arabic versions. [u] Siti insitione, Junius and Tremellius, Piscator. [w] Super plenitudinem, Montanus, Mercerus.

time," in Eph. i. 10, Gal. iv. 4; and now, from the first making of the everlasting covenant, down throughout the whole Old Testament dispensation, Christ's eye was fixed on this fulness: waiting, watching, as it were; longing till the time was come, when he should appear in human nature, and do the work which his heart was so much set upon; witness his many appearances in a human form before his incarnation, and the frequent notices he gave of his near approach. 3. Christ's eyes are set, or sitting upon his fulness, the church, whom in the fulness of time he came into this world to redeem; the church is called so, in Eph. i. 23; which " is his body, the fulness of him that filleth all in all;" and then is she, and will she appear to be so, when all his elect ones are called by grace; and these all filled with these gifts and graces of the Spirit designed for them, by him who is ascended to fill all things; and more especially when they are all grown up in proportion, unto the measure of the stature of the fulness of Christ; now Christ's eye is upon his church, and upon every member of it, until all this is done: and will be so when time shall be no more. 4. His eyes were, and still are set, or sitting upon the fulness of the Gentiles, until that is brought in; his eye was upon them in the everlasting covenant; therefore both he and his Father thought fit that he should be not only the Redeemer of Israel, but a light to the Gentiles also, and be God's salvation unto the ends of the earth; his eye was upon them during the Old Testament dispensation; and therefore gave out many promises and prophecies concerning their calling; his eye was upon them when he died and suffered: and therefore he became a propitiation, not for the Jews only, but also for the Gentile world; his eye was upon them when he gave the commission to his disciples to preach the Gospel; and therefore bid them " go into all the world, and preach it to every creature;" which he owned for the conversion of thousands; and his eye is still upon them, and will be so, until all those other sheep are brought in which are not of the Jewish fold. 5. His eyes are set, or sitting, on his own personal fulness as God; for " in him dwelleth all the fulness of the Godhead bodily ." his eye was upon this when he undertook the work of redemption, and so it was when he was actually concerned in it; therefore he failed not, neither was he discouraged; this supported him under it, and comfortably carried him through it. 6. His eyes are set, or sitting upon his fulness as Mediator; which is a dispensative, communicative fulness put into his hands, to be distributed to his people; and his eye is continually upon it, to supply the wants of his people out of it, under all their straits, difficulties, temptations, sorrows, and afflictions; and where Christ's eyes are fixed,

there should ours be also; we should be continually looking to, and be strong, not in ourselves, but in " the grace which is in Christ Jesus."

Verse 13. *His cheeks are as a bed of spices, as sweet flowers; his lips like lilies, dropping sweet smelling myrrh.*

In these words are the fourth and fifth particular instances of Christ's beauty; for having described him by his head, locks, and eyes, she here describes him by his cheeks and lips; still keeping in a beautiful and regular order in her description of him. And,

First. She describes him by his *cheeks*; which, she says, "are as a bed of spices, as sweet flowers;" by which we are to understand, not the smooth and naked cheeks, but with hair growing upon them, which best suits with the metaphor of a bed of spices; for as aromatic plants and sweet-smelling flowers bud out, and spring up from a bed of spices, and make it look very beautiful; so the hair of a man's beard puts itself forth, and grows upon his cheeks, or jaws,[x] as the word may be rendered, and makes him look very graceful and majestic: R. Aben Ezra understands by his cheeks, his beard; as also do many Christian Interpreters.[y] And this was literally true of Christ; who was not " an infant of days," but a man grown up, when he suffered in the room and stead of sinners; as is manifest from his " giving his back to the smiters, and his cheeks to those that plucked off the hair." The cheeks rising, and being a little elevated, are fitly described by beds in a garden; or fragrant flowers, or fruit trees, reared up in the form of towers, as some render the word, or pyramids; or by a dish of sweetmeats placed in such a figure; and the hair of the cheeks or beard, are aptly represented by spices, rising up from a bed of them; and all denote the beauty, savour, and majesty of Christ: or, as the Vulgate Latin version, " as beds of spices set by confectioners;"[z] not as aromatic plants, set in rows by the gardener; but as the spices themselves, set in rows, by the confectioner in vessels, or placed in such a manner in his shop to be sold,[a] which being of various colours, especially red and white, the cheeks, for colour and eminence, are compared to them. And being taken in a mystical and spiritual sense, may intend, either,

1st. Believers, who are the hair of Christ's cheeks, as well as of his head; these grow upon him, receive their life and nourishment from him, and are ornamental to him: these are as " a bed of spices and sweet flowers:" for, being, "perfumed with the myrrh and frankincense," of his grace, they ascend upwards in the exercise of faith, hope,

---

[x] לחיו maxillæ ejus, Pagninus, Montanus, Marchius, Michaelis. [y] Sanctius, Cocceius, Ainsworth, Marckius, Michaelis. [z] Sicut areolæ aromatum consitæ a pigmentariis, V. L. similes sunt areolis aromatum and turribus seplasiariæ Officinæ, Tigurine version. [a] Vid. Fortunat. Schacc. Eleochrysm. Sacr. l. 1. c. 18. p. 90.

and love, as " towers of perfumes,[b] as the words translated *sweet flowers* may be rendered ; they are fruitful in themselves, like a spicy bed, odoriferous to Christ ; and delightful to each other. Or else,

2ndly. The graces of the Spirit which are in Christ as Man and Mediator : these, like the hair of a man's beard which grow upon his cheeks, adorn the man Christ Jesus, and render him very lovely and graceful ; these grow in large numbers on him ; he is " full of grace and truth ;" and though there is a large communication of grace made daily to believers from this fulness which is in Christ ; yet it is no way lessened thereby, even as the hair of a man's beard, which the oftener cut, the thicker and faster it grows. Now these lovely cheeks thus adorned, may be said to be " as a bed of spices, as sweet flowers," because of their beauty and loveliness ; no spicy bed, set and filled with aromatic plants and sweet-smelling flowers, can be more lovely and delightful to the eye of sense, than Christ, with all his grace, is to the eye of faith ; the reason why he appears to a believer, " fairer than the children of men," is, because grace, in all its fulness, " is poured into his lips :" also they may be compared to these, because of the sweet odour of them ; the effluvias of the sweet flowers and most fragrant spices growing in large numbers, in beds of them, cannot be more grateful to the smell, than the graces of Christ are to believers ; and therefore they are compared to ointments, the savour of which cheers the minds, and attracts the hearts of his people to him : this oil of gladness being poured plentifully on his head, runs down his beard, and so to every part of his garments ; which makes them all " smell of myrrh, aloes, and cassia ;" and renders him, and all that belong to him, sweet, savoury, and delightful to his saints. Likewise they may be compared to " a bed of spices and sweet flowers," because of the variety of them ; as in an aromatic garden there are various beds, and in those beds various spices, plants, and flowers ; so there is in Christ a variety of the gifts and graces of the Spirit ; there are diversities of gifts, and all sorts of grace, which make up that fulness, from whence believers receive grace for grace. Or else,

3rdly. This may be expressive of the manliness and courage, prudence, gravity, and majesty of Christ ; when the beard appears in men like " a bed of spices," thick and well-grown ; it is a manifest indication that they are grown up to the estate of men, and are at years of discretion. Now Christ's manliness and courage appeared in his boldly refuting the errors of the Pharisees and Sadducees ; and in preaching the everlasting gospel, though he often ran the risk of his life in doing it ; and to the very last he bore a noble testimony to it, and " witnessed a good confession" of it before many witnesses ; as also he gave a manifest discovery of it at the time of his being taken by his enemies ; as well as in Pilate's hall, where he was smitten, buffeted, scourged, mocked, and spit on ; and yet in the midst of all, discovered the greatest undauntedness and composure of mind ; but never more than while he was bearing his Father's wrath, and the strokes of divine justice, grappling with his and our enemies, and undergoing a painful and ignominious death : for under all this he failed not, neither was he discouraged. His " cheeks being as a bed of spices," show him to be endued with manliness and courage, which he thus discovered ; as they also show his prudence and gravity, which he manifested in all his discourses, questions, and answers ; for " in him are hid all the treasures of wisdom and knowledge ;" for at twelve years of age, when the lovely down scarce appeared upon his cheeks, he discoursed with so much wisdom and gravity, put such questions to the doctors, and returned such answers to theirs, as filled them with wonder and surprise : and much more did he so, when his " cheeks* were as a bed of spices ;" when he was grown up to man's estate, and was entered upon his public ministry ; he spake with so much wisdom and authority, that his audience was amazed at him ; he dealt so prudently, according to the prophecy of him, that the subtle Scribes and Pharisees did not care to meddle with him ; for as they could not answer his questions, so they dare not put any to him ; his enemies themselves being witnesses, " never man spake like him." And this prudence and gravity of his appeared throughout the whole conduct of his life ; his words were with power and authority ; his deportment was grave and serious ; and his walk and conversation, as it was in all holiness and righteousness towards God, so it was in all wisdom and prudence towards men.

But if by cheeks, we understand that part of the face as smooth and naked, without the additional consideration of hair upon them ; then by them may be meant, either,

1st. The scriptures of truth.[c] The Targum understands them of the two tables of stone, which were written in ten lines, like the rows or beds of an aromatic garden, productive of acute and delightful senses ; much to the same purpose does R. Solomon Jarchi give the sense of them : but it seems better to understand them of the whole word of God, the scriptures both of the Old and New Testament. These are as it were the cheeks or face of Christ, which represent and set forth the glory of his person, the virtue of his blood, the excellency of his righteousness, and the riches of his grace : these may be said to be " as a bed of spices, as sweet flowers," being in several distinct plots or beds : for this garden of the scriptures

---

[b] מגדלות מרקחים turriculæ pigmentorum, Mercerus ; turribus pigmentorum, Marckius ; condimentorum, Schmidt, Michaelis.   [c] So Foliot and Tit. vers. in loc. and Carpathius in Sanct in loc.

was not thrown up at once, and formed in that beautiful order in which now it is; but first one spicy bed was made, and then another; for "God at sundry times, and in divers manners, spake in times past unto the fathers by the prophets;" these beds are set with a variety of "exceeding great and precious promises," and excellent doctrines; which the meditating soul, like the industrious bee, sucks much sweetness from: all those excellent spices, and sweet-smelling flowers which grow here, have their different usefulness; for "all scripture is given by inspiration of God, and is profitable for reproof, for correction, and for instruction in righteousness," 2 Tim. iii. 16. And as aromatic plants and fragrant flowers are delightful to the eye, sweet to the smell, and refreshing to the senses, so are these truths and promises; they are like "apples of gold in pictures of silver" to the eye of faith; diffuse a delightful odour to the smell, give a savour of Christ's knowledge, when and wherever explained; and being held in the hand of faith, refresh all the spiritual senses, and are "the joy and rejoicing of the heart." Or else,

2adly. By Christ's cheeks, may be meant his presence with his people, and the manifestation of himself unto them in his word and ordinances. Thus the presence of God is frequently called his face in scripture; as when saints are said to seek his face, or he is said to hide his face from them: which are to be understood of God's withdrawing his presence from them, and their desire of enjoying it: thus Christ's presence with his people may be set forth by his cheeks or face; which, when they enjoy, they see him in his beauty, behold him in his glory, and are ravished with his love: and this may be said to be "as a bed of spices, as sweet flowers;" for nothing is so desirable and delightful to believers as this; walking in the light of Christ's countenance, is far preferable to walking among beds of spices, where the most fragrant plants and odoriferous flowers grow: nothing that is earthly and sensual, with all its affluence and pleasure, can so strike the carnal senses, as the presence of Christ does the spiritual ones. Or else,

3rdly. The cheeks being the seat of modesty, bashfulness, and blushing, may intend the humility of Christ; which appeared in his assumption of our nature, and throughout the whole course of his life, and more especially at his death: and this is a very great ornament to him, and renders him very delightful to his people. How lovely does the meek and lowly Jesus look! how beautiful are those blushing cheeks of his, who, though he was "equal with God, yet was found in fashion as a man!" and though possessed of all divine perfections, and transcendent excellencies, yet always spoke modestly of himself; and did not seek his own, but his Father's glory, and the good of his people.

Secondly, Which is indeed the fifth particular instance of his beauty, she describes him by his lips; which, she says, "are like lilies, dropping sweet-smelling myrrh:" lips being the instruments of speech, and those compared to lilies, may be expressive of florid language and eloquence; so Lucian[d] describes the Trojan orators as having a lilian voice, that is, a florid and eloquent one. And by lips may be meant the words of Christ; which are like lilies, 1. For purity; "the words of the Lord are pure words, as silver tried in a furnace of earth purified seven times:" Christ's words are free from all pollution and defilement, from all scurrility and raillery, from all deceit and hypocrisy, and from all human mixtures whatever; and therefore his word is called "the sincere milk of the word." 2. His lips are compared to lilies for the beauty of them: and I suppose that not white lilies are here meant, but purple or red lilies; of which Pliny[e] speaks, the flower of which, he says, some call the rose lily; so Maimonides[f] speaks of red lilies, by which he interprets ורד, the rose: which, he says, have a good smell, and of them it is said, his lips, like lilies, Cant. v. 13, and also R. Alshech on the text: the best of these grew in Syria, in Antioch, and Laodicea;[g] and these best suit with lips; for not white, but red lips,[h] are accounted the most beautiful; and therefore Christ compares the church's lips to "a thread of scarlet," in chap. iv. 3. There is a beauty and loveliness in all Christ's words; they are pleasant ones; they are gracious words, or words of grace, which drop from his lips; and indeed how can his lips drop any other? his speech cannot be but always with grace, and with gracefulness, when grace itself is poured into his lips. 3. They may be compared to lilies for the fineness, thinness, softness, and delicateness of them: thinness, as well as redness, adds a beauty to the lips: Christ's voice was not heard, his lips did not move in setting forth his own praises; for he sought not his own, but his Father's glory; he did not speak for himself, but his words and actions spoke for him; he did as Solomon advised, Prov. xxvii. 2, "Let another man praise thee, and not thine own mouth, a stranger, and not thine own lips." 4. They may be compared to lilies for the sweet odour of them: Christ's lips drop "sweet-smelling myrrh;" his words, his gospel, and the doctrines of it, diffuse an agreeable savour; to some they are "the savour of life unto life;" and though they are "the savour of death unto death" to others, yet that does not arise from Christ's words in themselves; but is owing to their being rejected,

---

[d] In Hercul. Gall. [e] Lib. 21. c. 5. Theophrast apud Athen. Deiphnosophist. 1. 15. c. 8. p. 681. So Tertullian speaks of both lilies, that is, the white and red, De Corona, c. 14. [f] In Misn. Sheviith, c. s. [6] Midrash Esther, fol. 61. 1. [g] Dioscorides in Fortunat. Schacc. Eleochrysm Sacr. 1. I. c. 27. p. 134. so in Eygpt. Herodot. Euterpe, sive 1. 2. 9. 92. [h] Rosea, labra, Martial. roscum os, Virgil.

slighted, and contemned by men. 5. They may be compared to lilies for the glory and majesty of them: Christ says that "Solomon in all his glory was not arrayed like one of the lilies of the field;" Christ's words come with authority, and are clothed with power; "the voice of the Lord is powerful, the voice of the Lord is full of majesty," Psalm xxix. 4.

Again these lips of Christ are said to drop "sweet-smelling myrrh;" for the construction is not with lilies, but with lips; for myrrh does not drop from lilies, but may be said to do so from Christ's lips; though some¹ think, the allusion is to the crowns, made of red or purple lilies, worn at nuptial feasts, on which were poured oil of myrrh, and so dropped from them; but it is from the lips and not lilies, the myrrh is said to drop. And here we may consider, 1st. The matter of those words which drop from Christ's lips, which is said to be as "sweet-smelling myrrh." 2ndly. The manner of the delivery of them, which is dropping.

1st. The matter of Christ's words is like "sweet-smelling myrrh." 1. Grateful and acceptable as such; Christ's lips drop the "sweet-smelling myrrh" of peace and reconciliation to rebellious sinners, pardon to guilty ones, rest to those that are burdened, comfort to the distressed, and life to all his people; this he did in the days of his flesh, and still continues to do by his ministering servants; who are his lips, by whom he speaks, and are thought by some[k] to be chiefly intended here; and so will his lips drop "sweet-smelling myrrh," the words of eternal life, when he shall say, "come, ye blessed of my Father, inherit the kingdom prepared for you from the foundation of the world." 2. His lips drop words, for matter like "sweet-smelling myrrh," preserving from rottenness, putrefaction, and corruption: Christ's words preserve from the corruption of sin; his doctrines are "according to godliness;" they are so far from having a tendency to encourage persons in sin, that they are the best antidote and preservative against it: the doctrines of grace teach us "to deny ungodliness and worldly lusts;" they are the means of implanting and maintaining principles opposite to them: they also preserve from the corruption of false doctrines, which are pernicious to souls, and "eat as do a canker:" but Christ's words are wholesome ones; and those whose hearts are established with them, are not "carried about with divers and strange doctrines;" nor are they "tossed to and fro with every wind" of error, but retain their stedfastness in Christ Jesus: likewise wherever Christ's words come with power, they preserve from going down to "the pit of corruption;" for Christ says, that whosoever "keeps his sayings, shall never see death," that is, the second death.

2ndly. The manner of the delivery of Christ's words; which, as the matter of them is grateful, this is grateful, and is said to be dropping. 1. Gradually, and not all at once: Christ did not speak all at once to his disciples, but by little and little, as they were able to bear it; they had not their light, knowledge, and comfort all at once; no more have saints now, nor must they expect it; we are first babes, then young men, and then fathers in Christ. 2. Seasonably, at proper times, as the wants and necessities of his people require; for "God hath given him the tongue of the learned, that he may know how to speak a word in season to him that is weary," Isa. l. 4. 3. Constantly; his lips dropped sweet-smelling myrrh when on earth, and still drop it now he is in heaven; "see that ye refuse not him that speaketh;" that now speaketh, continues to speak, and will do so until all his people are gathered in. 4. Powerfully and effectually; though his words do but drop, yet they drop with power; they make and leave impressions where they drop; they work effectually in them that believe. 5. Yet sweetly and gently; not like hasty and sudden showers of rain, which beat down the grass and corn; but as rain that drops gently and mildly, and so is acceptable to the earth, and makes it fruitful: "my doctrine shall drop as the rain, my speech shall distil as the dew," &c., Deut. xxxii. 2. Now this graceful and agreeable manner of his delivery, as well as the grateful matter of his words, render him very acceptable to his church, and show him to be a most excellent Person, and "the Chiefest among ten thousand;" which is what she attempts to demonstrate, in this description, to the daughters of Jerusalem. The kisses of Christ's lips, or the manifestations of his love, may be taken into the sense of these words; which are as delightful as sweet-smelling myrrh; see chap. i. 2; and such a sentiment is expressed in the same language by others.¹

Verse 14. *His hands are as gold rings, set with the beryl: his belly is as bright ivory, overlaid with sapphires.*

THESE words contain the sixth and seventh particular instances of Christ's beauty, or distinguishing characters of him, whereby he might be known from all other beloveds, and wherein he was preferable to them.

I. She describes him by "his hands;" which, she says, "are as gold set with the beryl."

II. By "his belly or bowels;" which, she says, "is as bright ivory overlaid with sapphires."

I. She sets forth the beauty and loveliness of his hands, by comparing them with "gold rings set with the beryl;" which is the sixth particular instanced in: it was usual in former

---

¹ Schaccus. ut. supra, l. 1. c. 28. p. 138, 139.
[n] [k] Ambros. in Ps. cxviii. octon. 18. col. 1047. Psellus apud Theodoret. in loc. Carpath. and Ru-pert. in Sanct. in loc. ¹ Olent tua basia myrrham, Martial. Epigr. l. 2. ep. 10.

times, as now, for gold rings to be set with one precious stone or another,ᵐ and particularly with the beryl.ⁿ And by his hands may be meant, either,

1st. The munificence and liberality of Christ, manifested in the distributions of his grace to his own people: all grace is in Christ's hands, being put there by God the Father, as an instance of his love to Christ, as Mediator, and his regard to those whom he made his care and charge; "the Father loveth the Son, and hath given all things into his hands," John iii. 35; all fulness of grace is in Christ, of justifying, sanctifying, pardoning, and adopting grace; all the blessings and promises of the covenant are in his hands; all fulness of wisdom and strength, light and life, peace, joy, and comfort, is with him; which is all lodged in his hands, in order to be distributed to God's chosen ones: Christ, as the ascended Lord and King, "received gifts for men," and as such, gives them to them; the daily experience of souls testify it, for "of his fulness we all receive, and grace for grace." Christ does all this liberally, and upbraideth not; he does not do it with a reflection on our unworthiness; nor does he hit us on the teeth of our manifold sins and transgressions; as he does not withhold the blessings of grace from those they belong to; so when he gives, he does not do it grudgingly, but freely and cheerfully; not sparingly, but plenteously; he openeth his hands wide, and largely communicates to his people: all which he does wisely and prudently, at such times and in such ways, as will best suit with their wants and necessities; for as a "wise and faithful Steward" of God's grace, he gives to every one "their portion of meat in due season." And now these hands of Christ's, which so faithfully and wisely, so liberally, freely, and largely distribute the blessings of grace to the saints, are as beautiful and lovely as hands adorned with gold rings, set with the most valuable precious stones: how glorious does he appear to the eye of faith, "as exalted to be, a Prince and a Saviour, to give repentance unto Israel, and forgiveness of sins," with his hands full of grace, and a heart to give it! how beautiful do both his right and left hand look, in whose "right hand is length of days," and in whose "left hand are riches and honour!" Or else,

2ndly. By his hands may be meant his power in working: Christ's hands have always been active; "my Father worketh hitherto, and I work;" that is, I have been working, and I continue to do so. Those hands of Christ, which are said to be "as gold rings," &c., laid the foundation of the heavens and the earth, formed all things out of nothing, reared up the beautiful structure of the universe, and filled it with proper inhabitants; for "without him was not any thing made that was made:" and in doing this his hands look like gold rings; there is a shine, a lustre on them; the glory of the divine perfections appears in them: "the heavens declare his glory, and the firmament showeth his handy-work;" these hands also bear up and support the pillars of the earth; and in this he appears to be the brightness of his Father's glory, and the express image of his Person, in that he upholds all things by the word of his power: these hands likewise hold the reins of government; the government of the whole universe in general, as well as of the church in particular, is in the hands and upon the shoulder of our Lord Jesus Christ: but in nothing does Christ's hands appear more beautiful and lovely, like gold rings set with the beryl, than in grasping, holding, and retaining the saints; who are put into his hand by God the Father, where they are safe and secure; for out of his hands none can pluck. How beautiful do the hands of Christ look, in holding those bright stars, the ministers of the gospel there! for he "holdeth the seven stars in his right-hand:" and more do they appear so, when we view all the saints there; who are so many gold rings, jewels, pearls, and precious stones in Christ's esteem. Or else,

3rdly. By his hands may be meant, his works performed by his almighty power: his lips being the instruments of speech, intend Christ's words in the former verse; so hands being the instruments of action, may intend his works in this; such as the works of creation and providence, which are all formed in a beautiful order, in a delightful connection with, and an agreeable subordination and subserviency to each other; his works of miracles here on earth, on all which were a shine of deity, and were a demonstration of his being the true Messiah and Saviour of the world; and more especially his works of grace and redemption, which may be said to be "as gold rings set with the beryl." 1. For the perfection of them: the circular form is accounted the most perfect, and therefore they are compared to gold rings, which are of such a form; Christ is a Rock, and his work is perfect, and particularly that of redemption; he does none of his works by halves; and especially this, which he never left till he could say, it is finished; and so being made perfect himself through sufferings, having perfectly fulfilled both the preceptive and penal parts of the law, he became the complete author of eternal salvation to all them that obey him. 2. For the excellency and glory of them; gold rings are valuable, beautiful, and ornamental: all Christ's works of grace are glorious and honourable; and more especially this of redemption, in which the glory of all the three Persons, and the glory of all the divine perfections, is manifestly displayed, and eternally secured; "his glory is great in thy salvation," Psalm xxi. 5. 3. For the variety of them; gold rings, in the plural number, are here

---

ᵐ Annuli gemmati, Liv. Hist. l. 1. c. 11. Gemma ornat manus, Propert. l. 3. eleg. 6. v. 12. Vid. Macrob. Saturnal. l. 7. c. 13. ⁿ Et See litum digito beryllum adederat ignis, Propert. l. 4. eleg. 7. v. 9.

mentioned: Christ's works of grace are many and various, they are more than can be reckoned up; and even in the work of redemption, there is an admirable variety; many are the things which he has wrought out, brought in, and procured by his precious blood; such as a justifying righteousness, pardon of sin, peace, and reconciliation, liberty of access to God, deliverance from all enemies, sin, Satan, hell, and death, &c. 4. Christ's hands in working out redemption, may be said to be as gold rings set with the beryl: this is one of the precious stones in the high priest's breastplate, mentioned in Exod. xxviii. 20; and is one of the pearl foundations of the new Jerusalem, Rev. xxi. 20; the appearance of the wheels in Ezekiel's vision, is said to be like it, Ezek. i. 16; and the body of that great person who appeared to Daniel, chap. x. 6, is said to be as this stone: so that it is no wonder that Christ's hands should be said to be as gold rings set with it.

The Hebrew word Tarshish, here used, is sometimes the name of a person, and at other times the name of a place, and is used sometimes to signify the sea; and naturalists° tell us, that the best beryl is that which most resembles the colour of the sea; thus all the three Targums on Exod. xxviii. 20, call it כרום ימא, *crum yamma*, from its being of a sea colour: and Junius and Tremellius here render it, *beryllus thallassius*, the sea-coloured beryl: this stone is found in India; and being carried about by persons, is said[p] to inspire them with courage to help them to conquer their enemies, and to put an end to strifes and controversies. Christ, whose hands are said to be as gold rings set with beryl, in working out man's redemption, discovered the utmost courage, resolution, and magnanimity of mind; when he was bearing his Father's wrath, suffering the severe strokes of justice, and grappling with all his and our enemies; when he was deserted by his friends, forsaken by his God, and insulted by his enemies, he failed not, neither was he discouraged; when he saw that there was none to give him the least assistance, his own arm brought salvation to him; he stood the field, fought the battle alone, got an entire victory over all enemies, sin, Satan, and the world; saved us out of the hands of them all, and put an end to that grand controversy between God and us, occasioned by sin; he repaired that breach, made up that distance, and reconciled those two contending parties, by making peace between them, through the blood of his cross. 5. Some think that the chrysolite is here meant, as Ainsworth and others; which is a precious stone of a golden colour,[q] from whence it has its name; it is mentioned in Rev. xxi. 20, and is said[r] to be good against melancholy, fear, and folly, and to fill the mind with courage, cheerfulness, and wisdom; which, being applied to Christ's hands in working out redemption, may show that Christ not only performed this work with courage, but with cheerfulness, and also with the utmost wisdom: his wisdom appears in all the works of his hands, as the Psalmist says, Psalm civ. 24, "O Lord, how manifold are thy works, in wisdom hast thou made them all!" but in none more than in this of redemption, wherein he hath abounded towards us in all wisdom and prudence; this was so well contrived, and so fully effected, that all the divine perfections are glorified in it; he has herein secured the glory of justice and holiness, as well as given the greatest display of his grace and mercy; he has satisfied a broken law, and destroyed sin, and yet saved the sinner; herein appears the manifold wisdom of God; there is such a variety of it, and such a glory in it, that angels are amazed at it, and desire to look into it. Christ, as the great Redeemer, is not only the power, but also the wisdom of God; for in him are hid all the treasures of wisdom and knowledge; of which he gave the fullest proof when he was concerned in this work. 6. Others think that the hyacinth or jacinth is here intended: Pagnine renders it, "full of precious stones, like hyacinth;" the Vulgate Latin and Tigurine versions render it the same way, this is likewise mentioned in Rev. xxi. 20; it is of a violet or purple colour, for which reason the flower so called has its name;[s] also it is said[t] to be good against the bitings of venomous beasts; and being worn on the finger, and put about the neck, keeps strangers safe, and renders them grateful to their host: the bluish and purple colour of this stone, and its ruby veins, which some say it has, may represent a crucified and bleeding Christ; when his precious hands, which are as gold rings, wrought out man's salvation; by whose blue wounds and purple streams of blood, souls have a cure for every disease; and particularly for those wounds which their sins, those scorpions within, and Satan, that old serpent without, have made in them; for by his stripes we are healed; it is the precious blood of Christ, and spotless righteousness, and glorious redemption wrought out thereby, which being applied by the Spirit, and laid hold on by faith, preserve souls safe from all enemies and evils, as sin, Satan, law, hell, and wrath; and which only render them grateful and acceptable to God; for saints are only accepted in the beloved on the foot of redemption, and upon the account of his justifying righteousness; for the Lord is well pleased for his righte-

---

° Plin. l. 37. c. 5. Solin. c. 65. Ruæus de Gemmis, l. 2. c. 8. De Boot. Hist. Gemm. l. 2. c. 70. Βερυλλς γλαυκην λιθον, Dions. Perieg. v. 1012. [p] Albertus Magnus, l. 2. tract. 2. c. 2. de Rebus Metal. Ruæus, l. 2. c 8. [q] Plin. l. 37. c. 9. 11. [r] Albertus Magnus l. 2. tract. 2. c. 3. de Rebus Metal. Ruæus de Gemmis, l. 2. c. 7. • Plin. l. 37. c. 9. Solin. c. 43. [t] Fernel. Method. Medend. l. 5. c. 21. Albertus Magnus, l. 2. ract. 2. c. 8. de Rebus Metal.

ousness sake, because he hath magnified the law, and made it honourable, Isa. xlii. 21. 7. Others have thought that the sardonyx is intended, as Cocceius; this is an Arabian gem, and one of the principal ones; it is a composition of the sardius and onyx stones,[u] as appears from the name; it is of a white and ruddy colour, and much resembles the nail of a man's hand, set in flesh, both for colour and smoothness; and it used to be set in rings, and worn on the hand; hence a hand adorned with one, is called *sardonychata manus*;[w] and a ring set with this stone, was called *sardonyche*:[x] this is also mentioned in Rev. xxi. 20, and may represent the glorious Deity, innocent humanity, and bloody sufferings of Christ, whose hands have obtained eternal redemption for us; it was necessary that he should die, in order to satisfy for our sins, which he could not have done, had he had any sin of his own; neither would the sufferings of this innocent person have been sufficient, had he been a mere creature, and not truly God: it is by the precious blood of Christ that we are redeemed, and by the blood of Christ, as of a Lamb without spot and blemish; and what made this blood powerful and efficacious to such a purpose, is the influence of the divine nature: and all these three may be observed in one verse, Heb. ix. 14.

II. She describes him by his belly, which, she says, is as bright ivory overlaid with sapphires. The generality of ancient interpreters [y] understand by *belly*, the human nature of Christ, which is expressed by this part, because of the frailty and weakness of it: Christ's human nature, though not attended with sinful, yet with all sinless infirmities; he was encompassed with them · and was a man of sorrows, and acquainted with griefs; and yet, like ivory, was firm, constant, and immoveable in sufferings, being supported and strengthened by the divine nature, he appeared to be the man of God's right hand, the son of man whom he made strong for himself; and, like bright and white ivory, pure, holy, innocent, and spotless; and now like bright and white ivory overlaid with sapphires, being glorified and exalted at God's right hand. Ivory is used to express the beauty of persons; see chap. vii. 7; so the beauty of Æneas is described by it;[z] even by such as has been in the hands of a workman, smoothed and polished by him, and so become bright, as here called: the sapphire is used to express the glory and majesty of the Divine Being, in Exod. xxiv. 10.

The Septuagint render it thus, " his belly is an ivory box upon a sapphire stone,"[a] and this serves very well to represent the body, and may very aptly be applied to the human nature of Christ, in which " the fulness of the Godhead dwells?" and displays its glory: but the words may be better rendered, " his bowels are as bright ivory," &c.; so the same word is translated in ver. 4, and may express the love, grace, mercy, pity, and compassion of Christ to poor souls; which may be compared to bright ivory. 1. For the valuableness and excellency of it: the ivory is the tooth of the elephant, and is very valuable; Solomon made himself a throne of it, and overlaid it with gold; that is, studded it, and enamelled it with gold, as this is said to be sapphires: nothing is so valuable as Christ's love; the brightest ivory, the richest jewels, most precious stones, and excellent sapphires, are not to be compared to it; his " loving kindness is better than life," or all the things which render life comfortable and delightful. 2. For the purity, sincerity, and chastity of it; there is no spot, stain, or blemish of hypocrisy and deceit in it; but like pure bright ivory, is without the least sully or tarnish: nor is there any reason for jealousy of it; both the ivory and the sapphire are observed to be preservatives of chastity; and though God's children are often jealous of Christ's love, yet they have no reason for it; for as he loves them above all others, so he loves none but them in that way; and he " rests in his love " towards them, and is the " same yesterday, to day, and for ever." 3. For the firmness, constancy, and durableness of it; ivory is firm and lasting; Christ's love is so; it is from everlasting to everlasting, always the same, never varies, and will continue so for ever; for " having loved his own which were in the world, he loved them unto the end." 4. For its reviving, refreshing, and strengthening nature; ivory, to which Christ's bowels are here compared, is said [c] to be a great strengthener of the bowels and inward parts: Christ's love being shed abroad in our hearts, revives our fainting souls, puts new strength into our graces, and makes us not ashamed or confounded, even in a day of trouble. 5. It is like bright ivory " overlaid with sapphires;" that is, either covered with them, as the word signifies, or rather enamelled with them: of this precious stone frequent mention is made in scripture; it is used to express the glory of God, Exod. xxiv. 10, and the throne of his majesty is said to be as the appearance of it, Ezek. i. 26, the beauty of the Nazarites is represented by it, Lam. iv. 7, and the glory of the church in the latter day, Isa. liv. 11; it was one of the precious gems in the high-priest's breast-plate; and one of the foundations of the New Jerusalem: some of the Jewish writers [d] say, that the two tables on which the law was engraven was made of this; it is a very clear and transparent gem,[e] of a cœrulean or sky colour, shining with golden

---

[u] Plin. l. 37. c. 1, 6. Solin. c. 46. Ruæus de Gemmis, l. 2. c. 5. [w] Martial. Epigr. l. 2. ep. 25.
[x] Juvenal Satyr. 7. v. 144. Persii. Satyr. i. v. 16.
[y] Isidore, Foliot, and Alcuin in loc. and omnes in Sanct. in loc. [z] Quale manus addunt ebori decus, Virgil Æneid. l. 1. [a] Κοιλία αυτη πυξιον ελεφαντινον επι λιθυ σαπφειρυ, Sept. [b] מֵעָיו viscera ejus, Marckius, Michaelis. [c] Fernel, Method. l. 5. c. 21, 23. [d] Targum Jon. in Exod. xxxi. 18. Targum in Cant. i. 11. and R. Sol. Jarchi in Exod. xxxiv. 1. [e] Plin. l. 37. c. 9. Ruæus de Gemmis, l. 2. c. 2. Dionys. Pericg. v. 1105.

specks; it is said ᶠ to help those that are bitten with scorpions, to defend the heart from the infection of poison, and to cure intestine ulcers: this may all serve to set forth the glory and excellency of Christ's love; it is this oil of love, grace, and mercy, which being poured in by the good Samaritan, heals the wounds that sin has made, and preserves from the dreadful effects of its poison and venom. Albertus Magnus ᵍ says, that the sapphire creates peace and concord, and renders the mind pure and devout to God; but whether this be true or no, it is certain that the love of Christ, discovered to a poor distressed sinner, produces calmness and serenity of mind, creates " a peace which passeth all understanding ;" removes that enmity, and weakens the remains of it, which is naturally in the heart of man against God, Christ, his gospel, people, ways, and ordinances; there is nothing attracts our love to Christ as this does; " we love him because he first loved us :" nor is there any thing that more engages our hearts in acts of obedience to him than this; it is this which lays us under obligation, constrains us to, and enforces on us a regard to all his commands and ordinances, and makes us most cheerful in our observance of them.

But there are some interpretersʰ who think that not any part of the body is here described, as the belly or bowels, but rather that some covering of those parts is intended; and indeed it does not seem so agreeable with the rules of decency, nor consistent with the spouse's modesty, to describe her beloved by those naked parts to the daughters of Jerusalem; any more than it does with the scope of the place, which is to give some distinguishing marks and characters of him to them, that they might know him from another; but these parts being out of sight, and not exposed to public view, a description of them could be of no service to them in this respect; nor indeed does what is said serve so much to commend the belly, as it does some covering of it; R. Aben Ezra thinks the girdle about the loins is here meant; and if so, it may intend either Christ's royal girdle, which is a girdle of righteousness and faithfulness; all his regal administrations being performed, as well according to the strictest rules of justice and equity, as with the utmost wisdom and prudence; or else, his priestly girdle, which is called a golden one, Rev. i. 13, and is no doubt an allusion to what the high-priest wore; or else, the covering intended may respect the embroidered coat of the high-priest, which covered his whole body; whose embroidery were holes or incisures, in which, as Jarchiⁱ says, were put jewels and precious stones; and so as the church described Christ as a prince before, she is thought to describe him here as a priest; or rather, the ephod with the breast-plate is here alluded to, in which were twelve precious stones, and, among the rest, the sapphire, on which were engraven the names of the twelve tribes of Israel; and it is certain, that the Targum on this place has reference to it; for it mentions the stones one by one, with the several names of the tribes engraven on them: and this may represent Christ, as the great high-priest, bearing all his elect ones upon his heart in heaven, having entered there in their name to appear and plead for them, and to take possession of glory for them in their stead, until they are brought into the actual enjoyment of it themselves.ᵏ

Verse 15. *His legs* are as *pillars of marble, set upon sockets of fine gold: his countenance* is *as Lebanon, excellent as the cedars*.

THESE words contain the eighth and ninth particular instances of Christ's beauty, given by the church to the daughters of Jerusalem, or distinguishing characters of him, whereby they might know and discern him from all others. And,

I. She describes him by "his legs," which, she says, " are as pillars of marble, set upon sockets of fine gold."

II. By "his countenance;" which, she says, is, 1st. " As Lebanon." 2ndly. " Excellent as the cedars."

I. She describes him by his legs; which she says, " are as pillars of marble, set upon sockets of fine gold;" which is the eighth particular of this glorious description of Christ. The word translated *legs*, may as well be rendered *thighs*; which may very well be compared to marble pillars, both for form and colour; especially when we consider, that it does not appear that the ancient Jews did in common wear any thing upon their thighs and legs, but only sandals upon their feet: or perhaps, by thighs may be meant, the femoralia,ˡ or garments on the thighs, which were worn by the priests when they ministered in holy things. I have observed that some interpreters think, that some garment of the high-priest, either his girdle, or his embroidered coat, or the ephod with the breast-plate, is intended by the belly, in the latter part of the preceding verse; so that as Christ was described as a prince before, he is now described as a priest; which description may be still carried on here. These *femoralia*, or garments for the thighs, were made of fine linen, Exod. xxviii. 42; and so are very aptly represented by white marble; they are also said to be made of fine twisted linen, Exod. xxxix. 28, which the Jewish Rabbinsᵐ say, was of thread six times doubled; and therefore these breeches must sit

---

ᶠ Fernel.Method. Medend. l. 5. c. 21. Ruæus, ibid. ᵍ Lib. 2. tract. 2. c. 17. de Rebus Metal Ruæus de Gemmis, l. 2. c. 2. ʰ Lyra, Soto Major, Sanctius, and Bishop Patrick in loc. ⁱ In Exod. xxviii. 4. ᵏ See a discourse of mine, called Levi's Urim and Thummim found with Christ, p. 34. 35.

ˡ Bishop Patrick in loc. ᵐ Vid. R. D. Kimchi, in lib. Shorash, rad. שׁשׁ Maimon. Cele Hamikdash, c. 8. s. 14. and Jarchi in Exod. xxvi. 1.

very full and stiff, like pillars of marble: and this may set forth the pure and spotless righteousness of Christ, which is called, in Rev. xix. 8, "fine linen, clean and white;" it is this which covers our nakedness, hides the impurities of our nature, and renders us acceptable unto God. Moreover, below these breeches of the priest, was the hem of the holy robe, round about which were set pomegranates and golden bells; which perhaps may be meant by the "sockets of fine gold," on which those pillars of marble were set; and may intend the glory and excellency of the righteousness of our great high-priest, Christ Jesus.

Moreover, in this description, the church seems to take in thighs, legs, and feet; his thighs and legs are compared to pillars of marble, and that very aptly; his feet are intended by "the sockets of fine gold;" which either respects the sandals bound about the feet with golden ribands; or the custom of some who used to adorn their shoes with gold and precious stones:[n] and that nothing may be wanting to set off her beloved as the most excellent, she represents him as having such sandals or shoes upon his feet; golden sandals on his snow-white marble feet and legs;[o] for white marble is meant, such as Parian marble, so Aquila and Theodotion render it; or shoes gilt in the upper part, as noblemen in Spain wore, as Lyra on the place observes. And now Christ's legs being said to be "as pillars of marble," &c., may denote,

1st. The strength and power of Christ to bear up and support what is or has been laid upon him; much of a man's strength is in his legs; these are by Solomon called "the strong men," Eccl. xii. 3, and are the pillars and support of the body; which, when they begin to bow themselves, it is an indication that this earthly tabernacle is ready to be dissolved; Christ is the Rock of ages, in whom is everlasting strength; his legs are as pillars of marble, set upon sockets of fine gold, firm and immoveable, lasting and durable. 1. To bear the weight of the whole universe;[p] the earth, with all the inhabitants thereof, would soon be dissolved, did not he bear up the pillars of it; as he made all things, so he upholds all things by the word of his power; both worlds, with all the created inhabitants of it, have their dependance on him, and are upheld by him: for as "he is before all things, so by him do all things consist." 2. To bear the whole weight of the covenant of grace; it was the business of the Levites to bear the ark of the covenant; but Christ is the covenant itself; he is so both materially and fundamentally; he is the matter, sum, and substance of it; he is the basis and foundation of it; all the blessings of it are upon him; and all the promises of it are in him, yea and amen: it is this which makes the covenant of grace, with all its blessings and mercies, sure, and renders it preferable to the covenant of works because it is "established upon better promises;" which promises are upon a better foundation, and that is the Lord Jesus Christ. 3. To bear all the persons of the elect; as the legs of a man bear and support the whole body, so Christ's legs, which are as pillars of marble, bear up and support his whole body, the church; thus Christ bore and represented the persons of the elect in the everlasting covenant, and received all grace for them; and so he did when he hung upon the cross, when he died and rose again; and so he does now he is in heaven, even as Aaron bore the names of the children of Israel upon his breast-plate, for a memorial before the Lord. 4. To bear all their sins and transgressions; so Aaron bore the iniquity of the holy things of the children of Israel; and so did the scape-goat bear upon him their iniquities unto a land not inhabited; and therein were both types of Christ, who was manifested in our nature for this purpose; on whom God the Father laid the iniquity of us all, and who actually bore it in his own body on the tree; and by so doing, made satisfaction for it. 5. To bear all the punishment due to sin; sin being laid on him, he, as the sinner's Surety, bore the whole weight of his Father's displeasure for it; he had not the least abatement of his wrath, but suffered the severest strokes of his justice; and yet he failed not, neither was he discouraged, or was not broken; it was enough to have broken the strength of men and angels: but he stood up under it, "his legs being as pillars of marble, set upon sockets of fine gold;" when God banished Cain from his presence, as an indication of his displeasure for his sin, he cried out, "My punishment is greater than I can bear;" and indeed, who can stand in his " sight when once he is angry?" and yet, what was this to what Christ bore in the room and stead of the elect? 6. "His legs are as pillars of marble," &c., to bear the whole care and government of his church; the government of the church in general is upon his shoulder; and indeed no other shoulder is capable of it but his, who is "the mighty God, the everlasting Father, and Prince of Peace:" it may be said of him, in a much more eminent sense, what Paul said of himself, 2 Cor. xi. 28, that "the care of all the churches was upon him;" the care of every particular believer, as well as of the church in general, is upon Christ: for they cast their care upon him, who careth for them. 7. They are so, and need be so, to bear all the burdens of his people: there was a complaint of the Jews in Nehemiah's time,

---

[n] This is mentioned by Pliny, l. 9. c. 35. and l. 37. c. 2. [o] Perque caput ducti lapides, per colla, manusque, and pedibus niveis fulserunt aurea vincla, Manilius de Margaritis l. 5. Littora marmoreis pedibus signanda puellæ, Ovid. Amor. l. 2. eleg. 11. v. 15. [p] Several Jewish writers, by the pillars of marble, understand the six day's work of creation (though the Targum interprets them of the righteous) on which the world is founded; and by the sockets of gold, the doctrines of the law, Shirhashirim Rabba in loc. Bemidbar Babba, parash. 10. Vajikra Rabba, parash. 25.

Neh. iv. 10, that the strength of the bearer of burdens was decayed, but this cannot be made of Christ, who is the bearer of his peoples' burdens; for "his legs are as pillars of marble," &c., he he has said, Psalm lv. 22, "Cast thy burden upon the Lord, and he shall sustain thee;" he has both willingness and ability, a heart and a hand to do it. 8. To bear up his people under all their afflictions, trials, and temptations: " in all their afflictions he is afflicted; he supports and upholds them with the right hand of his righteousness; he suffers "no temptation" to befal them, but what he gives strength proportionate to it, "that they may be able to bear it;" he comfortably carries them through all the difficulties of life, and will not leave them till he has brought them to glory; for even "to hoary hairs" he will carry them; he has made, and he will bear them. 9. To bear them up and keep them from falling: he is able to do it, and he will do it; he is that "sure foundation," on which their souls being built, "the gates of hell" cannot prevail against them; and though they may be attended with many failings and infirmities, yea, with many slips and falls, yet they shall never fall totally and finally; for he "upholdeth them with his hand." 10. His legs are as "pillars of marble," &c., to bear "all the glory of his Fathers's house;" for as he "builds the temple," it is proper that he should "bear the glory:" Adam had a great deal of glory put upon him, in being made after God's image and likeness, and in being the representative of, and a federal head unto all his posterity; but "being in honour," did not abide long; the crown was too heavy for him, it soon fell from his head, he being a mutable creature; but Christ is "the same yesterday, to-day, and for ever;" and will for ever continue to bear the glory of the God-man and Mediator, which no mere creature is capable of, being no ways able to effect the work. And now, when we consider all these things, Christ's legs had need be, as indeed they are, "as pillars of marble, set upon sockets of fine gold."

2ndly. By Christ's legs may be meant, his ways and paths,[q] which he has trodden in; for as legs are for the support of the body, so they are likewise the instruments of walking; and may intend, either, 1. Christ's ways of love, grace, and mercy in the covenant; "whose goings forth" in it were "from of old, from everlasting;" these were, like "pillars of marble," firm and constant: his "counsels of old are faithfulness and truth," and like such, "set upon sockets of fine gold," glorious and excellent; the steps which were then taken, the measures and methods that were then concerted, were all to advance the glory of the three Divine Persons, as well as to bring about and secure the salvation of sinners. Or, 2. The path of the incarnation which he trod in, as never any did before or since: it was a wondrous stoop, a surprising instance of his mighty grace, that he should come down from heaven, and converse with mortals on earth in our nature; and the manner in which this was done is no less amazing, as well as it is an indication of his love to his people, to be a partaker of the same flesh and blood with them. Or, 3. His walk and conversation here on earth, which, like "pillars of marble," was always upright, even and constant: he never went away, or stepped aside from the path of righteousness and holiness; but always acted in a perfect conformity to the law of God, which he made the rule of his obedience; and upon the whole of his conduct and conversation, there appeared a beauty, glory, and lustre; so that his legs looked like "marble pillars set upon sockets of fine gold." Or else, 4. His walks in his churches, which are his "golden candlesticks;" among whom he delights to be, and to whom his presence is very beautiful and glorious, delightful and desirable. Or, 5. His providential dispensations to his people, which are sometimes "past finding out;" for his "way is in the sea, and his path in the great waters," so that his "footsteps are not known;" he seems sometimes to come forth against his people in a way of anger and displeasure; and then "his feet are like unto fine brass, as if they burned in a furnace," as they are represented in Rev. i. 15. But yet these are, 1. Like pillars, straight and upright, for he "is righteous in all his ways, and holy in all his works;" and though wicked men, and sometimes God's own children, through peevishness, impatience, and unbelief, may say that "the Lord's way is not equal," yet his is always equal, and theirs unequal. And, 2. Like "pillars of marble," are firm and constant; for "he is in one mind, and who can turn him?" and "what his soul desireth, even that he doeth." And, 3. They are like such pillars, "set upon sockets of fine gold;" the basis and foundation of them are his eternal purposes and decrees; for he "worketh all things after the counsel of his own will:" and this will all appear exceeding beautiful and glorious, when the book of purposes, and the book of providences are opened, and saints behold that delightful harmony and agreement which is between them; then will they sing the song of Moses and the Lamb, saying, "Just and true are thy ways, thou King of saints, who shall not fear thee?" &c., "for thy judgments are made manifest," Rev. xv. 3, 4.

3rdly. These legs may set forth the power of Christ, in treading under and trampling upon all his and our enemies; so his legs were like "pillars of marble," &c., when he hung upon the cross, who then trampled upon and triumphed over sin, Satan, and the world; and so they are now he is in heaven, "for he must reign until he hath put all his enemies under his feet:" Christ's legs and feet, in the government of his church, and in the subduing of his enemies, are not like the legs and feet of Nebuchadnezzar's image, in Dan. ii. 33,

---

q So St Thomas and Beda in Sanct. in loc.

whose legs are said to be "of iron," and "his feet, part of iron and part of clay," which were easily demolished and destroyed; but Christ's kingdom being a more glorious, durable, and lasting one, yea, an everlasting one, as in ver. 44, therefore his legs are here compared to "pillars of marble," and his feet to "sockets of fine gold;" his head and his feet are both of fine gold, which shows that his kingdom is glorious and excellent, and preferable to all others; and because Christ's legs and feet are such, hence the saints are "more than conquerors," and shall have all enemies trodden under their feet.

4thly. Some* by these legs understand Christ's apostles, and the ministers of the gospel: who bear the name of Christ, carry his gospel, run to and fro, and diffuse "the savour of his knowledge in every place;" are pillars in his house, are instruments to support and strengthen his interest; and are marble ones, constant and immoveable in their work, cannot be diverted from it, either by the frowns or flatteries of the world: and in the discharge of their work, are very beautiful; "how beautiful are the feet of him that bringeth good tidings!" and what makes their feet so beautiful? because they are as it were shod with gold; they are "shod with the preparation of the gospel of peace," with the golden truths of the gospel; and this makes them look like "pillars of marble set upon sockets of fine gold."

II. She describes him by "his countenance;" or "his appearance,"* look, or aspect; which is the ninth particular instanced in: by this is meant, not his countenance or look by which he beholds others; but that by which he is visible to, and beheld by others, and which recommends him to them; as his grand and majestic form, his tall stature, his graceful mien and deportment, and stately walk. And this she says, is,

First. As Lebanon; which intends, either,

1st. The mountain of Lebanon; which was a large and goodly mountain, abounding with fruitful and fragrant trees, situated on the north side of the land of Canaan: to which Christ may be compared, 1. For the height of it: Christ, as God, "is over all, blessed for ever;" as God-man and Mediator, he has "a name given him above every name; he is higher than the kings of the earth," or than all the angels in heaven; he is of a more excellent nature, and has "obtained a more excellent name than they." 2. For pleasantness; Lebanon is called by Moses, that goodly mountain which before his death he had a great desire to see; Christ's countenance, form, or personage, is more glorious and excellent that Lebanon, or any other mountain whatever; he is "the brightness of his Father's glory, and the express Image of his Person." 3. For the fruitfulness of it; Lebanon was a fruitful mountain for vines and cedars: on Christ all those "trees of righteousness" grow, which are the Lord's planting; from him they receive their life and nourishment, their verdure and fruitfulness; and by him they are supplied with all needful grace; for in him all fulness of it dwells. 4. For the fragrancy of it; hence we read that the saints' smell is as Lebanon, Hosea xiv. 6; the trees and plants which grew there, were very odoriferous, and diffused a grateful smell to passers-by: Christ's Person, grace, righteousness, sacrifice, and all that belong to him, are exceeding savoury to believers; and hence it is, that he is in this song compared to spikenard, myrrh, camphire, the rose and the lily, &c. Lyra interprets this, not of the mountain of Lebanon, but of the aromatic tree, *lebanah*, or frankincense; so Theodoret.

2ndly. It may be meant of the forest of Lebanon. Some think, that she has a regard in this part of the description to the attire of the high-priest, in whose garments were curiously wrought the figures of animals, trees, and flowers; so that when he had his robes on him, he might be thought in some measure to resemble a forest, and particularly this of Lebanon, which was esteemed the most excellent; and so may be expressive of the glory and excellency of Christ, as our great High-priest, so far exceeds Aaron and all his sons. Or else,

3rdly. It may be meant of the temple, which is sometimes called Lebanon, as in Zech. xi. 1; and it may be very well called so, because it was chiefly made of the wood of Lebanon: and Christ may be very well compared unto it, for the stateliness and magnificence of it; as well because that all that belonged to it, or were performed in it, were eminently typical of him, and did gloriously prefigure him; and hence he calls his body the temple, in John ii. 19.

Secondly. She says, that his countenance is, or "he is excellent or choice as the cedars" which grow on Lebanon; and her meaning is, that as the cedars in Lebanon were the choicest, and were preferable to all other trees, so was Christ her beloved to her: saints are compared to cedars; see Psal. xcii. 12, and Numb. xxiv. 5, 6; but Christ is the chief cedar, the choicest of all the cedars; in him these are planted and take root, and by him they are made fruitful; to these sort of trees Christ may be compared, for their tallness, stateliness, fragrancy, and durableness; but these and all other things falling short to express his beauty, and set off his greatness, she concludes the description in the following words.

Verse 16. Former part. *His mouth is most sweet: yea, he is altogether lovely.*

In these words we have,

I. The tenth and last particular instance of Christ's beauty, or distinguishing character of

---

* Foliot in loc. and Ambros. in Ps. cxviii. octon. 5. col. 914. and Carpathius in Sanct. in loc.

* מראהו ειδος αυτε. Sept. species ejus, Vulg. Lat. adspectus ejus, Montanus, Michaelis, &c.

him, whereby he might be known from all other beloveds; "his mouth is most sweet," or "sweetnesses."

II. A comprehensive summary of all his excellencies and glories; "yea, he is altogether lovely."

I. She here describes him by his mouth, which, she says, is most sweet;" yea, sweetness itself, and that in the highest degree of it; sweetnesses, as the word may be rendered.ʷ And by Christ's mouth here may be meant, either,

1st. The words of his mouth.ˣ In this sense is the word used, in Prov. v. 3, and viii. 7; and by them may be meant, the "doctrines of the gospel;" which are "the gracious words that proceed out of Christ's mouth; and are sweet to a believer's taste, administer spiritual refreshment to his soul, and are preferred by him to his "necessary food:" likewise the "precious promises" of it are the words of Christ's mouth; which, if ever spoken to any purpose to a believer, they are spoken by Christ; and when they are so, they are exceeding sweet, and fill the soul with an unspeakable satisfaction. The kind invitations of the Gospel also are not to be excluded, such as Isaiah lv. 1, Matthew xi. 28, Rev. xxii. 17; which manifestly speak out the love and grace of Christ to sinners; and when applied with power by the blessed Spirit, are exceeding sweet, comfortable, and refreshing to the consciences of distressed sinners. Moreover the comforts which Christ speaks to his people, either by his Spirit or by his ministers, may be included here; as well as his commands, which also are the words of his mouth, which he has enjoined us the observation of, and which are no ways grievous, but joyous to a believer; especially when he has the presence of Christ, the discoveries of his love, and is under the influences of the Spirit of grace, whilst he is engaged in acts of obedience to them: these " statutes and judgments of the Lord," as they are right and just in themselves, so they are to believers " more to be desired than gold, yea, than fine gold; sweeter also than the honey or the honey-comb;" for such is the grace of Christ, that what he has made the believer's duty, he also has made his privilege; and hence it is, that all wisdom's ways are " ways of pleasantness " to him, and the words of Christ's mouth are carefully regarded by him. Or,

2ndly. The kisses of Christ's mouth may be here intended, or the sensible manifestations of his love and grace to souls, which are what the church earnestly desired, in chap. i. 2; than which nothing can be more delightful to the saints: these give them more pleasure and satisfaction than all the things this world can afford; but both these seem to be intended before, namely, the words of his mouth by his lips, and the manifestations of his love by his cheeks; and therefore perhaps something different from these is designed here. And,

3rdly. Someʸ think, that Christ's voice in his ministers is here meant; this is not omitted in that glorious description of Christ which John gives, in Rev. i., and which bears some resemblance to this, and is there said to be as the sound of many waters: now if it is not intended here, it does not appear in this whole description; and whether the word be translated, " the throat, mouth," or " roof of the mouth," as it may be either, they are all the instruments of the voice, and so may be expressive of it: moreover, nothing is more common with lovers, than to admire each other's voice; Christ was taken with the church's voice, and therefore desired to hear it, in chap. ii. 14, saying, " Let me hear thy voice—for sweet is thy voice;" and no wonder then that the church should admire Christ's voice, and that it should make such sweet music in her ears, as it seems from hence it did: his mouth or voice is most sweet; I am charmed with it, and so would you, O ye daughters of Jerusalem, did ye but hear it.

The voice of the law is harsh and unpleasant; it pronounces guilty curses and condemns; it is a voice of wrath and terror; it is a soul-cutting and soul-killing one; it is a voice of words, and of words that are not grateful; and therefore those who had once heard it, entreated that it might not be spoken to them any more: but the voice of Christ in the Gospel is exceeding sweet, delightful, and alluring; and no wonder it is so, for it is a voice of love, grace, and mercy; it speaks peace and pardon, and brings the agreeable news of life and salvation by Christ to lost sinners; it is also the voice of the church's beloved, of him whom she loves with all her heart and soul, and therefore must needs be sweet unto her; it is what she is well acquainted with, perfectly knows, and can distinguish from a stranger's; nor is she ever more delighted than when under the sound of it; hence, in chap. viii. 13, she says, as it is commonly understood, " O thou that dwellest in the gardens? where the companions hearken to thy voice," and are charmed and ravished with those warbling notes of thine, cause me also to hear it; for no concert of music whatever is equal to it.

4thly. The word translated *mouth*, may be rendered *taste*, as it is in chap. ii. 3; or rather, " the palate or roof of the mouth," which is the instrument of tasting, as it is in chap. vii. 9; and as the roof of the church's mouth is there commended by Christ, why may not the roof of Christ's mouth be here commended by the church? Christ has a palate or taste, that, as Job says, chap. vi. 30, can discern perverse things; dis-

---

ʷ So this phrase is used of lovers by Solon, in Plutarch, in Erotica. p. 751. and in Apulril Apolog. p. 192. &c. Theocrit Idyll. *. v. 82. ▪ ממתקים

dulcedines, Pagninus. Montanus, Marckius, Michaelis.   ˣ So the Targum and R. Solomon Jarchi in loc.   ʸ Greg. Nyssen. in Cant. Homil. 14.

tinguish between the precious and the vile, knows the difference between the good and bad, and can tell what food is best for his people, and what a portion of it is necessary for them; and therefore gives to every one of them their portion of meat in due season: he has a taste that disrelishes all carnal and earthly things, even in his own people, as well as others; that savours nothing but what is spiritual; a believer being a compound of flesh and spirit, the spiritual part of him savours the things of the spirit, and the carnal part the things of the flesh, but Christ having no flesh, no carnal part in him, savours nothing but the things of the Spirit; hence he provides no food for his people but what is wholesome in itself, and savoury to them; and they may very safely eat of it, when Christ, whose taste is most sweet, has prepared it for them, set it before them, and bid them welcome; nay more, he himself sits at the table, and sups with them, and they with him. And, "his taste is most sweet," that is the taste of him is so; "Come, taste and see," says the Psalmist, Psal. xxxiv. 8, "that the Lord is good;" and every regenerate soul finds him so: Christ and all of Christ is sweet to a believer's taste, his person, grace, and righteousness; what he is in himself, and what he has done for his people, are all so; and hence the church could say, in chap. ii. 3, by good experience, his fruit was sweet unto my taste. Or else,

5thly, and lastly. By Christ's mouth may be meant, the breath of his mouth:[a] which being most sweet, wonderfully recommends him to the church's love and affection. Job's breath was strange to his wife; but Christ's is sweet to his people, nay, sweetness itself; and by it we may understand, either, 1. The expressions of Christ's love to his people: wicked men breathe out threatenings, cruelty, ruin, and destruction to God's children; but Christ breathes out nothing but love, grace, and mercy: fury is not in him, but mercy is; for with the Lord is mercy, and with him is plenteous redemption; it is true, "the breath of the Lord is like a stream of brimstone," even an overflowing stream to destroy the wicked, for with the breath of his lips shall he slay them; but it is like an overflowing stream of love, grace, and mercy, which abounds and superabounds towards his people in their everlasting salvation. Or, 2. It may be understood of Christ's mediation: the prayers of believers are called their *breathing*, in Lam. iii. 56. Christ's prayers, mediation, and intercession, upon the account of his people, may bear the same name. Now this is most sweet, and is therefore compared to incense; it is sweet and acceptable unto God, and what sweetens and perfumes the saints' sacrifices of prayer and praise; and hence it is, that the prayers of the saints are called *odours*; see Rev. v. 8, and viii. 3, 4. Though, 3. A late writer[a] thinks, that this may as well be referred to Christ's breathing upon his apostles, when he bid them receive the Holy Ghost: which was one of the finishing actions of his life on earth, as this is the finishing part of his description here: and indeed, Christ's breathing the gifts and graces of his Holy Spirit upon his apostles then, and upon his churches and ministers in all ages since, he having the fulness of it with him, renders him exceeding amiable and lovely to them.

II. She sums up the whole character, and closes the description of him, in saying, "Yea, he is altogether lovely; or, he is all desire,"[b] as the Septuagint read it; or, "all desires," as it is in the Hebrew text: he is exceeding desirable to believers; there is none in heaven or in earth they desire besides him; and one of the characters which he was known by, under the Old-Testament, was, "the desire of all nations." And now what makes him so desirable to the church and to all believers, are, The divine excellencies and perfections which appear in his person; for, "in him dwelleth all the fulness of the Godhead bodily:" there is no perfection or excellency in the Deity, but what may be found in Christ; and if so, there can be nothing that is excellent in any creature, either in heaven or earth, but what is eminently so in him; and therefore, he must needs be a desirable person. 2. The mediatorial qualifications he is possessed of; he has a fulness of the gifts and graces of the Spirit in him, which qualify him as Man and Mediator for his office; he has a fulness and fitness for it, and a fulness of abilities to carry him through it; which render him a suitable and a desirable High-priest unto us. 3. The fulness of grace, life, and salvation in him, makes him altogether desirable to souls; when they can see nothing in themselves, and all in Christ, an emptiness in the creature, and a fulness in him; that it is in vain to expect salvation elsewhere; but that there is enough in him to answer all their wants, present, and future; every thing that will make them comfortable here, and happy hereafter; how can he be otherwise than exceeding desirable to them? 4. His agreeable carriage and deportment towards souls render him so; which is so wise and prudent, so loving, tender, and compassionate, so meek and humble, so courteous and affable, and attended with such an air of familiarity; that it at once fixes our eyes upon him, attracts our affections to him, and makes him all desires unto us. 5. The names and titles which he bears: he has a name that is above every name, which awes and commands our fear, being full of majesty; and he has a name which draws our love, being full of sweetness, which is that sweet and precious name Jesus; which is as ointment poured forth, and therefore do the virgins love him; and so are all those names which are given him, in Isa. ix. 6.

---

[a] So Sanctius in loc.
[b] וכלו מהמדים K.u. ὅλος ἐπιθυμία. Sept. totus ipse
[a] Bishop Patrick in loc.
desideria, Mercerus, Montanus, Marckius; totus desiderabilis, Vulg. Lat. version, Cocceius.

6. The characters he bears, and the relations he stands in to his people, make him exceeding desirable to them; and indeed, how can he be otherwise than so unto them, when he stands in the relations, and bears the characters of a tender Husband, an indulgent Father, a loving Brother, and a faithful Friend? He is all things to them,[c] even all in all.

Again, if we read the words as they are translated in our bibles, " he is altogether lovely," we may observe, 1. That Christ, and all of Christ is lovely to believers; he is so in his person, in all his offices, in his people, and in his ordinances; nay, the worst of Christ, or what may seem the most scaring and frightful to others, is lovely to the saints; as the cross of Christ, reproaches and sufferings on his account; for though they are not lovely in themselves, yet they are for his sake; and are therefore preferred by believers to the pleasures of sin, and profits of this world; see Heb. xi. 25, 26. 2. That there is a perfect loveliness in Christ, every thing in him is lovely, and there is nothing lovely but what is in him; he is comprehensively so: if the church is a perfection of beauty, and is perfectly comely, "through the comeliness" which Christ has put upon her; he must needs be so from whom she has it, even "altogether lovely." 3. That he is so to all: he is lovely to his Father, as he is his own Son, the dear Son of his love; and as he is Man and Mediator, engaged in our cause, as having assumed our nature, and obtained eternal redemption for us; he is so to all the holy angels, many of whom descended at his incarnation, and sang his praise, ministered to him in his state of humiliation, attended on him when tempted in the wilderness, and when in his agonies in the garden; and gazed with wonder and delight upon his glorious person, as they accompanied him in his ascension to glory: hence this is said to be one branch of the " great mystery of godliness," that God, who was "manifest in the flesh, was seen of angels," and appeared lovely to them: and so he is to all the saints, for " to them that believe, he is precious;" and indeed he is so to all but Christless sinners; who see no beauty, form, nor comeliness in him, wherefore they should desire him. 4. As Christ is lovely in himself, and lovely to all others, so it is he that makes all the saints lovely to God: there is nothing in them, nor done by them, that can make them grateful to him; they are only accepted with him " in the beloved;" he is pleased with Christ and his righteousness, and with them as considered therein: He must needs be lovely, yea, " altogether lovely," that makes all the saints lovely too.

Now the church having given such an ample description of her beloved to the daughters of Jerusalem, they might from henceforward cease to wonder, why she, who was " the fairest among women," was so deeply fallen in love with Christ; why she made such a stir about him, was so much concerned at his absence, was so diligent in her search of him, and gave them so strict a charge concerning him: as well as they need not now be any longer at a loss to know who and what he was, he having given such distinguishing characters of him: and having done this, she closes all with claiming an interest in him, and appropriates him to her own soul, in the latter part of this verse; she having a clear sight of him, and her faith more strengthened in him.

Verse 16. Latter part.— *This is my beloved, and this is my friend, O daughters of Jerusalem.*

THE church having given a large description of Christ, in the preceding verses, to the satisfaction of the enquiring daughters of Jerusalem; closes the account of him with a comfortable appropriation of him to her own soul, and a holy boasting of him before others; which she does, by considering him under those two characters:

I. As her beloved.
II. As her friend.

I. She points him out to the daughters of Jerusalem, and distinguishes him from all other beloveds; and boasts of him in the views of her interest in him, under the character of her beloved: which shows, 1. That her love and affection to him were strong and ardent, such as many waters could not quench nor any thing separate from; though she was forsaken by him, and had suffered much from the watchmen and keepers of the wall for the sake of him; she had sought him with a great deal of care and diligence to little purpose; she had called aloud, and with great importunity herself, and had made use of the interest of others with him, and yet could not prevail upon him to show himself; she could neither see him, nor hear him, nor get any tidings of him: yet notwithstanding all this, he is her beloved still. 2. It bespeaks the strength of her faith in him; for notwithstanding the sense of sins and infirmities, which she now had, the desertions, temptations, sufferings, &c., which she was attended with, yet she could say, " This is my beloved;" this is the trial of faith, and herein lies the glory and excellency of it, when a soul can believe in the dark, or as Abraham did, believe "in hope against hope ;" herein the church acted in some conformity to Christ, her Head; who, when upon the cross, in the agonies of death, deserted by his friends, and forsaken by his God, yet nevertheless could say," " My God, my God, why hast thou forsaken me ?" 3. This shows that Christ only was her beloved; that she had singled him out from all others; and that he was in her esteem preferable to all others: there is none among all the angels in heaven, nor any among all the sons of men on earth, neither is there any creature-enjoyment whatever, comparable

---

[c] Omnia Cæsar erat, Lucan. Pharsal. l. 3. v. 108. id unum dixero, quam ille omnibus omnia fuerit Paterculus, l. 2 και συντελεια λογων το παν εςτιν αυτο. Ecclesiast. c. 43. 29.

to him, and it is as if she should say, Let others take their beloveds to themselves, the idols of their own hearts, their carnal lusts, and sensual pleasures, whom they have chosen; for my part, I ingenuously confess that this excellent person, whom I have just now described unto you, is only "my beloved;" him I have chosen, and I desire no other; and now I leave you to judge whether there is any comparison between him and others.ᵈ But having met with his character already in this song, I shall not any longer insist on it now; but proceed,

II. To consider the other character which she gives of him; "this is my friend."ᵉ There is a mutual friendship between Christ and believers; he calls them his friends in v. 1 of this chapter, as the church calls him in this; and it is worthy of observation, that the very same characters of beloved and friend, which Christ gives to his church there, are given to him by his own church here; it being usual for them in this song to take up each other's words, and return them. This character of a friend, undoubtedly suits well with Christ; in opening of which, I shall endeavour, First. To give some instances and proofs of Christ's friendship to his people. Secondly. To show the transcendent excellency of this friend. And Thirdly. Consider in what manner the church here delivers herself.

First. It will be proper to give some instances of Christ's friendship to his church and people; from whence it will manifestly appear, that he justly deserves such a character. And, 1. His engaging as a Surety for them, is a manifest indication of it; when our cause was desperate he engaged in it: when justice was ready to give the blow our transgressions deserved, he interposed and averted it, and took it upon himself; when he knew that we should run through all our stock, and become bankrupts, he became our Bondsman, and engaged to pay the whole debt: when he saw that we should fall into the depths of sin and misery, he undertook to bring us out of them, cleanse us from all sin, clothe us with his righteousness, and safely conduct us to glory; and must not all this be esteemed a proof of Christ's friendship to us? 2. His dying for us is another; this is the greatest act of friendship among men, for one man to die for another; "Greater love hath no man than this," says Christ, John xv. 13, "that a man lay down his life for his friends;" but Christ has given a greater instance of friendship than this, in that he has laid down his life for his enemies; for "when we were enemies, we were reconciled to God by the death of his Son;" O matchless love! unparalleled friendship! 3. He has paid all our debts; our sins are called so in scripture; and a large score of them we have run; we owe "ten thousand talents," and have not one farthing to pay; and to prison we must have gone, where we should have lain until we had paid "the uttermost farthing," had not Christ engaged to do it; which he has actually done, by making satisfaction to law and justice; on the account of which, God the Father has cancelled the bond, crossed the debt-book, and discharged both sinner and surety: it was an act of friendship now to be bound for us, but still a greater to pay the whole debt. 4. He has purchased our persons, and procured all things needful for us; we are "not our own," but "are bought with a price;" which price is not "corruptible things, as silver and gold," but the "precious blood" of Christ Jesus, which he has shed for the ransom of us: for a king to give a large sum of money for the ransom of any of his subjects out of Algiers, or any other place of slavery, is an instance of his beneficence, humanity, and friendship to them; but was he to give himself a ransom for them, it would be an unheard-of one; but Christ has done this for his people, and thereby redeemed them from the slavery of the law, sin, Satan, and the world; and not only this, but has washed them from their sins "in his own blood," stripped them of their "filthy garments," and clothed them with "change of raiment:" nay, has procured an inheritance for them, of which he now gives them the pledge and earnest, and ere long will put them into the full possession of it: and now, to do all this for persons who are entirely undeserving of it, is an instance of friendship indeed! 5. Not only so, but he is also gone to glory, to take possession of it in our name, room, and stead; that so we may not be under any fear of losing it, nor of being by any means deprived of it: and in so doing, acts the part of a loving brother, a trusty co-heir, and faithful friend; as well as he is gone thither also to prepare a place for us, that it may be ready for us, when we, by his Spirit and grace, are made ready for that. 9. His acting the part of an Intercessor and Advocate for us with the Father, is another instance of his friendship: "he appears in the presence of God for us," presents our services and petitions to him: pleads for every blessing we stand in need of, for converting, pardoning, adoption, sanctifying, and glorifying grace, and answers all Satan's charges and accusations: and in so doing, shows himself friendly to us. 7. He supplies all our wants: he has all grace treasured up in his person for this purpose, and he does not withhold it from his people: but at proper times, cheerfully and freely distributes it, according as their wants and necessities require: and this he does, not merely for their importunities sake, but because they are his friends: when disconsolate, he comforts them; when tempted, he succours them; when distressed he relieves them; when hungry, he feeds them; when sick and wounded, he heals them, and dis-

---

ᵈ Suus rex reginæ placet, Plautus in Sticho, act. 1. sc. 2. v. 76.   ᵉ וְזֶה רֵעִי και αυτος πλεσιον μȣ, Sept. and ipse est amicus, meus, Vulg. Lat. version; und iste socius meus, Montanus, Mercerus; and is est meus consors, Tigurine version.

charges all the good offices of a friend unto them. 8. He shows his friendship to us, and maintains it by the kind and comfortable visits which he makes to us; for though he may absent himself for some time, yet he will not leave us comfortless, but will come and see us, and visit us with his salvation: which is such an astonishing piece of friendship, that we have reason to say as the Psalmist, Psalm viii. 4, "What is man that thou art mindful of him? and the son of man that thou visitest him?" 9. Whenever he pays those visits, it is with such an air of freedom and familiarity, as renders them exceeding delightful, and justly entitles him to this character: it was his free, courteous, and affable deportment to men in the days of his flesh, which occasioned the Pharisees, by way of reproach, to call him "a friend of publicans and sinners;" and so free and familiar are his converses with his people in a spiritual way; he talks with them, as one friend may with another; he walks with them, nay, he sits down at table with them, sups with them, and they with him. 10. He shows himself to be a friend unto them, and that he looks upon them to be his friends, by disclosing the secrets of his grace unto them; hence says he to his disciples, John xv. 15, "I call you not servants, for the servant knoweth not what his lord doeth; but I have called you friends, for all things that I have heard of my Father, I have made known unto you," he lay in his Father's bosom, and so was privy to all his secret thoughts, counsels, purposes, and decrees, and makes a discovery of them to us, so far as is needful to advance our good and his glory; for "the secret of the Lord is with them that fear him; and he will show them his covenant," Psalm xxv. 14.

And lastly, his friendship appears in the good and wholesome counsel which he gives unto us; which being taken, is always useful, and infallibly succeeds, being given with the utmost wisdom and the greatest faithfulness; of which see an instance in Rev. iii. 18. Nay, his reproofs for sin, as well as his advice in distress, are exceeding friendly, and ought to be taken so; for, as the wise man says, Prov. xxvii. 5, 6, "Open rebuke is better than secret love; faithful are the wounds of a friend, but the kisses of an enemy are deceitful." Thus much may suffice for some instances and proofs of Christ's friendship to his church and people. I come now,

Secondly. To show the transcendent excellency of this friend; "this is my friend:" he is a nonsuch; there is none like him, nor to be compared with him; for, 1. He is a "friend that sticketh closer than a brother:" which may be expressive of that near union there is between Christ and believers; they are as if but one soul actuated them; and indeed but one Spirit does, which is in Christ without measure, and in believers in measure; for "he that is joined unto the Lord is one Spirit:" Christ stands in a nearer relation than that of a brother to his church; he is her Head and Husband, her Bosom-friend; she is "flesh of his flesh, and bone of his bone;" though all these relations fall short of fully expressing the nearness, strictness, and indissolubleness of this union. Or else, this character may intend that sympathy and affection, which Christ bears to his people, in all their afflictions, sorrows, sufferings, temptations, desertions, sins, and infirmities; as well as signify his close adherence to our cause; who having once undertaken it, never left it till he had completed what he had engaged to do; all which shows the transcendent excellency of this friend. 2. He is a constant friend, one that "loves at all times;" he was a friend to us, when we were enemies to him; and merely by his love and acts of friendship to us, he overcame us, slew the enmity of our natures, and of enemies made us friends; and continues to be a friend to us in all the adversities and afflictions of life: when men are in prosperity, they have usually many friends; but when the day of adversity comes upon them, they soon forsake them: but Christ does not treat his people so; he is a friend to them in adversity, as well as in prosperity; he knows their souls then, when nobody else will; he owns them for his own, and treats them as his friends, and so he will continue to do, even until death; and at that time will not fail to show himself friendly to them, no more than he will at the day of judgment, when he will publicly own them, before angels and men, to be his friends; set "the crown of righteousness" upon their heads, and give them an admittance into his Father's kingdom and glory. 3. He is a faithful Friend; we may safely tell him all the secrets of our hearts, he will not betray us; we may trust him with one all, he will never fail us; and though the prophet says, Mic. vii. 5, "Trust not in a friend, and put not confidence in a guide;" yet we may safely trust in this our friend, the Lord Jesus Christ, who will be our almighty God, and our trusty and faithful friend and "guide, even unto death." 4. He is a rich friend, such an one is often useful and needful; a man may have a friend that has a heart to help him, but not in a capacity; but Christ, as he is heartily willing to help us, so he has an ability to do it; he is possessed of "unsearchable riches," and these he distributes among his friends; for it is from those "riches in glory" which are in Christ's hands, that all the wants of his people are supplied. 5. He is an everlasting friend: a man may have a friend, but this friend may die, and then all his dependence on him is gone; but Christ ever lives, and ever lives to be a friend unto his people; death parts the best friends, and puts them into an incapacity of serving each other; but there is no fear or danger of this in Christ, over whom death shall no more have the dominion. 6. He is an unchangeable friend; he is always the same, "yesterday, to-day, and for ever;" sometimes little things "separate chief friends," but nothing can separate Christ and believers; his mind never changes, his affections never cool, nor are the communications of friendship ever cut off; his ears are not open to every idle story, nor is he tempted to break off friendship with his people, by their unkindness and ingratitude unto him. But,

Thirdly. A little to consider the manner in which the church delivers herself in these words; which appears to be, 1. In the strength of faith; she could comfortably appropriate Christ to herself, under each of the characters here mentioned; and though she had not the sensible manifestations of Christ's love to her, which she was desirous of, and had not those visible instances of his friendship she had formerly experienced, yet she did not doubt but that he was both her beloved and her friend. 2. She seems to speak in an exulting and rejoicing manner; her soul was filled with joy unspeakable and full of glory, as an effect of her faith in an unseen Jesus; and indeed she had all the reason in the world to rejoice in the views of her interest in such a beloved, and in such a friend, whom she had before described. 3. She seems also to speak in a kind of boasting manner "This is my beloved, and this is my friend:" and indeed believers may do so; for though they may not glory in themselves, nor in any thing done by them, yet they may in Christ, and what he has done for them: and so the Psalmist David did, Psal. xxxiv. 2, who says, "My soul shall make her boast of the Lord:" and thus the church did here before the daughters of Jerusalem, and what effect this whole discourse of hers had upon them, may be seen in the following words.

CHAPTER VI.

The discourse between the church and the daughters of Jerusalem is continued in this chapter; they inquire whither her beloved was gone in order to seek him with her, ver. 1; she tells them where he was gone, and for what purpose he went thither, and what he was doing there, and claims and asserts her interest in him, ver. 2, 3. Then follows a commendation of the church by Christ; who admires her beauty, and describes her by her eyes, hair, &c., ver. 4—7; and prefers her to all others; being a singular and choice one to him, and being praised by others, ver. 8—10; and next he gives an account of his going into his garden, and of his design in it, and of what happened to him there, ver. 11, 12. And the chapter is concluded with a charge to the Shulamite to turn herself, that she might be looked upon; which occasions a question, to which an answer is returned, ver. 13.

Verse 1. *Whither is thy beloved gone, O thou fairest among women? Whither is thy beloved turned aside? that we may seek him with thee.*

THE church having answered the former question of the daughters of Jerusalem to their satisfaction, by giving them an ample account of her beloved, what he was; they proceed to another question, and ask, whither he was gone, which we have in this verse. In which may be considered,

I. The title or appellation they give her, or their manner of addressing her, "O thou fairest among women."

II. A question proposed by them to her, which is also repeated; "Whither is thy beloved gone? whither is thy beloved turned aside?"

III. The end of their asking this question; "that we may seek him with thee?"

I. The title or appellation which they give her, is, the "fairest among women:" which is, no doubt, designed to express the exceeding greatness of her beauty; women being the fairest of human race, and she the fairest of all that sex; she was in their eye the "perfection of beauty," and therefore they give her this character; and they were not mistaken in it, for Christ gives her the very same encomium, and that in the same words, in chap. i. 8. But now we must not understand this of her, as considered in herself; neither did the daughters of Jerusalem so understand it, who had been better informed from her own mouth; for she had told them, that she was *black* in herself, though *comely* in Christ: nor is it to be understood of her outward appearance in the world: for under that consideration she appears also black with reproaches, scandals, persecutions, and afflictions: but this character suits her as she is considered in Christ, her Head; as justified by his righteousness, washed in his blood, and sanctified by his Spirit. It may also be observed, that these persons continued in their esteem of her; for the same character they give her here, they gave her when they proposed the first question to her, in chap. v. 9, nay, perhaps their esteem of her, and value for her, might rise higher than heretofore, they having a clearer knowledge of Christ than they had before; for as our knowledge of Christ and love to him increase, so do our love unto, and our esteem for his people: and it is very probable, that the beauty and loveliness which they saw in her, drew their pity and compassion towards her; so as to take notice of her case, condole her misfortunes in the loss of so excellent a person, and offer their service to assist her in the search of him. Likewise, no doubt but the veneration and esteem which they had for her person, made them more carefully attend to what she said concerning her beloved: for thus it is with persons under the preaching of the gospel; if they come prejudiced against the person who ministers, they take but little notice of what is said, unless it be to calumniate and reproach, and so reap but little advantage from it; when, on the other hand, if persons come, not only unprejudiced against, but having a veneration and respect for the minister of the gospel, they generally give the greater heed unto, and are most likely to profit by his ministrations.

Moreover, the daughters might make use of this title or appellation in their addresses, to assure her that they were serious and in good earnest in asking this question, as well as in the former; and that it was not to indulge a vain curiosity in themselves, nor designed for her disadvantage, but rather the contrary.

II. Here is a question put by them; "Whither is thy beloved gone?"[a] Which way did he take? what course did he steer, on which hand did he turn, when he withdrew from thy door? which question is repeated, though another word[b] is used, yet to the same purpose "Whither is thy beloved turned aside?" Which way did he look? which way did he turn his face when he turned it from thee? Now, 1. The putting of this question, and not insisting any longer upon the former, or upon the explication of any branch of her answer to it, supposes that they were entirely satisfied with it; therefore the question is not now, *who* or *what* her beloved was, for they knew that full well from the description she had given of him; but now the question is, "Whither is he gone?" This may teach us, that when younger Christians have any doubts, scruples, cases of conscience, or questions relating to faith or experience; to the person, office, and grace of Christ, or to any part of the great mystery of godliness, to be resolved, they should make their application to elder ones: this method these young converts, or daughters of Jerusalem, took here; which God was pleased to bless and succeed, for their increase in light and knowledge, and for the stirring up of their affections and desires after the Lord Jesus: and may serve to encourage the private conferences and conversations of the saints with each other: which, when carried on in an agreeable manner, when filled with spiritual discourses, and taken up with asking and answering proper questions relating to faith or experience, are highly well pleasing to God, and tend much to the edifying of one another: this may also serve as a direction to ministers to insist chiefly upon the glories and excellencies of Christ; for this is the way of preaching which God owns and blesses, for the conversion of sinners, and consolation of saints; the church's insisting on this subject, was made of great use to these persons, to draw out their love to Christ, and to make farther enquiries after him. 2. It may be observed from this question, that when Christ is known, who he is, and what he is; the next question is, where he is, and how he may be come at? whilst persons are insensible of their wretched state by nature, they see no need of Christ; and whilst they are ignorant of him, they have no value for him, nor desire after him; *ignoti nulla cupido*; there is no desire after an unknown thing; an unknown Christ is an undesired Christ; the reason why souls, in a state of nature, seek not after God is, because they have no understanding of him: "there is none that understandeth," says the apostle' Rom. iii. 11, "there is none that seeketh after God:" the same reason holds here, with respect to Christ; for, whilst souls remain strangers to the beauties and glories of Christ's person, they will have no value for him, nor make any enquiry after him; but as for those that know the Lord they will "follow on to know him," and make use of all means appointed for that purpose, for the more a soul knows of Christ, the more it desires to know; mere speculative notions of his person, without knowledge of interest in him, communion with him, will not satisfy them; an account of him by hearsay, though exceeding ravishing and delightful to them, is not enough without seeing him; for where Christ's worth is once known, there is no contentment without the enjoyment of him; when he is once discovered as "the pearl of price," the soul is willing to run all risks, endure all hardships, part with every thing that is near and dear, so it may be possessed of him: its language is, Give me Christ, or I die; ten thousand worlds, if I had them, for an interest in this glorious person: this seems to be the case of the daughters of Jerusalem here. 3. The repetition of this question, shows that they were serious and in good earnest, and did not speak sarcastically:[c] and that they were impatient until they received an answer; "Whither is thy beloved gone? whither is thy beloved turned aside?" prithee give us an answer speedily, keep us not in suspense; thou hast given us such a character of his person, that we long to see him, and are uneasy until thou givest us some notice of the place whither he is retired, that we may, along with thee, be searching after him. 4. There may be some knowledge of Christ, love to him, and desires after him, when there is but little faith in him that is discernible; all the graces of the Spirit are implanted at one and the same time, but they do not all appear at once in their actings upon Christ; love and affection to Christ, and desires after him, appear before faith does: so they did in these persons: they had got some farther knowledge of Christ from the church's description of him; were filled with greater love and affection to him, and had more ardent desires after him, and yet had but little faith in him; for they could not say, that he was their beloved; and therefore as one[d] well observes, they do not say, where is *our* beloved gone, but where is *thy* beloved gone? 5. It appears that they were willing to take the least hints, nay even conjectures, that if it was possible they might improve them towards finding him, "Whither is thy beloved gone?" Canst thou not give us some hints of it? canst thou not guess which way he took? which shows how intent they were of using all means, so that they might but

---

[a] אנה הלך πη απηλθεν, Sept. quo abiit, Vulg. Lat. version, Montanus, Tigurine version, Junius; quo ivit, Mercerus; quorsum ivit, Cocceius. [b] אנה פנה πη α περβλεψεν, Sept. quo declinavit, Vulg. Lat. version, Pagninus; quo respexit, Montanus: quo se vertit, Junius, Mercerus. Tigurine version; quorsum flexit, Cocceius. [c] So R. Sol. Jarchi in loc. [d] Durham in loc.

find him; let it be which way it would, they were resolved to pursue it; could they but have the least notice of it, whether it was to the right hand or left, backwards or forwards. 6. Their putting this question to her, shows that she was, or at least that they thought she was, capable of giving them some directions, though she was at the same time destitute of his presence; and it seems she was, by the answer she gives them in the following verse. The church knew where Christ usually retired, and granted his gracious presence to his people; and though he was not willing at present to show himself to her, yet she did not know but he might to them, and therefore directs them: nay, sometimes believers are capable of advising and directing others, when they cannot take advice themselves.

III. The end they propose in asking this question, is, that they might seek him with her: which may be considered as a motive to prevail upon her to comply with their request; for this shows that they were serious and in good earnest; that their end was not mere speculation, but practice, which indeed ought to be the end of all our enquiries; that it was their purpose and resolution to seek him; they had agreed and resolved among themselves to do it; for so the words may be read, " and we will seek him with thee;"ᵉ and if thou wilt tell us which way he went, it will lay us under an obligation to make good our resolution: nay, it shows also that it was her good they had in view, as much as their own; and self-interest goes a great way; so that, put all together, it is no wonder that she readily, and without any hesitation, answers the question. Now this being the frame of soul that these daughters of Jerusalem were brought into through her discourse concerning Christ; and seeking Christ being the thing which they had in view, and were desirous of being directed in; may lead us to observe the following things. 1. That the end of setting forth the excellencies of Christ, whether in private conversation, or in the public ministry, is to set souls a seeking after him; for this purpose the ministers of the gospel insist upon the glories of Christ's person, the excellency of his righteousness, the efficacy of his blood, and the fulness of his grace; it was with this view that the church took so much pains, and spent so much time, in discoursing concerning this excellent person, her beloved, which had its answerable success. 2. It is very discouraging to seek Christ, and not know where he is; it is true, the church knew where Christ used to retire, when he withdrew himself, and therefore knew where to seek him, in hopes of finding him; but the daughters of Jerusalem were unacquainted therewith; and therefore it was very proper for them to put such a question, previous to their seeking him. 3. This should be the principal thing we should have in view in all religious duties, seeking and seeing Jesus; this is that one thing that should be uppermost in our hearts and desires, when concerned in the duties of hearing, reading, praying, meditating, and conferring, that we may " behold the king in his beauty." 4. Our seeking Christ should be jointly and together; we should seek him, not separately, but with the church: though this does not exclude our seeking him alone, in our closets and in our families; yet there is a social part of worship that we should be concerned in jointly; in which we are to worship the Lord with one shoulder and one consent, and " not forsake the assembling of ourselves together, as the manner of some" too often is. 5. We should seek Christ in his ordinances, and where his church seeks him: we cannot expect the presence of Christ, when we run away from his church and ordinances, or when we seek him elsewhere; we should seek him with the church, and where the church seeks. 6. Their saying that they would seek him with her, was no doubt to encourage her in hopes of finding; they do as good as desire her not to be cast down at his departure; for they hoped he was not gone far, and that he would be found again, and at the same time promise her all the assistance they were capable of giving; though there is also reason to believe, that they were in hopes of sharing with her in so valuable a blessing; and indeed it was but reasonable, that if they bore part with her in the fatigue of the search, they should also participate with her in the enjoyment of the blessing; which no doubt she was willing to, and therefore immediately gives the following answer.

Verse 2. *My beloved is gone down into his garden, to the beds of spices, to feed in the gardens, and to gather lilies.*

THESE words contain the church's answer to the second question of the daughters of Jerusalem; they had asked her what her beloved was more than others; she told them: they then proceed to ask, whither he was gone; to which she here replies. In which may be considered,

I. The place whither she says he was gone; " my beloved is gone down into his garden, to the beds of spices."

II. The end of his going down, or what his business and employment was when there; which was twofold: 1st. " To feed in the garden." 2ndly. " To gather lilies."

I. The place whither she says he was gone, " into his garden;" and more particularly, " to the beds of spices." And,

1st. It may be enquired what was meant by his garden, into which he was gone down. Someᶠ understand it of the heavenly paradise, whither

---

ᵉ ונבקשנו עמך και ζητησομεν αυτον μετα ση, Sept. and quæremus eum tecum, Vulgate Latin version, Montanus, Cocceius, Mercerus, Marckius; ut quæremus eum tecum, Junius; ut tecum perquiramus eum, Tigurine version, agreeable to our version.

ᶠ Piscator and Diodat. in loc.

Christ was gone to share the everlasting joys thereof, and converse with angels and saints; who may be said to be the "trees of righteousness," those spicy plants and precious flowers which are planted there; and in the midst of which stands "the tree of life," Christ Jesus, the glory of the whole garden; and into this, Christ's lilies, when fully ripe, are transplanted by him. This sense is favoured by R. Aben Ezra's gloss upon the text, who says, "This is he who ascended on high," to feed in the gardens, and to gather lilies, "because he dwelleth with the angels, who are the righteous ones." But if the words design Christ's ascension into heaven, they should rather have expressed thus; "my beloved is gone up into his garden," than as they are, "my beloved is gone down into his garden:" therefore I rather think, that the church of Christ here on earth is meant; which is as a garden separated by Christ from this world, whose inclosure is sovereign and distinguishing grace; in which are various trees, plants, and spices, set and planted there by Christ himself, and where he takes his walks and pleasure; but in what sense the church may be compared to a garden, see more on chap. iv. 12.

2ndly. It may be observed, that this garden is said to be his; and so it may very well; for of all others he has chosen this to be his garden; he asked it of his Father for this purpose, and he gave it to him; he has also purchased it by his own blood, and distinguished it by his own grace; he takes the care of it, waters it, and watches over it; it is he that hath brought it to its present perfection, and will bring it to a far greater; so that Christ retires and takes his walks here, not as one either upon trespass or sufferance, and by the leave of others; but as having an undoubted right and title to it, and as being sovereign Lord and owner of it; but of this, see more on chap. iv. 16.

3rdly. Christ is said to be gone down into his garden: which perhaps may be an allusion to Solomon's gardens, which lay lower than his palace: and it is probable that those stairs, which went down from the city of David, the palace-royal of the kings of Judah, were made to go down into the king's gardens, of both which you read in Neh. ii. 15; and so "the garden of nuts," in ver. 11, seems to be in the valley. or the allusion may be to what Solomon himself was wont to do, as Josephus[s] relates; who used to go very early in the morning, in great pomp, to Etham, about two miles from Jerusalem, a pleasant place, abounding with gardens and flows of water, which might lie lower than Jerusalem. And in the spiritual or mystical sense, may point out, 1. The low estate of Christ's church here on earth: the saints are compared to myrtle-trees; and these are said, Zech. i. 8, to be "in the bottom," that is, in a low estate, being depressed with many sorrows, afflictions, and persecutions; they are doves, but "doves of the vallies," mourning under a sense of their iniquities, being burdened with the weight of sin; and they are not only in a low estate, but also low and humble in their own eyes: and with such Christ delights to dwell; he often goes down into his garden to those humble souls, pays them a visit, grants them his presence, and bestows larger measures of his grace upon them. 2. It is also expressive of Christ's condescension in doing this: it was a wonderful stoop, and an amazing instance of his condescension, to come down from heaven, clothe himself with our nature, and converse with sinful mortals here on earth; for a king to come from his royal palace, and enter into the cottage of a beggar, and to eat, drink, and lodge there for a time, would not express so much humility and condescension as this does; and next to this is his granting his presence to his churches, and to particular believers here on earth; so that we have reason to say, when we consider the greatness of his Majesty, and our vileness, sinfulness, and unworthiness, with Judas, not Iscariot, "How is it, Lord, that thou wilt manifest thyself to us, and not unto the world?" John xiv. 22. And if,

4thly. It should be asked, how she could tell the daughters of Jerusalem where her beloved was, when she was at a loss for him, and in the search of him herself? it may be answered, 1. That though she had sought him, and found him not; though he was not pleased to manifest himself to her at that present time; yet having had large experiences of these things, she knew where Christ usually was, and would be found of his people; therefore she directs them where formerly she had, though now she could not find him, in hopes that they might. Or, 2. It may be supposed that the case was altered with her, that she was no longer at a loss for him; but having sought him, had found him, or at least had gotten some intelligence of him; which she no sooner had, but she informs them of it. Or, 3. Their inquiring whither he was gone, might bring to her remembrance what she had formerly heard him say, in chap. v. 1, "I am come into my garden, my sister, my spouse," &c.; but falling asleep immediately, entirely forgot it; until her memory was refreshed by the enquiries of these persons. Thus you see that weaker Christians may be useful to stronger ones; and even the very questions they put for information-sake, may prove the quickening of believers, and be the means of increasing light and knowledge, or at least of reviving past experiences. But,

5thly. It may be observed, that she not only says that he was gone down to his garden, but that he was gone down "to the beds of spices:" by which I understand particular believers, who are so many beds in Christ's garden; in which are planted those precious spices, the graces of

---

[s] Antiquitat. l. 8. c. 7. s. 3.

the Spirit, which, for rareness, excellency, and fragrancy, are called so : and these more especially intend growing, thriving, and flourishing souls; lively believers, whose " spices flow out," whose grace is in exercise ; such Christ has a particular regard unto, and delights to be with.

II. She declares the end of his going down into his garden, or what it is he employs himself about when there. And,

1st. She says, it was " to feed in the gardens." By gardens, I understand particular congregated churches ;[h] for though there is but one " general assembly and church of the first-born, which are written in heaven ;" which is redeemed by Christ's blood, and will be presented "a glorious church, without spot or wrinkle, or any such thing," and therefore before called a garden, in the singular number ; yet there are many distinct and particular churches; such as those of Rome, Corinth, Galatia, Ephesus, Colosse, Philippi, Thessalonica, and the seven churches of Asia, were; which were as so many distinct gardens, or plots of earth, that the one garden was subdivided into. And by feeding here, is meant, either, 1. His feeding himself ;[i] which is to be understood of that pleasure and delight which Christ takes in being among his saints, and seeing their graces exercised upon their proper object ; for as believers feed themselves by exercising their grace on Christ, so he feeds or delights himself in observing this; this is his meat and drink ; this is his supping with them, as the other is their supping with him ; and this Christ is invited to, in chap. iv. 16, to which he complies, in chap. v. 1. Or else, 2. It may be understood of his feeding his flock, as R. Sol. Jarchi observes ; for " he feeds his flock like a shepherd," though in such places as other shepherds do not ; he feeds them in the gardens, which are unusual to feed sheep in ; commons or enclosed grounds, and not gardens, being the most usual places for that purpose : and she makes mention of gardens, in the plural number, to show that Christ is not tied to one particular church, but feeds in all his churches, in all his gardens ; where he feeds his people with himself, who is " the Bread of Life, the hidden manna ; whose flesh is meat indeed, and whose blood is drink indeed : O precious food ! delicious fare ! he feeds them by and with his ordinances, which are those " breasts of consolation " which convey much strength and nourishment to them ; those green pastures into which he leads them, and " the fatness of his house " with which he feeds them ; and particularly the Lord's Supper is that " feast of fat things," by which he sweetly refreshes them, he feeds them also by his ministers, who are his under-shepherds, to whom he has given a commission and also ability, to feed his people " with knowledge and with understanding :" and so he does likewise by his Spirit ; who takes the things of Christ and sheds it in us; and the promises of Christ, and applies them to us ; for which reason he is called " the Spirit of promise." And now this may serve to direct poor hungry souls where to go for food, and where to expect it, even in Christ's gardens, in his churches and in his ordinances, where he himself feeds.

2ndly. Another end of his going down into his garden, is " to gather lilies or roses, as the Targum renders it ; to crop them with the hand ;[k] lilies are liable to be cropped; hence Horace[l] calls the lily, *breve lilium*, the short-lived lily : by which may be meant, either the good works of the saints, which he is well pleased with, and takes notice of ; insomuch that he writes them down in " the book of his remembrance," as R. Solomon Jarchi observes ; for he " is not unrighteous to forget their work, and labour of love, but will reward them in a way of grace : or else, by them is meant, the sweet-smelling graces of his own Spirit, growing in his churches, as Ainsworth thinks, with which he is wonderfully delighted : or rather, the persons of the elect, and members of his church, who may be compared to lilies, for the glory, splendour, and beauty in his righteousness ; of which see chap. ii. 2.

Now there was, 1. A gathering of these lilies at Christ's death : as all the sins of the elect were collected together and were laid on Christ, when he hung upon the cross ; so all their persons were collected and gathered together in one Head, Christ Jesus; they all met in his person, and were represented by him ; for this purpose Christ came down from heaven, took our nature, and suffered in it : see John xi. 51, 52, Eph. i. 10. 2. There is a gathering of these lilies in effectual calling through the ministry of the word, by the mighty power of divine grace : and this work Christ is daily concerned in, in his church, and will be until all his elect are gathered in. 3. There is a gathering of them into church-communion, which is also Christ's work ; who takes " one of a city, and two of a family," and brings them to Zion; and in doing this, he shows his regard to the good of souls, and at the same time "glorifies the house of his glory ;" see Isa. lx. 7, 8. 4. There is a gathering into nearer communion with himself, which he often does after great desertions ; see Isa. liv. 7. 5. This may be expressive of that great delight and pleasure which Christ takes in

---

[h] The Jews, in Shirhashirim Rabba in loc. by gardens understand their schools and synagogues, as do also R. Sol. Jarchi and Alshech in loc. The whole is expounded in the Talmud thus, My beloved, this is the holy blessed God ; is gone down into his garden, this is the world; to the beds of spices, these are the Israelites; to feed in the gardens, these are the nations of the world; and to gather lilies, these are the righteous that spring up among them, T. Hieros. Beracot, fol. 5. 2, 3. Vid. Yalkut in loc. [i] Ut ubi pascatur in hortis, Vulg. Lat. version, Munster, Mercerus. [k] Ευννεα λειρια κερσοι, Theocrit. Idyll. 19. v. 32. Aut candida lilia carpit, Ovid. Metamorph. l. 5. fab. 6. Liliaque alba legit, and Fasti. l. 4. [l] Carmin. l. 1. ode 36. v. 16.

his people: no man can take more delight in plucking fruit, or gathering flowers in a garden, than Christ does in his own people, and in his own grace in them; see Cant. v. 1. 6. This may be meant of their being gathered by death; so Abraham and Isaac, when they died, are said to be " gathered unto their fathers," Gen. xv. 8, and xxxv. 29. Christ comes into his garden, the church, sometimes to plant new lilies, and sometimes to crop and gather old ones, when they are fully ripe; not to destroy them, but to remove them into his Paradise above; and at the last day, by the means of angels, he will gather in all his elect ones from the four winds, as wheat into his barn, and as lilies into his garden; see Matt. iii. 7, and xiii. 48, and xxiv. 31. This sense of the word is given by several Jewish writers.[m] And now, lest any should think that this was a mere surmise, conjecture, and imagination of hers: or if any should call in question her knowledge in this matter, she declares in the following verse, that she was not only well acquainted with him, but was nearly related to him; and therefore was capable of informing any person where he was, and what he was about.

Verse 3. *I am my beloved's, and my beloved is mine; he feedeth among the lilies.*

THAT these words are expressive of that mutual interest and property which Christ and his church have in each other, of that strict and inseparable union that there is between them, and also of that mutual affection and complacency which they have to and in each other, as well as of her knowledge and assurance of her interest in Christ, has been shown in chap. ii. 16; but it may be farther observed, that the order of the words is here inverted; that whereas in chap. ii. 16, the order of the words is this, " My beloved is mine, and I am his;" from whence has been observed, that Christ is first ours, and then we are his, which is an undoubted truth: for Christ first gives himself to us, before we are capable of giving ourselves to him; but that which was first there is here last, and what was last is first; for the first says, " I am my beloved's," and then "my beloved is mine:" from whence it may be observed, that though Christ is first ours in fact, yet our being his, may come first to our knowledge, may be first in discovery; that is to say, that we may know that he has called us by his grace, and enabled us thereby to give up ourselves to him: so that we can say, Lord, we are thine, thou hast conquered our souls by thy grace, and hast taken possession of us, which thou wouldest never have done, had we not been thine; and from this work of grace upon our souls, we conclude that thou art ours. Thus the cause may be known by the effect; and our interest in Christ, by the displays of Christ's grace to us, and in us; likewise, if we consider the words as connected with her former carriage and behaviour to Christ, and what she had met with from him, they will lead us to observe; that all the infirmities, sins, and miscarriages of God's people, do not destroy their union with, and interest in Christ Jesus: she had treated him very rudely, when he, in the most moving manner, and with the most tender language, entreated her to arise and let him in; she put him off with idle excuses, which he so much resented, as to absent himself from her, and left her to seek him in vain, and to be abused by the watchmen and keepers of the walls; and though he thus visited her transgressions with this rod of correction, his own absence, for this is so to God's children; and with those stripes and blows which she received from the watchmen; yet he did not take away his loving-kindness from her, nor break his covenant with her; and she was satisfied of this, and therefore could say, notwithstanding all this, " I am my beloved's, and my beloved is mine;" and if, with R. Aben Ezra, we connect the words with the preceding verse, there will appear a beauty and glory in them, " My beloved is gone down into his garden," &c. It is true, he is so; but though he is gone, and I am left alone, he is departed from me, and when he will return, I cannot tell; perhaps I may never see his face more here on earth, in a way of sensible communion and fellowship with him, as I have heretofore done, though I hope I shall; yet if I never do, I am satisfied as to my covenant-interest in him, and union to him; I know that I am my beloved's, and that my beloved is mine; here lies the glory and excellency of faith, thus to believe in an unseen Christ: though it may be as the Targum intimates, that she had now the presence of Christ, the glorious Shekinah, with her; he had once more shown himself to her, and, upon the sight of him, she says, as Thomas did, my Lord, and my God: but however, whether she had or had not the visible tokens of Christ's presence, her faith was certainly in exercise upon him, nay, she had not only faith, but the joy of faith; she not only knew her interest in Christ, as her salvation, but also had the joys of this salvation, restored to her. And again it may be observed, that though she excludes all other beloveds from having any share in her affections, or from being in competition with him; yet by saying what she does, she does not exclude others, particularly the daughters of Jerusalem, from having an interest in him as well as she, as R. Sol. Jarchi thinks; who paraphrases the words thus, " I am my beloved's, and ye are not his, and therefore shall not build with us," and then explains it by Ezra iv. 3; but though the church knew that a whole Christ was hers, yet she knew that he was others also; and would therefore never say so to the daughters of Jerusalem, to discourage them in seeking of him.

Moreover she adds, as in chap. ii., " he feedeth among the lilies:" which may be considered, either as an apostrophe to him, " O thou that feed-

---

[m] Zohar in Gen. fol. 44. 3. Bereshith Rabba, parash. 62. Shirhashirim Rabba, and Alshech in loc.

est among the lilies;" or as descriptive both of him and of the place where he was; that others might readily know where her beloved was; and where he was to be found: but of this we have spoken, on chap. ii. 16, and shall not here repeat it; only observe, that Christ having been a long time absent from his church, and would not make himself known, nor speak one word a great while, at last breaks silence, and, like another Joseph, cannot refrain himself any longer from her; but must make himself known to her, and bursts out with words of love and joy, in the following commendations of her.

Verse 4. *Thou art beautiful, O my love, as Tirzah; comely as Jerusalem, terrible as an army with banners.*

THESE are the words of Christ; who having absented himself from his church for a considerable time, to show his resentment of her former carriage to him, now manifests himself unto her, and declares that he has the same love and affection for her as ever he had, and therefore addresses her with this title or character, " O my love!" nay, that she was as beautiful and comely in his eye as ever she was, notwithstanding all her failings and infirmities; which beauty of hers he describes first more generally in this verse, and then more particularly in the following ones. In this general description of her beauty are three parts:

I. He says, " that she is as beautiful as Tirzah."
II. " Comely as Jerusalem."
III. " Terrible as an army with banners."

I. He declares her to be as " beautiful as Tirzah." The Septuagint do not take it to be the proper name of a place, as we, with R. Aben Ezra, do, and therefore translate the word, and render it thus, ὡς εὐδοκια, *as good-will*, or *good-pleasure;* which may be expressive of the sweetness of her temper and disposition, which is heightened by using the abstract; she was all over good-will and good-nature, not only sweet, but sweetness itself, as she says of him, in chap. v. 16. Moreover, this may be spoken of her, as she is the object of God's good-will and pleasure; and so she appears to be, as chosen in Christ by him, to be a partaker of grace and glory with him; which was not done upon the foot of works, but by an act of his sovereign good-will and pleasure, who, " will have mercy on whom he will have mercy:" also, as she is redeemed by Christ: in which there was such a discovery of " the exceeding riches of God's grace," such an appearance of his "good-will to men," that the angels could not but take notice of it, when they celebrated with a song the birth of an incarnate Saviour, Luke ii. 14; likewise, as called and sanctified by the blessed Spirit of grace, who " worketh in us both to will and to do of his good pleasure." And now if we thus consider the church as the object of God's good-will and pleasure, in those several instances of it, she will appear beautiful and lovely. Or else, this may be said of her, as she is filled with good-will to God, to Christ, his people, gospel, worship, ways, and ordinances: the church and all true believers in Christ bear a good-will to God; they " love him because he first loved them," not only for what he is unto them, and what he has done for them, but also for what he is in himself; for he is in his own nature, in his own perfections, amiable and lovely: they bear a good will to Christ, he is altogether lovely to them; they have none in heaven but him, nor is there any on earth they desire besides him; every thing that belongs to him is exceeding precious to them; " his name is as ointment poured forth, therefore do the virgins love him;" they bear a good-will to his people, who have his image enstamped upon them, and to his gospel, which they prefer to their necessary food; and to his worship, ways, and ordinances; they love the habitation of his house; his tabernacles are amiable; his ways are ways of pleasantness; his commands are not grievous, but exceeding delightful to them. Now if we consider the church as being of this sweet and loving disposition, which is wrought, influenced, and maintained by divine grace, how beautiful does she appear!

Again, the word Tirzah comes from a root which signifies to be grateful, or to be accepted; and so R. Solomon Jarchi paraphrases the words, " Thou art beautiful, O my love, seeing that thou art acceptable to me;" and so he says it is explained in an ancient book of theirs, called Siphre:[n] and if we take the words in this sense, they set forth the beauty and glory of the church, as she stands before God, " accepted in Christ, the beloved." God is well pleased with Christ, and with the church in him; he is well pleased for his righteousness sake, and with her as she appears in that; for so considered, she is a complete beauty, fair, and without spot, lovely to look upon, delightful to Christ, and acceptable to God.

The Targum paraphrases the words thus, " How beautiful art thou, O my love, in the time it is thy will to do my pleasure. Our righteousnesses are indeed as filthy rags, and we ourselves as an unclean thing;" yet when we are made " willing in the day of God's power," to act according to his will, and that in faith, from a principle of love, and with an eye to his glory, it is accepted by him, the same way as our persons are.

But I see no reason why we should not take the word as the proper name of a place; seeing it is certain that there was such a city as Tirzah, in the land of Judea, which was a very pleasant and delightful place, as its name manifestly shows; for which reason, no doubt, it was made choice of by one of the ancient kings of Canaan, to be the place of his residence; see Josh. xii. 24; as it was

---

[n] It is explained the same way in Shirhashirim Rabba in loc.

afterwards by Jeroboam and his successors, until Zimri's time: who, when the city was taken, burnt the king's house with fire. Now either for its pleasant buildings, or beautiful situation, or some such thing, the church is here compared unto it, being arrayed with Christ's righteousness, and adorned with the graces of his Spirit. But,

II. Lest this should not be sufficient to commend her beauty, he says also, that she is as "comely as Jerusalem;" which was not only the chief city in Judea's land, but, as Pliny* says, was the most famous of all the cities in the east; nay, more, it was "the joy of the whole earth:" the church goes under this name, both in the Old and New Testament; for which, see the following texts, Isa. xl. 2, and lii. 1, Gal. iv. 25, 26, Heb. xii. 22, Rev. xxi. 2. Now she may be said to be "comely as Jerusalem," for the following reasons. 1. Jerusalem was a well-built city, its houses were closely joined together, and its streets uniform; hence the Psalmist says, Psalm cxxii. 3, "Jerusalem is builded as a city that is compact together:" so the church of Christ, and the members of it, as they are built upon the same foundation, and are closely joined to the same Head, Christ; so they are strictly united one to another, and are like "a building fitly framed together," or like a human body that is "fitly joined together, and compacted by that which every joint supplieth;" all the members being set in their proper places, in a just symmetry with, and subserviency to each other; see Eph. ii. 20, 21, and iv. 16. 2. Jerusalem was not only the metropolis of Judea, but was the chief city in all the world, as has been observed: and this may set forth the super-excellency, glory, and comeliness of the church, above all the world besides; which will more manifestly appear, when the mountain of the Lord's house shall be established in the top of the mountains, and be exalted above the hills, and God's Jerusalem be a praise in the earth;" see Isa. ii. 2, and lxii. 7. 3. It was a very beautiful city;ᵖ it had many beautiful structures in it, particularly the temple, which was the finest building that ever was seen in the world; it was also very beautiful for situation, as well as for buildings, and therefore was called the perfection of beauty; as the church also is, being beautified with the garments of Christ's salvation. 4. It was a very rich and opulent city; especially in Solomon's time, who "made silver to be in Jerusalem as stones:" in the church, not only the unsearchable riches of Christ, are preached, but also the immense riches of divine grace and mercy are expended upon the members of it; so that every inhabitant of this Jerusalem is a king and a prince. How rich must that city be, all whose inhabitants are kings and princes? such are the saints, the members of Christ's church, who are made by Christ kings and priests to his Father. 5. It was not only the place of the residence of the kings of David's line, where they had their palaces, and kept their courts; but also, what made it more glorious and comely than all the rest, it was "the city of the great king;" even of him who is the King of kings, who was set up by his Father, as king over his holy hill of Zion: so the church is Christ's palace, where he keeps his court, grants his presence, shows himself, and entertains his friends as courtiers; it is his rest, his habitation, where he dwells and delights to be, having chosen it for that purpose. 6. What made Jerusalem also exceeding comely, was, that the worship of God was kept up there: here was the temple; here sacrifices were offered up; hither the tribes went up to worship; and therefore is called the city of our solemnities: Christ's church is the place of worship where saints assemble together, where God is reverenced and adored by them; where the sacrifice of prayer and praise are offered up; where the word of God is preached, and his ordinances administered, to the comfort of his saints, and to the glory of his name. 7. Jerusalem, as it was beautiful in its inward buildings, so it was likewise in its outward fortifications, which were both natural and artificial; it had not only many towers and bulwarks, which were its artificial fortifications, but had also mountains around it, which were natural ones; and for this reason the church and people of God are compared to it, in Psalm cxxv. 2, "As the mountains are round about Jerusalem, so the Lord is round about his people, from henceforth, even for ever:" God himself is a wall of fire around his church; Christ is a strong tower in the midst of it, and salvation has God appointed for walls and bulwarks about it. 8. Jerusalem was a free city, as is Jerusalem, which is the mother of us all; it had many privileges and immunities, as has also the church of Christ, and all the members of it; all who are "fellow-citizens of the saints, and of the household of God," are all Christ's freemen, and enjoy the liberty of the gospel, and can never lose their freedoms, nor be deprived of them; they shall never be arrested by divine justice, nor come into condemnation, nor be reduced to a state of bondage.

III. He also says of her, that she was "terrible as an army with banners." This comparison manifestly shows, that it was not any single person that is intended in this song; not Pharaoh's daughter, nor any single inhabitant of Jerusalem; but a considerable company of persons, a collective body, such as the church of Christ is; for a single person cannot well be compared to an army with banners. Now this shows that the church of Christ on earth is militant; she is in a warfare state, and has many enemies to fight with, as sin, Satan, and the world; she has enemies within and enemies without; "a great fight of afflictions" to endure, and "the good fight of faith to fight," after which she is to receive eternal life: the use of banners, has been taken notice of, on chap.

* Lib. v. c. 14. ᵖ It is highly commended for its beauty, in T. Bab. Kiddushin. fol. 49, 2.

ii. 4. Moreover, this comparison may lead us to observe, that the church was as an army in good order, well-disciplined, having proper officers and good armour: Christ is the chief general; the ministers of the gospel are the under-officers; the banner is love; and the armour they are accoutred with, what you read of in Eph. vi.; nay, not only so, but that she was in a posture of defence, ready to fight, whenever the enemy should attack her: she appeared like an army, having its general at the head of it, its colours flying, drums beating, and sword in hand; and being so, she was terrible to her enemies, sin, Satan, and the world.

Now the terribleness of the church of Christ, here spoken of, may be understood, either, 1. Of that awe which godly persons have over the wicked; the good examples and pious conversations of the saints often distress the conscience, and strike an awe upon the minds of the ungodly; they are deterred sometimes by them from evil practices, especially when in the presence of them, and are awed by them from doing them any hurt; thus Herod feared John the Baptist, because he was a holy man, Mark vi. 20. Or, 2. Of the invincibleness of the saints, when united together; when they are at peace one with another, and have no discord and mutiny among themselves, but keep close to each other, and endeavour " to keep the unity of the Spirit in the bond of peace," they are like an army in battle-array, that cannot easily be broken in upon by the enemy. Or, 3. Of her constancy and undauntedness in seeking of him; and it is as if he should say, When I parted from thee, what difficulties didst thou meet with? How wast thou abused by the watchmen and keepers of the walls? who smote and wounded thee, and took away thy veil from thee; and yet thou wast not discouraged, but still went on in search of me, marching like an army with banners, bearing down all before thee, surmounting all difficulties until thou hadst obtained what thou soughtest for. Or, 4. Perhaps Christ may say so of her, as regarding himself: who had felt the power of her arms, and was conquered by her; like another Jacob, she " had power with God, and prevailed." Her love to Christ was so great, her faith so strong, she so diligent in her search, and so importunate in her desires, that he could not withstand her; and therefore, as one that had found her to be " terrible as an army with banners," says, in the following words,

Verse 5. Former part. *Turn away thine eyes from me, for they have overcome me.*

IN this and the two following verses, Christ gives a more particular account of the church's beauty, and begins with her eyes in these words; for though they are delivered in such a manner as they be, yet they serve to commend that particular part of her, here mentioned; which is never taken notice of by Christ in this song but with commendation; see chap. i. 15, and iv. 1, 9, and vii. 4. And in these words may be observed,

I. Something that is enjoined the church by Christ; which is, to " turn away her eyes from him."

II. The reason of it; " for they have overcome me."

I. Here is an injunction laid upon the church by Christ, to turn away her eyes from him; in which may be inquired, 1st. What is meant by her eyes. 2ndly. What by turning them away from him.

1st. By her eyes may be meant, as has been observed on chap. i. 15, the ministers of the gospel, who are that to Christ's body, the church, as eyes are to a human body; they are placed in a more eminent part of it; their business is to watch, inspect, and overlook the several members of the body, and therefore are called *watchmen* and *overseers*; they pry, search, and penetrate into gospel truths, and discover them to others; they guide and direct those who are under their watch and care, " teaching them to observe all things" which Christ has commanded them. The Targum, by eyes, understands the Rabbins, and wise men of the great congregation: and R. Aben Ezra, by the turning of them away, the removal or ceasing of prophecy in the second temple. Or else, by eyes may be meant, the enlightened eyes of the church's understanding; the eyes of her faith, love, and knowledge; that eye of faith which looked upon Christ in the dark, and was the evidence of an unseen Jesus to her; so that she could say, " I am my beloved's, and my beloved is mine:" this eye of faith, I say, had pierced the heart of Christ, won it, and gotten an entire conquest over it; which obliged him to say these words, " Turn away thine eyes from me," &c. That love which she had shown unto him, though absent from her, discovered in a variety of expressions to the daughters of Jerusalem, appeared exceeding fair and beautiful to him; her strong and constant affections to him, being attended with solid judgment, and an exact knowledge of his person and grace, took much with his heart, struck the passions of his soul, which showed and gave themselves vent in such expressions as these. And these eyes of faith and love, I take to be principally intended here. But,

2ndly. It may be inquired what is also meant by turning away these eyes from him. Some read the words thus, " Turn about thine eyes over against me;" so Ainsworth: and this is favoured by the Targum or Chaldee paraphrase upon the text; and so indeed the word signifies, to *turn to*, as well as to *turn from*. And this, 1. Suits well with the mind and will of Christ: which is, that his church and all believers should be continually looking to him for life and salvation, righteousness and strength, peace and pardon, joy and comfort; and, in short, for every needful supply of grace, until they are brought

R

safe to glory: his language is, "Look unto me, and be ye saved, all the ends of the earth; for I am God, and there is none else," Isa. xlv. 22. 2. It suits with the experience of God's children; who often have their eyes taken off from Christ, and set either upon their own righteousness, their duties, and their frames; or else upon creature-enjoyments, the transitory and perishing things of this world; and therefore have need to be called off from them, to look to him: and perhaps this was the case of the church here; she had had her eyes intently fixed on Christ for some time, and now on a sudden they are diverted from him, and therefore he gives her this exhortation, to turn them again to him. Which shows, 3. That he was well pleased and exceedingly delighted with them: faith is a precious grace; it is so in its own nature, and in the actings of it upon the Person of Christ; it is a precious grace to believers, being very useful to them in dealing with Christ, and receiving from him; and it is also precious to Christ, seeing it brings all the glory back to him: how much Christ is delighted with both these eyes of faith and love, may be seen in chap. iv. 9, 10. 4. This version, or reading of the words, may lead us to observe, that Christ would have us not to take side-looks only of him, but full views; "turn about thine eyes over against me," right over against me; look me full in the face: it is true, Christ's countenance is as the sun, when it shineth in its full strength; which we, in this imperfect state, cannot so fully and directly look at; yet there is a vast difference between faith's looking at Christ at one time and at another: sometimes we have only a glance, a side-look at Christ; at other times, faith, with open face, beholds, "as in a glass, the glory of the Lord;" our eyes, as Solomon directs, Prov. iv. 25, "look right on, and our eye-lids look straight before us;" and this is what Christ would have his church do here. 5. It gives us an intimation, that we should look all around Christ, and take as it were a survey of his Person, and the glories and excellencies of it; turn about thine eyes; look all around me, view me from head to foot, on all sides: it is true, thou hast been viewing me, as if he should say, and giving an excellent description of me; but turn thine eyes about me again and again, thou wilt find more glories still, fresher beauties, and be able to make new discoveries of my Person and grace. 6. This being the first time of their meeting together, after she had so shamefully and basely treated him; she might be filled with so much shame and confusion at the thoughts of it, that she could not lift up her eyes, and look him in the face; which agrees with the experience of the Psalmist, when he said, Psal. xl. 12, "Mine iniquities have taken hold upon me, so that I am not able to look up." And this now being her condition, Christ speaks these words to her, for her encouragement, turn thine eyes unto me; look up with a holy and humble confidence to me, for thine iniquity is done away.

But then, if we consider the words as our translators have rendered them, we are not to understand them, either, 1. As a reprehension of her curiosity, in prying and searching into the glory and greatness of his Majesty, which is the sense that some[q] give of the words; for though Christ, as God Almighty, cannot be found out to perfection; nor can we comprehend his Person and grace as God-man in this imperfect life; nor see him as he is, which is reserved to another and more perfect one; yet this does not forbid our search and inquiries, in order to obtain a more perfect knowledge of him; though a check should be given, and a restraint laid upon all vain curiosity: but this does not appear to be the case of the church here; Christ was not displeased with her, nor had he absented himself from her on such an account as this, but because of her slothfulness and negligence in duty; besides, it does not appear likely that Christ, when he is extolling and commending his church in such a manner, should give so severe a rebuke unto her. 2. Nor were these eyes of hers carnal and sinful, haughty and lifted up, or wanton and unchaste, and therefore disagreeable to him; no, her eyes are said to be doves eyes within her locks, modest, humble, and chaste; which are well-pleasing to him, and are always commended by him. Nor, 3. Are we to understand the words as if Christ did not approve of her looking to him by faith; for there is nothing more grateful to him; faith always meets with a kind reception from him, and is always commended by him: souls need not fear its being accounted a piece of boldness or presumption in them to believe in Christ, for he gives all encouragement to it; "Ye believe in God," says he, "believe also in me," John xiv. 1. But, 4. It is expressive of the exceeding great passion of love he was in with her; he could stand it out no longer, but must acknowledge he was overcome by her, and therefore bids her turn away her eyes from him; not through any dislike, but as having his heart overpowered with love by them: the expression is designed to signify the exceeding greatness of Christ's love to the church, as well as her surpassing beauty. Unless, 5. We would rather understand it as his will, that she should cease petitioning to him, seeing he had granted her request; thus, lifting up the eyes to God, signifies prayer to him; see 2 Chron. xx. 12, Psal. cxxiii. 1; and if we take it in this sense here, it is as if he should say, thou hast been lifting up thine eyes to me, and petitioning me, that thou mightest have some discoveries of my grace, enjoyment of my presence, and communion with my Person; and now thou mayest turn away thine eyes from me, or cease petitioning; for thou hast the thing thou

---

[q] Foliot and Alcuin in loc. Thom. and Beda in Sanct. in loc.

hast been praying and looking up to me for.

II. The reason of Christ's saying so to his church, or bidding her "turn away her eyes from him," is because they had overcome him. These words are very differently rendered. 1. Some read them thus, "for they have lifted me up," so Ainsworth; or, "that they might lift me up,'" so Junius; that is, make me cheerful, comfort, and encourage me: there is a near union between Christ and his church, from whence arises a very great sympathy; he has a fellow-feeling with his people in all their afflictions, both inward and outward, temporal and spiritual; when they are afflicted, he is afflicted; when they are cast down, he is as it were cast down with them; and when they are cheerful, he is so too; he "weeps with them that weep, and rejoices with them that rejoice:" the church being in a comfortable frame, and in the exercise of faith and love upon him, he is as it were cheered by it, and rejoiced at it; but this must be understood only as expressive of that near sympathy there is between them, and not as implying weakness or alteration in him, who is subject to no change. 2. Others read the words thus, "for they have strengthened me;"* and so our translators have rendered the word, in Psalm cxxxviii. 3, and then the sense is, they have strengthened my desire towards thee, and confirmed me in it, as R. David Kimchi* observes; and it is as if he should say, It is true, as I am thine, and thou art mine, I always had a desire towards thee, and to thy company; and it is not long since I signified it to thee; but since thine eyes have been so intently fixed on me, thy faith and love have been so exercised upon me, methinks my desire towards thee is strengthened and increased; but this must be understood as expressive of that great reward which Christ had to her, and be taken with the same caution as before. 3. Others," as R. Sol. Jarchi, read the words thus, "for they have made me proud;" the word is rendered, "to behave one's self proudly," in Isa. iii. 5, by our translators: Christ, as I may so say, is proud of his people, whom the Father has given him, and he has purchased with his own blood; he takes a kind of pride as well as pleasure in them; he is proud of that beauty which he himself has put upon them, and of those graces which he has wrought in them, and especially that of faith, when it is in exercise. What notice did he take of the centurion's faith? and in a kind of boasting manner, as being proud of it, say to his followers, "I have not found so great faith, no, not Israel:" here is an instance of faith for you, such an one as is not to be matched in Israel. 4. Others" read them thus, "they have made me fierce;" not with anger and indignation, but with love; for there is a power,

a force, a fierceness in love, as well as in wrath; "love is strong as death;" it is so not only in Christ's people towards him, but more especially in him towards them; his affections are very strong towards them, and are sometimes let out with a greater force upon them than at other times, as they seem to be here. 5. R. Aben Ezra* renders them thus, "they are stronger than me," or, "they have taken away my strength;" so that I am as one that is dead, and have no life and spirit in me; these sparkling eyes of thine have transported me into a kind of extasy, that I am scarce myself: and to this purpose the Septuagint render it, "they have made me to fly away;"y that is, out of myself; which agrees with our version, "they have overcome me," I am not master of myself; the sense is the same with chap. iv. 9. Now this shows us, (1.) The power of faith; which not only "subdues kingdoms, stops the mouths of lions, and puts to flight the armies of the aliens," but conquers God himself. (2.) This is owing very much to the importunity of it, which is increased by seeming denials: faith will not let Christ alone, nor let him go, nor will it cease petitioning, till it has got the blessing; and the repulses it meets with, do but increase its importunity; see Gen. xxxii. 26, Exod. xxxii. 9, 10, Matt. xv. 24—28. (3.) Christ's being overcome by the church, does not imply any weakness in him; but is a discovery of his astonishing, condescending love and grace, that he should be willing to be held, as it were a captive, by a poor sinful creature; that He should be willing to be overcome by us, who has conquered all our enemies, sin, Satan, hell, and death for us, is surprising and amazing; and perhaps on this account, as well as upon some others, we may be said to be "more than conquerors," because we are the conquerors of him who has conquered all.

Verse 5. *Latter part—Thy hair is as a flock of goats that appear from Gilead.*

Verse 6. *Thy teeth are as a flock of sheep, which go up from the washing, whereof every one beareth twins, and there is not one barren among them.*

Verse 7. *As a piece of pomegranate are thy temples within thy locks.*

These commendations of the church's beauty are delivered in the same words in chap. iv. 1—3, but the repetition of them here is not vain and idle, but may be for the following reasons: 1. To show the reality and certainty of her beauty; that it was no imaginary beauty, but a real one: so things are sometimes repeated, for the confirmation of them. 2. To put her in mind of it, that she

---

ᵗ Ut illi efferant me, Junius; illi enim me extulerunt, Mercerus. * הרהיבני corroborant me, Marck'us. *ᵗ* In lib. Shorash. rad. *ᵘ* Me superbiorem faciunt, Tig. version, Piscator. &c.

ᵛ Ipsi reddiderunt efferum me, Montanus; ii ferocire fecerunt me, Cocceius. *ˣ* Fortiores fuerunt me, Pagninus, Mercerus. *ʸ* Ἀνεπτερωσαν με, Sept. ipsi me avelare fecerunt, Vulg. Lat. version.

might value it, and herself upon it, as coming from Christ; who had made her perfectly comely, through the comeliness which he had put upon her. 3. To assure her that her beauty was still the same, and that he had the same opinion of it as ever he had, notwithstanding all her failings and infirmities; and therefore expresses it in the very same words he had used before her backslidings from him. 4. To manifest the unchangeableness of his love towards her; that he is "Jesus, the same to-day, yesterday, and for ever:"¹ that is "the Lord that changes not, and therefore the sons of Jacob are not consumed." But having explained these words in chap. iv., I shall not consider them any farther here; but only just observe some variations and differences between them, though they are not indeed very material. In ver. 5, the word mount is omitted, which may be supplied from chap. iv. 1. In ver. 6, the word sheep is expressed, which is understood in chap. iv. 2, as are the words even shorn omitted here, though expressed there. In ver. 7 is wholly omitted that part of the description which concerns the beauty of the church's lips and speech; though it is added at the end of the sixth verse by the Septuagint; but is not in the Hebrew copies; neither is it taken notice of by the Targum on the place: nay, the Masora on chap. iv. 3, remarks some words as only used in that place, and therefore this was not repeated here in the copies then in use.

Verse 8. *There are threescore queens and fourscore concubines; and virgins without number.*

Verse 9. *My dove, my undefiled, is but one; she is the only one of her mother; she is the choice one of her that bare her: the daughters saw her, and blessed her; yea, the queens and the concubines, and they praised her.*

Christ having commended the church's beauty, both in general and in particular instances, as she might be considered by herself, without respect to others, in the preceding verses; now commends her, as she might stand related to, or be compared with others. And,

I. The persons with whom she stands compared, and to whom she appears preferable, are "queens, concubines, and virgins without number."

II. The things in which she appears to be preferable to them, are, First, That she "is but one." Secondly, "The only one of her mother." Thirdly, "The choice one of her that bare her." And then,

III. Her beauty is commended by the notice the "daughters, queens, and concubines" took of it; who, as soon as ever "they saw her, blessed and praised her."

I. The persons with whom she stands compared, and appears preferable to, are, "the threescore queens, and fourscore concubines, and virgins without number," mentioned in ver. 8, which words may be considered, either as an assertion that there are so many, a certain number being put for an uncertain one; or else, as a supposition, though there may be so many, yet "my undefiled is but one," &c. Queens are those who were the principal wives of kings, who brought portions with them; whose children inherited, and they themselves with their royal husbands, had the management of affairs. Concubines are secondary wives, or half wives, as the word² may be rendered; they were such who brought no portions with them;ᵃ and though they were admitted to the fellowship of the bed, yet their children did not inherit, but had only some gifts given to them; nor had they themselves any share in the government of the house, but rather acted like servants under the other; such were Hagar, Zilpah, Bilhah, &c. "The virgins without number," are unmarried persons; these were the maids of honour, who waited and attended upon the queens. Now there are in the words an allusion either to the custom and practice of kings and great persons, who had more wives than one, had many concubines, and a large number of virgins to attend upon them; and this was not only the practice of Heathen, but also of Jewish princes, as David and Solomon; which latter, more especially, had a large number; and it is thought that a regard is had more particularly to his queens and concubines in this text; for which reason some have thought that this book was written before he gave so great a loose to his lusts, as we find he did; for we are told, 1 Kings xi. 3, that he had "seven hundred wives, princesses, and three hundred concubines." Or else, the allusion is to a nuptial solemnity, and the ceremony of introducing the bride into the bridegroom's house, who used to be attended with a large number of persons of distinction: so four times sixty virgins are said to attend the nuptials of Menelaus and Helena:ᵇ see Psal. xlv., between which and this song there is a very great resemblance; and perhaps that was the plan of this: there the queen is represented as standing in "gold of Ophir," which answers to Christ's church and bride here, and means the same there: also "king's daughters," which answer to the queens here, are said to be among her "honourable women" who were attendants on her; and the "virgins, her companions," are said to "follow her," when she was introduced into the king's presence.

Now by these "threescore queens, fourscore concubines, and virgins without number," may be meant, either,

1st. The several kingdoms and nations of the

ᵃ פילגשים quidam vocem compositam volunt ex פלג divisit, and אשה uxor, quasi uxor divisa vel dimidia, Buxtorf. secundariæ uxores, Michaelis.
ᵃ Vid. Jarchium in Gen. xxv. 6. Schindler. Lex. Pentaglot. fol. 1508. David de Pomis, Lex. Heb. fol. 143. 1. and Kimchi lib. Shorash. in voce פילגש.
ᵇ Theocrit. Idyll. 18. v. 24.

world: and by queens may be meant those kingdoms and countries, which are more large, rich, and flourishing; by concubines, those which are inferior to them, either in largeness, riches, or numbers: and by virgins, the vast multitude of inhabitants which fill them: and then the sense is this: though there are many large, rich, and populous nations in the world; yet my church is preferable to them all: these all put together, cannot equal her; for "as the lily is among thorns," and is preferable to them: "so my love is among the daughters," the nations of the world, and is preferable to them all. Or,

2ndly. By them may be meant false churches, who pretend to be the true spouse of Christ, but are not so: by queens may be meant, those who boast themselves of their riches and numbers, and would be esteemed on that account the true bride of Christ; as the church of Rome, who "saith in her heart, I sit a queen, and am no widow;" and yet is an harlot, nay, "the mother of harlots." By concubines such who are inferior in wealth and numbers, but equally corrupt in principles, and which make the same pretensions the others do; such are the Arian, Socinian, &c., churches: and by "virgins without number," the large multitude of poor, weak, and ignorant people, who are seduced and carried aside by them. But now Christ's church, though it does not make so great a figure in the world; nor does it appear in so much external pomp and splendor; nor has it the riches and numbers that these may have; yet in Christ's esteem is preferable to them all. Though,

3rdly. Others[c] think, that the several sorts of preachers in the church are here intended: and that by queens, are meant ministers of the first rank; who are faithful to Christ and his Gospel, and are instrumental in bringing forth many souls unto him: and by concubines, such who "corrupt the word of God, and handle it deceitfully:" who are "false apostles, deceitful workers, transforming themselves into the apostles of Christ:" who seek not Christ but themselves: not his honour, but their own applause: and by virgins, such who, though regenerated, yet at present are not fit for the ministry, but are training up for it in the several churches or schools of learning: and may be such, whom the apostle calls novices: *not a novice, νεοφυτον, a young tender plant*; one that is newly planted in Christianity, and has arrived to some knowledge of the Gospel, but as yet not fit for the office of a bishop. But,

4thly. The words seem rather to be understood of the several degrees of believers.[d] By queens, may be meant believers of the highest form; such whom Christ has honoured with greater gifts and larger measures of grace; in whose hearts and lives grace reigns more gloriously than in others; and who have a greater nearness to Christ, and more communion with him than others have: and by concubines, believers of an inferior sort, who are of a more servile and legal spirit, have more of "a spirit of bondage than the spirit of adoption;" but yet these have fellowship and communion with Christ at times; and by virgins, young converts, new-born babes, that have not so much experience as either of the former: so that this distribution of believers unto "queens, concubines, and virgins," seems to suit with the division of them into "fathers, young men, and children," which is made, 1 John ii. 13, 14; and what seems to strengthen this sense of the words, is their blessing and praising the bride in the following verse. In an ancient tract of the Jews, called Midrash Hanneelam,[e] the queens, in the next verse, are said to be the fathers or patriarchs; the concubines, the proselytes of righteousness; and the daughters, the daughters of Jerusalem. Now Christ's church, considered as a collective body, is preferable to single believers, even to the greatest of them: and it is also well observed by one,[f] that there are more concubines than queens, and more virgins than either of them; for there are more weak believers and babes in Christ, than there are strong ones; those of the highest rank and form are very rare; there are but few to be found in comparison of the other; but Christ's bride comprehends them all, and is preferable to them: which is the next thing to be considered.

II. Christ, in ver. 9, commends his church above all those queens, concubines, and virgins; he gives her two excellent titles, which show her to be superior to others; the first of which, "my dove," has been explained in chap. ii. 14; and the other, "my undefiled," in chap. v. 2, and therefore need no farther explanation here. The things in which she appears to be preferable to all these fore-mentioned persons, are,

First. That she is *but one*, and they are many; which may be expressive, 1. Of the church's fewness in number; who, if compared with the nations of the world, which is the first sense given of the former words, she is but like one to sixty or eighty, nay to an innumerable multitude; there are but few that are chosen, though many are externally called: Christ's church is a remnant, according to the election of grace; it is but one of a city, and two of a family that Christ brings to Zion; they are but a little flock, to whom the heavenly kingdom is bequeathed. 2. Of the church's unity in herself. (1.) She is but one body as there are various members in a human body; and yet but one body; so likewise is the church, though consisting of many believers; as there are many sheep and lambs in a flock, and yet but one flock, under the care of one shepherd; many beds in a garden, and a variety of spices, flowers, herbs, and plants in these beds, and yet but one garden; even so, though there are many particular congregated churches, and in those churches many be-

---

[e] Alcuin in loc. Thom. and Bede in Sanct. in loc.
[d] So Durham in loc. and Nyssen. Homil. 15.
[e] Theodoret. in loc. Psellus and Tres Patres in ib.
* in Zohar in Gen. fol. 77. 1.
[f] Durham in loc.

lievers, yet there is but one " general assembly and church of the first-born, which are written in heaven." (2.) She has but one Spirit, which actuates and influences this body, the same Spirit that dwells in the head, Christ dwells in his body the church; and the same that dwells in the body dwells in every member of it; for though there are diversities of gifts, and various graces, yet there is but one Spirit who distributes them to the several members, for their use and profit. (3.) She has but one Head and Husband, Lord and Saviour: she has but one Head, to whom she holds, and from whom she receives life and nourishment, and so increases with the increase of God; but one Husband, whom she owns and acknowledges as such, and to whom she is " espoused as a chaste virgin;" but one Lord, under whose government she is, and to whom alone she yields obedience: and but one Mediator, that she regards, and makes use of, and that is, " the man Christ Jesus." (4.) Though the church consists of many members; yet being but one body united to one Head, and actuated by one and the same Spirit, they enjoy the same privileges; they are built upon one and the same foundation, Christ; they are washed in the same blood; they wear the same righteousness, and receive from the same fulness, " grace for grace." (5.) They make a profession of one and the same faith; for as there is but one Lord, so there is but one faith; the doctrine of grace is invariable, it is like the author of it, "the same yesterday, to-day, and for ever;" there never was another gospel, nor never will be; the faith which the church now professes, is what was "once delivered to the saints," to be kept by them; and which they, standing fast in one spirit, should strive for the purity of; which cannot be, unless they are " perfectly joined together in the same mind, and in the same judgment." (6.) They are one in worship: the object of worship is one and the same: and so is the Spirit who assists them in it, as well as the form of it; for as there is but one Lord, and one faith, so there is but one baptism: whose subjects and mode of administration should continue the same, without any variation, until the end of time; and but one Lord's supper: and so it may be said of every other ordinance, and of every part of religious worship; for saints, as they worship one and the same God, under the influences of one and the same Spirit, and in the same way; so likewise should they, with one consent, which they cannot be said to do, when an ordinance is administered by some one way, and by some another. (7.) They are one in affections, or at least ought to be; their chief business should be to "keep the unity of the Spirit in the bond of peace," and that from the aforesaid consideration: for this is one end of their calling, the glory of their profession, and a distinguishing character of their being the disciples and church of Christ. 8. This may be also expressive of her being the only spouse and bride of Christ: " my dove, my undefiled, is but one;" that is, though other princes may have their sixty queens and eighty concubines, and an innumerable company of virgins to wait upon them, yet I have but one, and am well satisfied with her; I desire none but her; my one is preferable to their many; as she says, " I am my beloved's:" that is, I only am his, he has none beside me, and " his desire is towards me," and to none else.

Secondly. He says, that " she is the only one of her mother." By *her mother* is meant " Jerusalem, which is above, which is the mother of us all;" and by her being " the only one of her mother," we are to understand that she had no other but her: for though we read, in chap. i. 6, of " her mother's children," yet we are to understand them of carnal professors; who had the name, but not the nature of children; were not true sons of the church, were bastards, and not sons. Or else the meaning is, that she was to him as a mother's only child; no mother could more tenderly love an only child, than he did her: so that it may be expressive of that strong affection and tender passion which he bore to her.

Thirdly. He says, that " she is the choice one of her that bare her," which is a periphrasis of her mother; and her being the " choice one of her," shows how much she was valued and esteemed by her; of all her mother's children, she was loved the best. Moreover, the word may be translated, " the pure or clean one:"[g] and so she is as clothed with that " fine linen, clean and white, which is the righteousness of the saints," as washed in Christ's blood, which " cleanseth from all sin;" as sanctified by the Spirit, purified by faith, and sprinkled with clean water, the grace of the everlasting covenant; also, as she was free from the pollution of error and false worship; was of an unspotted conversation; and was now, or at least had been lately, in the furnace of affliction, where Christ had purified her, and made her white and clean.

III. Christ commends her beauty, by observing what notice the daughters, queens, and concubines took of it, and how much they praised and commended her for it: " The daughters saw her, and blessed her, the queens and the concubines, and they praised her:" it may seem strange that concubines should praise a queen; but it was not unusual in the eastern countries; with the Persians, as the queen admitted of many concubines, by the order of her lord the king; so the queen was had in great veneration, and even adored by the concubines.[k] Which may be understood, 1. Of the great esteem which the church had or should have in the world, and that

---

[g] ברה היא munda ipsa genitrici suæ, Montanus; pura est genitrici suæ, Cocceius, Mercerus; puram illam apud genetricem suam, Junius. [h] Dinon in Persicis apud Athenæi Deipnosophist. l. 13, c. 1. p. 456.

from the great men of it; which will appear more visibly in the latter day, when those prophecies shall be fulfilled, of which we read in Isa. xlix. 23, and lx. 3, 10, 11, when kings shall be her nursing fathers, and queens her nursing mothers; and God's Jerusalem, the church, shall be the praise of the whole earth. Or, 2. Of the great value and esteem which professors, and especially young converts, have of the church; in whose eyes she is "the fairest among women:" who, as soon as ever they saw her, were ravished with her beauty, loved her, and wished themselves as happy as she: for, 3. They blessed her; that is, accounted her happy; as well they might, seeing she was "blessed with all spiritual blessings in Christ;" and indeed whether we consider the saints, either as to their entertainment in God's house, or their employment there, it may be said of them what the queen of Sheba said of Solomon's servants, 1 Kings x. 8, "Happy are thy men, happy are these thy servants which stand continually before thee, and hear thy wisdom." And, 4. They wished all happiness to her, and prayed for it, which also may be the sense of the words, "they blessed her;" see Psalm cxxix. 8; they prayed for the peace of Jerusalem, which was their duty; and in doing which, they show their affection to the church: nay, 5. They not only thought well of her, and wished well to her; but they also praised her, that is, they spoke well of her, and highly commended her beauty: so that Christ was not alone in his opinion of her; for others thought her to be an accomplished beauty, as well as he: and this, as it serves to commend her beauty, so its being taken notice of by Christ, shows how much he was pleased with it, for as those that touch his people, "touch the apple of his eye:" and whatsoever is spoken against them, he takes as spoken against himself; so, whenever they are praised and spoken well of, he is well pleased with it.

Verse 10. *Who is she that looketh forth as the morning, fair as the moon, clear as the sun, and terrible as an army with banners?*

THESE are either the words of Christ, commending and wondering at the beauty of his church, and confirming the daughters' praises of her; which shows that they were neither wrong, nor were they alone in their opinion of her; for she was an astonishing beauty in the eyes of him, who seeth not as man seeth, neither judges after the outward appearance: or else, they are the words of the daughters of Jerusalem continued; and this I rather incline to, for the following reasons: 1. The connection between this and the preceding verse is very easy; especially if we supply the word *saying*, as it is sometimes done, as in Jer. xxxi. 3, and so read the words thus: "the daughters saw her, and blessed her; the queens and the concubines, and they praised her," saying, "Who is she that looketh forth as the morning?" &c. 2. This gives a ready answer to such a question that she might be asked, What was it the daughters, queens, and concubines said of her, when they gave her commendations, declared her the happy person, and sung her praises? why, it was this, "Who is she that looketh forth as the morning?" &c. 3. It confirms what Christ had said of her, in ver. 4, that she was "terrible as an army with banners;" that they had just the same opinion of her as he had, and therefore used the same words: but if they were supposed to be the words of Christ, it would make a manifest tautology, which is scarce to be allowed of in the same commendation. 4. It best agrees with other parts of this song, which appear to be the words of the daughters of Jerusalem, as chap. iii. 6, and viii. 5. 5. The Targum, or Chaldee paraphrase upon this text, takes them to be the words of the people or nations of the world, which, in this paraphrase, are sometimes understood by the daughters of Jerusalem. And though the words are interrogatory, yet they are not the effect of ignorance, but of wonder and surprise. These daughters were not ignorant of the church; they knew who she was, but were surprised at her glory and beauty: the way of speaking is much like that in Isa. lxiii. 1, "Who is he that cometh from Edom," &c. Having now considered whose words they are, I shall in the next place consider the words themselves, and the meaning of them: and they may be expressive,

First. Of the state and condition of the church in the several ages of the world; especially in those three remarkable ones, that before the law, that under the law, and this under the gospel. There is a manifest gradation in the text; and this appears in the church, in those several periods: in which there was an increase of her faith, light, knowledge, and glory. And,

1st. The state of the church before the law was given, from Adam to Moses, may be intended in the first expression, "Who is she that looketh forth as the morning?" And here give me leave to observe, 1. That Adam's sin brought not only a night of darkness upon his own soul, but also upon all the world besides: man, who in his first creation was endued with light and knowledge, is now become a poor, dark creature, by the fall; nay, in darkness itself: he is born and brought up in darkness, and walks on in it, not knowing whither he goes, until he is called by divine grace; when he appears to be a child of the day, and not of night, nor of darkness. 2. The first display of grace to fallen man, which was in the garden, after the night of darkness had invaded his soul, was like the dawn of the morning; when the seed of the woman, the glorious Messiah, was made known to Adam: as who should break the head of the serpent, and so redeem him, and those of his fallen race, whom God had set apart for himself: this struck the light of joy and comfort into his soul; those dark and dreadful apprehensions he had of things, in a great measure then vanished and disappeared; this breaking up of covenant grace unto him, was like the break of day, or like the first appearance of a glorious morning; and as for Satan, whose works are works of darkness, and cannot bear the light; like a beast of prey he leered off, and lurked into his den, when this morning light thus first broke out: this was the first appearance and revelation of grace to fallen man. 3. This light of grace, which now began to show itself, like the morning light, increased yet more and more: there were greater breakings forth of it afterwards; not only to Adam himself, who was taught by God the way of sacrificing, and therein to look by faith to the great sacrifice, Christ, who was to be offered up for the sin of man; but also to succeeding patriarchs, particularly to Noah, who found grace in the eyes of the Lord, became a preacher of righteousness; and that not of moral righteousness only, but also of evangelical, even the righteousness which is by faith: but more especially to Abraham, to whom it was promised, that the Messiah should be of his seed, and in that seed all nations be blessed; there was so great a discovery of grace made unto him, that the gospel is said to be preached unto him: and then to his grandson Jacob, there was a greater discovery made; for not only the Messiah was revealed unto him as God's salvation, which he says he waited for, and that he should be of Abraham's seed; but also more particularly, that he should spring from the tribe of Judah: the time of his coming is pointed out by him, as well as the glory and magnificence which should attend him, by a mighty confluence of people to him, in that famous prophecy of his, Gen. xlix. 10; thus the morning-light of the gospel went on apace, and increased exceedingly. But, 4. Though here was light broken forth, and that increasing, yet it was but small, in comparison of what appeared in after ages: the first display of grace seems rather to be by way of threatening to Satan, than by way of promise to fallen man; and though it was made known to our first parents, that the Messiah should be the seed of the woman; yet perhaps it was not so clearly revealed, till Isaiah's time, that he should be born of a virgin; which might be the reason that our mother Eve was so mistaken in the birth of her first son, as to imagine that she had got the Messiah; for so those words, in Gen. iv. 1, according to some, may be read, " I have gotton a man,[i] the Lord;" and Jonathan Ben Uzziel, in his Targum on the place, paraphrases it thus, " I have got the man, the angel of the Lord;" but she could never have thought so, had she known that he was to be born of a virgin. Moreover, the greatness of his person, his several offices, of Prophet, Priest, and King; the nature, efficacy, and end of his sufferings; his resurrection, ascension, and session at the Father's right hand; are more clearly spoken of by David, in his book of Psalms, and by Isaiah, in his prophecy, than were before; and no doubt but there was more light in the church, in David's, Solomon's, and more especially in Isaiah's time, than there had been in ages preceding. But yet, 5. Those discoveries of grace, which were made before the law was given, like the cheerful morning, brought joy and comfort along with them, particularly to Adam; who stood trembling, expecting every moment to have the awful sentence of wrath pronounced, and the severe stroke of justice given; when on a sudden grace appears, a Saviour is revealed; and the darkness of guilt and horror which filled his soul disappears, and in the room of it an universal joy and pleasure diffuses itself. The Jews[k] tell us of ten songs that are sung in the world; and the first, they say, was that which Adam sung when the Lord pardoned his iniquity; and indeed he had a great deal of reason for it. Nay, it was not only joy to Adam; but also to all the angels in heaven, who stood astonished and surprised to see all human nature lost at once, and that to all appearance irrecoverably; but whilst they were waiting to see what the issue of things would be, a glorious display of grace is made; the way of salvation, by the incarnate Son of God, is opened; which caused these bright seraphs to clap their wings, and these morning stars to sing together, " Glory to God in the highest:" for if they rejoice at the conversion of a single sinner, much more would they at the tidings of salvation to Adam, and to so many of his race; and so all after-discoveries of grace, to succeeding patriarchs, were more or less attended with joy and pleasure; it is particularly remarked of Abraham, John viii. 56, that he saw Christ's day, and was glad.

2ndly. The state of the church under the law, may be represented under the second expression, "fair as the moon;" which, though it receives its light from the sun,[l] yet splendour and brightness are ascribed to it, Job xxxi. 26, and by other writers,[m] it is represented as fair and beautiful; and the beautiful form of persons is expressed by it.[n] Such was the nature of divine worship under that dispensation, that, it may very aptly be set forth by this phrase; and I cannot but be of opinion, that the ceremonial law is intended by the moon, which is said to be under the church's feet, in Rev. vii. 1, for though it was abolished by the death of Christ, yet it was kept up and maintained by many of the Jews, even of those that believed; so that it was one of the greatest difficulties that

---

[i] Vid. Reuchlin. Cabbal. l. 1. p. 739. [k] Vid. Targum in Cant. i. 1. [l] Luna distat a sole, cujus lumine collustrari putatur, Cicero de Divinatione, l. 2. c. 43. [m] Tanto formosis formosior omnibus illa est, Ovid. Leander Heroni, v. 73. Pulchrior tanto tua forma lucet, Seneca Hippolytus, act. 2. chorus, v. 740. Aurea luna, Ovid. Metamorph. l. 10. fab. 9. [n] Vid. Barthii Animadv. ad Claudian. de Nupt. Honor. v. 2. 3. So particularly the beauty of Hero is described by the white-cheeked, rising morn, Musæus de Hero, &c. v. 57.

the Christian church had to grapple with; for though it was under the feet of Christ, yet it was a long time before it was under the feet of the church; and a wonder it was when it was accomplished; for persons are naturally fond of ceremonies; and many had rather part with a doctrine, or an ordinance of the Gospel, than with an idle ceremony, or an old custom, though never so ridiculous; and this was in a great measure the case of the Jews; "Thou seest, brother," says James to Paul, Acts xxi. 20, "how many thousands of Jews there are which believe, and they are all zealous of the law." Now the ceremonial law may be very aptly represented by the moon; for, 1. It consisted much in the observation of new moons; its solemn feasts were governed by them; see 2 Chron. viii. 12, 13, Isa. i. 13, 14, Amos viii. 5, Col. ii. 16. 2. There was some light in it, and it gave light to the saints in the night of the Jewish darkness; it pointed out Christ unto them; and was their schoolmaster, to teach and lead them to him. But, 3. Like the moon, it was the lesser light, that which ruled by night, and not by day: the light it gave was inferior to that which saints have under the Gospel-dispensation. 4. As the moon has its spots, so had this its imperfections; had it been faultless, there had been no need of a new dispensation, to have succeeded; but God had provided some better thing for us, New Testament saints, that they, the Old Testament saints, without us should not be made perfect: for this law could not make them so; it could neither perfectly sanctify, nor justify, nor expiate sin. 5. Like the moon, was variable and changeable: it is done away; this middle wall of partition is broken down: this hand-writing of ordinances is blotted out; it is not only like the moon in the wane, waxen old, but is also entirely vanished away. But now, notwithstanding all this, the church, as considered in her observance of the ceremonial law, was fair; there was a beauty in that kind of worship; the laws of it, being the ordinances and institutions of God, and when performed in faith, and according to the will of God, were amiable and lovely. But,

3rdly. The state of the church under the gospel-dispensation, may be said to be " clear as the sun:" for now the glorious " Sun of righteousness" is risen, that great " light of the world" has appeared, and made " that day," which, by way of emphasis, is so often spoken of in the books of the prophets; now the shadows are fled, and gone, Christ, the substance, being come; greater light, and more knowledge, with clearer faith, are the saints possessed of than they were under the law; " the least in the kingdom of heaven, is greater than John the Baptist:" now saints, not with faces veiled, but with open face; not through cloudy shadows and cloudy sacrifices; but as in a clear, transparent " glass, behold the glory of the Lord, and are changed " into it. Some Jewish writers* interpret this of the coming of the Messiah, and redemption by him, before whom darkness will flee away.

Moreover, as there is one glory of the moon, and another glory of the sun, and that of the sun far exceeds that of the moon; so the glory of the Gospel dispensation far exceeds that of the legal one: if the church was then " fair as the moon," she must be now " clear as the sun." The excelling glory of the gospel dispensation is set in a true light by the apostle, in 2 Cor. iii. 7—10. Now,

4thly. The church, in all these several periods, whether she be considered before the law, or under the law, or under the Gospel, is " terrible as an army with banners;" the church was always militant in all ages of the world; and as she never wanted enemies to fight with, so she never wanted a leader, and a commander to march before her; nor proper officers to keep her in order: nor suitable armour to put on and use; nor did she ever fail of victory, but was always " more than a conqueror through him that loved her;" and so was like a well ordered or well-disciplined army, terrible to her enemies.

Secondly. The state of the Christian church, from the times of Christ and his apostles, until his second coming and presentation of her to himself in glory, may be here represented. And,

1st. The primitive church, or that in the age of the apostles, may be intended by the first expression; " Who is she that looketh forth as the morning ?" for then the morning of the Gospel light broke, and swiftly and suddenly spread itself over the nations of the world; it produced joy and gladness wherever it came; and moved on irresistibly, maugre all the opposition that was made against it; and could no more be stopped in its progress, than the morning-light can.

2ndly. The state of the church, in some after ages, may be set forth by the next phrase, " fair as the moon," it being variable and changeable; and like the moon, had different phases and appearances; sometimes lying under sore trials and grievous persecutions, and at other times enjoying rest and peace; sometimes retaining the doctrines and ordinances of the Gospel in their power and purity, at other times overrun with errors and heresies.

3rdly. The church being said to be " clear as the sun," may either be descriptive of her state and condition in Constantine's time, when she was " clothed with the sun;" was in a great deal of splendour and glory; had the moon, the ceremonial law, " under her feet," and " a crown of twelve stars upon her head," the glorious doctrine of the twelve apostles; and were as terrible to her adversaries " as an army with banners:" or else, the state of the church in the latter-day-glory; when " the light of the moon shall be as the light

---

* Vid. Yalkut in loc.

of the sun, and the light of the sun shall be sevenfold;" or else, as glorified in heaven, enjoying consummate happiness with Christ in the kingdom of his Father; where "the righteous shine forth as the sun," and are out of the reach of all their enemies.

Thirdly. These words may also be expressive of the state and condition of particular believers, who, in their first conversion, may be said to "look forth as the morning;" their light and knowledge being but small, and their faith weak; but yet like the morning-light, increasing; for "the path of the just is as the shining light, which shines more and more unto the perfect day:" as also her being compared to the morning, may intend the beauty[p] and glory of believers, both in their faith and walk; "she looks forth as the morning:" the look of faith is exceeding beautiful in Christ's eye; see chap. iv. 9; or, "goes forth as the rising morn,"[q] as the Vulgate Latin reads it; that is, her talk and conversation is exceeding comely. Moreover, believers, as to their sanctification, may be said to be "fair as the moon," which has its spots in it; and what light it has, it derives from the sun: so the sanctification of believers is imperfect, and all the light, grace, and holiness they have come from the Sun of righteousness; but then as to their justification, they are clear as the sun, all fair, and no spot in them; and in their faith and conversation are terrible to their enemies, as an army with banners.

Verse 11. *I went down into the garden of nuts, to see the fruits of the valley*, and *to see whether the vine flourished*, and *the pomegranates budded.*

THESE are either the words of the church, or of Christ. Some[r] take them to be the words of the church, who not finding Christ on earth, sought him in the heavenly paradise, which they understand by this nut-garden; and by her going down into it, the lively exercise of her faith on the unseen joys and glories of it, in looking to them, seeking of them, and pressing after them: though others,[s] who also understand them as the words of the church; think that they represent her as giving a reason why, upon his departure from her, she went not only into the city, but also into the fields, and that in the night-season, which might not appear so reputable to one of her sex: therefore to wipe off all reproach, and remove all suspicion of evil designs in her, as well as to inform him how she had employed herself during his absence, she tells him that she went into the nut-garden, to inspect the fruits of it, and to see in what case the vines and pomegranates were. Though I rather think that they are the words of Christ declaring to his church where he went, and what he employed himself about, when he departed from her; and that he was not even then altogether unmindful of her; but narrowly looked into the state and case of her, and her members, when she thought he was at a distance from her; and this agrees with what Christ had said, in chap. v. 1, "I am come into my garden," &c., and also confirms what she had said, v. 2, of this chapter, "My beloved is gone down into his garden," &c. Besides, it best suits with him, who is the owner of the garden, to look after the fruits of it, and to see in what case it stands: moreover, this was the usual place of Christ's residence. Taking them then to be the words of Christ, there are two things to be considered.

I. What is meant by this "garden of nuts," into which, Christ says, he "went down."

II. The end of his going there; which is threefold. 1st. "To see the fruits of the valley." 2ndly. "To see whether the vine flourished." 3rdly. Whether "the pomegranates budded."

I. I shall inquire what is meant by this "garden of nuts," into which Christ is said to go. Some Jewish[t] interpreters understand by it, the second temple, which was built by the commandment of Cyrus king of Persia; but it seems better to understand it of the church of Christ, which is compared to a garden, in chap. iv. 12, and for what reasons has been there shown: and Christ being said to go down into it, may be an allusion to Solomon's gardens, which lay low, and required a descent unto them from his palace; and this not only is expressive of the state and condition of Christ's church, but also of his condescension in visiting it, as has been observed on ver. 2. Now this garden here, is said to be a "garden of nuts;" a garden where nut-trees only grew; for the ancients had places appropriated to such trees,[u] and with propriety might be called nut-gardens; though, by what follows, there seem to be vines and pomegranates, and other fruits, as well as nuts, in this garden; nuts might be the principal tree, whence it had its name,

---

[p] So of Helena, in Theocrit. Idyll 18. v. 26. it is said, Λὼς ἀντελλοισα καλον διεφαινε πρόσωπον, that she showed her beautiful face as the rising morn.
[q] Homer often describes the morning by her rosy fingers, ῥοδοδακτυλος ηως, Iliad. 1. v. 477. and passim; so Theocritus, ῥοδοπηχυν, Idyll. 2. and as clothed with a saffron garment, ηως κροκοπεπλος, Iliad. 8. v. 1. and 19. v. 1. so, aurora lutea, Virgil. Æneid. l. 7. v. 26. and as beautiful and divine, Iliad. 18. v. 255. and fair-haired, Odyss. 5, v. 390. and as on a golden throne, and comely, Odyss. 15. v. 56, 250. A shining brightness is ascribed to it, Nitor aurorae, Lucret. l. 4. v. 512. Rubescebat aurora, Virgil. Æneid. l. 3. v. 521.   [r] Diodat. in loc.   [s] Theodoret. in loc.
and Tres Patres in Ib. So Athanasius Synops. Sacr. Script. l. 16. interprets it of Jerusalem, the church, who observing the faith of the children, and the philanthropy of the Word, says this; and by the garden of nuts, he understands the scriptures, which are hard without, but spiritual within: and the Ethiopic version renders the words, My beloved is gone down, &c.   [t] Targum and R. Sol. Jarchi in loc. Lyra interprets it of the temple of Solomon: but the Cabalistic doctors interpret it of malcuth, or the congregation of Israel, Lexic. Cabal. p. 24, 240.
[u] Quicquid nobile ponticis, nuuncetis Statii Sylva. l. 1. ode 6. v. 12.

The words are by some[w] translated, "the pruned gardens," or "the gardens of pruning or shearing:" deriving the word from a root, which signifies to cut or sheer; and so signifies that it is a garden well-dressed, and pruned, and kept in good order: and so indeed is Christ's church; and therefore is opposite to, and different from the field and vineyard of the sluggard, Prov. xxiv. 30, 31, which was neither in good order, without nor within; without, its stone-wall, its fence, was broken down; and within, it was all overrun with thorns and nettles: but Christ's garden is in a much better case; for, 1. It is well fenced with sovereign, powerful, and distinguishing grace; nay, God himself is "a wall of fire" about it, and has appointed "salvation for walls and bulwarks" all around it; so that it is strongly enclosed, and well secured from the "boar out of the wood" wasting it, and from "the wild beast of the field" devouring it. 2. It is well planted; it is not an empty garden within, but is well stored with plants of all sorts, and those the most excellent, as appears from chap. iv. 13, 14, it is filled with "trees of righteousness," which are laden with the fruit thereof, and therefore are very valuable. 3. It is well pruned; for as Christ is the vine, the principal plant in this garden, on which all others grow, and from whence they receive their life and nourishment; so Christ's "Father is the Husbandman," the Vine-dresser, the Keeper of the garden, and he keeps the plants in good order;" for "every branch that beareth not fruit," he lops it off, and taketh it away; and "every branch that beareth fruit, he purgeth," or pruneth it, "that it may bring forth more fruit," John xv. 1, 2. 4. It is well watered; as the Lord is the keeper of it, so he "waters it every moment" with refreshing dews and delightful showers of divine love and grace; there is a fountain in the midst of it to water all the beds, and this is Christ himself; who therefore, in chap. iv. 15, is called the "fountain of gardens;" who also is the "well of living waters;" and whose grace is as "streams from Lebanon:" so that every particular believer, every plant here, is "like a watered garden, and like a spring of water whose waters fail not." 5. It is well weeded; there are tares growing up in Christ's field, and weeds in his garden, such as hypocrites and carnal professors; and Christ sometimes weeds his garden of many of these; and that by causing the sun of persecution to arise upon them, which scorches and burns them up, they not having root in themselves; he sometimes takes his fan in his hand, and with it purges his floor of the chaff, and clears his churches of such sort of persons as these; but this he will do more effectually at the last day, when he shall send his angels to "gather out of his kingdom all things that offend, and them that do iniquity," Matt. xiii. 41.

Moreover, by these well-dressed or pruned gardens may be meant, those particular churches of Christ, which are regularly formed, are in good order, and are well disciplined; whose members are lively in the exercise of their faith, walk agreeably in their lives and conversations; are zealous for the truths of the gospel, and for the maintaining the ordinances of it in their purity; and are not remiss in dealing with offenders, whether they be immoral in their lives, or erroneous in their principles, such were, in a great measure, the churches of Ephesus and Colosse, see Rev. ii. 3, Col. ii. 5, and with such churches Christ delights to be: and these may expect his presence.

But the word,[x] though only used in this place, is by Jewish writers generally rendered a *nut*; and so it is by the Septuagint, as well as by our translators and others; this is very properly taken notice of in this love-poem: it being usual for new-married persons to get nuts, and throw them among children to make pastime; and to signify, among other things, that they now renounced childish things.[y] And by the garden, is meant the church of Christ, as has been observed before; and by the nuts which grow in this garden, from whence it has the name of a nut-garden, are meant believers; who may be called so, for the following reasons: 1. Because though they are mean and abject without, yet are glorious and valuable within: the "king's daughter is all glorious;" the inside of a believer, like that of the nut, is the best part of him; the outward appearance of saints is but mean, and the world judging according to that, not capable of seeing any farther, look upon them as the offscouring of all things: but Christ, who knows their inside as well as their outside, knows what they are by his grace, as well as what they are by nature, that though they are black in themselves, yet are comely in him; he reckons them the excellent in the earth, in whom is all his delight. 2. Because of their several coverings: in the nut there are the husk and shell, and besides these, an inward covering: believers have several coverings; they have the robe of Christ's righteousness to cover them, which may answer the shell of the nut; being lasting and durable, will abide for ever, and will bring the soul that is enwrapped in it safe to glory: there is also "the new man," or garment of sanctification, which is put on by the believer; and this may answer the inward covering of the nut, as being more thin and tender, weak and imperfect; and then there is likewise the outward

---

[w] Ad hortos putatos, Junius and Tremellius; tonsionis, Piscator; hortum putationis, Marckius.
[x] אל גנת אגוז *εἰς κῆπον καρυας*, Sept. in hortum nucum, Vulg. Latin version; ad hortum nucum, Cocceius, Tigurine version; in hortum nucis, Mercerus; ad hortum nucis, Montanus. [y] Sparge marite nuces, &c. Virgil. Bucolic. eclog. 8. v. 30. Da nuces pueris, Catulli Juliæ Epithalam. ep. 59. v. 131. Et nucibus relictis, Persii Satyr. l. v. 10. Vid. Plin. l. 17. c. 22. Chartar. de Imag. Deorum, p. 87. and Kipping. Antiq. Rom. l. 4. c. 2. p. 697.

garment of a gospel-conversation; and this may answer the husk of the nut, as being the coarser and more imperfect covering, which, continually needs washing in Christ's blood. 3. Because of their hardiness in enduring afflictions; they wade through a sea of troubles in this world, before they enter the kingdom; and this they do with becoming cheerfulness, patience, courage, and magnanimity of mind; they "are troubled on every side, yet not distressed; are perplexed, but not in despair; persecuted, but not forsaken; cast down, but not destroyed," 2 Cor. iv. 8, 9, and that because they are supported under all these trials and exercises, and carried above them by a superior power. 4. Because of their hiddenness; the best part of the nut is hidden: the saints are hid from everlasting, in the bosom of the Father, in the hands of the Son, and in the everlasting covenant of grace; until they are made openly to appear to be the people of God, by powerful and efficacious grace in conversion, and therefore are called God's "hidden ones;" and after conversion they are hidden from the men of the world; the work of grace upon their souls is hid from them, and therefore called "the hidden man of the heart;" their joys and comforts are hidden from them, and so indeed is their whole life of grace here, as well as their life and glory hereafter: for though they are "the sons of God, yet it does not appear" so fully to themselves, much less to the men of the world, "what they shall be." 5. Because of the safety and security both of their persons and their graces: nuts, in the greatest showers of rain, have only their outside washed the more, but their inside remains untouched, and is no ways hurt; so saints are safe and secure, notwithstanding all the floods, storms, and tempests of temptations, persecutions, and afflictions, being built upon the rock, Christ Jesus, and hid in him, the ark of the covenant; the inward principle of grace in them cannot be lost; that hidden seed is incorruptible, and will abide so for ever. 6. Nuts often grow in clusters; which may not only denote the multitude of believers, and their close adherence to Christ, his gospel, cause, and interest; but also their unity among themselves: and as it is a very pleasant and delightful sight to see nuts grow in clusters; so it is much more to see "brethren dwell together in unity." 7. Saints being compared to nuts, and to those of the best sort which grow in gardens, shows, that they have not only the shell of an outward profession, but also the kernel of true grace; some have only "the form of godliness, but deny the power thereof;" profess to know God in words, but in works deny him; have a name to live, but yet are dead; but such are not these who are here compared to nuts. 8. Their being compared to nuts, may denote their preservation from the pollutions of the world, though in the midst of them; as a nut, though it may fall into the mire and dirt, yet the inside is no ways defiled therewith; so R. Solomon Jarchi, out of the Midrashes,[a] explains these words of the impollution of the works of the Israelites, when they were in captivity among the nations of the world. 9. The kernel of the nut does not appear,[b] until the shell be broken: the graces of God's children generally show themselves most when they are under afflictions: for "tribulation worketh patience, and patience experience, and experience hope;" that is, makes those graces to appear more in their lively exercise; even as spice smells most when beaten in a mortar: moreover, this rich treasure of divine grace, which is put into our "earthen vessels," will not be so clearly seen, until these vessels are broken in pieces; nor will the soul appear so beautiful and glorious, being clothed with Christ's righteousness, and adorned with the graces of his Spirit, as when it is dislodged from "the earthly house of its tabernacle," and is joined with the "spirits of just men made perfect." 10. Some[b] think, that not the common nuts, but the fruit, which we call nutmegs, are here intended; but such nuts grew not in those parts: rather, walnuts are meant, which the Arabs call *gauz* or *geuz*, which is the same word that is here used; as walnuts were in great esteem in the eastern countries, among the gardens Solomon had, Eccl. ii. 7; one might be appropriated to these: and at Etham, about two miles from Jerusalem, Solomon had gardens, into which he had used to go early in a morning, as Josephus[c] relates: pistacia-nuts were well known in Syria,[d] which joined to Judea, and which might have a part in this garden; nuts grew in Judea, of which Josephus[e] makes mention, as in great plenty; and they are reckoned among the best fruits of the land of Canaan, Gen. xliii. 11, and if nutmegs were designed, they might be expressive of the fragrancy and sweet odour of the saints, as they are clothed with Christ's garments, which "smell of myrrh, aloes, and cassia;" and as they are perfumed with "his ointments," which is exceeding savoury. But,

II. Let us consider the end of Christ's going down into this garden of nuts; which is,

1st. "To see the fruits of the valley." By fruits, are meant the graces of the Spirit; the growth, actings, and exercises of which, Christ went down to take notice of: and these are said to be the "fruits of the valley," because they grow upon humble souls, with whom Christ delights to be, and on whom he bestows more grace; though it is a wonderful instance of his grace and condescension to vouchsafe a regard to such poor, low, mean, and worthless creatures: see Isa. lvii.

---

[a] Vid. T. Bab. Chagigah, fol. 15. 2. and Shirhashirim Rabba in loc. [b] Vid. R. Aben Ezra in loc. who also applies the words to the Israelties. [b] Diodat. and Ainsworth in loc. Nux. odorata, nux myristica, Buxtorf. Talmud. Lexic, col. 21. [c] Antiquitat. l. 8, c. 7. s. 3. [d] Plin. Nat. Hist. l. 13. c. 5. Athenæi Deipnosophist. l. 14. c. 17. p. 649. [e] De Bello Jud. l. 3. c. 9. s. 8.

15, and lxvi. 1, 2. Some interpreters translate the words, "the shoots or fruits of the brook or river;" agreeable enough to the Hebrew word, which signifies a torrent, as well as a valley: and so are expressive of the fertile soil in which believers are planted, and which is the occasion of their fruitfulness; see Psalm i. 3.

2ndly. "To see whether the vine flourished." In what sense particular churches or believers in Christ may be compared to vines, has been shown on chap. ii. 13, who may be said to flourish, when they increase in number, gifts, and grace, and become fruitful in every good word and work, which Christ much looks after in his churches and in particular persons.

3rdly. To see whether "the pomegranates budded." By pomegranates are meant believers; see chap. iv. 13, and by their budding, the beginnings or first puttings forth of grace in them; which Christ takes much notice of, and is highly well pleased with. And from all this may be observed, 1. The particular care and notice which Christ takes of his plants; he misses none, but goes from one to another; observes them all in what case they are, takes notice of the meanest, as well as the greatest; the fruits of the valley, as well as the vines and pomegranates. 2. That Christ is well pleased with the fruitfulness of them; he has been at a great deal of labour and expense to make them so; for this purpose he has made, planted, dunged, and watered this garden; and now it must be some pleasure to him, to "see of the travail of his soul, and to have the pleasure of the Lord prosper in his hands;" for as herein is his Father glorified, so herein is he well pleased, that his people "bring forth much fruit;" see John xv. 8, Col. i. 10. 3. That he particularly takes notice of the first appearances and buddings of grace in young converts; these he has a tender regard for, and takes more than ordinary care of; see chap. ii. 15, Isa. xl. 11, and xlii. 3. 4. That Christ has plants of various sorts and different growths in his garden; some vines, some pomegranates, and some nut-trees: all have gifts and grace differing one from another; some have ripe fruit upon them, others are blossoming, and some are but just budding forth. 5. Yet they are all fruit-bearing trees in Christ's garden: there are none else mentioned here; and there are none in it, which are of his planting, but what are fruitful. Seeing then that Christ does so narrowly inspect the plants and trees in his garden, and expects fruit from every one of them; how much should we be concerned to be "filled with the fruits of righteousness!" lest when he comes into his garden, and finds no fruit upon us, neither in the blossom nor in the bud, he should give orders to cut us down for cumber-ground; Luke xii. 6, 7.

Verse 12. *Or ever I was aware, my soul made me like the chariots of Amminadib.*

THESE are either the words of the church, or else the words of Christ: if we consider them as the words of the church, then they may be expressive, either,

1st. Of that rapture which her soul was in, in the views of those heavenly joys, which, some think, she had been taking notice of, and meditating upon in the former verse; which, whilst she was doing, "or ever she was aware," her soul took wing, and fled as swiftly in thought towards those happy regions, as ever the chariots of Amminadib ran: she seems to be in much such an extasy as the apostle Paul was, 2 Cor. xii. 2—4, when he was "caught up into the third heaven, and heard unspeakable words, which it is not lawful for a man to utter;" who then knew not whether he was "in the body" or "out of the body," and therefore in his account of it leaves it as a thing only known to God; so she here says, "or ever I was aware," or, as it is in the Hebrew text "I knew not;" that is, scarce where I was, or, whither I was going; or whither I was in the body or out of the body, I cannot tell; so sudden was the snatch, so surprising the rapture, that I cannot tell what better to compare it to, than the swift run of Amminadib's chariots. Or,

2ndly. Of her ignorance where Christ was, and yet her diligence in seeking of him; "I knew not" that is, where my beloved was: he departed from me, and was absent a considerable time, and I could hear no tidings of him; it is true, I had heard him say that he was come into his garden; but, alas! through my drowsiness and sleep I had entirely forgotten it, until discoursing with the daughters of Jerusalem about him, it came fresh into my mind; but even then, when I knew not where he was, "my soul made me like the chariots of Amminadib;" I ran about here and there in search of him until I found him, as swiftly as ever his chariots did; see chap. iii. 1, 2, and v. 6—9. Or else,

3rdly. Of that prodigious haste she made, as soon as ever she knew where he was; and it is as if she should say, As soon as ever I understood that my beloved was gone down into his garden, to take a view of the trees and plants which grow there, and of the fruits of it; immediately, on a sudden, as it were at unawares, such was the strength of my love and affection to him, that I moved as swiftly after him as if I had been in one of the chariots of Amminadib. Or,

4thly. Of her courage and resolution in sur-

---

f לראות באבי הנחל ιδειν εν γεννημασι τυ χειμαρρυ, Sept. ιδειν τον καρπον των χειμαρρον, Al. Interp. apud. Flam. Nobil. Not. in Var. Lect. Sept. Interp. Ut spectarum virentes plantas ad torrentem, Tig. Version. g בנחל vallis torrens per vallem dicurrens, Buxtorf.

b Diodat. in loc. i Nihil celerius mente, Cicero. k לא ידעתי ουκ εγνων, Sept. ουκ οιδα, Symmachus; nescivi, Vulg. Lat. version, Mercerus; nescio quid rei sit, Tigurine version; non novi, Montanus; me nescientem, Cocceius.

mounting all difficulties for the sake of him; love makes persons bold and daring: "perfect love," as the apostle says, 1 John iv. 18, "casts out fear:" and so it did in her; for she feared nothing that might befal her, and what did, did not discourage her; for though she was abused by the watchmen, and unveiled by the keepers of the walls, yet she drove on as briskly and as courageously as ever Amminadib drove on his chariots in the field of battle. Or,

5thly. They may be expressive of the modesty and humility of the church, in not thinking that such praises as those which had been given her, both by Christ and by the virgins in the preceding verses, belonged to her; "I knew not;" I did not think, being conscious to myself of my own imperfections, that such commendation belonged to me; but finding that they did, my soul made the greater haste to answer those characters, and to enjoy the company of him whom I dearly love; and therefore she takes her leave of the virgins, her companions, who had hitherto accompanied her in the search of her beloved, that she might be alone with him; which occasioned them to say, in the following words "Return, return, O Shulamite, return, return, that we may look upon thee." Though I rather think, that these are the words of Christ, as those in ver. 11 also are, who having gone down into his garden, to observe the fruitfulness of the trees and plants of it, declares in these words in what case he found them, or rather, in what he did not; "I knew not," or I did not perceive them to be in a fruitful and flourishing condition: and to this purpose Junius and Tremellius read the words, *Nondum percipientem hæc*, "Not yet perceiving these things;" that is, the vines to flourish, or the pomegranates to bud: therefore his soul put him upon using speedy methods to bring his garden and the plants of it, into a more fruitful condition. From whence we may observe, 1. That sometimes there may be but little fruitfulness appearing in the churches of Christ: faith may be very low, as to its actings and exercise; the life and power of godliness, may be much decayed; there may be but little warmth, zeal, and activity for Christ, his gospel, cause, and interest; the ministry of the word may meet with but small success; so that there may be no pomegranates budding, as well as no vines flourishing. But, 2. Christ will not always leave his churches in such a condition, but will make haste unto them, and bring them into a more fruitful state; he will come and revive his work upon the hearts of his people, and make them fruitful in every good word and work, he will bless the ministry of the word, not only for comfort and edification, so as his vines shall flourish, but also for conversion, so that the pomegranates shall bud forth. And, 3. It may be observed, that it is Christ's presence that makes churches fruitful: as his absence causes a winter season, both with churches and particular believers, so his presence is as the returning spring which renews the face of the earth, causes the flowers to appear above ground; the pomegranates to bud, and the vines to put forth their tender grapes; he is that "Sun of righteousness," by whose warm and quickening beams of light and love, souls "grow up as calves of the stall."

Moreover, these words may be expressive of that transport of love, with which Christ was filled towards his church, which caused him so speedily to return to her, as is here intimated; "or ever I was aware," that is, on a sudden, and in a surprising manner, my love and affection to my church broke out and discovered itself; which powerfully moved and inclined me to make speedy haste unto her, and afford her all the assistance I could, as well as grant her my presence, which she was so desirous of: not that we are to suppose that any thing comes to Christ at unawares, or is done inadvertently by him; but this he says to show the strength of his love, and in what a sudden and surprising manner it brake forth towards his church and people. And in these words may be considered these three things:

I. What it was that put him upon this speedy return to his church; "my soul made me," &c.

II. In what manner this was effected, or what his soul made him to his church, in his return to her; it made him "like the chariots of Amminadib."

III. Whose chariots these are which Christ's soul made him like unto, or set him upon; or rather, who the persons are to whom his soul made him as chariots.

I. In these words we have an account of what it was that moved him to, or put him upon this speedy return to his church; which was not any worth or worthiness, love or loveliness in her; it was not her grace, nor the exercise of it, considered in themselves, but his own soul that moved him to it; that is, that love and affection which he bore in his own heart towards her; it was this that moved him first to undertake her cause, assume her nature, and die in her room and stead; and it is this which causes him to manifest himself in a way of grace, and pay those love-visits to her, which he frequently does.

II. The manner in which this was effected, or what his soul made him to his church and people, may be here also observed; it made him "like the chariots of Amminadib." 1. Like these chariots he moved swiftly to her: Christ is a "present help" to his people in their time of need; he helps them, "and that right early;" he makes haste, and delays not to afford them his assistance; for which reason he is said to be as "a roe or a young hart, leaping upon the mountains, and skipping upon the hills," in chap. ii. 8, 9. 2. He is like chariots to support, bear up, and carry his people; he takes them up in his chariots of salvation, and carries them through all the troubles and difficulties of this life, safe to glory, as he himself declares he will, in Isa. xlvi. 3, 4. 3. He is as chariots to them, to protect and defend them from their enemies. That which chariots and horses are to others, that is Christ to them, and much more so; whilst "some trust in chariots, and others in horses, they trust in the name of the Lord their God; who comes with his chariots like a whirlwind, to render his anger with fury, and his rebuke with flames of fire," Isa. lxvi. 15. 4. It may denote the majesty and glory in which he visited her; which, as it was an instance of his condescension, so it was putting an honour upon her; that one so great as he, who is the King of kings, and Lord of lords, should visit one so poor and mean as she.

III. It may also be considered whose chariots these are which Christ's soul made him like unto, or who the persons are to whom his soul made him as chariots. Some take Amminadib here to be the proper name of a person;[1] who perhaps was one of Solomon's chariot-drivers, and was famous in that way; was an artist in it, and who, Jehu-like, drove on swiftly, and furiously; and therefore Christ, speedily returning to his church, compares himself thereunto. Though I rather think, with R. Aben Ezra, Jarchi, and others, that it should be considered as two words, thus, *ammi*, which signifies my people, and *nadib*, willing or princely; and so the words may be rendered, "the chariots of my willing or princely people."[m] And this may be understood, either,

1st. Of angels, who are Christ's willing people; who are always ready to do his pleasure, obey his orders, and execute his commands with the utmost cheerfulness and alacrity imaginable; see Psalm ciii. 20, 21; and therefore, one of the petitions in that prayer, which Christ directed his disciples to, is, that God's will might "be done on earth, as it is in heaven." These are also the chariots of the Lord, as is manifest from Psalm lxviii. 17, "The chariots of the Lord are twenty thousand, even thousands of angels." These are made use of by him in a providential way, to execute his will, and do his pleasure: see Zech. vi. 1—5, and so they are in a way of grace; they are made use of by him to carry messages of grace to his people; for they are "all ministering spirits, sent forth to minister for them who shall be heirs of salvation." These are his chariots, which he sends out to bring his children home; in these Elijah was conducted, body and soul to glory; for the chariots and horses of fire, which carried him thither, were no other than angels, who appeared in such a form; by whom also Lazarus was carried into Abraham's bosom; and perhaps Christ might here make use of the ministry of angels, and ride in these chariots in this discovery of himself to his church. Or else,

2ndly. It may be meant of the ministers of Christ; who preach Christ and his gospel freely; "not by constraint, but willingly; not for filthy lucre, but of a ready mind." These may be called the chariots of the Lord; as Elijah, in 2 Kings ii. 12, is called the "chariot and horsemen of Israel:" and they may be called so, because they bear the name of Christ, and carry and spread his gospel throughout the world, and are his chariots to bring home souls unto him, as the trophies of his grace; see Isa. lxvi. 20; and in which Christ frequently rides and shows himself unto his people. Though,

3rdly. I should rather think, that the people of Christ themselves are here intended, whom Christ is as chariots to; for so I think the words may very well be rendered, "or ever I was aware, my soul made me as chariots to my willing or princely people;" and so it points out the persons who shared in this instance of his grace: and these are said, in Psalm cx. 3, to be "a willing people in the day of his power;" and they may be called so, 1. Because they are made willing to part with sin. This God requires, but man is naturally loth to do it; for sin is a sweet morsel in his mouth; "he hides it under his tongue, he spares and forsakes it not, but keeps it still within his mouth;" but when the Spirit of God convinces him of the exceeding sinfulness of it, then what was before sweet, is now bitter; and what was delightful is now odious; and what his soul adored, it now abhors, and says, as in Hos. xiv. 8, with Ephraim, "What have I to do any more with idols?" 2. Because they are made willing to part with sinful companions. This is what God calls his people to; but is a thing that is not so easily complied with, until by mighty grace they are made willing to it; for it is no other than a forsaking a man's own people, and his father's house; besides a great deal of reproach is cast upon them for so doing: for "he that departs from evil, maketh himself a prey;" but when the Spirit of God convinces the soul of the necessity of parting with such company, and the danger of continuing in it; it is not only willing to do it, but also laments that it has been so long in it, saying, as in Psalm cxx. 5, 6, "Woe is me that I sojourn in Mesech, that I dwell in the tents of Kedar!" 3. Because they are made willing to part with their own righteousness; not in point of obedience, but in point of dependence; not as ornamental to the Christian, but as constitutive of him; not as it glorifies God, but as it is made use of as a plea with him, either for grace here, or glory hereafter: again, not as it is a guard or fence against the reproaches of men, but as matter of boasting before God; not as it is agreeable to God's law, but as it is opposite to God's revealed method of justifying sinners by his Son's righteousness: but this, man is not naturally willing to; it goes against him to part with it, because this is most agreeable to nature; it is his

---

[1] מרכבות עמי נדיב ἅρματα Ἀμιναδάβ, Sept. quadrigas Aminadab, Vulg. Lat. version; currus Aminadib, Tigurine version. [m] Quadrigæ populi mei munifici, Montanus; quadrigæ populi mei spontanei, Paginus: curribus populi mei ingenui, Junius: curribus populi mei voluntarii, Cocceius, Piscator, Marckius, Michaelis.

own offspring, the effect of great labour and toil, and what affords matter of boasting to him; but when the Spirit of God convinces him of the weakness and insufficiency of it, and shows him the glory and fulness of Christ's righteousness; he then desires with the apostle Paul, Phil. iii. 9, to be "found in him, not having on his own righteousness, which is of the law, but that which is through the faith of Christ." 4. Because they are willing to be saved alone by Christ: man is naturally for bringing his own works, either as the sole cause of, or as partners with Christ, in salvation-work; but when souls are made to see the imperfection of these, and that salvation is only by Christ, and in no other, their language is, "Ashur shall not save us;" we desire to be saved no other way than by Christ; and therefore they say, with Job, chap. xiii. 15, 16, "though he slay us, yet will we trust in him; he also shall be our Salvation." 5. Because they are as willing to serve Christ as they are to be saved by him; and this, not from fear of punishment, but from a principle of love; the love of Christ constrains them to it; nor do they perform it in a servile mercenary way, but freely; not as a task, but as a pleasure: for to them wisdom's "ways are ways of pleasantness, and her paths are paths of peace." 6. Because they are willing to bear the cross of Christ; this Christ requires of them, and this they readily and voluntarily submit unto: Christ's cross is to them preferable to crowns and kingdoms: with Moses, Heb. xi. 25, 26, they choose "rather to suffer affliction with the people of God, than to enjoy the pleasures of sin for a season." Now to such a free and willing people as these Christ makes himself as chariots.

But again the word may be rendered, "my princely people;" and such are the people of Christ; see Psalm cxiii. 7, 8, they are all princes, being the sons of a king; they are all heirs to a kingdom, have a crown of life, righteousness, and glory laid up for them, and a throne of glory prepared for them to inherit; they wear princely robes, enjoy princely fare, and have a princely equipage; the angels of the Lord attend them continually as their lifeguard. So the church is said to be a prince's daughter, in chap. vii. 1, and to her Christ here makes himself as chariots, and takes her up along with him, that she might enjoy his delightful company, which she had so long sought after, and so much desired; which occasioned the daughters of Jerusalem, who had hitherto accompanied her in the search of him, to say, in the following words:

Verse 13. *Return, return, O Shulamite, return, return, that we may look upon thee: What will ye see in the Shulamite? As it were the company of two armies.*

THESE words consist of two parts:

I. A call, either of Christ, or of the daughters of Jerusalem, to the church, to return, that they might have a full view of her.

II. A reply to that call, which is made by proposing a question, and returning an answer to it.

I. Here is a call, either of Christ, or of the daughters, to the church, to return, that they might have a full view of her : 'in which may be considered,

First. The name she is called by, or the title and appellation which is given to her, Shulamite. Secondly. What she is called upon to do; and that is, to return, which is repeated over and over. Thirdly. The end of it, which is, that they might "look upon her."

First. The name she bears, or the title and application which is given her, is, Shulamite; and she may be called so, for the following reasons:

1st. Because she was an inhabitant of Salem or Jerusalem:ⁿ as the woman with whom Elisha lodged, is called a Shunamite from her dwelling in Shunem; so the church is here called a Shulamite or a Jerusalemite, from her dwelling in Salem or Jerusalem: Jerusalem was formerly called Salem; so it was in Melchizedek's time, as is thought, who was king of that place; which ancient name of it is mentioned by the Psalmist, in Psalm lxxvi. 2, "in Salem also is his tabernacle." And now it is no wonder that the church, or any particular believer, should be called a Shulamite, seeing the church, both in the Old and New Testament, frequently bears the name of Jerusalem; so that to be a Shulamite, is to be a "fellow-citizen of the saints, and of the household of God," and to share in all the privileges and immunities thereof, as they do; who, besides the company of angels, and conversation of saints, enjoy the presence of Father, Son, and Spirit; and share in all the blessings of the everlasting covenant; for to the Shulamites, these natives of Zion, or inhabitants of Jerusalem, do these properly belong; see Isa. xxxiii. 24, Zech. xiii. 1.

2udly. Because she was the wife of the true Solomon, Christ Jesus. This is thought by some,º to be the same with Solomon, having a feminine termination, which suits well with her: and as it is a common thing for the wife to have the same name with the husband; so it is no unusual thing for the church to be called by the same name as Christ is. Is he the Solomon; she is the Shulamite. Is he Jehovah our righteousness? this is also the name wherewith she is called: see Jer. xxii. 6, compared with chap. xxxiii. 16; hence it is that she shares in all the blessings he is possessed of, and in every thing he has a property in : for Christ being hers, all that he has is hers.

3rdly. The word ᵖ from whence this is derived, signifies both perfection and peace; so that she may be called the Shulamite, from that perfection

---
ⁿ So R. Aben Ezra in loc. and R. David Kimchi, in lib. Thorash. rad. שלם give the sense of the word.
º Vid. Durham in loc. and Menochium de Repub.
Heb. l. 3. c. 21. n. 14.   ᵖ שלם compleri, perfici; pacem heabere vel colere, Buxtorf.

and peace which she enjoys in and through Christ. 1. She may be called so from that perfection, which she is or shall be possessed of; " Return, return, O Shulamite;" or, " O thou perfect one;" who art an accomplished beauty, being the perfection of it: whose renown is gone forth among the heathen for it; for thy beauty is perfect, through the comeliness which the Lord hath put upon thee. Now the church may be said to be a Shulamite, a perfect one, these several ways: (1.) Not as she is in herself, but as she is in Christ; as she is in herself, she is black, but as she is in Christ, she is comely; as she is in herself, she is imperfect, but as she is in him, she is complete; as she is in herself, she is full of spots, but as she is in him, " she is all fair, and without spot." (2.) She is perfect; not as considered in her own righteousness, but as considered in Christ's; as she is considered in her own, she is imperfect, that being so; which she frankly acknowledges, saying, Isa. lxiv. 6, " we are all as an unclean thing, and all our righteousnesses are as filthy rags;" but as she is considered in Christ's righteousness, she is perfect, being completely justified, acquitted, and discharged thereby from all sin; and so may be justly reckoned among the number " of the spirits of just men made perfect." (3.) She may be said to be perfect: not absolutely as in herself, but comparatively, with regard to others: so saints may be said to be perfect, when compared either with themselves before conversion, or with hypocrites and carnal professors, or with the profane men of the world; so Job, though he may be said to be " a perfect and an upright man," on the account of his having Christ's righteousness upon him, and the truth of grace within him; yet he may also be said to be so, as being compared with the men of that generation in which he lived; and therefore the Lord says of him, " there is none like him in the earth, a perfect and an upright man." (4.) She may be said to be perfect, with a perfection of parts, but not of degrees; it is true, the believer has a complete sanctification in Christ, but not in himself; moreover, every part, power, and faculty of the soul, may be sanctified, but not wholly, or to that degree as it shall be: the new creature is formed in all its parts, but it is not yet grown up to be " a perfect man in Christ;" it is not adult, it is as yet in its nonage, in its infancy. (5.) She may be called the Shulamite, or " the perfect one," not as she is now, but as she shall be hereafter; for though saints " are now the sons of God, it does not yet appear what they shall be;" they are now in some measure like to Christ, but then they shall be perfectly like unto him; they have now spots upon them, but then they shall be without " spot or wrinkle, or any such thing;" they will then appear to be complete in Christ, and to be " the fullness of him," as the church is called, in Eph. i. 23, which then she may be said to be, when all the elect are called by grace, and not one member of the body is missing; and when all these members are filled with all the gifts and graces of the Spirit in their measure, and are all grown up to a just proportion in the body. 2. She may be called the Shulamite,¶ from that peace which she does or shall enjoy in and through Christ. (1.) She may be called so from that peace which she has through Christ: who is her peace, and has made peace for her through the " blood of his cross," and thereby has reconciled her unto God: so that being now " justified by faith" in his blood and righteousness, she has " peace with God, through our Lord Jesus Christ." (2.) From that peace which she has from Christ; who gives unto her such a peace as the world can neither give nor take away: " Peace I leave with you," says Christ, John xiv. 27, " my peace I give unto you, not as the world giveth, give I unto you;" which is such an one as the believer can experience, even in the midst of the world's frowns, troubles, and persecutions: this is a peace which " passeth all understanding;" and which is spoken only by the blood of Jesus, that " speaketh better things than that of Abel;" and which the God of peace gives to men, by leading their faith to the person, blood, and righteousness of Christ. (3.) From that peace which she does or should enjoy in her members: who ought to endeavour " to keep the unity of the spirit in the bond of peace;" which they will do, if " the peace of God rules in their hearts," as it should do; for hereunto are they called. (4.) From that peace which she is entitled to, and shall enjoy hereafter; for though this world is a world of trouble to the believer, yet he is no sooner out of it, but " he enters into peace;" and into such an one as will never be interrupted and broke in upon, either by sin, Satan, or the world; for " mark but the upright and perfect man," the true Shulamite, " for the end of that man is peace." But,

Secondly, let us now consider what is said unto this Shulamite; and that is, " return, return:" which, if we understand as the words of Christ, may be expressive, either, 1. Of the spiritual return of his church and people to him after sin and backslidings; which sense is favoured by the Targum or Chaldee paraphrase upon this place; and also suits with the former state and condition of the church, who was fallen into a piteous frame of spirit, was sleepy and drowsy, negligent of her duty, and slighting Christ, for which reason he departed from her: but now returning himself, invites her to return also to him: which shows the exceeding greatness of his love unto her, and tenderness for her; and therefore to answer all objections and remove all discouragements, he not only speaks to her in such loving and endearing language; but

¶ *Eirencousa*, Aquilla; this is interpreted of a nation that both makes and enjoys peace, in Shirhashirim Rabba in loc. and in Bereshith Rabba, parash. 66.

also repeats the call over and over, to show how earnestly desirous he was of it, as well as the haste and speed he would have her make in it: see Jer. iii. 1—12, Hosea xiv. 1—4. Or, 2. Of the conversion of the Jews.[r] The name by which the church is here called, may more especially intend the Jewish church; and the words, "return, return," aptly represent the present state of the Jews, who are in a state of blindness, impenitence, and unbelief; and have not only veils over their heads, but also over their hearts, when the law of Moses is read and expounded among them; they have their backs turned upon God, and their hearts set against the true Messiah, Christ Jesus: moreover, their conversion is expressed both in the Old and New Testament, by a turning or returning unto the Lord: see Hosea iii. 5, 2 Cor. iii. 16; and the repetition of these words, "return, return," not only shows the power and haste in which this shall be accomplished; for then shall that prophecy be fulfilled, which is mentioned with so much wonder and surprize, in Isa. lxvi. 8, "Who hath heard such a thing? Who hath seen such things? Shall the earth be made to bring forth in one day? or shall a nation be born at once?" but also their being repeated four times,[s] may denote the collection of the Jews, at the time of their conversion, from the four corners of the earth: see Isa. xi. 12. I rather think, that these are the words of the daughters of Jerusalem, who, perceiving that the church was going away from them, call after her to return from them; they first meet with her in the time of her beloved's absence from her, and had accompanied her in her search after him hitherto; but not having met with her beloved, who had made himself unto her as "the chariots of Amminadib," she takes her leave of them, and in all haste goes along with him; which they observing, call to her after this manner; or else, these daughters having observed how the church, through modesty and shamefacedness, being conscious of her former treatment of Christ, hung down her head, and hid her face, as blushing and being ashamed to look up, being now in his presence, they call to her to turn, as some[t] render the word; that is, to turn her face, that they might behold the beauty and glory of it. Which leads us to consider,

Thirdly. The end of this call, which is, that they might "look upon her:" and if we take them to be the words of Christ, then the *we* are either the Trinity of Persons, Father, Son, and Spirit; who are all well pleased with returning sinners, look upon them with delight and pleasure, and grant them communion and fellowship with them: or else, Christ and his angels, who, together with Christ, not only rejoice at the conversion of profane sinners, but also at the return of backsliding ones: or else, he and the daughters, her companions;" who, as well as he, were in love with her, and with wonder gazed at her. Though they seem rather to be the words of the daughters themselves; who here express their desire of seeing her, and therefore call to her to return unto them:" they had heard very great commendations of the church's beauty, in the preceding verses, which had excited desires more narrowly to look upon, and take a fuller view of her, than hitherto they had done: as also, that they might again enjoy her company and conversation, which had been so useful and instructive to them; and which, they might imagine, would be more so, seeing she had so lately met with Christ, and had some fresh experiences of his love to her. So much for the first part of the words.

II. Here is a reply made to this call of Christ, or of the virgins to the church, to return; which is done, 1st. By proposing a question, "What will ye see in the Shulamite?" 2ndly. By returning an answer to it, "as it were the company of two armies."

1st. A reply is made, by proposing this question, "What will ye see in the Shulamite?" which is done either by Christ, who was best able to answer it; and this he does, not as being ignorant of what was to be seen in his church, nor with a design to lessen his church's glory and excellency; but rather to heighten it, and to animate and excite the desires and affections of these virgins more strongly towards her: or else this question is put by the virgins, one to another; some of them wished for her return, and others asked what they would see, or what they expected to see in her. Though I rather think, it is put by the church herself; who, perceiving that the daughters were so very importunate with her to return to them, that they might look upon her: ask what they could expect to see in her, who was in herself and in her own opinion, such a poor, mean, and unworthy creature; not fit to be looked upon, there being nothing in her that was extraordinary, or indeed valuable, or worth seeing.

2ndly. An answer is returned unto this question, thus, "As it were the company of two armies;" which is either given by Christ as an answer to his own, or to the daughters' question, and that with a design to set forth the glory and majesty of the church: should it be asked, as if he should say, What is to be seen in my church? I answer, a great deal of glory; for though she is militant, yet she is "terrible as an army with banners;" nay, there is as much stateliness and

---

[r] Vid. R. Aben Ezra and Brightman in loc. and Carpzov. Critica Sacra, par. 3. p. 904. [s] in Shirhashirim Rabba and Bereshith Rabba, ubi supra. it is interpreted of the four kingdoms the Jews had been carried captive into. [t] Verbum Heb. שוב sub, pro quo, Vulgatus, revertere, etiam converere significat; and ita vertunt LXX. (*epistrephe*) and legit Ambros. libro de Isaac. cap. 8. and Hieronymus in Epistola ad Algasiam, Sanctius in loc. Though it ought to be observed, that the Hebrew word is not שובי but שובי which is Sanctius's mistake. [u] Vid. Sanctium in loc.

majesty to be seen in her, as in two armies set in battle array; or else, they are the answer of the virgins, one to another, declaring what they expected to see in Christ's spouse; and that is, either such a glorious and joyful meeting between Christ and his church, as is often between great persons, which is frequently attended with singing and dancing; for the word translated *company*[w] signifies a company of those who dance and sing; and therefore is rendered by the Septuagint, χοροι, *choirs*; an instance of which spiritual joy, signified by such metaphors, see in Psal. lxviii. 24, 25, or as an army at the reception of their prince, for the sake of greater honour and majesty, divides itself into bands: or else, it was an angelic glory which they expected to see in her, or to see her face as the angel of the Lord; which would be as delightful and refreshing a sight unto them, as that was which Jacob had, when he had just parted with Laban, and was in danger from his brother Esau; who, Gen. xxxii. 1, 2, saw the angels of God as two bands, the one to go before, and the other behind him; and therefore he called the name of the place *Mahanaim*, which signifies *two hosts* or *two armies*, and is the same word that is here used; and to this history the allusion seems to be here made: or else, by this company of two armies, which these virgins expected to see, and were desirous of seeing in the church, may be meant, the union of Jews and Gentiles in one body: which will be effected in the latter day; and when it is, it will be a glorious and delightful sight. Though I rather think, that both the question and the answer are the church's; who first asks what they could expect to see in her; and then replies, that nothing could be seen in her, but as it were the company of two armies; that is, flesh and spirit, grace and sin, which were continually warring against, and opposing each other; see Rom. vii. 23, Gal. v. 17, and this surely could be no pleasant or desirable sight, as she thought to them: but notwithstanding she had such a mean opinion of herself, yet very large and noble commendations are given of her in the following chapter, which fill up the greatest part of it; and thus it begins:

CHAPTER VII.

In this chapter Christ gives a fresh commendation of the beauty of his church, in a different order and method than before: beginning with her feet, and so rising gradually upwards to the hair of her head, and to the roof of her mouth, ver. 1.—9. And then the church asserts her interest in him; and declares his desire towards her, ver. 10; and invites him to go with her into the fields, villages, and vineyards; and offers various reasons, by which she urges him to a compliance with her invitation, ver. 11—13.

Verse 1. *How beautiful are thy feet with shoes, O prince's daughter! the joints of thy thighs are like jewels, the work of the hands of a cunning workman.*

THESE are either the words of the daughters of Jerusalem, who having desired the church to return unto them, in the latter part of the preceding chapter, that they might take a view of those incomparable and astonishing beauties, for which she had been commended; to which request she complying, they now with wonder look upon her, and give those large commendations of her, which are in this and some following verses: and what seems still more to strengthen this sense of the words, Christ is spoken of in verse 5, as a distinct person, both from the person who is described, and also from the persons by whom the description is made. Though I rather think, that they are the words of Christ; who, observing his church think so meanly, and speak so modestly of herself, enters afresh upon the commendation of her beauties; to the end, that all her discouragements might be removed, her objections answered, and she be fully assured that she was as beautiful in his eyes, and as much the object of his love as ever she was, notwithstanding her unkind treatment of him, and behaviour to him. Moreover, it may be observed, that the title, which is given the church, in verse 6, does not suit well to come out of any other's mouth but Christ's, whose love peculiarly she is: nor indeed would it appear so proper to any as to Christ, to give such commendations of the church as here are given. And it is also worthy of our notice, that the order in which Christ proceeds here, in the description of the beauty of church, is not only different from that method which she took in setting forth his glory, in chap. v., but also from that which he himself took, when upon the same subject, in chapters iv. vi.; for as he there began with the hair of her head, her lips, teeth, cheeks, and temples, and so proceeded downwards; he here begins with her feet and rises upwards: which may be, 1. To show that he takes notice of and has a value for the meanest members of his mystical body, the church; he takes notice of her feet, which, though they have the lowest place in the body, yet are not without their usefulness; "for the head cannot say to the feet, I have no need of you;" and as they are not without their usefulness, so neither are they without Christ's notice; who has a real value, and has made provisions of grace for them, as well as for the other members of his body, and therefore appears in a garment down to the feet; which garment of his justifying righteousness, covers the feet and toes, as well as the other parts of the body: nay, Christ not only takes notice of, and has a value for the meanest saints, but also for their meanest performances; he hears and despises not the prayers of his destitute ones: he bottles up

---

[w] כמחלת המחנים ως χοροι των παρεμβολων, Sept. nisi choros castrorum, Vulgate Latin version; velut chorum castrorum, Mercerus, Montanus, Cocceius; quæ similis est choreæ castrorum, Tigurine version; velut chorum machanaimorum. Junius. Vid. R. Aben. Ezra in loc.

s 2

their tears, and forgets not their labour of love towards his saints: such as visiting them when sick, feeding them when hungry, and clothing them when naked, nay, even the giving them a cup of cold water in the name of a disciple; all which he looks upon as done to himself, and will remember, and speak of them when they have forgotten them, and at a time when they little thought to have heard of them. 2. It may be also to lead the church, together with the daughters of Jerusalem, gradually, by little and little, into the glory and beauty which she received from him; and so bring them to consider what glory and beauty he must be possessed of, from whom she received all hers; for if her feet with shoes were so beautiful, what must the other parts of her body be, which were still more gloriously adorned! and if she in all her parts was so glorious; what must he be who made her so! 3. He takes notice first of her feet, because she was now upon the return unto him after her backslidings from him, which was exceeding grateful to him: the returning prodigal was not more welcome to his father; who, seeing him afar off, ran and fell upon his neck, and kissed him; than a poor backsliding sinner is to Christ Jesus. 2. He inverts his former order and method, to show that the manifestations of his love are not always alike; he sometimes takes one way, and sometimes another; and whether a believer is considered either one way or another, he is always beautiful in Christ, and in his eyes. But let us now consider the words themselves; in which may be observed,

I. The noble and excellent title which is given her; " O prince's daughter!"

II. The commendations of her; which are, 1st. Of her feet, and these are said to be " beautiful with shoes." 2udly. Of " the joints of her thighs;" which are said to be " as jewels, the work of the hands of a cunning workman."

I. Here is a new and noble title given to her, " O prince's daughter!" Christ finds new names and titles for his spouse; and that not only to set forth her excellency the more, but also to express the largeness of his love and affection to her; who may be well called a prince's daughter, as she is the king's daughter in Psal. xlv. 13, and that because she is the daughter of the King of kings, and Lord of lords: and so she is, 1. By covenant grace, which makes her so; for God has in covenant made over himself unto his people, and declared that he will be their Father, and they shall be his sons and daughters; for even thus saith the Lord Almighty: and now that 'same grace, which has taken them into that relation, will make it appear manifestly that they are so, by bestowing all that grace which is laid up in covenant for them, and all that glory which is there provided for them. 2. By birth, or by the grace of regeneration: the church of Christ is a prince's daughter by birth, being born again,

" not of blood, nor of the will of the flesh, nor of the will of man, but of God;" the original and descent of the children of God is not base, mean, and low, but high and noble: those that are born again, are born ἄνωθεν, from above, as that word may be rendered; they are born heirs to an inheritance, that is not of this world, which is fading and perishing, but to one that is incorruptible, undefiled, and which fadeth not away, reserved in heaven for them: and as they are born, so they are brought up as the sons and daughters of kings and princes; they are brought up in the king's palace; they feed at his table, and participate of all his royal dainties; their clothing shows them to be such, which is all of wrought gold, as does also their equipage and retinue: who besides the virgins or maids of honour to wait upon them, have also a guard of angels continually to attend them. 3. By adopting grace: angels are the sons of God by creation; but saints by adoption: they are predestinated to it; and by the Spirit of God, who is the Spirit of adoption, are put into the possession of it, and reap the benefits, and enjoy the comfort of it, through his witnessing with their spirits, that they are the children of God; which is such a surprising instance of God's grace, that all who share in this privilege have reason to say, with the apostle John, 1 John iii. 1, " Behold what manner of love the Father hath bestowed upon us, that we should be called the sons of God. 4. By marriage: The church is married to Christ, the eternal Son of God; whose titles are, " The Prince of peace, and the Prince of the kings of the earth:" so that she is both a prince's daughter, and a prince's wife; and is the former, by becoming the latter; she is espoused as a chaste virgin to Christ, who is the only Son of the king, eternal, immortal, invisible, the only wise God.

Moreover, the words may be rendered, " O noble, or princely daughter!"[a] that is, who art of a noble and princely spirit: and this is, (1.) A free spirit, in opposition to a servile one: and so the word is translated, in Psalm li. 12, " Uphold me with a free [or princely] Spirit:" and such a spirit believers have, being freed from the servitude of sin and Satan; and being delivered from a spirit of bondage to a law of works, serve the Lord with all cheerfulness and readiness, being made a willing people in the day of his power. 2. To be of a princely spirit, is to be of a free, noble, generous, bountiful, and liberal spirit: and such a spirit saints have, not only in distributing their temporal things to the necessities of the poor, but also in communicating their spiritual things to the mutual comfort and edification of each other; so the word is rendered in Isa. xxxii. 5, 8.

II. Having considered the title, it will be now proper to take notice of the commendations given her: 1st. Of her feet, which are said to

---

[a] בת נדיב puella nobilis, Castalio; principalis, nobilis and ingenus virgo, sc. filia. so some in Michaelis.

be beautiful with shoes. 2ndly. Of the joints of her thighs, which are said to be "as jewels, the work of the hands of a cunning workman."

1st. Her feet with shoes are here commended: it is no unusual thing to describe the comeliness of women by their feet, and the ornaments of them; so Hebe is described by Homer,[b] as having beautiful feet; and Juno, by her golden shoes: particular care was taken of, and provision made for the shoes of queens and princesses in the eastern countries; Herodotus[c] relates, that the city of Anthylla was given peculiarly to the wife of the king of Egypt, to provide her with shoes: the Targum here is, purple shoes; and those of a red, scarlet, or purple colour, were in esteem with the Jews, Ezek. xvi. 10, and with the Tyrian virgins, their neighbours;[d] and also with the Romans,[e] with whom likewise white shoes[f] were much in use. By these feet with shoes may be meant, either, 1. The ministers of the Gospel,[g] whose feet being shod with the preparation of the Gospel of peace, are exceeding beautiful, according to Isa. lii. 7, "How beautiful upon the mountains are the feet of him that bringeth good tidings, that publisheth peace," &c. These are the church's feet, which run to and fro in the world, whereby the knowledge of Christ and his Gospel is increased; which was eminently true of the apostles and first ministers of the Gospel, who swiftly ran over the Gentile world; and wherever they came, diffused the savour of Christ's knowledge, and were instrumental in the conversion of thousands of souls; for their sound went into all the earth, and their words unto the ends of the world. And now these feet being said to be beautiful with shoes, may denote, (1.) The promptitude and readiness of Christ's ministers to preach the Gospel: as the people of Israel, having their shoes upon their feet, when they eat the passover, just when they departed out of Egypt, showed their readiness for their journey; so these feet of the church, having shoes on, show the readiness of the ministers of the Gospel to preach it in every place where they are called to it, though in the face of the greatest opposition; "I am ready," says the apostle Paul, Rom. i. 16, "to preach the Gospel to you that are at Rome also:" his feet were shod with it, and he was prepared to preach it; even where not only the seat of the empire, but the seat of persecution was, where it was the hottest, and raged the most furiously; and the reason he gives is, for, says he, "I am not ashamed of the Gospel of Christ;" no, not in Cæsar's palace: faithful ministers are ready to preach it any where, and at any time; and are "instant in season and out of season;" they preach, "not by constraint, but willingly; not for filthy lucre, but of a ready mind." (2.) It shows their intrepidity in preaching the Gospel; a man that has his feet well shod, regards not the roughness of the way, nor the sharp stones which lie in it, nor the pricking briars and thorns through which he walks: the ministers of the Gospel, whose feet are well shod with it, regard no difficulties that lie in their way, so as to be discouraged by them, and desist from their work; but, with the utmost courage and magnanimity of mind, bear and surmount them; with scorn and contempt they trample upon all the briars and thorns of reproaches and scandal that are cast upon, and persecutions which are levelled against them; none of these things move them, neither do they count their lives dear to themselves; so that they may finish their course with joy, and the ministry, which they have received of the Lord Jesus, to testify the Gospel of the grace of God. (3.) It is expressive of their beauty and glory: the ministers of the Gospel are not only beautiful in the eyes of those to whom they are made useful, either for conversion or consolation, but also in the eyes of Christ; especially when they faithfully discharge their work; though they run the risk of losing of their credit, honour, and reputation in the world, nay, their lives also. Or else, 2. By these feet, may be meant the affections of the church towards Christ;[h] which are that unto the soul, as feet are to the body; these carry it up and down, hither and thither, at pleasure: and being said to be beautiful with shoes, show that they moved in an orderly way; constrained her to turn her feet to his testimonies, and enlarged her heart to run the way of his commandments; which made them appear exceeding beautiful to him, so that his heart was ravished with them; see chap. iv. 9, 10, the eyes of Holofernes are said to be ravised with the sandals upon Judith's feet, which she had put on, on purpose to deceive persons; see Judith x. 4, and xvi. 11, and this shows it to be the custom of women to adorn their shoes or sandals, that they might enamour their lovers; to which custom perhaps the allusion is here made. Or else, 3. By them may be meant the actings of faith on Christ, in saints coming to him and walking on in him, as they have received him; as faith is the eye of the soul, which sees Christ, and the hand which receives him, so it is likewise the foot which goes to him and walks in him; and nothing is more pleasant and delightful to Christ, than for souls to come unto him, and venture their all upon him, in expectation of receiving life and salvation, righteousness and strength, peace and comfort, grace and glory; all from him and through him; for such he

---

[b] Odyss. 11. v. 602, 603. Auratos pedes. Ovid. Amor. l. 3. eleg. 12. [c] Euterpe, sive l. 2. c. 98. [d] Virginibus Tyriis mos est, &c. Virgil. Æneid. l. [e] Vid. Persii Satyr. 5. v. 169. Virgil. Bucolic. eclog. 7. v. 31. [f] Pes malus in nivea, &c. Ovid. de Arte Amand. l. 3. Vid. Martial l. 7. epigr. 27. [g] So Mercerus, Cocceius, and Not. Tigur. Vers. in loc. [h] So Sanctius in loc.

willingly receives, and has promised never to reject: and as their first coming, so their continued walking in him, by fresh repeated acts of faith, is well pleasing to him; these feet are beautiful with shoes. Though, 4. By them may be meant, the outward conversation of the saints;[l] which is frequently expressed in scripture, by walking in the ways, commands, and ordinances of Christ; see Luke i. 6, Eph. iv. 17, Col. iv. 5, which may be said to be beautiful with shoes. (1.) When they appear to be ready to every good work; who, no sooner are enlightened with an ordinance, or called to a duty, but they readily comply with it, being beforehand furnished and prepared for it, having their shoes upon their feet, in a posture of readiness to do it. (2.) When the conversation is so ordered, as that the shame of our nakedness does not appear to the eyes of the world. To walk barefoot, was accounted shameful; see Isa. xx. 4; and so it is to have an ill-ordered conversation: but a well-ordered conversation is like shoes to the feet, which cover them, so that the shame thereof does not appear. (3.) When it is conformed to God's law; which is "a lamp unto the feet, and a light to the path." (4.) When it is becoming Christ's Gospel. (5.) When it is guarded against the reproaches and offences of the world: as shoes upon the feet keep off the thorns and briars from pricking; so does a good conversation, in some measure, keep off the reproaches of the world, or at least keep them from being disturbed at them; for great peace have they which love God's law, and nothing shall offend them: and though it does not afford matter of boasting before God; yet a believer, whose conversation is becoming the Gospel, may say, as Samuel did, chap. xii. 3, "Whose ox have I taken? Whose ass have I taken? Whom have I defrauded?" so that hereby he is fenced and guarded against the world's calumnies and contempt. (6.) Then is it so, when there is such a lustre in it as cannot but be seen by, and is conspicuous to all beholders; which raises their admiration, and gives them occasion of glorifying God; see Matt. v. 16, and this, as it is commendable among men, so it is beautiful in the eyes of Christ; for to such who order their conversations aright, that is, whose feet are beautiful with shoes, will he show the salvation of God.

2ndly. "The joints of her thighs" are said to be "as jewels, the work of the hands of a cunning workman." By which may be meant, either 1. Some ornaments of gold, silver, or precious stones, which were used to be worn about the legs or feet by women in those times; which was a custom not only used among the Heathens,[k] but also among the Jews, as is manifest from Isaiah iii. 18, where among the rest of the attire of the Jewish women, "the bravery of their tinkling ornaments about their feet" is mentioned; and so may be expressive of the greater glory, lustre, and beauty of the church's conversation. Or, 2. The garments which covered the thighs;[l] for it is not agreeable to the rules of decency and modesty to describe the naked thighs: the word[m] signifies "the compassing of the thighs;" which does not intend the ambient flesh, or the thickness of it about them, as R. David Kimchi[n] supposes; but rather, the *femoralia*, or garments about the thighs, which encompassed, and covered them; by which may be meant, "the garments of salvation, and robe of Christ's righteousness," whereby the persons of God's elect are covered, so that "the shame of their nakedness" does not appear; and with which they are as richly adorned, as the bridegroom is with his ornaments, and the bride with her jewels, on their marriage-day. Moreover, this is not the bungling work of a creature, but "the work of the hands of a cunning workman;" even of one that is God as well as man, and therefore is called "the righteousness of God. Or, 3. The girdle about the loins," according to some,[o] which was wont to be worn in those times; thighs being put for loins, as in Gen. xlvi. 26, and may intend that girdle of truth with which the loins of believers are girt, and is joined with "the preparation of the gospel of peace," with which their feet are shod, in Eph. vi. 14, 15, which metaphor is frequently made use of, when a gospel-conversation is directed and exhorted to; see Luke xii. 35, 1 Pet. i. 13. Or, 4. By these "joints of the thighs," may be meant young converts. The Targum expounds it of the children which sprung from the thighs or loins of the people of Israel; see Gen. xlvi. 26, Exod. i. 5, Judg. viii. 30, where this phrase, "to come out of the loins," or, as it is in the Hebrew text, "the thighs," is expressive of generation; and therefore these words, in a mystical and spiritual sense, may have reference to those many souls that are born again in the church; who are as jewels in Christ's esteem: and are the curious workmanship of the blessed Spirit, "created in Christ Jesus unto good works." Or else, 5. By these "joints or turnings of the thighs,"[p] by which they move orderly and regularly, may be meant the principles of a believer's walk and conversation, as one[q] well observes, without which it is little worth, nor can it be ordered aright; for principles denominate actions to be either good or evil. Now the principles of grace, from whence a believer acts in his conversation, and by which he moves in his Christian walk, are as valuable and as precious as jewels; and are wrought by no less a hand than the Spirit of God, who

---

[l] So Durham and Ainsworth in loc. [k] Vid. Plin. l. 9. c. 35. and l. 33. c. 3, 12. [l] So R. Aben Ezra, Sanctius, and Bishop Patrick in loc. ירכיך ambitus femorum, Buxtorf. Mercer. Junius.
[m] In lib. Shorash. rad. חמק. [n] So Junius and Cocceius in loc. [p] Vertebræ, Pagninus, Montanus, Vatablus; signat illam agilem versatilem juncturam, qua capita femorum in suis foraminibus expedite moventur, Brightman. [q] Durham in loc.

"worketh in them both to will and to do of his good pleasure."

Verse 2. *Thy navel* is like *a round goblet* which *wanteth not liquor:* thy belly is like *an heap of wheat, set about with lilies.*

CHRIST here continues the commendation of his church, and gives two other instances of her beauty: and as in the former verse, he had commended those parts, which may be expressive of her outward walk and conversation, and of the principles of grace from whence she acted; so here he may be thought to set forth her inward glory by these, the navel and belly, which are more hidden and less conspicuous; for this "king's daughter" is all-glorious within, as well as her conversation is honourable without; her adorning not being the "outward adorning, of plaiting the hair, and of wearing of gold, or of putting on of apparel; but is the hidden man of the heart, in that which is not corruptible, even the ornament of a meek and quiet spirit, which is in the sight of God of great price:" but what is particularly intended by these parts, will more manifestly appear from a distinct consideration of them. And,

I. Her navel is said to be "like a round goblet which wanteth not liquor."

II. Her belly as "an heap of wheat, set about with lilies."

I. Her navel is compared to "a round goblet, which wanteth not liquor:" by which some[r] understand, not that part of the body itself, but some covering or an ornament of it; as some jewel or plate of gold, which was so called, either, because it was the shape of the navel, or else because it covered and adorned it; as also, because the word translated *round*, in the Chaldee language, signifies the *moon*, it has inclined them to think that this ornament may be the same which the Jewish women are said to wear, in Isa. iii. 18, where mention is made of their "round tires like the moon;" which figure is also understood by the Targum upon our text; though others,[s] who are also of opinion that some covering of these parts is intended; yet think that the reference is made unto that "clothing of wrought gold," with which the church is said to be arrayed, in Psalm xlv. 13, in the midst of which, or in that part of it which covered the navel and belly, was a raised or embossed work, which resembled an heap of wheat, or rather, sheaves of wheat, round about which was an embroidery of curious flowers, and especially lilies; and in the midst of the whole work, a fountain or conduit, running with several sorts of liquors, into a great bowl or bason; Fortunatus Scacchus[t] interprets it of a garment covering those parts, embroidered with lilies. By all which, the glory and beauty of the "garments of salvation, and robe of Christ's righteousness," with which believers are adorned, may be represented to us. R. Aben Ezra, by the navel, understands the great Sanhedrim; as he does by the belly, the lesser:[u] R. Sol. Jarchi, *lishcat gazit*, or the paved chamber, in which they sat. Moreover, nothing is more frequent with the Jewish writers, than to call the land of Canaan, and particularly Jerusalem, the navel of the earth; which they suppose to be in the very midst of it, for which reason they call it so; and it was from this navel of the earth, that the gospel of Christ went forth into all the world: "for out of Zion shall go forth the law, and the word of the Lord from Jerusalem:" The Targum or Chaldee paraphrase on the place, applies it to the "head of the school; by whose righteousness the whole world receives nourishment, even as the child receives nourishment through its navel in its mothers bowels." And I am inclined to think, that by it we are to understand the ministers of the gospel; who, in the administration of the word and ordinances, are that to Christ's body the church, as the navel is to an human body: and, 1. As the navel is placed in the more eminent part of the belly, so are the ministers of the gospel in the highest place in the church; who, being called to the greatest work, have the greatest gifts, and largest measures of grace bestowed upon them, to furnish them for it: to whom others are exhorted to submit themselves, they being set over them "in or by the Lord." 2. As the navel they are placed in the midst of Christ's body, the church: it is in the midst of the church they do all their work, preach the gospel, and administer ordinances, in imitation of and conformity to their great Master and Prophet in Israel, Christ Jesus; who said, "In the midst of the church will I sing praise unto thee," Heb. ii. 12. 3. As the navel is the strength of the intestines; so the ministers of Christ, are not only strong themselves, in the power and grace of Christ, as they had need be, but are also strengtheners of others; one principal part of their work being to "strengthen weak hands, and confirm the feeble knees;" as our Lord said to Peter, "when thou art converted, strengthen thy brethren," Luke xxii. 32. 4. As the navel conduces much to the health of the body, so do the ministers of the gospel to the health of the church: Solomon speaking of the fear of the Lord, says, that "it shall be health to thy navel, and marrow to thy bones," where, by the navel, he means the whole body; that being in a good plight, and a healthful condition, has much influence upon the whole body to make it so. The ministers of Christ in preaching the everlasting gospel and feeding souls with the "wholesome words of our Lord Jesus Christ," are very serviceable for the increasing and maintaining the health of the church; many things in the book of Proverbs are applicable to them in

---

[r] R. Aben Ezra and Sanctius in loc.   [s] Bishop Patrick in loc.   [t] Eleochrysm. Sacr. l. 3. p 1016.   [u] So likewise do the Jews, in T. Bab. Sota. fol. 45. 1. and Sanhedrim, fol 14. 2. and fol. 37. 1. and in Shirhashirim Rabba in loc. and in Bemidbar Rabba, parash. 1.   [w] Vid R. David Kimchium in Ezek. xxxviii. 13. and. Jarchium in loc.

this case; see chap. xii. 18, and xiii. 17, and xvi. 24. 5. The navel is that part through which the child receives its nourishment in the womb; the ministers of Christ as they are instruments in begetting souls again, so they are useful in the nourishing of them, even when in embryo, as well as in feeding them with " the sincere milk of the word;" which they, as " new-born babes," are desirous of, with which they are nourished and brought up.

Moreover, the navel of the church is compared to a "round goblet, bowl, or bason." I need not observe how aptly the metaphor agrees with this part of the body, it being like a bowl or bason, both round and hollow; though the mystical writers among the Jews render it, the pit of the breast or stomach;[x] a phrase which we also use, and rather seems to answer better the description given: which, in a mystical sense, may be expressive of, 1. The perfection of gospel-ministers: the round or circular form is accounted the most perfect; these, though they are not absolutely perfect, yet may be said to be comparatively so, having a more perfect knowledge of the Gospel, and the mysteries of it, than private believers usually have; see Phil. iii. 15; for having a larger acquaintance with the scriptures of truth, they are thereby in a sense made perfect, and "thoroughly furnished unto all good work," as the apostle observes, in 2 Tim. iii. 17. 2. It may also be expressive of that workmanship which is bestowed upon them; who of themselves are not "sufficient for these things," until, by the gifts and graces of the Spirit, they are made "able ministers of the New Testament," and in some good measure qualified for the work of the ministry; and then are they like " a round goblet," turned and formed by some curious artist. 3. It may likewise serve to set forth the capacity which they are endowed withal, to hold and retain gospel-truths; they are not like colanders, which immediately let out whatever is poured into them; but like round goblets, bowls, or basons, which hold and retain whatever they receive; and this is esteemed as a necessary qualification of a Gospel-minister, by the apostle Paul, in Titus i. 9, that he be such an one as holds fast the faithful word, and does not let it slip nor go from him: but continues in the things which he has learned, knowing of whom he has learned them.

Also, it is worthy of our notice, that this navel of the church is not compared to an empty goblet, but to one that " wanteth not liquor:" by which may be meant, 1. The grace of the blessed Spirit, which is more or less in all believers; which much conduces to their healthfulness, as the moisture of the navel does to the body; it is no unusual thing in scripture for the grace of the Spirit to be compared to water, and to an abundance of it; even to rivers of living water, which are said to be in the belly of a believer, and these are never-failing ones; for grace is in them, as a " well of water springing up into everlasting life." Or, 2. The church's cleanness may be intended by this expression; who being washed in Christ's blood, and sprinkled with the clean water of the everlasting covenant, needed no other liquor to be washed with; and thus, as a navel not cut and unwashed, represents the impurity and corruption of nature, in Ezek. xvi. 4; so a navel cut and washed, as the church's is here, may be expressive of her purity and cleanness, through the blood and grace of Christ; so that she needs no other liquor to make her clean. Or rather, 3. It intends those large and never failing supplies which the ministers of the Gospel continually have from Christ; who is " ascended on high to fill all things," and particularly ministers; so that they may never want the liquor of Gospel-truths to communicate to others; for which reason he has promised to be with them unto the end of the world; as he accordingly is, and continues filling these golden pipes, as fast as they empty the golden oil of Gospel-truths out of themselves. And, 4. The Hebrew word translated *liquor*, properly signifying, a mixture, or a mixed liquor,[y] may be expressive of that variety of Gospel-grace and Gospel-truths, which they are possessed of, and distribute to others; which is a mixture, not of human inventions, and the doctrines of the Gospel together; but of wine and milk, which are joined together, in Isa. lv. 1; to which souls are invited to partake of: and which perhaps is the mingled wine, in Prov. ix. 2—5; such a mixed liquor[z] being what was drunk in those countries as appears from Cant. v. 1; and such a mixture as this, for thirsty, distressed, and fainting souls, will never be wanting in the Gospel, or with Gospel-ministers.

Likewise it may be observed, that the words may be read as a wish for a continued supply of this mixed liquor in this vessel, thus, " Let there not want liquor:"[a] and so is expressive of Christ's strong affection to his church, and tender concern, that there might be a continued supply in the ministry of the word for her nourishment; as well as implies a promise that it should be so.

II. Her *belly* is said to be as "an heap of wheat, set about with lilies;" which, as the former expression sets forth the nourishment which she has through the ministry of the word, this may be expressive of her fruitfulness thereby; it was usual with the Jews to scatter wheat on the heads of married persons, at their weddings, three times, saying, *Increase and multiply;*[b] for the allusion

---

[x] Lex. Cabal. p. 99. [y] המזג mistio, Mercerus; mixtio, Junius and Tremellius, Piscator: mixtura, Marckius, Michaelis; though Gataker interprets it of pure wine, and that the most generous, Adversar. Miscel. p. 44. [z] The Jews say, it was two parts water and one wine, Shirhashirim Rabba in loc. and Bemidbar Rabba, parash 1. as the wine of Sharon was mixed, Misn. Nidoah, c. 2. s. 7. [a] Ne deficiat illius mixtio, Jdnius; so Ainsworth. [b] Vid. Selden. Uxor. Heb. l. 2. c. 15. p. 195. and Addison's Present State of the Jews, c. 5. p. 52.

seems to be a woman with child, as one[e] well observes; she is fruitful and big, not with wind, but with wheat: by which may be meant, either, 1. The word or Gospel of the grace of God, which is comparable to wheat: "he that hath my word," saith the Lord, Jer. xxiii. 28, "let him speak my words faithfully; for what is the chaff to the wheat?" there is as much difference between a teller of dreams, and a faithful preacher of the Gospel: or between the dreams which the one tells, and the word which the other preaches, as there is between the chaff and the wheat. The Gospel may be compared to wheat for the excellency of it: wheat is the most excellent of grain; it is not only preferable to chaff, but to all other grain whatsoever: so the Gospel is preferable to all other doctrines whatever; and ought to be valued by believers more than their necessary food, seeing that those who are fed therewith, are fed with the "finest of the wheat:" and therefore may not only be compared to wheat for its excellency, but also for the nourishment it conveys. Besides, wheat is a solid, weighty, and substantial grain; as are also the doctrines of the Gospel; which are not like wind, but wheat; and is a quite different food than what Ephraim fed upon; of whom it is said, Hosea xii. 1, "Ephraim feedeth on wind." Moreover, this is an heap of wheat, which the church's belly is compared to here; such an one as is upon the corn-floor, ready threshed and winnowed, and cleared of the chaff; see Ruth iii. 7; and so may intend the purity of the Gospel, and its being clear of all human inventions and mixtures: it is wheat that is clear from, and not mixed with the chaff: for as faithful ministers will not set forth such to feed upon, so neither will enlightened and experienced souls receive it; also, this heap may be expressive of the variety and multitude of soul-comforting doctrines, and exceeding great and precious promises, with which the Gospel abounds; there are many of them, a heap of them, and fulness of the blessing in every one; they are full of spiritual blessings and consolations, especially when they come "in power and in the Holy Ghost." Or else, 2. By it may be meant the graces of the Spirit of God, with which she was filled; which may also be compared to wheat for the excellency of them, being more valuable than, and to be preferred unto, all the desirable things of nature; and to a "heap of wheat" for the variety of them, which souls receive from Christ, of whose "fulness they receive grace for grace;" that is, grace in some measure answerable to the grace in Christ, or grace in abundance; "grace for grace,"[d] that is, heaps of grace; for there cannot be one grace, but there must be every grace, even heaps of grace: as also for the purity of them, being free from all mixtures of hypocrisy: their faith is a faith unfeigned; their hope, which is fixed on Christ's person, blood, and righteousness, is of a different nature than that of the hypocrites; their love to God, Christ, his Gospel, ordinances, and people, is without dissimulation; in short, sincerity runs through all their graces; they are like a heap of wheat, winnowed and cleared of chaff: moreover, these may be compared to wheat for their permanence; they will abide the sieve of Satan's temptations, as Peter's faith did; for though it was shaken much, it did not fail, because Christ prayed for it; and they will also abide the world's fan of persecution, and likewise the awful scrutiny and discrimination, which will be made at the day of judgment; when the florid profession and external works and righteousness of others will be as chaff, which "the wind shall carry away, and vanity shall take," these will abide and appear in their greatest glory and full perfection. Though I rather think, 3. That by this heap of wheat, to which the church's belly is compared, are meant young converts:[e] who are not only born in the church, but are also brought forth by her; "for as soon as Zion travailed, she brought forth her children:" and these are the wheat which Christ will gather into his garner, when he will burn up the wicked, "the chaff, with unquenchable fire:" as wheat is the noblest of seeds, is full of meat, is solid and substantial, these are born "not of corruptible, but incorruptible seed," and being full of faith and of the Holy Ghost, and continually receiving from Christ's fulness, are solid and substantial believers; and will abide the force of persecution now, and stand the trying and discriminating time hereafter; " when the ungodly shall not be so, but shall be like the chaff which the wind driveth away; for they shall not stand in the judgment, nor sinners in the congregation of the righteous;" but even then this wheat will continue on the floor, and be gathered into Christ's barn. Moreover, this heap of wheat signifies the large number of souls that shall be born again in the church; and when those scriptures, in Isa. xlix. 19—21, and lx. 8, have had their full accomplishment, then will this description of the church be exactly answered, and appear very glorious.

Moreover, this heap of wheat is said to be "set about with lilies," or, as in the Hebrew text, hedged with lilies:[f] which would incline one to think, that not a heap of wheat upon the corn-floor, but a field of standing wheat is here intended; whose enclosure is not an hedge of thorns and briars, but of lilies: by which lilies may be meant, either the precious promises and comfort-

---

[c] Durham in loc. [d] Gratiam super gratiam, q. d. gratiam gratia cumulatam, Beza in John i. 16.
[e] The Jews in Sharhashirim Rabba in loc. and in Bemidbar Rabba, parash. 1. interpret it of the Israelites, whom for many reasons they compare to wheat, and the nations of the world to chaff; and R. Alshech, of young disciples. ‏מונה בשושנים‎ πεφραγμηνη εν κρινοις, Sept. septus liliis, Montanus, Junius, Mercerus, Cocceius, Marckius and alii; vallatus liliis, Vulgate Latin version; circumseptus liliis, Tigurine version.

able doctrines which abound in, and encompass around the word of God, or else, the sweet odour which the graces of the Spirit emit on every side, or rather, "the beauties of holiness," in which men appear as soon as they are born again; and may be expressive of their secrecy and security, as well as of their beauty and glory.

There is one thing more which I would not omit the mention of, and that is, that some interpreters ᵍ think, that by these two parts, the navel and belly, here described, are meant the two ordinances of baptism and the Lord's supper; by the former, the ordinance of baptism, which is the first ordinance administered to believers; and which none but those who are born again, receive any comfort, nourishment, or benefit from: and by the latter, the Lord's supper; which like a heap of wheat, affords solid and substantial food to believers; where Christ, who is the Bread of Life, whose flesh and blood are meat and drink indeed, is set forth to them; who are kindly invited, and are heartily welcome to his table; which table of his is graced and adorned, or at least should be, not with the weeds, or thorns and briers of scandalous and profane sinners, who eat and drink unworthily; but with the lilies of precious saints and true believers, who sit as oliveplants, or rather are set as lilies about it. Though I should rather think, that these are intended in the following verse.

Verse 3. *Thy two breasts* are *like two young roes, that are twins.*

THE breasts are the fifth part, which is here commended by Christ; what is intended by them, has been shown in chap. iv. 5, where we have met with the same commendation, and that in the same words; only here is an omission of a clause which is added there, namely, "which feed among the lilies." The Targum here again makes mention of the two Messiahs, whom the Jews vainly expect: R. Aben Ezra expounds those words of their two laws, oral and written, as he had done in the chapter and place abovementioned: as R. Solomon Jarchi does also of the two tables of the law; though he likewise produces another sense of the words, which is, that by the two breasts are meant the King and the High-priest, but for the understanding of the words, the reader is referred to chap. iv. 5, where they are more largely insisted on.

Verse 4. *Thy neck* is *as a tower of ivory: thine eyes* like *the fish-pools in Heshbon, by the gate of Bathrabbim: thy nose* is *as the tower of Lebanon, which looketh toward Damascus.*

CHRIST continues his commendation of the church's beauty; and adds, in these words, three other instances of it to the five former, mentioned in the preceding verses. And,

I. He compares her neck to a "tower of ivory."
II. "Her eyes to the fishpools in Heshbon, by the gate of Bathrabbim."
III. "Her nose to the tower of Lebanon, which looketh toward Damascus."

I. He compares her neck to a a tower of ivory. Two things recommend the neck, erectness and whiteness; both are here expressed, the one by a tower, the other by ivory; hence a fine beautiful neck is called an ivory one;ʰ and for the same reason it sometimes has the epithet of snowy,ⁱ and sometimes of milky,ᵏ and sometimes of marble.ˡ R. Aben Ezra, by the neck, understands the King Messiah; but he is not the neck, but the Head of the church; R. Solomon Jarchi interprets it of of the temple and altar, or of the *lishcat gazit*, or paved chamber, in which the Sanhedrim sat. The Targum would have *ab beth din*, *the father of the house of judgment*, or chief of the Sanhedrim, intended but it seems better by it to understand, either,

1st. The ministers of the gospel, who hold unto, bear up, and exalt Christ, the Head; and are instruments in bringing souls near unto him, and of conveying spiritual food to the several members of his body, the church: who are likewise beautifully adorned with the gifts and graces of the Spirit, whereby they are fitted for the work they are called unto: these may also be said to be like towers for their strength and impregnableness; they are set for the defence of the gospel, and are as immoveable as towers; they stand the battery of Satan's rage and malice, and abide the force of the world's persecutions and reproaches; and none of these things move them to desert the work they are employed in. Moreover, this neck of the church is compared to a tower of ivory; whether there was a tower built of ivory, or that was so called, we have no account in scripture; the Targum, on this place, speaks of an ivory tower, which king Solomon made, but the scripture is entirely silent about it; unless by it we understand that great throne of ivory, which is mentioned in 2 Kings x. 18, and which may as well be called a tower, as the pulpit on which Ezra and others stood, is, in the Hebrew text, in Neh. viii. 4. Now the church's neck may be said to be a tower of ivory, 1. To express the purity of gospel ministers, both in doctrine and life; who at once answer that character, of holding the mystery of the faith in a pure conscience; and so become examples to others, both in faith and purity. 2. These may be said to be as towers of ivory for their strength, which they receive from Christ, to hold fast the doctrine of faith, to confirm and establish others in it, and to withstand

---

ᵍ Vid. Cotton and Bishop Patrick in loc.
ʰ Ελεφαντινος τραχηλος, Anacreon. Eburnea cervix, Ovid. Epist. 20, v. 57. eburnea colla. Ib. Metamorph. l. 3. fab. 6. v. 422. and l. 4. fab. 5. v. 335.   ⁱ Nivea cervice, Ovid. Amor. 1. 2. eleg. 4. v. 41.
ᵏ Lactea colla, Virg. Æneid. l. 8. v. 661.
ˡ Marmoreo collo, Ovid. Fasti, l. 4. v. 135. marmorea cervice, Virgil. Georgic. 4. prope finem.

the force and power of Satan's temptations. 8. They may be compared hereunto, for the smoothness and evenness of those doctrines which they preach; by which I mean, not those smooth things, which carnal persons would have prophesied to them, such as are tickling to the carnal ear, taking to the carnal fancy, and suited to the carnal hearts of unconverted ones; but such as are agreeable to the word of God, consistent with themselves, being all of a piece, and not yea and nay, as well as suited to the experiences of God's children. Or else,

2ndly. By the church's neck may be meant, the scriptures of truth; which lead and direct souls to Christ, the Head; and are the means of conveying spiritual breath, life, and food to God's children; and are beautifully hung and adorned with soul-refreshing doctrines, and comfortable promises. Now this neck may be said to be as a tower which is very high: seeing that it contains things which are sublime, and out of the reach of carnal sense and reason; and is also as impregnable and immoveable as a tower; for though Satan and his emissaries have attempted to remove the scriptures out of the world; yet their efforts have hitherto, and ever will be in vain: and these may likewise be very well compared to a tower of ivory, for the purity and glory of them; for, " the words of the Lord are pure words; as silver tried in a furnace of earth, purified seven times, Psalm xii. 6. Or else, 3rdly. By the church's neck may be meant, the grace of faith, which lays hold upon and keeps close to Christ, the Head; it is that grace which exalts and glorifies him, and by which saints live upon him, and receive grace, strength, and nourishment from him; and is never without the other graces of the Spirit, and the becoming fruits of righteousness, which serve to adorn it; This may be compared to a tower of ivory, 1. For the strength of it; which appears both in believing the promises of God, which sometimes seem to be attended with difficulties insuperable to sense and reason, and in resisting and withstanding Satan's temptations; this fort and tower of faith Satan could never take and demolish; it has stood and will stand against all the posse that he is able to collect together against it; because Christ, who is the Author, will be the Finisher of of it; and continually prays that it fail not. 2. For the purity, beauty, and glory of it; as the church's neck being compared to a tower, is expressive of its strength; so its being compared to ivory, shows its beauty and fairness: faith, that is pure and unfeigned, is a beautiful grace in the eyes of Christ; he is sometimes ravished with this neck of the church, and with one chain thereof; see chap. iv. 9. 3. For the preciousness of it; as ivory is very precious and valuable, so is this grace of faith; it is called precious faith, in 2 Peter i. 1; and so it is in its nature, object, and actings; it is more precious than ivory, yea, than gold; hence the trial of it is said to be " much more precious than that of gold that perisheth," 1 Pet. i. 7.

II. The eyes of the church are here compared to fish-pools in Heshbon, by the gate of Bathrabbim: in this comparison the allusion may be to the humours in the eye, one of which is called *aquea*; which are enclosed as water in a fishpool, and in which the eye seems to swim; hence the eyes are called by Virgil[m] *natantia lumina*; and the same word in Hebrew, signifies both a fountain and the eye; and fishpools, in the plural number, are properly observed, because there are two eyes. Some think that Heshbon is not to be taken here as the proper name of a place, but to be read in construction with fishpools thus, " thine eyes are like to fishpools, artificially made;" that are curiously formed, and according to art; such as were about the sheep-gate, which is here called *the gate of Bathrabbim*, because it was much frequented, and through it abundance of people passed to and fro: but it seems most agreeable to understand it of the city of Heshbon, which was the seat of Sihon king of the Amorites, as appears from Numb. xxi. 26, and Bathrabbim was one of the gates of this city; which was so called, either because it led to Rabbath, a city near unto it, and therefore are mentioned together, in Jer. xlix. 3, which, as is manifest from 2 Sam. xii. 27, was a city of waters; or else, because of the vast multitudes of people which went in and out thereat; for it may be rendered " the gate of the daughter of many, or of great ones." Near this gate, it seems, were some very excellent and delightful fishpools, to which the eyes of the church are here compared; and by which may be meant, either,

1st. The ministers of the gospel;[p] who are to the church, as eyes are to the body; for which see chap. i. 15, and these may be compared to fishpools, 1. For their clearness of sight into gospel-truths: it is true, in comparison of that light and knowledge which saints have in glory, they now " see but through a glass darkly;" but yet, with respect to the legal dispensation, in which there was much darkness and obscurity, they may be said to " behold with open face the glory of the Lord;" and their light will still be considerably increased, when the " watchman shall see eye to eye;" and that will be, " when the Lord shall bring again Zion." 2. Like fishpools full of

---

[m] Æneid. 1. 5. so Ovid. Fasti. 1. 6. animique oculique natabant. [n] עיניך כברכות בחשבון oculi tui piscinis artificiosissimis, Junius, Piscator. In Bemidba Rabba, parash. 14. the words are paraphrased thus; " Thine eyes are like fishpools, which are finished with consultation and thought." [p] The Targum by them understands the scribes: Jarchi, the wise men, or such who delight in sublime wisdom: so in Zohar, in Numb. fol. 89. 2. Aben Ezra, the prophets: in Shirhashirim Rabba in loc. and in Bemidbar Rabba, parash 14. they are interpreted of the Sanhedrin, and elders of the congregation; and so in Yelammedenu and Siphri in Yalkut in loc.

water, they are filled with "the fulness of the blessing of the gospel of Christ;" the means of grace, the ordinances of the gospel, and particularly the ministry of the word, are in scripture compared to waters; see Isa. lv. 1, where souls are kindly invited, and where they often meet with that which is as refreshing as cold water to a thirsty man; and of this Christ's ministers are full, being filled by him, who "fills all things;" they are not like those, in 2 Peter ii. 17, who are said to be "wells without water," but are like "the fishpools in Heshbon," clear and full. 3. They may be compared to those fishpools which were "by the gate of Bathrabbim," because of the multitude of people which flock to, and attend upon their ministry, and which receive benefit more or less thereby; and then more especially will they answer this metaphor, when that prophecy, in Isa. ii. 2, 3, shall have its full accomplishment. 4. The word which is here translated fishpools, comes from a word which signifies to bless, because pools of water were esteemed blessings; see Judges i. 15, and so are ministers of the gospel to the churches of Christ; they are promised by God as such, Jer. iii. 15, and he sometimes threatens to remove them as such from his churches, when they are grown carnal, lukewarm, and indifferent, and do not prize and use such mercies and blessings as they should; see Rev. ii. 5. Lord's days, ordinances, and opportunities of hearing the gospel preached, are the only blessings and comforts of life that some enjoy; God gives them "the bread of adversity, and the water of affliction;" this they are sure to have, with this they are fed all the week long; but on Lord's-days, they have sweet and comfortable meals for their souls; and this great blessing God favours them with, though he denies them many temporal ones, which is, that their teachers are not removed into corners, but their eyes behold their teachers; they have Christ's fishpools to come unto. 5. They are like fishpools, whose waters are still, quiet, invariable, and constant; and are not like troubled waters, such as false teachers are, who are continually casting up the mire and dirt of their own inventions, and the "divers and strange doctrines" of men; but these abound with those truths, which, like Christ, the Author of them, are "the same yesterday, to-day, and for ever." Or else,

2ndly. By these eyes of the church, may be meant "the eyes of her understanding," which are enlightened by the Spirit of God, particularly those of faith and knowledge; which may be said to be as fishpools, 1. For their perspicuity: faith can behold things clearly, which are invisible to, and are out of the reach of carnal sense and reason, and therefore is called "the evidence of things not seen;" it can look "within the veil," and view an unseen Christ, with all the invisible realities of another world. 2. For their steadiness and unmoveableness: the eye of faith is fixed, not upon the duties, services, and performances of the creature; but upon the person, blood, and righteousness of Christ; it looks off of all things else alone to him. 3. For their abounding with the tears of gospel-repentance; Jeremy wished that his "head were waters," and his "eyes a fountain of tears;" the believers eyes are so; for repentance is a tear that drops from faith's eye: souls first look, and then they mourn; nor do they ever more so, nor in a better manner, than when they can view their righteousness, peace, and pardon in a bleeding Saviour; it is under a sense of this, they both mourn, most and best, both for their own sins, and the sins of others; their eyes are as fishpools, abounding with these waters; "rivers of water run down their eyes, because they keep not God's law," Psalm cxix. 136. 4. For the modesty of them; these are not rolling waters, to which wanton and immodest eyes may be compared; but quiet, still, and standing ones: faith is a very modest grace; and he that is possessed of it, and has the greatest measure thereof, is the most humble soul; it exalts Christ, magnifies his grace, and gives all the glory to him; it abases the creature, takes away all boasting from him, and ascribes nothing to him; for which reason the church's eyes are also said to be as "dove's eyes within her locks." 5. For their proportionable size, exact symmetry, and delightful beauty: perhaps the allusion may be to fishpools;" which, being discerned at some distance, between trees or groves, look very sparkling and dazzling; and so did the church's eyes to Christ; with which he seems to be ravished, as he says he was, in chap. iv. 9, and vi. 5.

III. Her nose is said to be "as the tower of Lebanon, which looketh toward Damascus." Very properly is the nose mentioned next to the eyes; since as Cicero[s] says, "it is so placed, as that it seems to be as a wall between the eyes; and here it is compared to a tower, not for the largeness of it, which is not reckoned comely, but for its position and use; though it may be rendered, "thy face;"[t] and may denote her aspect bold and courageous. This tower of Lebanon seems to be one that was built in or near the forest of Lebanon; and was a frontier tower for that part of the country which lay towards Damascus; it was a tower on that part of mount Lebanon which fronted Damascus, that lay in a valley; and so open to view, as well as exposed to winds, hence called by Lucan[u] *ventosa Damascus*; which tower was so high, as Adrichomius[w] says, that from thence might be seen and numbered the houses in Damascus: Vitringa[x] observes, that many travellers relate that, on the extreme part of this mountain, in a craggy place, to which

---

[r] Vid. Sanct. in loc. [s] De natura Deorum. l. 2. c. 57. [t] תני פניך tua facies, Pagninus: frons, Clarius: so Jarchi. [u] Pharsal. l. 3. v. 215. [w] Theatrum Terræ Sanctæ, p. 109. so Jarchi in loc. from the Midrash. [x] Comment. in Jes. 37. 24.

the plain of Damascus is subject, is a small building; which though it is of an Arabic original, as is said, yet he thinks it is the place where a tower formerly was, looking to Damascus, to which Solomon here alludes. To this the church's nose is compared: by which may be meant, 1. either, The ministers of Christ, as before; for it need not be thought strange, that one and the same thing should be expressed by different metaphors for different reasons, especially this: seeing there are different parts and branches of the work and office of ministers; who are not only eyes to see, but as the nose to smell; having a spiritual discerning into gospel-truths beyond others, they not only savour them themselves, but diffuse the savour of them to others, and are themselves to many "the savour of life unto life:" they are, in some measure, both the ornament and the defence of the church; the former is intended by their being compared to the nose, which is the ornament of the face, as well as the seat of smelling; and the latter, by "the tower of Lebanon;" and this as "looking towards Damascus," the inhabitants of which were always enemies to the people of Israel: and so it denotes the courage and vigilance of faithful ministers; who continually have their eye upon the church's enemies, watch all their motions, observe all their steps, and, with a manful courage, face and attack them. Or, 2. By this part thus described, may be intended in general, the stateliness and majesty, courage and maganimity of the church; her stateliness and majesty by her nose, which, when of a good size and well-proportioned, adds much grace and majesty to the countenance; her magnanimity and courage, by its being compared to the invincible and impregnable tower of Lebanon, which looks towards Damascus; intimating, that she was not afraid to look her worst enemies in the face; and so answers the character which is given of her, both by Christ and by the daughters, in chap. vi. 4, 10, which is, that she was "terrible as an army with banners." Or else. 3. It is expressive of her prudence and discretion in spiritual things, which she is capable of discerning from carnal; she can distinguish truth from error, and can espy dangers afar off, and so guard against them; for which her nose may be compared to this tower which was thus situated.

Verse 5. Former part. *Thine head upon thee is like Carmel, and the hair of thine head like purple.*

These words contain the two last, which are the ninth and tenth instances of the church's beauty.

I. Her head upon her is said to be like Carmel.

II. The hair of her head like purple.

I. Her head is compared to Carmel. And it will be proper to inquire, First. What is the church's head. Secondly. Why it is thus compared.

First. I shall inquire what the church's head is; which is not the civil magistrate; he may indeed be a member of the church, but not the head of it. The princes and great men of the world may be of much service to the church; as in the latter day, kings shall be her nursing fathers, and queens her nursing mothers; but then they shall be so far from being her head, that they shall bow down unto her, and lick up the dust of her feet. The Targum indeed understands it of the king who is set over the people.

Some[y] think, that by the head, is meant the soul or mind; which is indeed the chief part in man; and being filled with the graces of the Spirit, and the precious fruits of righteousness, may much resemble the top of Carmel, covered with pleasant plants and fruitful trees: but it seems better to understand it of Christ, who only is the Head of the church; she is compared to a body, because consisting of various members, of which body he is the Head; see Col. i. 18; "and he is the Head of the body, the church." Christ is,

1st. A representative Head of his church; as such he acted in the everlasting covenant of grace; where what he did he did in her name, and what he received he received for her; hence the elect are said to be blessed with all spiritual blessings, and grace is said to be given to them in him before the foundation of the world: thus also he acted as their representative, when he was crucified, buried, rose again, and entered into heaven; they were then crucified, buried, and raised, and are now made to sit together in heavenly places in him.

2ndly. He is a political head; in the same sense as a king is the head of his people, Christ is the Head of his church: and this regards his kingly office, as the other did his surety-ship engagements: Christ is given to be "an Head over all things to the church;" and he is Head over the church, thine Head, עליך, which is over thee and above thee; and which may be understood in the same sense, and may be interpreted by his Father's setting him as King over his holy hill of Zion: which office he executes, by enacting laws for the good of his people, which are written not upon tables of stone, but upon "the fleshly tables of the heart:" by subduing their enemies, protecting their persons, and supplying them with all necessaries as a Head and common parent to them.

3rdly. He is an economical head. He is a Head to his church, in the same sense as a husband is to his wife, Eph. v. 23, she being espoused and married to him, ought to be subject to him, as her head; and in the same sense as a father is to his children. Christ is the everlasting Father; saints are his children, which God

---

[y] Alcuin and Sanctius in loc.

has given him, and are born unto him in his church; and him they ought to honour, as their Head. Also he is so in the same sense as a master is to his servants; and it is under this consideration that Christ becomes the head of angels, who are servants in his family: he is not indeed the Redeemer of angels, because they never were in a state of slavery and captivity; nor is he the Mediator of them, they having never been at variance with God, nor rebelled against him; but yet he is the head of them, according to Col. ii. 10, " which is the head of all principality and power."

4thly. He is a natural head; even as an human head is to a human body; and it is in allusion to this that he is often called the head; of which many things may be said: as, 1. That he is a true and proper Head; and that which is so, must, (1.) Be of the same nature with the body; so is Christ; he has partaken of the same flesh and blood, and has been in all things made like unto his church, sin excepted; hence arise that strong affection to her, sympathy with her, and care of her. (2.) It must be united to it; a head separate from the body, cannot be a proper head, nor do the service of one to the body: there is a spiritual and indissoluble union between Christ and his church; which is represented by that conjugal union there is between a man and his wife, by which they become one flesh; and also by that natural one, of the vine and branches; but nothing does more express it to the life, than that of head and members; for " we are members of his body, of his flesh, and of his bones." (3.) It must be superior to the body, as well as of the same nature with it, and united to it: so is Christ: and that not only in his highest nature, as he is God, and in his office, grace, and power: but even in our nature, being " crowned with honour and glory," and set at his Father's right hand in it, " far above all principality and power." (4.) It must be a living head, and endued with the same vital spirit as the body is: such an one is Christ: he and his church live one and the same life: he is the believer's life: he lives, but it is Christ that lives in him: one and the same vital Spirit actuates both head and members, and that is the Spirit of God, which is in Christ the head, without measure, but in his members in measure; " for he that is joined to the Lord, is one spirit." 2. Christ is a perfect Head; there is no deficiency in him, nor any thing wanting that may render him a suitable one to his church. (1.) Here are no parts nor sense wanting; he has eyes to see with, which are continually fixed upon his people; he sees their persons and their circumstances, and accordingly relieves them; his ears are open to their cries, which are not disregarded by him; and he has a tongue to speak a word in season, both to them and for them; he smells a sweet savour in the persons, garments, and graces of his people, and has tasted death for them all. (2.) Here are no vicious humours which fall from hence to infect the body: Adam was a federal head to all his seed; but nothing is derived from him but sin, corruption, and death, and such vicious humours, which have infected all human nature; but from Christ is nothing derived, but holiness, grace, and life; for he himself is " holy, harmless, and undefiled." (3.) Here is no deformity at all; but every part is in its proper place and just proportion; there is a surpassing beauty in all: " he is fairer than the children of men;" there is none to be compared to him; " he is white and ruddy, the chiefest among ten thousand." (4.) Here is a fulness of every thing to supply his body with; " he is full of grace and truth:" there is a fulness of justifying and sanctifying grace in him; all our righteousness, holiness, grace, strength, life, and nourishment, come from Christ, our Head; " it is in him we live, and move, and have our being." and he has a sufficiency of all grace to supply his members with. 3. Christ is the only Head of his church; there is no other; if the church had more heads than one, she would be a monster. The civil magistrate is no head of the church; neither is the pope of Rome; Christ only is. As there is but one body, though consisting of various members; and one spirit, which actuates them all; and one faith, by which they hold to the Head; and one baptism, in which they make a profession of him; and one God and Father of us all, who, by adopting grace, has made and owned them for his children; so there is but one Lord and Head unto them, " who is over all, God blessed for ever." 4. He is an everlasting Head. The church never was, nor never will be without an Head; she has a living one, and one that lives for ever; and this is matter of joy and consolation to God's people: hence they need not fear a supply of all grace, life, and strength; for, because he lives as their Head, they, his members, shall live also. But,

Secondly. I shall now consider why Christ, who is the church's Head, is compared to Carmel; that is, mount Carmel, as the Arabic version expressly renders it. And, 1. This was a mountain in the land of Judea, where Elijah contended with and slew the prophets of Baal; and which the Targum on this text takes notice of: and for the height of it, Christ, the church's Head, may be compared unto it; " who is higher than the kings of the earth," " nay, than the angels in heaven: for he " is set far above all principality and power;" nay, " He is higher than the heavens themselves." 2. This was a very fruitful mountain, whose top was covered with vines, cornfields, and fruitful trees; see Isa. xxxv. 2, and Amos i. 2. The word is sometimes used for green ears of corn, as in Lev. ii. 14, and xxiii. 14, and is sometimes rendered, by our translators, a fruitful field, as in Isa. xxxii. 15. A bushy, well-set head of hair, which may be here referred to, since hair is mentioned in the next clause, may be fitly compared to a mountain or to a field, covered with trees and grass, as such to a head of hair,[a] and this may be expressive of Christ, the church's Head, on whom her hair grows; and who is her green fir-tree, from whom all her fruit is found. 3. The word is by some[a] rendered crimson; and the rather, it may seem to be so taken here, because purple is made use of in the next description; and which go together, and are thus rendered, in 2 Chron. ii. 7, and iii. 14. And this may serve to set forth, (1.) The royal dignity and majesty of Christ; this being a colour usually worn by the kings and great men of the earth; one of Christ's titles, is " the Prince of the kings of the earth," Rev. i. 5. (2.) His ardent love to his church; whose flaming affection to her may be very well represented by this colour. Or, (3.) His passion and bloody suffering for his church and people; by which their sins, though like scarlet, become as snow; and though red like crimson, are as wool: so that here is a crimson Saviour for crimson sinners. Thus may Christ, the church's Head, be compared to Carmel.

Though some think, that not the head, but some covering of the head, is intended here: R. Solomon Jarchi thinks, that the *tephillin* or phylacteries, which the Jews wore about their heads, are here meant; but this is not probable: rather, with others,[b] the allusion is to the nuptial crown or garland, made of flowers, &c., which was worn by the bride on the marriage-day: and this may denote the graces of the blessed Spirit, which are "an ornament of grace to the head, and chains about the neck;" which may very well be thought to resemble the fruitful top of mount Carmel: and as one[c] well observes, by this covering of the head more particularly may be meant, the grace of hope, which is the believer's head piece, 1 Thess. v. 8; as Christ who is our Head is called our hope; so our hope which is our head-piece by a figure which is not unusual, may be called the head; it is supported and sustained by faith, which is the neck; and has its life and liveliness from the death, sufferings, and resurrection to Christ; and therefore may be compared to crimson.

II. The *hair* of her head is said to be like *purple*: purple coloured hair was in great esteem; of this colour was the hair of king Nysus, according to the fable;[d] and so the hair of Evadne and of the muses were of a violet colour;[e] the hair of Ulysses is said to be like to the hyacinth flower,[f] which is of a purple or violet colour; and Milton[g] calls the first Adam's hair, hyacinthine locks; and here in a figurative sense, the second Adam's hair is said to be like purple. By which may be meant either the thoughts of her heart, which are many and numerous, and which proceed from thence, as the hair does from the head; and when these are fixed upon, and are employed in the contemplation of a crucified Christ, then may they be said to be like purple; and then are they taken notice of by Christ and are exceeding delightful to him. Though I rather think, that believers are here meant, as I have observed on chap. iv. 1, and v. 11; who grow on Christ, the Head, and receive their strength and nourishment from him; and these may be said to be like purple. 1. Because of that royal and princely dignity they are advanced to by Christ; who has made them "kings and priests to God and his Father;" for this is a colour that is usually worn by great personages,[h] such as all believers are. 2. Because of their being washed in Christ's purple blood; for so are both their persons and their garments: they are tinctured with it, and are of this die. 3. Because of the sufferings which they undergo for the sake of Christ and his Gospel; and especially such dear and precious servants of Christ may be said to be as purple, who have spilled their blood, and laid down their lives on his account.

Though some[i] think, that not the hair, but either the hair-lace, or the pins, or some such small things, by which the hair is tied and dressed up in a beautiful order, are intended; and indeed the word is never used elsewhere for hair, and it properly signifies something small, thin, and tender: and this may teach us what notice Christ takes of the meanest grace and performance of believers; every little thing that is in, or is done by a believer, looks very beautiful in Christ's eye; so far is he from despising the day of small things.

Verse 5. Latter part—*The king is held in the galleries.*

Verse 6. *How fair and how pleasant art thou, O love, for delights?*

CHRIST, having given a description of the church's beauty, in ten particular instances of it, does here,

I. In the latter part of the fifth verse, discover his great love and affection to her, though in a very abrupt manner; "the king is held in the galleries."

II. Gives a general and comprehensive summary of her whole beauty, in verse 6, thus: "How fair and how pleasant art thou, O love, for delights." And,

---

[a] So of hair, it is said, Humeros ut lucus obumbrat, Ovid. Metamorph. l. 13. fab. 8. Comanti humo, Statii Thebaid. l. 5. v. 502. comata sylva, Catullus, 4. 11. arboreas comas, Ovid. Amor. l. 2. eleg. 16. v. 36.
[a] Velut coccinum, Pagninus, Vatablus, Mercerus: simile est coccineo. Junius and Tremellius: est ut coccus, Piscator, so Ainsworth: sicut carmesinum. Schindler, so R. Aben Ezra in loc. and R. David Kimchi, in lib. Shorash. in voce כרמל.
[b] Sanctius and Bishop Patrick in loc.
[c] Dur-ham in loc.
[d] Ovid Metamorph. l. 8. fab. l. v. 301. De Arte Amandi. l. 1. and de Remed. Amor. l. 1. v. 68. Hygin. Fab. 198. Pausia. Attica, p. 33.
[e] Pindar. Olymp. ode 6. and Pythan. ode l. v. 2.
[f] Homer. Odyss. 6. v. 231. and 23. v. 158.
[g] Paradise Lost. book 4.
[h] Paludamentum erat insigne pallium imperatorum, cocco purpuraque et auro distinctum, Isidor. Origin. l. 19. c. 24.
[i] Durham and Bishop Patrick in loc.

I. I shall consider this abrupt expression, "the king is held in the galleries;" which seems to have no dependence upon or connection with, either the preceding or subsequent words, but only with the affections of Christ's heart; who, being as it were, surprised and astonished at, captivated and ravished with the church's beauty, breaks out in these words, even before he had well finished the account he was giving. And it may be here inquired, 1st. Who is meant by the king? 2ndly. What those galleries are in which he is said to be held? And, 3rdly. What by being held in them?

1st. By the king, we are to understand the Messiah, the Lord Jesus Christ; who is the Governor of the whole universe, has a sovereign dominion over all creatures, is the Prince of the kings of the earth; who sets up and pulls down at pleasure, and exercises an uncontrollable power over all created beings; and who is in an especial manner the King of saints; who are committed to him as Mediator by his Father, to rule and govern; whom he has purchased by his own blood, and conquered by the mighty power of his grace; in whose hearts he reigns, by putting his Spirit, implanting his grace, and writing his laws there; whom he continually protects, subdues their enemies, and supplies with all things necessary; this kingdom of his is not of this world; it is not supported by worldly power; nor carried on with worldly interest; nor does it appear in worldly pomp and splendour: but is of an invisible and spiritual nature; it is managed according to the strictest rules of justice and equity, and is upon such a foundation as will last for ever.

2ndly. By the galleries in which this great king is held, we are to understand the ordinances of the gospel; the same word, which is here rendered galleries, is, in chap. i. 17, translated *rafters*; which are of much use for the strength and support of buildings, as the ordinances are for the strengthening of weak hands, and confirming of feeble knees; the word is also, by some, here rendered *canals*,[k] as it is *gutters*, in Gen. xxx. 38, 41, and *troughs* to water cattle in, Exod. ii. 16, which also is applicable to the ordinances of the gospel; through which, as through so many canals, conduit-pipes, or gutters, is conveyed to souls the grace of the Spirit, which is in scripture frequently compared to water; but we render the word *galleries*; as does R. David Kimchi,[l] and after him Junius and Tremellius. In the eastern countries, galleries ran along by the sides of great houses, and were a common passage to the rooms in them;[m] and which will well suit with the ordinances, which are those galleries where Christ and believers walk and converse together; where he discovers the secrets of his love, and leads them into a farther acquaintance with his covenant grace: from whence they have delightful views of his precious person; who having been some time absent from them, they now from hence behold him coming towards them, "leaping upon the mountains, and skipping upon the hills;" here they are oftentimes indulged with Pisgah views: and not only see the King in his beauty, but also behold the good land which is very far off. But,

3rdly. I shall next consider what is meant by this great person's being held there. The word signifies a being *bound*, as a prisoner, with chains and fetters: R. Aben Ezra and Alshech acknowledge, that the Messiah is here intended; and tell us, that it was the opinion of their ancient Rabbins, that he was born the day that Jerusalem was destroyed; and if you ask the modern Jews, why then they are so unbelieving concerning him? they will tell you, that though he was then born, he is not yet revealed; and if you ask where he now is, some of them will tell you, that he is in paradise, where he lies tied and bound with the locks of womens' hair, which are like to the frizzles and curling of water in canals; to support which whim of theirs, they torture this text of ours, and read it thus; "the hair of thine head is like purple, with which the king is tied or bound in the walks" or canals;[n] that is, in paradise. But though the King Messiah is here represented as one bound as a prisoner, yet not in this ridiculous sense: but his being held or bound in the galleries or ordinances of his house, shows, 1. How much his heart was ravished and captivated with the beauty of his church! it struck him with so much wonder, and filled him with so much pleasure, that he was like one bound in chains, and could not stir hand nor foot; had no power to move along, nor could he take his eye off her; but stood and gazed upon her, as one surprised and astonished at her. Or, 2. It is expressive of Christ's fixed habitation in his house and ordinances; for though believers do not always perceive him, yet he always is there; he has promised so to be, and he is as good as his word; nay, he takes delight and pleasure in being there, and that, as much as any man can, to be in his own house, and to walk in the galleries of it; "This is my rest for ever," says he, Psalm cxxxii. 14, "here will I dwell, for I have desired it;" he is, as it were, tied and fastened to its rafters, and bound in its galleries. Or, 3. It may be meant of any earthly king or prince whatever: and then the sense is as Junius gives it—There is no king so great and glorious, if he should behold thy beauty and glory, but would stand amazed at it: and would be held with a perpetual desire of seeing it; esteeming it far above his own or the glory of the whole world; and indeed, the earthly glory and grandeur of the greatest prince and monarch in the universe, is far inferior to that of Christ's church; if Solomon, in all his glory, was not

---

[k] So Montanus, Brightman, Cocceius, Mercerus, Tigurine and Vulgate Latin versions: and so the Jews understand it in Shirhashirim Rabba in loc. and in Vajikra Rabba, parash. 31. and the Targum and Aben Ezra in loc. [l] In lib. Shorash. rad. רהט. [m] See Shaws Travels, p. 273. [n] Vid. Buxtorf. Synag. Jud. c. 50.

arrayed like one of the lilies of the field, much less is any king or prince to be compared with Christ's lily, the church; but, though this sense serves much to set off the church's glory, and beauty: yet I rather choose the other, which best expresses the affection of Christ, and the astonishing beauty of his church.

II. In verse 6 Christ gives a general and comprehensive summary of his church's beauty; and at the same time expresses the strongest affection for her, saying, "How fair and how pleasant art thou, O love, for delights." Where may be observed,

1st. The title he gives her, "O love." The church is Christ's love, both objectively and subjectively; she is the object of his love, whom he loved from all eternity; loves in time without any change or variation, and will love to all eternity, without the least interruption; she is also one who dearly loves Christ, in whose heart that grace dwells and reigns; which she discovers by her regard to his person, value for his ordinances, and respect to his commands: of this title, see more on chap. i. 9; though indeed a different word is here made use of, and that more full and expressive, both of Christ's love to her, and hers to Christ, than is there; she is called love in the abstract; as being all over love, love itself, nothing else but love; and altogether lovely in his esteem.

2ndly. The commendations that are given of her, are, 1. That she is fair; and so she is, not in herself, but in Christ; not in her own nature and righteousness, which are unclean, but in his own person and righteousness, which are without spot and blemish; not as she is now considered in this imperfect state, but as she shall be hereafter, when she shall be presented "a glorious church, without spot or wrinkle, or any such thing;" though now, in Christ's eye, she is all fair, and there is no spot in her; but this commendation we have frequently met with. 2. She is also said to be pleasant: which epithet is by her given to Christ, in chap. i. 16, which he here returns to her; it being usual in this song for these two excellent lovers so to do. The church now was pleasant to Christ, and that for delights; he having loved her, not only with a love of benevolence, but with a love of complacency and delight, and that before the foundation of the world, as appears from Prov. viii. 31. The church, I say, is pleasant to him, as she is his spouse and bride; for though she is as the loving hind, and pleasant roe unto him; and as she is the portion and inheritance, of which he says, "the lines are fallen to me in pleasant places;" and also as she is his friend and intimate acquaintance, she is pleasant to him, as Jonathan was to David. Moreover, she is so as she is clothed with his righteousness and adorned with the graces of his Spirit; her countenance is comely; her voice, both in prayer and praise, is sweet; her faith and love are ravishing, and her company delightful: in short he takes abundance of satisfaction and pleasure in her: she was all delight° to him; her countenance, voice, actions, and gesture. And therefore,

3rdly. Expresses it after the manner he does, "How fair and how pleasant art thou!" that is, thou art incomparably and inexpressibly so; none can tell how fair thou art in my eye, and how pleasant and delightful thou art unto me; it is beyond all human thought and expression. What astonishing love and grace now appears in all this, that one so great and glorious, as this royal person is, should be so much in love with, and take so much delight and pleasure in such poor, vile, and sinful creatures, as we are!

Verse 7. *This thy stature is like to a palm-tree, and thy breasts to clusters of grapes.*

CHRIST, having gone through the ten particular instances of his church's beauty, in the five first verses of this chapter, and given a comprehensive summary of the whole in ver. 6; one would have thought he had done; but as not satisfied with the commendations he had given, and as not knowing when nor how to give over, the subject being so delightful to him, begins anew in these words; where he,

I. In general commends her stature, by comparing it "to a palm-tree."

II. Her breasts in particular, which are likened to "clusters of grapes."

I. He compares her stature to a "palm-tree." Her stature is what arises from and is made up of the abovesaid parts, which he had commended, as is manifest from the relative *this*; which being all set in their proper place, and in a just proportion, as the members of the church are by God, see Cor. xii. 12—18, look very beautiful and comely: the word properly signifies height, tallness, and straightness: to be of a tall stature, was accounted very honourable, and an indication of majesty; such an one was fit to be chosen a king, as Saul was, who "was higher than any of the people, from his shoulders and upwards;" and when Samuel came to anoint one of the sons of Jesse, as king in his stead, the first-born, Eliab, was presented to him; who, when he saw his comely countenance, and the height of his stature, judged him to be the Lord's anointed; but the Lord bid him not look on these things, nor judge according to them as man does, for he was not the person he had his eye upon. As the tallness of men is expressed by the palm-tree; thus Moses is said to be admired by the Ethiopians for his beautiful stature, like the palm-tree;ᵖ so the simile of a tree, as here of a palm-tree, is not an improper one to express the tall stature of a woman; so Galatea is, for height and tallness, compared to an alder and to a plane-tree;ᵠ and

---

° Meæ deliciæ, Plauti Stichus, act. 5. sc. 5.
ᵖ Sepher. Dibre Hayamim, fol. 7. 2.   ᵠ Ovid.
Metamorph l. 13. fab. 8.

Helena, to a cypress-tree in a garden,' on the same account: and if Solomon here has any reference to Pharaoh's daughter, his wife, since the Egyptian palm-tree is said to be the best,ˢ he might think of that, which is described " of body straight, high, round, and slender;"ᵗ and fitly expresses a good shape and stature, which recommended a person to their lovers.ᵘ Now the church being here represented as tall of stature, may be expressive of her royal majesty and greatness; and so the Septuagint render the words, " This thy greatness is like to the palm-tree."ʷ Moreover, tallness of stature was ever accounted no small addition to beauty; and therefore women have, in former as well as in latter ages, worn ornaments upon the very top of their heads, as well as high shoes on their feet, to make them appear the taller; and perhaps this was the reason why the Jewish women walked " with stretched-forth necks," as is observed in Isa. iii. 16; so that this may be taken notice of by Christ, as a commendation of the church's beauty. The palm-tree is a beautiful tree; and some have been compared to it for their beauty; thus Homerˣ compares the beauty of Nausicaa to the tender branch of a palm-tree; here the church is compared to it for her stature: and to be of a tall stature, is in many cases useful, and such, in many instances, have the advantage of others: Zaccheus, because he was low of stature, was obliged to climb a sycamore-tree, or he had lost the sight of Christ, which he was so desirous of gratifying his curiosity with. But to proceed: by the church's stature, is meant no other than that " measure of the stature of the fulness of Christ," mentioned in Eph. iv. 13, which the church and all true believers are growing up to, and shall arrive at; for which reason the means of grace, the ministry of the word, and the ordinances of the gospel, are instituted and continued: and then will the church have arrived to this stature, when all the elect are gathered in, and every member joined to the body; and these all filled with the several gifts and graces of the Spirit designed for them; and are all grown up to a just proportion in the body; and in this state and condition Christ seems to view his church here, and therefore gives her this commendation. Now to this stature no addition can be made, but by the grace and Spirit of God; as no man, " by taking thought," or projecting ever so many ways and methods, " can add one cubit unto his bodily stature," so none can, by any methods of their own, add to their spiritual stature, nor to the stature of the church of Christ: it is the Spirit of God that convinces and converts sinners; he works upon their wills and affections, and powerfully inclines their hearts to give themselves first to the Lord, and then to the churches; and when they are planted there, it is he that, by the effusions and influences of his grace, makes them grow up as " willows by the water-courses."

Now this stature of the church, is by Christ compared to a " palm-tree:" a tree well known in Judea, where great plenty of them grew; and as Plinyʸ says, the noblest and best of this sort of trees, and especially about Jericho; which is frequently in scripture called " the city of palm-trees;" as is Engedi sometimes called Hazazon-tamar, from the palm-trees which grew there; and someᶻ have observed that this tree, in future times, became an emblem of that country; and therefore the coin of several of the Roman princes had the figure of a palm-tree upon them, and particularly Vespasian's, and the medal of the emperor Titus was struck with the figure of a captive woman, sitting under a palm tree, with this inscription on it, *Judæa capta*, " Judea is taken:" the metaphor is taken, as are usually all the metaphors, similes, and comparisons, in this book, from what was well known in this country; and it is no unusual thing in scripture for saints to be compared to palm-trees; in Psalm xcii. 12, it is said, " the righteous shall flourish like the palm-tree;" and in Solomon's temple, which was a figure of the church of Christ, were palm-trees carved upon all the walls of the house round about, and upon the doors of the oracle; to teach us, that none but saints ought to have a place in God's house below, or shall be admitted into heaven above, signified by the oracle, or holy of holies: also in Ezekiel's temple, which was shown him in a vision, were palm-trees and cherubim; between every cherub and cherub was a palm-tree; which temple was either a figure of the gospel-church, or of the church-triumphant in glory; and if that is true, as someᵃ have thought, that the places of the fallen angels are filled up with men redeemed by Christ; that the same number are redeemed among the one, as fell among the other; this description would give a beautiful illustration of it; for as a cherub and a palm-tree, a cherub and a palm-tree, were placed in this order throughout the house; so an angel and a saint, an angel and a saint, an equal number of each according to this notion, will be in the heavenly glory. But, to consider a little particularly why the church, and all true believers, may be compared to palm-trees: and they may for these following reasons. 1. The palm-tree grows up very tall, straight, and upright;ᵇ and therefore the idols of the Gentiles are compared unto it, in Jer. x. 5, " they are upright as the palm-tree:" and saints may be said to be so in a spiritual sense; and that if we consider them

---

ʳ Theocrit. Idyll. 18. v. 30. ˢ A. Gell. Noct. Attic. l. 7. c. 16. Vid. Strabo, l. 17. p. 563. ᵗ Sandy's Travels, b. 2. p. 76. ᵘ Arno forma pulchram, statura procerem, Theophilus apud Athen. Deipnosoph. l. 13. c. 2. p. 563. ʷ קומתך μεγεθος σα, Sept. statura tua, Vulgate Latin version.

ˣ Odyss. 6. v. 163. 164. ʸ Lib. 13. c. 4. ᶻ Soto Major and Biskop Patrick in loc. Vid. Flurduini Opera. p. 331. 2. 332. l. 731. l. 2. 735. l. 743. 2. ᵃ August. de Civit. Dei. l. 22. c. 1. and in Enchir. c. 29. ᵇ Levin. Lemnii. Herb. Bibl. Explic. c. 20.

either in the exercise of their faith, or in the motions of their affections, or in the tendency of their desires, or agreeableness of their conversations; their faith looks straight upwards to a Christ above, and fixes its eye upon his person, blood, and righteousness; and does not look downwards to its frames, duties, services, or performances: their affections move heavenwards, and are set on things above, and not on things on earth; and therefore are compared to pillars of smoke, which move straight upwards, and which rise up in the form of palm-trees, as has been observed on chap. iii. 6; their desires also steer the same course, and move after Christ; they want to have a larger knowledge of him, more communion with him, and a nearer conformity to him; they are breathing after the heavenly joys; and having seen the vanity and emptiness of this world, and the things of it, desire the better country and continuing city, which God is the Builder and Maker of; and long to be unclothed of this mortal body, that they might be clothed with their house from heaven: thus, like the palm-tree, their souls move upward in their faith in, love to, and desires after Christ, and those unseen glories which he is preparing for his people: and as they are upright in their hearts, so they are in their conversations, which are often in heaven, and employed about heavenly things, even whilst they are here on earth, which renders them becoming the gospel of Christ Jesus. 2. The palm-tree will grow straight and upright, even though many weights are hung upon it;[c] saints have many weights and pressures upon them; the apostle says, Heb. xii. 1, "let us lay aside every weight;" which shows that they have more than one; they have a body of sin and death, which presses them hard, and makes them groan, being burdened with it; as also a variety of afflictions which attend them; as well as a load of reproaches and censures thrown upon them by the world, which often fall very hard and heavy; besides the many persecutions of various sorts which they endure; and yet, as the apostle says, 2 Cor. iv. 8, 9, though they "are troubled on every side, yet not distressed;" they "are perplexed, but not in despair; persecuted, but not forsaken; cast down, but not destroyed;" they are supported under all, and still grow upright like the palm-tree; "none of these things move" them, to turn or bend either one way or another; nor tempt them to desert the cause they have espoused; but continue in it with an unshaken mind, and a courageous and magnanimous spirit; so R. Solomon Jarchi applies this to the Jewish church, which stood as upright as the palm-tree, refusing to be guilty of idolatry, in Nebuchadnezzar's time, when other nations bowed and fell down before his golden image: nay, saints not only bear up under all these weights and pressures, but oftentimes grow the more in their faith, love, knowledge, and experience, under them; as the children of Israel, who the more they were afflicted, the more they grew and multiplied. 3. The palm-tree is a fruit-bearing tree; it bears the fruit which is called dates, which is not only of a beautiful aspect, but of a delightful taste, and it is fit both for food and drink;[d] and this perhaps was the reason why the children of Israel pitched their camp at Elim, Numb. xxxiii. 9; because there were not only "twelve fountains of water" there, but also "threescore and ten palm-trees:" the saints, being implanted and ingrafted in Christ Jesus, and abiding in him, bring forth fruit; they are laden with all the blessings of the everlasting covenant, the graces of the Spirit, and the precious fruits of righteousness; all which fruit they have from Christ, who is their "green fir-tree." 4. Naturalists[e] tell us, that the vital force or power of the palm-tree is not in its root, as in other trees, but in its top, which they call the cerebrum, or brain; and that if its top is lopped off, it immediately becomes barren:[f] the saint's life is not in themselves, but in their Head, Christ Jesus; is from him they receive all their grace, and strength, their life and nourishment, their fruit and fruitfulness; and if it was possible that any separation could be made between them and their head, they would not only become barren and unfruitful, but entirely dead and lifeless. 5. The leaves of the palm-tree are always green; it has on the top of it a tuft of leaves four feet long, which never fall off, but always continue upon it in the same verdure; it is a tree which never rots:[g] the saints are frequently compared to trees in scripture, and that to such whose leaves do not wither, as in Psalm i. 3, Jer. xvii. 8; when hypocrites and carnal professors are called δενδρα φθινοπωρινα, "trees that are withered in autumn;"[h] at which time not only the fruit is gone but the leaves fall: but saints being ingrafted in Christ, and planted by the rivers of divine love and grace, continually retain their verdure, shall never perish, but persevere for ever. 6. The palm-tree is very long-lived,[i] and continues flourishing a long time; it is, as Dr. Shaw[k] was informed, in its greatest vigour about thirty years after it is planted, and continues in full vigour seventy years more, bearing all this while every year about three or four hundred pounds weight of dates; and Symmachus renders the words here, "this thine" age is like unto the palm-tree: hence the flourishing of the righteous is compared unto it, in Psalm xcii. 12; in opposition to that of the wicked, in v. 7; which is said to be as the flourishing of grass, which is soon over, and continues but a short time; but the palm-tree abides so for many years, as before observed:[l] and this may be expressive of the perseverance of the saints, whose grace is immortal and incorruptible; whose persons shall

---

[c] Levin. Lemnii Herb. Bibl. Explic. c. 20.
[d] Ibid. [e] Plin. l. 13. c. 4. and Dalecamp. in idem. [f] Plin. l. 17. c. 24. [g] Plin. l. 16. c.
20. Lemnii Herb. Bibl. Explic. c. 20. [h] Jude 12.
[i] Plin. l. 16. c. 44. [k] Travels, p. 244.
[l] Vid. R. Aben Ezram in Psal xcii. 12.

never perish, nor ever be subject to the second death, but shall live for evermore. 7. The palm-tree grows and flourishes best in hot and sunny places;[m] it will not grow in cold countries, and therefore we have it not here: so saints, being "planted in the house of the Lord," where in the ordinances, they sitting under the warm and quickening beams of the "Sun of righteousness," Christ Jesus, "flourish in the courts of our God;" these are the best places for them, namely, the house and ordinances of God; here they delight to be, and here they thrive most, because here "the Lord is a sun and a shield" unto them. 8. Branches of the palm-tree have been used as tokens of joy and emblems of victory; the Jews had a feast of tabernacles, which they kept as a time of rejoicing; and among other demonstrations of joy, this was one, to carry palm tree branches in their hands, Lev. xxiii. 40, as did also much people of the Jews, when Christ rode in triumph to Jerusalem, as an indication of the joy they were filled with at his coming, and to welcome him into their city, John xii. 13; so likewise the saints are described, who were come out of great tribulations, and had gotten the victory over all their enemies, as "clothed with white robes, and palms or palm-tree branches in their hands," Rev. vii. 9; saints, of all persons in the world, have reason to rejoice in the views of an atoning sacrifice, a justifying righteousness, and peace and pardon by Christ Jesus, through whom they are made "more than conquerors" over sin, Satan, and the world; and a number of these, with palm-tree branches in their hands, will look like so many palm-trees. But,

II. The church's breasts in particular are commended by Christ, and compared to "clusters of grapes:" this part has been already commended in chap. iv. 5, and is repeated in ver. 3 of this chapter; but here a different metaphor is made use of; there they are compared to "two young roes that are twins," here to clusters of grapes. The word *grapes* is not in the Hebrew text; though the Targum supplies it, as our Translators do: R. Aben Ezra thinks, that clusters of the vine are meant, which might be planted by, and run up upon the palm-tree; though I should rather think, that "clusters of dates," the fruit of the palm-tree itself, are here intended; especially seeing this fruit, as Pliny[n] observes, grows in clusters, hanging upon the shoots, like bunches of grapes: moreover, her breasts are compared to "clusters of the vine," in the following verse; and it does not appear so probable, that Christ should use the same metaphor, to commend the same part in two verses together. What we are to understand by the church's breasts, has been shown on chap. iv. 5, but seeing a different metaphor is made use of here, it may not be improper to observe the agreement between them. And,

1st. By her breasts may be meant the ministers of the gospel. R. Solomon Jarchi would have Daniel, Hananiah, Mishael, and Azariah, here understood, who were as breasts to others in captivity: but it is much better to understand them of gospel-ministers; who not only direct men where they may have food, invite them to it, and dissuade them from every thing that would be pernicious to them; but also feed them themselves, with "the sincere milk of the word, and bread of life; they rightly divide" or cut the word of truth; and, as wise and faithful stewards, give to every one their portion of meat in due season. These may be compared to clusters, either of grapes or dates, 1. Because of their number: it is a great mercy to the churches of Christ, when there are plenty of gospel-ministers; Christ advised his disciples to pray for it, because the "harvest was plenteous," and labourers were but few, Matt. ix. 37, 38. 2. Because of their unity, likeness, and agreement; for though they have gifts and grace differing from each other, one has more than another has; yet they have one and the same commission, and preach one and the same Christ as the only way of salvation, though they may not be attended with equal success. 3. Like clusters of dates, the fruit of the palm-tree, they are the fruit of the church; and such are the best ministers, who are educated and brought up in churches, and approved and sent out by them. Or else,

2ndly. By the church's breasts may be meant, the Old and New Testaments; which, like breasts, are full of the "milk of the word;" than which, no two breasts are more like one another; like the two cherubim upon the mercy-seat they look towards each other: these may be compared to clusters, because there are in them clusters of excellent doctrines and precious promises; there are not only here and there a berry, but clusters of them; which being pressed and squeezed by hearing, reading, meditation, and prayer, yield both delight and nourishment to men. Or else,

3rdly. By them may be meant the ordinances of baptism and the Lord's supper, which are "breasts of consolation" to believers; and when they have the presence of Christ in them, and the discoveries of his love to them, then they are not "dry breasts;" they cannot say, they have "no cluster to eat;" but as when there is "new wine found in the cluster," and one saith, "destroy it not, for a blessing is in it," Isa. lxv. 8, so have they much pleasure, satisfaction, and delight therein: and the church's breasts being thus like clusters, full in themselves, are also delightful and beautiful in Christ's eye, and therefore are thus commended by him.

Verse 8. *I said I will go up to the palm-tree, I will take hold of the boughs thereof: now also thy breasts shall be as clusters of the vine, and the smell of thy nose like apples.*

CHRIST having compared the church to a palm-

---

[m] Plin. l. 13. c. 4.

[n] Plin. l. 1. 3. c. 4.

tree, and her breasts to " clusters of dates," the fruit thereof, does here,

I. Make a resolution or promise to go up into it, and "take hold of the boughs thereof."

II. Mentions several effects following upon his putting this resolution into practice, or fulfilling this promise; two of which we have an account of in these words: as, 1st. That her breasts should be filled, and become like " clusters of the vine." 2ndly. " The smell of her nose" should be " like apples."

I. We have in these words Christ's resolution or promise; which consists of two parts: 1st. He resolves to " to go up to the palm-tree." 2ndly. When there, to "take hold of the boughs thereof."

1st. He signifies it as his will, to " go up to the palm-tree." Some popish[o] writers have fancied that the cross of Christ, or at least some part of it, was made of the wood of the palm-tree; to support which they have no sufficient proof or evidence; though it is not very unlikely, seeing there was such plenty of those sort of trees in Judea, as has been observed on the former verse: and therefore, some[p] have thought, that by Christ's going up to the palm-tree, is meant his crucifixion, which he expresses by being lifted up, in John xii. 32. Moreover, his going up to it may signify his voluntary submission unto death, even the " death of the cross:" besides, the palm-tree being an emblem of victory, may represent the conquest which Christ has obtained over all his and our enemies; he has destroyed sin, overcome the world, abolished death, spoiled principalities and powers, and made a show of them, openly triumphing over them on the cross.

Though others[q] have thought, that by Christ's going up to the palm-tree, are meant his ascension into heaven, his conjunction with his church there, and that unspeakable pleasure which he will take in her for evermore: it is true, Christ not only ascended to his God and our God, to his Father and our Father; but also went up to the church triumphant, which may very fitly be compared to a palm-tree; the saints there appearing with " white robes and palms, palm-tree branches in their hands;" as a token of that joy they are possessed of, and of that victory over all their enemies, which they are sharers in, through Christ Jesus: and it was the delightful company of these persons, which Christ had in view in becoming a Surety for them, assuming their nature, and dying in their room and stead; it was this " joy that was set before him," which caused him so patiently to " endure the cross, despising the shame" which attended it. Though I am rather inclined to think, that by the palm-tree here, we are to understand the church militant, as in the foregoing verse; and Christ's going up into it, is ex-

pressive, 1. Of his right unto, and property in his church: she is his by the gift of the Father, and by the purchase of his own blood, as well as by the conquest of his powerful and efficacious grace; on which account he claims an interest in her, and says, " I have redeemed thee, I have called thee by thy name, thou art mine;" and she is very free to own and acknowledge this rightful claim unto her, as it is her honour, interest, and duty so to do: this palm-tree is of his own planting; he waters it every moment; he keeps it night and day; he prunes it, and makes it fruitful; and therefore has a right to go up into it when he pleases. 2. Of his presence with her; so Christ is said to be " among the myrtle-trees," in Zech. i. 8, as he is here said to go up into the palm-tree: and this is the grand reason why the church is at any time in a flourishing condition, and like the palm-tree, grows, though never such weights and pressures are upon it; because Christ is in the midst of her, and grants his gracious and supporting presence to her. 3. Of his delight in her; he loves to be in her presence and company, as men do to go up into their trees, and handle the boughs thereof. His saints are " the excellent in the earth," in whom his delight was before the world began, and now is, and ever will be: the mutual delight which appears in the bride and bridegroom, falls short of expressing that which Christ takes in his church; he " rejoices over her with joy; he rests in his love towards her, and joys over her with singing," Zech. iii. 17.

Now from Christ's going up into his palm-tree, the church, we are not to imagine that the church is higher than Christ, for he is far superior to her; and it is an instance of his grace and condescension, that he will take notice of her and grant his presence to her; he is her Head and Husband, her Lord and King, and therefore she is inferior, and ought to be in subjection to him; and though he was in our nature, and that by reason of suffering in it, made " a little lower than the angels;" yet he is vastly higher than they, yea, higher than the heavens themselves. But this expression here is suited, and is very agreeable to the metaphor here made use of. The palm-tree is a very tall tree; and its boughs and branches do not grow out of the sides, as in many other trees, but only on the top of it; so that whosoever would lay hold upon them and gather the fruit, must go up into it: moreover, the trunk and body of it is made with rings in the bark of it, like steps; so that it may be very easily climbed, which is done by the eastern people, with an incredible swiftness:[r] these steps are made of the knots or polices, as Dr Shaw[s] calls them, being gradually left upon the trunk of the tree, serve, like so many rounds of a ladder, to climb up the tree, either to

---

[o] Vid. Soto Major in loc.   [p] Foliot and Alcuin in loc. Tertull. and Cyprian. in Soto Major in loc.   [q] Diodat. in loc.   [r] Plin. l. 13. c. 4. so Sandy's Travels, b. 2. p. 79.   [s] Travels, tom. 1. p. 142. ed 2.

fecundate it, or to lop it, or to gather the fruit: Lucian[t] observes that "those who have seen how men get up into palm-trees, in Arabia, Egypt, and other places, much needs understand what he says, about climbing the Phalli in the temple of Hyrapolis in Syria, he is describing."

2ndly. Going up into the palm-tree, is in order to take hold on the boughs of it. The palm-tree has no boughs or branches growing out of the sides of the trunk of it, as before observed, but shoots upon the top of it, on which its fruit hangs; and the Septuagint renders it, "I will take hold of the heights of it;" some render it, the *fruit* of it, as the Vulgate Latin version; to which Kircher inclines: and this ascent to the top of it was, either to gather the fruit, or to crop the shoots themselves, and eat them; for the tops of them, which are of the first year's growth, are very tender and sweet, and may be eaten;[u] so the top of the palm-tree, which some call the cerebrum, or brain, is very sweet;[w] and is spoken of as very pleasant and nourishing.[x] Christ's end in doing this may be twofold: 1. To gather the fruits of it; which he has an undoubted right unto; they are his: whether we understand by them the blessings of grace, which believers are possessed of; or the graces of the Spirit, which are implanted in them; or the good works which they are enabled to perform; these all come from him; he is the "green fir-tree," from whom all the believers' "fruit is found;" therefore he may lay hold on the boughs and gather the fruit when he pleases, in doing which, he takes much delight and pleasure, and is kindly invited by his church thereunto: see chap. iv. 16. 2. His other end in laying hold on the boughs, may be to prune them, that they may bring forth more fruit; this he does sometimes by his word, and the preaching of it: by which sin is corrected, error refuted, and sharp reproofs and admonitions given on the account of both; for as the word is as an axe to cut down sturdy and obstinate sinners; so it is as a pruning-knife in Christ's hand, to remove all "superfluity of naughtiness," which hinders the growth of his trees and plants: sometimes also Christ prunes his churches by the ordinance of excommunication; by which he lops off unfruitful branches, such who are unfit for communion in his churches; which awful sentence is executed sometimes more mildly, and sometimes more severely, according to the nature of the offence; sometimes it is expressed in scripture by a withdrawing from disorderly persons; at other times, by a rejecting of heretics; as also, by putting away such who are notoriously vile and wicked: again, Christ prunes his people likewise by afflictive providences, by which their iniquity is purged, their graces are tried and exercised, and they made under those sharp trials, to yield the peaceable fruits of righteousness: moreover Christ sometimes effects this work by suffering persecution to befal his churches; this sun scorches up those plants, which are not of Christ's planting, and are not rooted in his person and grace; this is the fan which Christ sometimes takes in his hand, and "thoroughly purges his floor," the church, of hypocrites and formal professors; this is his pruning-knife, with which he lops off those fruitless and withered branches. This is an awful way of pruning the boughs of his palm-tree.

It may be observed, that these words are delivered in the form of a purpose or promise, "I said I will go up," &c., Christ thinks, and then resolves, before he acts: he does all things deliberately, and according to the counsel of his own will, and always for his own glory and his church's good: moreover, this being a promise of Christ's, the performance of it may be expected by his people; for "he is faithful who has promised;" it may also be pleaded by them: Has he promised to go up into his palm-tree, or grant his presence in his church? He will be as good as his word; his people may expect his presence there; and they are allowed to put him in mind of such a promise, which they need not doubt the fulfilment of. But,

II. Let us now consider the effects of Christ's going up into his palm-tree; and we find two of them mentioned in this verse, and a third in the following one:

1st. The church's breasts become like "clusters of the vine;" that is, of grapes which grow in clusters on the vine:[y] which words may be considered, either as a wish, and be read thus, "and now let thy breasts be as the clusters of the vine;"[z] or else, as a promise that they should be so; which accordingly was effected by his granting his presence to her, which filled her breasts, and made them like clusters of the vine. By which may be meant, either, 1. The ministers of the gospel: who not only direct men where the wine and milk of gospel-grace may be had, and invite them to it, but do also themselves feed them with "the sincere milk of the word;" with which they are filled, by Christ's granting his presence to them in their studies and meditations; and are brought forth by him at proper opportunities, laden with "the fulness of the blessing of the gospel of Christ;" so that these breasts look like clusters of the vine. Or, 2. By them may be meant the ordinances; which are "breasts of consolation" to God's people, when they have the presence of Christ in them, otherwise they are but dry breasts; it is that which fills them with milk for nourishment, and with wine for refreshment. Or, 3. The two Testaments, with those

---

[t] De Dea Syria. [u] Vid. Buxtorf. Lex Talmud. rad. קור col. 2005. [w] Plutarch. de San. Tuend. vol. 2. p. 133. Plin. 1. 13. c. 4. [x] Athenæi cipnosophist. l. 2. c. 28. p. 71. [y] Liventibus a racemis, Propert. l. 4. eleg. 2. v. 13. ipse racemum iferis uvis, Ovid. Metamorph. l. 3. v. 666. [z] שָׁדַיִךְ וִיהְיוּ נָא and sint quæso mammæ tuæ, Tigurine ver- Mercerus; and sint agedum ubera tua, Cocceius; and sint nunc ubera tua, Brightman, and so Ainsworth.

clusters of excellent doctrines and precious promises that are in them; which, when men have the presence of Christ, either in the hearing or reading of them, yield them much delight and comfort, though at other times they are but as a dead letter. Though, 4. This may in general intend that influence, which Christ's presence has on the fruitfulness of his people; it is this which makes them fat and flourishing, brisk and lively, in the exercise of grace, fruitful in every good word and work; so that they grow and thrive in every grace, and are not barren and unfruitful in the knowledge of Christ Jesus.

2ndly. Another effect of Christ's going up into his palm-tree, or of his presence in his church, is, that "the smell of her nose" thereby becomes like that of apples. Formerly it was usual to anoint the nostrils,[a] which was reckoned very healthful and refreshing to the head; as well as was done, that they might give the more agreeable smell: and some sort of ointments, it seems, gave a smell like that of apples, which in some is very grateful and delightful; and Cicero[b] observes, that the plenty and variety of apples, their pleasant taste and smell, show that they were only made for men: and indeed there was an ointment made of them, called melinum; so that the nostrils being anointed with it, might well be said to smell like apples; and which was accounted one of the best.[c] By which apples may be meant, either 1. The refreshing doctrines of the gospel from Christ's ministers; who are the church's nose, and are capable of distinguishing truth from error: these doctrines which they preach, when fitly spoken, seasonably applied, and attended with the power and presence of Christ to poor souls, are like "apples of gold in pictures of silver;" nay, not only like apples for sight, being beautiful to look upon, but also for smell; for these diffuse a sweet savour of the knowledge of Christ in the souls of his people. Or else, 2. The fame and report of the church's faith, piety, and courage, which was spread far and near; her faith, for its strength and purity, is compared in ver. 4, to "a tower of ivory;" and her courage and magnanimity in defending this faith against all opposition, is expressed by her nose, being "as the tower of Lebanon, which looketh towards Damascus:" now the smell, fame, or report of all this, like the smell of apples, was diffused abroad, and gained her credit and reputation, even from others: she having, like those heroes, in Heb. xi., "obtained a good report through faith." Or, 3. It may be expressive both of her outward conversation and inward constitution, which were both sound and healthful; she had an inward principle of grace, from whence proceeded a savoury conversation without; the hidden man of her heart, was that which is not corruptible, which sent forth, not a nauseous, but a grateful odour; no rotten nor corrupt communication proceeds from hence, but what is not only edifying to others, but grateful to Christ; and nothing has a greater influence than the presence of Christ, to make her inward constitution and outward conversation so. Though, 4. This may intend the savouriness of those things which she smelt, which were as grateful to her as the smell of apples: thus spiritual and heavenly things, the divine truths and excellent doctrines of the gospel, are exceeding savoury to believers, especially when they have the presence of Christ, the discoveries of his love, and the quickening influences of his Spirit. The third effect follows in the next verse.

Verse 9. *And the roof of thy mouth like the best wine, for my beloved, that goeth down sweetly, causing the lips of those that are asleep, to speak.*

THESE words contain the third effect of Christ's going up into his palm-tree, or granting his presence to his church: in which may be considered,

I. What is meant by the "roof of her mouth."
II. Why it is compared to "the best wine."
III. The commendations of this best wine, to which it is compared; which, 1st. Is commended from the person, for whose use it is: "for my beloved." 2ndly. From the property of it; "it goeth down sweetly." 3rdly. From its effect; "causing the lips of those that are asleep to speak."

I. It will be proper to inquire what we are to understand by the roof of the church's mouth. And, 1. By it may be meant her taste; the same word is so rendered in chap. ii. 3. The church's taste is good, and not like that of unconverted persons; whose taste remains in them, as it is vitiated and corrupted by sin; so that they are not capable of discerning the difference of things; and therefore call evil good, and good evil; put bitter for sweet, and sweet for bitter; but so is not the church's taste; she can discern perverse things; her taste is like the best wine, she can tell whether it is good or no: though perhaps this expression is not so much intended to signify the goodness of her sense of tasting, as the things which she tastes of, which are the person of Christ, and the words of his mouth: tastes that the Lord is good in his person, grace, and office; and finds the doctrines which proceed out of his mouth, and the fruit which drops from him, sweeter to her taste than the honey or the honey-comb. 2. R. Aben Ezra thinks that the saliva, or spittle under the tongue, is here meant; and what may be intended by that, may be learnt from chap. iv. 11, where it is said, that "honey and milk are

---

[a] Ευαλειφεται τας ρινας, &c. Alexis apud Athen. Deipnosoph. l. 2. c. 7. p. 46. Et crocino nare myrrheus ungat onyx, Propertius, l. 3.   [b] De natura Deorum, l. 2. c. 63. Vid Plutarch. Sympos. l. 5. p. 883.   [c] Athenæus, ut supra, l. 15. c. 11. 12. p. 688, 689. Plin. Nat. Hist. l. 13. c. 1. and l. 23. c. 6.

under her tongue;" that is, the doctrines of the everlasting gospel, which she lays and keeps there, and rolls them as a sweet morsel in her mouth, having tasted the goodness of them; herein she appears to be exceeding different from carnal and unconverted persons, under whose lips the poison of asps is said to be, Rom. iii. 13. 3. Others[d] think, that by the roof of her mouth, is meant her breath; which proceeds from thence, was sweet and of a good smell, like the best wine; and not like the breath of carnal persons, whose throats are like an open sepulchre; from whence are daily belched out horrid oaths, dreadful curses and imprecations upon themselves and others, with cruelty and threatenings to the saints and people of God; but as for the church's breath, it is of a different nature; no rotten communication proceeds out of her mouth, but what may be for the use of edifying; she breathes out nothing but peace and love among her members, and also to others: and as for her prayers to God, which may be justly called the breathings of her soul; these are as sweet odours, being perfumed with the incense of Christ's mediation. Though, 4. I rather think, by the roof of her mouth, is meant her speech, or the words of her mouth; for the roof of the mouth is an instrument of speech, as well as of tasting; and the same word is frequently rendered the mouth, as in chap. v. 16, Prov. v. 3, and viii. 7, which may either intend her speech in common conversation: which, like the best wine, is warming, comforting, and refreshing to souls, as well as grateful to Christ. How many have been cold, dull, and lifeless, when they have first come into the conversation of the saints; and by it have been warmed, quickened, and refreshed, so that they have gone away with joy and comfort, blessing and praising God for such opportunities! Or else, by it may be meant the speech of the church in prayer or praise, which are both delightful and well-pleasing to Christ; her voice in either is sweet unto him, makes delightful music in his ears; though the prayers of the saints are but like the chatterings of a crane or swallow, yet they are gratefully received by him; as are also their praises, which are more esteemed by him, than the sacrifices of an ox or a bullock that has horns and hoofs: though I am most inclined to think that the gospel, which proceeds out of Christ's mouth, and is put into the mouth of his church which is preached in the midst of her, and by her ministering servants, is here intended. Which brings us to consider,

II. Why this is compared to the best wine: Perhaps the wine of Sharon may be referred to, which was so strong, that they mixed it two parts water and one wine;[e] though there were other places in Judea that had the first name for wine;[f] the wine of Lebanon was very grateful for taste and smell, Hosea xiv. 7, where was a city, called Ampeloessa,[g] from the excellency of its wine. 1. That is the best wine which is pure and free from dregs and mixtures; that which is upon the lees, well refined: such is the gospel, as preached by the faithful ministers of it, who are not as some, which corrupt the word of God; they do not mix it with their own inventions, but deliver out this wine of the Gospel, neat and clean, as they have received it. 2. Wine that has age, is also accounted the best: thus saith Christ, Luke v. 39, " No man having drunk old wine, straightway desireth new; for he saith, the old is better:" the gospel is no novel doctrine; for though it is more clearly made known under the New Testament dispensation, than it was under the Old, yet it was known then; it was wrapped up in the types, shadows, and sacrifices of the old law; it was preached before unto Abraham, nay, to our first parents in the garden; and was spoken of more or less, ever since, by the mouth of God's holy prophets, which have been since the world began. 3. The best wine is that which is of a good flavour, and delightful to the taste, as well as that which is of a good colour: such is the gospel, it is like milk for nourishment, and like wine for pleasantness; nay, like Ezekiel's roll, as honey for sweetness; yea, the psalmist says, Psalm cxix. 103, that the words of God's mouth were sweeter than honey to his mouth. 4. Wine is of a cheering and reviving nature; it is what makes glad the heart of man; and therefore is proper to be given to those that be of heavy hearts, that they may drink and forget their poverty, and remember their misery no more: of such a nature is the gospel; it being received by persons in distress, like the best wine, it cheers and revives their spirits; it makes them forget their spiritual poverty, and puts out of their minds their former misery and distress; whilst they behold what riches of grace are treasured up in Christ, and what ample provisions are there made for them; nay, it not only revives distressed and drooping souls, but such is the virtue and efficacy of it, that it will bring dead sinners to life; for it is the savour of life unto life to many. 5. The best wine is very refreshing to weary persons, who have been fatigued with labour and travel; the gospel is a word in season to him that is weary; it not only directs the weary soul where it may have rest, kindly invites unto it, but is also the instrument of bringing him into it. 6. Wine is reckoned a comforter and strengthener of the stomach; therefore the apostle Paul advised Timothy, 1 Tim. v. 23, to use a little wine for his stomach sake, and his often infirmities: the doctrines of the gospel have a tendency to comfort souls; they are often blessed for that purpose; the ministers of it are employed herein on that account; and the Spirit of God

---

[d] Sanctius in loc.   [e] Misn. Niddah, c. 2. s. 7.
[f] As Kerutim, Hatulim; and next to them, Bethrima in Bethlaban in the mountain, and Cephar-signah in the valley, Misn. Menachot, c. 8. s. 6.
[g] Plin. l. 5. c. 18.

does his work, and executes his office as a Comforter by them. Thus the gospel, the word, which is in and proceeds out of the church's mouth, may be compared to the best wine.

III. I shall now consider the commendations given of this best wine of the Gospel. And,

1st. It is commended from the person, for whose use it is, for my beloved; and therefore must needs be the best; it is such wine as a man would give to his friend, whom he dearly loves; who, when he pays a visit to him, if he has any wine in the house, he shall be sure to have it; and if he has any better than the rest, it shall be at his service. But who are we to understand by this beloved, for whose use this wine is? And, 1. We may understand these words as the words of Christ, speaking to and of his church and people, whom, in chap. v. 1, he calls his beloved, and his friends: and these he treats as such, with his best wine, the gospel, which is chiefly designed for their good, comfort, and establishment. 2. If we take these words to be the words of the daughters of Jerusalem, as some do, and that not only these, but all that is spoken in the preceding verses; then the beloved is Christ, whom they call their own: having now arrived to a greater knowledge of him, and acquaintance with him, than they formerly had; see chap. v. 9, and vi. 1; nor need it be wondered at, that it should be expressed in the singular number, my beloved: seeing it may well be supposed, that but one of them spoke, and delivered these commendations of the church. Though, 3. I rather take them to be the words of the church, speaking to and of Christ; who, hearing such great things spoken in the commendations of herself, could hold no longer; but, as one[h] expresses it, snatches the word out of Christ's mouth, breaks in upon his discourse before he had done, and thrusts in his words, referring all the glory to him; it is as if she should say, Is the roof of my mouth like the best wine? it is for my beloved; it is of his making and providing, and in which his glory is much concerned, as well as my comfort; " for we preach not ourselves, but Christ Jesus the Lord;" he is the subject, the sum and substance of the gospel; it is designed for the manifestation of his grace, and the advancement of his glory; and its being so, makes it so comfortable and delightful to souls. Junius and Piscator render the word, *most lovingly* or *most lovelily*; and so understand it of the manner of this best wine, going down and being received by persons: but this is sufficiently expressed in the next clause, which I shall now consider.

2ndly. This wine of the Gospel is commended from the property of it, which is here mentioned; it goeth down sweetly, which words may be differently rendered and as differently understood. And, I. They may be translated thus, *that walketh* or *moveth aright*; as they are in Prov. xxiii. 31; where wine is also spoken of, and denotes its sparkling in the cup; which shows it to be a generous wine, of a good body, and that it has life and spirit in it; therefore the wise man, in the forementioned place, advises not to look upon the wine when it is red, when it giveth his colour in the cup, when it moveth itself aright, because when it is so, it is very ensnaring; but here is no such danger in this wine of the Gospel; the pleasantness of which, both in the eyes of Christ and of his church, may be here intended. 2. The words may be rendered thus, *which goeth to my beloved straightway* or *directly*;[i] and so may denote the direct tendency of the Gospel to lead souls to Christ, and to advance his honour and glory; for the whole of it consists in this, Christ in us the hope of glory. Or, 3. Thus, it goeth or leadeth to righteousnesses:[k] for it is one principal part of the Gospel to lead souls to the righteousness of Christ, which is clearly revealed therein; that disclaiming all pretences to their own righteousness for justification, they may wholly and alone look unto, and depend upon that for their acceptance with God, and justification in his sight; moreover, it also teaches them, that denying ungodliness and worldly lusts, they should live soberly, righteously, and godly in this present world. Or, 4. They may be thus rendered, that goeth or walketh to upright persons;[l] for so the word is rendered in chap. i. 4; and indeed it is to such persons that the gospel is of real service and advantage: to them that believe, it is the power of God unto salvation; it works effectually in their hearts: these receive it in the love of it; by them it is highly valued and esteemed; and to them it yields much solid comfort, pleasure, and satisfaction. For with such, 5. It goeth down sweetly, as our translators have rendered the words. This wine of the Gospel is received and taken down with all readiness by all those who have once tasted the sweetness, and felt the power of it: with them the gospel is no hard saying, and who can bear it? but, like the best wine that is very delightful: with some persons, the doctrines of the gospel, such as those of an eternal, personal election, particular redemption, powerful and efficacious grace in conversion, final perseverance, &c., are very disagreeable; but to believers in Christ, they are like wine that goeth down sweetly.

3rdly. This wine is commended, from the effect it has upon those who drink of it; " it causeth the lips of those that are asleep to speak." In which may be considered, 1st. The persons on whom it has this effect, " those that are asleep." 2ndly. The effect itself, which it has upon them, " it causeth their lips to speak."

---

[h] Alcuin in loc.   [i] למישרים directe, Mercerus: rectissime Brightman, Junius.   [k] Εις ευθυτητα, Sept. ad rectitudines, Montanus; ad ea quae rectissima sunt, Tigurine version.   [l] Ad rectitudines, i. e. rectos homines, Marckius, Michaelis.

1st. The persons on whom this wine of the Gospel has this effect: and they are such who are asleep. The Hebrew word,[m] here used, is by some rendered ancient persons; for persons, when they are grown old, have not their senses so quick, nor are they so full of talk, but are more slow of speech, than when they were in their youthful days; yet Cicero[n] says, *senectus est natura loquacior;* and therefore this serves much for the commendation of this wine, that it should have such an affect upon such persons: for that must be noble and generous wine that invigorates old men, and fills them with a juvenile heat, warmth, and sprightliness: it makes them loquacious,[o] which is one effect of wine, when freely drank;[p] and it softens the moroseness of ancient men;[q] wine is even said to make an ancient man dance.[r] But the word may very well, and perhaps better, be rendered as it is, "those that are asleep;" by which may be meant, either, 1. Sinners, who are in the dead and deep sleep of sin. These, (1.) As persons asleep, have not the free exercise of their senses; they do not see their lost, miserable, and undone state by nature, nor their need of Christ, and the value of him: their ears are stopped, they cannot hear, so as to understand the joyful sound; they have no taste nor savour of divine things: and many have arrived to such a prodigious pitch of wickedness, as to be past feeling, having their "consciences seared with an hot iron:" nay, in this they exceed persons that are asleep; who, though they have not the free exercise of their senses whilst asleep, yet are not destitute of them; but these have no spiritual sense at all, but are "dead in trespasses and sins." (2.) Like persons asleep, they are strengthless, and are not in a capacity to do any thing that is spiritually good of themselves: they cannot redeem themselves from destruction; they cannot fulfil the righteous law of God, nor satisfy divine justice; they have not power to begin, nor carry on a work of grace upon their souls; they cannot subdue their corruptions, nor withstand Satan's temptations, nor perform the duties of religion; these things are not effected by the might and power of man. (3.) Like persons asleep, they are inactive: "their strength is to sit still:" they have neither power nor will to do that which is good; "there is none that doeth good, no, not one;" they have no true knowledge of what is good; for though "they are wise to do evil, yet to do good they have no knowledge;" and if they had knowledge, they have no inclination; and if they had that, yet still they have no power; "for the Ethiopian may as soon change his skin, or the leopard his spots, as they do good that are accustomed to do evil." (4.) Like persons asleep, they are subject to illusions and mistakes; they are mistaken about the nature of the Divine Being, whom they either imagine to be such an one as themselves, who will either connive at sinful actions, or take little or no notice of them; or, else presume upon his absolute mercy, to go on in sin: and they are as much deceived about the nature of sin itself, which they now roll as a sweet morsel in their mouths, but will ere long find to be as gravel-stones: and so they are likewise with respect to the ways of God, and people of Christ; in the former of which they suppose there is no true pleasure; and in the latter, no enjoyment of true felicity; but in nothing are they more mistaken than in themselves and their state; which they imagine to be good, when at the same time they are poor, and wretched, and miserable, and blind, and naked. (5.) Like persons asleep, they are insensible of danger; they are walking in the broad road to destruction, and are upon the brink of it, and yet know it not; they are crying peace, peace, when sudden destruction is at hand. Or else, 2. By those that are asleep, may be meant drowsy professors: the wise as well as the foolish virgins slept. Christ's church may sometimes be in such a condition, as she was in chap. v. 2, this sleep is not a dead sleep, as the former; there may be life notwithstanding this, "I sleep, but my heart waketh:" this consists in a non-exercise of grace, an indifference to religious duties, a lukewarmness and want of zeal for the glory of Christ and his gospel, occasioned by the prevailings of sin and corruption; see more on chap. v. 2. But,

2ndly. Let us consider what effect the wine of the everlasting Gospel has upon the abovesaid persons; when it comes in power, and is received in the love of it, it causes their lips to speak. In the former of these persons, that is, in carnal and Christless sinners, it produces humble confessions of sin: it makes them speak in the praise of Christ and his grace, whereby salvation is procured for such lost and perishing creatures, as they by nature were; it brings them to the gates of Zion, there to declare to the saints the great things which God has done for them: it makes the tongue of the dumb to sing, who before had not one word to say for Christ, and of his grace; and those who were stammerers at these things, it makes them ready to speak plainly: as for the latter sort of persons, that is, sleepy and drowsy professors, it makes them speak meanly and modestly of themselves, and very highly of Christ and his grace; for such souls who have drunk the largest draughts of this wine, and have the greatest share of knowledge in gospel-truths, are the most humble; they are ready to acknowledge themselves the least of saints, and the chief of

---

[m] שפתי ישנים labia veterum, Pagninus: antiquorum, Vatablus.   [n] De Senectute, c. 16.
[o] Plutarch. Sympos. l. 7. p. 715.   [p] Philoxenus apud Athen. Deipnosophist. l. 2. c. 1. p. 35. Vid. Sanhedrin T. Bab. fol. 38. 1.   [q] Philoxen. apud Athen. Deipnosoph. l. 11. c. 3. p. 463.   [r] Ibid. l. 4. c. 4. p. 134. and l. 10. c. 7. p. 428.

sinners: and none more frequent than they in magnifying Christ, and exalting the riches of his grace.

Verse 10. *I am my beloved's, and his desire is towards me.*

CHRIST having spoken largely in commendation of his church's beauty, vouchsafed his presence to her, and made her drink of his best wine, which causes the lips of those that are asleep to speak: she, after a long silence breaks forth, as an effect of it. And,

I. Claims her interest in him: " I am my beloved's."

II. Takes notice of his love and affection to her; " and his desire is towards me."

I. She signifies the satisfaction which she had in her soul, with respect to her being Christ's; which is an affair of the utmost concern; about which saints have often a great many doubts and fears; and a satisfaction in which he is exceeding desirable to them. The church has expressed herself in the same words twice before in this song; see chap. ii. 16, and vi. 3: therefore less will be required in the explication of them here. However, some things respecting the present frame and disposition of her, the agreement of these words with the context, and what has not been so carefully observed in the former texts, may be taken notice of here. And,

1st. These words may be considered as expressive of that assurance of faith, which the church had of her union to and in Christ; it is as if she should say, After all these expressions of love unto me, and the sweet enjoyment of his presence which he has indulged me with, surely I may venture to say, that *I am his*; nay, I am sure that I am. From hence may be observed, 1. That the grace of assurance is attainable in this life; instances of which we have, not only in the New-Testament-saints, such as the apostle Paul, and others, who knew that Christ had loved him, and had given himself for him: was well satisfied both in his ability and fidelity, to keep what he had committed to him against another day, and was persuaded that there never would be a separation from his love; but also in Old-Testament-saints, as David, who could claim his interest in an everlasting covenant, and was assured of it, even in his dying moments, and that in the prospect of the present and future ill state of his family; and Job, who knew that his Redeemer lived, and that for him, even when he was under the most severe, afflictive dispensations of providence; as also Habakkuk, who discovered the strength of his faith in God, as his salvation, even when all outward and temporal enjoyments failed him. 2. That there may be a continuation of the exercise of this grace: a person may not only be able to express his satisfaction as to his interest in Christ once, but also to repeat it, as the church does in this song; this is the third time she expresses her assurance in this very form of words, and oftener still in other language: nay, this grace is often exercised by believers, after much sleepiness and drowsiness, many slips and falls, great weakness and infirmities, as may be observed in the church's case frequently in this book; and it is likewise worthy of remark, that those persons who have been the greatest sinners before conversion, and have been suffered to fall the foulest after, have been blessed with this grace of assurance, as David, Paul, Peter, &c. 3. That the exercise of this grace often follows upon the enjoyment of Christ's presence; the church had been lately indulged with it; Christ went up into his palm-tree, the church, filled her breasts, the ordinances, with his grace and presence, and had made her drink of the wine of his consolation, which occasioned these expressions of hers. 4. Her frequent repetition of these words shows, that much of her comfort depended upon the knowledge she had of her interest in Christ; for, though assurance is not of the essence of faith, there may be true saving faith, where there is not the assurance of faith; yet to have it, makes much for the comfort of a believer: for if a glimmering sight of Christ fills the soul with so much joy, what must a full view do? if only an hope of interest gives much satisfaction, certainly a full assurance of it must give much more. 5. It may also be observed, that this grace has no tendency to promote or encourage licentiousness: that is the sealing word of the Spirit, who performs it as the holy Spirit of promise; and at the same time he seals, he leaves a greater impress of holiness upon the soul; this does not make persons careless, indolent, and inactive as to duty; but rather excites and stirs them up to be more careful and constant in it; of which here is an instance in the church in the following verses; " Come, my beloved, let us go forth into the field; let us lodge in the villages," &c.

2ndly. These words may be considered as a modest acknowledgment of the church's, that all she was and had were Christ's; " I am my beloved's," and it is " by his grace I am what I am:" all that he had said of her in the former verses, she does in this one expression return to him again; she acknowledges that all her beauty, which he had so much commended, was his, and not her own; that she was by nature black, and only comely through that comeliness which he had put upon her; that those several graces, with which she was adorned, and which he might have a regard unto in the several parts described, were his; he was the Object, Author, Owner, and Preserver of them: that particularly it was owing to grace and strength received from him, that her walk, her outward conversation, was in any measure agreeable, and was so beautiful as he was pleased to declare, in ver. 1. That all her fruitfulness, either in the exercise of grace, or in the performance of good works, or in having many souls born again in the midst of her, which may be intended in ver.

2, were all from him, and to be referred to his mighty grace and divine blessing. That her ministers and ordinances were of his providing, appointing, and filling, expressed by her breasts, in ver. 3. That all her strength, which appeared in the exercise of her faith on him, and in the discharge of her duty to God; her light and knowledge in divine truths, the savour and relish which she had of them, together with her zeal, courage, and magnanimity to keep and defend them, signified by her neck, her eyes, and nose, in ver. 4, were all communicated to her from him: as also that he was her only Head, both of eminence and influence; and that it was owing to that grace, life, strength, and nourishment, which he afforded, that her hair, true believers, grew so well, and appeared so beautiful as they did, in ver. 5. Moreover, that she was his palm-tree, which he might go up into, and gather the fruit of, when he pleased; and that it was his grace which caused her to grow so straight and upright, and made her so fruitful as she was, in ver. 7—9; wherefore she concludes in this verse, saying, "I am my beloved's;" that is, the glory of all this is to be referred to him, and not to myself.

3rdly. These words may also contain in them a voluntary surrender of herself, and all she had, into Christ's hands. This is what he requires of us; "my son," says he, Prov. xxiii. 26, "give me thine heart:" but this we are unwilling to do, until the day of his power passes upon us; and then we are made willing to give ourselves unto the Lord, and all we have, that we may therewith serve and glorify his name. This the church was enabled to do, knowing that she was not her own, but his; and therefore was desirous to glorify him with her body and spirit, which were his.

4thly. They are likewise expressive of that open profession she made of Christ before others; she was not ashamed to tell whose she was, and to whom she belonged. It is our duty to make a public profession of Christ, as well as to believe in his name; "for with the heart man believeth unto righteousness, and with the mouth confession is made unto salvation," Rom. x. 10, a believing in Christ may be sufficient for our everlasting security; but a profession of that is necessary and requisite to show forth a Redeemer's glory, which we ought to be concerned for; and when we have made a profession of Christ, we ought to hold it fast, without wavering, and adorn it by a suitable conversation. But,

II. The church in these words takes notice also of the love and affection of Christ towards her; "and his desire is towards me." The words may be rendered, thus, because or seeing his desire is towards me; so Junius reads them; and then they may be considered as a reason of the former expression of her faith in Christ, acknowledgment of his grace, and profession of his name; for Christ's love manifested to us, is a considerable evidence of our interest in him, and in his everlasting love; this will make us free and ready to acknowledge that we have nothing but what we have received from him; it is this which fills us with love to him, constrains us to obey him, encourages us to make a profession of him, and to maintain it, notwithstanding all discouragements thrown in our way, or opposition made against us. But let us consider a little the import of this phrase, and what is intended by it: it seems to be very much like, and perhaps the allusion is unto those words, in Gen. iii. 16, and "thy desire shall be to thy husband;" but here the husband's desire is towards his wife; so that what was inflicted by way of punishment upon the woman, being inverted, is a blessing of grace unto the church. The phrase may be expressive,

1st. Of Christ's love and affection to his church; his desire was towards her, 1. From everlasting; for having loved her, he desired her of his Father for his spouse and bride, which was granted him; for God gave him his heart's desire in this thing, and did not withhold the request of his lips from him. 2. His desire was towards her in time, that he might procure everlasting salvation for her; as an instance of his love, he undertook it; in the fulness of time assumed her nature; in order to effect it; was straitened in his mind, and as it were uneasy until it was accomplished: so great was his desire after it; hence he expressed himself thus to his disciples, at his eating the last passover, "With desire have I desired to eat this passover with you before I suffer," Luke xxii. 15; the chief reason was, because his time was at hand, the hour was now come, so much desired by him, when he should give the strongest evidence of his love to the church, in laying down his life for her. 3. His desire is towards his people, even before conversion, though dead in trespasses and sins; that they may be quickened, called by grace, and brought to the knowledge of himself; and, notwithstanding all their backslidings and revoltings from him, still his desire is after them, to do them good; neither will he turn away from them, but rests in his love towards them. 4. His desire is continually after his people's company, grace, and beauty; they are the excellent in the earth, in whom is all his delight; he is well pleased with that beauty which he himself has put upon them, and his desire is after it; "so shall the king greatly desire thy beauty," Psalm xlv. 11; he is ravished with those graces which he has implanted in them; he is exceedingly delighted with their looks and words: and therefore says, Cant. ii. 14, "let me see thy countenance, let me hear thy voice; for sweet is thy voice and thy countenance is comely:" nay, he has signified his desire that his church and people may be the place of his residence and habitation, and that for ever; "for the Lord hath chosen Zion, he hath desired it for his habitation," Psalm cxxxii. 13, 14. Hence, 5. He will be not satisfied until he has the whole church with him in glory; this was the joy that was set before him in his sufferings; what he is now making preparation for in heaven, and what he is continually pleading for, as being exceedingly desirous of, saying, John xvii. 24, " Father, I will that they also whom thou hast given me, may be with me, where I am, that they may behold my glory." Thus Christ's desire is towards his church.

2ndly. This phrase may be expressive of that power which the church has over Christ, so that she can have any thing of him, when she pleases; he is so kind and indulgent an husband, that he will not deny his spouse anything that may be for her good and his glory. The strength of faith in prayer is very great: an instance of this we have in Jacob, who had power with God, and prevailed: and it is upon this score that God said to Moses, let me alone: knowing what interest Moses had in him, and how prevalent his petitions were with him; so that speaking after the manner of men, he could scarcely deny him any thing; "the effectual fervent prayer of a righteous man availeth much," James v. 16.

3rdly. The import of this expression may be, that Christ was her husband; " I am my beloved's, and his desire is towards me:" that is, he is my husband, I am his, and he is mine: so the wife is called " the desire of the eyes," Ezek. xxiv. 16, 18, and this was a very great blessing that she was favoured with, and an unspeakable comfort, that she could claim her interest in Christ under this sweet and endearing character and relation. Or,

4thly. It may be expressive of the whole care and concern of Christ for her, as her husband;* who as such bears and sympathizes with her under all her weaknesses and infirmities; protects from all dangers and enemies; and provides every thing for her, as food and raiment, grace and glory, all things necessary for her, both for time and eternity. Whatever may conduce to her comfort here, and eternal happiness hereafter: as a loving husband, he has given himself for her, rescued her from slavery and thraldom, procured an inheritance for her; and is now preparing that for her, and her for that, and will ere long put her into the possession of it. All which manifestly make appear, how much his desire has been and is towards her; which she having had some knowledge and experience of, ventures to invite him, as in the following words, saying,

Verse 11. *Come, my beloved, let us go forth into the field: let us lodge in the villages.*

Verse 12. *Let us get up early to the vineyards; let us see if the vine flourish; whether the tender grape appear, and the pomegranates bud forth; there will I give thee my loves.*

In these words are,

I. A general invitation given by the church to Christ, to go along with her; " Come, my beloved."

II. Some particular things mentioned which she invites him to: 1st. " To go forth into the field." 2ndly. " To lodge in the villages." 3rdly, " To get up early to the vineyards."

III. The things she had in view in so doing: 1st. To see whether " the vine flourished." 2ndly. Whether " the tender grape appeared." 3rdly. Whether " the pomegranates budded forth."

IV. A motive which she makes use of to prevail upon him; " there will I give thee my loves."

I. In these words is a general invitation given by the church to Christ to go along with her, " Come, my beloved;" on which may be made the following remaks: 1. That this word, *come*, is by the church taken out of Christ's mouth; it is a word much used by them, not only with reference to themselves, but to others also; see chap. ii. 10, 13, and iv. 8, Rev. xxii. 17, and is expressive of much familiarity, hearty desire, and tender affection. 2. We must not suppose that Christ needed stirring up, or was unwilling to go along with her, but he sometimes stays until he is asked: not only to make his church sensible of her duty, and that she may prize his presence the more: but also because he loves to hear her ask for his company, and say, " come, my beloved," let us walk together into the fields; let me there enjoy thy company, and let us take our fill of love. 3. These words may be considered as the church's calling upon Christ, to make good his promise, in verse 8, where he had given her reason to expect his presence; " I said I will go up to the palm-tree;" that is, I will grant my presence to my church and people, which are comparable to the palm-tree; I will be in the midst of them; she now says to him, " come, my beloved," do as thou hast said: though none of Christ's promises shall ever fail, yet they may not be immediately fulfilled; and it very much becomes believers to plead them with him in prayer, and not let them lie long by them; they ought to put Christ in remembrance of them, as they are allowed, that he would remember to them the word upon which he has caused them to hope. 4. They also contain an earnest desire after the presence of Christ, and the manifestations of his love unto her; nothing is more desirable to believers than Christ's presence; and there is a great deal of reason for it: for this only makes their lives comfortable whilst here; fills them with true solid joy and pleasure, makes a heaven upon earth, supports them under all their trials, carries them through all their difficulties, and gives them pleasing prospects of death and eternity. 5. They show the sense she had of her own insufficiency for the work she was going about, without the presence of Christ; for without him we can do nothing: hence, says Moses, Exod. xxxiii. 15,

* Vid. Fuller Miscell. Sacra, l. 3. c. 16.

"If thy presence go not with me, carry us not up hence:" the church here knew full well that her visiting the several congregations of the saints, to see in what condition they were, would be to little purpose, unless Christ went with her, and therefore she requests the favour of him. 6. It may be farther observed, that the clearer views a soul has of its interest in Christ, the more desirous it is of communion with him: this may easily be observed in the church's case, by comparing these words with the preceding verse: some, the more they are known, the less their company is desired; but the more and better a soul knows Christ, the more desirable his company is; and when they once have it, would never part with it; but say, with Peter, Matt. xvii. 4, " Lord, it is good for us to be here:" hence it is that they often long to depart out of this life, that they might be with Christ; which to them is far better than this life, and all the enjoyments of it. 7. The church's affixing this endearing character, " my beloved," to the invitation *come*, thereby signifying her affection to him, as well as her interest in him, may be considered as a powerful argument to induce him to go along with her: for with whom should, or indeed will loving husbands go, but with their wives, and especially when their company is importunately desired? one saint cannot tell how to deny another, when their company and conversation is desired on spiritual accounts; so engaging is it to each other; much less can Christ deny his church, when she entreats him after this sort.

II. The particular things she invites him to, are now to be considered. And,

1st. She desires him to " go forth into the field with her:" which may be expressive, 1. Of her desire after Christ's presence, both at home and abroad; she would not stir out of doors without him; when at home, nothing so delightful as his presence; and, having some business in the field, she is loath to go without him; O happy soul, that is thus blessed! of such an one it may be truly said, Deut. xxviii. 8—6, " Blessed shalt thou be in the city, and blessed shalt thou be in the field; blessed shalt thou be when thou comest in, and blessed shalt thou be when thou goest out." 2. Of her desire after solitariness, or of being alone with Christ: thus, Gen. xxiv. 63, " Isaac went out to meditate in the field;" where he could be retired, and have his thoughts more free, composed, and fit for such an employment: the field is also a place of more secrecy, as well as retiredness; and therefore, 1 Sam. xx. 11, " Jonathan said to David, come, let us go into the field;" that they might more freely tell their minds, and impart their loves to each other: thus the church desired Christ to go with her into the field; that there being alone with him, she might tell him all her heart, and let him know how much she loved him; which she could not so freely do in company. 3. She might design some recreation by it; it may be an allusion to persons who keep their country-houses, who, being retired from the city, take their walks in the field, to see how the fruits of the earth grow, as well as to enjoy the benefit of the country air: so the church: she is for going abroad into the fields; but then she would have Christ go with her; for no recreation is so, unless he be with her; walking abroad in the fields will yield her no pleasure, unless Christ be there. 4. It may signify her desire to have the gospel spread in the world, especially in those parts of it, in which it had not been as yet preached; and which looked very much like an uncultivated field: thus the field in the parable, Matt. xiii. 38, is said to be the world; which, being overrun with the thorns and briars of sin and corruption, moves her pity and compassion, and excites desire in her to have the gospel planted there, that so it might become a fruitful field: and therefore she is desirous to have her husband, and the true husbandman, go along with her, to manure, cultivate, and plant it; and perhaps the Gentile world may be particularly intended.

2ndly. She farther invites him to lodge in the villages with her. There is a manifest gradation in these words of hers, which shows her end and design in all; she first invites him to go forth into the field with her, and that is in order to lodge with her in the villages; and their lodging there, is in order to get up early next morning to the vineyards: Junius and Tremellius read the word thus, " let us lodge by the cyprus-trees;"¹ for the Hebrew word בכפרים, *cepharim*, signifies both *villages* and *cyprus-trees*; see chap. i. 14, and iv. 14; by which may be meant the saints; who may be compared thereunto, for their excellency, fragrancy, and fruitfulness; and an invitation to lodge by or with these, could not be unwelcome to Christ; seeing they are with him, " the excellent in the earth, in whom is all his delight:" though the word may as well be rendered villages, as it is by the Septuagint and others. From whence may be observed, 1. The villages being places of mean entertainment, both for food and lodgings; that a mean condition of life, with Christ, is more eligible and much preferable to the greatest affluence of the good things of this world without him: the church had rather have hard lodgings in a country village with Christ, than to dwell in a city, have her lodgings in a king's palace, or lie upon a bed of down without him: as one ⁿ once said, " Brown bread and the gospel are good fare;" so it may be also said, " A country lodging with Christ is good lodging." 2. Villages being places of retirement, and free from the noise and hurry of the city, and might occasion her desire to lodge there; she wanted to be at liberty from the world, that she might have some solitary communion with Christ; so David, being almost worn

---

¹ נלינה בכפרים pernoctemus ad cypros, Junius, Piscator, Brightman, Michaelis. ⁿ Mr. Dod.

out with the fatigues of the camp, the hurries of the court, thus passionately wishes, saying, Psalm lv. 6, 7, " O! that I had wings like a dove, for then would I flee away, and be at rest; lo, then would I wander far off, and remain," or as in the Hebrew text, " lodge in the wilderness, Selah." The cares of this life, and the hurrying employments of it, do much interrupt and break in upon a believer's comfortable communion with Christ; and therefore, with the church, he desires sometimes to be retired from them, and lodge with him in the villages. 3. She desires not only communion with Christ, but that it might be continued; she would lodge with him all night, as she says, in chap. i. 13, " He shall lie all night betwixt my breasts," it is not merely for an hour or two, that she would have his company, but all night: believers, who have got some knowledge of Christ's person, and have tasted the sweetness of communion with him, are like the Samaritans, John iv. 40, who " besought him that he would tarry with them;" they are never weary of his company, and do not care how much they have of it. Though, 4. These words may signify her desire to have the gospel preached in the villages, as well as in the cities: thus our Lord Jesus Christ, in the days of his flesh, "went about all the cities and villages, preaching the Gospel of the kingdom," Matt. ix. 35; as did also his disciples after him; though, as one [w] well observes, the Gospel was first preached in cities mostly, and from thence spread itself in time into the neighbouring villages, where the heathen idolatry lasted longer than in cities; from whence it had the name of paganism, *pagus* signifying a village; which the church here observing, desires Christ to go along with her, and spread the Gospel there.[x]

3rdly. She signifies her desire also to " get up early to the vineyards," for which reason she thought it most proper to lodge in the villages, and not in the city; from whence she could not have been so early at the vineyards, as she desired to be. By the vineyards, the Targum, R. Solomon Jarchi and Alshech understand the synagogues and schools of the Jews; and so it is explained in the Talmud:[y] though it seems much more probable, that by them are meant, the several particular churches and congregations of the saints; which are distinguished by sovereign grace, planted with a variety of fruitful vines, watered every moment by Christ, and fenced about with his almighty power; and by her getting up unto them, may be meant her visiting of them; which is much such an act of kindness and friendship as that of Paul's, who said to Barnabas, Acts xv. 36, " Let us go again and visit our brethren, in every city where we have preached the word of the Lord, and see how they do." And what still more shows how intent she was upon it, and how much her heart was in it, she is for getting up early; that is, betimes in the morning, or in the most seasonable time, as the word early is sometimes used: she is for losing no opportunity, and making use of the most suitable one to visit the churches; and that her visit may not be in vain, she is for taking Christ along with her; she is not willing to go alone; she knew of what service Christ's presence would be to the churches, and to what little purpose hers would be without him; and therefore she says, "let us get up early," &c. But,

III. She mentions the several things she had in view in giving this invitation to Christ, or the several ends of it. And,

1st. It was to " see if the vine flourished;" and she might well think that this and what follows would take with Christ, and go a great way to prevail upon him to go along with her; seeing her ends here are much the same with his in going down into his nut-garden, chap. vi. 11, and which, no doubt, she had some reference to. By the vine, the Targum understands the Israelites, who may be compared thereunto; and I think, true believers in Christ, who are Israelites indeed, may very well be meant. These indeed, like vines, are weak and worthless creatures of themselves: yet being engrafted in Christ, the true vine, and growing upon him, they bring forth fruit, and are exceeding valuable and precious: and by their flourishing may be meant, both their fruitfulness in the exercise of grace, and in the performance of good works: and though the believer is not always in a flourishing condition; there is sometimes but a small appearance of fruit upon him; his life, his grace, is hid unto him; and his fruitfulness does not appear to others; yet he shall flourish again, because he is planted in a fruitful soil, by the rivers of divine love and grace; is well rooted in Christ Jesus, and whom he takes care of, waters every moment, and purges and prunes, that he may bring forth more fruit; this the church was sensible of, and therefore is desirous that Christ would go along with her.

2ndly. Another end she had in inviting Christ to go with her into the field, villages, and vineyards, is, to see " whether the tender grape appear, or whether the flower of the grape opened itself."[z] By which may be meant young converts; who are weak and tender, have but little knowledge, a small degree of faith, and have not arrived to that solidity and establishment, as many others have; and are therefore compared to new-born babes, lambs, and kids of the flock: as also to a bruised reed, and to the smoking flax; but as Christ does not despise the day of small things, so neither does the church overlook them, but shows a very great

---

[w] Bishop Patrick in loc.   [x] In Shirhashirim Rabba, in loc. By the field and villages, the nations of the world are understood.   [y] T. Bab. Erubim, fol. 21. 2.   [z] סתה הסמדר ηνθησεν ὁ κυπρισμος, Sept. si flores fructus parturiunt, Vulg. Lat. version; ap- erueritse uva parva, Montanus; an aperta sit gemma, Mercerus; ac florem protrudat, Tigurine version; exeruerit se uva prima, Cocceius; an aperiat se prima uva, Junius; aperuerit uva prima, Brightman.

concern for them; she is very desirous of seeing these appear in churches: this is a very great encouragement to churches, when souls are born again among them; it is a sign that the Lord designs to continue them, and to make them yet more flourishing and fruitful.

3rdly. Her other end is to see whether "the pomegranates budded." By pomegranates may be meant stronger believers, who are taller and more fruitful than the former; why they are so compared, may be seen in chap. iv. 13; and by the buddings of them, may be meant the actings and exercise of grace in them. We may observe that the church is concerned for the comfortable wellbeing and good estate of believers of all ranks and sizes; of the vines and pomegranates, as well as of the tender grapes; and of the buddings of the one, as well as of the blossoming or opening of the other.

IV. The motive which she makes use of to prevail upon Christ to comply with her invitation, is, "for there will I give thee my loves;" that is, when we are alone in the field, or out at lodgings in the villages, or when we are together in the vineyards, visiting the vines and pomegranates, I will show thee my love; I will open all my heart to thee, and thou shalt know how much I love thee. And, 1. We are not to suppose that this is the first time of her loving Christ, or of her manifesting it to him, for she loved him long before; but she mentions this now to gain her end; for she knew very well what would take with Christ's heart, what was grateful to him, and that nothing was more so than expressions of her love to him, and this she had learned from his own words, in chap. iv. 10, "How fair is thy love, my sister, my spouse! how much better is thy love than wine!" Christ knew very well she loved him; but yet he loved to hear her say she did. What made Christ ask Peter so often whether he loved him or no? it was not because he doubted of it, but because he loved to hear him express it. 2. By her loves, may be meant the manifestations of her love to him, in the observance of his commands; the offering up the sacrifices of prayer and praise unto him; as well as all other branches of religious worship and service in his house, which she promises to him there; and this sense the Targum inclines unto. 3. This, being expressed in the plural number, may intend not only the excellency of her love to Christ, and the various ways of manifesting it to him, but also the abundance of it: here was an overflow of it in her soul; her heart was brimful of it, and she seems to want an opportunity of venting it; for which purpose she desires to be alone with Christ, as Joseph did with his brethren, that so she might, with the greater freedom, let out her affections to him. 4. Communion with Christ, and the flourishing condition of his churches,

tend much to enlarge a believer's heart with love to Christ, and to draw out his affections towards him, "we love him, because he first loved us," 1 John iv. 19. I see not why the word for loves, may not be rendered, my lovely flowers; as a word nearly the same, in the following verse, is by some rendered, "those lovely flowers give a good smell," as Junius and Tremellius; which seem to refer to the flowers here; such as were to be met with in plenty in fields and vineyards, and among vines and pomegranates, as lilies, violets, &c., and may be an allusion to lovers, who used to give to those they loved, sweet smelling flowers;[a] and here may signify the graces of the Spirit, and the actings of them, which are fragrant and acceptable to Christ.

Verse 13. *The mandrakes give a smell, and at our gates are all manner of pleasant fruits, new and old; which I have laid up for thee, O my beloved.*

IN these words the church makes use of another motive or argument to prevail upon Christ to grant her his presence and company, taken from the variety of fragrant flowers and pleasant fruits, which she abounded with, and had ready at hand, and which she had carefully laid up and reserved for his use and service; all which are commended.

I. From the fragrancy of them; "the mandrakes give a smell."

II. From the comprehensiveness of them; "all manner of pleasant fruits."

III. These are said to be "new and old."

IV. Not afar off, but at the very door; "at our gates."

V. They are all for his use and service; "which I have laid up for thee, O my beloved."

I. The fragrancy of those flowers or fruits with which she abounds, is here expressed; "the mandrakes give a smell." The Hebrew word דודאים, *dudaim*, translated mandrakes, is only found in this place, and in Gen. xxx. 14—16; in this sense; but what plant or herb is intended by it, is not very easy to determine; Junius and Tremellius have rendered it, in both places, by "flores amabiles, lovely flowers:" which they think best agrees with the etymology of the word: others[b] render it, Jessamin; others[c] lilies; others violets: R. Solomon Jarchi would have it rendered baskets here, and refers it to Jer. xxiv. 1; where the people of Israel are represented by two baskets of figs; where a word derived from the same root, and of the same form is used; and that both sorts of people, there represented, may be here said to give a good smell, because now they all sought the face of the Lord. Ludolphus, in his Ethiopic history,[d] takes it to be the fruit which the Arabians call *mauz* or *muza*, (called, by some, the Indian fig) which, in the Abyssine country, is as big as a cucumber, and of the same form and

---

[a] Naias amat Thyrsin, Glauca Almona, Nisa Theonem, Nisa rosas, Glauca violas, dat lilia Nais: Cythereus Sidonius apud Auson. [b] R. Sol. Jarchi in Gen. xxx. 14. [c] Vid. Jun. in Gen. xxx. 14. [d] L. 1. c. 9. n. 23.

shape; fifty of which grow upon one and the same stalk, and are of a very sweet taste and smell; from which cognation of a great many upon the same stalk, he thinks it took the name of *dudaim*. Some think, the fruit of the lote-tree is here intended; which, according to Homer,[e] Herodotus,[f] Ovid,[g] and others,[h] was a very sweet and delicious fruit; sweet apples, as some call them; there were a people in Africa, called Lotophagi, who lived upon it, as observed by the same authors; the mandrake of the Chinese is the famous root they call *ginseng*; which, with them, is a sovereign remedy for all weaknesses of body or mind: a preservative of health; and they call it the plant that gives immortality. Ravius, in his dissertation concerning the *dudaim*, thinks the words should be rendered, "the branches put forth their sweet-smelling flowers;" and that the branches of fig-trees are meant, which give a good smell, agreeable to chap. ii. 13; and which, he supposes, to the use of the word, in Jer. xxiv. 1; and to this sense Heidegger[i] agrees; only he thinks the word branches, is not to be restrained to a particular species, but may signify branches of sweet-smelling flowers and fruits in general. But the generality of translators and interpreters render it, mandrakes; as do the Septuagint, both the Targums of Onkelos and Jonathan, on Gen. xxx. 14; though the Targum on this place renders it, balsam, but then it is questionable whether the same plant which is known among us by the name of mandrakes, is here meant, because of its strong smell; but of this more hereafter. Let us consider what may be intended hereby. And,

1st. By these mandrakes may be meant, the saints and people of God; who are plants of God's right hand planting, are both fragrant and fruitful; and may be compared unto them, 1. Because the mandrake is a cold plant, and therefore used for the assuaging inflammations, and healing ulcers:[k] the people of God, though they ought not to be cold in divine things, nor lukewarm in the cause of Christ, and vindication of his truths and ordinances: yet are, or at least should be, of cooling spirits, to allay those heats, and heal those divisions which too often appear in the churches of Christ; which they may be instrumental in, by a prudent carriage, a moderate temper, and by using soft and "pleasant words:" which, as Solomon says, Prov. xv. 1, and xvi. 24, "turn away wrath, and are sweet to the soul, and health to the bones:" and when they appear to be of hot and fiery tempers and dispositions, it is what is opposite to the principle which is wrought in them and that profession which they make. 2. Because the mandrake is supposed to excite love; hence the apples of it are called "apples of love;" and the Hebrew word here used comes from a root which signifies love: the saints may well be represented by them on this account; for though they do not provoke Christ to love them, by the love they show him, or the obedience they perform unto him; yet these often draw out Christ's affections to them; and what he himself has wrought in them, and put upon them, render them lovely in his eyes: besides, it is their incumbent duty, and should be the great employment of their lives, to provoke one another "to love and good works." 3. They have been also thought to help barrenness,[l] and to make fruitful; which some have imagined to be the reason of that great contention between Rachel and Leah concerning them; and the same opinion of their prolific virtue remains in those eastern parts still, and they are applied for that purpose; and the plant is described as having a large leaf, bearing a certain sort of fruit, in shape resembling an apple, growing ripe in harvest, but of an ill savour, and not wholesome:[m] hence the phrase here may intend the fruitfulness of the church in the first times of the gospel, through the vast numbers of souls which were born again therein, when that prophecy was fulfilled, Isa. liv. 1, "Sing, O barren, that thou didst not bear; break forth into singing, and cry aloud, thou that didst not travail with child: for more are the children of the desolate, than the children of the married wife, saith the Lord;" which fruitfulness of the church may be considered as a very good argument used by her here, to prevail on Christ to grant her his presence and company. 4. The mandrake is a narcotic, has a sleepy virtue in it, as Pliny[n] observes, and much inclines thereunto; Levinus Lemnius[o] writes of himself, that being in his study, he was suddenly taken with a sleepy fit, which he could by no means account for, until he espied a mandrake-apple upon one of the shelves, to which he ascribed it; and Plutarch[p] relates, that mandrakes, which grow by vines, give the wine made of them such a virtue, that those who drink of it sleep more sweetly; the saints are often in sleepy frames themselves; the wise virgins slept as well as the foolish; and conversation with sleepy professors makes others so likewise. 5. It not only inclines to sleep, but makes persons sluggish and slothful; hence those phrases, "to drink the mandrake, and to sleep under a mandrake,["q] are proverbially used of persons who are

---

[e] Odyss. 9. v. 94. [f] Melpomene, sive l. 4. c. 177. [g] Tristium. l. 4. Epist. 1. v. 31. and De Ponto, l. 4. eleg. 10. v. 18. [h] Vid. Strabo, Geograph. l. 17. p. 574. Athenæi Deipnosophist. l. 14. c. 18. Plin. l. 13. c. 17. and Pomponius Sabinus in Virgil. Georgic. l. 2. p. 210. [i] Hist. Patriarch. tom. 2. exercit. 19. s. 9. 15. [k] Fernel. Method. Medend. l. 6. c. 1. and Plin. l. 26. c. 9, 10,—14, 15. [l] Avicenna apud Castel. Animadv. Samar. in Gen. xxx. 14. [m] Maundrel's Journey from Aleppo. &c, p. 61. edit. 7. [n] L. 25. c. 13. So Plutarch. Sympos. l. 3. p. 652. and Medici in Theodoret. in loc. Vid. Philostrat. Vita Apollon l. 8. c. 3. [o] Herb. Bibl. Explic. c. 2. [p] De Audiendis Poetis, p. 15. [q] Μανδραγοραν πεπωκοσιν, *Demosth. Orat. Philip.* 4. Ύπο μανδραγορα καθευδεις, *Lucian. in Timon s. 1. Vid. Julian. Ep. 21. p. 139.*

sluggish and inactive in the discharge of their office: the saints are too often so themselves, and the cause thereof in others: being "slothful in business, and not fervent in spirit, serving the Lord," as they ought to be. 6. The apples of the mandrake are very delightful to look upon, being of a yellow or golden colour; and so are the saints in Christ's eye; to them he looks, and with them he is well pleased, they being beautified with the garments of his salvation, and adorned with the graces of his Spirit. 7. These mandrakes are said to "give a smell;" it is true, it is not said that they give a good smell; but it may be reasonably supposed that such an one is intended, because their commendation is designed; and they are taken notice of by the church, as what might be inviting to Christ; and so no doubt Reuben's mandrakes, which Rachel took such a fancy to, were fragrant, and of a sweet smell: or we may reasonably suppose the boy would not have gathered them, nor Rachel have taken such a liking to them, no more than Leah would have contended with her about them, unless it was for a reason before given. But then the difficulty is to know what plant is intended, seeing our present mandrakes are of an ill and offensive smell; and so is the plant now shown for it, as before observed: and such an account also Pliny[r] gives of it; though Dioscorides, Levinus Lemnius,[s] and Augustine,[t] who says he saw the plant, and examined it, says, that it is of a very sweet smell; which though it does not agree with the plant which now bears the name, suits well with that intended here; for which reason the saints may be compared unto it, whose persons are of a sweet smell, being clothed with Christ's garments, which "smell of myrrh, aloes, and cassia," and anointed with the savoury ointments of the Spirit's grace: whose prayers are so, being perfumed with Christ's mediation: and their good works being accepted, with their persons, "in the beloved;" so the Jews[u] interpret the mandrakes, of the young men of Israel; who have not tasted the taste of sin, pure and holy persons, free from vicious habits. Or,

2ndly. By these mandrakes, which give a good smell, may be meant the doctrines and promises of the gospel; which, 1. Like mandrakes, are of a healing and cooling nature: the law is a fiery law; and when it works, in a sinner's conscience, it makes fiery work there; it worketh wrath, which is only assuaged through the application of gospel doctrines and promises, by the blessed Spirit. 2. Like mandrakes, these excite love; for though it is the law which enjoins and requires love both to God and to our neighbour; yet it is the Gospel which moves and presses us to it, with the noblest motives and most powerful arguments; such as those which are taken from the love of God and Christ to us. 3. Like mandrakes, are the means of fruitfulness: it is by the gospel, as the instrumental means, that souls are begotten again to Christ; for though they are born of an incorruptible seed, and are begotten again according to the sovereign will of God, and as an instance of his abundant mercy, yet it is by the word of truth, which liveth and abideth for ever. 4. As the mandrake-apples are delightful, so are the doctrines and promises of the gospel; which words being "fitly spoken, are like apples of gold in pictures of silver." 5. As the mandrakes give a good smell, so do these; for to them that are saved, they are "the savour of life unto life."

3rdly. By these *dudaim* or lovely flowers, as Junius translates the word, may be meant the graces of the Spirit; such as faith, repentance, love, thankfulness, hope, humility, &c. 1. Faith may be one of those lovely flowers which give a good smell: this is a flower that does not grow in nature's garden; but is sown and raised in the believer's heart, by the power and Spirit of God; which at first is but like a grain of mustard-seed, that is the least of all seeds; but afterwards grows in some more, in others less; but in all it is "alike precious faith," which emits a sweet fragrancy to God and Christ. 2. Repentance may be another of those lovely flowers; this grows in the same garden as faith does; they are sown and raised up together, and that by one and the same hand; and when attended with fruits becoming it, is highly valued by Christ Jesus. 3. Love may be another of those lovely flowers; this precious flower springs from, is raised up and influenced by, as well as scented with the love of Christ: and of all the flowers in the believer's garden, none is fairer in Christ's eye, or gives him, with its smell, more pleasure and delight; for of this he says, in chap. iv. 10, "How fair is thy love, my sister, my spouse!" &c. 4. The grace of thankfulness is another of these flowers; nay, a certain Expositor[w] thinks, that it is chiefly intended: the exercise of this grace is required of us, for every mercy, both spiritual and temporal; and in every condition, state, and circumstance of life: this is more pleasing to God; and he smells a sweeter savour of rest in it, than in all burnt-offerings; and a contrary disposition is highly resented by him, as appears from the case of the ten lepers that were cleansed, of which but one returned to give God thanks. 5. The grace of hope may be another of those lovely flowers: this is none of the meanest flowers which grow in the believer's garden; this is raised by powerful efficacious grace; is watered with divine love; is made to abound through the power of the Holy Ghost; and in which Christ takes no small pleasure and delight; "for the Lord takes pleasure in them that fear him, in those that hope in his mercy." 6. The grace of humility is another precious flower; "the ornament of a meek and quiet spirit is in the sight of God of great price:" this grace so much adorns

---

[r] Odor gravis ejus, sed radicis and mali gravior, l. 25. c. 13.   [s] Herb. Bibl. Explic. c. 2.   [t] Contr. Faustum, l. 22. c. 56.   [u] T. Bab. Erubin, fol. 21. 2.   [w] Dr Guild in loc.

believers, that Christ says, "to this man will I look, that is poor, and of a contrite spirit;" neither can he take his eye off them, nor will he remove from them, but dwell with them for evermore. I might have mentioned many more of those lovely and sweet-smelling flowers, as patience, self-denial, &c., but these may suffice.

II. The church's fruits are commended from the comprehensiveness of them; she is possessed of "all manner of pleasant fruits." Which may denote, 1. The plenty of them: believers have not only abundance of grace in Christ, but also abundance in themselves; for "where sin abounded, grace does much more abound;" they have also a fulness of all spiritual blessings in Christ, as well as a plenty of gospel-doctrines, and exceeding great and precious promises. 2. This may likewise denote the variety of them: the graces of the Spirit are many and various; as are the blessings of the gospel, such as redemption through Christ's blood, pardon of sin, justification by his righteousness, adoption, sanctification, &c., so are the doctrines and promises of the gospel, which are all suited to the several cases and circumstances of believers. 3. It also denotes the excellency of them; for here are not only plenty and variety of all manner of fruits, but all manner of pleasant fruits; such as do not grow every where, nor in any garden, but only in the garden of the church; whose "plants are an orchard of pomegranates, with pleasant fruits," &c. The allusion, no doubt is to the most excellent fruits, with which the land of Judea abounded, as apples, figs, dates, pomegranates, &c.; the word used includes every precious thing; not fruits only, but gold, silver, jewels, garments, &c.[x]

III. These fruits are said to be both new and old, which still heightens and increases the commendation of them; there is such plenty and fulness of them, as that the former year's produce is not gone, when the new is gathered in; here is some of both years increase, which is in indication of great plenty, as well as of the goodness of the fruit that will keep so long. By these fruits new and old, 1. Some[y] understand the gifts of the Spirit; which Christ, after his ascension, received for his church, and bestowed on it; together with those temporal blessings which she enjoyed before. Though, 2. Others think that by them are intended moral and natural virtues, which may be found in an unconverted man; and the graces of the Spirit, which are only in renewed souls. But, 3. It seems much better to understand them of those fresh supplies of grace which believers have from Christ; for they cannot live upon their old stock, but must have a new supply; which they are graciously indulged with from Christ, from whose fulness they continually "receive grace for grace." Though 4. I am rather inclined to think, that the doctrines of the Old and New Testament, which, for matter and substance are one and the same, are here meant, with which the church, and particularly her scribes and faithful ministers are furnished, so as they can "bring forth out of their treasure things new and old," Matt. xiii. 52.

IV. These fruits are also said to be at their gates; which is mentioned, 1. In opposition to the mandrakes which grew in the field; which appears to be a field-plant, from Gen. xxx. 14, where it is said, that "Reuben went in the days of wheat-harvest, and found mandrakes in the field," but these fruits here grew at their very doors. 2. It may be an allusion to a custom of the eastern countries, in garnishing the doors of new-married persons with fruits and flowers; and not only at nuptial feasts, but at other festivals also;[z] which made it very inviting to go within. 3. It may also signify, that these fruits were near at hand; there was no occasion to go far for them; they were even at the door, as the judge is said to be, James v. 9. 4. It may denote the publicness of them: they are not hid in secret, but exposed to public view; as the graces and good works of the saints should be; "Let your light," says our Lord, Matt. v. 16, "so shine before men," &c., as well as the doctrines of the gospel, which are not to be spoken in a corner, but to be divulged upon the house-top. 5. By these gates may be meant, the means and ordinances of the Gospel, where those fruits may be had; and it is therefore an encouragement to souls to "watch daily at wisdom's gates, waiting at the posts of her door:" so some Jewish[a] writers interpret them of their synagogues and schools.

V. All this plenty and variety of pleasant fruits which were just at hand, the church declares were all laid up for Christ; "which I have laid up for thee, O my beloved:" respect may be had to a custom with lovers, to lay up fruits for those they love; at least such a custom may be compared with this.[b] Christ had bestowed a large store and great plenty of fruit upon the church, which she had carefully reserved for him; she laid it up in her heart; she bore it in remembrance, which this phrase is sometimes expressive of: thus it is said, Luke i. 66, that all that heard of the surprising circumstances which attended the birth of John the Baptist, "laid them up in their hearts," that is, bore them in remembrance; so should we lay up the word of God, and the doctrines of it in our minds, and not forget them; thus David

---

[x] Vid. Schindler. Lex. Pentaglott. col. 970.
[y] Bishop Patrick in loc. [z] Vid. Plutarch. Amator. vol. 2. p. 755. and Barthium ad Claudian. de Nupt. Honor. v. 208. Longos erexit janua ramos. Juvenal. Satyr. 12. v. 91. Necta coronam postibus. Ib. Satyr. 6. v. 51, 52. ornantur, postes, v. 79. ornatas paulo ante fores, &c. v. 226, 227.

janua laureata, Tertullian. ad Uxor. l. 2. c. 6. Vid. Ovid Metamorph. l. 14. fab. 17. [a] Targum in loc. and Zohar in Gen. fol. 129. 3. [b] Sunt poma gravantia ramos; sunt auro similes longis in vitious uvæ, sunt and purpureæ; tibi and has servamus and illas; Ovid. Metamorph. l. 13. fab. 8.

said, Psalm cxix. 11, he did: "Thy word," says he, "have I hid or laid up," it is the same word that is here used, "in mine heart, that I might not sin against thee:" so likewise should we treasure up in our minds all the instances of God's grace and favour to us, and record the several experiences of his loving-kindness; not as a stock to live upon, but to be brought out at proper times, to magnify the grace of Christ, and to advance his glory: "for of him, and through him, and to him, are all things." Now this appears to be a very great attainment and a mighty instance of grace in the church, to have a stock of promises and experiences, and yet not live upon them herself, but upon Christ, the Author and Donor of them; to lay them up for his service, and lay them out for his honour and glory: and her adding this endearing character, "O my beloved," shows not only the strength of her affection to him, but may also serve to assure him of the truth of what she said; as well as be an inducement to him to comply with her request, which she passionately renews in the beginning of the next chapter.

CHAPTER VIII.

This chapter begins with an ardent wish of the church, for a free and intimate converse with Christ; declaring what she would do to him, and for him, should she have an interview with him, ver. 1, 2; what familiarity should be between them, ver. 3; charging the daughters of Jerusalem not to give him any disturbance, ver. 4. Upon which they inquire who she was, that was in such a posture as they saw her in, ver. 5, when the church, instead of giving them an answer, says some things concerning her beloved on whom they saw her leaning; and makes some requests to him, for more nearness to him, and manifestations of his love to her; urged from the strength of her love and affections to him, which were invincible, v. 6, 7. Next follows a speech of the church about her little sister: expressing a concern for her, and what she would do to her, and with her, ver. 8, 9; and the answer of the little sister, declaring what she was, and what she enjoyed, ver. 10; then the words of the church again, concerning her husband's vineyard, the place, keepers, and profits of it, ver. 11, 12. And the chapter, and with it the Song, is concluded with a request of Christ to the church, that he might hear her voice, ver. 13, and with a petition of hers to him, that he would come quickly to her, ver. 14.

Verse 1. *O that thou wert as my brother, that sucked the breasts of my mother, when I should find thee without, I would kiss thee: yea, I should not be despised.*

These words are a continuation, or rather a renewal of the church's desire after communion with Christ; they contain these three things:

I. An ardent wish for a free and familiar converse with Christ; that he would show himself to her as her brother, and act the part of one unto her: "O that thou wert as my brother:" and her meaning herein is more strongly expressed, by adding, "that sucked the breasts of my mother."

II. A resolution of hers to kiss him when she found him without; "when I should find thee without, I would kiss thee."

III. The opinion which she entertained, that she should not be despised for such an action; "yea, I should not be despised."

I. These words contain a hearty wish of the church's: the words may be read thus, "Who will give thee as a brother to me?"c Such forms of wishing may be seen in many places; see Isa. xiv. 7, Job xxiii. 2; and the meaning is, that Christ would show himself to her in the relation of a brother, act the part of one towards her; and that she might as freely converse with him, as a brother and sister may and used to do. Several Jewishd writers acknowledge, that the King Messiah is intended by the brother here: in what sense Christ stands in such a relation to his church and to all true believers; as also what this wish of hers is expressive of, I shall now consider. And, 1. Christ is the church's brother by virtue of his incarnation, or the assumption of her nature; they are nearly allied in the bonds of consanguinity; he is of the same flesh and blood with her; and she is flesh of his flesh, and bone of his bone; there is a very great nearness, affinity, and likeness between them, for "in all things it behoved him to be made like unto his brethren;" and it is upon this score that he becomes a brother to them: the words may be considered as the wish of the old church for Christ's incarnation. 2. Christ and believers are of one and the same Father: God is the Father of Christ, and so he is of all his covenant-people; of whom he says, 2 Cor. vi. 18, "I will be a Father unto you, and ye shall be my sons and daughters;" which is an instance of his boundless and amazing grace: hence because Christ and believers are sons of the same Father, though not in the same way of filiation, he bid Mary Magdalene go to his brethren: and as an evidence of their standing in that relation to him, say unto them, John xx. 17, "I ascend unto my Father and your Father, and to my God and your God;" it is also upon this account that saints become "heirs of God, and joint-heirs with Christ;" they are heirs of God, because his children; and joint-heirs with Christ, because they are his brethren, he being the first-born among them. 3. Persons may be said to be brethren, by being concerned in one and the same covenant: thus there was a brotherhood between Judah and Israel, which was dis-

---

c מִי יִתֶּנְךָ כְּאָח לִי *τίς δῴη σε ἀδελφιδέ μυ*, Sept. Quis mihi det te fratrem meum? Vulgate Latin version; O si quis daret te ut fratrem esse mihi! Junius: Quis det te ut fratrem mihi? Montanus, Mercerus; Quis dabit te tanquam fratrem mihi? Brightman. Utinam quasi frater mihi sis! Tigurine version; Utinam fias mihi ut frater! Cocceius.

d Targum in loc. Zohar in Gen. fol. 104, 1. Caphtor Uperah, fol. 5. 2. and Tzeror Hammor, fol. 73. 3.

solved by God's breaking his covenant with them, Zech. xi. 10, 14; Christ and his people are in one and the same covenant, and in such an one as can never be broken; though as he has the preeminence in all things, as he ought to have, so he has in this; for he is the Mediator, Surety, and Messenger of the covenant; nay, he is the Covenant itself; he is the Foundation on which it stands, and the matter of which it consists; he is the saints' Representative in it; and because it is made with him, their elder Brother, in their name, room, and stead, therefore said to be made with them, and they share in all the blessings and comforts of it. 4. Persons that are of like nature, temper, dispositions, and practices, are said to be brethren: thus Simeon and Levi are said, Gen. xlix. 5, to be brethren; not because of their natural relation, but because of their agreement in their tempers and practices: Christ and believers are brethren in this sense; they are much of the same nature; Christ has assumed their nature, and they are in some measure made partakers of his; principles of grace and holiness from him are wrought in them; nay, he is formed in their hearts; his image is enstamped, and his features are drawn there; there is a very great likeness between them; they are conformed to the image of him who is the first-born among many brethren: hence it is said, Heb. ii. 11, that "he that sanctifieth, and they that are sanctified, are all of one, for which cause he is not ashamed to call them brethren;" and to the same purpose those words of Christ might be produced, in Matt. xii. 50, "for whosoever shall do the will of my Father which is in heaven, the same is my brother, and sister, and mother." 5. Those who are partners and companions in afflictions, may be also called brethren; hence Job says, chap. xxx. 29, on the account of his sorrowful and afflicted condition, that he was "a brother to dragons, and a companion to owls:" Christ and believers are brethren in sufferings; though it is true, they were not companions with him in his sufferings, yet he is in theirs; the afflictions of the churches are the afflictions of Christ; he bears the heaviest part of them: for what is done to his people he takes as done to himself; and as they suffer with him, so they shall reign with him hereafter in glory, and that for ever. 6. Persons may be called brethren on the score of friendship: thus David, in 2 Sam. i. 26, calls Jonathan his brother; not so much because he had married his sister, but on the account of the mutual friendship that had been between them: in this sense Christ and believers are brethren; he is a friend to them, and such a "friend that sticks closer than a brother;" of which friendship of his towards them, he has given many open and undeniable proofs; he accounts them as his friends, and therefore treats them as such, by frequent visiting of them, disclosing of his secrets to them, and making noble entertainments for them. 7. The church might wish that Christ would manifest himself to her, under this relation of a brother, because of that intimacy, freedom, and familiarity, which she might use with him as such; she would kiss him in the open street, take him by the hand, and lead him into her mother's house, and there keep a free conversation with him; as a sister might do with an own brother, and not be reproached for it. 8. Her meaning also may be, that he would act the part of a brother to her; that is, that he would be pitiful and compassionate to her, and sympathize with her under all her exercises, as a tender-hearted brother would; and such a one is Christ; he has a fellow-feeling with his people in all their temptations, and gives them all needful succour and relief; in all their afflictions he is afflicted, and has bowels of compassion for them in all their distresses. 9. A brother not only sympathizes with, but condescends to the weaknesses and infirmities of his brethren, it is a wonderful condescension in Christ to stand in this relation to his people, as also not to be ashamed to own it; and being in it, he is capable of showing a great deal of condescension to them in many instances; which the superiority of a father, in which relation he also stands, would not admit of; to which the church might have regard in this wish of hers. 10. The love and affection of a brother is very great, and much to be valued, as Christ's is by the church; for "his loving-kindness is better than life," and all the comforts of it; the manifestations of which the church may well be supposed to desire here, as she did in chap. i. 2, where she says, and what is much the same with this request here; "Let him kiss me with the kisses of his mouth; for thy love is better than wine."

Again, the church's meaning, in this ardent and pathetic wish of hers, is more strongly expressed by adding, that it was such a brother she wished for, "that sucked the breasts of her mother;" in which may be considered, 1st. What this phrase in general intends. 2ndly. Who is meant by her mother. 3rdly. What by sucking of her mother's breasts.

1st. This phrase in general may intend either, 1. The truth of Christ's human nature; she wishes for his incarnation in the former phrase, and in this, that it might appear to be true and real; of which his conception and birth, his being the child born, and the infant of days, his eating butter and honey, and sucking the breasts of his mother, were sufficient indications. Or, 2. The near relation Christ stands in to his church, being a brother by the mother's side; which relation is accounted the nearest, and the affection of such an one is also the strongest; of which we have an instance in the case of Joseph, to whom Reuben, Judah, Simeon, &c., were brethren, though only by his father's side; and to whom he had a brotherly love, but not so strong an affection as he had to Benjamin, his mother's son; who was such a brother that had sucked the breasts of his mother, as may be seen in Gen. xliii. 29, 30, 34, such a brother, so nearly related, and of such an affection, the church wisheth for.

2ndly. It may also be inquired who is meant by her mother: and this may be, either the church, who may be called so, on the account of the many converts which are born in her: thus Zion is said to travail in birth, and bring forth children, Isa. lxvi. 8; and the Gentile church is said to be the mother of many, Isa. liv. 1, and regenerate souls are frequently called the church's children, in that prophecy; or else, by her mother, we are to understand the covenant of grace, "the Jerusalem which is above, which is the mother of us all," Gal. iv. 26, for every converted soul is the birth of an everlasting covenant; hence such are called, in Rom. ix. 8, the children of the promise; and it is no unusual phrase with the Jews, to call themselves the children of the covenant.

3rdly. By sucking the breasts of her mother, may be meant, either, 1. The enjoyment of the grace and blessings of the everlasting covenant; so this phrase of sucking the breasts is used for the enjoyment of blessings, Isa. lx. 16, and in this sense Christ may be truly said to suck the breasts of her mother; for all grace is in his hands; every blessing of the covenant he is in possession of; we have all our grace from him, and are blessed with all spiritual blessings only in him. Or else, 2. By these breasts may be meant the word and ordinances; which are breasts of consolation to believers, in whose hearts Christ is formed; so that when they suck the breasts, and are nourished with the sincere milk of the word, and grow thereby, Christ may be said to suck of them, and be nourished by them. Or else, 3. This phrase may be expressive of that familiar intercourse and delightful communion which is between Christ and his church; which is frequently expressed by eating, feasting, and supping together; see chap. v. 1, and Rev. iii. 20.

II. The next thing in the words, is the church's resolution to kiss Christ, whenever she found him without: in which may be observed, 1st. The resolution itself, to kiss him. 2ndly. The time when she would put this into practice, "when I should find thee." 3rdly. The place where she would do this, and that is, without.

1st. We may consider the resolution itself, which is to kiss him; which is no other than what was her duty to do, and what is enjoined all believers; Psalm ii. 12, "Kiss the son, lest he be angry." Which may be understood these several ways: 1. There is a kiss of approbation; in this sense the word is used, Prov. xxiv. 26, "Every man shall kiss his lips, that giveth a right answer;" that is, shall approve his sayings, and highly extol and commend him for them: Christ is a person to be liked and approved, being "altogether lovely, and the chiefest among ten thousands;" and so he is by every believer; there is none in heaven or earth, that is so much valued by them as he is; they count all things but loss and dung, in comparison of him; they approve of him as their Surety and Saviour, and esteem him in every character and relation he stands in to them. 2. There is a kiss of love and affection, which is used by friends and relations, and that either at meeting or parting; thus the prodigal's father fell on his neck and kissed him, when he met him; as did Paul's friends, at parting with him; which kiss of charity, or love, was much used among the primitive saints; and with such a kiss as this, the church kisses Christ, whom she dearly loves, and has the strongest affection for, arising from his love and loveliness: as Christ's kisses, in chap. i. 2, are the lettings out and manifestation of his love to the church; so the church's lips are the lettings forth and manifestations of her love to him: with such a kiss as this, the poor woman kissed Christ, in Luke vii. 38, who "began to wash his feet with tears, and did wipe them with the hairs of her head, and kissed his feet, and anointed them with ointment; for she loved much," much being forgiven her. 3. There is also a kiss of faith and dependence; and then may souls be said to kiss Christ, when they, as perishing creatures, come and venture their all upon him, give up themselves to him, resolving to have no other Saviour but him; when they can roll themselves on him, relying on his grace, trusting to his righteousness; when, whilst they are coming out of the wilderness, are leaning upon their beloved; and more especially when they embrace him in the arms of faith, and say, with Thomas, "My Lord and my God." 4. There is a kiss of homage and subjection; so kissing the king's hand, as it is an instance of his grace and favour to his subjects to permit them to do it, so it is a token of their subjection to him; thus Samuel anointed Saul, and kissed him, 1 Sam. x. 1, which former act was a declaring him king, the latter an instance of his subjection to him: thus souls may be said to kiss Christ, when they acknowledge him to be their Lord and King, and submit to his laws and ordinances, refusing subjection to sin, Satan, and the world. 5. There is a kiss of worship and adoration: the custom of kissing idols very early prevailed among idolatrous people; thus Baal's worshippers kissed him, 1 Kings xix. 18, as did also the worshippers of Jeroboam's calves, Hosea xiii. 2, so kissing the hand at the sight of the sun or moon, was esteemed an act of adoration of them in Job's time, chap. xxxi. 26, 27; in the same sense it may be used here; for as Christ is the believer's Lord, he ought to worship him; and that not with a mere civil worship, which may be given to creatures, but with that religious adoration which ought to be given to the Most High God; for "all men should honour the Son, as they honour the Father." When therefore the church or any believer signify their love and liking to Christ, exercise faith upon him, subject themselves unto him, and give him all due worship and adoration, as well as make an open profession of him, then may they be said to kiss him. But,

2ndly. She declares the time when she would do this; and that is when she found him: From whence may be observed, 1. That Christ may be sometimes absent from his church and people, which is a very great affliction to them. 2. That they cannot be easy without him, but will be earnestly desirous of his company, but seek for him until they find him, as may be learned from the case of the church, in chap. iii. 1—3. 3. That finding Christ, is the comfortable enjoyment of his presence; it is souls having nearness to him, and sensible communion with him; which is the time that they can come so near to him as to kiss him.

3rdly. The place where she would do this, and that is, without: by which may be meant, either, 1. The Gentile world, which was without, the land of Judea; the inhabitants of which are said to be without afar off, aliens from the commonwealth of Israel, strangers to the covenants of promise, and without hope, and God and Christ in the world; so that it may be expressive of her desire to find Christ in the Gentile world, and how much her love and affections would be drawn out to him on that account. Or, 2. By without, or in the street,[e] as it may be rendered, may be meant the public ordinances, where wisdom cries, Prov. i. 20, and where the church sought Christ, chap. iii. 2, and where finding him, she owns him, gives him homage and adoration, and lets out her affection to him. Or, 3. It may point out the way, and manner in which she sought him, as well as the place where, which was by going out of herself: Christ is not to be found within but without; believers " go in and out, and so find pasture, food, and comfort. Or, 4. By it may be meant any open or public place, where she should not be ashamed to own his person, Gospel, ordinances, cause, and interest; for those who are ashamed of him and his words before men, he will be ashamed of before his Father and his angels, Mark viii. 38. Or, 5. By her finding him and kissing him without, may be meant her going forth to meet him, claiming her interest in him, and signifying her affection to him, before men and angels, at his second coming; see Matt. xxv. 6.

III. The opinion which she had entertained that she should not be despised and reproached for such an act as this; yea, " I should not be despised; or, they would not despise me;"[f] that is, the people of the land, as the Targum paraphrases it. Now this opinion of hers might arise, 1. From the relation Christ stood in to her as a brother; for how unseemly and immodest soever it might be for a maiden in the the streets to kiss a stranger, or one not related to her: yet nobody would reproach her for using this freedom with an own brother; which would be accounted as a chaste and a harmless action in her, as if she had taken a sucking child out of the nurse's arms, and kissed it; no more immodest and unbecoming is this act of the church's; and therefore she concludes, that she should not be despised for it. 2. From the reception she believed that she should meet with from Christ; who would not turn away his face from her, when she made such an offer to him; which would occasion shame and blushing in her, and others to laugh at her; but she was well assured of the contrary, and that it would be kindly accepted by him. 3. From her having so good an husband as Christ; which might be known by this familiarity between them; and whom she had no reason to be ashamed of, nor others to despise her for having none: not to have a husband, being matter of reproach in those days; see Isa. iv. 1, and liv. 4, 5. 4. From her prospect of future fruitfulness; she doubted not but that by being married to such a husband, she should bring forth fruit unto God, and so not be despised for being barren and unfruitful; it being accounted reproachful to be so: see 1 Sam. i. 6. 5. It may be expressive of her great love to Christ, and of her boldness and confidence in owning and professing him, without either fear or shame,[g] before men and angels; she knew that she could not be justly despised and reproached for it; and if she was, she did not value it. 6. She may have respect to those apprehensions which the wicked will have of the saints in the last day, however mean and despicable the saints may appear to the wicked now, being in a state of imperfection, loaded with reproaches, and attended with a variety of sorrows; yet they will appear otherwise, and that in their apprehensions too another day, when they would be glad to change places and conditions with them; though Lazarus was despised when he lay in his sores at the rich man's gate, yet he was not when in Abraham's bosom. Thus the church might conclude that how much soever she may be despised now for owning and professing Christ, yet she should not, when she should go forth to meet him at his second coming, and be set at his right-hand in gold of Ophir.

Verse 2. *I would lead thee* and *bring thee into my mother's house*, who *would instruct me: I would cause thee to drink of spiced wine, of the juice of my pomegranate.*

---

[e] חבוק εξω, Sept. foris, Vulgate Latin version, &c. in plateis, Montanus, Brightman, Marckius; or in any public place; in publico, Cocceius; εν αγρω, al. Interp εν αγορα al. Interp. apud Flam. Nobil. Not. in Var. Lect. Sept. [f] גם לא בזו לי και γε ουκ εξηδενωσουσι με, Sept. and jam me nemo despiciat, Vulgate Latin version; etiam non contemnant me, Montanus; non faciant contumeliam mihi, Cocceius, neque vero me despicient, Tigurine version; etiam non contemnerent me, Brightman, Marckius. [g] Audacem faciebat amor, Ovid. Metamorph. l. 4. Fab. 4.

THESE are still the words of the church, discovering the resolutions and desires of her heart after communion with Christ, and a discharge of her duty to him: in which may be observed,

I. Her resolution to "lead and bring him into her mother's house."

II. Her expectation of receiving instruction there; "who would instruct me."

III. The entertainment she promises to give him; "I would cause thee to drink of spiced wine, of the juice of my pomegranate."

I. She resolves to lead and bring him into her "mother's house:" wherein may be considered, 1st. What may be intended in those acts of leading and bringing. 2ndly. What by her "mother's house," whither she should lead him, and into which she would introduce him.

1st. It will be proper to consider what those acts of leading and bringing intend. We frequently read of Christ's leading his church and people; but never, as I remember, but in this place, of the church's leading Christ: Christ leads his church as a king does his subjects, or as a general does his army; for he is given to be a Leader and a Commander to the people; which he performs, by ruling them with wholesome laws, and protecting them in their rights and liberties from all their enemies: thus, Deut. xxxii. 12, "the Lord alone did lead Israel of old, and there was no strange god with them;" thus David, Psalm lxxviii. 72, the type of Christ, fed the same people, "according to the integrity of his heart, and guided them by the skilfulness of his hands:" He leads them also as a shepherd does his flock, gently, as they are able to bear it, to suitable pastures, and proper resting-places; and likewise as a master does his scholars, leading them by his Spirit into all truth, and showing them the fulness and glory of the everlasting covenant: moreover, Christ leads his people, as a guide does a stranger; for they know not the way everlasting themselves, and therefore commit themselves to his guidance and conduct; who, though he leads often in rough paths, yet always in a right way, to the city of their habitation: likewise he leads them, as a nurse does her child; taking them by the hand, he teaches them to walk by faith, and leads them into their Father's presence; and also as an husband leads his wife, when he brings her home, introduces her into his house, consummates the marriage, and makes her a partner of all his goods; hence the phrase, *ducere uxorem, to lead a wife,* is used to express the act of marriage: thus it appears to be no very difficult matter to understand how Christ may be said to lead his church; but how she may be said to lead him, does not appear so manifest and easy. The act seems to import these following things: 1. That she used much familiarity with Christ; for, for one person to take another by the hand and lead along, discovers this: Christ allows his church much freedom with him; which she may make much use of, without incurring the reproach and scandal of forwardness or immodesty; seeing it is her own brother, nay, her own husband, whom she thus treats. 2. It shows much tender love, affection, and respect, to Christ; as also a welcome of him to her mother's house: thus friends and relations show their respect and affection to each other, and a hearty reception of them into their houses, by taking them by the hand, and leading them in. 3. It also denotes honour given to Christ by her, becoming his stateliness and majesty; thus kings and great persons are usually led: she treats him according to high station, as she is in Psalm xlv. 14, 15, and leads him along, as kings and conquerors are led, when they march in triumph. 4. All this is done by prayer and entreaty in the exercise of faith: Christ is easily prevailed upon by his church, through the exercise of faith in prayer; he is, if I may be allowed the expression, to be led any way by believers, in things which are consistent with his revealed will, and what will make for their good and his glory.

Much in the same sense are we to understand the other act of bringing; which, (1.) On her part may denote the strength of faith in prayer; which held him, and would not let him go, until she had brought him into her "mother's house;" like Jacob of old, who, when the angel said to him, Gen. xxxii. 26, "let me go, for the day breaketh," answered, "I will not let thee go, except thou bless me:" thus, James v. 16, "the effectual fervent prayer of a righteous man availeth much." (2.) On his part much condescension, in allowing such mean and worthless creatures, as believers in themselves are, to take him by the hand, lead him along, and bring him where they would have him.

2ndly. The next thing to be inquired into, is, what is meant by her "mother's house," where she desired to bring him: which may be expressive, 1. Of her desire to have the marriage consummated; the introduction of the bride and bridegroom into their house, being the last and finishing ceremony of marriage; thus it is said of Isaac, Gen. xxiv. 67, that "he brought Rebekah into his mother Sarah's tent, and she became his wife:" agreeable to this ceremony, the church expresses herself here; only here is this difference, that it was usual for the bridegroom to lead and bring his bride into his "mother's house;" but here the church promises to lead Christ to her mother's house; Christ and the church's mother being one and the same. 2. Of her desire to have the knowledge of Christ spread among her near relations, those of her mother's house; for nothing is more common than for persons, when they are converted themselves, to desire the conversion of their near relatives; an instance of which may be observed in the apostle Paul, Rom. ix. 1—3. 3. Of her desire to enjoy his presence in the church, which may be meant by her "mother's house;" for the catholic and invisible church, or " the general assembly and church of the firstborn, which are written in heaven," may be said to be the mother to the visible church on earth in any age of the world; for this is " the Jerusalem which is above, which is the mother of us all;" as may also the visible church on earth be to the several particular and congregated churches; and every particular and congregated church may be said to be the mother of particular believers, or converted persons: so that, (1.) The church is their mother's house, where they are begotten and born again; for " of Zion it shall be said, this and that man was born in her," Psalm lxxxvii. 5. (2.) Where they are educated and brought up; for Zion's children, as they are born in her, so they are nursed at her side, Isa. lx. 4. (3.) For which they have a great deal of zeal and affection, as persons usually have for the place of their nativity and education; and this in imitation of, and conformity to Christ; of whom it is said, that " the zeal of God's house had eaten him up," Psalm lxix. 9. (4.) Where they take much pleasure and delight to be; are glad when asked to go up unto it; because there they meet with the presence of Christ, receive instructions from him, and are employed in delightful service by him. (5.) This is not only the church's mother's house, but also Christ's Father's house; nay, his own house; which might be an inducement to him to go along with her; see John ii. 16, Heb. iii. 6.

The reasons which might induce her to desire and endeavour the introduction of him in her mother's house, may be such as these: 1. That she might enjoy free and uninterrupted communion with him; which end was attained by her, as appears from the following verse. 2. That others, even those of her mother's house, might have the benefit of Christ's presence and company, as well as herself; which shows her to be of a free, noble, and public spirit: like those saints, in 1 John i. 3, who were concerned for the comfortable wellbeing of others, as well as of themselves. 3. That the ordinances of her mother's house might be blessed unto her; for she knew full well that those breasts of consolation would be but dry breasts without his presence, and, like the mantle of Elijah, be of little service and usefulness, without the Lord God himself. 4. That she might be assisted by him in the service of the house: there are a great many works of faith and holiness to be performed herein, which she knew she was not able to do of herself; but that through Christ strengthening her, she could do all things.

II. She expected instruction in her mother's house, upon the bringing of him there; and this she expected either from her, or else from him; for the word in the Hebrew text will bear a reading which will suit either sense.

1st. They may be read, " who teacheth me;"[h] referring it to her mother, who would do so; so Junius and Tremellius read them, to which our version agrees, and which is also favoured by R. Aben Ezra. From whence may be observed, 1. That the church is a school of instruction, where souls are instructed in the ways of Christ, in the doctrines of the Gospel, and in all the duties of religion; both how to carry themselves in the church, and how to behave themselves agreeably to Christ, in all acts of love and obedience to him; which she may here have chiefly a regard unto: it seems to be an allusion to a grave and prudent woman, who, taking her new-married daughter apart by herself, teaches her how to behave herself towards her husband, that so she may have his affections, and live comfortably and happily with him: some such instructions the church expected from her mother. 2. That the greatest believers are not above instruction, and the means of it; but count it a mercy to have both the one and the other; some persons who know nothing as they ought to know, think they know every thing better than others; and therefore are above ordinances, despise instruction, and contemn the ministry of the word; but those who know most of themselves and of Christ Jesus, desire to know more, value the means of instruction, and make use of the ordinances of the Gospel to improve therein: the difference of these two sorts of persons may be seen in Prov. ix. 8, 9.

2ndly. The words may be rendered, " thou shalt instruct me,"[i] meaning Christ; and this sense is favoured by the Targum upon the place, and is followed by many interpreters: for though the church is the school, and ordinances are the means of instruction; yet Christ is the Teacher, who teacheth as none else can: this the church knew, and therefore expected instruction from him in her mother's house; being there in the way of her duty, where persons may more reasonably look for it. Now when Christ and the church are in their mother's house together, he instructs her, and shows her her interest in all the goods of the house: acquaints her with her work and duty, and how she ought to behave herself towards him; he gives some such marriage-precepts as those in Psalm xlv. 10, 11, " Hearken, O daughter, and consider, and incline thine ear; forget also thine own people, and thy father's house; so shall the king greatly desire thy beauty; he is thy Lord, and worship thou him:" He informs her what respect and affection, homage and obedience, he expected from her; and that she should not now hanker after her own kindred and relations, being married unto him.

Now Christ teaches and instructs his church and people many ways: as, 1. By his Spirit; who being sent by him, teaches them all things, goes

---

[h] תלמדני quæ docet me, Junius; and doceret me, Mercerus; ut doceres me. Cocceius; doceres me, Brightman. [i] Docebis me, Vulgate Latin version, Pagninus, Montanus, Tigurine version; so Sept. in Theodoret. Ibi docebis me, Ambros, in Ps. cxviii. octon. 19, col. 1057.

before them, and leads them into all truth, as it is in Jesus, John xiv. 26, and xvi. 13. 2. By his ministers; who are both fathers and instructors to Christ's babes; and therefore are called " pastors and teachers:" pastors, as they have the oversight of the flock; and teachers, as they are the instructors in Christ's school. 3. By the scriptures; which " are profitable for doctrine, for reproof, for correction, for instruction in righteousness;" for there is nothing written there, whether promises or doctrines, words of advice and direction, or of exhortation and comfort, but what is " written for our learning; that we through patience and comfort of the scriptures, might have hope," 2 Tim. iii. 16, Rom. xv. 4. 4. By his ordinances; for as in his church he teaches men his ways, so he teaches them by them, and in their waiting and attending on them. 5. By afflictive providences; he sometimes takes the rod, and makes use of that to promote his people's learning, when need requires; and, "blessed is the man whom he chasteneth," and thereby teacheth out of his law, Psalm xciv. 12.

III. She promises him a noble entertainment; I " would cause thee to drink of spiced wine, of the juice of my pomegranate;" some think, here is an allusion to a custom at marriage; when a cup of wine, after a benediction of it, was given to the new-married couple, who both drank of it;[k] and in some places, the custom was[l] for a young woman to bring in a cup of wine, all her lovers being present, and deliver it into the hand of him she fixed on to be her bridegroom; and by this action declared him to be so: and so here the church, by proposing to give to Christ a cup of her spiced wine, as the Vulgate Latin version renders it, declared him, and acknowledged him to be her husband. This is a different kind of entertainment, than what the old synagogue gave Christ; who, when she found him in the street, did not kiss him, showed no respect to him, made no profession of him, nor did she exercise any faith upon him, nay, despised those who did so; she was far from leading and bringing him into the temple, which the Jews[m] here understand by her mother's house, that she thrust him out of it, and gave him gall for his meat, and in his thirst gave him vinegar to drink; or, as one of the evangelists says, Mark xv. 23, " wine mingled with myrrh;" which, though it is of a sweet smell, yet is of a bitter taste: but the church here promises him spiced wine, such as was accounted the most pleasant and agreeable; and " the juice of her pomegranate,"

for her plants were an orchard of pomegranates; from the fruit of which a delightful juice is squeezed, of which is made a pleasant wine; and the word which is here translated juice, signifies most[n] sweet, or new wine; and so it is rendered in Isa. xlix. 26, Joel i. 5, Amos ix. 13. Pliny[o] speaks of a wine made of pomegranates, which he calls rhoites: mention is also made of it in the Talmud,[p] and by Maimonides:[q] there was a city in the tribe of Dan, called Gath-rimmon, Josh. xxi. 24, " the wine-press of the pomegranate," or where they made pomegranate-wine; and the word here used comes from one which signifies to force, squeeze, or trade under; see Mal. iv. 3; spiced wine was much used by the ancients; it was thought less inebriating;[r] and therefore they sometimes put into their wine myrrh and calamus, and other spices;[s] sometimes it was a mixture of old wine, water, and balsam; and of wine, honey, and pepper;[t] sometimes wine and honey.[u] These sorts of wine were no doubt accounted the best, and therefore she resolves to treat Christ with them: by which may be intended, 1. The richness and plenty of this entertainment; a banquet of wine being accounted the richest banquet; hence the provisions of grace under the gospel, are represented by it, Isa. xxv. 6, as are also the joys of heaven, Matt. xxvi. 29; but here these metaphorical phrases intend the graces of God's people; which, when in exercise, are preferred by Christ to the richest wine. 2. The variety of it; here are spiced wine, and wine of pomegranates, different sorts of wine; which are expressive of the various graces of the Spirit, which are implanted in the hearts of Christ's people. 3. The delight and pleasure which Christ takes therein; for even one single grace, even that of love, is said to be " better than wine, and the smell" of such ointments than all spices; which delight and pleasure is expressed by his drinking of it; see chap. iv. 10, and v. 1. With the Hebrew writers,[w] pomegranates are said to be a symbol of concord: the tree was sacred to love.[x]

Verse 3. *His left hand should be under my head, and his right hand should embrace me.*

THESE words may be considered, either, 1. As a petition that it might be so, and be read thus, " let his left hand be under my head,"[y] &c; a phrase used by lovers,[z] and here repeated in this song. Or, 2. As expressing her faith, that it should be so; which sense is favoured by our version. Or, 3. As declaring her present enjoyment of

---

[k] Buxtorf. Synagog. Jud. c. 39. p. 632. &c.
[l] Phocenses apud Athen. Deipnosoph. l. 13. c. 5. p. 576. Vid. Plutarch. de Virtut. Mulier. p 258.
[m] Targum and R. Solom. Jarchi in loc.
[n] מעסים רמי and mustum malorum granatorum meorum, Vulgate Latin version; de musto mali punici meo, Cocceius; de vino dulci mali granati mei, Montanus. [o] Lib. 14. c. 16.
[p] T. Bab. Sabbat, fol. 143. 2. [q] Hilchot Maacolot Asurot, c. 17. s. 11. [r] Athen. Deipnosophist.

l. 11. c. 3. p. 464. [s] Plin. Nat Hist. l. 14. c. 16. 16 Plauti Persa, act. 1. sc. 3. v. 7. 8. [t] Munster. Dictionar. Chaldaic. p. 22, 27. [u] Aufidius forti miscebat mella Falerno, Horat. Satyr. l. 2. sat. 4. v. 24. and 2. v. 15. [w] Apud Chartar. de Imag. Deorum, p. 139. [x] Athenæi Deipnosophist, l. 3. c. 8. p. 84. [y] Sinistra ejus supponatur capite meo, Tigurine version, Marckius, some in Michaelis. [z] Circumdatequc me brachiis, Plauti Asinaria, act. 3. Sc. 3. v. 106.

the mercy which she had been seeking for, and had faith in; and so be read, as in chap. ii. 6, where they are more largely explained.

Verse 4. *I charge you, O daughters of Jerusalem, that ye stir not up, nor awake my love, until he please.*

These words are either the words of Christ or of his church; who, having the presence and company of, and enjoying communion with each other, forbid all interruption, as has been observed on chap. ii. 7, where the same words are used, as they are also in chap. iii. 5, but with this difference: 1. The phrase, "by the roes and by the hinds of the field," which is used in the two former texts, is here omitted; not because there is less vehemency and earnestness in this charge than in the former: for, 2. There is also a difference in the form of expostulation, which seems rather to express her earnestness the more; for the words may be rendered thus, "Why will ye stir up, and why will ye awake?"[a] &c., which seems to imply as if she is apprehensive that they were about to do it, and that there was no danger of it; as also that it was an unreasonable thing in them to do it; and what would be every way as prejudicial to them as it would be to her; and therefore they ought to be careful, as well as herself, not to disturb him, nor provoke him to depart: the allusion is to virgins, that sung songs at marriages; one in the evening, lulling to sleep; and another in the morning, awaked and stirring up from it:[b] the church would not have her beloved awaked by them in such a manner.

Verse 5. *(Who is this that cometh up from the wilderness, leaning upon her beloved?) I raised thee up under the apple-tree; there thy mother brought thee forth, there she brought thee forth that bare thee.*

In these words are,

I. A question put by way of admiration, concerning the church, who is here described: 1st. By her ascent out of the wilderness. 2udly. By her posture in coming up from thence; "leaning upon her beloved."

II. Some things asserted, either by Christ or by his church; "I raised thee up," &c.

I. Here is a question put by way of admiration, "Who is this," &c. Not by the angels, as some[c] think; though it is true, they admire the grace that is bestowed upon mortal men, and rejoice at the faith and conversion of sinners: but it is much more likely that these are the words of the daughters of Jerusalem; who being strictly charged, in the former verse, to give no disturbance to Christ and his church, who were enjoying communion and fellowship with each other; look more earnestly at her, whom Christ had so much honoured and indulged with such earnestness to himself, at which they seem astonished and surprised. Though others[d] have considered them as the words of the Jewish church, wondering at the conversion of the Gentiles, and their sudden reception into the embraces of Christ. Others[e] have taken them to be the words of the bride herself, declaring what Christ said to her when he first met her, as she was coming up from the wilderness; or else, expressing her great love and affection to Christ, which appeared by her coming out of the wilderness, forsaking all for him, encountering with all difficulties, running all risks, that she might enjoy his company; and therefore says, "Who is this," &c., or where is there another that has done the like, or shown the like love to him as I have done? which is not to be understood as though she boasted in herself; for she acknowledges, that it was by his grace and strength that she had been enabled to do this, which is expressed in the very next words, "leaning upon her beloved;" for she could never have been able to come up from the wilderness had she not had his arm to lean upon. Though they seem rather to be the words of Christ himself; not as being ignorant of her, or as not knowing who she was; but as admiring at the graces of his Spirit in her, and especially that of faith, signified by her "leaning on her beloved;" as he had admired her love and affections to him, in a like form of speech, in chap. iii. 6, which are there compared to "pillars of smoke."

The person who is here inquired of and wondered at, is either the Gentile church, which, before the Gospel was brought thither, was much like a desert and wilderness; to which it is frequently compared in the prophecies of Isaiah; see chap. xxxii. 15, 16, and xxxv. 1, 6, and her coming out of the wilderness, may signify her conversion to the faith of Christ: or else, the springing up of a new church may be here intended; and, because an Arabic word is here made use of, Brightman thinks it intends the conversion of the eastern part of the world, Arabia, Persia, Egypt, Assyria, and refers it to the prophecy in Isa. xix. 23—25, though rather the bride, who is all along spoken of in this song, is here meant; who had attained to a greater degree of faith, and had larger experiences of Christ's love, and was allowed a more intimate communion with him; and is described here,

1st. By her ascent from the wilderness. The Septuagint read the words thus, "Who is it that cometh up in white,[f] or clothed in white?" though there is nothing in the Hebrew text to favour

---

[a] מה תעירו ומה תעררו Quid excitaretis, aut quid expergefaceretis? Junius, Brightman; Quid expergefactitis and quid excitatis? Cocceius. Quid excitabitis, and quid expergefacietis? Mercerus; Cur suscitabitis, cur evigilare facietis? Montanus.   [b] Vid. Theocrit. Idyll. 13.   Schmidt.   [c] Sanctius and Diodat. in loc.   [d] Alcuin in loc.   [e] Junius in loc.   [f] λελευκανθισμενη dealbata, Sept.

such a version; yet this appears to be the apparel of the church in other places, especially in the book of the Revelation, chap. iii. 4, 5, and xix. 8; where she is said to he " arrayed in fine linen, clean and white ;" which fine linen is said to be " the righteousness of the saints," &c., that which Christ has wrought out for them, and is by an act of God's grace imputed by them; for their own righteousness doth not deserve the name of " fine linen, clean and white ;" that being at best but as " filthy rags, and as an unclean thing." But the words are better rendered, " Who is this that cometh up from the wilderness ?" by which may be intended, either, her conversion from a state of nature, her being called and chosen out of the world; or her deliverance out of some great affliction; as the saints are said to " come out of great tribulation," Rev. vii. 14. But of all this, see more on chap. iii. 6.

2ndly. She is described by her posture, in this her ascent out of the wilderness, " leaning upon her beloved ;" which is expressive of much confidence in him, and familiarity with him; which she was allowed by him to use, and which she might without justly incurring either shame or reproach; for he, on whose arm she leaned, stood in a near relation to her, being both her husband and her brother. The word translated *leaning*,[f] is only used in this place, and is differently rendered : 1. Some, among which are many Jewish interpreters,[g] from the use of the word in the Arabic language, render it, joining or associating, or cleaving to her beloved : the church had given up herself to Christ, to be his for ever; was resolved, through grace to abide with him, and to go with him, whithersoever he went: that act of faith in God's people, which in the New Testament, 2 Cor. viii. 5, is expressed by a giving up of themselves to the Lord, to serve, honour, and glorify his name, is frequently expressed in the Old Testament, Isa. lvi. 3, 6, Jer. l. 5, by a joining of themselves unto him; which, when they have done, they cleave unto him with full " purpose of heart :" resolving, with Ruth, that where he goes, they will go; where he lodges, they will lodge; that his people shall be their people, and his God their God; nay, that in the strength of his grace, they will abide with him, and by his interest even unto death. 2. Others read the words thus, rejoicing or delighting herself " in her beloved ;"[h] which sense the Vulgate Latin seems to have a regard to, as well as expresses the sense of our version, by reading the words thus, *deliciis affluens, innixa super dilectum suum,* " flowing with delights, leaning upon her beloved ;" as does also the Targum, which thus paraphrases the words, " and they shall delight themselves in the mercy of the Lord :" Christ and his church take mutual delight and pleasure in each other, as she is fair and pleasant for delights in his esteem, so he is in hers: saints delight themselves much in taking a view of his personal glory, in his comparable beauty, transcendent excellencies, inexhaustible fulness, and unsearchable riches; it is not only their duty to " rejoice in the Lord always ;" but this interwoven in the very make, frame, and constitution of their souls, as renewed by grace : hence they are said to be, " the circumcision which worship God in the Spirit, and rejoice in Christ Jesus, and have no confidence in the flesh," Phil. iii. 3. 3. The Septuagint render it, " strengthening herself upon her beloved," that is, being conscious of her own weakness and inability to perform the duties of religion, withstand the temptations of Satan, escape the snares of this world, and hold on and continue in her Christian race, she applied herself to Christ : in whom she saw both " righteousness and strength " for her ; and from whom she received both; the one as her clothing, the other as her armour; the one as her title for glory, the other to enable her to hold out until she arrived thither. 4. Others translate the words, thus, " casting herself upon her beloved ;"[k] sensible souls will cast themselves at the feet of Christ for mercy, and into the arms of Christ for safety, shelter, and security; they will cast their burdens upon the Lord, to be eased from them by him, who has promised to sustain them : and they will cast their care upon him, knowing that he careth for them ; nay, they will venture their souls upon him, and commit the whole affair of their salvation to him; as undoubtedly the church did here. 5. Our version reads it, leaning on her beloved ;"[l] which is the use of the word in the Ethiopic language :[m] confidence and trust in our own strength, wisdom, and righteousness, is sometimes expressed by leaning thereunto, as in Job xviii. 15, Prov. iii. 5 ; and so is faith in our Lord Jesus Christ, by leaning on him ; see Isa. l. 10. By faith believers lean upon Christ's person, for their acceptance with God; upon his righteousness, for their justification before him ; upon his fulness, for every day's supply; and unto his blood, for pardon and cleansing: who is such a staff or prop as will never deceive them : upon which they may venture to lay the whole stress of their salvation, as it seems the church did here. The attitude in which the church was seen, seems to be this: she appeared coming up from the wilderness, arm in arm with her beloved, her arm under his arm-hole ; for a word from this here used, signifies " the arm-hole ;"[n] which was expressive of great freedom, familiarity, and fellowship with

---

[f] R. Sol. Jarchi, R. Aben Ezra in loc. R. Joseph Kimchi, in R. David Kimchi. in. lib. Shorash. rad. רפק and R. Sol. Urb. Ohel. Moed, fol. 19, 1. Adjungens se, Montanus; adjiciens se, Cocceius; associans se, Brightman, Schmidt, Marckius, Michaelis. [h] R. David Kimchi. lib. Shorash rad. רפק Targum and Vulg. Lat. vers. [k] Injiciens se super dilectum suum, Cocceius. [l] Innitens, Mercerus; innixa, Vulgate Latin version, Pagninus, Tigurine version. [m] Vid. Hottinger, Smegma Oriental. l. 1. c. 6. p. 106. [n] מרסק axilla, Buxtorf. Talm Lexic. col. 2281.

her beloved, and of her close affection to him, firm trust in him, and dependance on him.

II. In the following part of this text are some things asserted; either by Christ concerning his church, or else by the church concerning Christ; "I raised thee up under the apple-tree," &c. These words may be considered as the words of Christ;[o] showing by whom and by what means the church was raised out of her former mean condition, and was brought to that honour and dignity which she now enjoyed.

1st. Says he, I raised thee up under the apple-tree: which may either intend the work of faith and conversion, which is the quickening or raising up a soul that is dead in trespasses and sins unto a newness of life; or else, the awakening of a sleepy and drowsy saint. If we consider the words in the former sense, they will lead us to observe, 1. The state and condition that the church was in before conversion; which Christ, it may be, remarks unto her, to teach her humility, that she might not be puffed up with spiritual pride, and forget what she once was; she was dead in sin, and must have continued so, had not Christ raised her up; she was like the wretched infant, in Ezek. xvi. 6, which was "cast out in the open field, to the loathing of its person in the day that it was born; in which condition Christ found her, being like a new born infant, thrown under an apple-tree, and there left naked and helpless; where he took compassion upon, and said unto her, whilst in her blood, live: moreover, some regard may be had in this place unto the manner how she came to be in this condition; which was through Adam and Eve's eating the forbidden fruit, which some have thought to be the apple; whereby "sin entered into the world, and death by sin; and so death passed upon all men, in whom all have sinned," Rom. v. 12. 2. That the work of faith and conversion is a resurrection from the dead; which for ever secures persons from being hurt by the second death; see John v. 25, Rev. ii. 11. 3. That this work belongs to Christ, is performed by him, and the glory of it to be given to him; " I raised thee up," &c.; this work cannot be effected by the free-will and power of man, but by the mighty and efficacious grace of Christ; hence he is said to be the resurrection and the life, John xi. 25. No less a person than he, who said to Lazarus, come forth, can raise dead sinners; and no less a power must be exerted in doing this work, than was in the resurrection of Christ's dead body; see Eph. i. 19. 4. Christ's doing of this work upon the hearts of his people, is a very great indication of his love to them; he speaks of it here as a peculiar favour done to his church; see Eph. ii. 4, Jer. xxxi. 3. But,

If we understand these words of the awakening of her when asleep, they may teach us the following things. 1. That she was fallen asleep; which is sometimes the case of God's own people, as in chap. v. 2. 2. That this befel her when she was under the ordinances, under the shadow of the apple-tree, chap. ii. 3. 3. That Christ will not suffer his people to continue so; but will, by some means or other, awake them out of it.

2ndly. He says, that there her mother brought her forth,[p] &c. Here he expresses her conversion by a regeneration, as he had before by a resurrection; by both which names it is very well known in the New Testament; which work, though it is effected by the grace and Spirit of God, yet the ministry of the word and ordinances are the instrumental means thereof, which Christ has placed, continues, and blesses in his church for that end.

But the words seem rather to be the words of the church,[q] speaking these things concerning Christ; for though there is nothing in our version to determine the sense this way, yet the suffixes in the Hebrew text being of the masculine gender, manifestly show that they are spoken of a man, and not of a woman. And,

1st. The church says, that she raised Christ up under the apple-tree; that is, she sitting under the ordinances of the gospel, which are the shadow of the apple-tree, to which Christ is compared in chap. ii. 3, and finding no communion with him, he being as it were asleep all the while, did, by earnest prayer and entreaty, at length raise him up; so that she enjoyed a large degree of nearness to him, and familiarity with him.

2ndly. That there his mother, which is the church and every true believer; see chap. iii. 11, and Matt. xii. 50, brought him forth: as did, 1. The Old Testament-church, who long waited for him, and was often in pain, as a woman with child, on that account, until this man-child was born; which was at length accomplished, to the joy of all those who waited for the consolation of Israel. 2. With much pain did the apostles bring Christ forth into the Gentile world, by professing him, preaching his gospel, and suffering for his sake: thus did they travail in birth, until Christ was formed in the hearts of men. 3. It is with much pain, even like that of a woman in travail, that the new birth, or the work of regeneration on the heart, which is no other than Christ formed there, is wrought; all, more or less, who are called by grace, pass under a work of the law, which is a killing letter; which puts the soul to a great deal of pain; pricks it to the heart, and makes it cry out, What shall I do to be saved? 4. The New-Testament church, which is also Christ's mother, in the exercise of faith and prayer, is waiting for his second coming; nay, is not only looking for it, but is hastening to it; is uneasy, and as it were like a woman in travail, until he makes his appearance; which he will shortly do, through the incessant and continued cries and entreaties

---

[o] Theodoret. and Tres Patres in Ib. Foliot and Alcuin in loc.   [p] Genet ix is often used for a mother, in poetical composures.   [q] So Mercerus, Cocceius, Marckius, Michaelis.

of his people: and this may be the reason why the phrase is doubled;" there thy mother brought thee forth;" that is, the Old Testament church, who waited for his manifestation in the flesh; "there she brought thee forth that bare thee;" that is the New Testament church, which looks for his second appearance. R. Aben Ezra interprets these words of the raising, loosing, and bringing forth of the King Messiah, through the prayers and entreaties of the Jews; who fancy that he now lies bound and fast asleep, but will ere long be awakened and loosed through their prayers, and appear for their deliverance from present exile and captivity; which is all vain and delusive.

Verse 6. *Set me as a seal upon thine heart, as a seal upon thine arm: for love is strong as death; jealousy is cruel as the grave: the coals thereof are coals of fire, which hath a most vehement flame.*

THESE words may be considered either as the words of Christ, or of his church. Some[r] think that they are the words of Christ expressing his desire to be set as a seal upon the heart and arm of his church; and the argument, reason, or motive, which he makes use of to prevail upon her to grant him this request, is taken from the exceeding greatness of his affection to her; which is compared to the strength of death, the cruelty of the grave, and the vehemency of flaming coals of fire.

I. He makes a request to her, that he might be "set as a seal," both upon her *heart* and *arm:* by which he may intend, 1. An inward and abiding principle of love and affection in her towards him: the church's love to Christ is highly valued by him, especially when it comes from the heart; for mere expressions of love, without an inward principle of it in the heart, are not satisfying to him; for what he requires, is, to "love him with all thy heart, and with all thy soul, and with all thy mind;" let us love therefore, not in word, neither in tongue," that is, only "but in deed and in truth;" for this is what he seeks for, and is highly esteemed of by him. 2. A manifestation of this affection to him outwardly; it should not only have a place in our hearts, but also be shown by our actions, which should be in conformity to his will; "for if ye love me," says he, John xiv. 15, "keep my commandments;" Christ should have both our hearts and our hands. 3. A constant remembrance of him, and continual looking to him: as seals worn upon the arm, or in a ring upon the finger, are continually in sight, and put in remembrance whose they are, and whose image they bear; and so would Christ be always in his church's sight and mind; for we should, as David did, "set the Lord always before us," and continually look unto him, which is both pleasant and profitable; pleasant, because we behold him "full of grace and truth;" and profitable, because we receive from him "grace for grace." 4. A greater likeness to him: conformity to Christ's image is one great end of predestination; which is begun in the hearts of his people by his Spirit; is increased by those transforming views he gives them of the glory of Christ's person; and will be completed in heaven, when they "shall be like him, and see him as he is;" believers have the image of Christ instamped upon them; for as they "have borne the image of the earthly, they shall also bear the image of the heavenly;" which is, to have Christ set as a seal upon the heart and arm, so as that he leaves an impress of his image there; which conforms both heart and life unto him, and cannot but be desired by him; for every like loves its like. 5. A close adherence to his person, Gospel, cause, and interest; having made an open and public profession of him, we should "cleave to him with full purpose of heart," as Ruth did to Naomi; or as a signet does to a man's right hand on which it is worn. 6. and lastly, In this request of Christ to the church, his design may be, that she might appear to be his, and only for his use and service; as things are known to be such a man's property by his mark or seal being upon them; so the church is known to be Christ's, by his seal being upon both her heart and arm; which is himself; who is inwardly received, and outwardly professed by her; for whose use and service all she is and has are; being "a garden inclosed, a spring shut up, a fountain sealed."

II. The argument, reason, or motive, which he makes use of to induce her to take notice of his request, is taken from the ardency of his love and affection to her, which is signified by those several following expressions:

1st. He declares that his love to her was strong as death: he loved her so, that he died for her; he preferred her to his own life, and chose death rather than to go without her; which is a full proof and evidence of his love to her, and shows the exceeding greatness of it; for, as in John xv. 13, "Greater love hath no man than this, that a man lay down his life for his friends;" which may very well be improved by him, as an argument or reason why she should love him again; manifest that love, bear him continually upon her mind, cleave close unto his cause and interest, seek after a nearer conformity to him, as well as reserve herself and all she had for his use and service.

2ndly. He asserts his "jealousy to be cruel as the grave:" by which may be meant, either, 1. His zeal for his church's good and his Father's glory; so this word is sometimes rendered; see Isa. ix. 6, and lxiii. 15; which zeal of Christ's, like the inexorable, cruel, and devouring grave, consumed his time and strength, and at last his life; as appears from his own words, "the zeal of thine house hath eaten me up," Psalm lxix. 9. He, as the great prophet in Israel, showed a becoming zeal for the gospel; which appeared by

[r] Alcuin, Foliot, Sanctius, Not. Tig. in loc.

his warm and lively preaching of it; his assiduity and constancy in it, the frequent and wearisome journeys he took to do it; the risks and dangers he ran upon that account; as well as the many miracles he wrought to confirm it, and the care he took to free it from calumnies, aspersions, and prejudices: He likewise showed the like zeal for the discipline of his Father's house; as is manifest from his severe reflections on human traditions; his asserting the purity of worship to be in Spirit and in truth; as also his frequent inveighings against the vice of professors; as well as his great courage in clearing the temple from the defilers of it; which heroic action of his is particularly recorded in John ii. 14—17; which put the disciples in mind of what was before written of him: moreover, his zeal was no less fervent for the salvation of his people, and the glory of his Father, concerned therein; which plainly discovered itself in his voluntary assumption of human nature, and cheerful submission to the death of the cross on their account. Or else, 2. By it may be meant his vengeance on his and their enemies; and in this sense the word is used, Deut. xxix. 20, Isa. lix. 17; what was a day of grace and salvation to his people, was a day of vengeance to his enemies; for no sooner was the year of his redeemed come, but the day of vengeance was in his heart; which he executed upon them without any mercy, pity, or compassion; his jealousy or vengeance was cruel as the grave; he spared them not: he made an end of sin, abolished death, destroyed Satan, and spoiled principalities and powers. Or else, 3. By it may be meant, the jealousy which he justly entertains of his people's faith in him, love and duty to him, who frequently turn aside from him to other lovers, of which he often complains, being jealous over them with a godly jealousy; which is no other than the height of his love and affection to them; there being nothing that he is more anxiously concerned for and jealous of, than the faith, love, and obedience of his people, lest they should be given to any other.

3rdly. This strong affection of his to his church, he compares to coals of fire, which hath a most vehement flame; by which he would signify the ardency and vehemency of his love; how tottering it was to him, and how uneasy he was until he had given it vent; thus the prophet Jeremy, chap. xx. 9; being reviled and reproached for prophesying in the name of God, made a resolution not to make mention of him, nor speak any more in his name; but, says he, his word was in mine heart, as a burning fire shut up in my bones, and I was weary with forbearing, and I could not stay: so Christ's love was like burning coals of fire in his bosom, which gave him much uneasiness until he had given it vent; as appears from Luke xii. 50: I have, says he, a baptism, meaning his death and sufferings, to be baptised with, and how am I straitened, distressed, tortured, and uneasy, till it be accomplished? and now this zeal of Christ's for the salvation of his church, his vengeance upon her enemies, his anxious concern that her faith, love, and obedience, might not be alienated from him; as also his uneasiness until her salvation was accomplished; may well be used by him, as so many arguments, to prevail upon her to grant him the abovesaid request. Thus much for the first sense of the words, as they may be considered as the words of Christ to the church; but the generality of interpreters understand them as the words of the church, requesting of Christ that he would set her as a seal, both upon his heart and arm, because of the greatness of that love which she bore to him; which she compares to death, the grave, and coals of fire: and this I take to be the most genuine sense of them, as being most agreeable to the suffixes in the Hebrew text; I shall consider it much in the same method as I did the former. And,

First. The church requests of Christ that he would set her, as a seal upon his heart, and as a seal upon his arm: in which she may desire, 1. Nearness to him; as a seal must be near, that is worn next the heart, or upon the arm: the saints are a people near unto the Lord: with respect to union, they are members of his body, of his flesh, and of his bones: Christ and believers are like the old primitive Christians, of one heart and of one soul: and they would be near to him with respect to communion; they would not only, with Job, come even to his seat, but also into his arms; would lie in his bosom; nay, are not content without a place in his heart. 2. She seems to be desirous of abiding in Christ's heart, and that she might be as a signet upon his arm; from whence she might never be removed, but there always continue; of which believers may be assured, though they are often attended with fears about it; for, as in Psalm cxxv. 1, "they that trust in the Lord shall be as mount Zion, which cannot be removed, but abide for ever;" they can never be removed from off Christ's heart, on which they always are; nor out of his arms, in which they are continually inclosed; for "they shall never perish, neither shall any man pluck them out of his hand." 3. She desires a share in his heart's love and affection, and that she might be valued and esteemed by him as a signet upon his right-hand; see Jer. xxii. 24, Hag. ii. 23; for there is nothing more desirable to believers than the love of Christ and the discoveries of it; for his loving-kindness is better than life; may they but have a share in Christ, an interest in his favour, be but valued and esteemed by him, they care not how they stand in the world's esteem, what they say of them, or can do unto them. 4. She seeks for a continuance of his love, which may be depended on; for, "having loved his own which were in the world, he loved them unto the end," John xiii. 1; Christ's love is like himself, "the same yesterday, to-day, and for ever;" from whence it is impossible that any separation should ever be made. 5. She also wanted and sought after an assurance of Christ's love, which is the Spirit's work, and is expressed by sealing in scripture; see Eph. i. 13, and iv. 30; which he performs, either more generally, by that work of grace which he has begun, and is carrying on in the hearts of believers; for from his drawing of them to Christ with loving-kindness, they may conclude and be assured of their interest in his everlasting love; or else more particularly, by some special testimony of his, which he bears together with their spirits, that they are the children of God. 6. In this request she likewise presses after a manifestation of his love to her soul, by the arm of his Almighty power, delivering her out of all temptations, and supporting and bearing her up under all afflictions, trials, and exercises; which had wrought out salvation for her, and plucked her as a brand out of the burning. 7. She desires a continual remembrance of him; and seems to allude to the high-priest, who had the names of the children of Israel engraven, like the engravings of a signet, upon precious stones; which were born by him, both upon his shoulders and upon his heart, for a memorial before the Lord continually; which was typical of Christ,[x] our great High-priest, who represented the persons of all the elect upon the cross, and now bears them upon his heart before the throne in heaven; whither he is gone to appear in the presence of God for us. 8. She desires to be always in his sight, and under his care and inspection, as his people always are; for they are graven upon the palms of his hands, and their walls are continually before him: they are as the apple of his eye, his jewels, and peculiar treasure; which he has his eye always upon, and continually watches over, lest they should be lost, or any hurt come unto them.

Secondly. The reason of this request of hers, she declares to be the exceeding greatness of her love unto him; which she compares to death for its strength, to the grave for its cruelty, and to burning coals of fire for its insatiable and devouring nature.

1st. She asserts her love to Christ to be as strong as death: the meaning of which is, 1. That as death conquers all, kings and peasants, high and low, rich and poor, bond and free, young and old, weak or strong; there is no disputing his authority, nor controlling his power; but all ranks and degrees of men must, whether they will or no, be subject to him, the king of terrors: so her love to Christ overcame all things, and surmounted all difficulties which stood in the way of her enjoying him; she could part with, and bear all or any thing for the sake of Christ; father, mother, wife, and children, houses and lands, a good name, credit, and reputation, are nothing to the believer in comparison of Christ, which he cheerfully quits when they stand in competition with him; nay, things that are the most frightful in nature, cannot scare him from Christ, nor separate him from the love of him: such as tribulation, distress, persecution, famine, nakedness, peril, and sword; nor death itself in its most formidable appearance;[t] for in all these things he is more than a conqueror, through Christ that has loved him. Perfect love casts out fear; it dreads nothing, runs all risks, encounters and surmounts all difficulties, that it may enjoy the object loved. 2. As her love, like death, had conquered all things, so she herself was conquered by it;[u] it had wounded her sore; so that she was as one gasping, panting, dying, just ready to expire, unless she had the sight and enjoyment of him whom she loved. 3. Such was her love to Christ, that death itself was nothing to her, so that she might but win Christ and be found in him: the book of martyrs furnishes us with many instances of those bold, daring, and heroic lovers, who loved not their lives unto the death, for the sake of Jesus; the most exquisite torments, and most cruel deaths they have been put to, have rather inflamed, than lessened their love to Christ; so that their love to him has not only been as strong, but even stronger than death. 4. Her meaning may be, that love had so captivated her and worked so powerfully in her, that she was as a dead carcase, that might be moved and drawn by him whithersoever he pleased; the love of Christ constrained her to live to him, and not to herself; for love, as one [w] expresses it, is a kind of a civil death; lovers rather live at the will and pleasure of others whom they love, than at their own; and so the church did here; for a frown, or an angry look or word from Christ, was as death unto her.

2ndly. She says, that her jealousy was cruel as the grave; by which may be meant, 1. Jealousy of Christ's love unto her; either as it intends the height of love, love at its $\alpha\kappa\mu\eta$; or else that evil, groundless suspicion of not enjoying another's love, or of having a rival in it, which Solomon calls, Prov. vi. 34, 35, "the rage of a man," and may be said to be cruel as the grave; for such an one, "he will not spare in the day of vengeance; he will not regard any ransom; neither will he rest content, though thou givest many gifts;" now if jealousy is taken in this sense here, it intends those fits of unbelief, which sometimes attend the people of God; who are often jealous of Christ's love to them: and ready to suspect his regard for them; which exceedingly tortures and afflicts them, and must not be reckoned their excellency,

---

[x] See more of this in my sermon, called, "Levi's Urim and Thummim found with Christ."
[t] Nostros non rumpit funus amores, Lucan Pharsal. l. 5. v. 761, 762. [u] Omnia vincit amor, and nos cedamus, amori, Virgil. So Plato represents love as the strongest of all things; since that which rules over the strongest of other things, must be the strongest of all; Symposium, p. 1189, 1190.
[w] Sanctius in loc.

but their weakness; for of all people in the world, they have the least reason to entertain such thoughts of him. 2. By it may be meant the envy of the wicked against the saints, which is very great; for they would, as much as in them lies, deprive them of the common rights and liberties of mankind, as well as debar them the free enjoyment of their religious exercises; which is a great affliction to the people of God; for Prov. xxvii. 4, "wrath is cruel, and anger is outrageous; but who is able to stand before envy, or jealousy?" it is the same word which is here used; in this sense the Targum or Chaldee paraphrase on our text understands it. Or,^y 3. By it may be meant her zeal^x for Christ, his gospel, cause, and interest: thus Elijah is said to be, 1 Kings xix. 10, jealous for the Lord of hosts, that is, zealously affected to him, and concerned for his glory; which, like the grave, is of a devouring and consuming nature; for, says David, Psalm cxix. 139, "my zeal hath consumed me, because mine enemies have forgotten thy words;" Virgil_z gives the epithet of cruel to love.

3rdly. The church expresses the ardency and vehemency of her love to, and zeal for Christ, by comparing them to coals of fire; live coals, such as have their coruscations, which flash and flame, and are bright and vehement; and to these her love may be compared, for the following reasons: 1. In such coals of fire there is light; so there is in the church's love to and zeal for Christ, for though she believes in, and has love for an unseen Christ; yet not for an unknown Christ; for *ignote nulla cupido*; her zeal is not a blind, misguided zeal, but is according to knowledge. 2. In such coals, there is heat as well as light: it is true, sometimes the love of God's people waxeth cold, through the prevalency of corruption, and the cares of the world; it is like coals of fire covered with ashes; which seem to have no life nor heat in them; but then at other times it is re-kindled and re-inflamed by the Spirit; either under the hearing of the word, or in meditation upon the glory of Christ's person, love, and grace; "my heart," says David, Psal. xxxix. 3, "was hot within me; while I was musing, the fire burned; then spake I with my tongue:" nothing sooner raises it into a flame, than fellowship and communion with Christ Jesus; agreeable to what the disciples said to one another, Luke xxiv. 32, "Did not our hearts burn within us, while he talked with us by the way, and while he opened to us the scriptures?" Again, though they are sometimes cold, lukewarm, and indifferent in their frames, yet at other times they are fervent in spirit, serving the Lord. 3. Fire is insatiable;

it is one of those "four things which say not, it is enough," Prov. xxx. 16: so is love; for it would always have more of Christ; it is never satisfied with communion with him; but, like the horse-leech at the vein, continually crying, "Give, Give;" and for the same reason love is compared to death, and jealousy to the grave, in the preceding sentences; see Hab. ii. 5.

Moreover these coals of fire are said to have a most vehement flame; nothing is more common with other writers^a than to attribute flame to love, and to call it a fire; and here a most vehement flame is ascribed to it; or, as it is in the Hebrew text the flame of Jah, or Jehovah:^a by which is meant, either, (1.) An exceeding great or most vehement flame, as our Translators have well rendered it; for when the Hebrews would express the superlative degree, or increase the signification of a word, they sometimes use some one or other of the names of God; as mountains of God, and cedars of God, for most high mountains, and most excellent cedars. Or, (2.) It may mean a flame that is kindled by the Lord;^b for it is by the Spirit of the Lord, who is compared to fire in scripture, that this flame of love is first kindled in our souls. Or, (3.) It may be in allusion to the fire upon the altar of burnt-offerings, which was always kept alive; and so a fit emblem of love, which is of an abiding nature; see Lev. vi. 12, and ix. 24; and can never be extinguished, as is expressed in the following words.

Verse. 7. *Many waters cannot quench love, neither can the floods drown it; if a man would give all the substance of his house for love, it would utterly be contemned.*

In these words are some further commendations of love, which, 1. Is represented as inextinguishable and insuperable; many "waters cannot quench it, neither can the floods drown it."

II. As exceeding valuable and inestimable; "if a man would give all the substance of his house for it, it would utterly be contemned;" which may be understood, either of Christ's love to his church, or of the church's love to Christ; for as these words stand connected with the former, and are spoken by the same person, they must be interpreted the same way; and I shall first consider them as they may be expressive of the excellency of Christ's love: which,

I. Is inextinguishable and insuperable: it cannot be quenched by many waters: nor drowned by all the floods.

1st. Of sin and corruption, which have overflowed all human nature; for "all have sinned and come short of the glory of God:" like a mighty

---

^x Junius and Tremellius, Piscator, Cocceius, Marckius. ^y Crudelis amor, Bucolic. eclog. 10. v. 29. Musæus de Hero, &c. v. 245. ^z Vid. Barthii Animadv. ad Claudian de Nupt. Honor. v. 16. and de Laude Stilico, v. 74. So love is said to kindle a more vehement flame than Vulcan's forge, Theocrit. Idyll. 2. v. v. 133, 134. Vid. Idyll. 7. v. 56. and Musæi Leand. v. 245, 246, 247. ^a שלהבתיה flamma Dommi, Mercerus, Montanus; vastantis flammæ, Domini, Brightman; flammæque divinæ, Junius; flamma Dei, Cocceius, Tigurine version; flamma Jah, Marckius. ^b Cujus Carbones sunt iguiti a flammæ Dei, Tigurine version, so Castalio; quam Dominus accendit, Glassii Philolog. Sacr. l. 5. tract L c. 10.

x

torrent, or rather inundation, has entered into the world, and brought death along with it, upon all the posterity of Adam; it has drowned them in destruction and perdition, as all hurtful and foolish lusts do. Now the elect of God themselves are not exempted from this universal deluge; but though these waters of sin have come into their souls and overrun all the powers and faculties thereof; yet they have not extinguished Christ's love towards them; nor in the least alienated his affections from them: it is true, when he first loved them, he saw them in all that glory and perfection, which his Father designed to bring them to, and which they will appear in, in another world; yet when the great council was held concerning their redemption, they were presented to him as plunged into the depths of sin and misery; which was so far from setting his heart against them, that it rather moved his pity and compassion for them, and gave him an opportunity of showing the exceeding greatness of his love towards them: for upon this, he readily and cheerfully became their Surety, engaged to assume their nature, lay down his life for them, and thereby satisfy law and justice in their room and stead; all which agreements were to a tittle made good by him, in the fulness of time, for all the elect of God, notwithstanding their after-fall in Adam, and their actual rebellion against him, as they appeared upon the stage of the world; nay, though their innumerable evils compassed him about like floods of water, and brought death and the curse upon him; these being imputed to him, and laid upon him by his Father; and with which, standing charged by divine justice, he suffered to the uttermost that they deserved; yet his love continued the same towards his people; for, " having loved his own which were in the world, he loved them to the end," John xiii. 1. For,

2ndly. By these " waters and floods," may be meant the several afflictions and sufferings which Christ underwent for the sins of his own people; by which they are expressed, Psalm lxix. 1, 2; where Christ is introduced thus speaking, "Save me, O God, for the waters are come in unto my soul; I sink in deep mire, where there is no standing; I am come into deep waters, where the floods overflow me." Hence it is, that his sufferings are called a baptism, in Luke xii. 50; under which may be comprehended these following things: I. " The floods of ungodly men," which compassed him about; some of whom reviled him, other spit upon him, others buffeted him, others crucified him, and pierced his hands, feet, and side; yet his love to his people remained firm and unconquerable: nay, though the whole infernal posse of devils was let loose upon him, and exercised all their rage and cunning; yet as neither " life nor death," that is, all his sufferings, both in life and death, could separate his people from his love: so neither could angels, wicked angels, nor " principalities and powers." 2. Floods of reproaches were poured into his bosom on the account of his birth, parentage, and education, his public ministry, the miracles which he wrought, and the free, courteous, and affable conversation he used with sinners. He was spit upon in Pilate's hall, and mocked at when upon the cross in the utmost misery; yet he bore all this " contradiction of sinners against himself," with an uncommon patience; despising all the shame that attended these reproaches, for the " joy that was set before him," of having all his people with him in glory. 3. The vials of his Father's wrath were also poured forth upon him; for though, as God's Son, he was always the object of his love, yet, as the sinner's Surety, suffering in their room and stead, he was '"cast off and abhorred;" for God was wroth with his anointed or Messiah; " terrors took hold on him as waters ;" when only some few drops of divine wrath fell upon him, he " began to be sore amazed, and to be very heavy; his soul became exceeding sorrowful unto death; his sweat was as it were great drops of blood falling down to the ground;" then was it that " the waters began to come into his soul," which kept flowing in until the measure was quite filled up; yet all these waters and floods could not quench or drown his love towards his people; his affections to them, as well as his regard to his Father's will in their salvation, continued the same; as appears from those words of his to his Father, in the midst of his agony, " not my will, but thine be done." 4. All the sorrows and sufferings of Christ, from his cradle to his cross, may be included herein; for his whole life was one continued series of suffering, which ended in an accursed and ignominious death, to which he voluntarily submitted; that so his people might be set free by justice, and delivered from death and condemnation.

3rdly. As the love of Christ cannot be extinguished and overcome by all the waters and all the floods of sin and corruption in them, nor by all the sorrows and sufferings which he has undergone in his own person for their sins: so neither can it, by all their water-floods and billows of sufferings and afflictions which pass over his members; these indeed make them appear mean and abject in the eye of the world, and render them the object of their scorn and contempt: yet nevertheless, though the sun of persecution has looked upon them, and made them black, they are comely in Christ's eye; his heart is not set against them, nor his love alienated from them upon that account; for when they " pass through such waters," he will be with them; nay, he chooses, approves of, and delights in them, when " in the furnace of affliction," and will purify them thereby; so that though they " have lain among the pots," and are become black and sooty; yet they " shall be as the wings of a dove, covered with silver, and her feathers with yellow gold," Psalm lxviii. 13.

II. This love of Christ to his church is also

exceeding valuable and inestimable: " if a man would give all the substance of his house for it, it would utterly be contemned." For, 1. This is not to be procured by money, if any should offer to purchase the favour of Christ at any such rate, he would be treated with the utmost contempt, as Simon Magus was by the apostles, of whom he would have bought the gift of the Holy Ghost with money; to whom Peter said, Acts viii. 18—20. " Thy money perish with thee, because thou hast thought that the gift of God may be purchased with money." Christ and his love are of greater value, than to be obtained in such a manner; for not only the substance of a single person's house, but even the riches of the whole world, and the most precious things in nature, are not equal to them; see Job xxviii. 12, 13, 15—19, Prov. viii. 11, 19. 2. Riches will not entitle men to the love and favour of Christ; he does not regard them on the account of these; though perhaps too many, like Haman, are apt to say, Esther vi. 6, " to whom would the king delight to do honour, more than to myself?" and so " trust in their wealth, and boast themselves in the multitude of their riches," to a neglect of divine Providence, and concern about their immortal souls; such would do well to consider, that " not many noble are called, but God hath chosen the poor of this world," whom it hath pleased him that the Gospel should be preached unto. 3. Riches will not procure Christ's love, favour, and regard, neither at the hour of death, nor in the day of judgment: when " he takes thee away with his stroke," that is, of death, then " a great ransom cannot deliver thee;" all thy bags of money will not buy off thy life one hour, much less secure his favour to eternity; for, " Will he esteem thy riches? no, nor gold, nor all the forces of strength," Job xxxvi. 19, 20; which will be much the same case at the day of judgment; for the righteous judge, who will then sit upon the bench, will not be bribed, nor can his favour be procured by any such methods: " riches profit not in the day of wrath;" for if a man " gain the whole world, and lose his own soul," there will be no recovering it; for nothing will be given, nor will be taken " in exchange for it." 4. Therefore the love and favour of Christ should be preferred by us to all temporal enjoyments; for if his " loving-kindness is better than life," then it is better than all the temporal comforts and enjoyments of it: we should not covet to have our portion here, nor boast ourselves of our wisdom, strength, or riches; but " glory in this," that we know the Lord, who " exerciseth loving-kindness in the earth." Thus much may suffice for the first sense of the words. I shall now proceed to consider them as they may be expressive of the church's love to Christ; which also is,

First. Inextinguishable and insuperable; it cannot be quenched nor drowned by many waters, nor all the floods, 1. Of wicked and ungodly men; the people and nations of the world, who are frequently compared to many waters; see Isa. xvii. 12, 13, Rev. xvii. 1, 15, and so most of the Jewish[c] writers understand them here: for the nations of the world and the great men thereof, have not been able, either by force or flattery, by cruel edicts or fair promises, to alienate the church's love from Christ, nor tempt her to desert his cause and interest. 2. It cannot be quenched nor drowned by all the waters and floods of persecutions,[d] which wicked men, by the instigation of Satan, have brought upon the people of God; thus we read, in Rev. xii. 15, that the serpent, which is the devil, " cast out of his mouth water as a flood, after the woman," which is the church, " that he might cause her to be carried away of it:" by which flood cast out of the serpent's mouth, must be meant, either a flood of heresies brought into the church to disturb her, and draw her off from Christ, her Head, through the cunning craft of Satan; or else, a flood of persecutions, introduced by wicked and ungodly men, through his instigation, in order to affright, scare, and turn her aside from the pure ways of Christ, but all in vain; for, Rom. viii. 35, 37, " Who shall separate us from the love of Christ? Shall tribulation, or distress, or persecution, or famine, or nakedness, or peril, or sword? nay, in all these things we are more than conquerors, through him that loved us:" nay, death itself attended with the most exquisite torments and barbarous cruelties that hell can devise, cannot do it; for saints count not their lives dear to themselves, so that they may but " finish their course with joy," and bear a noble testimony to " the Gospel of the grace of God." 3. The love of believers to Christ is not quenched nor drowned by all the waters and floods of affliction, which God is pleased to bring upon them: they generally have a large share of them; " waters of a full cup are wrung out unto them:" yet these, though they are not " joyous, but grievous," do not alienate their affections from Christ, but rather fix them more strongly on him; whilst they view all their afflictions as covenant-mercies, the effects of wisdom, love, and faithfulness, and designed for their good, profit, and advantage. 4. Neither can their love be quenched nor drowned by the many waters and floods of their own sins and corruptions: it is true, these are most likely to extinguish this fire and flame above all things else, and often do strike a damp upon it; for through the " aboundings of iniquity," love oftentimes waxed cold; but yet it is not drenched and drowned; there may be a leaving the first love; some degrees of heat in it may be remitted, but there is no such thing as losing the grace of love entirely; for it is an immortal seed, of a lasting, yea, of an everlasting nature. 5. Nor

---

[c] Targum, Shirhashirim Rabba. R. Sol. Jarchi, and R. Aben Ezra, and Yalkut in loc. Shemoth Rabba, parash. 49. [d] So R. Alshech in loc.

can it be quenched nor drowned by all the waters and floods of Satan's temptations; this enemy of believers oftentimes "comes in like a flood" upon them, by filling their souls with blasphemous thoughts, vile suggestions, and wicked insinuations; in all endeavouring to draw off their love, and alienate their affections from Christ; which he sometimes attempts by fair words, showing them "all the kingdoms of the world, and the glory of them," as he did Christ, and promising to give them to them, which is more than he can perform, if they will but turn their backs on Christ, and his ways; at other times he sets before them all the hardships, difficulties, reproaches, and persecutions, which they will be exposed unto, if they persist therein; and yet all these floods cannot quench nor drown their love to Christ. Nor, 6. Can this be effected by divine desertions, which are compared to "waves, billows, and water-spouts," Psalm xlii. 5—7, for though these much weaken the faith, and disturb the peace of God's children, yet they do not destroy their love: Christ's absence gives much uneasiness to believers, brings much darkness upon them, and raises many doubts, fears, and misgivings of heart in them; they cannot, it may be, say at such times with the church, "My beloved is mine, and I am his;" yet they can say with her, when in the same condition with them, "Saw ye him whom my soul loveth?" 7. The terrors of the law, and the apprehensions of God's wrath, which believers are sometimes filled with, are set forth by waves and floods of water, in Psalm lxxxviii. 6, 7, 15—17, under which, though there may be but little faith, and less joy; yet there may be much love to Christ, great longings and earnest desires after the enjoyment of his presence; as appears from the case of the Psalmist, now referred to. 8. and lastly, all the hardships, difficulties, pressures, and reproaches, which may attend believers in their Christian race, are so far from destroying their love to, and alienating their affections from Christ, that they do but rather endear him the more unto them; and make heaven, and the enjoyment of Christ there, the more desirable to them now, and the more welcome to them hereafter.

Secondly. This love of believers to Christ is exceeding valuable; for "if a man would give all the substance of his house for it, it would utterly be contemned:" for, 1. This is not to be bought with money, no more than the love of Christ is; no gift nor grace of the Spirit can be procured any such way, it is true, grace is compared to "gold tried in the fire," which we are advised to buy of Christ; but then it is to be bought "without money and without price." 2. As this grace cannot be bought with money, so neither will it be parted with for it: a Judas indeed, for thirty pieces of silver, forsook his Master, and betrayed him into his enemies hands; as Demas also deserted the apostles, and cause of Christ, "having loved this present world; but these things cannot prevail upon true believers to do the like. For, 3. The offers of a man's whole estate, nay, of the riches of the Indies, or vast treasures of the whole globe, if made on terms, and conditions of parting with Christ, or deserting his cause and interest; would be treated with the utmost disdain and contempt; they would "utterly be contemned;" or, "in despising they would despise" it, as the words may be rendered from the Hebrew text. For, 4. The things of this world appear but mean in the believer's eye; who "counts all things but loss and dung, for the excellency of the knowledge of Christ Jesus:" nay, he is willing to part with all for Christ, and does, when called to it, "take joyfully the spoiling of his goods, knowing that he has in heaven a better and a more enduring substance." 5. The sense of this clause is thus given by some:[e] that those who spend their substance, their time, their strength, nay, their very lives, for the love they bear to God, Christ, his ways, cause, and interest, are but laughed at, despised, and set at nought by those who are destitute of it; which sense is favoured by the Septuagint version, which renders the words thus; "If a man would give all his living away in love, or charity, in despising they would despise him." Now the constancy and insuperableness of this precious and valuable grace of love in her soul to Christ, is improved by the church to obtain the former request; "set me as a seal upon thine heart," &c., for my soul is all in flames of love for thee, which cannot be extinguished by all I suffer on thy account, nor will be parted with for all that the world can give me; which love of hers discovers itself, not only in a regard to Christ, but also in a concern for others, as appears from the following words:

Verse 8. *We have a little sister, and she hath no breasts: What shall we do for our sister, in the day when she shall be spoken for?*

THESE are either the words of the daughters of Jerusalem[g], who were concerned for the welfare of the church; or else of Christ,[h] being solicitous for the conversion of the elect uncalled; or rather of the church,[i] who, having in the preceding verse discovered a very strong affection to Christ, here signifies her hearty concern for the good of others, which go under the appellation of a little sister: an own sister, near and dear to her,[k] a loving expression; by whom may be meant, either the unconverted elect in general; or else, some new church that was to be set up in some certain age or period of time; or rather, the whole Gentile church, who is called so by the Jewish church, so that they seem to be the words of the Jewish church, signifying her affection to and concern

---

[e] So Theodoret. in loc. [f] So Sanctius in loc.
[h] Alcuin in loc. [i] So Theodoret. Tres Patres, and alii in loc. [k] Germana mea sororcula, Plauti Fragment. Cistellar. v. 15.

for the Gentile church, which was then uncalled. In which may be observed,

1st. That the Jewish church asserts and owns the relation that the Gentile church stood in, both to her and Christ, at that present time; " we have a little sister."

II. She describes her, 1st. By her being little. 2ndly. By her having " no breasts."

III. She manifests her concern for her; " what shall we do for our sister, in the day when she shall be spoken for?"

I. The old Jewish church asserts and owns the relation, in which the Gentile church, though uncalled, stood in both to her and Christ; " we have a little sister." In which may be considered, 1st. In what sense the Gentile church is sister to the Jewish church. 2ndly. How she appears to stand in the same relation to Christ. 3rdly. How she could be so at that present time.

1st. The Gentile church may be said to be a sister to the Jewish church, for these following reasons: 1. In a more general sense; because Jews and Gentiles are both of one and the same blood; for God " hath made of one blood all nations of men for to dwell on all the face of the earth," Acts xvii. 26. 2. On the account of their being neighbours: Thus Samaria and Sodom are said to be sisters to Jerusalem: the one the elder, the other the younger, Ezek. xvi. 46. 3. Because, in a spiritual sense, those who are Christ's, whether they be Jews or Gentiles, or Abraham's seed, Gal. iii. 28, 29. 4. The elect of God, whether among the Jews or Gentiles, belong unto, and are interested in one and the same covenant of grace, Isa. xlii. 6, and xlix. 6. 5. Believers in Christ, of either race, are born of one and the same Father, brought up in one and the same family, and are heirs together of the grace of life, Eph. ii. 19, and iv. 4. 6. Christ stands in the relation of an elder brother to the Gentile, as well as to the Jewish church; and therefore these two must be sisters, Rom. viii. 29. 7. The church catholic or universal, with respect to its several parts, is called a mother, and that frequently in this song: see chap. i. 6, and iii. 4, and viii. 2, and so agreeably the parts of it, with respect to themselves, may be called sisters, being mother's children. 8. They are of the same faith and religion, as to the substance of it: it is true there is some difference as to the circumstantials of worship, which are now laid aside; but the true spiritual nature and object of it are the same; the Old-Testament saints " ate the same spiritual meat, and drank the same spiritual drink" as saints do under the New; the articles of their faith are the same; for converted Gentiles believe "none other things than those which Moses and the prophets did say should come," relating to Christ's person, grace, work, and office.

2ndly. The Gentile church is not only a sister to the Jewish church, but also to Christ; therefore she does not say, I have a little sister, but *we* have one; which way of speaking perhaps she purposely makes use of, that she might stir up his affection and concern for her the more, she being as much related to him as she was herself, and it may be observed, that Christ is not ashamed to own his church, whether of the Jewish or Gentile race, as standing in this relation to him; nay, rather seems to take pleasure in viewing her under this consideration, as appears from his frequent use of it, in chap. iv. 9, 10, and v. 1, 2; where this character is more largely opened.

3rdly. There remains a difficulty in this clause to be removed; and that is, how the Gentile church could be said before calling to stand in the relation of a sister, either to Christ or to the Jewish church; for she expresses herself in the present tense, we *have* a little sister: which difficulty will be removed, if we consider these following things; 1. She was so in divine predestination; just as the elect uncalled are said to be Christ's sheep before conversion; John. x. 16, " Other sheep I have, which are not of this fold; them also I must bring in;" by which are particularly meant the Gentiles; who were sheep, though wandering, though not yet brought in by grace, nor folded in a church-state; the same are called, " the children of God" before conversion, John xi. 52, though scattered abroad, and not openly and visibly appearing to be fellow-citizens of the saints, and of the household of God;" for though they are not in the possession of adopting grace, yet they are " predestinated unto the adoption of children;" on the account of which they may truly be said to be related to the saints, who are called by grace. 2. The Gentile church was brought into this relation in the everlasting covenant; in which Christ not only stood as an elder Brother and glorious Representative to both churches, but also espoused them both to himself; so that they stood in the relations of sister and spouse to him, and of sisters one to another; thus Christ is said to be the husband of the Gentile church, before her calling and conversion; Isa. liv. 5, " Thy maker is thine husband, the Lord of hosts is his name." 3. The calling of the Gentiles being sure and certain in God's promises, all whose " promises are yea and amen in Christ," it is represented as if it was already done: as things only promised and prophesied of, though not yet fulfilled, frequently are in scripture; see Isa. ix. 6, and liii. 3—5. 4. The Gentile church was a sister in the faith of the Jewish church, who viewed her future calling as present; which agrees with the nature of faith, defined by the apostle, Heb. xi. 1, to be " the substance of things hoped for, and the evidence of things not seen."

II. She describes this sister of hers: 1st. By her littleness. 2ndly. By her having no breasts.

1st. She calls her "a little sister;" so the Gentile church was to the Jewish church, 1. In respect of age, being a younger sister: the Jewish church was first called, and then the Gentile; which is very fully and aptly expressed in the parable of the two sons, the elder and the younger, as is thought by some, Luke xv. 12—25, the elder signifying the Jewish church at that time, which murmured at the grace of God bestowed upon the Gentiles; the younger, the Gentiles, who had lived in all manner of sin and wickedness, and was disregarded of God, but was now embraced with all demonstrations of joy, affection, and tenderness. 2. She is called so as being in some respects less honourable than the Jewish church; "Who are Israelites," as the apostle says, Rom. ix. 4, 5, and iii. 1, 2, "to whom pertaineth the adoption, and the glory, and the covenants, and the giving of the law, and the service of God, and the promises; whose are the fathers, and of whom, as concerning the flesh, Christ came:" therefore, as he says, the Jew has the advantage of the Gentile, and that much every way; but chiefly, because to them were committed the oracles of God. 3. The Jewish church calling the Gentile church "a little sister," may express her pity and compassion towards her, being like a young and tender infant, that is in a forlorn and helpless condition; see Ezek. xvi. 4, 5. 4, She may be called so with regard to her number of converts, either at that time, which were very few, few proselytes being then made among the Gentiles to the Jewish religion; or else, at the time when the gospel first came among them; "for this sect was everywhere spoken against;" and indeed the whole number of Christ's sheep, either among Jews or Gentiles, are but a "little flock," when compared with the world. 5. She was then more especially, as also at her first calling, but little in spiritual stature; her light, knowledge, and faith, being but small, not having as yet arrived "to the measure of the stature of the fulness of Christ," she was to grow up unto.

2ndly. She says, that "she has no breasts;" that is, 1. She was not arrived to years of ripeness; she was not marriageable; her "breasts were not fashioned," as in Ezek. xvi. 7; the time of her open espousal to Christ, by the preaching of the gospel, was not yet come. I call it the time of her open espousal to him; for she, as well as the Jewish church, her elder sister, was secretly espoused to Christ in the everlasting covenant; see Isa. liv. 5; but she was not yet espoused to him in that sense in which the apostle Paul says, 2 Cor. xi. 2, of the Corinthian, which was a Gentile church, "I have espoused you to one husband, that I may present you a chaste virgin to Christ;" the time fixed upon for it in ancient council not being yet come. 2. She had "no breasts;" that is, at this time she had no ministers nor ordinances, from whence she might suck and be satisfied, with the sincere milk of the word: moreover, it was some time after the gospel came among the Gentiles, that they had a settled ministry; which was fixed by the apostles, who "ordained elders in every city."

III. The Jewish church signifies her very great concern for the Gentile church, being thus little, and without breasts, saying, "What shall we do," or "shall be done for our sister?" Which shows, 1. That this little sister was in a state of nature, uncalled, unconverted, poor, miserable, forlorn, and helpless. 2. That the Jewish church was concerned for her, was moved with pity and compassion towards her; and would gladly contribute all she could towards her everlasting salvation; as the apostle Paul was for his unconverted kinsmen and relations, Rom. ix. 1—3. 3. That she not only wished her well, but was willing to do anything for her that lay in her power; though she seems, in some measure, to be at a loss what to do; and indeed the converted Jews were very much assisting to the spreading of the Gospel among the Gentiles: they were Jews who first carried the Gospel into the Gentile world; for it was proper that "out of Zion should go forth the law or doctrine, and the word of the Lord out of Jerusalem;" and when tidings of the Gentile's reception of the Gospel "came to the ears of the church at Jerusalem," they sent forth others also on the same errand; nay, supplied them with money, that so they might not be burdensome to the Gentiles, nor give them any occasion to reproach the Gospel; for the fund or stock, which was raised at Jerusalem by the believing Jews, who knew that their land would be laid waste, and their city destroyed in a little time, and therefore sold their land and possessions, and put the money into the apostle's hands; this, I say, seems to be designed, not only for their own use, but for the service of God in spreading the gospel among the Gentiles; who, when they had churches settled among them, upon that consideration were called upon to make collections for these poor saints at Jerusalem. 4. She is not forgetful of the main and principal agent in this work, who is Christ; therefore she says, what shall we do? she was willing to do what she could; but she knew that all her endeavours would be of little significance, without his agency and blessing: she could send her ministers; but if Christ did not go along with them, and bless them, they would meet but with little success: as it is said, "Who then is Paul, and who is Apollos, but ministers by whom ye believed, even as the Lord gave to every man? I have planted," says Paul; "Apollos watered, but God gave the increase," 1 Cor. iii. 5, 6.

The time that the Jewish church had in view, and is concerned what should be done for her then, is, "the day when she shall be spoken for, or with."[1] By which may be meant, either, 1. The time of the first preaching of the Gospel among them, which, to them, was the "accepted time

---

[1] ביום שידבר בה εν ημερα η εαν λαληθη εν αυτη, Sept. In die qua fiet sermo in ea, Montanus; quando ei colloquendum erit, Tigurine version.

and day of salvation;" when Christ, by his ministers, spoke to and for them, wooed and beseeched them; treated and communed with them, as David with Abigail; about openly espousing them before the world: it seems to be an allusion to persons treating either with virgins themselves, or with their parents,[m] about their marriage. Or, 2. It may refer to the fame that was spread abroad of the conversion of the Gentiles: when it was first effected, it made a great noise in the world; the faith of a single church, the church at Rome, was "spoken of throughout the whole world:" thus the clause may be rendered, "In the day when she shall be spoken of;"[n] that is, when her fame shall be spread far and near: and some will say one thing of her, and some another: now the Jewish church seems to be concerned how she would behave herself under all this noise and talk about her. Or else, 3. The words may be rendered, "When she shall be spoken against:"[o] this has been the common lot of God's children; this sect, as it is called, has been in all ages and in all places spoken against; and no wonder, for Christ himself is "set for a sign, which shall be spoken against:" now the old church might be concerned for this new church of the Gentiles; that she might be able to stand firm and constant to her profession, notwithstanding all the revilings, reproaches, and persecutions of men. Or, 4. They may be read thus, "When she shall be spoken to;"[p] that is, when the great men of the world, as Nero, and other heathen emperors, shall call her before them, and tempt her, either by fair words or severe menaces, to desert the faith of Christ. O! that she might stand fast then, as if the church should say, and not be moved away from the hope of the Gospel; neither be frightened by their threatenings, nor deluded by their promises: she was jealous of her, as the apostle Paul was of the Corinthian church, lest she "should be corrupted from the simplicity that is in Christ." Now this should teach us in general, from the example of the Jewish church here, to be concerned for all the elect of God uncalled, and particularly for those among the Jews; we should earnestly pray for them, and use all proper means and methods to bring them to the knowledge of Christ; the time is coming when they shall be spoken for, shall be called by grace, and openly espoused to Christ; and seeing they were so much concerned for us, when we were little, and had no breasts, we should be as much concerned for them, they being now in the same case and circumstances.

Verse 9. *If she be a wall, we will build upon her a palace of silver: and if she be a door, we will enclose her with boards of cedar.*

THESE are the words of Christ, in answer to the solicitous concern of the old Jewish church for her little sister, the Gentile; declaring what should be done for her on such and such considerations.

I. If, or "seeing she is a wall, we will build upon her a palace of silver."

II. "And if she be a door, we will enclose her with boards of cedar:" all which is expressive of what strength and ornament should be added to her, and what grace and glory should be conferred upon her.

I. He promises, that if or seeing she was a wall; that is, well walled, built upon a sure foundation, and firmly established in her faith in and love to Christ, and is constant therein, and stands as a wall against the attack of enemies;[q] a palace or tower of silver should be built upon her: by which may be meant, either, the scriptures of truth, with which she should be furnished; which, for their impregnableness and store of spiritual armour that is in them, may be compared to towers; and for their purity, richness, and excellency, to silver ones; or else, the ministers of the Gospel may be intended, who are set for the defence of it: or this phrase may in general signify, that she should be fortified and put into a posture of defence against all her enemies, having on the πανοπλια, or whole armour of God; walled towns and cities, to which the allusion is here made, usually have towers built upon the walls thereof; so Zion is said to have such, Psalm xlviii. 12, 13; which also this little sister, the Gentile church, should not be without: though the word may as well be rendered, *a palace ;*[r] and signifies, that she should be built up an habitation for Father, Son, and Spirit, who would come and make their abode with her; and being such noble and uncommon guests, a silver palace must be erected for them. The persons who were to do this work, are either the Jewish church, with her ministers as instruments, and Christ as the principal agent; for Psalm cxxvii. 1, "Except the Lord build the house, they labour in vain that build it:" or else, by the we, are intended the blessed Trinity, as in chap. i. 11; who were all jointly concerned in raising up a church-state in the Gentile world. From the whole may be observed, 1. That he that begins the good work, whether it relates to a particular person, or to a church, must and will finish it; the same hands which lay the foundation, must raise up the superstructure, and complete the whole building, by bringing in "the head-stone with shoutings, cry-

---

[m] Vid. Aben Ezram in loc. [n] Dei quo sermo fiet de ea, Mercerus, Junius, Brightman ; in dei quo verba fient de ea, Cocceius.
[o] Vid. Targum, Shirhashirim Rabba, and Jarchi in loc. and Bereshit Rabba parash. 39. fol. 34. 1.
[p] In die quando aloiquenda est, Vulgate Latin version. [q] So Ajax is called the wall of the Grecians, Homer, Iliad. 6. v. 5. and 7. v. 211. and Achilles also, Graium murus Achilles, Ovid. Metamorph. 1. 13. v. 281. [r] שירה כסף επαλξεις αργυραι, Sept. propugnacula argentea, Vulgate Latin version ; propugnaculum argenteum, Tigurine version.: arcem argenteam, Mercerus ; castellum argenti, Michaelis.

ing, grace, grace unto it." 2. This verifies the saying of our Lord, Matt. xxv. 20, that "unto every one that hath shall be given, and he shall have abundance:" grace is usually but very small at first, but it afterwards increases much; frequently from small beginnings great things arise; this Gentile church at first had but a very small appearance of a building; a foundation was just laid, and a side wall erected; but in a short time, a noble structure, a silver palace for God is built up.

II. Christ also assures her, that if she was a door, she should be inclosed with boards of cedar: the meaning of which may be, either, 1. If the Gentiles had the door of the Gospel opened among them, as they had in many places, see Acts xiv. 27, 1, Cor. xvi. 8, 9, 2 Cor. ii. 12, this should be succeeded for the building up of a holy temple for the Lord; which should be of such ornament and strength, so well fenced and enclosed with the grace and power of Christ, that it should not be in the power of all their enemies to deface or demolish it. Or, 2. If the door of their hearts was opened to Christ, as Lydia's was, Acts xvi. 14, so as to receive and let in this king of glory, with his numerous train of graces; then she should be adorned and beautified with a larger measure of them. Or, 3. If when they came into a church-state, the door was set open, that so "the righteous nation which keepeth truth, may enter in," and yet at the same time careful to exclude others; this should make much for their honour, comfort, safety, and security. Or, 4. This phrase is expressive of the building being completed; but only it wanted some farther decorations and ornaments, which it should not be long without: so the setting up of gates or doors to towns or houses seems to signify; see Neh. iii. Though, 5. It seems rather to intend the mean, low, and weak state and condition the Gentile church was first in, when there was but very little appearance of a building: there was only as it were a door set up; which afterwards grew up to be a magnificent and stately temple, built up of cedar-boards of the wood of Lebanon; of which Solomon's temple was made, and to which an allusion here seems to be. But, 6. Some* have thought that these words carry in them some intimations of her inconstancy to Christ, and the wandering of her affections after other lovers; as also the methods which Christ would take to restrain and prevent her: "If she be a door;" that is, if she will not keep at home, but will gad abroad, and go in and out at pleasure, we will use some methods to keep her in; "we will enclose her with boards of cedar;" or, as it is expressed in Hosea ii. 7, "I will hedge up thy way with thorns, and make a wall, that she shall not find her paths." Though, 7. The meaning rather seems to be, that however mean and abject she might appear to be, even as a door, yet she should be adorned with grace here, and enjoy glory hereafter; both which, for their perpetuity and incorruptibleness, may be compared to cedar-boards; besides, the safety and security of the church in this present state, her walls being salvation, and her gates praise, may be here intended; as well as the delights and pleasures of the heavenly state, signified by the fragrant cedar, which she should, ere long, be enclosed and surrounded with.

Verse 10. *I am a wall, and my breasts like towers: then was I in his eyes as one that found favour.*

THESE are either the words of the Jewish church, asserting herself to be what her little sister was not; namely, that she was a wall well fenced, and firmly established, was indulged with ordinances, and blessed with ministers; whilst the Gentiles lay open, were "without Christ, being aliens from the commonwealth of Israel, and strangers from the covenants of promise, having no hope, and without God in the world," Eph. ii. 12; as also confirming what Christ had said in the former verse; as well as assuring her little sister, the Gentile church, that she should also find favour in Christ's eyes, when she came into the same state and condition: unless we should rather choose to consider them as expressing that additional glory, peace, and prosperity, which should accrue to the church by the calling of the Gentiles; which would not be inconsiderable, and no small indication of her finding favour or peace in Christ's eyes; who would then "extend peace to her like a river, and the glory of the Gentiles like a flowing stream." Though I rather think, that they are the words of the little sister herself, the Gentile church; either signifying her desire to be in such a well-settled state and condition, "O that I was a wall!" &c., or else, asserting herself to be in such a case,¹ which Christ had intimated in the former verse.

I. She asserts herself to be a wall.

II. That her breasts were like towers. And,

III. Being so, was in his eyes as one that found favour.

I. She asserts herself to be a wall; that is, 1. Well walled. God himself is a wall of fire about his people; Christ's salvation is appointed for walls and bulwarks to them; nay, faithful ministers and Christian magistrates may in some sense be said to be so, being placed for the protection and defence of the church. 2. She is one of those two walls, to which Christ is the corner-stone, as he is called, Eph. ii. 20, the Jewish church is one, and the Gentile the other; which both meet and make up one building in Christ, the middle wall of partition being broken down. 3. She is a wall built up of lively stones, cemented together in love; the elect of God, by nature, lie in the same quarry, are taken out of the same pit, and hewn from the

---

* Vid R. Aben. Ezram and Sanctium in loc.
¹ Hoc est, nolite dubitare utrum murus sum. Ambros. Enarrat, in Psal. cxviii. octon. 22. p. 1087.

same rock, as others are; but being separated from them by distinguishing and efficacious grace, are hewn and fitted for the building by the Spirit of God, where they are laid by him, and knit together in the bond of love. 4. She was firmly built on Christ, the Foundation; which God has laid in Zion, and is sure, firm, and lasting, against which the gates of hell can never prevail; and which will be sufficient to bear up and support the church and all believers, who lay the whole stress of their persons, and the salvation of them upon it. 5. She was well established in the doctrine of faith: the Gentiles received the gospel with all readiness of mind, when the Jews rejected it; and though it was in much affliction, yet it was with much joy in the Holy Ghost; and when they once got it, they could not be moved away from it, by all the frowns and flatteries, promises, and threatenings of men; which, to their adversaries, was an evident token of perdition, but to them, of salvation, and that of God; so the Targum and R. Solomon Jarchi interpret these words of the steadfastness of the congregation of Israel, in the religion and laws of God. 6. She was constant and immoveable in her love to Christ; she was a wall; she was proof against all temptations and insinuations, and not a door, that easily let into her affections every one that knocked: she loved Christ dearly, and kept her love inviolate and pure for him; nothing could separate her from it; the greatest pleasures and profits of life could not tempt her to desert him; nor the most dreadful sufferings and torments deter her from expressing her affections to him; she was like a wall that stood invincible and impregnable.

II. She says, that her breasts were like towers; which may in general denote her ripeness for marriage; her breasts were fashioned, were round and plump, and rose up high like towers; she was now marriageable; the time of her being presented as a chaste virgin to Christ, and of her open espousals to him, was come. Or else more particularly,

1st. By her breasts, may be meant the ministers of the gospel; who like nurses, 1 Thess. ii. 7, give the breast to "new-born babes," and feed them with the "sincere milk of the word;" and like towers, are set for the defence of the gospel: such ministers the first church among the Gentiles had; whose ministry was not only edifying and nourishing, but they themselves also were faithful, zealous, and courageous in the discharge thereof; and could not be moved from their station, nor be made to desist from their work, by all the violence and oppression of men. Or else,

2udly. By these breasts, may be meant the two Testaments, the Old and the New; which are both full of the milk of excellent doctrines and precious promises; which are all useful for the comfort, edification, and instruction of God's people; and from whence, as from towers, they may be supplied with all needful armour, to repel Satan's temptations, refute erroneous doctrines, and defend the gospel; and though efforts have been made by Satan and his emissaries to remove them out of the world, yet they still remain impregnable and invincible: now with these breasts the Gentile church is blessed.

3rdly. The two ordinances, of baptism and the Lord's supper, may be intended; which are peculiar to the church under the New Testament dispensation; and are as breasts of consolation to believers, especially when they have the presence of Christ in them, and his love at the same time manifested to them; these are like towers, have stood firm and immoveable against all the efforts of men, to change, deface, subvert, and abolish them. The Jews[u] interpret the wall of the congregation of Israel, and the "breasts as towers," of the synagogues and schools; also the former of the law, and the latter of the scholars.

III. Being so, she says, she "was in his eyes as one that found favour;" which may either respect,

1st. The time[w] of her becoming a wall, and having breasts like towers; then was I, or from the time that I was in his eyes, "as one that found favour or peace;" that is, I became a wall, was firmly built on Christ, established in the doctrine of faith, and formed into a church-state; had breasts, a settled ministry, and gospel ordinances; which have continued with me ever since I found peace with Christ, which he made for me by the blood of his cross. Now this is certainly matter of fact, that from the time that Christ became "our peace," Eph. ii. 14, the ceremonial law, which is there called "the middle wall of partition," which stood between Jew and Gentile, was removed: so that they both coalesced in one church-state, ver. 14—16, and equally shared in all Gospel ordinances and privileges, ver. 17—22, from that time the Gentile church began to be a church in Gospel order. Or else,

2ndly. It may respect the time of the open manifestation of Christ's love, which was when she became a wall, and had breasts. It is true, he loved her before, even from eternity, with an everlasting love; but that was hidden and secret both to herself and others: but now her "breasts are fashioned;" he looked upon her, and her "time is the time of love:" he openly espouses her to himself, and lets all the world know, as well as herself, what favour she found in his sight: and it manifestly appears that she was sensible of it; and by expressing it, would signify, 1. That her being a wall, and having breasts, were instances of his kindness to her: and indeed, it is an unspeakable mercy to have a gospel-ministry and gospel-ordinances; Psalm cxlviii. 19, 20, "He showed his word unto Jacob, his statutes and his judgments unto Israel: he hath not dealt so with any nation; and as for his judgments, they have not known them: praise ye the Lord:" if it was so

---

[u] T. Bab. Bava Bathra, fol. 8. 1. and Pesachim, fol. 87. 1.   [w] Vid. Alcuin in loc.

great a favour for the people of Israel to have the law, on the account of which they were called a "great nation;" what an instance of surprising and distinguishing grace is it, that we Gentiles should have the Gospel and the ordinances thereof! The church here esteemed it a favour, and so should we. 2. She ascribes all these blessings and privileges which she was possessed of, to his grace and favour. Was she a wall? it was owing to him; and had she breasts? she acknowledges it is an instance of his regard to her; and was ready to say, with the apostle, 1 Cor. xv. 10, "By the grace of God, I am what I am:" an excellent example for us to follow. 3. This phrase may be expressive of her gracious acceptation with Christ; thus Noah is said to have "found grace in the eyes of the Lord," Gen. vi. 8; the Gentiles, who were proselyted to the Jewish religion before the coming of Christ in the flesh, were like Esther, "standing in the court" alone, for they might not worship with the Jews; whom, when Christ looked upon, they "obtained favour in his sight," and he held out the golden sceptre of his grace, and admitted them to nearer communion with him; built them into a church-state, furnished them with gospel-ordinances, and graciously accepted both them and their services: he "took pleasure in these his people, and beautified the meek with salvation." 4. The enjoyments of the presence of God and Christ, is a very considerable instance and evidence of finding favour in his eyes: Moses desired to be ascertained of his having found grace in God's sight, by the enjoyment of this blessing, Exod. xxxiii. 15, 10, which he was graciously indulged with; and perhaps it is this which the church here had particularly in view; and a great mercy it was to have ordinances, and the presence of Christ along with them, than which nothing can be more desirable and delightful. 5. The words may be rendered, "then was I in his eyes as one that found peace;" meaning that inward peace of conscience, and tranquillity of mind, which "passeth all understanding;" which she enjoyed in the midst of all her tribulations and sufferings for Christ; which he only gives, and which the world cannot take away? for if he "giveth quietness, who then can make trouble?" 6. This word "favour or peace," may comprehend all these spiritual blessings, wherewith she was blessed in Christ Jesus, such as peace, reconciliation, justification, pardon of sin, sanctification, adoption, &c., for he is "a Sun and Shield; he will give grace and glory, no good thing will he withhold from them that walk uprightly," Psalm. lxxxiv. 11. 7. The manifestation of Christ's love, which is the greatest blessing in life, may be here intended: hence says the Psalmist, Psalm cvi. 4, "Remember me, O Lord, with the favour that thou bearest unto thy people;" and no wonder that he should be so desirous of it; for "in his favour is life;" but not to enjoy it is death. O! how miserable will those be to all eternity, in whom that scripture will be verified, Isa. xxvii. 11, "He that made them, will not have mercy on them; and he that formed them, will show them no favour!"

Verse 11. *Solomon had a vineyard at Baal-hamon; he let out the vineyard unto keepers: every one for the fruit thereof was to bring a thousand pieces of silver.*

IN these words the little sister goes on to give an account of the success of the Gospel, the planting of churches, and establishment of Christ's interest in the Gentile world; together with the advantages which accrued to Christ thereby, under the metaphor of a vineyard, and the fruit thereof: where we have to consider,

1. The vineyard itself, and what is intended by it.

II. The owner of it, who is Solomon.

III. The place of its situation, at Baal-hamon.

IV. The letting of it "out to keepers," and who are meant by them.

V. The price it was let at, or the rent which they were to bring in: "every one for the fruit thereof was to bring a thousand pieces of silver."

I. It will be proper to consider what is meant by this vineyard; which I think is to be understood of the church of Christ; the Israelitish nation and the church of God therein, sometimes bears this name; see Psalm lxxx. 8, 9, 14, 15, Isa. v. 1, 7; and it is very usual with Christ to express the New-Testament church-state by the same metaphor; see Matt. xx. 1, and xxi. 33; which was thus prophesied of by Isaiah, chap. xxvii. 2, "In that day, sing ye unto her, a vineyard of red wine." Now the church of Christ may be compared to a vineyard, for these following reasons: 1. A vineyard is a spot of ground, separated and distinguished from others; so is the church of Christ from the rest of the world by electing, redeeming, and efficacious grace; believers are a chosen generation, a royal priesthood, an holy nation; and being so are a peculiar people; they are fenced about with sovereign grace, whereby they are made to differ from others. 2. A vineyard is a spot of ground set with plants of various sorts, and especially vines: it is manifest, from chap. i. 14, and vii. 12, that it was usual to set other plants in vineyards besides vines; for which see also Luke xiii. 16. In the vineyard, the church, stands in the first place Christ, the true and most noble vine; and next to him true believers, who are there planted by him, engrafted on him, and grow up in him: now these are of various sorts, of different growths and fruitfulness; some are larger and more fruitful than others; but are all "the planting of the Lord, that he might be glorified:" but besides these, there are some who are only externally planted here, and grow up only in a mere outward profession; who are not planted by Christ's heavenly Father, and therefore shall be rooted up; because instead of bringing forth right fruit, they bring forth wild grapes. 3. Vineyards are valuable to the owners of them; one part of their wealth and riches consisting therein: the church of Christ is highly esteemed of by him, it being his inheritance, his portion, and wherein great part of his riches, as Mediator, lies; his Father gave it to him, and he values it upon that account: as Naboth did his vineyard, because it was "the inheritance of his fathers," and therefore would not part with it to Ahab upon any consideration whatever: moreover, Christ's esteem for his vineyard, the church, is farther manifest from the great price he gave for it, which was his own blood, as also from the exceeding great care he takes of it. 4. A vineyard is a very fruitful spot; so is the church of Christ and all believers, who are "filled with the fruits of righteousness by Jesus Christ:" who is "the true vine," on whom they are engrafted; and "the green-fir-tree," from whom their fruit is found: all that are "planted in the house of the Lord," being watered by divine grace, "flourish in the courts of our God," and bring forth fruit, whereby he is glorified. 5. Vineyards are delightful and pleasant; thus among the several methods which Solomon took to gratify and indulge himself in pleasure, this was one; he "planted himself vineyards," Eccl. ii. 4. The church is a delightful vineyard to Christ, where he delights to walk, and observe how his several plants grow and thrive; for this purpose he often goes down into it, as in chap. vi. 11; and the church, knowing how much pleasure he takes therein, invites him to it, in chap. vii. 12. 6. Vineyards are not only delightful, but also profitable; there is much fruit produced by them, to the advantage of the owners thereof; so Christ has much fruit from his vineyard, as appears from this and the following verse; which makes for the advancement of his honour and glory in the world: for as all their fruit comes by him, and from him, so all the glory redounds unto him; and "his glory is great" in every branch of their salvation. 7. Vineyards are exposed to beasts of prey, which often break in and do much damage to them; the church of Christ is not only exposed to the "boar out of the wood," the openly profane world, which often makes great havoc of it, by its oppression, and persecutions: but also to those foxes, false teachers, heretics, who cunningly bring in their pernicious doctrines, to the great annoyance and disturbance of the peace, comfort, and faith of God's people; hence it is said, in chap. ii. 15, "Take us the foxes, the little foxes, that spoil the vines; for our vines have tender grapes." 8. A great deal of care must be used in promoting the fruitfulness of vineyards; the vines must be watered, pruned, and propped up, as well as the stones gathered out, and a fence set about them; see Isa. v. 2. Christ does all this and much more to his vineyard; he waters it every moment with his grace, prunes and lops off the unfruitful branches, supports the weak and tender vines with his Almighty power; gathers out all things that offend, and fences it about with divine favours; in short, acts the whole faithful part of a a vine-dresser to it.

II. The owner of this vineyard is Solomon, by whom the Messiah is meant: for it may be truly said, that "a greater than Solomon is here." Christ bears this name because Solomon was an eminent type of him, as has been shown on chap. iii. 7; he now is the owner of this vineyard; it is his, 1. By choice; he has pitched upon this spot of ground, and separated it from all others for his use and service. 2. By his Father's gift; he asked it of his Father, and he gave it him: "thine they were," says he, "and thou gavest them me," John xvii. 6. 3. By purchase; he has bought this vineyard with his own blood, Acts xx. 28. 4. It is of his own planting: all the vines in it are of his setting, and are made fruitful by him. 5. He takes the whole care of it, and has the advantage of the fruit thereof.

III. The situation of this vineyard, at Baal-hamon; perhaps the same with Baal-gad in the valley of Lebanon, Josh. xi. 17, and xiii. 5; since they are of the same signification, "the master of a multitude, or of a troop. By which may be meant, either, 1. The city of Jerusalem;[y] which may be called "Baal-hamon, or the master of a multitude," because it was a very populous city; as it is said, in Lam. i. 1, "How doth the city sit solitary that was full of people?" where was the principal seat of the Jewish church-state; the letting out of which to keepers, the priests and Levites, may seem to suit well with the legal and mercenary spirit which much attended the Old-Testament dispensation. Though, 2. I rather think the Gentile world is here intended: among the nations of which Christ has a Gospel church planted; whereby the promise is fulfilled to Abraham, that he should be a "father of many nations;" which his name signified, and is of much the same import with this in our text. Unless, 3. It should be thought only to intend in general, the fruitfulness of the soil in which Christ's vineyard was planted; at "Baal-hamon, the Lord or master of a multitude,"[q] that is, where a multitude of vines grow. Thus it is said, in Isa. v. 2, "My well-beloved hath a vineyard in a very fruitful hill:" the church of Christ, and so all believers, are planted in a very fruitful soil, being "rooted and built up" in Christ, and watered with the continual dews of divine grace; the believers are like to "a tree planted by the rivers of water, that bringeth forth his fruit in his season; his leaf also shall not wither, and whatsoever he doeth shall prosper," Psalm i. 3.

IV. The letting out of this vineyard to keepers, is next to be inquired into. By the keepers,

---

[y] So the Targum and R. Sol. Jarchi in loc. interpret it.

[q] In ea quæ habet populos. Vulgate Latin version, in domino multitudinis, Piscator.

we are to understand the ministers of the Gospel; who have their several parts and different employments assigned them in this vineyard of Christ. 1. The business of some of them is to plant: this work the apostle Paul was much concerned in; "I have planted," says he, 1 Cor. iii. 6, 8; and indeed it is hard to say how many churches, and how many souls in those churches, were planted by him; and especially at Baal-hamon, in the Gentile world, with whom he was chiefly concerned. 2. Others are employed in watering this vineyard, as was Apollos; of whom Paul says, "I have planted, Apollos watered:" some ministers are more useful for edification than conversion; their ministry succeeds most for the watering of Christ's plants, for promoting the comfort and faith of those who are already planted; their "doctrine drops as the rain, and their speech distils as the dew, as the small rain upon the tender 'herb, and as the showers upon the grass," Deut. xxxii. 2; so that they become fruitful. 3. The work of others is to prune the vines; they have an excellent talent at reproof, both on the account of erroneous doctrines, and immoral practices; they can give gentle admonitions where the case only requires them: and rebuke with sharpness, cut deeper, where there is a necessity for it; not being afraid of the faces of any, but having the good of Christ's vineyard at heart; these excel in that branch of their office, which concerns the discipline of the church. 4. Others are useful in supporting and upholding weak believers; who like vines, stand in need of it; which they do, by putting into their hand the staff of the promises, and refreshing them with the reviving cordials of gospel-doctrines. 5. The employment of others is to protect and defend; their business is chiefly to take the foxes, to refute heresies, and defend the doctrines of grace, and preserve the church from all innovations, both in doctrine and worship. Now I would not be understood, as though I thought that ministers were so confined to one or other of these particular branches of the ministerial work, that they had no concern in the rest: for one and the same minister may be more or less useful in them all; but yet, generally speaking, he excels in some one of them.

The letting out of this vineyard to them, agrees with those parables of our Lord, in Matt. xx. 1, 2, and xxi. 33, where he seems to allude to the words of our text; which is no inconsiderable evidence of the divine authority of this book. The phrase shows, I. That though Christ takes care of the vineyard himself, yet he also makes use of his ministers: Christ is not separated from his ministers; he acts as the owner, they as the servants; he is the chief and principal vine-dresser; which work he performs mediately by his ministers, who are not to be slighted and laid aside; hence the apostle writing to the Corinthians, among whom were many divisions about their ministers; some being for Paul, in opposition to Apollos, and some for Apollos in opposition to Paul, and others for Cephas in opposition to them both, and others for Christ in opposition to them all; they were for Christ without his ministers; but, says the apostle, 1 Cor. i. 12, 13, Is Christ divided? that is, from his ministers; no, they are not to be separated from him, though subordinated to him. 2. It shows, that Christ entrusts his vineyard with his ministers; he makes them overseers of it; he sets them to watch over it, and faithfully discharge the several branches of their duty beforementioned; which is meant by the letting it out unto them: and it ought to be observed, that Christ has the sole power of letting out his vineyard, and he lets it out to whom he pleases; therefore none ought to usurp it: it is indeed a great honour to be intrusted with it; but no man should take this honour to himself, but he that is called of God to it; persons should not run into this work before they are sent, nor perform it negligently when they are in it. 3. Christ in some respects makes his ministers owners of this vineyard: he let out, or gave^a the vineyard to keepers; hence, in chap. ii. 15, it is said, our vines, have tender grapes; ministers have in some sort an interest in the vines, the churches; their joy, comfort, life, and glory, lie much in the fruitfulness and well-being of them; which is a very great and powerful argument to induce them to vigilance, diligence, and carefulness, in the discharge of their work.

V. The price this vineyard was let at, or the rent which these keepers were to bring in for the fruit of it, is a thousand pieces of silver: which may denote, 1. The exceeding great fruitfulness of this vineyard, that the fruit of it was worth so much: thus in Isa. vii. 23, it is said, "and it shall come to pass in that day, that every place shall be, where there were a thousand vines, at a thousand silverings, it shall even be for briars and thorns;" that is, those places, which were so exceeding fruitful before, shall now be barren and desolate. 2. It may denote the usefulness of a Gospel-ministry; which is to bring home souls to Christ; to gather in the fruit of his labours, and travail of his soul, which are as dear and valuable to him as a thousand pieces of silver; at which he rejoices as much as the poor woman did, Luke xv. 8, 9, at the finding of her lost piece: Christ's ministers are her rent-gatherers, and the collectors of his fruit; "I have chosen you, and ordained you," says he, John xv. 10, "that they should go and bring forth fruit;" and then do they bring it in, when souls are converted under their ministry. 3. The sum to be brought in from every one of them is alike, every man his thousand pieces: Christ's ministers have indeed one and the same commission to preach the Gospel; but they have not all the same abilities for the work, nor are they alike

---

^a נתן ἔδωκε, Sept dedit, Marckius, Michaelis.

succeeded in it; but yet, in the faithful and honest discharge of their work, they are all so blessed by him, as to answer the end of their ministration designed by him; so that he reckons that every one, even the meanest, brings in his thousand pieces, as well as the more able and successful. 4. It shows that there is a reckoning-day coming, for ministers as well as others; who must give an account of their talents, what use they have made of them in Christ's vineyard, and what success has attended their labours; which, if they can do with joy, and not with grief, will turn to their account, as well as be of advantage to others.

Verse 12. *My vineyard, which is mine, is before me: thou, O Solomon, must have a thousand, and those that keep the fruit thereof two hundred.*

The former part of these words seem to be the words of Christ, asserting his interest in his vineyard, the church; thereby explaining and confirming what the church had said in the former verse. The latter part of the text appears to be the words of the church, allotting proper portions to the owner and keepers of the vineyard.

I. Christ asserts his claim, right, and property in his vineyard, the church, " my vineyard, which is mine, is before me:" in which may be considered,

1st. The vineyard itself, which is the church of Christ, and is called so for several reasons, which have been shown on the preceding verse.

2ndly. This is expressed in the singular number, a vineyard for Christ's church is but one, as he asserts in chap. vi. 9, though it is true, we read of vineyards, in the plural number, in chap. vii. 12, because there are several separate, distinct, and congregated churches; though these all make up but one catholic church, one " general assembly and church of the firstborn, which are written in heaven."

3rdly. Christ asserts his right and property in his vineyard, " My vineyard," says he; whereby he confirms what the church had said in the foregoing verse; where has been shown in what respect he is the owner of it, and what kind of right he has to it.

4thly. He doubles this claim of his unto it; he not only says, " My vineyard," but adds, which is mine;" whereby, 1. He excludes all others from having any right unto it; the vineyard is his, and only his; he is the sole proprietor of it: none has any thing to do with it but himself. 2. By repeating his claim, he shows the certainty of it; that his title is unquestionable and indisputable. and indeed what can be more sure and evident, seeing his Father has given it to him, who had an undoubted right to dispose of it? nay, he has purchased it with his own blood, and has it now in possession; he is right heir to it,

according to God's own appointment; though the wicked Jews, the chief priests and Scribes, who were the keepers of the vineyard, when our Lord was here on earth, when they saw him, " said among themselves, This is the heir, come, let us kill him, and let us seize on his inheritance: and they caught him, and cast him out of the vineyard, and slew him," Matt. xxi. 38, 39. 3. He may use this additional phrase, " which is mine," to distinguish it from all other vineyards; as also to show the excellency of it, it being preferable to all others; this world, when compared with Christ's church, is a mere desert and wilderness; all other vines are " of the vine of Sodom, and of the fields of Gomorrah; their grapes are grapes of gall, their clusters are bitter," Deut. xxxii. 32, 33. 4. He repeats it, to signify the great delight he took in his vineyard; as it is in itself preferable to all others, so it is exceeding valuable and delightful to Christ; he says of it, " the lines are fallen unto me in pleasant places; yea, I have a goodly heritage," Psalm xvi. 8.

5thly. He says, that this vineyard was before him; which may denote, 1. The omniscience of Christ; which in general extends to all persons and things, that ever were, are, or shall be; " Lord, says Peter, thou knowest all things," John xxi. 17; but in a more especial manner he is concerned about his own people, whom he knows by name, and is acquainted with all their wants and necessities; he knows his own flock, and the state of it, which the Father has committed to him; he knows every sheep and lamb therein, in what condition they are, and what is most suitable for them; he knows his vineyard, and the several vines which grow there; there is never a plant escapes his notice and watchful eye; he is acquainted with every one of them, and in what case they are. 2. The omnipresence of Christ; he is the Lord that " fills heaven and earth" with his presence; the whole world is before him, but more especially his church; where, in a peculiar manner, he grants his gracious presence, there he dwells, and will abide for ever; who " holds the seven stars in his right-hand, who walks in the midst of the seven golden candlesticks," Rev. ii. 1. 3. The delights and complacency which Christ takes in his church; it is ever before him; his eye is continually upon it; he cannot bear it out of his sight, so dear and valuable is it to him: thus it was from everlasting and has continued ever since, and so it ever will; his delight from all eternity " were with the sons of men," the elect of God, " rejoicing in the habitable part of his earth, where he knew " in time, he should have a vineyard planted. 4. The care of Christ over his people, " who are engraven upon the palms of his hands, and whose walls are continually before him !" though Christ does indeed let out his vineyard to keepers, yet he does not neglect it himself; he is present with them, and works by them; it is still in his own hands, and under his watchful eye; "I the Lord," says he, Isa. xxvii. 3, "do keep it; I will water it every moment, lest any hurt it; I will keep it night and day." Thus these words may be expressive of Christ's claim unto, affection for, and care over his vineyard, the church. Though,

There are some interpreters who take them to be the words of the church, speaking of her vineyard; by which may be meant, her own soul, and the particular concerns of it: thus every one has a vineyard to look after; and in what condition that of the slothful man's was, may be seen in Prov. xxiv. 30, 31, which "was all grown over with the thorns, and nettles" of sin and corruption; its stone wall or fence was broken down, so that he was exposed to every snare and temptation. Or else, by this vineyard may be meant, the church in general; for believers have a mutual interest in each other's persons, gifts, graces, prayers, &c., and being all members of one and the same body, should, as the apostle says, 1 Cor. xii. 26, "have the same care one for another." Though perhaps the several gifts and talents, whether of nature or grace, which God bestows upon his people, may be intended; which are all to be used for the glory of Christ, and the good of his church: for as every one has a vineyard of his own, or a particular work assigned him in the vineyard, the church; so he has his particular gift, talent, and capacity for that work, which ought to be used by him; for he must one day give an account thereof. Now the church here says, that her vineyard was before her, thereby signifying her care, watchfulness, and diligence in it, of which we have an instance, chap. vii. 12, and shows that she was now in a different frame from that of which she complains, in chap. i. 6. Though I think that the former sense of the words is most agreeable. Yet,

II. The latter part of the text, "Thou, O Solomon, must have a thousand, and those that keep the fruit thereof, two hundred," manifestly appears to be the words of the church allotting proper portions. First. To the owner of the vineyard, Solomon. Secondly. To the keepers of it, the ministers.

First. She allots to "Solomon a thousand," that is, a thousand pieces of silver, as in the former verse: where is to be considered,

1st. Who is meant by Solomon; by whom, no doubt, the Messiah is intended, as is acknowledged by R. Aben Ezra,[b] and other Jewish[c] writers; though Maimonides[d] says, that "wherever the name of Solomon is mentioned in the Song of Songs, it is holy, and is as the rest of the names," except that, "a thousand unto thee, O Solomon:" to which some[e] add also, chap. iii. 7: but that Christ, and not Solomon, is here intended, is most agreeable to the nature and design of this song.

2ndly. The church's manner of addressing him, "Thou, O Solomon," shows that she was now in his presence, had much nearness to him, and used much freedom and familiarity with him, as she was by him allowed to do.

3rdly. The allotment which she makes to him, is, "a thousand;" which, 1. Is the sum agreed upon in the former verse: for the church is willing that Christ should have all that he demands or desires; she would have no abatement made, but would have him have his whole due, and full revenue of glory from his people. 2. It is a far greater share than what is assigned to the keepers; and good reason there is it should be so; for he is the Head and Master of them, as well as the Owner of the vineyard; he is "all and in all, and God over all, blessed for ever;" his is the vineyard, and all the fruit thereof; he has a right unto it, and takes the chief care and oversight of it; so that "neither is he that planteth any thing, neither he that watereth, but Christ, "who gives the increase;" and therefore should have all the glory. 3. This shows the fruitfulness of this vineyard, that it yields so large a profit both to the owner and keepers of it.

Secondly. The share allotted to the keepers is, "two hundred;" from whence may be observed,

1st. That the ministers of the gospel shall have their reward; every one that labours in the vineyard shall have his penny; and every man as the apostle says, 1 Cor. iii. 8, "shall receive his own reward, according to his own labour;" whether he be employed in watering or in planting.

2ndly. That their having their reward is no lessening of Christ's; for he has his whole thousand, though they have their two hundred; nay, Christ comes at a considerable part of his revenue, through their having theirs; for "he that receiveth you," says he, Matt. x. 40, "receiveth me;" where ministers are valued and honoured, Christ also is.

3rdly. As one[f] well observes, where Christ gets his due among a people, there and there only do ministers get their due; where Christ is heartily received, the feet of them that "bring glad tidings," will be beautiful; where Christ has his thousand, ministers will have their "two hundred;" but if Christ comes short of his due, no wonder that ministers should of theirs; but what is this "two hundred, which is due to the keepers?" Why, 1. An honourable maintenance for themselves and their families; for "the labourer is worthy of his reward," which is his due according to God's ordination: hence the apostle, 1 Cor. ix. 7—14, establishing the truth of this, from several in-

---

[b] In loc. and in Præfat. ad Comment. in lib.
[c] Vid. Shirhashirim Rabba, and Alshech in loc. and R. Abendan. Not. in Miclol Yophi in Psal. lxxii. 20.
[d] Yesod. Hattor. c. 6, s. 12. Not. in Maimon. ibid. Vid. T. Bab. Shebuot. fol. 35. 2.
[e] Vid. Vorst.
[f] Durham in loc.

stances in nature, from the reasonableness of things, as well as from proofs out of the law of God, adds, "even so hath the Lord ordained, that they which preach the gospel, should live of the gospel;" but this is but the least part of their "two hundred." 2. Honour and esteem among the people, to whom they minister, is another part thereof; for, 1 Tim. v. 17, 18, "the elders that rule well, are to be counted worthy of double honour;" by which the apostle means, first an honourable maintenance, as is manifest from his following words; and then, that duty and respect which are due to them from their people, who ought to "esteem them very highly in love," not for their persons, but "for their work's sake." 3. The conversion of sinners is another part of his two hundred; and indeed, godly and faithful ministers think that they have a very large share of their reward, when their labours are succeeded this way; for, "what is our hope," says the apostle, 1 Thess. ii. 19, 20, " or joy, or crown of rejoicing? are not even ye in the presence of our Lord Jesus Christ, at his coming? for ye are our glory and joy:" and as the conversion of sinners, so the comfort and edification of saints; their stedfast adherence to, and continuance in the doctrines of the gospel, are likewise a great satisfaction to them; "for now we live," says the same apostle, 1 Thess. iii. 8, "if ye stand fast in the Lord." 4. Eternal glory is the compliment of it; they will have their full two hundred in heaven, how much short soever they come of it here; where, instead of it, poverty, disrespect, and reproach frequently attend them; then "they that turn many to righteousness shall shine as the stars for ever and ever," Dan. xii. 3, who when they have "fought the good fight of faith," 2 Tim. iv. 8, they shall receive "the crown of righteousness," which is laid up for them, and shall be given, not only to them, "but unto all them also that love Christ's appearing."

Verse 13. *Thou that dwellest in the gardens, the companions hearken to thy voice: cause me to hear it.*

I ONCE thought, as some have,[g] that these words were the words of the church of Christ, whose dwelling-place is in his gardens, the churches; to whose voice in the everlasting gospel, the companions, or young converts, listen with great attention and affection; which the church observing, stirred up in her earnest desires to hear the same with more power and efficacy, life and liveliness: but having considered the original text, I find it will by no means bear this sense; for the word translated, "thou that dwellest," is in the feminine gender, and so regards the bride, and may well be rendered, "O thou inhabitress of the gardens!"[h] though the Septuagint and Ambrose render it in the masculine gender,[i] but wrongly, for the word is certainly feminine: hence it appears that the words are the words of Christ, directed unto his bride, the church. In which may be considered,

I. The title and appellation which is given her; "thou that dwellest in the gardens."

II. The notice which the companions take of her; "the companions hearken to thy voice."

III. The request which Christ makes unto her: "cause me to hear it."

I. The title and appellation given her by Christ, is, "Thou that dwellest in the gardens;" or, "O thou inhabitress of the gardens!" Whereby the gardens, must be understood particular congregated churches, as has been observed on chap. vi. 2; of which the church universal is made up, and wherein it may be said to dwell; the Jewish[k] writers interpret them of the schools and congregations where the law was taught. Now her dwelling in those gardens is expressive, 1. Of the work she is employed about there; she does not dwell there idle; there is work for her to do, which is the reason of her dwelling there; and that is, to plant, water, prune, and dress the gardens, which she does by her ministers: her business here also is to attend upon the ministry of the word, and all other ordinances of the gospel, where she frequently meets with her beloved; for "he feeds in the gardens, and gathers lilies." 2. It denotes her diligence, constancy, and assiduity, in attendance on public ordinances; she not only attended now and then, but always; she dwelt in the gardens; and like the first Christians, "continued steadfastly in the apostle's doctrine and fellowship, and in breaking of bread, and in prayer," Acts ii. 42. 3. It shows the delight she took in being there, seeing she had taken up her dwelling there: "the tabernacles of God were amiable to her; a day in his courts was better than a thousand elsewhere; this was the one thing she desired of the Lord," Psalm xxvii. 4; and what, with a great deal of application she sought for; namely, to "dwell in the house of the Lord all the days of her life, to behold the beauty of the Lord, and to enquire in his temple;" because, with the disciples, she judged it was good for her to be there; where she enjoyed the presence of Christ, had the assistance of his Spirit, and the discoveries of his love. 4. It also appears evident from hence, that she made an open profession of Christ; she did not creep into those gardens now and then, as it were by stealth, but she dwelt in them; she was not like Nicodemus, who came to Christ by night; nor those other Jews, who believed in him,

---

[g] So Theodoret. and Tres Patres in loc.
[h] הישׁבה בגנים quæ habitas in hortis, Vulgate Latin version, Michaelis: O quæ habitas in hortis! Pagninus, Brightman; O quæ habitas in istis hortis! Junius: quæ, O tu quæ in hortis habitas! Mercerus: quæ sedes in hortis, Cocceius. So the Targum.
[i] O καθημενος, Sept. qui sedes, Ambros. in Psal. cxviii. octon. 22. col. 1088. but Symmachus and Aquila, as he observes, quæ sedes. [k] Targum, Shirhashirim Rabba, Jarchi, and Alshech in loc. Vid. T. Bab. Sabbat. fol. 63. 1. and Gloss. in Ibid.

but were afraid to confess him, for fear of being put out of the synagogue; nor like many in our days, who will not enter into church-communion, because of being exposed to the reproach of the world; " though with the mouth confession should be made unto salvation, as well as with the heart man should believe unto righteousness," Rom. x. 10; for as the one is necessary for the comfort of the believer, the other is as necessary for the glory of Christ. 5. Her dwelling here expresses her steadfast adherence to the professions she had made, as well as her constant attendance on Gospel-ordinances; she was not as many who "forsake the assembling of themselves together;" but cleaved unto the Lord and to his churches with full purpose of heart, having an affectionate concern for them all; and in this respect she dwelt in them: it may be said of her on some accounts, as the apostle said of himself, 2 Cor. xi. 28, that the "care of all the churches was upon him;" as appears from chap. vii. 12, and viii. 8.

Moreover, from Christ's giving her this title, may be observed, 1. That her dwelling in the gardens, was what he approved of, and was well pleasing to him; it is his will that saints should incorporate into churches, and those who are converted, give themselves up to them and continue with them; as appears from his blessing of them, when they are there, with greater measures of grace, light, and knowledge, larger supplies of his Spirit, and sweet enjoyments of his presence. 2. That this is a title of honour, and is expressive of what dignity she was advanced unto; and indeed it is no small honour which saints have, to " have a name and a place in God's house, which is better than sons or daughters:" David thought so when he envied the very sparrow and swallow, which had made their nests, as he says, " even near thine altars, O Lord of hosts, my king and my God!" and then adds, " blessed are they that dwell in thine house, they will be still praising thee," Psalm lxxxiv. 3, 4; their work, their employment, as well as their place, is honourable and glorious. 3. That it was for her profit, as well as for her honour, to dwell here; for these gardens are stored with all manner of precious fruits; and above all, there stands in the midst of them the apple-tree, Christ Jesus, which is richly laden with a variety of excellent fruit, mentioned chap. ii. 3; under the shadow of which the church frequently sits with great delight, and plucks and eats, and the fruit thereof is sweet unto her taste. 4. That she should always continue and abide there; he does not say, " thou that didst dwell, or shalt dwell in the gardens;" but " thou that dwellest," denoting her continued abode there: there is no fear of her being turned out of these gardens, as Adam was out of his Eden, " so he drove out the man," Gen.

iii. 24; nor are there any cherubim, nor a "flaming sword to keep the way of the tree of life;" but all free and open, and nothing terrifying and menacing; it is true, every plant which Christ's heavenly Father has not planted, shall be rooted up; all those who are in churches only by a mere visible profession, without the truth of grace, shall be turned out, with a " Friend, how camest thou in hither?" but as for all true believers, they shall continue and abide, until they are transplanted into the heavenly paradise above.

II. The notice which the companions take of her; they hearken to her voice: in which may be inquired, 1st. Who are meant by the companions? 2ndly. What by their hearkening to her voice?

1st. These companions may be taken either in a bad sense or in a good sense. If in a bad sense, as in chap. i. 7, then by them we are to understand false teachers, who pretend to be the companions and friends of Christ; who artfully insinuate themselves into churches, and would have them believe, they are aiming at the advancement of the same cause and interest, and mean the same thing as they do; and thus, with feigned words, they introduce their damnable heresies, and make merchandise of the souls of men; they listen to the church's words and doctrines, to catch and carp at, wrest and pervert, use and improve to answer their own ends and purposes: now these words may be considered as a caution given by Christ to the church to beware of them, as he did to his disciples, Matt. vii. 15, and as Paul did to the elders of Ephesus, Acts xx. 29—31; seeing they were listening to what she said, not out of good, but ill-will; yet, notwithstanding he would not have her be silent, but, says he, cause me to hear it, or cause to hear me; that is, preach me boldy and openly, in no wise being afraid of them; for he would not have her speak so softly to him, that the companions which listened might not hear, as R. Aben Ezra on the text observes; no, for, says he, " what I tell you in darkness, that speak ye in light; and what ye hear in the ear, that preach ye upon the house-tops," Matt. x. 27; but, yet with a proper guard upon themselves, both with respect to open and secret enemies. Though I rather think, that we are to understand these companions in a good sense: by whom may be meant, either, 1. God the Father, and God the Holy Ghost,[1] who are both the companions of Christ; for " there are three that bear record in heaven, the Father, the Word, and the Holy Ghost, and these three are one," 1 John v. 7, they are of one nature and essence, possess the same perfection, are partners in the same works, both of nature and grace, and equally share the glory which results from thence; now these divine persons listen to what the church and poor believers say; " they that feared the Lord spake often one to another, and the Lord hearkened and heard

---

[1] So Piscator in loc.

it," Mal. iii. 16. Or else, 2. The holy angels may be here intended, as many interpreters,ᵐ both Jewish and Christian, think; these are the friends and companions of the saints, as well as of Christ; they are reconciled to them through Christ; are willing to perform all the offices of friendship to them; they rejoice at their conversion, bring messages of peace and comfort to them; acknowledge themselves to be their fellow-servants, and are ministering spirits unto those who are the heirs of salvation: not to enter upon the consideration of that question, whether every man hath his angel to attend upon him; which I must confess I am somewhat inclined to believe, there being some scriptures which seem to furnish us with some proofs of it, as Matt. xviii. 10, Acts xii. 15; however, this appears certain, that the saints have the angels of God attending on them; he hath given his angels charge concerning them; they encamp round about those that fear him; they are the guardians and companions of the saints in life, and at death carry their souls to glory; now these listen to what they say in their closets, in their families, in their private or public conversation, as seems manifest from Eccles. v. 6; they wait upon the public assemblies of the saints, and hearken to the voice of the gospel, as delivered by the ministers of it; hence that direction is given by the apostle, 1 Cor. xi. 10, for the woman to cover her head in the time of public worship: the angels get much of their knowledge in, and acquaintance with the great mysteries of grace and salvation, from what they hear from the church, Ephes. iii. 10, and it is with much constancy, diligence, and earnestness, that they desire to look into these things, 1 Pet. i. 12. Or else rather, 3. By these companions may be meant the daughters of Jerusalem, who all along attended the bride in this song; who are the virgins, her companions, as they are called, Psal. xlv. 14, by which young converts more especially may be understood; who listen with a great deal of affection and attention to what the church, or older and more experienced Christians say; though all believers in general may well come under this title of companions, as it is given to them, Psal. cxxii. 8; for David, though he was so great a man, and in such an exalted station of life, yet did not disdain to be called " a companion of all them that fear God," Psalm cxix. 63. Now the saints may be said to be companions of each other for these following reasons: (1.) Because they are interested in one and the same covenant, of which Christ is the Head, Surety, and Mediator; and have an equal right and claim to all the blessings and promises of it. (2.) They have all one and the same Saviour, are all saved in one way, and share alike in the same salvation; for which reason it is called " the common salvation," Jude 3; not that it is common to all the world, but only to the elect of God, who are called to be saints. (3.) They are partakers of the same grace, particularly that of faith; for the meanest saint obtains like precious faith with the greatest: the same may be said of all other graces of the Spirit; for indeed as there is but one body, of which they are all members: so there is but one spirit which actuates them all, even as they are also called in one hope of their calling, Ephes. iv. 4. (4.) They are partners, and share alike in the same privileges of the gospel, to which they have all an equal right; for they are all " fellow-citizens with the saints, and of the household of God." (5.) As companions, they frequently converse together; " they that feared the Lord, spake often one to another ;" they meet in private, and take sweet counsel together, as well as walk unto the house of God in company; they sympathise with each other in all conditions, both outward and inward; they " weep with them that weep, and rejoice with them that rejoice ; they bear one another's burdens, and so fulfil the law of Christ." 6. They are here companions together in tribulation and sufferings, as John says, Rev. i. 9, and shall be partners together in heaven, where they shall enjoy that glorious inheritance which lies among them that are sanctified.

2ndly. Now these companions hearken to the voice of the church : by which may be meant, either, 1. The gospel, as preached by her ministers, which is a joyful sound, and makes delightful music in the ears of believers, which are opened and unstopped by the Spirit of God. Or, 2. The admonitions of the church, which ought to be hearkened to, Matt. xviii. 15—17, and will be regarded by all those who wish well to Zion, who have a value and esteem for the authority of churches, and entertain mean and humble thoughts of themselves, Psalm cxli. 5. 3. The voice of the church in all other ordinances, and particularly that of singing, may be here intended; for the church was now bearing her part in this song with Christ: with whose voice these virgins her companions were charmed; which made them get the nearer, and more carefully listen to her : thus saints should be " teaching and admonishing one another in psalms, and hymns, and spiritual songs, singing with grace in their hearts to the Lord," Col. iii. 16. 4. The voice of the church, and of true believers in private conversation, is listened to by young converts; because it is that which is good, to the use of edifying, and what ministers grace unto the hearers.

III. The request which Christ makes to his church, is; cause me to hear it; that is, thy voice, which is, exceeding sweet and charming to Christ, as appears from chap. ii. 14, where he says, " let me hear thy voice ;" a phrase exactly agreeable to this, and which is there more largely explained, and the reason there given, why he makes such a

---

ᵐ Shirhashirim Rabba, R. Sol. Jarchi, R. Aben Ezra, Isidore, Alcuin, Foliot Lyra, Sanctius. and Diodat. in loc.

request, is, " because sweet is thy voice:" so is the voice of the church, in praying to him, praising of him: speaking largely of his Person, grace, and office; as well as boldly confessing of him before men. Though the word here used may as well be rendered, " cause me to hear me;"ᵃ that is, *preach me*, as Junius translates it: and the meaning is, seeing the companions thus flock unto thee, and listen with the utmost attention and satisfaction to thy voice; take the opportunity of preaching me unto them; let my person, blood, righteousness, and grace, be the subject of thy ministry. And thus indeed it was in the primitive times; for, says the apostle Paul, " I determined not to know," that is, to make known, " any thing among you, save Jesus Christ, and him crucified," 1 Cor. ii. 2. The first ministers of the gospel did not preach themselves nor others, but Christ Jesus the Lord; he was the sum and substance of their ministry; and now though this way of preaching was to " the Jews a stumbling-block, and to the Greeks foolishness;" yet it was owned of God, for the conversion of sinners, and the comfort of saints; and has been more or less so in all ages of the world, and will be continued to be practised until the second coming of Christ; which he may perhaps here intend, and is what the church earnestly prays for in the following verse.

Verse 14. *Make haste, my beloved, and be thou like to a roe or to a young hart, upon the mountains of spices.*

THESE are the words of the church, earnestly imploring the presence of Christ. She begins and ends this song; and in both signifies her great affection to him, how much she valued his company, and how desirous she was of it: this appears throughout the whole song to lie uppermost in her heart, affections, and desires; she had had much nearness of access to Christ, and much communion with him, as appears from this chapter, and yet she wants more; she cannot be easy without the everlasting enjoyment of him on the mountains of spices. In the words may be considered,

I. The title she gives him, " my beloved."

II. The request she makes to him; " make haste," &c.

I. The title she gives him, is, " my beloved!" and is what she had often given him in this song: she seems to take delight in using it; in which she expresses her love and affection to him, with the continuance of it; she acknowledges that he was her beloved still; she claims her interest in him, a comfortable sense of which she now enjoyed; hereby she also distinguishes him from all other beloveds, and shows that she was not ashamed to own him as such; as indeed she had no reason; and perhaps she may have a particular view in giving him this title here, which is to improve her interest in him, as a motive or argument to obtain her request; for such suits that are founded upon the near relation which souls bear to Christ, seldom miss of succeeding. But having more largely explained this character elsewhere, I shall not insist longer upon it; but proceed,

II. To consider the request she makes: which may be regarded, either, 1. As a passionate wish for the incarnation of Christ, that he would speedily come and appear on mount Zion, and in the temple where the sacrifices were offered up, and the sweet smelling incense ascended, which were both typical of his sacrifice and mediation; nothing was more desirable or more importunately prayed for, or more impatiently longed for, by the Old-Testament-church, than this was, and yet nothing more slighted than it was, when brought about. 2. It may be understood as the desire of the church after the spiritual presence of Christ in his house, and upon the mountains of Zion, where he commands his blessing, even life for evermore: nothing is more satisfying to believers than Christ's presence; it is preferred by them to all the enjoyments of life; "if thy presence go not with me," says Moses, Exod. xxxiii. 15, " carry us not up hence;" this puts joy and gladness into the souls of God's people, more than when corn and wine increase; they are oftentimes impatient without it, pant for it, as the hart panteth after the water-brooks; for as his absence is death unto them, so his presence is life; this fills their hearts with comfort, diffuses an universal pleasure throughout their souls; banishes their doubts and fears, supports them under all the pressures, sorrows, and afflictions of life; sets them above the fears of death, and makes them that they can look into another world, and an awful eternity, with the utmost satisfaction and serenity of mind; so that it was no wonder that Christ's gracious presence should be so desirable to saints: besides, there was good reason for the church to make such a request here; seeing he had, in the preceding verse, enjoined her to cause him to hear her voice; that is, to preach his gospel, set forth the glory of his person, and open the treasure of grace to souls; which to perform aright, she knew that she was unable of herself; for who indeed is sufficient for these things ? for even those who are furnished with the greatest gifts and largest capacities for such a work, are yet insufficient to think any thing as of themselves, much less to go through so great a work; but their sufficiency is of God; and therefore the church here desires the presence of Christ with her, and that speedily, in order to do it: it is as if she should say, I am very willing to be found faithful and diligent in the discharge of this work, which thou hast called me to; but I am not able to perform it myself; do thou therefore hasten to my assistance, and grant me thy presence, without which I can do nothing; and this also Christ knows full well, and therefore he has promised his ministering servants to be with them always in their work, even unto the

---

ᵃ השמיעני predica me, Junius and Tremellius.

end of the world. Or else, 3. This petition of hers may regard the spreading of the gospel over all the nations of the world: the gospel shall not only be preached to all nations, but this precious box of ointment being opened, the savour of Christ's knowledge shall be diffused in every place: for the earth shall be full of the knowledge of the Lord, as the waters cover the sea, Isa. xi. 9, multitudes of souls shall be converted to Christ, and made subject to the sceptre of his grace; those voices shall then be heard in heaven, that is, in the church below; Rev. xi. 15; the kingdoms of this world are become the kingdoms of our Lord, and of his Christ: those nations which before were comparable to lions' dens, and the mountains of the leopards, may now be called the mountains of spices, for their fragrancy and fruitfulness; on which Christ appears in his glory; the time being come that the prophecy should be fulfilled, Zech. xiv. 9; and the Lord shall be king over all the earth; in that day shall there be one Lord, and his name one; and what can be more desirable to the saints than this? no wonder the church should be so importunate in her request. Though, 4. I rather think, that she intends the second coming of Christ; as the Old Testament saints breathed after his first coming, so the New-Testament saints earnestly desire his second coming; they love it, they long for it, they pray for it; nay, as the apostle Peter says, 2 Pet. iii. 12, they are hastening to it, that is, they desire Christ to hasten it; they do not care how soon that day comes; for though it will be awful and terrible to the wicked, yet it will be much to their profit and advantage; for Christ "will appear a second time without sin unto salvation:" his first appearance was "in the likeness of sinful flesh," and with all the sins of his people charged upon him; for which he made satisfaction to justice, and thereby procured eternal salvation for them; but his next appearance will be without any sin at all, in any sense whatever, being fully discharged from all, as the Head, Surety, and Representative of his people; when he will put them into the actual possession of that salvation he before procured. Now it may be observed, that this is the last petition of the church's: she closes the song with it, as John does his book of the Revelation; "surely I come quickly," says Christ; "Amen," says John, "even so come, Lord Jesus:" from whence we may observe, that the coming of Christ to take his people to himself, that where he is, there they may be also, is the completion of all believer's prayers and joys! when this is obtained, they have no more to ask for, nor any more indeed do they want; it may be said of them then, what is said of David in the 72nd Psalm; which whole Psalm regards the glory and peace of Christ's everlasting kingdom; "the prayers of David the son of Jesse are ended!" that is, all his wishes are granted, and his requests fulfilled, when this is effected. But now let us consider a little more particularly the several phrases, by which the church expresses her desire for the coming of Christ. And,

1st. She says, "Make haste my beloved:" not that she desired him to come before the time appointed of the Father: for as there was a set time, which is called "the fulness of time," which was agreed upon for Christ's coming in the flesh; so there is a time fixed and determined for his second coming; as the Person, so "the day is appointed by God, in the which he will judge the world in righteousness;" though "of that day and that hour knoweth no man, no, not the angels which are in heaven, neither the Son," as he is man, "but the Father;" therefore it is both vain and sinful for persons curiously to inquire into it, and bold and daring to attempt the fixing of it; for "it is not for us to know the times or the seasons which the Father hath put in his own power." Now Christ will not come before, nor will he stay longer than this time appointed; and this his church knew; nor does she desire him to come sooner; yet could be glad to see those things accomplished which must precede it; such as the conversion of the Jews, and the bringing in the fulness of the Gentiles; all which the Lord will hasten, but it will be in "his own time:" nor does the church mean any other; but by using this expression, she signifies the earnestness of her desire to have this accomplished, being as it were impatient until it was done; her language is much like Sisera's mother's, who said concerning him, "Why is his chariot so long in coming? why tarry the wheels of his chariots?" Moreover it may be observed, that the word here translated, "make haste," may be rendered, "flee away;"° the meaning of which is, not that the church desired to remove or depart from her; no, she valued his presence at another rate than to desire him to withdraw from her; those indeed who prefer their lusts, their pleasures, their profits, their swine before Christ, say, depart from us; but as for the church, when she has found him, she holds him fast, and will "not let him go:" so that when she desires him to "flee away," something else must be understood; which is, that she, being weary of a sinful and troublesome world, breathed after an everlasting rest with him upon the spicy mountains; and therefore she would have him remove from his garden below, where he was, and take her along with him to glory; where she might eternally enjoy him, without any disturbance or molestation.

2ndly. She desires that he would be "like a roe or a young hart upon the mountains of spices;" for what reasons Christ may be compared "to a roe or a young hart," has been shown on chap. ii. 9. Her meaning here is, that he would come quickly and speedily, and be as swift in his motion

---

° ברח φυγε Sept. fuge, Vulgate Latin version, Pagninus, Montanus, Mercerus, Cocceius, Brightman: fugito, Tigurine version occurre, Junius.

as the roe or young hart, and flee as swift as they;[p] which run upon the mountains, and other high places, where they delight to skip and leap: see Hab. iii. 19, and by these "mountains of spices," we are not to understand mount Moriah, and the temple built upon it, as R. Solomon Jarchi interprets them; but rather, the mountains of Zion, or the several congregations and churches, where she desired his gracious presence until his second coming; which may be compared to mountains for their height and sublimity, being established and exalted above all others, Isa. ii. 2, as well as for their permanence and immoveableness: for, "they that trust in the Lord shall be as mount Zion which can never be removed, but abideth for ever," Psalm cxxv. 1, and may be called "mountains of spices," because of those precious plants which grow there; and those fragrant graces with which they abound; as well as those sweet-smelling sacrifices of prayer and praise, which are there offered up. Though I rather think, that the joys and glories of the heavenly state are here intended; where the church desires to have everlasting and uninterrupted communion with her beloved; and that speedily, if it was his will; where she should be on high, and out of the reach of every snare and every enemy; where she would be safe, secure, and immoveable, and in the possession of pleasures that will never end. For, 1. These mountains may denote the height and sublimity of this happy state; it is above, it is an "inheritance reserved in heaven; a hope laid up there, a prize of the high calling of God in Christ Jesus." 2. May express the permanence and everlastingness thereof: it is a "city which hath foundations," and these immoveable; it is a building of God eternal in the heavens;" these habitations are everlasting, from whence there never will be a remove. 3. May signify the exceeding pleasantness and delightfulness thereof: that state may well be represented by spicy mountains, seeing in the presence of Christ there is "fulness of joy, and at his right hand there are pleasures for evermore;" no wonder then that the church should so passionately wish for the enjoyment of this happiness; and close this song in the manner she does, saying, "Make haste, my beloved, and be thou like a roe or a young hart upon the mountains of spices."

---

[p] Cervique fugaces, Virgil. Georgic. l. 3, prope finem. Vid. Plauti Pœnulum, act. 3. sc. 1. v. 26. 27.

THE BAPTIST STANDARD BEARER, INC.
A non-profit, tax-exempt corporation
committed to the Publication & Preservation
of The Baptist Heritage.

SAMPLE TITLES FOR PUBLICATIONS AVAILABLE
IN OUR VARIOUS SERIES:

THE BAPTIST *COMMENTARY* SERIES
Sample of authors/works in or near republication:
John Gill - *Exposition of the Old & New Testaments (9 & 18 Vol. Sets)*
(Volumes from the 18 vol. set can be purchased individually)

THE BAPTIST *FAITH* SERIES:
Sample of authors/works in or near republication:
Abraham Booth - *The Reign of Grace*
John Fawcett - *Christ Precious to Those That Believe*
John Gill - *A Complete Body of Doctrinal & Practical Divinity (2 Vols.)*

THE BAPTIST *HISTORY* SERIES:
Sample of authors/works in or near republication:
Thomas Armitage - *A History of the Baptists (2 Vols.)*
Isaac Backus - *History of the New England Baptists (2 Vols.)*
William Cathcart - *The Baptist Encyclopaedia (3 Vols.)*
J. M. Cramp - *Baptist History*

THE BAPTIST *DISTINCTIVES* SERIES:
Sample of authors/works in or near republication:
Abraham Booth - *Paedobaptism Examined (3 Vols.)*
Alexander Carson - *Ecclesiastical Polity of the New Testament Churches*
E. C. Dargan - *Ecclesiology: A Study of the Churches*
J. M. Frost - *Pedobaptism: Is It From Heaven?*
R. B. C. Howell - *The Evils of Infant Baptism*

THE *DISSENT & NONCONFORMITY* SERIES:
Sample of authors/works in or near republication:
Champlin Burrage - *The Early English Dissenters (2 Vols.)*
Albert H. Newman - *History of Anti-Pedobaptism*
Walter Wilson - *The History & Antiquities of the Dissenting Churches (4 Vols.)*

For a complete list of current authors/titles, visit our internet site at
www.standardbearer.com or write us at:

The Baptist Standard Bearer, Inc.
No. 1 Iron Oaks Drive • Paris, Arkansas 72855

Telephone: (479) 963-3831   Fax: (479) 963-8083
E-mail: baptist@arkansas.net
Internet: http://www.standardbearer.org

Specialists in Baptist Reprints and Rare Books

Thou hast given a *standard* to them that fear thee; that it may be displayed because of the truth. -- Psalm 60:4

www.ingramcontent.com/pod-product-compliance
Lightning Source LLC
Chambersburg PA
CBHW021801220426
43662CB00006B/147